No Brakes!

Bicycle Track Racing in the United States

Sandra Wright Sutherland, Ph.D. with
Legends of Bicycle Track Racing

Foreword by Greg LeMond

IRIS PRESS

Encinitas, California

Pre-press production by Sandra Wright Sutherland
utilizing Apple Macintosh Power PC 6100/66, Apple 17" monitor,
Apple LaserWriter II, SyQuest 200 (3), Microtek ScanMaker 35t,
Adobe Photoshop 3.0 and Aldus/Adobe PageMaker 5.0,
                    (next time, it will be QuarkXPress)
plus final pre-press prep with my friend at TNT Design.

First Edition
Printed in Canada

ISBN: 0-9645243-0-9

by
Iris Press
314 A St.
Encinitas, CA 92024

The Iris Press logo: the iris flower (nature); the iris of the camera lens (technology); the iris of the human eye (human endeavor).

Iris was the Greek goddess of the rainbow. The Rainbow Jersey is the highest prize in the world of bicycle racing.

Cover photos : *1994 Double World Champion Marty Nothstein rides the wheel of 1994 US National Champion Jeff Solt during Olympic Trials, 1992.*
Marty's face says, "Pull me up to turn four, Jeff, I'll take it from there!"
Top: *Panorama shot of the debut of the Vandedrome. Del Mar, CA 1995*

Back cover: *Four time World Champion Connie Paraskevin Young (right) goes into a "track stand" with fellow World Champion, Janie Eickhoff, during the 1994 US National Track Championships.*
This photo shows two types of equipment commonly seen on the track.

Table of Contents

To Jeanna Laffen
my mental gate to the velodrome.
Anything knowledgeable here
only reflects your influence.
Now the gate is open to
everyone else, too. (Uh-oh!)
(Now isn't this better than
a silly Go-Plug?)
Thank you!

and thank you supportive
parents, including mine.

Most people don't realize that I raced on the velodrome when I was young rider. I learned many important skills there, including how to ride straight, how to ride close, and how to grab and throw another rider without falling down (Madison).

In 1979 I was second in the Pursuit at the Junior World Championships in Argentina. In 1980 I was one of the riders who was unable to compete due to boycott of the Olympic Games. Finding frustration in the amateur ranks, I went on to a career on the professional road circuit.

Today's riders are not forced to choose between amateur and professional racing. If monetary support had existed early in my career in track racing as it did in road racing, I may have raced track too, instead of having a career solely on the road.

I loved racing Six-day races. Having an audience of thousands screaming their support throughout the race is as exciting as finishing the Tour through the streets of Paris. On the road, many hours are spent without this inspiration, but on a track, the fans are there the whole time. Crowd support is a huge motivator for an athlete.

The track is an excellent training ground for bicycle riders. Training on the velodrome complements road racing because it gives a different structure to work-outs, especially concentration on technical skills.

There are dangers on the road which are not found on the track. Aside from accidents and road hazards, some people just don't seem to want to share the road with others.

On a velodrome, there are no road hazards, no irate motorists, no red

racing on and off as it interests them while in constant view of their parents.

Parents don't need to worry about telling them to be quiet and sit still, things that can be problems at other sporting events. Children are not allowed on the track, so parents don't need to worry about that. Often at velodromes there are hills to roll down or other kids to play with.

It is common for families to bring

get involved in racing, from locations of velodromes, to events offered, to insights through the eyes of America's top riders -- some of whom I used to race against on the track.

With the 1996 Olympics on American soil once again, spectators will be better able to understand how really good our track racers are, in their specialties and when pitted against the rest of the world.

LeMond, second from front, in the 1986 World Road Championships, Colorado Springs, CO

lights to contend with and no potholes to avoid. True, nothing can match the magnificence of a beautiful countryside, and nothing can replace road riding, but there is a place for long rides and a place for technical focus.

As a family activity, the velodrome environment provides many benefits. Children who are not involved in racing can be with the family, but don't have to sit in one place. There are usually areas where they can move around and watch

picnic lunches and enjoy a relaxing social event with free or low cost entertainment constantly in view. It is fun for the whole family.

I'm happy to see a book written to help people understand velodrome racing. I've always enjoyed being there, both on and off the velodrome.

With this book, riders can learn how to

Welcome to the wonderful world of the velodrome.

Look for me in the crowd.

Greg LeMond

Preface

The Book I Wanted to Read

This is the book I wanted to read. I waited for some "expert" to write it. I knew someone would -- they had to. How could people learn about the most exciting bicycle racing on earth unless it was organized and presented in a stable format for others to follow?

I waited and waited, frustrated at seeing a job that someone needed to do. The last book was written in 1977 (*Bicycle Track Racing*, from Bicycle World). It was time for a new one and a major one. The whole base for present day track racing has been built since 1977. Here's how this book began:

Influences

It started with a road ride and the kindness of a bike shop mechanic who stopped to help with a flat tire. Hangin' at Laffen's Bike Shop, I was initially disappointed that they all seemed to be trackies, one of whom (Jean) used to go on AYH (American Youth Hostels) rides with Audrey McElmury. I was more interested in the roads. But I went to the track anyway, just to be sociable. I discovered that the track was a lot more fun.

San Diego Velodrome was a mecca for Olympic hopefuls in the early '80s. Dominguez Hills (LA) was being built and the '84 Olympics were scheduled 100 miles away. Ralph Elliott and Dan Gindling's efforts made San Diego a hot track. AYH, a major supporter of bicycle racing in San Diego for many years, actively supported a Juniors team. San Diego

Bicycle Club (est. 1946) and Hannah North were training people on the track. My friend Jean thought I might like to try it and so I did (after thinking "*Me*?"). The opportunity to learn this strange activity was pretty exciting.

My first time on the track made me feel like I was Neil Armstrong walking on the moon. Hannah had us practice "Flying 200s," "pacelines" and all the other typical track routines. I surely wouldn't have written this book without having experienced how really fun velodrome riding can be.

One clinic was held by some guy called "Eddie B" who was supposed to be this big expert. Another speaker at the event was some guy named Mark Gorski. I didn't know who they were, but Jean seemed to value their information. Most people are not so fortunate to be exposed to such a high level of expertise so early.

I printed a small booklet (1983), *Bicycle Training for the Triathlete *and Others* with World Champion Audrey McElmury and Pan Am Team Member Michael Levonas, my first coaches, who were teaching basic bicycle racing principles to triathletes (which I was not). Neil Bruington, a non-bicyclist graphic communications professor taught me enough about printing to make me functional (and helped with this book!)

My friend Jean helped me when I moved near Marymoor, another strong cycling venue, in 1985. She stayed to start a new bike shop in Seattle. She

dragged me away from my doctoral studies to do things like -- volunteer at the track! "Doc" training included production of educational materials with the assistance of subject matter experts ("SME"s). This enables the producer to develop expert level materials by drawing upon knowledge from those who possess it for the benefit of those who want to learn.

In 1991 (and again in '92), I began exhibiting my photos of track racing at the US National Championships with the assistance of Jerry Baker and Barclay Kruse (and Briggs Pharmacy). In 1993, I took a long look at the photographs I had exhibited and saw in them evidence of a sport that many more could enjoy. In 1994, I began taking photos with intent. "If no one else is going to write this book, (I said to myself) I guess I'll do it -- *so I can read it!*"

Sometimes life presents missions that you must pursue. Apparently this is one of mine. It may appear to be a choice, but it felt like an imperative.

Friends have been very important. Jeanna Laffen's feedback and shared knowledge is responsible for much of this book (if it's wrong, blame her -- just kidding, Jeanna!). In the end, this book would not exist if she did not -- no doubt about it. She got me hooked with both experience and education. Meg Berry taught me a lot, in the beginning and now. I was fortunate to meet Paul Swift at the 1990 Goodwill Games, who has helped me understand the agonies and ecstasies of the top-level competitor (some of which he wishes were not his to share.) It happens these are all Sprinters.

Audience

When asked "who is your audience?" my answer can only be: "spectators in the Olympic Velodrome in Atlanta in 1996," from neophytes, who may never have seen a bicycle race before, to longtime aficionados of the sport.

Every bike race fan needs a velodrome book which will:
1) organize and define track racing events, locations and top competitors,
2) offer insights into the tradition and specialty of bicycle track racing, and
3) share the fun and uniqueness of track racing with friends and family who know nothing about it (so, **hey! buy one for each of your friends and family!**)

Bicycling Wine

There's something unique and special about track racing and its enthusiasts which is not the same in other kinds of bicycle racing. Track racers are the elite, the fine artists of the sport. Specialization, simplicity and the confined space demand a fine-tuned excellence from each athlete.

Velodrome racing is like wine -- there are a million subtleties in each event that can't be appreciated at first. Its rich character remains lingering in the soul through the dead of winter. Understanding deepens with time, each season a higher plateau.

It helps to have a knowledgeable person fill in some of the details at first. The facts (i.e. how many laps is a Kilometer?) are easy to learn, but the inside tidbits (why is a Kilometer such a special challenge?) are only accessible through those who have been around for a while.

A Survey Book

I wanted this book to be a true survey book. The richness of the sport results from it's multiplicity, enjoyable by people with divergent orientations. History, craftsmanship, invention, specialization, physical exhilaration, mental challenge, volunteerism, plain old entertainment, from child to old folks -- there's something for everyone. I wanted this variety to be represented. Such a presentation did offer a challenge to book construction, which "shifts gears", evolving through information for beginners, rules of events, competitor biographies, views of support personnel to straight data. It's like a crystal with many facets.

My favorite sports books didn't just describe events, though that's helpful too. The books I loved best shared the athlete's perspective. I wanted to know what Rebecca Twigg had to say about that World Record and how Harvey Nitz won all those championships.

My selection of riders was guided by a review of the "Champions" section of the USCF RuleBook. To me, they speak from Mount Olympus. I wanted riders who either had ended or were nearing the end of their careers, yet who were still involved -- mature wisdom, uncompromised by fear of divulging secrets to encroaching competitors. I wanted a true variety of people, not cookie-cutter riders.

Certain riders were obvious choices, though I didn't always realize it at first. No one could be better for Match Sprint than Connie Young and no other choice for Keirin than Gibby Hatton. While I didn't want a rider as

young and mainstream as Janie Eickhoff, she is too spectacular and too strong a force in women's racing to omit.

Other experts were somewhat more personal choices, such as Ralph Elliott, the first announcer I ever heard, who knows his sport and always makes me laugh. While Audrey McElmury was not primarily a track racer, her international experience and World Championship at a time when women simply did not do that sort of thing has always been something I've admired. I wanted to know what my heroes had to say and share this with others.

Once I selected my "dream team" of riders and experts, I was gratified that not one turned me down Each seemed only awaiting the opportunity to share their love of the sport.

There is a strong representation of the 1984 Olympic Team in this book, including Coach Eddie Borysewicz. This completes a circle to the 1996 Olympics when once again a velodrome built in the US makes welcome international competitors.

Reviewing the various reflections, Great Wisdoms of sport emerge. One of these, that the most cherished accomplishments are often those early in an athletes' career which may appear insignificant to others. All were simply young dreamers once upon a time, nurtured by loving hands who gave time and energy to their futures.

There were other top riders and experts (Mike Walden!) who could have given terrific insights into their events and experiences. While I wanted to include many more, spending the rest of my life writing

this book would have been enjoyable only for the one-person audience of me. I forced myself to set limits, stop, and publish so others could share and learn what a great sport this is.

I like to think that each person interviewed for this book realized that I saw him/her as uniquely important to bicycle racing and to this book, because this is absolutely true. And so I present to you a selection of the legends, the movers and shakers of the sport.

Style

As an aside to style, I have taken the liberty of capitalizing key terms specific to velodrome racing in order to increase their visual impact as designators. They include names of particular events (i.e. Pursuit), names of rider designations (i.e. Sprinter), and names of particular places on a velodrome (i.e. Turn Four).

While this is improper from an editorial standpoint, I choose this method of communicating terms specific to velodrome racing, not simply general terminology. This is a cognitive organizational strategy (I knew theories from my doctoral work would sneak in here somewhere).

Experts' reflections were taped verbally, then "translated" into text.

The trouble with a first edition is that it offers an invitation to correct errors and add further information, but with no possibility of actually making these changes within that edition. I don't doubt that I will be set straight on many aspects of how this book could have been improved once it is available. That's okay, I welcome its improvement.

My time line of having this book available for audiences of the 1996 Olympic Games precludes my taking time to optimize this first attempt. The second edition will be an intriguing challenge which will likely begin with the publication of this book.

And so, I present to you the book I wanted to read. I hope you enjoy reading it as much as I enjoyed producing it.

Sandy Sutherland
Encinitas, CA
1995 for 1996

Steve Sims photo

"Wha . . . .? Where . . . . . .? What am I doing up here? I'm supposed to be out there taking pictures!"

(Well actually, they needed the body in the age division -- another job that needed doing. It was more fun for the winner to beat more people than less people.) "Okay, okay, I'll do it."

It was fun -- try it! Master's Nats, 1993

Marty Nothstein -- America's Champion
Sprint + Keirin = World Champion X 2

Marty Nothstein made his mark in bicycle racing history in 1994 at the tender age of 23 by winning World Championships in two events at the same competition.

Marty was not born a Champion. A short time ago he was just a kid looking for a challenge. He found it in track racing.

After winning Sprints as a Junior in 1988 and '89, Marty was part of a team dominating Tandem Sprinting, first as Stoker with Paul Swift, then as Driver with Erin Hartwell.

In 1993, Marty was U.S. Sprint Champion. In '94, with a broken heel, he barely lost Sprints to Jeff Solt after going to an unusual four rides, but still won the Keirin Championship.

Having a coach who won Junior Worlds in Sprints and competed in Keirin for eight years (Gibby Hatton) couldn't hurt.

Asked what would revitalize U.S. Track racing, old-time Sprint great Frank Kramer answered: "Only one good American rider." That man may have finally arrived.

Getting Started

Ever since I was young I was real competitive. I played baseball, football, wrestling, but I also started racing BMX. I grew up with my younger brother in a neighborhood where there weren't any kids our age. We were bored one day, whipping rocks around the yard. We wanted to see how close we could get to the neighbor's house. We bounced them off the roof and garage door of a house across the street. Our mom found out and made us go over to apologize.

It turned out that our neighbor was Heinz Wolter, who was managing the Murray Cycling Team, including most of the Olympians.

He said "I see you guys riding your bikes. How about trying this developmental program in Trexlertown sponsored by Air Products?"

I said "Hey, I don't care, I'll give it a shot." and that's how I got started.

The velodrome was about a mile and a half from my house and I had never been there. I knew it was a bicycle racing track. I could see the flags and I used to listen to the P.A. announcer. I knew guys from all over the world raced there, but I had never gone and watched. I wasn't curious about it because I was too busy with the typical American sports. Track racing never appealed to me. I liked BMX because it was over jumps and in the dirt. But once I got involved in cycling enough to appreciate it, I just loved it, because it was definitely a tough sport. I also liked it because it was an individual sport.

I started the developmental program when I was 15. They have teams, like one was the Hurricanes, one was the Comets, there were about five or six teams. My coach for that team was (Team Time Trial Champion) Joel Stetina. Other coaches were Gibby (Hatton) and Pat (McDonough) - - good coaches -- helping the younger kids out. We were all from different teams, but it was similar to the interscholastic team concept. They "drafted" us. We got out there and did a Time Trial and took a few tests and the coaches got to pick their teams.

Gibby was coaching in the program I was in. One day when I was about 16 we had to do 3km Pursuits. I had to ride against Gibby. Gibby said, "Okay, if I catch you, you're going to have to Sprint a 200m time."

I said "Alright, no problem."

He caught me with about a half lap to go (he admits he had to work hard to catch me). After only about a five or ten minute break, he said "Okay, now you've got to do a 200m Sprint."

"America has a lot of talented athletes. There are other guys like me out there who may want to consider track cycling, especially if they have an Olympic dream. There are a lot of kids who are into basketball, baseball, football, who just don't know about it.

A lot of people don't realize that track cycling is an Olympic event. It's fast, it's exciting, and it's all right there in front of you. I go to Six-day races in Europe and 15,000 people a night come to watch."

My Sprint turned out to be an 11.7 - after a 3km Pursuit - so he realized I had some talent. From that point on he took me under his wing. He was coaching a few other guys too.

I didn't really know Gibby too well at that point. I had watched him in races at T-Town and I knew he was a great rider. I used to cheer for him and for Mark Whitehead and Pat McDonough.

Whitehead was the villain of the track. If people understood bike racing and looked beyond the way he comes across sometimes, he was the best rider out there often, by far. He had style on the bike. He was really tough and never quit. That's the stuff I like seeing. Mark didn't like to lose. I find I'm that same way, I have that bad character to me. I keep it in, but I feel it. I learned a lot from watching those three riders. Since then they've all become my friends. When I started coming through the Junior ranks they started helping me out.

When I won my first National title in '88 (Junior Sprints) I was hooked. I'd gotten second in '87. It was in Trexlertown in '88, so I was the hometown boy.

I really don't know how I came to specialize in Sprints. Probably through the guidance of Gil (Gibby), Pat and those guys. I was State Road Champion and won many criteriums. Could do both road and track, which makes me a much different Sprinter than normal. I still ride criteriums and road races. I ride them to compete, too, not just for conditioning. Whenever I put a number on my back I'm competing.

At certain times of the year I won't ride road races or criteriums because I'm getting into my track shape, my track legs. I like riding both road and track. Maybe some day I'll go back to the criterium scene. It wouldn't take me much to do both, but to be World Champion in one thing you've got to concentrate pretty much on one event. You can't be World Sprint Champion and World Road Champion at the same time. It doesn't work.

Training

I enjoy the benefits of winning and the benefits of training really hard. That's how I won these titles. It wasn't just showing up and getting lucky, because it doesn't work like that.

If people saw how I trained and tried to train as hard as I do, most of the guys wouldn't be able to do it, when I really get down to it. It's a lot of really hard work, a lot of pain and sweat.

In training there are some things that I stick to every year, but we're always re-doing my program. In '93 I got second in the Worlds in the Keirin and fourth in the Sprints, something no American has ever done. But even then, we didn't copy my program for '94 because it was successful. We changed it to make it *more* successful.

One change was that I broke my heel! Seriously, I hit the weights heavier and I rode real hard on the roads earlier in the season. In Los Angeles in the Spring I was dominating every race. I was hungry. I said "I got second and now I can win.

Let's bump it up and train harder." and that's what I did. I hit the weights pretty hard all year. You've got to go in with the right attitude. Weights helped. I did a lot of road miles.

But I tell a lot of people, you win mainly on your heart and your head. You may have the strongest legs in the world, but you may not win. I was hungry at the Worlds and I'm always hungry to win. If I don't win I get really upset.

Some people think "Maybe if I get coached by Gil I can be a World Champion", but certain things work for certain people. Some people may not be able to train as hard as me. Others may have to do different things. Some guys might not be able to ride the roads like I do, it might screw up their track riding.

Everyone's a different person. If one program worked for everyone we would have had a program long ago from Frank Kramer (old time Champion).

Coach Gibby Hatton was a Champion in Sprint and Keirin. Now Marty is a World Champion in Sprint and Keirin. Hmmmm . . . wonder if there could be a connection there . . . hmm . . .

There is no one way to become a World Champion. I change my program every year even though it was the most successful it has ever been or could ever be.

Going to a World Championship I'll fine tune everything for about the last four weeks. Over that time it will be strictly track and speed work. With motorpacing, without motorpacing, power work, we mix it up.

Diet

I eat a lot of venison and a lot of low fat stuff, but I'm not a diet guru. I eat meat, a lot of steaks. I splurge and eat ice cream and Doritos, cheese, and the list goes on. You just have to train hard and get rid of the excess when it's time. I may take a multivitamin and a carbo-protein drink, but that's about it. I really don't believe in that stuff.

We get a body fat, composition, stuff like that. I have pretty low body fat. When I'm racing good I'm about

200 lbs and my body fat is about 5%. I'm 6'2". During the winter it's not abnormal for me to get up to 205, 210 lbs, but even then my body fat never gets above 8%. I'd like to race with a little more weight. I'm still young, I still have more body phases to go through. It'll probably happen eventually.

1994 Nationals

In '94 Nationals I could barely walk. I didn't know what to expect. At that point we were shooting for the World title. Then I came home, crashed, and the whole thing was up in the air. I almost wrote the whole year off. I was going to pack it in and say "Okay, let's just go for next year."

There were nights when I couldn't sleep because the pain was so bad. But I said to myself "between all the pain and all the nights of being up, all the training you've done through the years, you deserve to tough it out and get out there and go for it."

The only reason I went to Nationals was to get second so I could make the Pan Am Games. That's the only reason. The Olympic Committee would not allow me to go unless I placed at least second. I told them, "I'm one of the best in the world and by far the best American -- you don't want the best American representing the US in the Pan Am Games? The people of America want that."

They said "If you can't qualify, you can't go."

Doctors told me I was crazy. I told them that there was no other way I

"A great Sprinter is a patient Sprinter. You have to put the other guy into a position he doesn't want to be in."

could go to the Pan Am Games. I wanted to go and this was the only possible way. I had to give it a shot.

By that time Nationals started I was so hungry, I wanted to race so bad. I just knew I deserved to win and deserved to go to the Pan Am Games. The Olympic Committee doesn't like to make exceptions because they think it's favoritism, but the coaches don't really favor anybody, not really. They may favor the best guy, but he's the best guy!

If I were the one making the decision I would have some way to allow the best guy to race, especially if the Pan Am Games are eight months later. It would have been alright if I *couldn't* have raced. I wouldn't have wanted to go, even if I were going to race, if I were 75%. It's not the point to make the trip. Eight months down the road I was going to be 100%, guaranteed.

When Nationals was over I felt I got a lousy call (resulting in second place), but that's all old news now. I went there and did what I had to do.

American officiating is the worst in the world. They don't understand real bike racing. All events. I'm not so sure about roads, but on the track they're terrible. Inconsistent. There are a few good officials, but there are more bad ones than good ones. What's worse is that an official will make a call and then they get scared to back themselves up. If they made the call they need to stick by it.

The officials should listen to the riders, good riders, riders who race internationally, top racers in the country. We're the guys out there. You could just put everyone side by side and say "race" but that's not what Sprinting is.

They have to watch video tapes of good racing, not a race of local guys at Alpenrose or Houston, but the top guys in the World. They're going to think guys should have been DQ'd, when Worlds level riders and officials will say "Hey, excellent ride!"

Riders can't race one way in America and a different way in Europe. European riders feel the officiating in America is poor. They say "What's wrong with these people?"

On the other hand, if you make a mistake in a race, you can't blame officials because you got yourself in that position.

I do push the rules. I race to the limits. You've got to race to the limits

to win. At the Worlds I race aggressively. If you watch at the World Championships, so do the other competitors. It's do or die. You can't stand there and let yourself get pushed around. At least I won't. It wasn't the way I was brought up. You may let someone swing at you first, but then you take 'em. I may not throw the first punch, but if it comes at me, I'll deal with it.

Strategy

Sprints are tactics. Keirin is tactics. I'm not the fastest guy. I didn't qualify first at Worlds. I qualified sixth and I won.

I don't watch any video tapes. I'm really bad in that way. I don't write down what I do in training and I don't watch any video tapes of other riders. Some guys take notes on riders and what they do. Some guys study video tapes. Other guys document what people do in other ways.

I don't do that because I don't think you can judge a guy by that. You might think I'm going to do a certain move and I'm not going to do it. A good Sprinter is not going to keep doing the same thing.

A great Sprinter is a patient Sprinter. You have to take your time and wait. You have to put the other guy into a position that he doesn't want to be in. That means you have a lot of rage and you want to go fast, you want to explode on your bike, but you have to wait until you put him into a bad position. You force yourself to be patient when you don't want to be. **A great Sprinter is a patient Sprinter.**

My heroes were the riders who rode weekly at Trexlertown. You could go and watch the best riders in the world. I don't forget things. I'll remember things. Especially, if you lose to a guy, you're going to remember what he did to you! If you beat the guy, you know how to beat him.

I don't feel like anyone in the United States can give me a run for my money. There was Carpenter in '92, but I was still young and had just decided I was going to take cycling seriously. I got serious after '91. I decided I was not going to school. I decided I was going to train really hard and make cycling my occupation. That's when the results started to show. Ken was racing Keirin in '93. There's always got to be a time when someone's got to step in and take over.

If he came back there's no way he'd beat me. I look at two Rainbow Jersey's hanging on my wall and no one in the World can beat me! Actually, there are a few guys in the world who are tough competitors and tough racers. You've got to be in top shape to win.

There are probably about five to eight Sprinters in the world who are pretty much equal. A couple of Germans, an Italian, a couple of Australians, and that's about it. You could ask Huebner the same question and he'd say "Yes, there's these few guys." It's kind of whoever trained harder that year.

To get to that level you have to have a stepping stone to step up. No one comes out of the woodwork. Two years ago I "burst on the scene" when I was the first American to get second in the Keirin and fourth in the Sprints in one year, but throughout the year I

was placing well in the World Cup events in Europe. It wasn't like "Well, who's this guy?"

This year again I was racing real well in Europe. I broke a 16 year winning streak of East Germans placing top three in the Leipzig Gran Prix, the biggest Sprint title next to the World Championship. I ended up getting third without getting much track training at all. That's unheard of, for someone to get top-three in that.

It's a shame the American press and American cycling magazines don't publish that sort of accomplishment. That was history again, like my second and fourth, but it didn't make very many papers.

Keys for a Good Sprinter:

Attitude, good genetics -- you've got to be born with good legs. You've got to have natural leg speed. You've got to be aggressive. I feel you've got to be a bigger guy, lean, a total athlete, for Sprinting. I know some roadies I've played basketball with who are so uncoordinated they are lucky they can ride a bike.

On a track, bike handling is very important. You're always moving and swerving your bike, using your body to control your bike and yourself. Roadies don't tend to have that. No sense of balance. Track cycling develops your bike handling skills better because you <u>have</u> to.

As to what characteristics I don't

have, I really don't know. I haven't found my limits. I know I'm strong enough and fast enough, but I know I could be stronger, faster and quicker.

I don't pre-visualize races against other riders. I know what I think and what I have to do. I know I have to

"Sprints are tactics. Keirin is tactics. I'm not the fastest guy. I didn't qualify first at Worlds. I qualified sixth and I won."

win and will do anything to win.

Patience is important. If I say "I want to ride this guy from the back or take the front away from him" I must be patient. If two guys are going slow on the banking but the banking is too steep to hold you, if you slide down the track, you're patient. You go up and slide down again, just to make the point that "I'm going to ride from back

here."

Or you might say "I'm going to ride from the front because this guy's screwing around with me." And you're going to make him slide down the track and scare him. "Okay, I don't care!" A lot of it's head games and mental stuff, at least at the international level. It's different in the States. Guys never get into a battle like that here.

The mental challenge is much more at the World level. We pretty well know each other. I race them throughout the Spring and Summer. There are a few guys in America who play the game well, but a lot of them are impatient. If you go slow they'll take the front on you, so there's no one to play the game with.

Sprint and Keirin are the only two events for me. It takes too long and is too different a style of training to do other events. It would make no sense for me to say "I've won these two titles, now I want to win the Points race" or "I want to be a Team Pursuiter now." It just wouldn't work. It would probably take four years to become the best in that. I've been Sprinting since '88. In Sprinting you need a lot of experience. Experience counts a lot in that event.

If Tandem Sprints were still raced at the Worlds I'd race it if I had the right partner to win. Erin Hartwell and I begged the coaches to send a tandem over so we could race in Italy. They wouldn't bring it over. (*Nothstein and Hartwell were not current U.S. Na-*

tional Champions) We were there already. We asked and they wouldn't do it. We hadn't ridden it that year, but we just wanted to do it because it was the last year they were ever going to have it.

Ever since Erin and I broke away from the Tandem we've both become very good individual riders. Tandem is fun. It's a good crowd pleaser. It's a dangerous event. Every year guys crash. They crash hard and hurt themselves. I don't think the UCI wants to get involved in that. They want to be safe.

Olympic Sprint

Now they're going to bring in the Team Sprint, the "Olympic Sprint". It's a good event for the crowd and hopefully a good event for the U.S. I'll definitely take part in that. It will be Hartwell, myself, and then Hartwell! (*laughs*) That would be the best team! But we've got to find someone else. Erin and I are going to put a team together. Other riders can challenge us if they want.

Olympic Sprint will push a lot of Sprinters. It will give us another event to go for. It's actually an Italian Pursuit.

World Champion Status

Since winning the World Championships, it's busy and it's fun. I shouldn't say fun, it's so hectic. I have a lot more responsibilities now, sponsorships, stuff like that. Financially, it has changed incredibly. I'm real motivated to train now to defend my titles.

I want to win a few more World Championships. I have a great support team of coaches, friends and family. I

also have good genetics. My family is a tough family and people in the area where I live have great work ethics. People work very hard at what they do, no matter what the weather. It's the Pennsylvania Dutch. They're stubborn and they're hard workers -- tough individuals. Not much bothers them.

Touring with the Vandedrome

There is a possibility I may tour with John Vande Velde's portable track. I'd like to help him get that going. It's hard to say, it's going to take a lot of money to get it going, some good publicity. But, I tell lots of people, once it happens, I think it's going to be here. Those tracks are pretty amazing to watch.

If there's a show with it, good food and good drinks, a band, etc., you're not just going to go to see a bike race, you're going to go to have fun. You want to see good racing, but you also want to listen to music and have some beers!

John has my commitment if it gets going, I told him that already. Good television exposure can help too. Track racing is much more exciting than road racing, and that has been successful.

The Olympics

I think a lot of people don't realize that track cycling is an Olympic event. It's not as big in America as it is in Europe, in Europe, cycling's *big*. The track's more oriented to America. It's fast, it's exciting, and it's right there in front of you. America has a lot of talented athletes, more than the Europeans do. We're slowly finding that out with programs like we have

in Trexlertown, which found me.

There are other guys like me out there. They just don't know about it. There are a lot of kids who are into basketball, baseball, football, who may want to consider track cycling, especially if they have an Olympic dream. It's an individual sport, but people need to realize it's a tough sport. To become the best you've got to train harder than you'd ever imagine and harder than you ever would on the football field or Spring training in baseball.

Track cycling is a different breed of people, people who like to train hard. So far, for how hard you train, the benefits haven't been that good. If I trained this hard and was a pro football player, the benefits would be incredible. I think that's going to change, especially if cycling makes a big impact in the Olympics.

Track Racing

People don't realize that track cycling was THE sport in the '20s. Thousands and thousands of people went to see it. They didn't go to the baseball games and the football games, they went to Madison Square Garden to watch track cycling. Hopefully we can bring that back to America. We're bringing back Rainbow Jerseys! (Two of them!)

Sooner or later track cycling will come around. I plan on helping it, winning some more titles and getting it some more exposure. It's getting better, but you've got to be one of the best in the world to do it. Before I was getting paid really well, I won eight National titles. You're still a peon. It really didn't matter being the best in

your country, you didn't get paid as much as you would have if you were in another sport and were the best in your country.

Then you become the best in the world and things change dramatically, numbers I didn't think were possible in bike racing. Numbers I had only heard of. That happened when LeMond first broke the ice. So it's possible that people can do well, but they can't expect to win Nationals and make a lot of money, because it's just not going to happen. You've got to be one of the best in the world. Demand is greater.

I've got to turn down more races than I race in Europe when I'm offered easily over $1000 a day to race. I'm saying no because I want to stay home. It would be different if, for the next six days I had to go to Chicago. I'd definitely go then, but it's not available. It's not as fun to go overseas. You're around 15,000 people a night, but you still feel alone.

There are a lot of people hunting me down. This year has been a very good year. My foot still hurts, but I'm really motivated to train. I allow myself a two week break out of the year when I go hunting and I relax. That's my break for the year, then it's back to training really, really hard again.

I start by lifting weights, swimming -- I do quite a bit of swimming in my program. I also do road miles, cross training -- I tell Gibby that we have to make it interesting and fun to train.

I really enjoy training. We have a great training group. Gibby keeps us motivated. Most of the time you're dry heaving, thinking you're going to throw up, but you're enjoying it. Everybody jokes around and I train with my friends. After the work-out's over the only thing I do is shower and go to bed. I'm exhausted. I become a nasty person and crabby.

I haven't changed because of my success. Nothing has. I love the sport and winning so much that if I'd won the World Championships and got nothing out of it, I'd still race it again. Winning makes my life easier, but if I hadn't gotten anything out of it, just being able to label yourself the World's Fastest Man is something money can't buy.

When I travel I like to be alone. It makes me hungrier, meaner, and a better racer. I don't have to worry about things. I know what's at home and I know I'm going to get home and I know I'm going to be victorious. I do a lot of winning for my family.

When I go to compete I am very focused. It's usually just Gil (Gibby). He knows how to get me fired up and when to stay away from me. If my girlfriend or my mom or dad comes, they don't really realize -- well, Kristy races, she kind of knows, but other people don't understand that one second you might be nice and the next second, just stay away. It's hard to explain.

I don't know if other people are like that or not. There are people who want to go out and walk around, but that's absolutely crazy for me, I could never do that. I lay in my bed all day and get ready to race. I don't like to

be alone, but there's a time for it and that's when I'm racing.

The Future

I'd like to race another 10 years. I know I haven't hit my prime yet. I know I have some weaknesses to fix, mainly physical. I think I can get stronger, I think I can get faster. I've got to fix a few things in my riding style.

Mentally, everything's there. I've got that, and that's mostly what Sprinting is. At least half of it's mental. It's tough for me to say, being World Champion, but I know I can make myself even better and faster.

I want to help this sport. I want to promote track cycling. It's going to benefit me, but it's also going to benefit a lot of other riders. I think it's getting better recognition now. I've been in every publication for the last few issues, but it still needs more.

We still need good racing programs like we have in Trexlertown. It's a great spectator sport. It's very oriented toward American culture, especially the Sprints and Keirin, the fast paced events with lots of action. There's bumping and hitting. The Madisons are fun and neat to watch.

I've been to road races and watched Dupont. It's like "Zoom . . . there they go. Now, let's drive another 45 minutes to see them again." I didn't enjoy it at all, and I'm a cyclist!

I go to these Six Day races in Europe and go into the arenas. I look at this little 200 meter track with 52° banking and think "This is incredible! No wonder 15,000 people a night come and watch this!"

Marty and Jeff Solt raced to a most unusual four rides in 1994 due to protests on both sides. Finally, it was "winner take all". Though Solt took the prize, Nothstein qualified for the Pan Am team, his main goal (and got mad enough to win Worlds!)

July, 1994. "So Gary, where'd you say I could pick up one of those cool Rainbow jerseys? The World Championships next month? Oh, okay, I think I'll go do that. Thanks for the info."
By August, he had two.

The intrepid Sean and Bill. These guys did the lion's share of the grunt work putting the velodrome together. Those Midwesterners were amazing.

John Vande Velde is a person of great faith who loves his sport. The building and touring of a portable track has been a lifelong dream -- a dream that became a reality in 1995.

The Vandedrome was built in the belief that Americans are ready for a revival of the wooden track racing tradition so popular in the U.S. in the '20s and '30s. It is the world's first portable, expandable track and one of the steepest tracks in the world with 53° banking. Design concept revisions occur daily with an eye to future track construction. It could revolutionize the sport of bicycle track racing forever.

With two sports networks begging for offerings and viewers seeking new forms of entertainment, Vande Velde is ready to show America what it's been missing.

Track racing is the most media-friendly form of bicycle racing. In Europe, thousands of fans pack stadiums, thrilling to the wooden ovals. In Japan, velodrome racing is a multi-billion dollar industry. Vande Velde is convinced that this form of bicycle racing is the best kept secret in sports.

The Beginnings

Vande Velde began his journey into bicycle racing history at age 14, following his father and uncle in the family tradition. Finding the scenery at the bottom of a swimming pool boring, he found that bicycle riding offered freedom to enjoy the beauty of the world.

At age 19, John was the youngest member of the 1968 Olympic cycling team. By 1972, after winning three National Champion Pursuit titles, he was the oldest.

Vande Velde remembers the times of no advocacy in bicycle racing. In 1969, he went to Czechoslovakia as National Champion and Captain of the World's team only to find out he could not race due to a clerical error which omitted his name from the official roster.

Jerry Rimoldi, American coach that year, found himself in the position of negotiator, but was unable to rectify the situation. There was no recourse.

After placing 12th in the Pursuit at the 1972 Olympics (the highest placing by an American in the Pursuit up to that time) Vande Velde decided to turn professional. He was one of nine riders, including Jack Simes III, Skip Cutting, Tim Mountford, Doug Downing, Tom Snedden, Butch Stinton, Bill Best, and Ray Matthews, to bravely attempt this transition. At that time, going Pro carried big risks including loss of amateur status and no support.

In his first professional criterium in Holland, Vande Velde was blown away (and off the back) by the speed of the race. Not only could he not keep up, he got nothing for his efforts and there was no other economic support.

"In my first Six-day with Jack Simes, I won simply because the banking on the European tracks was so steep that I was terrified!" Humbling experiences for a three time National

"My Best Dream" starring John VandeVelde. My son the Pan Am Gold Medalist, my portable velodrome. Life is good.

The debut of the Vandedrome took place in February of 1995 in Del Mar, California. The National Team just happened to be in town. The Sprinter's camp was nearby. The Pursuiter's camp was a little farther away and included John Vande Velde's son Christian. Hmmm . . . wonder if there could have been a connection . . . hmmm.

From the Vandedrome, the National Team went to the Pan Am Games, where they showed the world that America is ready for 1996. Fans in Del Mar got to see the best racing America has to offer! Great performances were recorded on film for PrimeSports and aired in March -- maybe you saw it! Lucky you. It was <u>great</u> fun. And, they'll be back!

Champion.

In 1973, Vande Velde raced a six week Six-day circuit comprising Detroit on Monday, Berlin on Wednesday, Montreal on Thursday, a quick trip the next Wednesday for a brief 2nd anniversary with his wife, then concluding his tour with trips to Frankfurt, Munich, Muenster and Zurich. He was exhausted. Vande Velde continued racing the Pro circuit until 1978, when he retired.

It's a Family Tradition

Vande Velde's family financed two professional Six-day races in Los Angeles which failed in the hands of a fraudulent promoter. Vande Velde's uncle tried again in Detroit, but sacrificed the track when a union work crew demanded $50,000 to disassemble it.

Still, the Vande Velde clan trudged on undefeated, convinced that America was right in its early fanaticism with bicycle track racing.

When John Vande Velde took his business partner, Pete Ferro, to Europe to witness a real indoor bicycle track race first hand, they sat in a velodrome with 15,000 screaming fans. Ferro needed no further convincing and lent his support to this thrilling but little known (in America) sport.

Trackies don't give up. Velodrome racing gets in your blood and aficionados know that it's only a matter of exposure for others to love it as much as they do. For those in this category, the Vandedrome's success means we will all be able to enjoy our favorite entertainment more often.

In 1994, Christian Vande Velde, John's son, won the National Points race Championship while trying to qualify for the Junior Worlds Team. In 1995, he won Gold in the Team Pursuit at the Pan American Games. Christian now wears the family racing mantle into the next generation. Watch for him in 1996! It's a family tradition.

Zac Copeland shows how horizontal riders get as they scream through the corners at 40 mph. Notice: his left arm is <u>inches</u> off of the apron!

Chapter 1

ʘ⌐o *Getting Started* ʘ⌐o

You sit at a velodrome watching the races. "Hey, this looks like fun! How do I get involved?" You may not realize that there are presently only about 20 velodromes in the United States, but you probably intuitively know that you must find a facility like this back home if the velodrome you're sitting in is not near your house. How will you find this out? You can start with this book.

Getting involved in velodrome racing can take many different forms, from actual racing (ages 10-60+) to volunteering to officiating -- and a whole lot more. Some activities are attached to glory and some completely unknown, but whatever level of involvement you want, it's available.

Track -where the hot action is!

Track enthusiasts have a difficult time understanding why track is not as popular in the media as road racing. It has to be an oversight. Spectating is much more exciting at a velodrome.

We don't need to interrupt our food breaks and watch the riders go by for a few seconds at 40 mph <u>every half hour</u>. Instead we have the opposite problem -- "I need to eat, but I don't want to miss anything! Get me something, will you? When's the next break?"

On the road, without close proximity to an announcer to keep abreast of the action, race progress and strategy are impossible for spectators to follow -- they can't see any of it! On the track, you can see <u>all</u> of it -- <u>all</u> the time!

If you sit at a velodrome reading this book and want to know more about track racing, just listen to those around you for someone who sounds like they know what they're looking at. Ask them <u>one</u> question. They'll be glad to share their expertise and will likely tell you all sorts of things that you may (or may not) want to know. In fact, they may get so excited at the prospect of a new convert to their passion, that you may need to invent some excuse to move away so you can once again watch the race in peace!

One problem for spectators new to the track is trying to understand what's going on. One race has two people, the next has twenty. Like any sport, it's not much fun if you don't understand the rules. After going to races at the track a few times you will start noticing a consistency in many of the events. Different velodromes emphasize different things. But still, unless you have a guide, what you see may not be clear.

At the National level certain events (like Mass Start races) are classic competitive events for which weekly racing may prepare riders. Other events (like the Kilometer) are not usually held on weekly race nights because they tend to be less exciting to crowds unless a new record attempt is going on or a special event has brought top competitors who are trying to win local area championships. "Scratch" races, and other Mass Start events, are crowd pleasers and allow many riders

Bicycle racing is a sport of legacy. Mike Myles, announcer at 1994 Junior Nationals, watched a familiar bicycle roll by. He told rider Brian Blanchard, "Take that sticker off the frame -- it says "The Rack" underneath." Brian removed the sticker and -- sure enough. Mike received the nickname from announcer Ralph Elliott in his own Junior racing days when he repeatedly sprinted for, and won, a succession of Blackburn racks used as Primes in San Diego. Now his bike was being raced at Junior Nationals in Seattle. Mike wanted to buy it back! Lots of memories in that frame. Moral of the story: You can replace the equipment, but you can't replace the memories.

to race at the same time, so they are the most common events on the track.

A velodrome can be an intimidating place. If nothing is going on during your first visit to a velodrome, imagining why it is constructed as it is might be a challenge. What do the lines mean? Why is it banked? What's the point? Surely there's some reason for its design. It looks intimidating but mysterious. Learning the reasons for markings and rules of different events is part of the fun.

If a big event is going on, a velodrome is <u>really</u> intimidating and exciting, because no one is allowed on the track unless they have business there. If there is no passageway, people <u>run</u> across when they are given permission, as though some great harm might befall them if they linger too long on the track surface. This implication of danger is valid. Officials want neither riders nor pedestrians to be injured (or killed!).

In Europe, Australia and Japan track racing is extremely popular. In the United States, most people have no idea what a velodrome is, much less how exciting it can be. The exciting sport of velodrome racing has been kept a secret too long.

What people need is a book about velodrome racing that they can understand. Hey! Good idea!

Racing

Actually <u>riding</u> the track may initially seem like something only "other people" do. Probably just Olympians and people like that. You may imagine some long apprenticeship necessary before entry onto the Golden Doors of the velodrome is possible. It may be easier than you think.

Getting started in track racing requires a velodrome and a track bicycle. Other race equipment (shoes, shorts, jersey, helmet) is fairly standard until higher levels of competition which might warrant adaptation for the specialized track events.

Even if you don't live close enough to a track to begin there, you can start riding with whatever opportunities are available. Most cities have a hard-core group of bicycle enthusiasts. Find them and begin by riding the roads. Road riding can teach valuable bike-handling skills needed on the track (and vice versa).

Look in the yellow pages for

Parental support is very important. Andy and Chris Coletta have no greater fan and supporter than their dad. They have progressed from interested kids to top competitors. Chris is a three time National Team Pursuit Champion. In 1994 Andy and Chris both medaled in the Kilometer. Chris (rt) won Best All-around Rider (BAR).

bicycle shop ads using the words "racing," "professional," and "expert". Local bicycling publications often leave off their monthly editions at bicycle shops and/or race promoters post flyers about upcoming events.

Other sources of information are local clubs or national organizations such as the United States Cycling Federation (1-719-578-4581), the

governing body for cycling competition in this country. There's always a way to get information if you're persistent.

If you are fortunate enough to live near one of the 20 velodromes in the United States (see "The Velodrome") and want to give it a try, your first move is to contact personnel at the track to find out what kinds of programs are offered. Many tracks have velodrome associations or employees to provide a governing body for programs and policy decisions (including how to get money and how to spend it). Many have training programs which will assist in preparing for competition. Some

require your participation in these training programs before you will be allowed to race at the facility. Ask.

Check the activities sections of local papers for the cycling events run by clubs in the area. These clubs, for tourists, racers and novices, are the best starting point for the beginner. There, a rider can gain experience riding in a group, and take advantage of senior members' knowledge and advice. Most clubs have one or more "guru", a person who has been in the sport for a life time and knows a tremendous amount. There is so much to know. The more you know the more you realize there is to know, especially in track racing.

If you can't think of any questions to ask, just hang around and listen. Bikies often make little comments which are basic to racing. You will learn just by being there. After you've raced a little, questions will be easier. In fact, they will take on a life of their own, you won't have to think of them, they'll just come to you.

After you find the local facility, your first step is to go and watch what's going on in the racing scene. If racing is happening, you have a ready entry into the world of velodrome racing. If it is an off-season time (winter), go when racing starts again.

Meanwhile, find out which clubs are involved with training on the track, if any. If none are, start with road events until things start happening at the track.

To race, all riders must have a license from the United States Cycling Federation. All riders are assigned to "Category 4" when they first get their

17

licenses. They advance through the ranks as they improve their racing and riding. Next they are Category 3, then 2, and finally, at the top of the amateur heap, Category 1.

Professionals are just that and are not rated like the amateur rankings.

it's all here. Pick your poison (or in this case, oxygen deprivation).

If you want to compete, seriously or just for fun, this book will tell you all you want to know about velodrome racing and its possibilities. The rest is up to you.

catching, they are not reliable predictors of performance.

Watching a lean "little guy" like J'Me Carney versus a Goliath like Ken Carpenter may have led observers to bet privately on Carpenter. In a Sprint, they'd keep their money, but in a Points race their money would be gone long before the race was half over! What's surprising is that even in a Sprint, Carney would not be far behind because he is an incredible talent. Physical size or anticipated strength are deceptive when endurance and mental strategies come into play.

Age Categories

Within the past few years, age has ceased to be a barrier. National Championships exist for all ages, male and female. Juniors are 10 - 18 in two year categories. Seniors are from age 19 to 29 all competing together and Masters is from age 30 to 60+ and beyond in five year categories. Some National Senior Champions are in their early thirties, so competition is excellent at the Masters level.

Excitement

Don't want to race but looking for a fun and on-going activity? The track needs you! The seasonality of racing offers in an on-going series of revolving duties, so things are always changing and never boring. There's always work to do.

You may want to try riding the track just to learn and understand more about what you are watching. That's worthy

and valuable and will add to your viewing pleasure. Understanding deepens with a breadth of experience.

If you don't want to ride but are interested in participating in any way you can, think of what you have to offer. All sorts of jobs are available, and the ones which are most needed are sometimes jobs that are not in evidence (like my job -- writing this book!)

Almost every person represented in this book has had experience on the velodrome and each person shares their beginning with you. Some of them have had spectacular careers. Others have taken an alternate route, enjoying

This is definitely one of the most pleasurable jobs on the velodrome: awarding prizes to the winners. The loving faces on the left are Sprinter Greg Carlson's parents. They are some of Indianapolis' (and their sons Greg and Andy's) greatest supporters.

Volunteers are essential to great track racing events.

See the USCF RuleBook for how to advance. You don't need to worry about that in the beginning. The top riders will be Pros, "1"s, or "2"s.

Got a sprint? We've got races for you. Like strategy/mind games? We have races for you. Have good endurance? We've got 'em. Short distance, long distance, sprints, varied pace, team effort, individual effort,

There is no one "right" physical type for track racing. The variety of cycling events and the mechanical advantage of the machine means that anyone with the urge to ride hard (and the discipline to stick to a training program) can compete at some level on the bicycle. Spectators see all sorts of shapes and sizes on the track and while the differences may be eye-

Volunteers get to see the races for free (later).

their own level of participation as much (or maybe more) than the Champions. If you want glory, some of them can tell you a lot about that. But that need not be the purpose or the focus of your involvement.

Every track can use fund-raising assistance. There is a never-ending list of labors on the facility itself. The infield requires constant maintenance. Someone has to sign up the riders, someone must sell the refreshments and souvenirs. All tracks need officials if races are going on. If you hang out, you'll see things that are needed.

Each track event requires it's own routine and associated personnel, such as sponge monitors for Time Trial events. There's the sound crew, the ticket takers (if the track is active enough), the decorations folks, the clean-up crew and lots of miscellaneous jobs. Many hours of unknown people power go into planning every event before it ever happens. Volunteer -- you'll get a job.

Involvement with clubs and friends make for a lot of fun, whichever road you take. Programs have greatly expanded at many velodromes, so loaner track bicycles may be available for new riders, or the curious, to try at

set times. Some tracks even offer helmets.

For kids, track racing offers discipline and challenge. For them too there are jobs both on and off the track. They can be part of things or play nearby while you're enjoying the racing.

Whatever your level or interest, there's something for you to take seriously or just do for fun. As Announcer Ralph Elliott says, "It's not whether you win or lose, but how much fun you have!"

I waited for someone to write this book. Someone needed to do it but no one was. And so, I assigned it to myself as my job. See how easy it is? So, what's your job? What do you see that needs to be done?

Track racing becomes a life style. It's healthy, it's clean, and it requires intellect, knowledge and skill -- just the kind of activity to activate all the senses. The Sprints make your heart stop. When someone tries to lap the field, it's tension all the way. There's such heart in this sport; every year begins with new hopes and dreams. There's always something to do.

So now, if you develop the inclination, look around with your brain in gear. Hang out, ask questions that come to you. Listen, and observe.

What do *you* have to offer? It will come to you. And when it does, don't hesitate --

Velodrome racing needs you!

It can start here . . .

. . .and end (or begin again!) here.

Making the Olympic Team is many a track rider's dream. Carl Sundquist, a veteran Olympian, wastes no time in expressing his joy as Rebecca Twigg and Erin Hartwell work on their corks. Riders' celebrations belong to everyone who has made their dreams possible.

Chapter 2

०ᵛ०　*The Velodrome*　०ᵛ०

Dominguez Hills Velodrome was built in 1982-3 for the 1984 Olympic Games. The United States won eight medals on this track, an unprecedented victory. Dominguez Hills remains a world class track awaiting competition of Olympians of the future. Note the stage on the infield (right). Velodromes are seeking alternate income in order to survive. They are expensive facilities to maintain (and they're worth it!).

Velodromes get in your blood. The elegant sweep of the banking gives structure to the racing events, adding intellectual challenge to the speed and power of rider and machine.

Riders learn to use the banking and its various zones to pass and surprise the competition. It matters not only how steep the surface is, but also which turn the rider is in. Those who understand the strategies of the different events can use this knowledge to win, even against opponents who are superior in strength or speed.

Watching the different events with a knowledgeable announcer or a well-informed friend can quickly allow you to see how highly developed is the skill of experienced riders as they make the choices which succeed.

Part of the glamor of velodrome racing is the seeming simplicity of the challenge made complex by choices which will determine the victor. The machine alone, no matter how sophisticated, cannot determine the outcome.

Velodrome racers are proud to ride one of the simplest transportation devices ever invented. The challenge becomes man against man, woman against woman. While slight differences in the basic machine may make a small difference to those at the pinnacle of competition, most bicycles are pretty much the same. Any differences in horsepower result from the athlete him/herself.

Race strategies can be extremely sophisticated and often revolve around where the rider is, both on the track and in the race. This is the reason that, in track racing, a coach is very important; crucial for those wanting to achieve at top levels.

A Sprinter, for instance, will use all parts of the track while a Points racer will stay low. A Kilo rider does not have to worry about anyone except him/herself, but will stay at the bottom of the track at all times.

A Madison rider must not only move up and down the track in synch with his partner, he must also be aware of the speed and exchanges of other teams as they move up and down the banking. Successful Team Pursuit teams use the banking regularly and efficiently as an integral part of racing technique over each half lap.

To understand how the track itself is used in the races, you must first understand the structure of the arena. You must know what the lines mean and why they are drawn where they are. In order to understand the strategies in using track features to win races, you must understand the rules and goals for each event. This information is contained within the sections following this one.

All velodromes are basically set up the same because they must follow international rules. Variations may be seen in construction materials, layout and amenities, but lines must all be the same. Numbers and details may vary, but zones are always the same. This chapter contains the information needed to "read" the track.

Velodrome Structure

There are approximately 20 velodromes in the United States, most active, some technically closed. Half are 333.33 meters around. Two are 250 meters, one is 153m. The rest are varying sizes up to 400 meters. Banking varies from 17 degrees to 53 degrees. Two are owned privately, the rest are public and therefore must satisfy municipal demands which may be of disadvantage to the track's functioning.

All velodromes are set up similarly to the one pictured here. Lines are painted permanently on the track according to USCF rules, denoting various zones and start/stop areas. All lines are to be the same width, between 4 and 6 cm.

•Warm-up track

A **warm-up track** is a luxury not all tracks have. All tracks should have the other components shown.

•Apron

The **apron** is flat. Its purpose is for riding before and after a race to get into position and to exit from an event. Some aprons are very narrow. Others are extremely broad.

Parallel ovals:

•Blue band

A **blue band** is painted below the inner edge of the track and must be at least 20 centimeters wide. It can be wider and often is. The apron usually extends beyond this line.

•Measurement/Pole line

20 centimeters from the inside edge of the track is a black or white line (whichever contrasts more with

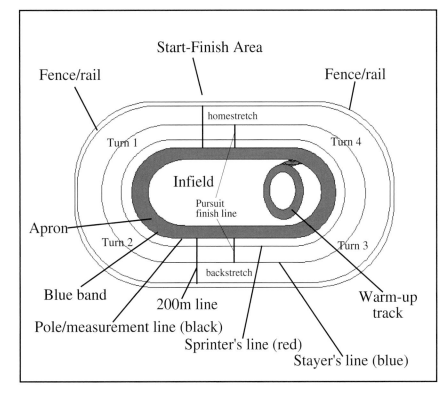

Start-Finish Area
Fence/rail
homestretch
Turn 1
Turn 4
Infield
Pursuit
finish line
Apron
Turn 2
Turn 3
backstretch
Blue band
200m line
Warm-up track
Pole/measurement line (black)
Sprinter's line (red)
Stayer's line (blue)

the color of the track) called the **Measurement Line.**

The distance of the track is measured on the inner edge of this line, also known among riders as the **Pole Line.** The track is marked at this line every five meters and numbered every 10 meters beginning at the finish line and moving counterclockwise around the track.

•Sprinter's line

90 centimeters above the inner edge of the track is the outer edge of the **Sprinter's Line,** painted red and so named because rules of the Sprint relate to a zone between this and the black line. The final 200 meters before

the finish line is used for timing Sprints over this distance during qualifying events. During competition, only one Sprinter is allowed in this zone during the Sprint. Once in it, s/he must stay unless s/he has "a clear lead".

•Stayer's line

The highest line on the track is the **Stayer's Line,** named for the vehicle used in the Motorpace event common in Europe but not in the United States. This line is not required by the USCF Rule Book, but is included as a guide to riding zones and is usually painted blue. Above this line, riders are expected to ride more slowly unless a race is actually taking place.

Perpendicular lines:

•Finish Line

The **Finish Line** is painted black on a white strip 72 centimeters wide in order that it be clear and distinct. This also helps in photo-finishes. The side of the track on which this line is painted is the **Homestretch.**

•200 Meter line

The **200 Meter Line** can be either black or white, whatever is in most contrast to the color of the track surface. No matter what size the track, this line will be placed 200 meters prior to the finish line. While the purpose of this line is officially for Sprint timing only, riders are constantly aware of this line as part of their race strategy. The side of the track upon which this line is usually painted is called the **Backstretch** (333m track).

•Pursuit finish lines

Pursuit Finish Lines are painted on each side of the track exactly in the middle, no matter what size the track. They are always red. They begin on the inner edge of the track and extend half way across the straight, no matter how wide the track. They are always on both the homestretch and the backstretch.

While these lines are used strictly as finish lines for the Kilometer and Pursuit events, riders are also aware of these lines as designators of the half-way point around the track.

Sometimes the Pursuit Finish Lines do not coordinate with where the start lines need to be in order to complete the 3000 meter and 4000 meter distance. In those cases, a red line is painted wherever the event is to start, extending from the inner edge of the track to the Sprinter's Line.

Riding the track

A velodrome can be a very safe place if all riders conduct themselves with a little thought and structure. Riding the track with someone who moves up and down the track unexpectedly and rides in the wrong zones can be quite dangerous. Track etiquette is therefore very important for everyone to understand.

If you commit a breach of track etiquette, riders will usually set you straight pretty quickly. It is for this reason that it is good to start out with a club or coach or some other group that will teach you the basics before you try to get out there and embarrass yourself, if not injure yourself and maybe others.

Track enthusiasts *want* you to take part, and safely, so they are happy to show you the ropes. All you have to do is find out who is conducting training and when.

All the lines on the track give structure to the track's surface in order for riders to understand where they are supposed to be in certain times of both training and racing.

During training times, **faster riders are expected to be at the bottom of the track** below the Stayer's Line if not the Sprinter's Line. **Slower riders are expected to stay above the Stayer's line or higher.**

Paceline

A **Paceline** is a long line of riders moving at a steady pace, each rider on the wheel and in the draft of the rider ahead. If a Paceline is going, it is usually at the bottom of the track.

Riders changing the lead will swing uptrack at the corner, riding straight instead of turning with the line. The Paceline is allowed to pass, then the rider swings down on the back of the Paceline, usually before the next corner. Each successive rider does this, usually in full or half-laps.

In training, riders swing off and on at will. The length of the ride just depends on who wants to do the pace of the group and for how long.

Riders joining the Paceline, move onto the back of it or move down into a gap. Riders leaving the Paceline usually quit after pulling uptrack during a change of lead.

Riders can just pull out, but that leaves the riders behind having to bridge the gap. Since Pacelines work best when speed is constant, this is not preferred.

A Paceline generally starts out very slowly. It is usually a smooth ride that becomes progressively faster, depending on who is in the group. At the end, there are usually only a few riders going very fast.

Motorpacing

If riders are **Motorpacing**, they ride in back of a derny or motorcycle in order to go faster in a larger draft (not to be confused with the Motorpace event which is not usually raced in this country.) Motorpacing riders often ride at the Stayer's Line unless a group is all doing Motorpacing as a workout, in which case they may use the bottom of the track where other riders will not

If other riders are training on the track, Motorpacing will usually be kept uptrack at the Stayer's line to keep out of everyone's way.

If riders are warming up or working out together, Motorpacing may be done downtrack on the measurement line. The pace increases steadily.

be trying to ride at the same time.

Since track bikes have no brakes and one speed, quick changes in acceleration and deceleration can be unnerving. Other riders appreciate gradual changes when wheels are inches from each other in a line up.

Quick moves are hazardous.

Training

In an organized track workout, coaches will divide the workout into different types of activities. It may be the kinds of things riders will be expecting to do in their events, it just depends on who the riders are and who is leading the workout. In general, lower level riders will do more generalized activities while top level riders will work on more specific things, just like in any physical training.

Workouts often begin with a Paceline because everyone needs to warm up and it only makes sense to do it slowly and steadily. Riding in a Paceline is also good training because it requires riding with other people in front of and behind you.

Everyone will learn to do "Flying 200s" at some point, both for training and as part of an interval workout. Other distances of intervals will relate to events for which the rider is training. Usually there is some kind of routine broken up into parts to teach bike handling skills, rules of particular races, practice competitions, etc., depending on the mission of the work-

out. It may change every week.

Different coaches emphasize different things and there will be no second guessing of that variety of activities here. Suffice to say, if your coach has been around for a while, has participated in coaching clinics, has been a competitor or has trained riders who have done well, you can learn a lot from him/her.

If you keep going to the track, you will know who to ride with and they will know you. One thing is true: you will never know it all.

Racing

When races are held, only competitors are expected on the track. If you usually train on a track where a National Championship is being held, you *may* get permission to ride when competitors are not there, but don't expect it and don't expect to do your own training during the time of the

event. Competitors have absolute priority. Officially, no one is allowed on the track but competitors.

Even competitors are restricted in the times they are allowed on the track during Championships. If warm-up time for Sprints is occurring, for instance, Madison riders are not expected to be practicing at that time. Priority is given to those whose event is pending. All others are to be off the track at that time. There may be training periods which are open to all competitors, usually early in competition or between sessions.

General Track Race Conduct

Certain standard "track race etiquette" rules apply which are the same for any Mass Start race. A leader is expected to stay below the Sprinter's line unless s/he chooses to move uptrack *when s/he can do so without impeding other riders.*

If the leader is below the Sprinter's line, other riders may not pass underneath. If the leader is above the Sprinter's line, others may pass underneath, otherwise riders overtaking are expected to pass on the right (uptrack). Riders behind must not be impeded by actions of riders in front.

The finish of a race is hotly contested. All riders are expected to ride a straight line on the homestretch, parallel to the edge of the track.

While riders may ride within the small zone below the black line, they must not ride on the blue band unless they are entering or leaving the track. Using the blue band to improve position in a race is prohibited.

Officials will watch with some degree of understanding that riders

may momentarily drop into the blue band in order to avoid a collision. Riders are going very fast. Judgement is on intent. If a rider is just disregarding rules, s/he will be penalized. If the move was for purposes of safety, officials don't want to discourage safe riding. Often officials were riders themselves and understand conditions.

If there is a crash which presents a danger to other riders, the race will be "neutralized" by the Starter. At this time, riders are to ride at the top of the track at a steady pace and maintain their position. When the crash is no longer a danger to others, the race can be restarted by the Starter. If officials feel that a crash is not a threat to others, the race need not be neutralized.

Riders who suffer a mishap (blown tire, equipment failure, etc.) may receive assistance in restarting within a reasonable time period. In all situations on the track which endanger riders, officials must walk the line between enforcing the rules and maintaining fairness to all competitors.

Part of the conduct of races involves the structure of the velodrome itself. Rules govern zones where certain activities are expected to happen. Riders are expected to cooperate for the safety of everyone.

Other rules apply for the specialty events. The rules quoted here are general rules for situations where many riders are on the track. See the individual events for track conduct during those events.

Once you understand the various zones and what the lines tell riders, much of what happens on the track makes more sense.

Slower riders are expected to ride above the Stayer's line while faster riders are expected to ride below it. Pacelines will be at the bottom of the track. This group is just forming a Paceline and will be dropping to the bottom of the track.

Velodromes in the United States

West:

1. Marymoor (Seattle)
2. Alpenrose (Portland)
3. Encino (Los Angeles)
4. Dominguez Hills (LA)
5. Hellyer Park (San Jose)
6. San Diego

Central:

7. 7-Eleven Oly/Co. Spgs (Denver)
8. Alkek (Houston)
9. Baton Rouge
10. St. Louis (closed, 1994)
11. National Sports Center
   Blaine (Minneapolis)

12. Washington Bowl Park /
   Kenosha (Milwaukee)
13. Brown Deer (Milwaukee)
14. Northbrook (Chicago)
15. Vandedrome Portable (Chicago)
16. Major Taylor (Indianapolis)
17. Dorais (Detroit)

East:

18. Kissena (New York City)
19. Lehigh (Allentown)
20. Dick Lane (Atlanta)
21. Piccolo Park (Ft. Lauderdale)
   Olympic Velodrome (temp) Atlanta
23-100 The "Mystery" Velodromes

West

① Marymoor Velodrome

Chris Smith
1535 - 11th Ave., #302
Seattle, WA 98122
(206) 389-5825

Marymoor Velodrome is named for the Park in which it was built in 1976 at a cost of $169,000. It is also known as "Redmond" for the town where it is located. It is owned by King County and governed by the Marymoor Velodrome Association. It has been quite active in recent years, partly due to good volunteers.

Marymoor is a 400 meter concrete track with 25 degree banking on the turns and 5 degree banking on the straights. Marymoor has an active track program with permanent seating, lighting and a warm-up track. Loaner bicycles are available for use in training classes, required before racing here. Racing Thursday and Friday nights. Concessions are temporary, infield access by gate, good parking.

Significant events: Senior National Championships in 1977, 1986, 1989, 1991 (Pan Am Trials). Goodwill Games 1990 (4000+ spectators). Master's Nationals 1992, Junior Nationals 1994.

② Alpenrose Velodrome

Mike Murray
4318 SE 8th Court
Gresham, OR 97080
(503) 661-5874

The Alpenrose Velodrome was rebuilt on the site of a dairy in 1967 to host the U.S. National Championships. Prior to 1967 there was a bumpy asphalt track on the site. It is a 269 meter (1/6 mi.) oval track, 22 feet wide, built of concrete with ±45 degree banking. Straights are long, corners short, guided by old Schwinn formulas which were further shortened, making transitions abrupt.

The velodrome is owned by Alpenrose Dairy and run by the Portland Velodrome Committee, with weekly racing events and a developmental track program offering loaner bicycles. It has seating for 250, parking, track access by ladder and temporary concessions. In a park complex with baseball, quarter-midget car track and rodeo. One of two privately owned tracks in the country.

Significant events: Senior Nationals, 1967 and 1971. Master's Nationals, 1989.

The "criterium course with banking" Jeanna calls it (but we love it), 400m Marymoor Velodrome, the largest track in America. Gary Neiwand (Australia) takes the lead at the start of a Sprint against Curt Harnett (Canada), during Goodwill Games, 1990. There has been, and continues to be, great racing here (when it's not raining!).

③ Hellyer Park Velodrome

Casey Kerrigan
985 Hellyer Ave.
San Jose, CA 95111
(408) 226-9716/ (510) 531-1400

The Hellyer Park Velodrome is named for the park where it is located, in the city of San Jose near San Francisco. It was built of concrete around 1962-63. The exact distance is 335.75 (336) meters with 22 1/2 degree banking. Infield access is by gate, seating for up to 600. Lighting allows racing Friday nights from May through August, Wednesday training races April through August.

The San Jose Mercury News used to have a reporter whose job was specifically to cover bicycle racing events (where is he?? Let's get him back!).

Significant Events: '71 Pan Am Trials, '75 Junior Worlds Trials, '86 Madison Nationals.

The sweep of the track has an elegance about it. Dominguez Hills, site of the 184 Olympic Games, is an excellent site with great racing and top competitors. A spring racing program is popular.

④ Encino Velodrome

Rick Denman
P.O. Box 16006
Encino, CA 91416
(818) 899-2648

Encino is named after the city where it is located, a suburb of Los Angeles. It was built around 1960-62. It is a 250 meter concrete track with 28° banking. Infield access is by gate. Concession stands are permanent and it has both lighting and parking.

Training is on the following schedule: USCF training on Mondays, motorpacing on Wednesdays, racing on Friday nights. Adult training: Tuesdays and Saturday mornings.

Encino has long been a very active track with top level training and racing programs and regular special events throughout the season.

Significant events: Pan Am Trials, 1963. U.S. National Championships 1965, 1968.
Far West Championships were BIG.

⑤ Olympic Velodrome California State University -Dominguez Hills

The Olympic Velodrome at Cal State Dominguez Hills was built in 1982-3 for the Olympic Games. It is a "standard" 333.33 meter concrete track owned by the University. It has track access by tunnel and two gates, excellent lighting, seating and parking, permanent concession stands, an active track program.

Nick Curl
1000 East Victoria
Carson, CA 90747
(310) 516-4000

In a search for varied funding, Dominguez has also hosted rock concerts on site and has plans for other varied activities to assist in supporting it's track racing program. Spring racing series are planned.

Significant events: Olympic Festival, U.S/U.S.S.R. Challenge, Nationals 1983, Olympic Games 1984.

There's been some great racing in San Diego, especially when 1984 Olympians were in training.

⑥ San Diego Velodrome

San Diego Velodrome Association
Walt Spieth, President
2221 Morley Field Dr.
San Diego, CA 92104
(619) 296-3345

San Diego Velodrome has never been called by any other name. It is a 333.33 meter track, built of concrete in 1976 with banking of 27 degrees. It is owned by the San Diego Parks and Recreation Department, run by the San Diego Velodrome Association. Infield access by gate, seating simple, but permanent, concessions are temporary. Parking is distant. Ralph Elliott announcing.

San Diego has various training programs including one with the Amateur Athletic Foundation for kids coached by Tony Olsen and Danny Van Haute. Racing season(s) are March to June, Aug. to Oct.

Significant events: Senior U.S. National Championships 1949 (old track) and 1980 (all categories), Master's Nationals 1990, 1991, Master's World Cup, 1990, 1991, Junior Nationals, 1990.
(and, new surface in 1995!)

Central ⑦

USOC 7-Eleven Velodrome

U.S. Olympic Committee
One Olympic Plaza
Colorado Springs, CA 80909
Mark Songer
(719) 634-8356 / 578-4894

The 7-Eleven Olympic Velodrome was named for it's main sponsor. It is a 333.33 meter track of concrete with 33 degree banking, built in Memorial Park in 1982-83. Infield access is by tunnel and gate. Lighting is excellent, concessions are temporary, parking is good, seating for 800, and a warm-up track. On site are a permanent complex with an office structure, seating, an officials tower, bicycle facilities and many other amenities for World class competition.

Colorado Springs is most noted for high altitude training and World Records, many of which were set during the 1986 World Championships. It is also home for the U.S. National Cycling Team while they are housed at the Olympic Training Center.

Significant events: Olympic Festival 1983, Master's Nationals 1984, World Championships 1986, Pan Am Trials, 1987, Junior Nationals 1989, Junior World Championships 1991, Master's Nationals 1993, World Cup Finals, 1994.

When an event is standing room only all around the velodrome, it must be a hot one. International events are always exciting. World Cup Finals, 1994

Colorado Springs has a reputation for being "the" place in the U.S. if you want to set a record. You can use a bigger gear due to less air resistance. The altitude bothers some people. Great racing here.

⑧ Alkek Velodrome

City of Houston Parks and
Recreation Dept.
Kathy Volski
18203 Groeschke
Houston, TX 77084
(713) 578-0693

Alkek Velodrome was named after Mr. Albert Alkek. It is located in Cullen Park, in Houston and run by the Parks and Recreation Department. It was built of concrete in 1986 at a cost of ± $1 million dollars. It is a 333.33 meter track with banking of 33°, 9 degrees on the straights. Infield access is by tunnel and gate. Alkek has lighting and parking with temporary concessions. Friday night racing runs from March to early June and mid-August to mid-October. It is open year 'round, parking available.

Alkek is one of the more active tracks in the country with USCF sponsor EDS nearby. Strong development programs and many top local riders.

Significant events: Olympic Festival 1986, Master's Nationals 1987, Olympic Trials, 1988, Junior Nationals 1991, USA/USSR Challenge 1991, EDS Grand Prix 1993-95, Junior Nationals, 1995.

⑨ St. Louis Velodrome

St. Louis Velodrome Association
1550 Eastham / P.O. Box 41011
St. Louis, MO 63146
(314) 434-7357

The Penrose Park Velodrome is named after the park where it is located. It was built in 1962 at a cost of $12,000. It is 1/5 mile (±323m), 28 degree banking, blacktop surface. It has no lighting and no concessions, but there is parking. There is no seating and no budget. Infield access is by crossing the track. It is owned by the St. Louis Park Department.

While there has been training and a race series from April to September in the past, the track has recently been officially closed due to lack of maintenance and crime in the area. Too bad. But -- where there's a track, there's hope! Sounds like a work crew job.

Significant events: Nationals 1962. Other Nationals were in St. Louis in 1925, '36, '53.

⑩ Baton Rouge Velodrome

East Baton Rouge Parks and
Recreation
Debbie Spica / Mark Landry
P.O. Box 15887
Baton Rouge, LA 70895
Debbie Spica - 504-273-6400
(504) 273-6404

Baton Rouge Velodrome is a 333.33 meter track, built of concrete with 33° banking. It is open for training for experienced riders Tues, Weds and Thurs nights; for developmental riding Saturday mornings and Tues and Thurs nights. Saturday night racing runs from April through October on alternate weeks. Track is open to in-line skating Tues eves and Sat aft. Open for radio-controlled cars Sat & Sun.

One of the newer tracks, it has been slower getting going than some. Activity has increased over the last year and a half. Here's a prime opportunity at a prime facility!

⑪ Edward Rudolph Meadowhill Velodrome

Northbrook Park District
Tony Calabrese
111 Waukegan Rd.
Northbrook, IL 60062
(708) 564-3993

Northbrook was built of asphalt in the early 60's with 17.5° banking. It has two measurement lines, one 382 m. (1/4 mi.) and another 400 meters. It has lighting, seating, concessions and parking. Infield access is by crossing the track.

Racing April to September is put on by the Northbrook Cycle Committee under the Northbrook Park District. Track bicycles are available to beginners in the development program. Northbrook's program continues to produce many top competitors. Great supporters there. Takes turns with Kenosha for weekly cream-of-the-crop riders.

Significant events: Nationals 1966, '73, '74, '75, '76, '79. Madison Championships, 1980.

⑫ **Washington Bowl Park Velodrome**

Marty and Carolyn Gauss
P.O. Box 836
Kenosha, WI 53141
(414) 652-7484
414-652-2522

The Washington Bowl Park Velodrome is named after the park in which it's located near Milwaukee. Locals call it "The Bowl" It is the oldest operating velodrome in the United States (1927) for continuous velodrome racing. The track is 333.3m with 23° of concrete, cigar shaped, with long straights and tight, shallow turns. It has lighting, parking nearby and natural seating on the hillside around the bowl in which it's built. Concessions are temporary and infield access is by gate. There is a warm-up track for riders. Takes turns with Northbrook for weekly cream-of-the-crop riders. Great supporters here, too.

Significant events: Nationals 1928, '30, '48, '57, '59, '72, '78, '82.

 ⑬ **National Sports Center Velodrome**

Barclay Kruse
1700 - 105th Ave. NE
Blaine, MN 55434
(612) 785-5600

The National Sports Center Velodrome was built for the 1992 Olympic Trials, designed like the velodrome in Barcelona where the Olympics would take place. It was built by the Schurmann brothers of Muenster, Germany of afzelia wood. It is a 250 meter track with 45° banking. Infield access is by tunnel, parking is nearby. Concessions are temporary. It has seating, lighting and a warm-up track along with track classes and loaner bicycles and helmets for beginners. Riders like this track because it's fast and smooth.

Significant events: Nationals/ Olympic Trials 1992; Master's World Cup, 1993, '94, '95. Collegiate Nationals, 1994 -- more soon!

National Sports Center Velodrome, Blaine, Minnesota. National Championships / Olympic Trials, 1992.

Indianapolis, "Indy's <u>other</u> oval," site of the 1993-95 National Championships

⑯ Dorais Velodrome

Mike Walden
P.O. Box 63
Royal Oak, MI 48068
(810) 545-1225

Named for a coach of the Detroit Lions, Dorais is not a rideable track at this time. It is 312m., 26° or so, built of concrete in 1969 for Nationals by a grass roots group from the Wolverine Sports Club (you too can build your own with local talent!) No amenities . Significant events: Nationals 1969.

⑭ Major Taylor Velodrome

Dick Kelly/Phil Stephens/Phil Rust
3649 Cold Springs Rd.
Indianapolis, IN 46222
(317) 926-8350

Major Taylor Velodrome was named for America's first black World Champion in 1899. It is a 333.33 concrete track with 28.5° banking, 11.5 on the straights. It was built in 1981 at a cost of $2.5 million. Infield access is by tunnel and gate. Permanent parking, lights, seating, TV lighting, satellite up-link and concessions. Good facility, great volunteers.

The velodrome is run by velodrome staff under the Indianapolis Parks and Recreation Department. Friday night racing May to September. Loaner bicycles and helmets are available, as is a development program for ages 8 and up. The U.S. National Track Championships found a home here through 1995.

Significant events: Madison Champs 1983, '85, '88, '89, Master's Nationals 1983, '86, '88, Nationals 1985, '93, '94, and '95. Junior Nationals '92, Collegiate Nationals, '93

It's exciting to watch riders warm up and know you'll soon be watching the best racing America has to offer. Like Dominguez Hills, Indy is opening the velodrome to other events in order to survive. In the foreground you can see the effects of having midget auto racing on the velodrome. The apron is extra wide, but it is now covered with the build up from the racing tires. It benefits the bicycle program, but takes its toll on the track.

Yes, it really is that steep! Some classicists (including Jeanna) consider this kind of velodrome the only <u>real</u> bicycle racing track. Vandedrome portable, Del Mar, 1995

⑮ Vandedrome Portable Track

John Vande Velde/F&V Spts Mktg
P.O. Box 156
Joliet, IL 60434-0156
(815) 726-6373 / fax: 726-5614

The newest track in America. Three time Pursuit Champion John Vande Velde and partner Pete Ferro are giving America what they know it needs: a true, steep, portable track. A variable 126 to 153 meters with 53° banking and 18 degree straights, constructed of 2" spruce.

Debut was February, 1995, and what a time we had! Vande Velde plans to do it right with Madison and Team racing, a beer garden and dining on site. Racing for three hours. Scheduled events: the best track racing you've ever seen. PrimeSports televised the first race March 5, 1995. Watch for more!! (see *Special Event*)

East

⑰ Dick Lane Velodrome

Lowell Hallams
1431 Norman Berry Dr.
East Point, GA 30344
(404) 765-1085
Joe Stallworth (404) 765-1077

This Velodrome was built in 1976 and named after Dick Lane. It is made of concrete, 323.13 meters and 33°. It has lighting, seating and parking nearby. Concessions are temporary. Access to the infield is by gate. There is no warm-up track. Showers and bicycle storage are available for athletes.

While this track is in disrepair, it has had good racing within the last few years.

Significant events: ESPN showed the Sundance Gran Prix racing here a few years ago with some top people (Carpenter, Swift, Harnett). No Nationals.

Lehigh Velodrome has been home to some of the greatest racing in the United States.

Donna H. Chiarelli photo, courtesy of Lehigh Velodrome

⑱ Kissena Velodrome

Peter Senia
44 Clifford St.
Lynnbrook, NY 11563
(516) 593-7939

Kissena is a 1/4 mile track with 17° banking built in 1963 in an industrial corridor. It is publicly owned, made of asphalt. It has no lighting, benches for seating, parking for 150 cars, sound system provided by Peter Senia. The track is bumpy and badly in need of repair. Yet Kissena still produces riders who perform well at the National level.

Kissena was built in an area slated for a future development which never occurred. Location: Parsons Blvd & Booth Memorial Ave., Flushing, Queens. The city has done little to keep up the velodrome or its surrounding area, yet the hard-core locals persist in using the facility for training and Wednesday night racing. This track is a survivor and so is Senia ('65 Jr. Champ).
Active 1963 - '85. Yearly highlight: Labor Day racing.

Significant events: Nationals 1964, '70

⑲ Lehigh County Velodrome

Nancy Neely/Pat McDonough
217 Main St.
Emmaus, PA 18049
(610) 967-7587

While named Lehigh County Velodrome, it is usually just called T-Town (Trexlertown). This is undoubtedly the most active track in the country, possibly the world, due to excellent sponsorship by Rodale Press, Lehigh Co. and others.

It was built of concrete for $500,000 on land donated by Robert Rodale in 1975. It is 333.33 meters around and 27°. T-Town has added lighting, seating, parking, concessions, and an overhead walkway for access to the infield. In addition, it has a scoreboard, grants for support and International racing. Great personnel turns out great riders. **Home of 1994 World Sprint and Keirin Champion Marty Nothstein and coach Gibby Hatton.**

Significant events: Madison Champs 1980, Professional 1983, Nationals 1981, '84, '87, '90, Master's Nationals 1985, Junior Nationals 1988, '93, Olympic Cup yearly, Fastest Man on Wheels, Tandem, Sprint, Keirin racing. **Site of the 1996 Olympic Trials/National Championships!!**

(20) Brian Piccolo Park Velodrome

Brian Piccolo Park
Pat Mason
9501 Sheridan Street
Cooper City, FL 33024
(305) 437-2600 Ed Hall 437-2626

This is America's newest permanent track, built of concrete in 1993 in Piccolo Park near Ft. Lauderdale at a cost of over $1 million. It measures 333.33 meters with 30° banking and a warm-up track. It had temporary seating for Master's Nationals. It has lighting, parking, an in-line skating track on the infield that doubles as a warm-up track, and a tunnel for access to the infield.

Significant events: Master's Nationals 1994.

(21) Brown Deer Park

Brown Deer Park is yet another velodrome that exists but is not very active at the present time. It is located near Milwaukee. It is 400 meters and 23°, made of asphalt and built in 1948 for the Olympic Trials.

It has no lighting, no seating, no concessions, and parking is a ways away. The velodrome is open, no fence or rail. There is no warm-up track. Sounds like another urban renewal project! Rumor has it that people still ride there, no organized racing.

Significant events: Nationals 1960, '61.

(22) 1996 Olympic Velodrome, Atlanta, Georgia (temporary)

Significant event: **The '96 Olympics!** The question is, where will it end up?

Charlie gets paid, but these other guys don't. The fellow at the bottom is Ed Wood, a local Minnesota bike race historian. The fellow in the middle is unknown, but the photo shows this: he's sure needed! All volunteers are.

(23-100)

The Mystery Velodromes

Looking for velodromes is like investigating a mystery -- leads are everywhere, but it's hard to nail anything down. Velodrome racing was so popular in the past that there were velodromes all over this country that are now fish ponds (San Diego), totally overgrown (Sacramento) and may now be a part of someone's barn or fence. But then there are the "rumored, secret" tracks. No one knows if these are real or just someone's overly active dreams.

Apparently everyone who loves velodrome racing wants a velodrome in their back yard so bad that they can see and discuss the reality before anyone else can. The desire appears to be there. It's the money that's lacking. Unfortunately, dreams do not drive the nails into the wood or pour the concrete. Today's rumors:

There used to be a velodrome owned by Dale Hughes of Michigan that was a portable wood track, Madison Velodromes, Ltd. It was stored in two semi's which disappeared one day. Rumors include: "track riders stole it and it is now being used in someone's backyard" and "the thieves probably didn't know what was in the semi's and they probably just tore it apart and used the wood." Dale's proposal to build the 1996 Olympic Velodrome was accepted!

Dave Bittenbender's dad bought the Hamar, Norway velodrome used in Worlds (where Rebecca Twigg set her '93 World Record). Now he must figure out how to move it to the US.

He offered its use for the '96 Olympics.

Mention of the new Vandedrome was met with skepticism ("Oh yeah, right, sure.") until they heard "I've seen the photos!" Then they said, "Oh, okay, that's different." (now they <u>know</u> it's real.) Vande Velde submitted a proposal for its use in '96.

Carl and Christine Sundquist are reportedly having a Vandedrome built in Arkansas. Maybe the Clinton's will take up track racing! Chelsea would like it.

There is supposedly a portable track stored in Boston Gardens.

Peter Jenic of Fonthill, Ontario is reportedly selling velodrome supports and plans with which the buyer can build his own velodrome.

John Waite is reportedly building a velodrome in his backyard (CA).

Tony O'Brien only needs a location for the San Francisco Velodrome.

In *Bicycle Track Racing* (1977, World Publications), nine cities were listed as proposing velodromes. Edmonton and San Diego were the only two to actually make it.

In the fifteen years since that reference, Colorado Springs, Dominguez Hills, Houston, Baton Rouge, Blaine, Indianapolis, Piccolo, and the Vandedrome have been built near the proposed locations. Rumors are still coming out of New Mexico of a planned velodrome, so people there haven't given up hope! A velodrome was even rumored for Anchorage.

See what Pat McDonough says (Ch. 17) about velodrome proposals.

Putting on all those races over the years requires a good volunteer support crew. There are many jobs to be done. It's not the glory in one occasion that makes a velodrome great, but the dedicated persistence, year after year.

Real Strength at Velodromes

No matter about the physical elements. At every track of any quality and action, it is not the facility which produces good racing but the support personnel. Certain velodromes have volunteer armies that work the long hours which translate into good racing over many years.

Fortunately, velodrome racing fans get hooked and can't give up the fun and excitement of a specialty where everyone is involved because they love it so much. If that were possible, bicycle track racing would have died long ago. Gibby calls it "family".

There are people who are the "rocks" upon which local racing is built. In San Diego, Ralph Elliott is such a rock. In Seattle, Jerry Baker is such a rock, assisted in some of Marymoor's great years by Barclay

Kruse, now the rock of Blaine. Robert Rodale passed the Trexlertown torch to Pat McDonough, but surely T-Town has a quarry full of "rocks" supporting that most dynamic program. The "rocks" are always there, supporting racing whenever and however they can. They endure all storms. Their service is their reward.

Building a successful volunteer base is virtually a gift which certain people seem to possess. Everyone has unique talents and abilities. The wise volunteer leader plugs the square pegs into their slots as they plug the round pegs into theirs. Success occurs when everyone contributes according to ability.

We all had to wear identical clothing to volunteer at Goodwill Games -- the cameras, you know. But, we would have done just about anything to be there and it was definitely worth it.. Thanks, Barclay, it was fun! Kinda looked like Texaco guys, didn't we?

Top level volunteers work together with an eye to the long term interests of the sport, rather than short term changes which only satisfy immediate objectives.

Many of the most devoted workers are the parents of racers who know that bicycle racing is a healthy, disciplined activity for their children. Other great workers are: old racers who simply love the sport, retired people who want to be involved, and kids who have aspirations or are just looking for something fun to do. The list is endless and bicycle racing cannot survive without every person who's willing to make a contribution.

Certain velodromes are known for their long term staff success. Good racing and training has been going on at Kenosha and North-brook for many years even though those velodromes are not parti-cularly known for their magnificent facilities. Kenosha is old and Northbrook is shallow, yet many top riders have been produced through racing opportunities at those tracks.

If you look at the prime suppor-ters, many of them are parents. Ask Danny Van Haute what his father was doing throughout his racing career -- planning race schedules at Northbrook! Ask Paul Swift's mom what kinds of things they did at Kenosha. Houston is producing top riders thanks to EDS, Kathy Volski, Nick Chenowth and others there.

Nationally prominent events help motivate people, too. Indian-apolis has put on great events the

Don't think of them as spectators, think of them as prospective racers and volunteers!

last couple of Nationals, partly due to their excellent volunteer organization. Where do the volunteers come from? Local bicycle clubs and organizations with people who love racing.

High level local Indy riders are already resulting from this effort, visible in local Sprinters Bill Clay and Greg Carlson. Roger and Connie Young and Nelson Vails' influence has also left its mark on Indy which will last well beyond their time there.

Now Dominguez Hills will benefit from the Youngs move to Los Angeles, joining Mark Whitehead at Dominguez Hills and Rick Denman at Encino. Los Angeles will be poppin'. With San Diego's new surface and the Vandedrome returning to Del Mar, San Diego will be poppin' too!

Colorado Springs is always hosting some new excitement like the World Cup this last summer ('94). Those folks at the USCF know how to hold an event.

However, the biggest success story of the United States can be seen at Trexlertown, home to World Sprint and Keirin Champion Marty Nothstein. This began with Robert Rodale and Jack Simes in the '70s. The legacy left through the construction and development of this venue will last many, many years to come.

Top riders make a yearly pilgrimage to Trexlertown for the best racing of the season. This country owes a debt to T-Town it can never repay for top level racing experience. Attempting to describe the contribution this track has made to the development of U.S. riders is futile.

It will be interesting to see the effects of an attempt to coordinate U.S. tracks into a national calendar presently being spearheaded by Pat McDonough. Thanks again, T-Town.

The point is this: Things happen in this highly technical sport when people are exposed to it for a long enough period of time to understand and appreciate it.

If you want your local velodrome to produce top riders, provide the opportunity, the expertise and the development and it will happen.

Someone in your area knows. Find that person and put them to this happy work. Building top level racing does not happen in a year or even two. It takes a while to get the momentum going. Once it's going, it takes on a life of its own.

Reading reflections of riders and experts here only reinforces respect for the many who have contributed to the velodrome tradition from its wild popularity early in this century, through the unsung years of dormancy in the 50s and 60s which evolved into the incredible resurgence of success of the 1984 Olympic Team and continuing to Marty Nothstein's blazing victories. People made this possible, some named in this book, many others who will remain forever unknown.

How can a country with so few active velodromes (16) produce a World Champion against countries who have so many velodromes? (Germany, 50+, Australia, 70-150, Japan, 70+, Italy, 40+, France, 120+ - - even little Great Britain has over 30.)

You wonder what might happen if the United States had near the level of development elsewhere.

We would surely be unbeatable.

	Marymoor/ Redmond	Alpenrose	Hellyer Park / San Jose	Dominguez Hills/ Olympic Velodrome	Encino	San Diego	Colorado Springs / 7-Eleven Olympic	Alkek / Houston	St. Louis	Baton Rouge	East Point / Dick Lane
State	Washgton	Oregon	California	California	California	California	Colorado	Texas	Missouri	Louisiana	Georgia
Dist	400	268	335.75	333.33	250	333.33	333.33	333.33	1/5mi	333.33	323.13
Bankg	25	±45	22.5	33	28	27	33	33	28	33	33
Mater	concrete	concrete	concrete	concrete	concrete	concrete	concrete	concrete	black top	concrete	concrete
Yr Blt	1976	1963/7	1963	1982/3	1962	1976	1983	1986	1962	1985	1976
Near	Seattle	Portland	San Fran	LA	LA	San Diego	Denver	Houston	St Louis	BatonRouge	Atlanta
Loc	park	priv	park	univ	park	park	park	park	park	park	park
Lights	yes	no	yes	yes	yes	yes	yes	yes	no	yes	yes
Seats	850+	250	600	yes	yes	yes	800	yes	no	yes	yes
Concess.	temp	temp	temp	2	yes	temp	temp	temp	no	yes	no
Parkg	near	near	near	near	near	far	near	yes	yes	near	near
Announ	yes	yes	yes	yes	yes	often	tower	yes	no	yes	yes
Access	gate	ladder	gate	tunnel	gate	gate	tunnel	tunnel	gate	tunnel	gate
Wmuptrk	yes	no	apron	yes	no	yes	yes	yes	no	yes	no
LoanBks	yes	yes	yes	yes	yes	yes	yes	yes	no	yes	no
SpecFea	1990 Goodwill Games active race prog	private: Alpenrose Dairy near amuse park active	racing Wed/Fri abrasive surface active	built for 1984 Olympics AAF prog active	active race prog AAF prog	AAF prog new srface active race prog	world class office complex WldRecords 1986 Wlds 1994 Wld Cup Finals	pub & priv EDS base strong program	closed due to crime	increased activity in last 1-1/2 years	showers bike storag

1996 Olympic Velodrome. Atlanta, 250m. 40+ degrees. (Temporary/portable)

Velodromes

	National Sports Center/Blaine	Brown Deer	Washington Bowl Park / Kenosha	Northbrook	Vandedrome Portable	Major Taylor / Indianapolis	Dorais	Lehigh / Trexlertown	Kissena	Piccolo	
State	Minnesota	Wisconsin	Wisconsin	Illinois	Illinois	Indiana	Michigan	Pennsylvna	New York	Florida	State
Dist	250	1/4 mi.	333.33	382	126-153	333.3	312	333.3	1/4mi	333.3	Distance
Bankg	45	23	23	17.5	53	28.5	26	27	17	30	Banking
Mater	wood	asphalt	concrete	asphalt	wood	concrete	concrete	concrete	asphalt	concrete	Material
Yr Blt	1991	1937/48	1927	1958/61	1994	1982	1969	1975	1963	1993	Year built
Near	Minneapls	Milwaukee	Milwaukee	Chicago	Chicago	Indianapls	Detroit	Allentown	NY(Qns)	FtLaudrdl	Nrst lg cty
Loc	*NSC	park	park	park	portable	park	park	county	city	park	Located
Lights	yes	no	yes	yes	yes	yes	no	yes	no	yes	Lighting
Seats	yes	natural	no	yes	arena	yes	no	3500	200	temp	Seating
Concess.	temp	no	temp	yes	yes	yes	no	yes	no	temp	Concessions
Parkg	yes	walk	near	yes	yes	near	near	near	yes	near	Parking
Announ	yes	no	yes	yes	yes	yes	no	yes	yes	yes	Announcer
Access	tunnel	open	gate	stepover	gate	tunnel	open	wlkway	gate	tunnel	Access
Wmuptrk	yes	no	yes	no	no	yes	no	yes	no	inline skat	Wm-up trk
LoanBks	yes	no		yes	n/a	yes	no	yes	no		Loaner bikes
SpecFea	*National Sports Ctr multi-sport facility active loaner bikes/ helmets	rideable speedskat no active racing program	"TheBowl" "The Hill" Oldest active track in the U.S. TuesRaces	no apron measured 1/4 mi & 400m scoreboard clubhouse Supported: Schwinn, Oschner ThursRaces	beer grdn dining team races more-- Watch it happen!	bike lockrs offices go-kart rac in-line skat showers TV hook-ups Nationals	great riding in the past M. Walden Wolverine	"T-Town" scoreboard grants Internat'l racing Supporter: Rodale **#1 track**	sound system no support run by dedicated	newest permanent velodrome. off to good start!	Special fea.

of the United States

Chapter 3

⚲ *The Equipment* ⚲

Whole books can and have been written on this subject. This chapter will offers information on how track bicycles are unique, the trends, and what items a rider might consider when competing in various track events.

The competition makes more sense if you understand, for instance why this person may be riding a disc wheel and that person may not. Specialists in each event share their preferences at the end of the chapter.

Riding the Track

While a velodrome can be ridden on any bicycle (with a bottom bracket and cranks high enough relative to the banking so the pedal doesn't hit), track racing is done on a special bicycle with no brakes, a shorter wheel base, one gear, and no derailleur.

This would seem to provide little control for the riders, but in fact these bicycles are exceptionally responsive. They are very light weight and may be smaller than the bicycle ridden by the same rider on the road.

If you're a new rider, don't bother with the high-tech equipment. While businesses will be happy to sell you whatever you want, you need no more than the basic track bicycle to enjoy good results. An old track bike with meaning is a lot more fun than a new bike with none, anyway. Time enough for the hot stuff when you're a Champion! *Anyone* can buy trick stuff, but knowing how to use it is a whole different thing.

Trackies are a highly sophisticated group and not easily fooled or impressed. They quickly recognize riders who don't know what they're doing and those who do. They are not nearly as impressed by elite equipment as they are by riding expertise. Track racing is highly technical, which is why it's so interesting.

First, gain expertise from those who know (then you can dazzle them with your brilliance.) You will gain the most respect by developing your racing skills. There are many things to know. **Start with the brain, not with the hardware.** But, true, you have to have a track bicycle to race, so here are some things to start you out.

The Track Bicycle

Until 1963, track bicycles were ridden in competition on the road. While derailleurs were around at the turn of the century, they were not common to road bicycles until the forties and fifties. By the sixties, they were common to road bicycles. Since 1963, the only competition opportunities for single gear, direct drive bicycles have been, and continue to be, on the track.

The easiest way to know if a bicycle frame was designed for road or track riding (aside from no brakes) is to look at the rear drop-outs (where the rear hub attaches to the frame). If they curve around toward the front of the bicycle like a fish hook, it's a road bicycle. If the drop-outs point toward

*Bobby Walthour IV rides a bicycle almost identical to that raced by his great-grandfather at the turn of the century. **No matter what other equipment you see in this book, this IS the basic equipment, and all you really need to get started.** Note: no brakes (!), no derailleurs, direct drive in one gear. Bobby is a Sprinter and uses toeclips and double toe straps, not clipless pedals. There is no more basic bicycle.*
The greater the simplicity, the higher the art, the more exquisite the challenge.

the back, it's a track bicycle.

Originally all bicycles were designed with dropouts pointed back, but all bicycles were also single-geared. With the derailleur's popularity in the late 40s, came a need to make rear adjustments easier. Pointing dropouts forward and slopped downward

allowed for increased freedom in adjustment and made it easier to get the rear wheel with a derailleur in and out.

Having no derailleurs, track bicycles did not require this change. Plus, a slopped drop-out would allow the bottom bracket to move closer to the track with wheel adjustment, an undesirable change for track riding.

There are other more obvious clues to the kind of bicycle if the bike is built up, such as no brakes, no derailleur and one gear, but this can be deceiving. The drop-outs reveal the purpose.

The Frame

The classic frame, the "diamond" design of tubing construction, is common to bicycles seen on the streets today. They have a head tube, a top tube, a seat tube, a down tube, and a set of "stays" which hold the back wheel. These sections are welded into a tight, strong unit to which the rest of the parts are attached.

The front of the bicycle has a fork held into the head tube by a "headset" which allows the fork to turn without falling out, surely an engineering marvel when first invented.

Until very recently, the greatest change in frame construction was in the tubing materials rather than the look of the bicycle. Vintage bicycle enthusiasts pleasure in distinguishing minute differences in bicycle construction over the last 100 years, but the average person usually thinks they all look pretty much alike.

Recently, innovative materials have become more common to variations in bicycle design, distinct shifts from the past. A new rider does not need to concern him/herself with these new style bicycles right now.

No matter what the design or materials, the following are primary considerations in a track frame:

1) a higher bottom bracket. The banking on a velodrome requires a higher bottom bracket due to the threat

of "digging a pedal", striking the track surface on the downstroke, which might send a rider crashing onto the track. The momentum of the bicycle is affected by this sudden jarring and change in speed. The impact is immediately transferred to the back wheel which loses stability.

The steeper the track, the more concern for pedal impact. Either the bottom bracket must be higher, the crank arm shorter, or both. Riders flinging their bicycles back and forth during Sprints do not need the worry of whether actions to increase speed will also cause them to crash. They have enough of that kind of stuff to think about during a race!

2) a shorter wheel base. Since responsiveness, not comfort of ride over hours, is the primary concern, the increased stiffness and handling of a shorter wheel base is desirable.

3) lightness. If a bicycle is made of less of a lighter material, its weight is reduced. Less energy is demanded from the rider, regardless of event.

4) probably, aerodynamics. Aerodynamics are a primary concern of the Pursuiter, but all riders are looking for that little advantage which will slow them less. Sprinters need power and responsiveness in their bicycles. They will sacrifice both lightness and aerodynamics for the sake of strength and stiffness.

Another part of the frame is the front fork, almost a separate factor to framebuilders. No matter which frame, the fork can have more or less "rake". Rake is the slope of the fork from out of the headset to where it connects to the front wheel. Rake affects stability.

Most distinctive is the "**Zipp**" style with the "Softride" seat support attached to the frame. These bicycles have no seat tube, making them look very unstable. In fact, they are quite stiff and responsive. If the rider wants attention, this one will get it. These bicycles are designed to be aerodynamic and ultra-light. There is debate as to the amount of flex with no support directly under the seat. Some riders say you just have to get used to them. Others say "Not me, thanks."

Another type of frame construction has been accepted with more enthusiasm by top riders, including 1994 World Sprint and Keirin Champion Marty Nothstein. This is a shift from traditional frame design to a "**uniframe**" construction of composite material reminiscent of a functional sculpture.

The USCF's "**Project 96**", designing the bicycle of the future with the 1996 Olympics in mind, unveiled a bicycle in 1994 which is fairly close to the classic design, but has certain changes for increased aerodynamics. Designers for Project 96 are not convinced that the "uniframe" design is the only possibility. Judging from the U.S. performance at the 1994 World Championships and the 1995 Pan American Games, they may be right.

Sprinters tend to prefer a straighter fork than others. Rake on a track bicycle will be less than on a road bicycle, contributing to the shorter wheel base preferred by track riders.

Wheels

Materials and design of wheels are undergoing massive change. In the last ten years, solid disc wheels and wheels with no metal spokes, have become increasingly popular. The solid discs are most often used on the back of the bicycle, but can be used on the front, if there is not so much wind that the bicycle is blown off course.

More often, riders will use three or four "spoke" wheels in the front. These are not spokes in the traditional sense, but three and four sections of material, often carbon fiber, which are built as supports from hub to rim. They are an integral part of wheel construction and not adjustable.

A new rider does not need a disc or "tri-spoke" wheel. These are expensive specialty items, designed for specific purposes. New riders begin with the standard spoked wheel.

Classic wheels with spokes are as much an art for wheel builders as tubing and angles are for frame builders. Kind of hubs, number of spokes and kind of rims and tires are all life breath for some fanatics.

Wheel builders take great pride in their work, performing it as a high art. Here too, the materials possibilities have more recently become diverse. Wheelbuilders want the wheel to be as light and strong as possible, while rolling as fast as possible, with as little resistance as possible. Lightness is found in choice of materials. Strength

depends on the wheel builder and his/her choice of "radial", "cross two" and "cross three" designs.

In a radial wheel, the spokes go directly from hub to rim, uncrossed. They have greater aerodynamic efficiency, but spokes are unsupported laterally for the added strength found in "cross" designs. Actual distance from hub to rim is the shortest, resulting in less spoke "mass" in the final product. The wheel is then lighter if all other factors are the same.

While this may sound like the best choice, these wheels must be built by a knowledgeable person so that this less stable wheel can be as stable as possible. Uneven spoke tension makes the wheels weak, increasing the possibility of collapse. Breaking a spoke is a major deal with a radial since the integrity of the overall wheel is then threatened.

"Cross two" and "cross three" refers to how many spokes cross each other from the hub to the rim. The more crossing, the more strength and the more weight due to increased numbers and length of each spoke in the increasing numbers of crossings. Heavier riders and more strenuous events demand heavier wheels.

Another factor involving spokes is their shear number. On a track bike, the fewer spokes the better. Likely they will be 24, 28, or 32. Tandems may require 40.

In Time Trials, discs are used for increased aerodynamics and a "flywheel" effect. More recently, tri-spoke wheels are gaining popularity in all events. They may make a significant difference in Time Trial

events, where competitors are attempting to shave off 100ths of seconds, but the classicists say they are not necessary in all events.

In bicycle racing, designers continually and literally try to "re-invent the wheel".

Tires

Tires might be "clincher", a tire with a tube held on by a bead which clinches onto the rim. Or it might be "tubular", also known as "sew-ups" a tire with a tube sewn into it which is attached to the rim with glue. Each tire requires a different rim.

The virtue of one tire over the other relates to weight and strength. Tubulars (sew-ups) are lighter and stronger so that riders can pump them up to higher pressures (120 vs. 160), decreasing their rolling resistance.

Clinchers have increased in lightness and strength, but most hard-cores will be using tubulars in elite races, usually silks which are very strong and dastardly expensive. (That's why bicycle riders need sponsorship so much!) Ask around for recommendations on tires -- which ones last longest, which stand high pressure better, etc. Experienced riders know and see this as an important issue.

Pedals

There are two important issues with regard to pedals. First, contact with the rider's foot must be solid, not "spongy". The less movement between pedal and foot, the more efficient is the transfer of power from leg to wheel. Second, the rider's foot must not come out during competition.

There are presently two types of pedals used in track racing, "clip" and

"clipless". The older of the two is the clip pedal (see pg. 36), with a strap pulled tight to secure the foot in the toe-clip and on the pedal. Track racers often use double toe straps, especially Sprinters.

More recently, pedals have been invented which clip into the bottom of the shoe (see pg. 16). There are several systems, "Look", "Time" "SpeedPlay" and others, all named after their manufacturers. The amount of tension in the clipless pedal can be adjusted so it is easier and harder to get the shoe out. While these pedals are quite secure, there seem to be more foot pulls with clipless pedals, according to my experts. It is possible that riders are still learning to maximize adjustment. In theory, the shoe should not come out unless the rider wants it to and makes a specific effort to do so.

Clipless pedals were invented for road riding. Riders' feet tend to fall asleep with the pressure of toe-straps across the arch over the many hours of riding typical of the road, plus, riders have a freewheel, allowing them to stop pedaling and re-insert their foot if they should pull it.

On the track, events are shorter, so feet falling to sleep is not a primary concern. Getting thrown off of a bicycle mid-Sprint because the rider lost control with one foot forced to continually revolve while the other suddenly has no support, is of great concern -- not only to the rider involved, but also to others who will now land on top of him/her.

On a track bicycle, if you're going any speed at all, it is difficult (if not impossible) to reconnect your foot onto the pedal without first slowing down. By the time the foot is reconnected and the rider picks up speed again, the other competitor or competitors are long gone.

Top riders, especially Sprinters, have tended to stick with the "toe-clip" variety because they feel they are more secure. In addition, many top riders have their feet taped onto their pedals at the starting line (for Time Trials) for maximum contact. This is easier to do with toe-clip pedals than with the smaller clipless pedals.

The subject of toe-clip versus clipless pedals is one of considerable controversy whenever someone pulls their foot out during a race, invariably losing the race for himself and anyone who is depending on him/her. Neither choice is immune to pulling a foot.

Handlebars

Classic track handlebars are slopped downward in a more gentle sweep than road handlebars. Track riders spend little time during races on the top of the bars and there will be no brakes mounted on them, so the shape does not have to accommodate these two factors. Hand grip is more likely to be forward on the lower part of the slopped area, not forward to grab the brakes, or resting on the bottom.

The increased slope allows more room between the top of the wrists and the bars while in the grips, especially useful whenever riders move the bicycle and handlebars side to side. Riders will often stay on the "drops" keeping as much of their bodies out of the wind as possible. Otherwise their torsos act like sails and slow them down.

If you look at the backs of top Time Trialists, they are flat. This body angle is assisted by the use of **aero bars**, the angles of the bicycle, the length of the stem, the drops, the placement of the seat and the length of the cranks. In Time Trial events, handlebars take many forms, all in a search for the lowest physical profile. Over the last 10 years, considerable handlebar variation has been explored.

'95 Pan Am Pursuit Gold Medalist Kent Bostick uses the most innovative equipment he can find. His latest handlebars are made for the Pursuit/aero position only -- there are no grips for side-to-side pull during the start.

Aero bars can take many more forms than will be addressed here. Suffice to say that these bars stick out in front of the handlebars, over the front wheel. They have support for the elbows and a grip for the hands. Some clip on to regular track bars and others are built with a special design.

Classic track handlebars can be used in any track event. **Aero bars are allowed in Time Trial events only.** In all other events, no aero bars are allowed. Those are the rules.

Seats

Seats are a personal thing, but can make a big difference in a rider's comfort. You will not see a wide seat on a track bicycle. Riders need to move into different positions for different efforts, so they must have a seat which allows for that.

In general, track seats are slim and streamlined, adjusted forward or back according to bike/body fit. Sprinters tend to sit more forward, Pursuiters more back.

Kent Bostick's equipment here is just about "the max" for Time Trialists. Two disc wheels, the smallest bike possible with aerodynamic tubing, the weirdest handlebars and helmet gear you ever saw. What's left? It's harder to get out of the gate with no lateral pull, but Kent seems make up any time loss over the distance. Not sure about that helmet. . .

You may try different adjustments to see what works better. If you're going to play around with this, get someone knowledgeable to help you.

Cranks

Size of rider tends to determine crank arm length. Cranks usually run from 165, 170 and 175 mm in length.

There are half lengths between and custom designs. 165 and 170 are the most common. Smaller riders tend to use 165s, giants tend to use 175s.

Different events might decide one choice over another. For Sprints a rider might choose 165s. and then switch to 170s for a Pursuit. It has to do with power and leverage. Beginning riders do not need to obsess about this. Find a coach or other knowledgeable person to help you.

Stems

The grip from the head tube onto the handlebars is called the "stem". While it is (usually) a nonadjustable item, it can be changed to accommodate a rider's needs. One rider may have a long stem while another has a short one. This relates to the length of the top tube and where the handlebars need to be in relation to the rider's body and the seat.

Once a bicycle is built, the top tube is no longer adjustable. The seat can be moved back and forth and a shorter or longer stem can be selected. These two adjustments enable a rider to change position relative to the wheels and cranks. Ask someone who knows about bike fit.

Gears

The subject of gear choice is a strong area of contention among racers. Most riders and coaches agree on one point in relation to gears: if the wrong one is selected, it can annihilate a rider's performance no matter what other factors are in place.

Gears are usually referred to in terms of "inches" in this country, based on the distance one may cover with each revolution of the pedal. "What inch gear do you have on your bicycle?" you might be asked. "78" is a small gear for a track bicycle, "98" is a large gear (for instance).

A combination of two numbers results in the magic "inches" figure. The front chain ring is the source of the first reference number, the rear wheel is the source of the other. For instance, 46 on the front and 15 on the back results in a 83 inch gear (actually 82.8 or so, depending on tire size).

If you don't know what gears you have on your bicycle and you cannot find the number (usually stamped on the chain ring), you can simply count the number of teeth on each. A gear chart will give you the resulting number of inches. Gear charts are found in many bicycle reference books. They often neglect to note what tire size they are figured on. To arrive at the <u>true</u> inches, you need to know your tire size. Then you can use the following formula:

Tire size (times) front chain ring (divided by) rear cog (equals) number of inches (or mm) covered per wheel revolution. Example: take two size tires with the same gears:
1) 26.5 in. tire: 26.5 x 46 ÷ 15 = **81.26**
2) 27 in. tire: 27 x 46 ÷ 15 = **82.8**

Get the picture?

You can make a chart for yourself, customized for your wheel circumference. If you're brand new at the idea of gear ratios, it is handy to mount a small chart on the handlebars of your road bicycle so you can monitor gears you use most often and what they feel like. (Audrey McElmury and Michael Levonas suggested that -- great idea.) Learning how the numbers <u>feel</u> is important.

The trick is to fit the bicycle with a gear that is:

1) large enough to cover a longer distance with each pedal stroke, while

2) not demanding so much effort that the rider loses the ability to be "on top of it" over the full distance.

If a gear is too small, the rider will simply not be able to turn the pedals fast enough to cover enough distance. If it is too big, s/he will not be able to get the bike moving fast enough, quickly enough, when sudden moves are made by opponents. Either turning the gear will be too difficult and/or the rider will tire too quickly over the course of the race to keep up.

A rider has the physical ability to push a certain range of gears without running out of RPMs or energy. This range changes as strength and fitness improve. Most riders begin with a smaller gear earlier in the season and move to bigger gears as they get stronger and in better shape.

In general, Time Trialists tend to ride "bigger" gears, while Sprinters tend to ride big, but not the biggest, gears. Time Trialists must maintain a constant tempo while Sprinters must be able to respond to quick moves with high RPMs. At altitude, riders are apt to use 2" larger gears than at sea level for the same effort due to less air resistance.

Junior riders 16 and under are restricted in their gear choices. In one complete revolution of the cranks, these riders may cover no more ground than 23 feet, 3 inches. At races, officials will do "roll outs" between two pieces of tape to verify the distance.

One reason for this is to even out competition and not allow young enthusiasts and their "Little League" advisors to pump big gears too early in their development, causing injuries and practicing poor technique. This is similar to cautions in weight training and other sports.

It is commonly advocated that all riders begin by pushing smaller gears (like in the 70s) at higher RPMs (±90) earlier in the season and then work up to bigger gears (80s, low 90s) when their coordination and strength improve. This is appropriate each season as well as over the length of one's career. The muscle needs to be trained to be agile and make circles quickly. Higher RPMs produce better racers because the riders learn to pedal faster with less fatigue. This quick endurance is built with smaller gears.

Bigger gears are for later or for riders who know their bodies and events so well that they can use whatever works best due to their training. Top riders tend to ride bigger gears, but they didn't start out that way. They built up to it. Typically, beginning riders, left to themselves, ride gears that are too big. Ask your experts, they'll guide you.

Brain first, <u>then</u> hardware. Watch and learn.

JERSEYS

Jerseys have a unique and special place in bicycle racing, whatever the venue. Jersey's identify team, status and achievement. There is a whole culture which has evolved around jerseys. If you want to be a bicycle racing snob and/or if you want to demonstrate your knowledge and appreciation for the sport, it is important to understand the full meaning of bicycle jerseys.

Bicycle shops often carry jerseys with famous logos, advertising, or for aesthetics. Some are simply bicycle clothing, but those aren't the fun ones. The fun ones, of course, are the ones with meaning.

To wear jerseys inappropriately demonstrates your ignorance of bicycle racing etiquette. If you have a nice jersey with nothing but multicolored stripes across the chest that you have been happily wearing on your breakfast road rides, you are committing one of bicycle racing's greatest faux pas (errors).

The Rainbow Jersey

The highest level jersey in the bicycle racing world is that of the World Champion. This jersey has a rainbow of colors, blue, red, black, yellow and green, descending in that order, across the chest and no advertising if worn by an amateur. If you see someone on the track in the Rainbow Jersey, you know they are the current World Champion in their event. Last year's Champion cannot continue to wear the Jersey. Marty Nothstein wears the Rainbow Jersey for Sprint and Keirin in 1995 as the current World Champion.

Connie Young has Rainbow stripes on the trim of her track jersey even though she is not the current World Champion. When the new Champion is crowned, former World Champions can wear Rainbow stripes on sleeves and collars to show their status. It is a privilege that now belongs to them and no one else.

A World Sprint Champion may not wear his/her Rainbow Jersey on the road. Likewise, the World Road Champion may not wear it on the track. This conduct is followed by all who participate.

National Champion/Teams

If you look around and notice several riders with "Stars and Stripes" jerseys, these are the jerseys of US National Champions and the US National Team.

Only current National Champions are allowed to wear the jersey of the National Champion, and in the same type of event (road vs. track) as the Championship win. Former National Champions can wear Stars and Stripes bands around their sleeves and collars (and only they can).

Not just anyone can be on the National Team, so the National Team jerseys are also status jerseys. National Team members must compete in their National Team jerseys in their appropriate venue: road in road events, track in track events. A National Team member can wear the National Team jersey in other events on the track besides his/her specialty. This jersey may only be worn while actually representing the US or the USCF.

The Winner's Jersey

The next level of status is the winner's jersey awarded to symbolize other victories. Probably the most famous of these is the Yellow Jersey awarded to the leader/winner in the Tour de France. You will not see a Yellow Jersey on the track because the Tour is a road event.

Winner's jerseys have symbols and the name of the event, sponsors and other special graphics. These can be worn indefinitely, not just for the year of the "reign". The year of the win is usually identified on the jersey.

Hot Team Jerseys

Every year there is usually a new hot team jersey, distinct to sponsored teams. Look around the track and you will likely see the same jersey on several riders. It may be the jersey of a local club, but it might be the jersey of a top national team -- a "hot team." (Clubs are discussed later.)

For instance, Saturn has some hot riders, among them Jessica Grieco, Robbie Ventura and Mike McCarthy. Fans look at the jersey and know it's a hot one because of who is riding for the team, not for its own flashiness.

Because the Saturn team is sponsored, only sponsored riders are likely to be able to get and wear the jersey. It might be available in stores at some point, most often a year or more after it is worn in competition,

Teams want their jersey to be worn by team members only so identification is certain when team tactics come into play. They don't want a team member in a Points Race, for instance, to ride the wheel of a person with a Saturn jersey who just bought it in the store and can't function as a team member. Jerseys are identifiers.

Once again, it goes back to meaning, not simply what may seem to be. Wearing an inappropriate jersey in competition or on the street becomes a matter of personal social conscience and ethics.

Image vs. Performance

Image and performance get con-fused in many peoples' minds, a fact that advertisers take advantage of all the time (look at any glamor ad). A rider may look at Mike McCarthy and think: "a) Mike McCarthy is a good rider. b) He wears a Saturn jersey. c) If I wear a Saturn jersey, I'll be a good rider like Mike" Not quite.

It isn't really the jersey that the rider wants, but the ability to perform at such a level that he can wear a jersey that says he is a good rider.

The next step is one that is not well thought of: "If I wear a Saturn jersey, people will think I'm a good rider like Mike McCarthy." He/she might get away with that one as long as anyone who sees them in the jersey doesn't know enough to know the difference.

Performance shows the truth, and it can be embarrassing to watch someone in a hot jersey show that they just got it because they knew some-one. When you wear a hot jersey, you wear a responsibility.

The Ultimate Jersey Elitism

Anyone can have a jersey printed, all they have to do is take the design and their money to a manufacturer. Don't be too impressed by a bunch of fancy graphics. It's who is in the jersey and what that person knows and can do that should be impressive.

Sometimes elite riders wear non-descript clothing (i.e. all black) to send a very intentional message: "I'm so cool I don't need to wear a cool outfit." That person is only looking to impress to those who know. It's kind of "ultimate meaning with the absence of meaning." It's the ultimate in bicycle racing elitism. Some top riders particularly enjoy showing the truth to those who are fooled by super-ficiality when they beat all the guys in the cool jerseys who can't ride.

Club Jerseys ("Normal People")

"Normal people" who start to ride and get interested in competition join a bicycle club, for comradeship, to learn from others, and other benefits that go along with club membership.

Club members can purchase club clothing if they want to, but it is not mandatory unless they intend to compete. In that case, they are expected to do so in their current year's club jersey. A rider may compete in no jersey except that of his/her club. Last year's jersey, from the current or last years club, may be worn in training rides, but in competition it must be the correct club and the correct year.

Usually there will be a new jersey every year. If the term of the jersey is two years, it is still the current jersey, the second year.

Club jerseys have sponsorship logos all over them. In a sense they are a visual log of who supports bicycle racing and how successful clubs are at getting sponsorship. Sometimes sponsors contribute cash. Often there are one or more "eateries" included due to the voluminous consumptive behavior of athletes. These restaurants, coffee houses and etc. usually offer discounts on their foods to club members.

Other sponsors may contribute the printing of the club newsletter, and so on. Club members may have busi-nesses which they decide to advertise (and tax deduct) through the club.

If you want to support bicycle racing and become instantly famous in the bicycling community, become a sponsor of a rider, a club, or a race! There is never too much sponsorship in this expensive sport. Money contributed supports club functions and may pay some expenses for club members to attend National events.

Other Jerseys

There are many jerseys available for purchase through catalogs, bicycle shops and other sources. If you're not competing, rules don't apply -- your personal preferences come into play. Will you wear a flashy jersey just for the fun of it? Does a La Vie Claire jersey make you feel like Greg LeMond? Jerseys are a lot of fun.

As far as wearing a Rainbow Jersey or a National Champion jersey, it isn't thought of as an appropriate thing to do unless you earned it. It demonstrates a lack of knowledge and a lack of respect. You won't be arrested but you'll be kicked out of races.

Meaning is the interesting part of jerseys. Now that you know what is appropriate, you can make knowledgeable choices. People who take pleasure in wearing old jerseys honor the tradition which has given so much to their lives. They don't need to impress those who don't know anything about bicycle racing. They enjoy sharing a secret with others who recognize the obscure jersey with a historical tradition.

It's fun to acquire jerseys that have special meaning, either from the graphics on them or because they belonged to someone you admire. Old team jerseys are particularly fair game. Since they are old, who wears them doesn't matter. Jerseys of manufacturers (i.e. Campagnolo) show you know something about equipment.

Old Pro jerseys are really fun. You can tell people about the meaning to demonstrate your knowledge of bicycle racing -- but of course, you have to know something, first -- and that's the whole point!

And last -- Shorts

Shorts are tight so they won't irritate! Black for tradition and dirt.

It's easy to buy a hot outfit, it's a lot harder to actually <u>know</u> something. And speaking of those who know --

EQUIPMENT FOR TRACK EVENTS

So far, general racing equipment has been discussed which you would acquire with the help of an informed person. Focusing on specialized events may warrant equipment for Championship competition.

Specialists in each Championship event share their views with you here:

SPRINTS

Match Sprints -- Connie Young

I've worked very hard at coming up with a well designed frame, the way it's built, the way it responds, the quickness. I've changed frame design constantly.

The weight of it is important once you've got your bike down in other ways. It's hard to get the frame light and, at the same time, stiff and responsive. Getting away from the frame itself, you want everything as light as possible, but you still need the strength.

I've been using 24 to 28 spoke wheels, real light wheels. I'll probably have radial spokes in the front, disc in the back, everything as light as possible.

If your body isn't prepared, I don't care what machine you put it on, it's only going to go so fast. That's why equipment is a focus for me now. I can't do anything more with my body. I got a little more satisfaction when I got a decent time on all conventional equipment. (*note: a classicist*)

It's pretty difficult to develop some of the things needed for a Sprint bike with new materials. The bottom bracket area needs to be stiffer and stronger. It's hard to come up with those kinds of changes. All the things that make a good Pursuit bike must, in addition, be strong enough in the right places to make a proper handling Sprint bike. That's more difficult.

If they spent time developing a Sprint bike they might be able to apply those same things to a Pursuit bike. The United States has never placed emphasis or attention on Sprint bikes.

I'd like to see what the wind tunnel tells me. I want it to help me figure out if I'm right on my bike. I'm trying to work with what I have, the design of bike I want and perfecting **me** on that bike, positionally and everything. I'm trying to get a little bit smarter about it. That is a big key right now.

Match Sprints -- Mark Gorski

I first used a disc in '86. I didn't use anything special in '84. Ted Kirkbride (Masi) built the bike that I rode '82 through '84. It had the Murray name on it, but Ted built it. It was Masi number 001. Then I signed with Fuji after the Olympics and I rode a Fuji for four or five years.

The bikes that Ted built were sturdy, strong bikes. There was never any sacrifice in weight at the cost of strength. I was using flat spoke wheels, a high tech thing for a couple of years until everyone had them. I used steel bars and stems. I didn't ride a real light bike. I much preferred the additional strength to lighter weight.

Aside from the disc wheels and the three-G wheels (the tri-spoke), over three hundred meters at 43, 44 miles per hour, I don't think equipment makes all that much difference. Maybe a tenth, at the most, over two hundred meters for a record-setting attempt, but otherwise that's not going to make or break anyone's career.

In the Sprint event there are no major position changes or technological changes that are impacting performance by, maybe, less than half a percent. We haven't seen times progress at all from the Hesslich days.

Keirin -- Gibby Hatton

No specialized equipment is required for Keirin other than a track bicycle. In the United States riders use a variety of equipment. In Japan bicycles are very basic and all exactly the same, only spoked wheels, and these must all be exactly alike. (see Keirin section)

Tandem Sprints -- Nelson Vails

Guys may be in synch, but they may not trust their equipment. The biggest problem is tires. If you don't have a good set, they get soft on you, you can feel it. You don't even think about blowing a tire, because you wouldn't be on tires you had to worry about. First tires, then wheels.

You need good wheels that won't flex. You'll feel a tandem wheel flex more than you would on an individual bike. It's more weight, especially the rear wheel. The front wheel too, on a steeper track, from the G-forces.

I always used four-cross on a high flange hub, preferably on both of them. The old way is the best way. Not all this new three spoke wheel stuff. I've ridden them before because they're strong, but with a good Conti (Continental) 175, too, that was glued on. Something that can take 160 pounds pressure. A good quality tire would take that much. A regular tire I would pump up to 150.

Tandem wheels have 40 spokes, front and back. A disc wheel in the rear is fine, but now they're going with three-spoke wheels because acceleration is faster. The gear we rode was about 103, depending on the track. On a small track, you need a smaller gear, less reaction -- you need quicker acceleration and leg speed.

If it was a big 400 meter track like Seattle, you'd want a big gear because you'd have a longer runway to get going. I'd probably use over 100 for Seattle, probably 98 for Minnesota. It's five to eight inches, a big difference in the feel.

MASS START RACES
Points Race -- Karen Bliss

The most important equipment for the Points Race is *good* wheels and tires. Everyone these days uses a rear disc, but it is not absolutely necessary.

I'm not an equipment fanatic. 49-15 is my standard Points Race gear. I'll ride anywhere from 53-16 to 46-14. Those are the three big ones. That's about 88.9.

Bobby (Livingston) sets things

up differently depending on whether tires are fat or skinny. For him that makes all the difference in the world. If I ride 49-15 with fat tires, that's a big gear. That's on par with 53-16 with skinny tires.

Points Race--Mark Whitehead

Points Races require a standard track bike and a disc wheel. That's important. A Points Race rider needs a light, light rear disc and can ride a little bit bigger gear.

Gears are individual. Some guys like to pedal a little bit better, some guys like to push a little bit better. I would say anywhere from a 90 to a 93 inch gear, it just depends on the rider.

My gear was a 51-15 which is a 91.8. That was the gear I rode in every event. I trained in a 49-15 and I raced in a 51-15. But now you have to train in much smaller gears, like 81, 82, 79 and work very, very hard in the gym.

Madison -- Danny Van Haute

Equipment has changed a lot in the last 10 years. To get started in Madisons you don't need any special equipment. It's probably the cheapest event you can get. You don't need any aero bars, no special wheels, nothing. You just get your bike out there and a set of wheels and go.

At T-Town people are using disc wheels for all events, including Madisons, but in the developmental programs they're going back to the basic spoke wheels for all riders because discs are expensive and not necessary for regular racing.

I've been riding a disc wheel more and more for all events since I'm putting in less miles on the road! I might put on a disc and a tri-spoke in

the front.

People in Europe are using rear discs for Madisons more now, too but that's in top level racing. In local weekly races, bladed or regular spoked wheels are fine.

Mark Gorski stands in a facility that is many a mechanic's dream -- the equipment room of the USCF Coaches building. All the highest tech stuff the USCF has to muster -- tools for every occasion. The year Mark won the Gold ('84) this room didn't exist.

TIME TRIALS
Kilometer -- Janie Eickhoff

I ride a 24 inch front wheel in the chance that it might be a little bit windy. I'm smaller, so I'd probably use a front disc with a smaller wheeled bike rather than with a large wheeled bike because it wouldn't blow me around as much. I like to hold a nice, tight line. I don't want to be distracted from my pedaling. If I don't use a disc, I may use my HED high rimmed wheel, carbon fiber with a high rim and short spokes.

I started using aero bars in '91. I didn't use them on my Kilo bike because was such a short event, I was always concerned with the transition time in going from the hooks to the drop-ins. In the Kilo there's no time to waste. I'm more comfortable with aero bars now.

Another concern I have had with aero bars is in the last lap. You're fighting off tunnel vision, having a hard time holding your line. It's easy to hit sponges in that last quarter when you have your hands on the regular hook part of your handlebars. If I'm in the aero position, I would hate to go down because I was heading into the sponges or something gets caught, but I still use them.

I still use toe clip pedals on the

track. I like the security you get from the toe straps. Sometimes the fabric on shoes will stretch, even though there might be straps on the shoes.

There's nothing like a nice leather strap or two around your feet because they just don't give. Your foot's not going anywhere. When you pull up everything's going into moving your pedals and nothing's going anywhere else. I didn't like that stretch that you get with the clipless pedals. I like to tape my shoes with duct tape for big competitions.

Kilometer -- Rory O'Reilly

My bikes always look like sin. I wouldn't buff things out, and I'd never, paint them. They were always rusted.

I use small wheels front and rear, both 24s. I went all the way down to 18 inch wheels, but I could just never get the stability wired out of the saddle with that small of a wheel.

I felt 24 was pretty near ideal. You end up with a lighter wheel, stiffer frame, a lighter frame. Some of the studies I've seen show lower rolling resistance with some of the 24s.

The idea behind rolling resistance was about the deflection of the tire itself as it met the road surface. You would have all the fibers of the tire deflecting at the sharper angle. When you crank your tires up to 200 lbs., they have so little deflection to start with, that it doesn't really matter.

(see stories of Rory's famous "goofy bikes", Ch. 10)

Pursuit -- Rebecca Twigg

I use aero bars in Pursuit. I was a little concerned when I came back in '92 that they weren't helping me. I didn't go that fast. I thought maybe it

was that these new aerodynamics were not good for my position on my bike. I'm thankful that was not the case.

Aero bars are important. I use Scott bars and a rear disc wheel. I may use one on the front, depending on the conditions. If it's a little windy, I'll use a deep dish (spoked) wheel.

Eddie always wanted me to switch to clipless pedals when I was Pursuiting before, but I wouldn't. When I came back that's what was on the bike, so I got used to them. You can tighten them down pretty hard.

I use the same style of helmet that I used in the past. I have opinions on what works for me, but I know that maybe the same helmet wouldn't work for someone else. It's kind of a "shape of my head" kind of thing, for Pursuit, strictly a timed event. In the road race you have to look for ventilation and color and stuff like that for the heat.

I did wind tunnel testing and it confirmed what I already knew. They said "We can't improve on it, you're already aerodynamic." That means I can't go faster by changing equipment!

Pursuit -- Carl Sundquist

I have a road bike, a Time Trial road bike, a track bike and a Pursuit bike. If it were up to me I would standardize equipment in Pursuit. I would just use a regular track frame, drop or aero handlebars, no bull horns, just bolt on a pair of aero bars on your Points Race bike.

It's interesting that the Japanese are technological maniacs, yet in the Keirin circuit every bike is the same - - they're all standardized. There's something to be said for that. They could come out with all sorts of exotic

stuff, but they're trying to make it dependent on the rider, not the machinery.

I use aero bars and double discs if it's safe enough, depending on the wind. If it's not safe enough I might use a tri-spoke, but I've usually used a 16 spoke wheel. My 16 spoke wheel is one of those thicker types with the carbon fiber rim. Otherwise you have to have a minimum of 24 spokes, radial if you want, bladed spokes if you want, but you have to have a minimum of 24 spokes on the front and rear wheel. My front wheel is 26. My tires are pressurized at about 12 atmospheres, 165 to 170 lbs. I use clipless pedals.

I can't see that there'd be a whole lot of difference in the rolling resistance between 165 and 200. A tire pumped up to 200 lbs is going to wear out faster just from wear and tear on the casing than a tire at 165.

Gearing at low altitude is usually 51 - 15. In Colorado I might go up to a 53 - 15. I've pretty much been using those gears for a long time. 50 - 15 or 51 - 15 typically, at sea level.

I don't have a separate Kilo bike. You could go into so many variations. You could have a Kilo bike, a Pursuit bike and a Team Pursuit bike. You could almost rationalize all of that, just from various positions and things like that. It's nice to see that it's the athlete and not just the technology.

If you're doing Pursuit, you've got to have the equipment. That's the one thing that sucks about doing Pursuit riding. You've got to have a road bike, a road Time Trial bike, a Pursuit bike, and a regular track bike. If you're

a good road rider, one good road bike is all you need. It's a humorous whine, but it gets to be a drag tottin' around three or four bikes.

Team Pursuit -- Harvey Nitz

Equipment for Team Pursuit is: disc in the back, tri-spoke in the front, a smaller front wheel, a light frame, ram horns and aero bars. Ram horns for the start and then aero bars for the rest of the ride. Geometry on a bike is personal, everyone needs it to be different though it might look similar.

My father was an industrial engineer, so his line of work was aeronautics. We discussed bicycle aerodynamics, but the way the rules were back then, they didn't allow you to use a lot of those things.

I had discussed aero equipment in '76, about tubing and stuff, but we came to the conclusion after reading the Rule Book that it would all be illegal. Everything that we discussed ended up happening anyhow!

We rode disc wheels nine months before Moser did his hour record. We came to the conclusion that if we showed up at a World Championship with disc wheels, that they would outlaw them.

It was kind of a funny time. Ed Burke worked with the Federation. He was a big part of the research and development of high tech equipment. If we had gone to the World Championships before Moser rode the hour record I believe that disc wheels would not exist today. If the Americans showed up with them, they would outlaw them. But since *Moser* showed up with them, it was okay. He was like a god.

Olympic Sprint --
Too soon to tell!
Finally

While local tracks may occasionally offer an event on the track strictly for road bicycles, National Track Championships include no events for road bicycles whatsoever. The two are never raced together due to speed-change differences which makes the combination dangerous.

One reason track bicycles have stayed direct drive is the demands of the close quarters of the track. Direct drive means that the rider cannot coast, but s/he also cannot stop as quickly as s/he could with brakes. Therefore the bicycle is under direct control of the rider at all times, like it or not.

Brakes can stop a bicycle much more quickly than another rider can react in close quarters. If "braking" time depends on the rider resisting the forward motion of the pedals, other riders will have more time to respond. Rider speed cannot suddenly be so different that inability to react causes crashes. Everyone must maintain or change speed more slowly and in closer concert with each other. Riders cannot be instantly tricky and they are unable to make sudden stops. This is good.

Equipment, most often a single brake, can be put on a track bicycle to ride the road, A road bicycle can be altered so that it functions as a fixed-gear bicycle. The theory is that riding a fixed gear improves leg speed and pedaling. Most likely you will notice considerable variation in the equipment on the track. Next year equipment may look completely different.

Many people say it's the motor (the rider) that's the important thing, not the equipment at all. Others seem to live life for the latest innovation. Some bicycles are truly works of art, and it seems a shame to ride them.

There is a romance about the independent nature of bicycle endeavors. Bicycle enthusiasts pride themselves on their gasoline independence and reliance on human power alone.

Even today, the lone crazed inventor working in his garage can come up with ideas and devices which revolutionize the classic bicycle and therefore the sport.

Unfortunately, along with this constant innovation comes risk and injury from great ideas which did not quite work out. Each component on a bicycle has it's own evolutionary history. To some extent, this constant search for the ultimate bicycle is part of the fascination with the sport.

Bicycle history is a history of art and engineering. Track bicycles are both machines that developed at a particular period time in history and machines which have remained primarily the same due to their specialized use.

No matter what equipment a rider has, the most important investment is in time, time in studying and time in training. Competition success is not found in having the latest super-light equipment. It is found in the quality training miles put in each week with the support of others to hone the winning edge.

It is also found in the mental ability to stick with both the program and the dream.

How equipment innovations happen:

Shawn Wallace knew what he was doing when he arrived at the starting line to ride the Kilo. He was testing international acceptance of an "Obree" style bicycle. He was denied the opportunity to ride on his controversial equipment. While he was offered another bicycle, he opted instead to talk to journalists about the situation. Controversies and acts by riders such as Wallace force equipment changes. Presently the Obree bicycle is not accepted, said to be too unstable and dangerous. Others say it's not accepted because it's too <u>fast</u>. When this controversy is resolved another will take its place. It's part of the challenge.

Chapter 4
꩜ A Mini-History of Track Racing ꩜

The highly prized Rainbow Jersey of the World Champion. This one belongs to Lance Armstrong and is displayed in the Coaching Offices of the United States Cycling Federation.

Only the current World Champion is allowed to wear this in competition in the same arena where it was originally won, road worn only on the road, track worn only on the track.

Don't buy one that looks like this to ride your bicycle anywhere! That is a major no-no.

Marty Nothstein has TWO of these! Marty's jerseys don't say "Motorola" -- that's just the name of Lance's team. Marty's World Champion jerseys say "EDS".

The overview of track racing history presented here is a bare skeleton of the rich heritage of personalities and events which makes the world of the velodrome so colorful and would easily fill a thick book. Perhaps someone out there is writing that history now.

Meanwhile, readers are referred to Ted Harper's *Six-days of Madness*, Major Taylor's autobiography, and Nancy Neiman Baranet's *The Turned Down Bar* for more in-depth glimpses into this history. Peter Nye's *Hearts of Lions* has track racing history intermingled with many other stories. A search of the Library of Congress would likely turn up many others.

Two books have been produced entitled *Bicycle Track Racing*, both in 1977. One is by Barbara George, geared toward children, the other by "Editors of Bike World Magazine". The latter is a particularly interesting view of the sport through reflections of racers of the 60s and 70s.

"Statistics" History
The most concise synopsis of U.S. cycling history can be found in the "Statistics" section of this book. It was assembled largely from the 1990 and 1994 USCF RuleBooks.

The 1990 RuleBook was the last to list full historical data of Champions of U.S. cycling dating from the late 1800s. Results from Master's and Juniors divisions added in the late 80s quickly swelled the shear size of the RuleBook way out of proportion, so

only the Champions of the last 10 years (all divisions) are now listed.

Records in the "Statistics" section have been organized in "chunks" to offer overviews of various segments of track racing history on each page. Readers can also see how American cycling has developed over an extended time period, from turn-of-the-century racing through present day Master's and Junior's competition.

Prior to 1965, all races were held on an "Omnium" basis: a grand total of points, usually for three races, and one Champion. Beginning in 1965, three events were contested on an individual basis. These listings show the addition of other events over the years. On another page is assembled all Pan Am and Olympic medals won by the United States, World Champions, and so on.

What is readily apparent on these pages is that track racing has always been active in this country. It is "The Sport that Wouldn't Die". When the indoor velodromes were torn down, racers made do on criterium courses, horse race tracks, indoor gymnasiums and dance halls and on the few surviving tracks like Kenosha until tracks were built again.

You can't keep a good sport down.

The Time is Now
In the year of track racing history called 1996, the revival of track racing may be at hand which has been so long predicted by those who know first hand what an exhilarating sport it is.

First, an American, Marty Nothstein, has not only won <u>one</u> World Championship on the track, but an unprecedented TWO. It is no accident that the many lives which touched Trexlertown, Marty's home velodrome, are well documented in the pages of listings of past track Champions, beginning with the most unique Jack Simes and continuing with Marty's coach, Gibby Hatton.

Second, another person in the listings with a family tradition of track racing and construction, three time Pursuit Champion John VandeVelde (son Christian is a 1995 Pan Am Gold Medalist) has built a portable track which began touring in 1995. For many who are too far away from a "dug in" velodrome, the novelty of a portable will bring renewed interest in this thrilling spectator sport. It is also no accident that this book is being published now. Track racing is on the move.

When you study history, what you notice is that when major movements occur, several things are happening at the same time in different areas which come together, seemingly fortuitously, gathering a momentum which no one of the single occurrences could match. This appears to be happening now in track racing.

A survey of trends over the last twenty years shows the development of support structures upon which track racing in the 1990's is based. Profiles of riders represented in this book

includes how that rider got started and who influenced their development.

As you read about each person, it becomes apparent that these are very unique individuals but, at the same time, their development was strongly influenced by significant members of the track racing world who had gone before. Many of the same names keep popping up in different people's lives. They are a virtual living history of track racing.

From the bare existence of track racing in the fifties and sixties came the riders of the seventies, who became the Olympians of the eighties, who are now riders and coaches of the nineties. The base is built.

The Beginning

A bare few minutes chat with "old timers" in the sport reveals that a history restricted to velodrome racing would make for many hours of good reading. Velodrome racing has its own character and its own characters. What one finds in delving into assorted "histories" is that each is only the tip of the iceberg. That's why this section is so short here -- too much to cover!

Only an overview will be offered here for purposes of reflecting general trends. Insights by three unusual people unique to their time periods adds historical flavor to this section.

Most histories of bicycle racing begin with the devise itself -- that is not necessary here. Track bicycles have always been pretty much the same as they are today, with some variations, as reviewed in the Equipment chapter.

The 1990 USCF RuleBook lists Championship track events dating back to 1895. At that time velodromes were being built *everywhere* in the United States. San Francisco had, reportedly, six velodromes in Golden Gate Park alone. By the first decade, most cities of any size had several velodromes promising hair-raising, death-defying events. In the Puget Sound area, between 1894 and 1904, more than a dozen velodromes were in operation. An 1894 map of Seattle shows a "Seattle Cycle Track" located in Woodland Park. The quarter-mile sand and gravel track had grandstand seating for 2,000 spectators, a clubhouse with lockers and showers for the riders, and stalls for storing wheels.

Track racing had novel popularity at the turn of the century, grossly glorious popularity in the 20s and 30s, and virtual dormancy in the 40s, 50s, and into the 60s. The growth of track racing from the 70s is almost a separate story which might begin with a bunch of Midwestern speedskaters looking for some off-season training.

No segment of history can be isolated from its environment. Taking a broad view of historical trends, bicycle track racing was only one of many forms of entertainment which blossomed from the turn of the century until World War II. A wide spectrum of technological and cultural changes brought massive innovations to the attention of the public. Bicycles, motorcycles, cars, and airplanes exchanged technological motivation and design, which continues today.

The parallel development of film and radio in the 20s and 30s heightened the frenzy for the new, the exciting, and the glamorous. Even classical arts such as ballet enjoyed many of the accompanying promotion and exposure techniques developed to bring a new audience to its visual delights and heroic performers.

Traveling circuits of entertainers with exotic names and images were everywhere and the audience lusting for thrills and spills appeared endless. Bizarre rituals included "barnstorming" events and other airplane and auto feats, as attractive for their blood and guts displays as for any real demonstration of skill.

Marathon dance and athletic events, designed to tax human endurance literally to death became a somewhat perverse form of entertainment, especially during the depression of the 1930's, when people became desperate for any monetary source. One of these marathon events had been born in America many years before.

In his book "Six-days of Madness" (1993), Ted Harper, a Six-day racer from 1936 to 1941, sets on record memories of the old, exciting days. A taste of Harper's discussion is given here, centering on America's gift to the world of track racing.

The Great American Madison

Back in 1891, at Madison Square Garden in New York, marathon velodrome bicycle racing had crossed the Atlantic Ocean from Europe. These races were professional, though amateur events were also held during this period. Both were overseen by the National Cycling Association.

In 1898, the state of New York passed a law which no longer allowed riders to race for 24 hours straight. If truth be told, some people were killing themselves in an attempt to succeed in this "sport", taking drugs, punishing themselves beyond reason, in hopes of glory that might pay off, but could, and no doubt did, also kill them. To discourage this behavior, the new rules restricted riders to a maximum of 12 hours of continuous riding.

After momentarily tearing their hair out at this new, encumbering rule, promoters came up with a solution that gave birth to a uniquely American race which today is ironically more popular outside the country of its birth than in its own home town.

Riders began riding in teams, 12 hours each, maintaining the 24-hour progress of the race. In order to maintain continuity, riders would hand-off or "exchange" participatory authority while temporarily on the track at the same time. Named for its most famous United States arena, this race became known as the "Madison".

The first true, modern day Madison contest with two man teams, began in 1899. It was won by the team of Miller and Waller who covered 2733.4 miles. Riders rode for a total of 12 hours each over a 24 hour period, with sufficient breaks to rest and recuperate. One rider was required to be on the track at all times but did not have to be on for 12 hours straight.

Initially, the Madison was a yearly event, but in 1920 the race proved so popular that two races were held, in March and December. Harper says that in the 1920s and 30s Six-day races were so common that riders barely had a week's rest between events during the indoor season. Riders came from all over the world for the Big Bucks. Much secrecy surrounded earnings at that time, but top riders were known to make approximately (according to Harper) $1000 per race, $10,000 to $15,000 per year. Some riders made even more. That was big money at that time. National Hockey League players were making about $7,500 maximum, and baseball players, $5,000. Bicycle racing was big time stuff and one of the most popular of the spectator sports.

Harper also writes that beginning riders earned a mere $150 to $600 per race and had to pay their own transportation and expenses during non-race times. Promoters paid for many expenses, however, including food during races, trainers and runners, and for jerseys and tires. All things considered, the 30's were a rough time and certainly $150 looked like good money to those who had none. Harper does not discuss injury. There was no such thing as health insurance for the riders. Since injury and death was part of the drawing card to excitement, riders were in real danger.

The largest amount Harper heard of a rider earning was $20,000, won by Franco Giorgetti in one race after he had won Six-day races in a row in New York. Other variations and incentives existed, depending on the promoter and fame of the rider.

Equipment was very similar to today's tube frame bicycles. Riders' feet were strapped in with toe clips as many velodrome riders are today. Bicycles were direct drive as they are today. Tracks were steeper than any of the stationary tracks in the United States today, approximately 55° (the Vandedrome is 53°) Riders had to maintain a high enough speed not to fall off the banking -- at least 20 mph.

Race strategy was similar in some ways to modern Madisons, but the time factor forced riders to maximize efficiency. Much of the time riders would simply "suck a wheel", that is, "sit on" behind the rider in front and coast in his slipstream. The excitement would occur when riders attempted to "steal" laps on the field (same as today), racing to get off the front of the main pack and ride fast enough to end up on the back of the pack, therefore being a lap ahead of the other riders.

While it was easier for riders to lap the field on a smaller track, it was also harder to "get away" in order to do that. Riders knew that strategy and fought hard to prevent any rider from getting "off the front". Once the rider lapped the field he had to become part of the main field, not just straggle on the back, in order for referees to award him the lap (same as today).

This challenge to "steal" laps with high speeds for relatively short periods was where the change in riders and maximum efficiency gave birth to perfecting the Madison "exchange". The rider who began the "jam", as this race period was called, was likely as fresh or tired, and of equal ability as many of other the riders. Maximizing efficiency demanded top speed for as long as possible after taking opponents by surprise.

The relief rider got pushed off by a trainer, waited for his partner to come abreast, then increased to maximum speed because the partner either grabbed his "jam-ball" (a roll of cloth in the hip of his shorts) or by a hand-sling. One rider increased in speed as the other decreased, an efficient exchange. With luck, their opponents were left behind and the team gained a lap on the field.

If a crash occurred, often due to blowouts, five bells sounded to notify other riders of the crash, slowing the race temporarily. Three bells told the riders "the race is on!"

The same overall race strategy has always been classic to Madison races, even today, though it is more difficult to lap the field on the larger tracks which are common now. Tracks

in the old days were 150 to 160 meters (like the Vandedrome). Most stationary tracks in the U.S. today are 333 meters, over twice the distance. Tracks today also tend to be concrete and less steep (25 to 43 degrees), so they are slower than the old board tracks. However, lapping the field is still not unusual among top riders and the heart that is displayed in the attempt is always exciting and admirable, successful or not.

Sprints of one and two miles were included as part of the Madison race. Since these were part of the most exciting portions of the race, it is no wonder that Sprints and the Kilometer have evolved into a race of their own today. Riders also accumulated points during the sprint portions of the race, a precursor to the Points races of today. Safe riding was encouraged by fines imposed on riders who were felt to impede others trying to pass or make other race attempts, along with an assortment of unsportsmanlike behaviors. This continues today, though instead of fines, racing privileges are suspended.

Another type of bicycle racing in the old days was the Motorpace event, where riders rode behind motorcycles at high speeds. Americans began placing in international competitions in 1899. Today, a variation on this idea, Keirin racing, has developed into a multi-billion dollar industry in Japan. Bicycles raced in modern day Japan are virtually the same as the classic Six-day machines, and the frenzy of modern Keirin fans must sound equivalent to the frenzy of American fans in the heyday of Six-day racing.

Motordromes

One variation on the entertainment theme which united motorcycles and bicycles in the earliest years, was motorized bicycle racing on "motordromes". Motordromes were banked tracks, larger, more circular, and steeper than velodromes.

Huge audiences thrilled to the spectacle of bicycles with motors mounted on them as an alternative to speed powered solely by human might. Daring young men went around and around, displaying the terrifying speed of a devise which eventually went its own technological direction.

As motorized bicycles became motorcycles, they became unsafe for the motordrome environment. The oil dispersed by the motorcycles onto the oily walls of the tracks further increased the danger for both vehicles.

On September 12, 1912 an accident occurred in Newark, New Jersey which changed the future of motordrome racing forever. Two racers, two spectators and four young boys were killed and the Newark Motordrome was subsequently closed down. By the 20s, motorcycle racing had pretty much moved to dirt tracks.

Bicycles, on the other hand, were not only perfectly suited for the velodrome environment, they took over where the motordromes left off.

Why Track Racing Thrived

Certain conditions early in this century were especially conducive to velodrome racing. First, good roads were scare. The velodrome allowed bicycles to race at high speeds over its lovely, smooth surface without the bumps and potholes so common to a newly developing road system. On a velodrome, people could go FAST. Second, there were no such things as radios and televisions to divert people from the thrills of live entertainment. For maximum thrills, they went to the velodrome.

For bicycle racers, the big circuits in the old days were Chicago, Cleveland, New York, New Jersey and, on the west coast, San Francisco. Ironically, the Madison developed as uniquely an American event as baseball, but has become more appreciated in international arenas than here at home.

So, what killed the Six-day circuit in the United States? According to Ted Harper, Six-day competition died because of World War II. According to James McGurn, it died in the thirties. According to Peter Nye, velodrome racing was struggling in the 30s, but so was the entire country. Nye also writes "When Bobby Walthour III came of age after World War II, all the wooden velodromes in this country were gone." Nye goes on to say that the Amateur Bicycling League of America held competitions on country roads and that this was all that remained of competitive cycling (though a few velodromes like Kenosha did remain.)

One factor in the death of the Six-day circuit was certainly World War II. Men and supplies were at a premium and no one had time for frivolities of the past. There was an attempt to reactivate the Six-day circuit after the war, but it did not "take". There were other factors involved which diverted potential fans from this focus.

First, America fell in love with

power. Power in the form of petroleum dependent machinery like the automobile, the motorcycle and the airplane. These were not only more powerful but also more glamourous than plodding away on a devise which actually forced its operator to break a *sweat*. Industries associated with those devices offered far greater profits than the lowly bicycle. Power machines got the push, even the <u>manipulation</u> by business (paving over trolley tracks in L.A. so people would have to buy automobiles), to make them king.

Another evolutionary change occurred in the form of mass media. With the advent of television, it was more difficult to get crowds out for events when people could sit in their living rooms with free entertainment.

Unfortunately, unlike some other sports, bicycle racing was not one which was offered to television audiences as were others. In the 50s and 60s, when television became the rage, there were very few tracks in existence, much less any who offered racing suitable for home entertainment. Track racing was simply not "happening" when television came to power. The "ball" sports took up as many time slots as became available over the years.

However, track racing has never been dead in the United States. When the wooden tracks were gone, clay and horse tracks remained. They weren't as glamourous or as well attended as the glory days, but track races were, indeed, held on tracks located in such places as St. Louis, Kenosha and Milwaukee. Track enthusiasts would not let them die.

They held their places like lighthouses, casting beacons of light in the darkness.

In the 70s, changes began occurring in the world of bicycle racing in general and in velodrome racing specifically. In 1973 the ABL selected the first National bicycling team. Track cyclists were Gary Campbell, Steve

If Ron Summer had his way, all riders would ride on bicycles like his 1900 Racycle. Marymoor, 1990

Woznick, Dave Chauner, Bobby Phillips, Roger Young, Ralph Therrio and Jeff Spencer. The next year ('74) riders became separated into categories according to ability, A, B, & C.

In the 70s, cycling blossomed. After Audrey McElmury won the women's World Road Championships (the first American to win a World Road Championship) in 1969, the pump was primed for women. Two speedskaters who began riding bicycles for off-season training began taking turns on the World Track Cham-

pionship podiums.

Sheila Young and Sue Novara won five World Championships, 13 World medals total, between them. They also provided training for an upcoming Sprinter named Connie Paraskevin who won her first National Sprint title as a "Midget" in 1975 and has since walked away with four World Championships (so far) of her own, dominating her competition for 20 years.

In 1974, a feisty little guy named Gibby Hatton, coached by 50s/60s Sprint great Jack Disney, stunned the track racing world by winning the Junior World Sprint Championships in Warsaw, Poland. While it wasn't the Senior division, the fact remains, Gibby was actually the first American male to win a World Sprint title since 1912. His eight years on the Japanese Keirin circuit was another first. In 1994, 20 years after Gibby won Junior Worlds, his student (Marty Nothstein) won the World Senior Championship in both the Sprints <u>and</u> the Keirin. It went around and it came around.

In 1975 and 1976 four new velodromes were opened. In 1975, fields began including both amateurs and professionals. A fourth category was added to competition ranks. The name "Amateur Bicycling League of America" was changed to the "United States Cycling Federation" (USCF).

With the steady increase in international success, America began to take itself seriously as a bicycle racing force. The USCF searched out and hired a Polish immigrant named Eddie Borysewicz to develop a <u>serious</u> bicycle racing team for the 1984

Olympics. All of a sudden, after **zero** Olympic medals in bicycle track racing, since the turn of the century, America won <u>five</u>, plus four more on the road. We were on the map at last.

Since those lean early years, bicycle racing has only gained momentum. In 1979, **Greg LeMond won a Silver medal in the Pursuit on the track** and a Gold on the road in the Junior World Championships. In 1981 he won Silver as a Professional in the World Championships on the road. The rest is history (time to look at the "Statistics" section!)

What if the same incentive had existed at that time to race track as there was to race the road? Might LeMond have been a track racer? Is it possible that, robbed of endurance to race the grueling roads, LeMond might consider turning to a newly lucrative track circuit for personal and financial rewards? An interesting idea. Successful or not, he could certainly activate an audience, regardless of role.

LeMond's achievements brought bicycle racing back into the media spotlight. In track racing, Marty Nothstein has taken up the torch. With his double victory, track racing enters another golden age.

While the power of petroleum driven machines remains a source of fascination for Americans, the media has again undergone a shift, this time offering new opportunities for expanding concepts in sports entertainment. With the prospect of a Keirin-type betting arena which may be emerging in the United States, audiences may also be able to feel they are participating from their armchairs (as well as their wallets).

ESPN, ESPN2 and other channels carrying sports programming, provide many "time slots of opportunity" begging for new and novel events to present to an audience thirsting for entertainment over the hundreds of channels now being proposed for every subscriber.

So far, camera techniques are not adequately translating the thrill of bicycle track racing to the TV screen. Television succeeds when a viewer receives the same excitement at home as at the sporting event and can see it better. Cameras are too far away, shots too disjointed. Techniques developed for football, baseball, etc., don't work. Even the most enthusiastic bicycle track racing fan finds home viewing unexciting, knowing that if they were there, their hearts would be in their throats!

Velodrome racing is more like *bobsledding*, and needs to be photographed appropriately. The Japanese likely know some secrets. If betting starts in this country, watch how fast coverage improves! Software giants like Microsoft search for ways to assist audiences in following the action. Maybe this is the key. When television learns to place the whoosh, the energy and the heart-stopping danger of bicycle track racing on film, sponsors will clamor to get in on the hot action.

Live entertainment is still a big draw. European, Japanese and Australian models show that people will attend velodrome racing in person and grow as addicted to its excitement as any other sport or entertainment -- if they understand what they're watching.

With the present merging of amateur and professional sports, an upsurge in velodrome possibilities becomes more practical than it has ever appeared in the past. As road racing and off-road racing have shown, bicycle racers will go where the money is. As audiences whet their appetites for exciting competition, track racing finds its glory.

While in the past Marty Nothstein would have had to guard his amateur status for the sake of Olympic dreams, today he and other aspiring Olympians can race for the Big Bucks without compromising that goal. Television, which once was prohibited from offering top athletes monetary incentives, can now treat everyone the same.

The opportunity is in place, complete with at least one television announcer who knows track racing like he knows no other sport (Brian Drebber). Others who have announced live and know the sport are waiting in the wings. Once again, we have converging factors which force the gathering momentum. Watching this modern history unfold is most intriguing.

And . . . the bicycle . . .

The independence of the bicycle as a form of transportation has long captured the imagination of free spirits. This ingenious devise has lead to many innovations in transportation growing up with the automobile, the airplane and the motorcycle. As the others became increasingly petroleum dependent, the bicycle alone remains dependent exclusively on human physiology for its power.

Basic instincts force us to investigate how fast this vehicle might go, how far, how to build the most ingenious model, who can triumph within any given set of race conditions, et cetera.

Aficionados of velodrome racing see racing track bicycles as very pure, demanding power and skill while cut to the most basic elements possible. There is no more simple bicycle than a track bicycle. No more simple a course than a velodrome.

Cutting the challenge down to utmost simplicity lends track racing incredible beauty. The task becomes dependent on the skill of individual riders, not on the machinery.

While engineers seek efficiency in aerodynamics and materials, the basic machine has not changed since the beginning of track racing. Attempting to improve on this most simple machine while maintaining its essential elements, has evolved into a high art.

Responding to a challenge to ingenuity is basic to the American spirit. Making petroleum dependent machines more complex has always been very easy. There is no greater challenge than coming up with ways to improve the ever-so-simple bicycle. The challenge of going faster on this vehicle with more skill than one's opponent will never diminish.

And on a velodrome, every thrilling moment is right before your eyes.

50 years of bicycle racing
Bob Bergen

Bob Bergen gets a push off from son Damon who raced "Midgets", "Intermediate" and "Junior" in the past. Damon now goes to school full time in Finland. This is not your usual duo (and proud of it). 1993.

Talk to Bob Bergen for more than about 10 minutes and you know you're having a chat with a most unusual guy. A retired lawyer and volunteer Sheriff, Bob has had one of the longest careers in track racing. He is a sponge for new and unusual information. Some of his stories belong in that history book someone is writing. He speaks of a kind of racing here that few people know.

The first velodrome I know of in San Diego was built in 1916. It went from Harbor Drive to Pacific Highway to Broadway. It was very steep. In 1917 when the United States got involved in World War I, they tore part of it down. What was left became the grandstand for Lane Field where the Padres played until Westgate Park Stadium was built.

The Morley Field velodrome was a dirt track when I first got into racing. I don't know when it began, but I know from 1936 to about 1948, including the war years when nothing was happening, that was the track that we had. The first bicycle race that I won was on that track in 1940, on September 14.

My First Bicycle

I got my first bicycle in 1936. I discovered I could ride that bicycle faster than other people. In 1937-1940 I went to Theodore Roosevelt Junior High School. I came home up the Morley Street hill. I was passing people walking their bikes up the hill. I could

never understand. I'd ask them, "What's the matter, did you get a flat tire?"

When they had the Nationals in 1983 I thought "Isn't this interesting, I used to ride up this hill every day coming home from school, and here we are, all these years later." I'd lived over in Golden Hills and I figured I'd been up that hill more times than anyone.

The present track is close to my old house. The irony of that is that Harry Backer, who was the top San Diego rider that I knew up to that era, lived right there on Arnold and Utah Street and there was no track. For him to get track experience he had to go to Europe. He was on the U.S. Olympic Team in 1952. He was the first guy from San Diego on the Olympic Team, and he had no track to ride in San Diego.

The tracks in the 30s and 40s were steep and short. Some of them were tiny, only 110 meters.

My First Bicycle Race

The first bicycle race I ever saw was when my mother took me to the Olympic Games in 1932. I was just a little boy in Pasadena. The reason we went there was because it was free. It

was the height of the depression and it was free.

I was awed by these big men on these little skinny bikes that came *screaming* by. We just saw them once as they came by in the road race, but I was really impressed.

In 1934 they made that movie Six Day Bike Rider that I've seen many, many times, with Joe E. Brown. I knew some of the guys who were in that movie. In 1936 the Olympics Trials finished in San Diego and I met Myers who won the race, and Charlie Morton was second. I was impressed when they went to Europe.

I was just reading Cycling USA where John Sinibaldi won the Time

Trial of the 80-year-olds in Florida. I stopped and said "I can't believe he's 80 years old!" He was the hot shot rider all over the United States in the 30s. I have a picture of him taken when he was 19. Now they wouldn't know who he is. This is a whole new generation. They don't know who these people are. John Sinibaldi is the last of the old Six-day racers. All the others have gone on.

My First License

I got my first license in 1940. It said ABL on it. My ABL license cost $.25 for Juniors and $.50 for Seniors. I was a Junior, so it cost me $.25.

Back in the old days there was no insurance, but there was always something happening, some sort of terrible spill.

I've got a picture somewhere in my scrapbook of the Wisconsin State Championships of 1933 showing a massive spill in progress with the front riders still in the air. Helmets cost $5.00.

"Hairnets" were the ones being used. I watched the hairnets getting skinnier and skinnier. When the Mexicans had them they were virtually nothing. There were hard shell helmets around, but they weren't nearly the same as the ones around today.

I think the ones today aren't that good. I saw a terrible crash in Brea last year where a young man on the French team went down and the whole front of the helmet just broke off. He had blood coming out of his ears, nose and mouth. He looked terrible. He really went down hard. It was in the Valentine's Day Massacre. The field came flying around with about 100 riders. After the field passed there was one rider left on the ground, who knows what happened? I was standing right there and I didn't see him go down, but he sure must have gone down hard.

Tracks

There was a track in Montebello, California, an asphalt velodrome. I don't know when it started, but they raced there in the 30s. I remember in '46 or '47 they had a work party that

"So, how is it, racing for 50 years?" I asked. "Well," he said, "Guys come along and beat you, then you beat them and then they're gone . . . "

tried to see about restoring it, but it was just hopeless. The asphalt was all chipped and the weeds were growing through. It was terrible.

The big racing in California was at the velodrome in San Jose, a board track. Now there's an asphalt track, one of the nicest ones on the Pacific coast. I don't know why they never bid on the National Championships, but it's one of the nicest ones we have. I don't know if the one now is on the same site as the old one, San Jose changes so much.

All the Italian-Americans lived around San Jose. They called them the "Wop Club". Many, many of the top riders raced up there. Sammy Rinella is one that comes to mind. Jimmy Perez is another one -- he wasn't Italian. The Gatto brothers were there, and all of the Gatto family raced on the

velodrome, Vince and Gus and all the other Gattos.

We raced at Culver City, which was the Midget auto racing track. We raced at the El Cajon Speedway for years. I raced on portable tracks at Sacramento, San Jose, Burbank -- the one at Burbank we called the "Flying Saucer". They also assembled it inside the Rose Bowl and we raced there a bunch of times. We raced in San Bernadino. It was connected with the Orange Show. I still have a big trophy from there. It's like an animated face of an orange.

I came in at the end of the 1930's. We rode those tracks all in the 1940's until the end of the 50's. When Encino came in, all the others in that same area just disappeared. There was one set up in San Fernando.

We raced on a lot of automobile tracks that people don't know about. When the midget auto racing was going on in the 30s, it was on dirt tracks, then they began paving and banking those dirt tracks.

There was a lot of bicycle racing going on. We raced in Balboa Stadium. The National Championships in 1949 were held in Balboa Stadium. It was a dirt track. I still have the bulletin from that and the newspaper article. Jimmy Lauf, was the National Champion in

San Diego on Balboa Stadium, I still see him. He shows up for races once in a while.

San Diego wasn't banked at that time. They talked about it being banked, but it was insignificant. Enough to make the water drain to the pole, that's about it.

The Pole Lane & Horse Tracks

The term "pole" came from horse racing. Some mathematician figured out that if two parallel lines were drawn in the shape of an oval, the shortest way around was the inside line. The start and finish line used to be the start and finish pole.

With all these dirt tracks, we raced horse racing tracks everywhere. I raced at Del Mar in 1942. Track bikes were all they had then. We raced at Santa Anita race track, Los Alamitos Speedway in Long Beach. There was bike racing everywhere.

Even the old High Wheelers used to race on horse tracks. There was bike racing everywhere. Everywhere there was a horse racing track there was bicycle racing on the dirt.

There was also balloon tire bike racing. People nowadays think the mountain bike was invented yesterday. We had those forever. My whole lifetime we had those. They had the spring fork, they had those going back a long way.

I've got a picture of Albert Champion. He won the Paris-Roubaix race in 1899 and he was riding a balloon tire bike. He later came to the United States and founded the Champion spark plug company.

They had races in the same

Olympic Stadiums as the old Olympics. In the Coliseum in Rome, in Lyons, France, there's one in Spain, in Timbuctu, in Africa.

The Olympic Games used to travel like they do now, but one year they were held in Lyons, France, another year they were held in Spain, a couple of times in Morocco, Algeria, all those old south Mediterranean stadiums. All anyone seems to know about today is the Coliseum in Rome, but that's just one of many.

Asphalt tracks were around, as far as I know, in the 40s, and probably earlier. Don't forget that asphalt is an ancient thing. It was invented by a Scotsman named MacAdam. That's where the term maccadam comes from. It was a process he invented using tar and sand. That very inferior process is still used around the world for paving. They're still using it in Russia, for example. The problem with that is that when the sun comes out, it gets soft.

In the 40s, most of them were dirt. Dirt track racing is an interesting concept. Whatever you race on, you get good at. You practice, practice and become very good. We became very skilled at dirt track racing. We used a heavier tire and a lower gear. It was a matter of bike handling.

When the guys from L.A. would come down to race on our track, we were beating them because we could go around our track faster than they could on the dirt, without sliding and being afraid and all that.

Flat Floor Racing

Another kind of racing I just happened to think of was the Flat Floor racing. In New York we raced on the flat floor in The Armory, which was like a dance hall. In many, many cities they had second story dance pavilions, dance halls. Then would make a big circle on the dance floor and the bike riders would race.

You'd ride with a tennis shoe on

"I've never really stopped racing. I did 54 races last year. I ride races people don't even know about. I get on an airplane and go to Wisconsin to ride a series of races that nobody in California knows anything about, Pennsylvania or New Mexico. I'm inundated with all sorts of things through the mail. I get entries that nobody else seems to know about. There's racing everywhere." Master's Nats, '93.

your left foot so you could put your foot down like the motorcycle riders put their knee down now. We would put one foot down with a toe strap just on the right foot, and we'd have Flat Floor racing. Sometimes you'd use a

shorter crank on your left than you would on your right.

I raced in New York when I was in the Navy, about 1945. Flat Floor racing. In New York was the first time I saw that. One day a week they'd have this Flat Floor racing in the armory, where the National Guard met. They'd do this in the winter time when there was snow on the ground and it was cold outside, windy and rainy.

The only difference with the bikes was the shorter cranks on the left and the rubber pedals off the stock bikes.

I'd just take my toe clip off the left crank and someone would loan me a short left crank -- your chain's on the other side anyway -- and you'd strap in one foot. You'd leave the other one free so you could put one down and drag it going around the corners.

The course was really tight, like a gymnasium. It worked out pretty well. We tried to avoid hitting the wall. Spectators were jammed in the corners. They put hay bales in the corners to protect them. Even smaller ones were the dance halls. There were dance halls everywhere.

There was a dance hall here in San Diego, but I never raced on it. They were very popular places. They'd bring in an orchestra -- they even had these dime a dance things with dance hall girls. Dance halls go clear back to the wild west, you know. It was the forerunner to the modern ballroom.

Anyway, I haven't heard of Flat Floor racing for years. It was an era and the guys got very good at it. If you were coming in for the first time you would have no chance against somebody who had been racing there regularly. I think they went on for about three decades. The New York Armory was the one I raced on, but I heard about others.

Barrel Racing

Another thing we raced on was in Long Beach, along the beach there, they called it "The Pike". There was a merry-go-round, a carnival atmosphere, a roller coaster, and all of those things.

There was a guy in there who had a huge barrel. He had barrel racing, with motorcycles going around inside of the barrel. He also had motorcycles going around inside a globe. I never tried that, but we raced on the barrel. It was straight up and down, 90 degree banking.

The way to do it was to ride it with stiff hubs (fixed gear) and a very, very low gear. The barrel was maybe 30 feet in diameter. The spectators would go up to the very top of the barrel and look down.

Some of the bike riders would use balloon tire bikes, but we used our regular racing bikes. Even the guys on the balloon tire bikes used stiff hubs - - everybody used stiff hubs.

We called fixed gears "stiff hubs" and we called our training tires "frog skins". We could use frog skins on the barrels. Because the gear was so low, it didn't matter.

When we rode on the barrel one event was to get three on the track at the same time with the middle guy going the opposite direction. Try to pass without colliding.

The frightening thing on that was that after a while you lost all sense of direction. You're balance and everything else was gone. It was kind of scary. To try to get off the track was scary.

There was a little platform that was maybe four feet wide. You'd go in the circle, ride around in the circle very slowly, then you'd jump on this 45 degree bank which is like the steepest track we have, then from there you'd try to go up on the 90 degree banking, getting up without falling and trying to get back down without

falling.

Interestingly enough I don't recall anybody falling. We also didn't wear helmets. That was racing inside a barrel.

The only place I ever did that was Long Beach. It was just between motorcycle acts. People would dare others to do it and they wouldn't even be able to get on the board.

There was not much difference between riding a dirt track and a clay track. The only difference was that the dirt track was loose, so you were in danger of sliding. If the clay track was ground out smooth, it wasn't too bad.

Other Racing

Another kind of racing that we haven't talked about is grass track racing. I've never raced on grass tracks, but the ones I've heard about are the ones in the Caribbean Islands. Trinidad, principally, and Barbados, Jamaica, Martinique. I understand those tracks are banked a little bit.

They have the other kinds of velodromes too, but there's always somebody good coming up from there, guys like Gene Samuels and a couple of others. They were very good.

There's a guy named Knute Knudsen who did all his training on a dirt high school track in Northern Norway and then he goes to the Worlds and wins the Pursuit title. He turned pro and rode the Tour de France.

When I was in high school we had interscholastic competitions. We raced in Balboa Stadium. That was considered a clay track. They had the running track going and they had the lanes painted. I raced for San Diego

High against Calipatria High, El Centro High, and so the interscholastic racing goes way back. Monte Vista High School, near where I live, has it's own bicycle team. I see them out riding.

You have to remember that many of the old records you see in the record books were set on dirt tracks, not the paved roads like today. On the old dirt tracks they would smooth out on the areas going into the turn on the pole. It would get a little bumpy and you had to be careful not to slip and slide.

I rode the dirt tracks with both a free wheel and a fixed gear. I haven't been on a dirt track in forever. I don't see any reason to race them now. The BMX bikes race on dirt. That was for

little kids, now you see older guys taking them over.

I've never really stopped racing. I did 54 races last year. I ride races people don't even know about. I get on airplane and go to Wisconsin to ride a series of races that nobody in California knows anything about, or to Pennsylvania or New Mexico. I'm inundated with all sorts of race entries through the mail that nobody else seems to know about. There's racing everywhere.

I need someone to help me organize my medals. I have over 1,000 and they're in boxes everywhere. I don't know what to do with all of them. They're all over the place!

Bob was the fourth member of a medal-winning Master's Team Pursuit Team in 1993 Master's Nationals. The team's age had to total 150 or more. Bob was a definite asset. (Bergen, Mark Rosenthal, Phil Buhl, and Tom Lee)

America's First World Champion since 1912 Audrey McElmury

Audrey McElmury was America's first World Road Champion of either sex, amateur or Professional, yet she is virtually unknown.

She won the World Road Championships in 1969. In 1966, she won both the National Pursuit title and first National Road Championship. In 1969 she won the track Omnium. In 1970 she again won the Pursuit and Road Championships.

Audrey may have been better represented in the annals of U.S. National Track competition if she had opted to compete at the National level rather than at the Worlds level. If there was a choice, she raced with men rather than compete in the women's division, even when she might have easily won. Her aim was excellence and World level experience at the sacrifice of easier competition.

While not primarily a track rider, Audrey is represented here to honor her World Championship which remains a milestone in American bicycle racing history and a most underrated achievement.

She held the U.S. National Hour Record on the track for over 20 years (1969 to 1990), along with several on the road. She is a modest Champion.

How it Started

Peter McElmury, (husband) Scott's brother got me started in bike racing. He started with American Youth Hostels (AYH) with Dr. Clifford Graves and his group. We went on a trip to Europe and then decided to start racing. It was strictly a social thing at first: "Well, Pete's doing that. That looks like fun, I think we'll start doing that." They had these qualification rides: 25 (miles) in 3 (hours), 50 in 5 . . it used to be a big thing everybody in San Diego rode.

I started racing roads in San Diego. I started racing track at Encino Velodrome because it was the only track in Southern California. They didn't have a State Championship for women back then. If you wanted to be State Champion, you had to ride the track.

Track racing was also the only National Championship for women in 1964 and 1965. It was a combination of Sprint, 1 Mile and 2 Mile races.

In 1965, they changed it to individual track events for men but it was still a combination event (Omnium) for women, with no road championship. It was held at Encino Velodrome in LA. I placed second.

It wasn't until '66 that they had the first National road race, which I won.

Audrey was America's first female World Champion and the first American of either sex to win a World Road title. She raced track at every Worlds she rode "just to get the nerves out." "Actually I enjoyed track racing a whole lot more than road racing, because it's more like being in the spotlight. Road racing is so lonely. You can't have hundreds of thousands of people watching you unless it's the World Championships."

The women's track included the Pursuit and the Sprint. I won the Pursuit and the road race.

In 1968, I rode the Worlds in Italy instead of Nationals.

In 1969, they changed the women's track Championship back to an Omnium consisting of a Sprint, Pursuit and a 1 Mile race. I won that event due to disqualification of the other rider who knocked me down.

I could not perform in the National road race, although I rode it, due to that accident.

1972 was the only year I didn't ride the track.

Records

I had the National record for Pursuit for a number of years, but I was never really that good at it. It was 4:06 or so.

I set the hour record at Encino. I got so dizzy because it's that little tiny 250 meter track. If you go around and around that thing for an hour, anybody's dizzy!

When I rode Encino, Jerry Rimoldi was coaching me. We used to work out in Quivira Basin in San Diego for Sprints. It was a long stretch of road. It's all built up now, but we used to use it for Sprints. We had it marked off for

UPI Photo, McElmury Collection

Audrey's win was totally unexpected. She waited over an hour in the rain for officials to find a copy of the U.S. National anthem for the awards ceremony.

various distances, like 1000 meters, which is about where you exit off. We all had to have brakes on our track bikes, no one would let you ride without brakes. You had to be able to stop if a car came by. We used track bikes, but with brakes. That's how we trained for the track, because we couldn't go to Encino during the week from San Diego, it was too far.

In those days I was married to Scott (McElmury). He rode the Worlds in Team Pursuit in Barcelona. We belonged to San Diego Bicycle Club. It was the only one around.
In the U.S. I've ridden Northbrook, Dorais, Kissena, Encino, the one in Chicago, and also in Mexico City. We never had time to set up record attempts in Mexico. Colorado didn't have a track at the time we lived there. We did the track events on the oval at Colorado State University. They had an oval driveway surrounded by trees. It was up hill and down hill. We also used it as a criterium course. It was about a mile around.

International Racing

I missed a lot of National Championships because the Worlds were at the same time, and I wanted to go to the Worlds instead of going to Nationals.

In 1973, I went to the Worlds in San Sebastian, Spain instead of to Nationals. I rode the track there in Sprints -- 48 degrees! It was concrete. It was real wide, too, because they built it for motorpacing. If you were up at the top you had a <u>long</u> drop to the bottom if you fell down!

I had to be taught how to take my bike all apart and put it back together. Every time we traveled to Europe we took everything off the bike and carried it. We had to think about weight limits on the plane. I don't know what they do internationally now, but it was weight that was important then, not the number of pieces. 20 kilograms per person. So, we took all the equipment off and carried it on, the handlebars, seat, cranks and everything.

Frankfurt was the only Worlds I didn't ride the roads. There was some question about how to get to it.

1965, '66, -- '67 I had Ian (my son),-- '68, '69, '71. 1972 was the one time I didn't ride the track. Michael and I were together and we didn't have a track bike with us. We rode the track at Varese. Michael hated it. It was a 500 meter track and steep, 40°! We'd get out there and all these Italian guys would be playing soccer in the middle of the track and the ball would fly up and hit the bikes.

I rode the track in Brno, Czechoslovakia the year I won the Worlds (1969). Track was before the road events. I was on a road bike set up as a track bike. It was very light.

I knocked Jackie Simes down on that track. I hit the crack on the banking and I wasn't going fast enough. I think it wrecked his wrist and screwed up his Worlds. His big event was the Kilo. I wasn't worried about winning anything on the track. I raced track to get the nervousness out.

Jackie threw a champagne bottle out of the 11th story window of the dormitory in Czechoslovakia and hit a tank. The tank turned it's guns toward the dorm. It was the first anniversary of the Russian invasion. They had tanks going all over. They kicked everybody out of the country except the bicycle racers. That was memorable!

I never got a medal on the track in the Worlds. I think my best placing was fifth. I almost got a medal in Rome, but Jerry (my coach) gave me the wrong lap and I was out of it. He told me one to go and it was two to go. I only did that event because I really enjoyed it. It was fun doing something that you know you're not going to do anything in, but you're good enough to be World class. There's no pressure and you get the nerves out.

Support

I always had to pay my own way. I got a few contributions from Kiwanis, like $100 or so, but really it was my dad who paid for my racing expenses. I couldn't have gone without his support. It used to cost about $10,000 to go. Plane fare, room, transportation, -- we used to stay for about six weeks.

The year after I won Worlds the Amateur Bicycle League (ABL) gave me some money and all the guys wanted me to give it to them! I was the only one who had money to go to England and they were mad! They gave me about half the fare.

At that time the way you went to the Worlds was to say "Hey Al, (ABL Director at the time) I want to go to the Worlds!" We always used to fight because they always wanted me to go to the Nationals, not the Worlds, and I wanted to go to the Worlds. We'd go 'round and round. Jerry (Rimoldi) handled it all. He was Treasurer of the national organization.

There was no real National Team at that time. If you went to the Worlds you were considered on the National Team, at least for that trip, and then that was it. Almost everybody rode for themselves.

San Diego Bicycle Club had a team, but most of your team work was driving to the races with somebody and sharing the gas money. Most racing was individual, you didn't help each other, you raced against each other.

Motivation and Winning

I got good because I raced with the men. It makes you better than you are when you race with people who are better than you are all the time.

Women weren't racing with men at that time. They wouldn't let them. Jerry helped me get permission. In the Denver Criterium, I didn't get anything -- sprint with men -- give me a break! The woman winner got a hot air balloon ride.

I was more interested in being good than winning prizes. I liked

Audrey & Michael (Pan Am Team, '71) goin' fishin'.

winning, I liked being in the spotlight, especially racing with the men. I was the only woman and there were two hundred men out there -- it was great.

Racing with the men made me the toughest of any training techniques. I just always raced with the men except in Europe. There were fewer races for women. I even did team races on the track at Encino with guys. I did Madisons and Italian Pursuit. It was fun.

When you read about some of the "imaging" people (Wayne Dwyer and others), that's exactly what I did with cycling. I would get an image of how I was going to win the race. Now that I'm reading things and listening to tapes, I pick up on what went on then. You image in your mind how you're going to do this and then you have alternate images if that doesn't work.

I won the Worlds because I visualized it, I believed I could do it. You get it in your head that you're going to win. I was fifth the year before. And, I thrive on adversity.

I don't think I'd do as well as a young person nowadays with all the regimentation. I like the fun of putting your own bike together or having to get your own tires and just deal with everything, because I never had a coach with me.

I did in Italy for a little while, but he left before the road race, and in Czechoslovakia he was there, but I paid his way. We'd already been there for a while when I sent him the money to travel and said "Hey, we need you, we're going crazy, we can't handle this." That was the most foreign country we'd ever been in and they were in chaos. They might as well have been having the Russian revolution!

Track Racing's the Best

Actually I enjoyed track racing a whole lot more than road racing, because it's more like being in the spotlight. Road racing is so lonely. You can't have hundreds of thousands

of people watching you unless it's the World Championships except for criteriums.

Track racing is more exciting. That's one of the reasons I always liked to do it, but I got started in it because that was all they had. It's a much more social thing than road racing, because you have to sit around and watch everybody else race. So, you talk and stuff.

The trouble is, you can have a road race anywhere there's roads, while track races can only be raced on a track, which is only certain places. Everybody has a road bike, but everybody doesn't have a track bike. Except for Six-day racing, track racing

is not as popular in Europe. Track racing was never very popular, it was always road racing. The event that's really popular is the criterium, where you see the riders more often.

I still only have one bike trophy. It's a marble, hill climb trophy from Italy. I donated most of my trophies to Monday International to be recycled in the Tecate-Ensenada Bicycle Race. I also still have a crystal vase from the Worlds, but it's not really a trophy, it's a vase. I still have a trophy given to me by AYH after I won Worlds and my induction plaque to the Bicycling Hall of Fame. I like plaques, they look nice. I get claustrophobia when there are too many things on the wall!

Audrey still keeps tabs on the bike racing scene when not fishing, whitewater rafting, backpacking and skiing. She and husband Michael Levonas are presently building a log house in West Yellowstone and plan to operate an adventure tour/ catering business. "Still crazy after all these years . . . "

Jack of All Bicycle Racing Jack Simes III

Jack Simes III must be the most unique individual ever to be involved in bicycle racing.

The name Jack Simes debuted in bicycle competition, with Jack's grandfather. The Simes name first appears in the RuleBook when Jack Simes Jr. won the National Omnium Championship in 1936 .

Jack Simes III won his first National Championship in 1959. In the 60s he engaged in an on-going battle with Jack Disney, winning the National Sprint title in alternate years.

He won Silver twice in the Kilometer at the World level, first in the Pan American Games in 1967 and again in the World Championships in 1968.

Jack was Trexlertown's first velodrome director. He coached national teams in the 70's. He won the 36+ Master's road race in 1979.

A pivotal force in United States Professional bicycle racing, Jack returned to competition in 1988, almost sweeping Master's competition in Sprint, Kilometer and Pursuit (he allowed Robert Lea to win the Points race), setting a Master's record in the Pursuit.

After seeing his USPRO organization become an official part of the USCF, Jack has taken a breather, "only" serving on boards of the USCF and UCI. But, there is no question, he ain't done yet.

How I Got Started

Both my grandfather and my father raced. My father was a really good racer, but he retired by the time he was 21 because he had a very bad accident. He won about 40 open events on the road in those days at a young age. He could have been much, much better. He was primarily a road rider, but he did both road and track.

When I started, cycling was pretty much an underground sport. I started in the fifties. At that point there were still a lot of people around who had been involved with cycling when it was a major sport in the 20s and 30s. Members of local clubs kept cycling alive in this country.

After World War II, cycling virtually went underground. People ran club races on the back roads all around the country and did their own activities. There wasn't any media coverage and the sport didn't have their own publications. My father was one of those people who helped keep cycling alive.

There was also a gentleman named Tino DeAngelis who donated some money to bring over some "midget racing bikes", twenty-four inch racing bikes from Italy. He gave them to some clubs on the east coast hoping that some kids would get these things and the sport would begin to grow. I was one of those kids and Mike Fraysee (USCF President) was one of those kids. Bikes at that time were all single gear bikes. Tino was kind of a controversial character.

I began as an amateur in 1952. I was about 8 1/2 at that time, riding on the back roads of New Jersey on the club level. We had no velodromes around at that time. The closest thing we had to a track was a half-mile, flat, paved oval where Shea Stadium now sits. That was the old 1939 World's Fairgrounds. It was used only for cycling. It was part of the Fairgounds and then it became a huge parking lot. There was nothing else there, and I guess some local clubs lobbied the city to pave it. That's sort of where I sort of cut my teeth. That was also where 1960 Olympic Trials were held, on this half-mile, flat oval. Tracks like Kenosha were 1000 miles away.

Kenosha was my first experience on a real bicycle track. I went to Junior Nationals in 1959. We went out a few weeks early so I could get used to it. That was my first real racing experience on a velodrome. It went well -- I won everything!

I raced as an amateur until 1969. When I was racing the most I was primarily a track rider, but I had other abilities. I had a lot of endurance when I was young.

Best Memories

My best memories are of times when I overcame great odds. That was a thrill for me. There were a couple of times. A couple of times which might not seem significant to other people. Once I learned it's never over until it's over.

It was the Tour of Somerville, which at that time was only about a 12 mile race. I had a track bike with one hand brake on it. It was 1959 and track bikes and road bikes raced together at that time. I got a flat after about one or two miles. It was the biggest race we had in the country if you were a Junior. Things go real fast, so when I got the flat, I watched the peloton disappear up the road. I had some spare bikes around the course.

My spare bike wasn't there. The guy didn't get there or something happened. I got off and thought "It's all over. This race that I really wanted, that I was all pumped for." It was very important to me and I watched these guys ride away, up the road. I just kept thinking "It's all over."

I looked across the road and saw this guy standing there with this 20" bike with stingray handlebars and a banana seat. I ran over and said "Let me have that bike!"

The guy just looked at me. I said "Take my bike! Meet me at the finish line! Give me that bike!" So I took the thing and started riding it for almost a whole lap until I could get on my other bike. By this time the whole peloton was out of sight. I was like possessed, I wasn't even thinking.

I got on my other bike and started chasing, thinking "I'm never going to catch these guys" but if I did catch them that would be a great accomplishment. I thought I'd just give it my best shot. I kept working and working and pretty soon I had them in sight. Inch by inch I rolled up into the back of the field with a lap and a half to go.

At that point I said "Wow, I caught these guys, that's terrific." I sat there a minute or so, then I moved right up closer to the front. Then I thought

"You know, I could get a piece out of this, maybe top 10. If I get in the top 10, that would be pretty good." So, I was trying for that.

Then, coming down the home straight, everything started really rolling on the straightaway. With about 400 yards to go, I was sitting in fifth or sixth place. It just flashed in my mind "Go for it!" and that's what I thought "I'm going for it. If anybody who can come by, can come by." I went for it, and nobody came by.

Much longer after that I realized that it was a situation I thought was really impossible. It's such a crazy thing, you just grab for what you can get, grab a small bite like that. It made me think you really can overcome seemingly impossible situations.

Much later I drew upon that when I got second in the World Championships. Situations that are impossible - - snatching victory out of the jaws of defeat.

When I was riding in the World Championships in 1968, I had gone to the Olympics and I was in pretty good form, riding with the top three in the world in my event, the 1000 meter Time Trial (Kilometer) at the Mexico Olympics.

I had, maybe second or third place and 200 meters or less to go, and I just died in Mexico City in the altitude. I didn't handle it well, and I just folded up completely. It wasn't due to any training or not being acclimatized to it or anything, I just didn't handle the altitude very well.

After that I thought "I can't beat these amateurs, how am I going to go Professional?" I was in the Army in that time, during Viet Nam. I got a chance to go down, from Mexico City, to the World Championships in Uruguay. So I went down there. Just a few guys from the United States went down. I didn't care. As far as I was concerned, I wasn't going to make it. I had done so bad in the Olympics where I had tried so hard to do well.

It rained the first day we got down there. We looked around town and

came back the next day, slept in late, ate my meal, went down to race and didn't feel nervous at all. I was just going through the motions. It was cold, wet, and damp out.

I drew number one position to ride the Time Trial, the first guy off the line. For me, that was a good sign. Most guys don't like being off first, but I always really liked it, because I was warmed up. I like going right into it, not waiting around.

I thought "Well, that's good. Look at these conditions, it's just like riding in training in Flushing, New York at the Kissena Park track. It was a terrible, rough track. That's where I came from. I don't feel bad here, I wonder how these other guys feel. I bet they don't like it at all."

"I bet I have one more chance. A last shot. And really, I owe it to myself for all the years training and trying for it. Remember what happened when I was a kid back in Somerville. It's not over until it's really over."

I thought about all the people who had supported me and the riders who could be there in my place. "I can't just blow this." I was really ready when the gun went off.

I did really well, I got Second in the World. That changed my whole cycling career. I was able then to realize that I had the ability to do it. From there I could go on.

Becoming a Pro was a sacrifice. You had to leave the country, you couldn't race here, they treated us like we were second class citizens, like you were a rebel for considering going into Professional racing. Then I was ready to take that step.

Getting second in the World's didn't have a lot of influence on my participation in Professional cycling. Each year the best of the best go into Professional cycling, and out of those not many make it. The second in the World's was important to me, but it wasn't important as a stepping stone toward Professional racing. In Professional racing they take the best of the best every year. Out of that group only a few succeed.

My Pro Career

The U.S. was far behind in road racing compared with the rest of the world and I began looking in that direction. It seemed like it would be easier to break in internationally on the track than on the road, and that turned out to be true. I had a very fast finish, so I started specializing in

Sprinting as time went on. Later in my amateur career I was riding a lot of criteriums and a few road races. When I became Professional, I rode Six-day races.

I turned Professional when I got out of the Army and went immediately to Europe. I got my license in early 1970. From 1970 to 1973 I raced Six-days, then I was back here. I was the first guy to turn Pro in about 25 years. There were no opportunities. When I turned Pro, the Federation said "We don't allow Pros to race in this country, so if you're going to turn Pro, you can't race here anymore." It was a lot to give up. There was a period around the early 80's where the USCF and USPRO were in all-out war for control of Pro cycling. I raced Pro from early 1970 until I retired in 1975. I just realized it was time.

In order to turn Pro, it's not much different than it is now. You applied for a license. Track cycling was a lot different than road cycling. You had to get into events in Europe where you could be seen by promoters and organizers of events. If you showed talent you would get in more important events, and you work your way up that way. The top events were difficult to get into. They still are. No American team has succeeded in Professional Six-day racing since VandeVelde and I did back in the early 70's. It's a very tough life.

I tried to turn Pro in 1969 but I couldn't get a license. At that time I didn't know that there was an organization called "PRO", the Professional Racing Organization of America. It was started by a guy named Chris Van Gent. That is the USPRO Federation. I couldn't get a license from the USCF because they weren't authorized to issue Pro licenses. It took me a little bit of time.

I went to Europe not knowing this. I got there in 1969 as soon as I got out of the Army, but I raced a race or two without a license first. I couldn't get real racing until January, 1970 when I found out about this Professional Racing Organization of America. I got ahold of Chris Van Gent and I got a license from that organization.

I knew a Dutch promoter named Charlie Ruys who promoted criteriums and Six-day races in Holland. He was the one who encouraged me to come over to Europe to race track. I had met him when I had been traveling on amateur teams here and there. I was in Denmark racing, at one point on my own as an amateur. I met him there again. I didn't know anybody, so I corresponded with him, asking him if he wanted to help me begin to get set up at that point.

I went to Holland first to meet with him. There were Six-day races in Amsterdam. It was cold, frost and snow on the ground. The first night I was there he set me up at a "rooms for students" type place, a room in an attic, above an apartment. They said I could cook in there. They had a Bunsen burner -- that's all it was. I stayed there for a couple of days then went down for the Six-day races.

I was watching races at track side. I met some other people, one of them an English cyclist named Norman Hill. He told me I should go down and stay in Antwerp, so I moved down there after a short period of time and got based at the Cafe Yachthaven. It was a hotel for longshoremen right on the harbor.

I had a friend, an Australian, who I had known when I first went over to Europe when I was real young, as an amateur. I sort of broke through that way. I had some really good results and some bad accidents, but I met some real interesting people. That was back in '62. A guy named Jorgan Byerholm from Denmark helped me get over there. I got his name and connections through a guy named Jack Heid (*1949 World Sprint Bronze medalist*).

Jack passed on a lot of things to me. He was about a half a generation ahead of me. I got to Denmark where I met other people. I met a guy named Ron Bench who was based in Antwerp. He had turned Pro and done well in the World Championships, though he was no longer racing by the time I got over there.

The Cafe Yachthaven was a stone's throw away from the Antwerp Sports Palace, which at one time was a real mecca of cycling. It was an old building with a lot of what looked like cabled structure on it. It kind of loomed up as you approached it. It's still in use.

Six-day racing, especially then when they went really long hours, was grueling. It was absolutely a grueling sport. The thing I liked about it was that it was a whole little microcosm of life. It's not like now when we don't stay in the building. In those days you went in to this building and you did not see the outside for a week. It was Six-days and seven nights.

You slept there, you ate there, you raced there. You had servants to take care of you. It was not an easy life, the food wasn't great, the sleeping quarters were, pretty much, lousy, it was drafty, either too hot or too cold. But when you were racing you had people who took care of you every minute of the time. That was good because when racing you got real irritable because of the long hours.

You had to fight for what you got. That type of racing was a real struggle. They had a group of riders known as "The Blue Train". The Blue Train was the elite riders. They kind of controlled the race. If you were new coming into it, they didn't just let you come in. They held you out, they taught you a lesson. You had to fight for every inch of it. I found it very interesting and challenging.

It was just the way it worked like when you go onto any profession. You come in new to a profession that is established. Politics, there's an established chain of command. When you come into it, you have to look around a little bit before you know what kind of a niche you're going to be able to work your way into. The elite riders were from different countries, just whoever was hot on the circuit at that time.

At the first day race I was in, when the race was over I owed $200! I was $200 further in debt than when I went into the thing. At that time we didn't have any races like that in the country, so I didn't have any promoter backing me up. I was an American so I was a novelty, so I could get in, but they know you're over there living hand to mouth fighting for every inch. So, they can give you a minimal contract. They can get away with giving you a real pittance.

The Six-day team is normally five people. There's the soigneur, the riders, the mechanic, and a runner.

The soigneur tells you what and when to eat, gives you massages, and takes care of the overall organization of what you're doing and when. The runner goes to get stuff and helps you on and off the bike.

The workers are contracted as private individuals. They're easy to find. They work all of the Six-day races. They're around. The Six-day races is an elite group. It's not easy to get into. You don't just sign up, you have to prove yourself. Everybody sort of knows one another. They were readily available.

When I went into it, I was running against the grain already. I said "I don't need one of these guys. I don't want a soigneur, I don't have the money to pay this guy. I'll just take a runner." They sort of hassled me about that. You had to pay for the kitchen, the kitchen charge, all the food you ate and probably half the food that some of the other guys were eating!

Then the mechanic. You had to pay for the crashes, you break equipment and this, that and the other thing. So you have to pay the runner, you have to pay the mechanic, and the contract was so small anyway, it was like nothing, so I wound up actually owing money.

There's no base pay on the con-tracts, it's all totally negotiable. There are exchanges going on, too. For instance, if I were from Belgium, there's a Belgian promoter, and he has his local guy, the home team, so to speak. He'll say to the Dutch promoter "Okay, you take my guys, I'll take yours." Some Belgians will go up to Holland to watch his guys, and so give them a little bit of contract. It's sort of a reciprocal thing like that. Or an Italian promoter might say "I'll take a couple of guys you have, you take a guy I have . . ." That's how it worked from the inside, but coming from the outside as an Australian or an American, you don't have that backing, so you take what you get until you establish yourself and get a real name.

They definitely knew who I was right from the beginning, I'll tell you that. It got easier as I acclimatized to that level of competition. At one point I came back to the United States, I had gotten mono and I couldn't shake it for a year, so I couldn't ride well. I came back here, but along came Charlie Ruys to run some races in the United States. That got me interested again. That's when I talked to VandeVelde. He decided to turn Pro and we started racing together.

It helped to have a good partner. When VandeVelde got tired, he could still hurt. We did pretty well in a couple of those races in the United States. We trained really hard.

We thought Six-day racing was really going to go. We didn't realize that Ruys didn't have the wherewithal for American business. We thought "Okay, this is really going to catch on." so we had a high morale. We rode as well as the best Europeans could ride at that point. That's when it becomes fun.

Even the last race we rode, we didn't go on any combines with other teams because we wanted to win. We didn't want to split prizes or pay anybody to win. We had a tough time of it and we had a great race. That's when I really wound it up for the Six-day racing, though I could see racing for another season. I was trying to get Professional racing established in the United States. You still weren't allowed to race Professional here. I kept hammering away at that.

How I Became a Race Promoter

USPRO ran two track Pro championships when Chris Van Gent ran it and I won those. They were held in three different locations. The first year all three were held at Encino, but then they were held at Encino, CA, Northbrook, IL, and Kenosha, WI. They were Omnium style racing in '73 and '74. A couple of times we held track championships at the Lehigh County velodrome. Those were not Omnium, they were specialized. The last few years there has been very little Pro racing going on on tracks.

When I started promoting Professional racing here in the U.S. I was finished with my own racing. There wasn't much of a time gap. I had done some coaching, even when I had been racing. When I realized it was time, that things weren't happening as far as Professional racing, I was still capable of winning races, my ability had not gone down, but I couldn't race here. I couldn't go to a criterium, I couldn't go to anything. I couldn't talk people into running Pro races, it was very difficult getting the Federation to move.

It was opening up, little by little, but I was practically a one-man campaign doing that. At that point I coached the 1975 Pan American team and stopped racing to do that. I did a very good job at that -- we won a lot of medals and did really well.

At that same time I had read about a velodrome being built by a guy named Bob Rodale. I wrote to him and went to work developing the velodrome at Lehigh County. When I first went there, it was being built. I went there to see it and had a meeting with Rodale. They had not quite finished it at the point. They ran a small training-type race on it in the fall of 1975.

By December of '75 I had been hired to develop it. Shortly after that they hired Dave Chauner. Chauner and I put a lot of ideas into practice there. It was a proving ground for us. It proved that track racing could be highly successful. We worked there for three years. During that time it became the largest spectator sport in the Lehigh Valley.

A professional soccer team came to us to ask us advice on what we were doing. Having a professional team from another sport coming to us to ask us how we're doing it, pleased us.

We did everything, we had a comprehensive program. From cycling right up to the top Pros. We brought over Patrick Sercu, Rene Pijnen, and other top riders from Europe. We brought Eddy Merckx over as a guest. They were people I knew when I was racing over there.

When we first opened we had to argue with the local board about whether we should charge admission. The first one we charged $1 each, the last one we had we charged $10, $6 and $4 each day for a two day meet. In those days, for bike racing, that was fairly expensive. We sold the thing out in a couple of days.

We weren't satisfied just doing it in Lehigh County. We wanted to see it grow elsewhere. Rodale gave us a choice. He said "I just want you guys working on stuff here (though he had said other stuff earlier) or you've got to leave." So we left.

We were going to start there and there was another company interested in having the Junior Worlds Championships there. They wanted to sponsor it, so we brought in the sponsorship in for that. We began to realize that it was not only hard to get sponsorship here, but on a National basis for track racing, because it was so centralized, localized in Pennsylvania. Nothing was going on anywhere else, so we wanted to get tracks going in other places to go national. We were just in the thinking stages.

We also thought the people we worked for wanted us to bring in many more sponsors, so we developed a plan to involve all the major corporations in the Lehigh Valley. Although the people we worked for said that, they didn't mean it. When we said "Look at this great plan we have, we can bring all these companies in and

you guys don't have to worry about being the only sponsors" they didn't like that. At that point they said "We have to throw these characters out!" They said "You guys just do it here locally and the way we want you to, otherwise leave."

Everybody expected us to stay because it was good and secure. Where are we going to go? What are we going to do? There's nothing else to go to. We said "Sorry, but we're leaving."

USPRO

After that we developed a series

of events called the American Bike Racing Circuit. We gave clinics and began to develop high-end Professional cycling because the sport was not going anywhere in the Pro class. No one was doing anything with Professional cycling.

We went to the USCF and realized that they didn't have it. Then we went back to the Professional Racing Organization, which had become dormant. Chris Van Gent said "Yeah, I'd like you guys to do it." So he turned it over to us, and that's how it started. That was in 1980.

We went to the USCF first, Dave Chauner, Arnie Greenberg and I flew out to meet with them. We said "We have a plan to develop Pro cycling." On our way out on the airplane, we decided that Dave and I were going to be the promoters and Arnie was going to be the technical person, running PRO once it got started. We were going to pitch the USCF and say "We have an idea how to develop an aspect of this game, can you support us?"

On the airplane, Greenberg is paging through old pages of documentation from the UCI and he keep seeing references to this Professional Racing Organization of America. He said "From everything I see, this is the real governing body of Pro cycling to the UCI, not the USCF." I said "Yeah, I got my license from them when I was racing Pros."

The original USPRO started because Chris Van Gent had been a track cyclist in Holland. He moved to this country and started a bike business. He wanted to get indoor racing going. He formed an organization sanctioning people at the UCI, so he got these affiliates to do that and the USCF wasn't interested in doing that. The USCF wasn't interested at all. We came along and we didn't really know what's going on, so "let's pitch it to the USCF anyway," so we did. They said "Good job, fellas." We knew they would take it away from us if it went anywhere anyway.

We then went back and did our homework. We went to the UCI and lined up everything, got all the paperwork in place. We went back to the USCF and said "You guys don't control Pro cycling, we don't know if you know it or not, but you don't. USPRO does now. We're representing them and want to work together with you."

They went nuts. They tried to stamp us out, make us go away, and they almost did. This was starting with no riders, no races, no teams, no support, nothing. The USCF told all the riders "If you get involved with these guys you will get suspended, you can't ever race with us again."

But, things were happening. Great talent was beginning to surface. A few individual riders, carry-overs from the "Lone Wolf", days when I went over, the same type of guys were going over and beginning to make inroads in road racing.

Mike Neel and Jacques Boyer went over around '77. Neel was actually Pro in '76. He was tenth in the Worlds. Then Boyer went over there. When we started this stuff, the Pro organization was reactivated. Lo and behold, Boyer was already on Renault-Gitane and getting ready to ride some major races.

LeMond won the World Junior Championship and turned Pro at 19. LeMond's dad was a character. He called us up and said "Look, I know you guys a little bit, I don't know anybody at USCF, we're supporting you." So we had four, five or six Pros that year, 1980. They wrote letters of support for us to the UCI.

There was a big squabble between USPRO and the USCF as to who actually controlled Pro racing. They challenged us in the UCI. It went back

and forth. One meeting they would say it was the USCF, the next meeting they would say "It's USPRO".

Finally, Chauner and I said to Greenberg "Jack has the contacts and he's the scrapper, so he'll go over and work on getting this thing for us." I did that quietly, behind the scenes, while Greenberg was the front man. Meanwhile Greenberg got killed in a car accident. People in the USCF thought "Well, that's the end of that." Greenberg was the front man, so they thought it was going to crumble, but I had already been doing all the work, for 6-8 months, so I slipped into it. I had to change into an organizer, though I kept doing that.

In the end, the UCI gave it to their Professional branch, the International Professional Cycling Federation, and in the end, when all the smoke cleared, they said that they had decided that USPRO was the rightful governing body of Professional cycling. At the same time, I was elected to the executive committee of the Professional World Federation. Then we had a little bit of momentum and ammunition and we had a few riders, but for no event.

Chauner and I, as part of the American Bicycle Racing Circuit, got a sponsor to run a Pro championship, with over 60 riders from Europe. We couldn't use any riders from here because they weren't allowed to race. We had our first race in Baltimore, Maryland. The next year we got a few more Pros and we brought over 40 guys. Then we had the first $100,000 prize list in cycling for a men's Pro road championship. That began to open eyes.

Then with the Olympics coming up, everything was geared around the 1984 Olympics. In 1983 I said "Look, where is Pro cycling? There's something out there." Everything was geared around the Olympics. 7-Eleven had team and they were building that up, and then what happens? Where do cyclists go? What is there? They saw the things we did in Baltimore and another race called the Tour of America (a name used by another group now). People from Capitol Sports in New York City made a deal with the society for the Tour de France.

Now there were two major events, the USPRO Championships in Baltimore and the Tour of America. Two major events in cycling sanctioned and run by an organization that licensed about 10 members!

Then Jim Ochowitz began looking into things: "Where am I going after '84? I want to keep my team going." and he began looking into Pro cycling. In 1985 he affiliated the 7-Eleven team as a Pro team. Then we had the best races and the best teams in the country. They started falling like dominos. When we started the whole thing, we based everything on the free enterprise system. America's a free enterprise system and professional sports is making money and being in front of the media. You can't stop that and this is a worldwide, professional sport.

This sport has all of those elements. It's exciting, it has huge money behind it in other countries. It's not developed here, but the laws of inertia say that it's <u>going</u> to be developed here. It's going to come

here -- it's like the tide coming in. That's what we based everything on, and that's surely what happened. All the major teams began falling like dominos, one by one they became Pro over the years. We had them all.

The Future

I think the American Track Racing Association will make a difference at the grass-roots level. If it creates activity, that's good. It's great potential, but it's very difficult to do. Cycling is not an easy sell, and when you do track cycling, that's even a more difficult sell. Nobody knows what that is.

Outdoor track racing in many areas of the country is very difficult because first, if you're competing it's got to be a summertime activity or in a warm climate. Then you're competing with so many other sports. You're competing with other aspects of the sports. Plus, rain-outs will kill it. You can't race in the rain. I think the only way it's really going to come back is to have indoor racing and I think it will.

Now that the USCF and USPRO is together, I'm on the Board of Directors and I'm on the UCI Professional counsel. It frees me up to do some things I'd like to do. Right now I'm considering what direction I want to go. I have a company called Major League Cycling.

I'm convinced that major league track racing is a viable sport. If I come back into cycling, that's probably where I'm going. It will be portable track, indoor stuff.

It's probably coming, whether I want to do it or not!

Chapter 5
○▽○ *Match Sprint* ○▽○

Match Sprint is a race over approximately 1000 meters which is not dependent on time. It is often called a "chess game on wheels" and "cat and mouse." The actual Sprint may be the least intriguing segment of the race, though it is usually the most dramatic!

History

Sprints of one sort or another have always been part of bicycle racing, but most usually within the context of longer distances. The Match Sprint separates raw power and speed into a race of its own, often revealing the win only at the finish line.

Match Sprint is the most technical of track races as far as direct interaction between riders over the course of the race. Riders are matched in both a psychological and a physical battle through out each ride. While the time of the last 200 meters is recorded, this is only the last in a string of contests which begin before riders are even on the track.

Spectators new to the track are surprised at the usual slow pace over the first lap of the Match Sprint. The most common question is: "If this is a Sprint, why are the riders riding so slow?" The answer to this question lies within the mental and physical intentions and abilities of each rider, varying in each race.

This race does not hinge on answering the question of who can cover 1000 meters (a frequent contest distance of the race) in the shortest period of time. That is answered in the Kilometer.

The Sprint involves outsmarting another rider, getting him/her to provide a draft in which the eventual winner can ride and "slingshot" to victory. This is the intrigue of the Match Sprint. Who will trick who into doing what and who will have the most power at the end of the race lends suspense to each contest.

This is why a Sprint offers optimal thrills beginning in the Backstretch (or before) and into Turn Four on the last lap when one rider is trying to hold off another who is trying to come around, both riding at maximum speed.

The rules for Sprints have developed in response to the dynamics of the event, including providing for as much safety as might be available in this kind of competition.

The race itself can occur among "a small number" of riders. The Rule Book says "the number and composition of the races is organized by the Chief Referee to meet the needs of the racing program for the number of riders." Translated, this means that provisions will be made for different levels of racing which require formats adapted for a variety of needs.

Great Sprinting is a joy to watch. Jeff Solt and Bill Clay, Dominguez Hills, 1994

At the Championship level, "two-up" Sprints are always seen in the finals. Local events may have six in a Sprint, which seems much more like a mass start scratch race.

Qualifying -- Flying 200s

In order to appropriately match Sprinters of comparable ability, a series of 200 meter Time Trials ("Flying 200s") is run. This may not be necessary in local, weekly races where rider abilities are pretty well known, and is not mandatory, but is done at the National Championship (and up) level since current levels of ability must be known.

The Flying Start is usually only used in Flying 200s, the Kilometer, and the 500 meter Time Trial, not in other track events.

In a Flying 200, riders line up successively. Usually two or three riders will be in the start area at one time. The rider "on deck" will get ready and usually be held by an official or other person. S/he is pushed off to begin the first of (usually) two laps during which the rider gets physically and mentally ready to do a maximum effort over 200 meters.

Riding the two lap preface to Flying Start events is almost a science in itself. Riders must gather both mind and speed into a maximum effort by the time they hit the start line. Knowing where to begin gathering speed and when to dive down the banking is a skill coaches work on with athletes over and over since this important preliminary can strongly effect the finish time.

As the end of the preliminary lap draws near, the rider's pace increases. Usually by Turns One and Two (maybe sooner) the riders will accelerate, diving down the banking on Turn Two. The best line should be from the highest point of the banking to get the greatest amount of downhill benefit, straight to the starting tape.

The Flying Start allows the fastest time possible over a given distance (all other things being equal) due to the fact that rider and bicycle are moving at top speed by the time they hit the starting tape.

The starting tape designates a specific zone within one meter of the lower edge of the track. It is a distinct factor for a rider in a Flying Start and can detract from the rider's concentration on speed alone.

If the target zone is missed, the Starter will signal a restart with either a gunshot or a whistle. The restart will take place immediately. If the race is an International event, the rider is disqualified on the spot.

Flying 200 times are not reliable predictors of Sprint success.

Sometimes competitors compete better than they Time Trial. It's another intriguing aspect of Sprints.

Distance

Match Sprints are held over three laps on tracks which are 333.33 meters or less. On a larger track, the race goes two laps.

The other distance of note in the Match Sprints is the last 200 meters before the finish line between the black and red lines. During the final Sprint, only one rider is allowed in this zone. This sounds like a simple rule, but it is the most disputed area in Sprinting.

Sprint Formats

Race announcements will disclose both format and seeding methods for this event. Riders must be instructed as to whether the event will be held in Championship or "round robin" formats.

Championship format

Championship format sets up rounds in such a way that the fastest riders will meet in the final race. There is are two formulas in the USCF Rule Book for Sprints, one for at least 36 competitors, the other for 24. These formulas will not be reviewed here.

Suffice to say, riders are matched in such a way that slow riders are eliminated quickly while fast riders who may have a bad race can still work themselves back into Champion level competition through the "repechage" (discussed later).

In theory, the two most highly competitive riders (not necessarily the fastest, but the most competitive) will meet in final competition. Championship format seeding is the same as

Queen of American Sprints Connie Paraskevin Young gets a good contest from fellow World Champion, Janie Eickhoff. U. S. National Championships, 1994

that used in World Championship races.

The Sprint seeding formulas looks like Greek to novices, but are extremely important for Sprinters to understand. Strategic planning can revolve around seeding. Once Sprinters know relative Flying 200 times, they know who will be racing against who, and the strategy begins.

Round Robin format

A "round robin" format allows each rider an opportunity to compete against all other riders. With large numbers, this would be a tedious process and so is only done in smaller events. The winner is determined by the total points accumulated. The Rule Book should be consulted for round robin procedures.

If any rider does not complete round robin competition, his/her points are cancelled. If points are tied, the win goes to the rider with the most points against the other tied riders or there can be a "ride-off" Sprint among all tied riders.

The advantage of round robin type matches is that this may be the only time new and lower level riders get an opportunity to try their skills against National and World Class Sprinters. For lower level riders, this is an unforgettable experience and a source of much bragging if the World Class Sprinter happens to have a bad or off day.

Exhibition Sprints

Exhibition Sprints must follow the format of Championship Sprints, but the number of competitors and distance of Sprints may vary. Certain other rules may vary, such as the necessity of "repechage" and the rider losing twice prior to being eliminated.

Repechage is a "second chance" where riders who would otherwise be eliminated may win their way back up to the higher ranks through competition with others who are in this same position. Repechages are not necessary in Exhibition Sprints, nor are two out of three losses before elimination.

The Start

Before riders line up for the start, they will pull a "lot" out of a bag held above eye level by officials, in order to randomly establish their position on the track for the start. If the race is run in two heats, riders alternate as leaders. If there is a third heat, lots are drawn again to decide position.

Sprinters draw lots for position.

Riders line up perpendicular to the black line and may position themselves at any reasonable place down or up track. The rider with the number "1" lot is the lead rider and will take the bottom position, whether actually at the bottom or half way up the track. Rules do not dictate this. Sufficient room must simply be left for the other riders uptrack.

Since the bottom rider must lead, it makes sense for the rider(s) uptrack to start up farther in case the downtrack rider should take a flyer. It is easier to accelerate moving down track.

Holders may be officials, but tend to be coaches, parents, or "handlers". Often holders will give their riders last minute reminders or other advice as the rider is preparing for the start. When a rider is ready, s/he notifies the official. No one is rushed and each rider determines on his/her own when the race shall begin. As in all races, if a rider intentionally delays a race, s/he can be disqualified. Holders may push riders at the start, and often do.

Sometimes riders practice relaxation techniques at the start. Other times they pray or try to clear their heads. As in Pursuits, sometimes they play "head games" with each other during this early stage. The mental part of Sprints seems to have no temporal bounds.

Sprints begin with a whistle. Whatever the riders would prefer, the rider at the bottom of the track must lead the first lap at a minimum of a walking pace. The appropriate pace is verified by officials literally walking parallel to the riders in their various zones around the track. If the pace is too slow, the gun will sound and the race will be restarted with the rider who went too slow leading again in the re-ride.

In this sense, the first lap is an integral part of the start. Once the lead rider's front wheel completely crosses the finish line, the true Sprint begins. All first lap restrictions are gone.

The rider(s) behind may <u>choose</u> to pass the lead rider and assume responsibility for the lead over the course of the first lap. This is less common since the rider in the back can watch the lead rider better from that position, (see what Connie Young says in the next section about position.)

"Kiloing"

Riders may go faster than a walking pace during the first lap, if they choose to. In fact, they can Sprint from the start if they want, but they usually don't. If they do, it is a high risk, a surprise, and it is usually done by riders who think they may have an endurance advantage and cannot match their opponent's Sprint or speed. It is legal. It is called "kiloing", named for the Kilometer race, a full speed effort over 1000 meters.

The problem with this strategy is that if the other rider can catch the

Tom Brinker "kiloed" Mark Garrett at Olympic Trials, 1992. If you can surprise your opponent and get a good lead, you <u>might</u> be able to "stay away".

draft of the rider who is trying to "kilo" him, it is an easy ride in this draft to the finish area. At that point, the opponent probably has a lot more energy left than the "kiloing" rider and will be able to come around at the finish, "slingshoting" out of the draft and taking the win while the kiloing rider is too tired from the effort to fight back.

For some riders, especially if they don't have a Sprint, this is the only reasonable strategy and it may work on a surprised "pure" Sprinter.

Then again, a rider just may want to defeat the unreliability of strategy and win through pure speed, especially if s/he believes that endurance over three laps can beat the other rider's speed over 200 meters. This requires dropping the other rider, though, and is risky. But, sometimes it works.

The Race

The most common action seen in Sprints is a "cat and mouse" routine between riders who, especially at a National Championship event, may have raced against each other many times and know each other well. Often they know each other's strengths and weaknesses and plan their strategy around matching their own strengths against their opponents weaknesses.

The race will typically go something like this: Riders begin with a slow first lap at a walking pace. At the completion of the first lap, the lead rider may try to force the following rider to take the lead by riding very slow or stopping into a "Track Stand".

If the following rider is skilled, s/he may also go into a Track Stand. There was a time when Track Stands could last indefinitely, a true challenge of grit, skill and determination.

The practicalities of modern bicycle racing have forced a ruling limiting Track Stands to three minutes. At this time, the official will signal the obligated (lead) rider that s/he must proceed.

In fact, this is signal is usually not necessary. Usually one rider will decide, for whatever reason, to proceed before this three minute limit is reached. Under the stress of competition sometimes even a skilled rider just doesn't have it to maintain a Track Stand for an extended period.

Even some good Sprinters have trouble with this skill and don't value it enough to develop it to a high level. It is a respected mark of a high level rider to be able to hold a Track Stand for an unlimited period, however, and some Sprinters feel it further demonstrates the depth and breadth of their abilities.

From this point until the finish, anything can happen, according to the skill, riding style and strategies of the riders. Sometimes the ride will proceed slowly (almost boringly) until the bell is sounded for the final lap, which usually stirs the blood of athletes and audience alike. It's almost like the bell of the starting gate for the race horse.

The second lap can see riders at high speeds, moving each other up and down the track like cats playing with mice. Trying to catch another rider off-guard and Sprint away is the most predictable part of the Sprint.

The problem is trying to predict *when* a rider will do this. Just when you think you can relax, a rider takes off and all hell breaks loose. From that point it's a matter of watching who can maintain or pull out what top speed from that moment to the finish.

It takes a lot of practice to ride straight while watching your opponent behind. This is the end of the first lap. The rider in front can go into a "Track Stand" to try and force the rider behind to take the lead so he can watch him more easily. Or he can keep watching, waiting for the Sprint to begin. He doesn't want to go too early and provide a ride on his wheel to the finish. The rider behind shouldn't leave too big a gap in case the front rider should "take a flyer". It's easier to watch your opponent from behind.

If a rider breaks away early in the race it is not unusual for him/her to pull up track and slow down again. During changes in pace riders can even more quickly change their minds and the speed picks up again.

In International races, things are even more unpredictable, as each country seems to have its own style. For this reason it is vital for American riders to compete in International arenas. The quick reflexes developed through unpredictable competition can only be developed during unpre-dictable competition.

Stopping a Match Sprint

Stopping a Sprint once the race has begun is addressed in a distinct section of the RuleBook. Sprint violations differ during the slow part of the race from those once the Sprint has begun.

Stopping a Match Sprint before the Sprint begins:

During the slow part of the race the starter may stop the race for the following reasons:

1) a rider backs up more than 8 inches (20 centimeters), most likely during a Track Stand,

2) a rider does a Track Stand on the blue band, a zone s/he should not be in,

3) a rider touches the track surface or the outside fence or railing.

A rider who does any of these things must lead when the ride is restarted.

Other reasons for stopping the race during the slow part:

4) if a rider suffers a mishap (blown tire, falls down, etc.) during the race had no chance to place, a re-ride is not necessary. If the race is restarted after a legitimate mishap, riders restart in the same positions.

5) if a rider appears to have a mishap which causes a restart and the mishap turns out not to be legitimate, the race will be rerun without the offending rider or the other rider will be declared the winner.

6) if an accidental collision occurs before the Sprint has begun, the race will be restarted with riders in the same positions.

Once the Sprint has begun:

When the Sprint has actually begun and riders are moving at full speed or near full speed:

1) a rider cannot overtake an opponent by using the blue band.

2) a rider must leave room on the right for others to pass.

A rider does not have to leave room on the left, but must not cut off an opponent when moving into the Sprinter's lane. If another rider is already there, the rider in front must have *a clear lead* in order to make this move. A rider may never force another rider off the track.

3) a rider who is below the

Early rounds may include "four-up" Sprints. Riders usually know each other well enough to know who the guy is to beat. In this case everyone seems to be watching the middle rider.

Sprinter's (red) line must stay there until the finish.

All riders behind a leader who is in the Sprinter's lane must pass on the right, outside of this zone. It is okay for the leader to come out of the Sprinter's lane if s/he has such a large lead that there is no hindrance to others.

4) a rider outside of the Sprinter's lane cannot make an abrupt motion to stop others from passing or move right, even if it is not an abrupt move, which could cause a fall or a move that exceeds 90 centimeters (the width of the Sprinter's lane). Riders in back of the leader may pass on either side.

5) the leader must not move into the Sprinter's lane without a "clear lead", especially when the rear rider is overlapped.

If the lead rider does this the RuleBook says s/he is to be relegated for foul riding. The lead rider is not penalized for accidentally riding below

the measurement line or even on the blue band at the finish line.

6) a rider must not deliberately cause a crash (disqualification). If s/he does, the race will be restarted without the offending rider or the win will go to the other rider.

A rider shall be disqualified if s/he causes another rider to fall. If a rider falls while attempting a move which is illegal, s/he will be relegated. The other rider may be declared the winner whether or not s/he crossed the finish line.

The biggest problem in these rules is determining the intent of riders. All riders want to win the race and Match Sprint is a race of high tension. If *your* rider goes down, you are apt to be touchy about his/her safety and tend to blame the other rider. If the other rider goes down, of course *your* rider would never deliberately do such a thing, so if s/he is called for dangerous riding you *know* they are wrong.

It shouldn't be necessary to say, but in case anyone has doubts, the Rule Book states that a rider who "deliberately" causes a crash will be disqualified. Interpretation of a rider's intentions, however, is often subject to dispute.

In the event an accident is determined by officials to be deliberate, a re-ride omitting the offending rider (disqualified) will be conducted. If the accident is deter-

mined not to be deliberate, the race will be rerun with riders in the same positions.

Other Sprint Rules
Blocking

Blocking of other riders is a common strategy in bicycle racing, but is not allowed in Sprints. If there are three or more competitors, a rider who is boxed in at the bottom may not force his/her way out. It is illegal to block or interfere with another rider. A rider who does so will be relegated or disqualified.

No-shows

If a rider does not show up at the starting line, the other rider must show readiness to race, but needs to do nothing more than show up at the finish line. That rider will have a bye to the next level of competition. The rider who did not show will still be eligible to ride in further competition, if appropriate.

Sometimes a riders may take advantage of this rule because they know they are up against a rider they cannot beat. They may decide it is wiser to save their efforts for a more appropriate level of competition.

Other times a rider may have some personal reason for not showing. Sometimes top level riders decide to save their efforts for other events where they feel they will be more successful, such as a Mass Start specialist who has a Madison coming up.

Dead Heats

If officials are unable to determine a winner in a particular heat, the race will be rerun with the competitors who were involved in the dead heat.

In National Championship races, there will most certainly be a finish line camera which will aid officials in this decision. If there is any doubt, if it was even close, officials will usually wait for the camera results to make a final determination.

In local events this will not always be the case and officials will really be making their best guess. Track racing crowds will often make their feelings known if there is no finish line camera and they disagree with the official decision.

Officials are under considerable challenge and pressure in judging all of the above rule violations. Perceptions are tricky and the human eye can be fooled. Incidents which looked one way from one vantage point looked another way from somewhere else.

When there are disputes, officials often group together and gather as many facts as possible before rendering a decision. Sometimes they are willing to review video tapes taken by spectators, coaches or TV crews, sometimes they are not. Human endeavors net human reactions. There have been many controversial decisions in bicycle racing, but nowhere are they more common than in Sprints. It is seldom an easy decision.

An additional problem for track officials is that Sprints happen so fast that they are difficult to judge without a highly skilled eye, preferably one developed over many years. Recently the USCF has begun designating track and road officials in separate categories partly due to demands which are specific to track events. No where is this more important than in Sprint events.

Most officials do try to make fair decisions under very difficult conditions. (*You won't see me volunteering for that job, but--*) If you believe you can make those kinds of judgments well (and take all the flack you get as part of the job), the world of bicycle racing needs you!

Race Equipment

Little special track equipment is used for Sprints. No sponges are used, though Sprinters are expected not to go below the measurement line and onto the blue band. Judgement of this type of violation is left to the officials, who are more highly utilized in this event to monitor the various phases of the race than in any other.

The Starter's pistol is an instrument of control for violations at any point in the race. Double gunshot stops the race. The end.

Bicycle Equipment

Equipment for Sprints is a standard track bicycle. This may include disc wheels and tri-spokes, but may not include bull horn bars or aero bars. Sprint bicycles are usually slightly heavier than other bicycles due to the added strength and stiffness desired by Sprinters. They also usually have steeper angles, all for better handling.

Summary

Weekly race series at local tracks often do not include Sprints due to their specialized nature. There may be too few riders who want to do them or too many to be reasonable. Latitude is given to officials to make decisions which are practical. An endless string of Sprints among non-Sprinters turns into a tedious training session which can just as well be conducted at other times. Promoters must consider pleasing crowds if s/he plans to have any.

On the other hand, Sprint competition between or among high level Sprinters is beautiful and thrilling to watch and will please the crowds. Every Sprint is a learning experience for every rider. Some velodromes respond by offering special Sprint series or events to fulfill this need.

So why do some Sprinters consistently Time Trial better than other riders who consistently beat them in the actual race? Defying the logic of mere speed, the Match Sprint is more consistent with the workings of the human heart. This is the classic mystery of this event, maintaining endless fascination for riders, coaches, and audiences alike.

Champion is as Champion does. Connie and Janie have each had lots of practice being Champions and always know what to do.

Match Sprint
Connie Paraskevin Young

Four time World Champion Connie Paraskevin Young has spent her life as one of the great Sprinters. She is part of the legacy of the Midwestern Speedskaters who have given so many Champions to bicycle racing.

Connie began winning championships in the 13-15 division, (1975 & '76). Since then she was U.S. Junior Women's Omnium Champion for four straight years (1975, '76, '77 & '78), Senior Women's Sprint Champion seven times over a ten year period (1982, '83, '85, '87, '88, '89, & '92) and again in '94.

Connie won World Champion Sprint titles in 1982, '83, '84 and '90. She was second in 1985 and third in 1986 and '87. In 1988 she won a Bronze Medal in the Olympic Championships in Seoul, Korea and in 1995 she won Silver in the Pan American Games. She holds the U.S. National track record for 200 M.

How I Got Started

I was born July 4, 1961. Initially I got involved in speed skating with the Wolverine Sports Club. They have a year 'round sports program that includes speed skating and cross country skiing in the winter and then cycling, bicycle racing and a big touring club, in the summer. It was just a natural thing.

Most of the club members were kids, at that time, 10 years old, nine years old. I was skating with them and did bike racing with them in the summer. I just kind of fell into it.

I always competed in both cycling and skating from the beginning in the mid-70s until 1984. After the '84 Winter Olympics, I continued just with cycling, but I had always done both. I was basically competing year 'round on National Teams and World Championship Teams since I was 15, so 1977, or so. I'd go to the World Championships for speed skating and then continue with cycling.

In the seventies the ABL would typically pay the way of the winner to the World's, but everyone else who wanted to go would have to pay their own way. There was a group of women who were training for Sprints, usually three or four -- I think four was the maximum that could go -- but several had to pay their own way.

I think 1981 was the first year that all four women got their way paid, and all four placed in four out of the top five. Sheila (Young), Sue (Novara) Pam Deem and I all made the top five. That's not that long ago.

I've been asked many times if I would pick one sport over the other, "Which do you like better?" I never had to make a choice because they're very different sports, from a racing standpoint.

Skating is a very individual, time trial situation. The workout's the clock. Whereas cycling (Sprinting) is the opposite. They're very different.

"I'm continually learning, that's what keeps it interesting. Maybe the key is that I don't really care what other people do, I just know what I need to do for me. I can be a better Connie, I can't be a better Erika. I get satisfaction out of the ability to be very consistent over a long period of time and, when it gets tough, mentally fighting my way through."

Though your physical training and preparation complement each other, they're very different, so I liked them both in different ways. If I'd had to choose one or the other I don't know which I would have chosen.

Eventually it came to the point where I wanted only one sport for time reasons. I had some injuries, too, that bothered me more in skating.

I wanted time off and I didn't want to spend so much time in Europe skating. You didn't have choices to compete in the United States.

I was ready to stop spending half my year in Europe. In cycling, I saw, number one, the opportunity to pick and choose where I competed. I could compete in the United States.

Number two, right around that time, 1984, cycling was improving, including women's cycling. There were more opportunities, more races, more things happening. Looking ahead and wanting to choose one, I saw more opportunities in women's cycling, so I took that avenue.

I could make a certain amount of money in cycling, whereas with skating there was absolutely no opportunity for income. There are a few people like Bonnie or Dan, a small group of skaters, who can make a living from skating. In a way it's like cycling, the depth doesn't go down very far for athletes to make a living.

With cycling I could do different races -- track races, criteriums -- this and that. I was doing a lot of criteriums, so it was fun, and I was looking for that too.

I never really did the roads. Criteriums, yes. They varied from year to year. There used to be good circuits like the Wheat Thins Circuit. Other years there wasn't a circuit, so to speak, but you had your solid, existing criteriums that the top riders went to, a top category race. I went to those. The last few years there haven't been enough good criteriums to make that worth my while.

In an off-Olympic year I'd love to do a criterium circuit. I'd have to train

a little bit differently. It takes away from the Sprint, which I don't mind doing, but it has to be worth it. Number one, there has to be enough of them.

Number two, they have to be worth something. I'm not going to travel and do all this stuff and get myself down in the hole. I don't see that. There's only a handful of them out there now. It has slowly turned over into road races. I'm not going to ride a road circuit, that'd be crazy. It's too intrusive on Sprint training. It wouldn't be bad if it was in November, December, even up to the end of January, but they don't exist at that time.

Coaches

You'd be surprised at how few people have coached me. There's always been a solid group of people that I could rely on. A very good and knowledgeable group of people starts with those at the club level.

A lot of the basic philosophies that I still follow are from Mike Walden and Clair Young. The reason Roger and I think so much alike is because that's what his background was -- Clair Young, his dad, and Mike Walden. We have taken those general philosophies, twisted and tangled them our own way with other influences and all our experiences.

In speedskating I've worked with two coaches that I respect very much. I've continued to consult with Peter Shie and Roger to this day. In the early years it was Clair and Mike.

What I've done throughout the years is my homework. I'm always

Clair Young was a nurturing hand for Connie in the early days. No one is more proud of her now. Indianapolis, 1994

looking and trying to learn different things. I talk to different experts in certain fields. I've dealt with and talked to different weight training specialists because Roger will be the first to admit, that's not his expertise.

I've formulated what works for me through the speed skating years and through different people, my "experts", people that I respect for what they do in their fields. A couple

of them are weight trainers. They've all helped me piece things together.

A lot of what I do comes from experience. I don't think "Oh, if somebody's doing *that* . . . maybe I should do that too!" I've researched and I've studied.

Even if Roger tells me to do something, I ask "Why? -- No, tell me and show me why that is good for me, what it does to me, what's its effect? -- *then* maybe I'll do it."

So I've got a few people, now maybe three people, that I consult with. If I think it makes sense, then we implement it into the program. That's how I do it.

Training

I go through periods where I visualize and then I don't. I can really notice the difference. You have to train that element along with everything else. If you don't, it's not going to work. You can't just show up July 2 and say "Okay, I think I'll start visualizing, concentrating, focusing." I guess it would work to a certain extent. Nothing is ever useless.

The time periods where I work hard on that element, I perform better. I daily train myself physically and if I'm going to be at my best, I also have to train myself mentally.

Visualization, relaxation techniques, focusing techniques -- it's one of the hardest things for me to do. If I'm "on" in a race, my opponent is the <u>only</u> <u>thing</u>. Nothing else is happening around me. Someone can be calling my name right next to me and I don't hear them. I honestly don't hear them. That's when I am ON.

I can go into a race and my opponent is all I see. I'm very much "in the moment". Nothing exists before, nothing after. I'm centered, which means body, mind, everything. You have to work at that, it doesn't just come. That's when I'm at my best, when I work on those techniques too.

I also watch a lot of videotapes. When I've been at my best I've "had it", but it's the quickest thing to lose. It's one of the hardest things for me to get into.

When I took a year off, I took a year off of that, too. It's one of the hardest things to get back. Not just to get back, but to feel that it's effective, that it's working. To have things second nature. It's hard, but it's fun. That's part of the game.

I do hill workouts, but a Sprinter doesn't want to go for, say, a two hour period or into the hills. As you do that you're taking away from the speed in your Sprint.

Sprinters need to maintain the

"Tell me, show me why that is good for me. What is its effect? <u>Then</u> maybe I'll do it."

ability for quickness and power. You need to develop that. Sprints require quick, explosive efforts, power efforts. This is work that you would do on the bike, in the gym, different ways -- quick, short efforts.

As you train your body to do "extended power ", the more you do a long duration, power type of effort, the more you're breaking down the ability to do one explosive effort.

You have to be able to repeat in a

Sprint series. That first explosive effort is going to be less if it's broken down. You're going to be able to get it up to the lesser level, not to the higher level. You're breaking down your power ability for the Sprint. It involves the training and the make up of the muscle.

Your slow twitch /fast twitch is part of it, you don't change that a lot. That's your make up. Sheila Young is a perfect example -- she has more slow twitch, but she was one of the best Sprinters ever. It just shows that she could have also been one of the best endurance athletes. She chose to put her efforts into the Sprint and Sprint training. It's more than muscle breakdown and how you're training yourself.

Early season, within base miles training I'll go for long rides, there's nothing wrong with long, even hilly rides, for the endurance base. You have to have an endurance-power base, that will allow you later to do repeated explosive efforts, not just one and die for the rest of the day.

That's where some international Sprinters are, great for one or two

Sprints, but have them do 10 Sprints within a day and they're out the back door. They slowly get a little bit slower and slower each time.

Maybe not even that noticeably, but all of a sudden they're not "just winning" their Sprints, they're "just losing" their Sprints. You have to have a certain endurance base in order to repeat that same high intensity effort over and over and over again.

In training for Sprints you have to train your endurance base, your power base, everything. You have to have a base built up which will allow you to start off early in your program and then put in the high intensity efforts you ask of your body.

It may be Sprints on the bike, in the gym, however you're training. My high intensity efforts are for Sprinting ability. If I don't first put in the mileage, the base and the endurance, I will only be able to do so much work. The more endurance base I have, the more work I can do throughout the year to prepare for the Sprints or any other event. That base should allow me to improve and get better.

Typically, the base is built in the winter months. For me, exactly when varies from year to year because of different ways I'm training and different things I'm doing.

In general, the World Championships are around August. Then the season continues through September, maybe into October.

Starting around November, intensity is fairly low. November, December, January, February, those months.

Around February and through May you're working yourself out of the endurance base phase into increasing intensity. I set out my year's plan: "This is what I want to work on, this and that and that" but I try to be very well rounded.

You'll hear riders say "He can only come from the front" or "from the back" or whatever. I train myself to be very comfortable in either position.

I train myself to be comfortable in *both* positions. I don't care. If my opponent doesn't like to ride from the front, I'll just put her up there, because I don't care either way. I'm going to make her ride there. I'll do the opposite of her preference.

Some people are driven up the wall by that because they can't handle it. They cannot win a Sprint from the front or from the back.

That's just one example of using her weaknesses against the other rider. I'm not going to focus on <u>my</u> weakness -- what is my strength against you? I'm going to try and play upon that.

I'm very analytical in how I perceive things to be happening and how I perceive people to be doing things -- why or where they do them, how they do them -- I pay attention, put it in the file. But you have to work on that.

Weights

My work with weights varies from year to year. The heavy weight season is during the off-season, the off-season through around May. Winter and spring, are real important.

Some years I will continue weights straight through. As you're doing more work on the bicycle, the work in the gym becomes maintenance and an enhancement to work you're doing on the bike. I'll continue it up until a few weeks before the World Championships.

Other years, due to injuries and other things, I might have stopped in April or even March. It varies a lot and will depend on what I feel I need to work on that year.

Do I need more power? How do I want to get that power? I'm a firm believer in changing things a little bit at times, -- although I have general training philosophies and guidelines that I continue to follow every year. I feel that the body adapts so easily that if I ask it to do the same thing the same way all the time, I'm going to adapt, level off. I'm not going to keep getting improvement from it.

I may do a little bit less heavy duty power work in the gym one year and I may do over-gear, power work on the bike. My philosophy is the same, I want "X" amount of power work, but I change around how I get it.

I shake up my body, I'm waking it up, preparing it a little bit better and more completely when I vary it a little bit from year to year.

I do the entire body. I mix it up. People don't realize how much you use your upper body in cycling, especially in Sprints. A road rider doesn't put on the bulk and the weight, but even for the road rider there's more upper body strength required in cycling than people realize.

In Sprinting, you're exaggerating the movements. You're going from zero miles per hour to top speed as quickly as you can. You're pulling up on the bars a lot, as much as you're using your legs. You want to have the ability to do that as smooth as possible and efficiently as possible, and it requires strength.

Everything needs to be coordinated and done in a straight line. You don't want to be off-balance and have your upper body working against what your lower body is doing.

The more balanced and solid you are on the machine, the bike, the more you'll be moving in a straight line, a power straight line instead of fighting yourself down the track. You'd never know it, but I work really hard on my upper body.

Squats is a standard. For cyclists who are working on their legs, it's an all-around leg exercise. For just about anybody who lifts, squats is a mainstay of the program. The basic exercises are squats, leg curls, leg extensions, variations of lunges, leg lifts with weights on the ankle and high knee lifts. Those are pretty much the mainstays for the legs.

From there I go to where my weaknesses are, what I'm working on. If the abductor is weak I may be trying to strengthen it due to an injury. I've had injuries the last few years. I may try working it more to compensate.

Sprints

Sprinting is like cutting to the chase. If you take all the track disciplines, what you have is a road race broken down and people specializing in each of the elements.

I became a Sprinter because I don't like all the stuff in between, I just want to go fast! I've always been like that "Let's just go!"

Roger has said this, and I guess I can see it, that's my personality. "What's the bottom line? Tell me what you want, what you're looking for." I guess that's how I am racing, too.

I love to ride, I love to be on my bike, but I get bored out there. I couldn't handle the "in between" in a road race -- "Let's get to the end and Sprint!" I think it's just part of my personality. I've always liked to go fast.

In Sprinting, because of the length of the race, you don't have time to make mistakes. Unlike a road race where you might try to break away or try to make a move, if you miss a wheel or make a mistake, you have time to reel it in. You're dealing with a different situation when you come down to the end. You have time to make mistakes and to correct them.

In Sprinting, if you make one mistake at a high level, you're dealing with people who are equal to or better than you. One mistake and you're out of there.

You have to be very focused, very aware, concentrating. That's stress. That's hard to do, not knowing what's going to happen. You go out there trying to make a certain thing happen, but "What are they going to do to me? How are <u>they</u> going to try and ride <u>me</u>?"

You can guess how somebody's going to try and ride against you, but you're out there and all of a sudden they're doing something else . . .

"Hmmm, this isn't quite working the way I thought".

But that's what's interesting to me, that's what I like about it. "Hey, let's cut to the chase!" if you do it wrong, you're out of there. That's the fun part of it and that's a very hard part of it. You have to train that aspect of it too.

Sprinting Today

Things have changed. Styles have changed. There's less finesse now, less bike handling less movements and ability to really handle the bicycle on the track. Sprinting has moved to more of this straight-line stuff.

Some of the top riders in the world cannot handle their bikes as well as they should. I don't say I'm great either, but they just don't do it. They don't ride that way and they don't train that way. They're powerful, they're strong, they're fast -- in a straight line.

You get them to start turning their bike and it's a different story. Since they don't train that way, they don't race that way. The races have become more straightforward as opposed to what I call "finesse" races.

That happened first, but there's also been a slow progression from the officials standpoint.

Officiating and Sprints

There have been increasing numbers of officials officiating track events who didn't have a track background. It's much easier for them to judge a race if they don't allow a lot of movement. That's one of the changes that has been made, so that you don't have the movement.

If it's a fair race, there's a way to move out of your lane that's dirty, that's dangerous. Then there's a way to do it that's clean and part of the game, to sucker somebody in to do something.

But if officials don't really understand the game, they don't see what's really happening. They see a movement and think that it's wrong.

It's a combination of both sides, the athletes in general and the officials situation, which has slowly changed the way the athletes ride.

The East Germans kind of started it because they were like machines that go. Just sit back and motor. They were so powerful, so fast. Gradually, to keep up or to try to beat them, we had to ride differently, we had to change. "Okay, we'll just have to be this motor that can go by these guys too."

When I say officials here, I'm not talking domestically, I'm talking internationally. I think that's why some of the rules have changed, to make it easier for some of the officials.

The problem that they're having now, domestically and internationally, for various reasons, is not so much the rule changes, but the inconsistencies. It's kind of the same problem both ways. They have to go one way or the other.

This doesn't only happen here in the States as opposed to in Europe, but here in the States from race to race. And not only domestically, but internationally too. There's that problem from race to race and even from one heat to the next! They're not consistent and that's where the problem lies.

Athletes feel both ways too. Some like that kind of riding. But a lot also want to have more of the game. It's kind of equal on both sides.

Right now, more than just feeling strongly one way or the other, both athletes and coaches are going nuts because _we want consistency!_ We're not the only ones, I've had discussions with Morelon and Zajickova -- pretty much all the countries feel this way, but what's the answer to the problem? I don't know. All I know is that it's not consistent.

The coaches want to know "Well, what do we tell the riders to do?" The athletes say "I'll go out there and ride this way or that way, just tell me which way!"

What happens is you go out and ride a certain way and it's judged good or bad or whatever. Then you go out for the next one or someone else does the same thing and they're DQ'd for it. Anyway, it's not the same.

Then, for the athlete, there's the bit of hesitation in you because of the confusion: "Do I do this move or don't I do this move?" Or you can just do it that way and "If you DQ me then you DQ me." That's the problem right now and it's being addressed.

People are starting, internationally, to express their concern. It's been made public at a UCI meeting. People recognize it, but I don't really see it changing. I wasn't at the World's last year, but I heard some of the same stuff was going on. Nothing happens overnight.

I guess a start is that coaches from the different countries are saying "Hey,

come on, get your act together!" They are starting to try to get an answer instead of allowing the officials to just do whatever they want.

Maybe we'll start to see a change. Only time will tell. It didn't happen overnight. Both domestically and internationally you saw it change very slowly until "Yeah, it's out of control" right now in both areas. It didn't happen overnight and it's not going to change overnight.

As far as my own racing and being officiated, I just do my best, and whatever happens, happens.

I learned a lesson in Barcelona ('92). I got disqualified on the first ride. I thought "Holy . . . I didn't even _do_ anything! I got disqualified! If she comes anywhere near me I've just got to back off, I just can't afford to do _anything_ here!"

So I based my racing decision on a hesitation. I didn't ride like me. I tried to ride how I had been officiated _against_.

I said "Gee, I don't know what to do out here because I didn't do anything! I did not _do_ _anything_. I've never done that ride differently, but now I've got to do it differently. What do I do?" I based my thinking, my decision, on that.

The only thing I could do now is just race, which is normally what I do. That was my mistake.

I've never been disqualified before. I've had a warning or whatever. In other rides after that, people were hooking and doing all kinds of things and nobody was getting DQ'd in anything.

I don't know -- who knows why or what? I started looking around at the officials' faces. I said, "Roger, I've never seen any of these guys in my life!" Every year since 1977 I'd seen the same faces out there officiating. I'd never seen any of those officials before and I've never seen any of them since.

The thing is, it was my mistake to allow myself to make a decision based on bad calls. That was my mistake. The only gratification or lesson I can

Connie and Erika at Goodwill Games, 1990. End of the first lap. Erika wants Connie to pass so she can watch her from the back. Notice the official making certain that they follow the correct rules for Track Stands (no backing up, no contact). Connie got close. Erika appeared unshaken. Good competition for Connie.

learn from Barcelona, the only *ounce* of gratification I can get, is having learned that.

I've got to just be in my own head next time, to just do what I do. At least I'll get satisfaction out of doing what I wanted to do the way I wanted to do it. That's what you have to do. You play the game with what you feel is fair and within the rules.

I can only think of figure skating. It's all judgemental. If they want to DQ you because you have green eyes, they're going to do it, so you can only do what you do.

Greatest Strength

I don't know what distinguishes me as a Sprinter. A strong point is probably my initial acceleration. I don't want to give someone a lead-out.

Greatest Weakness

My biggest weakness is probably my finishing kick. Not so much the

duration or the length, but to give that last push. It's kind of like you have a top end, but it's that last surge to the line. Which may be, who knows depending on the track, it may be 20 meters, 30 meters, that last section, is the weakest. It's hard for me to specify weaknesses and strengths because I think it changes so much from rider to rider.

I don't think so much of what might be *my* weakness but my weakness against my opponent. It doesn't mean so much that I don't think I have a weakness, have tons of them, but I don't think of things in those terms.

(Meanwhile, back at Greatest Strength) I could probably tell you quite a bit about other riders, but I couldn't tell you 110%. I'm trying to bring it back. I have a terrible memory. I like having it in my memory bank so

I don't have to think about it, it comes naturally.

Going into Barcelona, I studied SO many videotapes. I could have told you what anybody did before they did it. When I was sitting out there watching, I would go "Oh my God. Watch this. She's going to do this and this and this. See?! She did!" That's when I was very proud of myself and I was very in tune to what and how things happened, but I worked very hard at it. I saw the results from it, at least in the sense of knowing what was going on. That part of it's fun for me to. I'd feel like "Yeah! That's cool! That's right, I knew she'd do that!"

Maybe that's the key, I don't really care what other people do. I just do what I do my own way and I don't think about what other people are doing. It works for me. I hadn't thought about this before, but as I'm speaking

to you now, maybe that's it.

I see even some of the athletes that I'm around right now are so worried or interested in, concerned, about what everyone else is doing. To me, that's energy taken away from yourself.

It's not that I'm not interested but I can't question what I'm doing or my confidence in what I'm doing. Watching them is not going to make me change, so why should I pay attention? Maybe that's part of it.

Some people never lose the thought that some people may have a secret that they don't have. I think that's the difference. Some riders are good, but they never quite make it over the top. There's a point at which riders need to know themselves and stop always looking at other people's ways of achieving at the sacrifice of what really works best for them.

You have to believe in what you're doing and how you're doing it. If you don't believe in yourself, you're not going to excel to the fullest.

I don't care what or how you're doing something, I'll be the first to say that I think that athletes are the most insecure bunch of people you'd meet. It's very contradictory. If you have to be so confident, how can you be insecure? It's a good insecurity, I think, it's an insecurity more of the question -- "how can I do this better?"

My way of explaining it is like "It's not how are *they* doing it better - - it's how can *I* do this better? What am I doing today or what can I do tomorrow to change this, to make this a little bit better?" The insecurity is there because the questions are there, "Am I doing enough? Am I doing it right? Am I this, am I that?"

It's the confidence to say "No, you're not, this is better" but it's based upon what you yourself are finding, not so much on others. Sometimes you find athletes who are at a very high level but they still want to be a better version of someone else instead of a better version of themselves.

I can be a better Connie, I can't be a better Erika. I've never thought that way, but I would imagine that would be a little different.

If I worked hard and had certain expectations, didn't perform, and then people said they were disappointed in my performance, I'd probably think "Wow, they're right!"

It wouldn't bother me so much that they said that. What would bother me was that I didn't perform. It doesn't bother me what people say. If it did it would be because I gave 100% and I didn't come through. That's what would bother me.

In 1993, I didn't care, because I knew what I put into it and I'm realistic to know what I should have gotten out of that, so it doesn't bother me at all.

Plus, I don't listen to what people say. I really don't hear it. I'm off in my own world. I don't know half of what anybody says anyway. That's probably better.

Injuries

In 1990 I didn't even know if I was going to compete in '92. After '88, my goal was not the Olympics. My goal was to win the World Championships one more time before I retire. I wasn't <u>leavin'</u> until I won those World Championships.

I'd had some tough times. The stupid injury in '89 -- I was on crutches ten days before the World's. Stupid things -- come on! But it was like "I'm not going <u>anywhere</u> until I do this!"

1990 was when I first started having knee problems. I'd had "get sore", "pull a muscle", here and there. Normally any injury in the past had kind of warmed up. It might have bothered me at the beginning of a workout and it might have killed me afterwards, but the muscle warmed up. I would go through a period during the workout where "Hey, I feel normal again!" Then I might be dying afterwards.

To make a long story short, practically the whole beginning of the year, when I came over the top of the pedal stroke, <u>every</u> pedal stroke I took, it was just like someone put a knife through my knee. It drove me nuts.

I was getting therapy and I continued trying to work through it. We changed the training around, but it became very hard mentally. It hurt me every single pedal stroke. It became very frustrating -- how many times are you going to stick your finger on a hot iron? I had to do a lot of work with my mind game things, keeping my head on straight, to keep working through it.

I tried very hard to strengthen that area. I did a lot of work to prevent it from happening again. Sometimes you just can't help it, you crash and do the splits. Chances are maybe it wouldn't have been so bad if that was the first time it happened, but it was the same thing again.

What I was doing didn't work. I thought I was strengthening it through different exercises, but because of the injury, overcompensation by other muscles, scar tissue and other things that happened, the work that I was doing was not effective. I knew what was happening, but I didn't know why.

We'd try to change position and different things, but it would always end up "I'm not getting any power!"

I found a doctor who rode on the '72 or '76 Olympic Team, who had a cycling background. We've pinpointed problems and gotten things functioning properly again. It's amazing. I was totally blown away.

Now I'm using certain muscles that I have not used in a long time. Now I think back and think "Yeah, that's why this or that was happening! Now it makes sense." It's amazing, Now I have full power through the whole pedal stroke. I haven't had that in years. It's pretty exciting.

Why didn't I figure this out before? But then, that's good, I'm continually learning and that's what keeps it interesting, too.

Satisfaction

In general, if I think back, what I get satisfaction out of now (but maybe I didn't over the last few years) is the ability to be very consistent over a

long period of time. Personal satisfaction.

There were a few years where, maybe I was Third place in the World's or something, but I knew what was going on that year and how I went into it -- I worked hard for that.

I went into it thinking "Oh man, this is going to be a tough one!" and mentally fought my way through that competition. It's not even so much that I felt that at the time, but now, as I look back at stuff like that, I go "Yeah!"

I try and remind myself of things like that when it gets hard, that you can fight your way through things, the ability to have been consistent under certain conditions during those years.

Good Memories -- 1990

One of the things that helped also, was when I brought Erika (Salumyae) over. I wanted to help her, too. I wouldn't have done it if I didn't like her and if I didn't want to help her.

But also, it was good timing for me because I needed something to motivate me. She got me going and we had fun. If you can laugh and go through things and have a good time, it helps you not think about other things happening. The more you let yourself think about it, the worse it gets.

Erika had expressed interest in coming to the States for a couple of years to train and race a little, but she never could. The Soviet system prevented an athlete from going anywhere without a 50 million person entourage, so she never could.

In 1990 when the doors opened

up a little, almost overnight she could go. If she wanted to go, she could go. So she contacted me and said "Hey, I want to come!"

I went to different companies that I work with and said "Look, can you sponsor her program? Pay her expenses, pay for her program and make it so she can come and stay here, train, and ride."

She was riding in the Goodwill Games that year. It was more or less leading up to that. That would be the finale, so to speak. And they did. They were real cooperative and supportive.

That worked out really well. It helped her out, that's what she wanted to do, and it helped me out too. There's nothing better than being able to train with someone like that. You want it to be a good environment.

There are people I could train with right now that, from a physical standpoint would be great for me, but I don't want to be on a total downer the whole training time. For me, it's very important to have a certain kind of atmosphere.

Erika and I were very much alike, we train a lot alike, so it makes for a light, easy atmosphere. That worked out well. 1990 was good, not only because I won, but also because I went through a lot that year, I fought through a lot that year to win Worlds.

I get more satisfaction out of things like that, yet I raced well that entire year. There was a World Cup, or some cup race in T-Town earlier that year and I raced internationally. I don't always do that.

Each time I raced internationally

I raced really well. That was motivational too. It was a strange year because while I was having a lot of problems, I was still doing the work. I think what kept me going mentally was that I was performing well, and that was a boost. "Yeah, this is cool. If this keeps up I guess I can handle it."

I had a very solid year. I raced really well, but it wasn't easy from a training standpoint.

After six years since my previous World Championship, I reached my goal. Now I could quit. But, it's still fun, sometimes . . . sometimes. . . .

I came pretty close to quitting in 1993. I took an active year off. I started '93 out thinking I wouldn't even race. I was leaning in favor of not continuing.

But, I thought "Well, I still have contracts. Let's have an active year off. I'll train and I'll race a little bit." but I was doing a lot of other things too.

A race day came and I was keeping it very low key. I thought that if I decided to continue on it would probably be tough.

After the Olympics ('92), I took six months off straight. I didn't do a thing. I'd never done that in my life before. When I started training again, I had to dig myself out of a big hole, it was tough. But I thought "that's alright, if I'm going to continue, I need a break."

Physically, I'd been tearing my body down for years. Logically I realized that it would be tough when I started training again after that much time off, but in the long run, I believed it would pay off. And if I decided to

Connie and Estonian Erika Saloumiaee, Goodwill Games, 1990

quit, c'est la vie -- who cares? I'd done what I wanted to do.

So that's the way I went into it in '93. About half way through the year I got the real feeling back, just in my heart, that I wanted to race.

I took about five months off before I started training again in '94. I just thought "Okay, I'll just finish the year off" and now I'm straight through it, no more time off. I'm so tired.

This year I didn't expect to do great (*Connie won the 1994 National Sprint title*), I tried to be realistic, but next year, '95, I have a very strict time table, so I should come around about a year before the Olympics.

There's a definite place where I

want to be. I think I'm capable of doing it. I should have a strong Olympic year. But it was tough. I never took time like that off. I had to remind myself and be very patient.

There were so many starts and stops that I had. I would get training for a couple of weeks and something else would happen. "Geez, am I ever going to feel like an athlete again?"

I've had a solid stint of training now and I'm feeling good. Initially it was hard, because I kept going into the gym and looking at my past records.

I keep very accurate records of what I do. Normally I know -- January 2nd, this is where I'm at. I was in the gym going "I can barely lift this!" or "I can barely do this". I'd go out for a ride and do whatever and I was dying.

I knew how I used to feel, and it was hard. You just have to go "You did it, you decided to do that, it was your choice." Now I'm confident or solid enough in myself that I know that's happening.

Best Memories

I think my most fun time of riding was racing against Sheila. It was a lot of fun for a couple of years. I compare it to when Erika and I were training together.

We trained together, we could have fun, be friends, then go out on the track and try to kill each other, try to beat each other. Not just "kill you by beating you by this much -- I want to kill you by beating you by ten feet!"

Connie's favorite competition, husband Roger Young's sister Sheila; speedskater, twice World Sprint Champion and her brother's matchmaker.

We could do that and then get off the track and go "Okay, you won that one!" It was a lot of fun. After that it decreased a little bit and I'd have to find other things for motivation. No one has challenged me as much as Sheila did. Internationally there have been people.

My next favorite accomplishment would have to be '83 (Worlds).

The first Worlds I rode was in '77. In '82, my first World Championship, Sheila (Young) and I were in the finals together. She got a warning in the second ride. We were one-up. In the third ride, she got disqualified. I had

crashed, she had gotten DQ'd and they awarded the ride to me, which meant I had won.

To me, we only rode twice. We rode three times, but I crashed once. I wanted to re-ride. Jack Simes was the coach at that time. I said "No, go up there and tell them I want to re-ride." He's going "Are you nuts? You just won the World Championship!"

I said "Yeah, but this isn't right. We only rode twice, and this isn't right." They wouldn't do it.

So the next year, just for myself, I don't think anyone else noticed or

cared or whatever, but to myself, I got more satisfaction out of it because I actually won. I rode three rides and that was the way it went.

I was against Lomash, German, she doesn't ride anymore. She was the infamous Third. She got third so many years. A real nice person, I just saw her a couple of years ago. Three kids -- she came to a race in Germany.

Velodromes

Barcelona is my favorite velodrome of any. I really like that one a lot. It's built right. The transitions are right.

They say that the velodrome in Minnesota (Blaine) is the same, but it's not. The transitions are different, very different. It's the same dimension, the same banking, but it's built differently. Barcelona's my favorite, that's an easy one.

In the U.S. I would have to say Minnesota is my favorite at this point. I definitely like steep, small tracks like that.

Least favorite -- well, I don't know. There are some, like St. Louis, that I've never ridden.

Marymoor isn't a real fun track to compete on. It's like a washboard. It's slow, boring -- I guess if I had to say one I'd rather not compete on, it would

be one like that because it's not real fun.

It's not that I dislike Marymoor, or that there's anything I hate about it. It's just not as much fun to Sprint on a large, shallow track with such a rough surface that it's slow. You file the tread on your tires. It's bad on your equipment. It's just not fun.

That's the two extremes. It's more fun to ride a small track that's steep. You need better handling ability and it's more challenging. That's probably, for me, what decides what I like and what I don't like. The more of a challenge, the more fun it is. The less of a challenge, the less fun.

Advice to New Riders

My main advice to upcoming women riders and/or Sprinters is to get in as much racing as possible early in their development, all different types of racing -- anything and everything.

That's going to improve the mental game, awareness, handling ability, fitness, and make them more experienced. The more experience they have before they focus on one particular event, the better. They're going to have better race results.

In a training program, on a yearly basis, if they look at it as a career, they're going to have a better foundation to then decide to become whatever they want to be, a Sprinter, Pursuiter, or whatever. That's a real key.

Kids today are encouraged to specialize too young. That's not the best thing for their long term cycling, for their careers.

I've seen kids talking up in L.A.

and coaches encouraging them at 12 years old -- they want them specializing in Match Sprints! That's all they want to have them race and have them do. My gosh, 12 years old! -- sure go out and have some fun, do some Match Sprints with other kids your age, but that's not all you do.

You race and race and race, Mass Start stuff. You've got to have the ability and the awareness. That's going to physically make you better. That's a real key. That's one of the most important pieces of advice I have to give, because I see the opposite happening right now.

Changes

A key change to this sport would be for people in all facets of the sport to work together more. Everybody, from the retailer to the corporate executive, to the bike company -- everybody's just off on their own thing. Even from the bike company to the retailer, they're missing the boat on a lot of stuff. Everybody is very separate and not very supportive of one another. As a group, we can all be a little bit better if everybody tries to feed everybody else a little bit.

The industry itself is getting more sophisticated. They are doing things better. The relationship between the bicycle company and the retailer means that if they work together they'll sell more bicycles and both profit from it. It might be how they package it or whatever. They're doing that more rather than "Here's the bike and . . . later . . . "

But still, a lot of the time it's very up and down. Our sport has little consistency. There are a million and one different reasons why, but that's a real problem.

If you just take the race circuit, for example, there's a greater percentage of events that are new or short-term than have been around for a long time, like a Somerville. That's a very successful, wonderful event. It's been around a long time. It has tradition to it. We need more Somervilles!

For whatever reasons, that doesn't happen with too many races. They're gone in a year, two years, a flash in the pan. That's the big problem.

I want something that's going to be a Somerville, that's going to last, that has tradition. A much different event, maybe, but one that's going to be here 60 years from now. We don't have that. We need more of those.

There was Sundance Grand Prix, and before that the 7-Eleven Grand Prix. They were very much the same type of thing. But they're gone. Nobody took the ball. The person who had the ball dropped it and went somewhere else, and for very good reasons I won't go into. So we didn't get that tradition yet, and that's what happens so many times. They don't keep the ball rolling. You need somebody to drive the bus. Right now everybody wants to drive it for about a year!

Master's Racing

Will I race as a Master? I am a Master now, so the answer is yes! As far as the Master's categories, I don't know. Right now it's hard to say because I'm still competing in the Senior category.

I would tend to say that if I compete in something for fun after I finish my cycling career, it will be running or other things that I like to do, that I don't have time to do now. I do a lot of running for my training, but maybe I'll do that a little more seriously. Not seriously, but make that my motivational goal. Say "Ok, I'll do this 10 K or whatever, and make those my little goals to have fun and to get that competitiveness in myself out. To try to improve my running time. I could see me doing that and something else.

The Future

After '96 what I'd like to do is remain in the sport in some way, shape or form. I think there's a real lack of promotions. It's not an easy task. Of anybody, I know it's hard to get money. I work very hard at it. It's almost a full time job and cycling's secondary! Sometimes it feels that way. But, that's the way it is. Nobody's knocking on our door. It's not an easy task, but one of my goals would be to try and develop my ideas. I have a lot of them.

I'd like to bring choreography into the sport, making it a combination of hard-core, serious, true racing, competitive racing, and bring in an element of show. I've talked to some people who are very well known, choreographers, about doing some stuff. Choreographing some things to music with cyclists, just some neat stuff -- who knows? Maybe some stuff that is so hokey that nobody buys or sells it.

Velodrome racing is more exciting than roads, but what has happened is that if you look at who the good promoters are in the sport, roads is what they're choosing to promote.

When I'm talking "good" promoters, I'm talking professionals, guys from the professional races. The Thrift crowd, the Classic, the only two good promoters that we have right now are doing the Pro races. They're simply not focusing on the velodrome, for whatever reason. It doesn't matter whys or whats, nobody's doing it.

I'd personally like to do a combination of velodrome riding and criteriums. It's the sport in general, the amateur side. I think there are some very good Pro races that are being promoted. Maybe some of the people I've had relationships with in the past will support me in that.

I would definitely emphasize women's racing. I think there's enough of a quality field to showcase women's racing. There's a lot of opportunity. That will be it initially, to take velodrome, criteriums, the sport of cycling, and try to implement some of my ideas.

That decision will be determined by the financial backing. I'm a firm believer that things have to grow. I wouldn't do something like this over night. You get the bugs out. You perfect it and build on it slowly and then it has more of a chance of lasting. All of it takes time, homework, beating on those doors.

I wouldn't want to do something that was a million dollar event for one year. I'd rather have a $100,000 event for 10 years. I'd like to take something, try and work on it, perfect it, take it slow, and try and make it something that's going to last.

Match Sprint
Mark Gorski

Mark began his career by winning the U.S. Junior National Sprint Championship in 1978. He went on to become U. S. National Sprint Champion in 1980, '82, '83, and '85.

In 1984 he won the Gold Medal in Sprints in the Olympics. He was the Silver Medalist in Sprints in the Pan Am Games of 1987. He set a track record for 200 meters -- 10.314 (Co. Springs, 1985) which remained unbroken for five years.

Mark was a "pure Sprinter" (did not seek competition in other events). His World level experience has made him an excellent ambassador of cycling.

I was born January 6, 1960 and grew up in Roselle and Itasca, Illinois, western suburbs of Chicago.

How I Got Started

When I was 10 years old I used to travel down to Indianapolis with my sisters to stay with some family friends. The father of the family was a sculptor and an art professor at Indiana University. He was from Florence, Italy and was a huge cycling fan.

He planted the seed in my mind that I could be a bike racer. He looked at me and said "I think you've got the physical attributes of a cyclist." Little did I know at that time, he was a huge cycling fan, but he really didn't know much about cycling.

But, I believed him, so I started touring, just riding for fun, that year and the next couple of years. That was

around 1970, '71, '72. I rode "century"s and found myself becoming competitive.

I was always competitive in sports and was a very good athlete, so it was natural for me to evolve into the competitive side of cycling. The guy who planted the seed didn't coach me, I took it from there.

Ironically, we later moved to Indianapolis, they built a velodrome there, the Pan Am Games were there and we're still great friends. He's seen me race many, many times. They built Major Taylor velodrome about a half a mile away from the family's home. That's how I got started.

As I was looking for a more competitive aspect to the sport of cycling, I watched a bike race at Northbrook. I saw Danny Van Haute, who was probably about 16 years old at that time, and a lot of other top Midwest riders. That was the catalyst that started me racing the next year.

Although my parents were very supportive, they knew very little about cycling and could offer very little in the way of guidance or coaching or anything.

"I could tell you a lot about what I did, about Hesslich, what a lot of the top guys did, but just knowing that is insignificant compared to the ability, dedication, commitment, to do it. That's the most difficult thing about sports."

I really enjoyed the independence of cycling. I had played a lot of team sports, and I enjoyed determining my own destiny. If I wanted to get up at five o'clock in the morning, as I did in

the 7th and 8th grade, and go train in the morning, I could.

It was something I took pride in because it was something for me. I just decided I was going to do it. I think that's a common thread in a lot of individual athletes, compared to team sports.

I wasn't in a culture of bicycle racing. I wasn't in a club. I was very much on my own. I sort of sought out the races and other people but I trained pretty much by myself a lot of the time, from early on. I enjoyed that, depending only on myself.

I started racing in 1974 through '78-'79. I raced regularly Tuesday nights at Kenosha and Thursday nights at Northbrook from early June through the end of August.

Danny Van Haute was racing at that time but we didn't race together in the same category until '79. I was an Intermediate in '74-'75, a Junior in '76, '77 and '78 and a first year Senior in '79, so that was the first time we really would have competed. He's a couple of years older than me. I saw him all the time and he saw me all the time, we were just in different categories.

In 1975, when I was 15 years old,

I placed second in the National Championships for the 13-15 year old age category. I was getting some good National results and I started to learn that I had a real strong finishing kick. I started to realize that I was a Sprinter, though, for the next three years, I did a lot of road racing as well as track racing. I won a lot of races on the road.

In 1977, I placed fourth in the Junior National Championships. I still had one year to go in the Juniors category. We had Milwaukee Super Week in 1977 which was a major series of races at that time.

In the Junior category were people like Greg LeMond, Alexi Grewal, Ron Kiefel, Davis Phinney, myself, Greg Demgen, Jeff Bradley -- and I was leading the series with one race to go in a six or seven race road race series. I flatted in the last stage and finished up second overall, but I was very encouraged.

I was a very good road rider, particularly if we stayed together in a group and we had a sprint finish. There's a lot more of that in the Junior than there is in the Senior ranks.

Anyway, I did do a lot of road racing in my early years and I still feel today that a lot of the skills and the endurance that I developed at 16, 17, 18, on the road were ultimately beneficial for me as a Sprinter. Success in the Intermediate category was important.

In '78 I won the Junior National Championships in the Sprints and placed fifth in the Junior World Championships. Those put me at another level mentally. I realized that internationally I probably had the ability to do very well. When I got fifth in the Junior Worlds, there were a couple of East Germans ahead of me and an Italian, but I knew I was on my way to a place internationally that meant I had the potential of making the Olympic Team and riding the World Championships.

I began to specialize in Sprints when I made a conscious choice to dedicate myself to a discipline where I felt I had the potential to be the best in the world. I won races on the road in both the U.S. and Europe. The dream of being a pro road rider was in every American's mind at that time.

I certainly would have loved to pursue that, but I honestly felt that a better future for me lay in Sprinting. When you do something well, you enjoy it. I felt that I could win major events. There was no better feeling than winning bike races and I felt that I could do that more often and with more gratification, more satisfaction as a Sprinter. But I certainly appreciated and had a great love for the road as well.

Even from the time I was a small kid I dreamed of and envisioned myself doing things well, winning, and seeing myself on the podium and/or on Olympic Teams. I remember watching the '68 Olympic Games and '72 in Munich. It was one of my lifelong dreams to participate in the Olympic Games.

Support

People who helped me most during my career and development cannot be limited to one person. Roger Young was one, but there were a number of people.

A gentleman by the name of Alberto Bustimenti who still has a bike shop in Chicago, a very successful shop on the North Shore. He worked with me when I was 15, 16, 17 years old to a certain extent. Not real closely, but I had a lot of respect for him and if I did have a coach at that point, it was probably him.

Carl Leusencamp worked with me very closely in 1978 as a Junior, '79 and '80. I worked with Andrzej Bek off and on for a number of years. I traveled with him a lot, did a lot of European events with him as a coach.

But Roger helped me at key points in my career, which was '82, '83, '84, '85, that time period.

I always took a lot of pride in the fact that I was my own coach, to a great extent, for many things I did. No one was really the pupil with the teacher. I was more like on the same level as the coach and he would suggest things and if I didn't feel it was right I would tell him that. I'd tell him I think this is what I need more in the way of a particular exercise or days training or whatever it might be.

I'd have to say my mom and step-father helped me a lot. My parents were divorced. My mom, my stepfather and my dad all played a part, not in a coaching sense, but in a supportive role.

Finally, my wife, Mary, never told me what tactics to use, but from 1980, when we met, through all of my career after that, she's been the most important person in my life and had a major impact on what I did in cycling.

She was really responsible for my not retiring from cycling in 1981 after a serious crash in Japan. That was back in the days before hard-shell helmets.

I was in the quarterfinals of the Japanese National Championships. They invited Great Britain and the United States to their Nationals. It was their 50th anniversary, I think.

I got a flat tire in the front during a full-on sprint while diving below a guy. I went down on my head and right shoulder. I was unconscious for about an hour and a half. I separated my shoulder and had a severe concussion. I had long-lasting headaches and blurred vision for several weeks. I basically decided to hang it up at that point.

A couple of months later Mary and I went to Europe, camping and traveling around on bikes. One morning in France we got up in the morning as a bike race went right by our camp. I was watching this race longingly and Mary said "Gosh, you really miss this, don't you?"

I said "Yeah, I really do."

She said "Well, time to go back to work."

For several months time before that, I had thought "I'm going to go back to school, I'm going to get on with my life, get back to the real world . . . ". Mary was most responsible for motivating me to go back into the sport. I decided to take one more shot at cycling at least through the '84 Games, and that was how that all happened.

Sprints

Sprints are the most emotional of any cycling event. They are extremely intense, very aggressive, and you have to prepare for them like you're going into the ring with someone for 12 - 15 rounds. You have to learn to want to beat someone badly. That helps you perform well.

I didn't use any tricks to get myself up for Sprints. A lot of people looked at me as pretty easy going, but there was no one who wanted to win any race more than me. Some races were more important than others.

Keys to Match Sprinting

There are four key components to developing into a World Class Match Sprinter .

First, a basic, flexibility and stretching, for injury prevention, and to enhance your performance. The second component is weight training, but you have to have a lot of flexibility first to be sure you don't get tightened up from weight training. You also have to maintain your agility and flexibility on the bike. You *have* to maintain your flexibility. You can improve your pedaling on the bike just with improved flexibility.

That was something I paid a lot of attention to and the top Sprinters in the world paid a lot of attention to. These are guys who could squat 300, 400, 500 pounds, but could also nearly do the splits. That was a pretty powerful combination, that combination of agility, flexibility and power. So that's Number One.

Second is strength training to improve power and explosiveness.

You've got to spend a lot of time in the gym. Heavy squats, power cleans, bench press, bent-over rowing, just a variety of upper and lower body exercises, are critical to developing the kind of strength, the overall body strength you need to be one of the best in the Sprints.

Third is small gear training on the road. A lot of time in very, very small gears, 42-21, 42-20, 42-19. Early season, a lot of Sprints in small gears to develop that leg speed that you need to be able to turn an 88, 90 or 92 inch gear at 130, 140, 150 RPMs. That's particularly important.

Fourth would be your Sprint workouts on the track, which are very long, very tiring. A Sprinter doesn't go out and ride 100 miles, but he or she does three and four hour workouts on the track, multiple exercises at 100% with rest in between. When you're doing four sets of Flying 500s, and you're doing four to five sets of Flying 200s, and repeated short, 100 meter jumps, it's pretty tiring, but those quality workouts on the track are what I consider the fourth really important component to Match Sprint training.

Training

The real key to Sprints is not training, but racing.

The key for me was going out and racing, every week -- twice a week -- from fourteen years old on, and that's what I loved to do. Kids don't want to just train for weeks or months on end without racing, and I think that's what's fun about competing. It's not the practices, it's the games, for any sport. Finding racing opportunities is

important, convincing mom or dad, a friend or an older rider to take you.

The key is just to race, week in and week out. You learn more in one race than you do in five training rides because of your intensity level. Your effort level is 10% greater and the riding skills, the strategies, etc., that you learn in a race are the lessons from failure and success. They are so much greater than what you do in training, racing is the key. I just wish we had more of it, more opportunities to do it on the track for kids.

The key to road riding is doing it at a real developmental point in your career, which is in your teenage years as a Junior. I don't recommend that someone who's 22 or 24 or 26 do a lot of road training or road racing in order to improve their career as a Match Sprinter. What I advocate is a variety or a balance to your training and racing in your Junior years.

The problem is, now I see kids specializing too much as Juniors. When I was riding the Track Nationals in '76, '77, '78, Greg LeMond was riding the Track Nationals too. The point is that the good people were doing both things at that age.

I think that the skills that Greg learned on the track were very helpful to him as a road rider. The pack skills, the sprinting skills, time trial skills, a lot of the savvy he learned on the track. And, there are skills you learn from racing on the road that help you as Match Sprinter, but that's more in the developmental years as a Junior. When you get to 20, 21, 22, 23, you have to specialize if you want to be

one of the best in the world.

The Olympics

I will always remember the press conference before the final day of the Olympics. The Sprints took place over four days.

During the press conference they asked Nelson and then asked me, because they knew we were riding against each other for the Gold and Silver the next day, "You're guaranteed at least a Silver medal, how do you feel?"

Nelson said "Well, I'm just happy to be here. I've got at least a Silver now, what a great Olympics."

Then they said "Mark, how do you feel?"

I said "I don't want the Silver medal. I didn't work ten years of my life and sacrifice as much as I did to get a Silver medal. My job isn't done yet." That's why I won. The race was won there. It was over with at that point.

Getting the Silver I would have felt that I'd lost. Silver would have been no different to me than getting 20th. Maybe ten years later I would have felt better, but that's the kind of competitiveness which was a part of me -- still is a part of me in other ways. That is what the Sprints is all about.

That's the kinship that I felt with Hesslich and a couple of other people in the world, was that kind of intensity about winning and losing.

I got very nervous because of the intensity of Sprints, those four or five days of the Olympic Games. The races started at ten in the morning. I'm not an early morning person at all and I'd wake up at, like, four, five in the morning every one of those days.

At about six or six-thirty I would try to eat breakfast. Every one of those days of the Olympics I literally couldn't put anything in my stomach. That's nervous. I would drink fruit juice. I always drank a coke or coffee, usually coke, about an hour or so before competition to get me up a little bit.

I ate my meal after the competition, about four or five in the afternoon. I could get something down, I could get some relief. But I got very, very nervous.

Because of the magnitude of the Olympic Games, knowing what it meant, the older I got, the more nervous I got. But even the first two or three years I raced I got terribly nervous. I've just been like that as an athlete.

In Little League, I used to throw up before the game. The thing that kept me going is that the feeling when you win is so good. It becomes worth it. The up side is worth the down side. That's what it was for me.

The pain, and it really is almost painful, the nervousness, the nervous stomach. There are so many times when I just said "Why am I doing this to myself?" Then when I won, I knew why I was doing it to myself. I realized that that energy was almost useful.

There's a fine line there where it isn't useful, because it certainly can work negatively for people, but ironically, my nervousness, particularly in the Olympics, went away, to a certain extent, when I started warming up on the track. It went away almost completely when they started

the race. That's always, to this day, kind of amazing to me.

I almost felt a sense of calm once the race started. You'd think that would be the most nervous point. I felt a tremendous sense of confidence and calm once the race started, particularly in the Olympics and in most major competitions. I felt very "at home".

That comes with experience, I think. It comes from having done it many, many times successfully. You now know that you're in control and "I've done this before and I'm good at this."

You know this is what you're meant to do. The anticipation of that moment is a nervous time for me and I think it is for a lot of people.

I've never done anything special at those times. I've been with my family, been with my kids. I've never done anything in particular except for the last few days leading up to any major competition. I would go away from my wife and my kids and stay in a hotel, like during the Pan Am Games in '87.

We lived in Indianapolis a mile from the velodrome but I went and

Gorski was known as a "win from the front" rider (here with Scott Berryman). Marymoor, 1986

stayed at a hotel during my competition just because that mind-set, that extremely intense, nervous anticipatory kind of mind-set is one where I'm not real good at dealing with other people and other people's problems at that point.

I guess I just sort of deal with it in my own way, in a very focused way. I didn't go out and be with friends to sort of forget about things. I actually

tried to -- I probably made it worse by sort of isolating myself. But, I think I was able to focus better because of that.

My wife understood that it was part of what I needed, plus I wasn't a lot of fun to be around. That was the bottom line, actually, I think I was pretty tough to be around.

That's the side that people never saw. I'd be very easy going, but I had a very -- not a short fuse, but I was very focused. It wouldn't go on for a long period of time, but just for a day or two prior to competition.

It's kind of preparing for battle, is what it is. It's probably not a lot different than people preparing for war, in ancient times or even today.

I still don't think today that I truly appreciate fulfilling my Olympic dream, to a certain extent. You get to a point where you take it for granted, it becomes such a part of you. You don't truly appreciate fulfilling something that meant so much to you early on in your life.

Without question, the ability to envision accomplishments ultimately gives you a much better chance of actually doing them successfully.

Emotionally and mentally it prepares you for winning and being a Champion.

I think that works in a lot of things that you do, not just athletics, but anything that you do, creatively, in business, in what you do with your life. It certainly isn't limited to sports.

I never had to manipulate myself to want to win. I think that particularly in '84, that was just something that I wasn't going to be stopped from doing.

Best Moments

My most satisfying accomplishment came in 1984 in early June. It was about two months before the Olympic Games. We were just finishing a six week stint riding a number of the Gran Prix events.

I had finished third in the Soviet Union behind Huebner and Hesslich, but I had beaten Kopilov in the semifinals. Before that I won a Gran Prix in the Soviet Union, then I got third in the Gran Prix of East Germany again. The last Gran Prix we rode was in Czechoslovakia. At that point the East Germans and Russians knew they were going to be boycotting.

I got into the Quarterfinals and I had Rolf Kushy who, I think, was Bronze medalist a couple of times in the World Championships, and I beat him. I had Huebner in the semifinals -- I don't think I have to give you his resume -- and I beat Huebner.

In the finals I rode against Hesslich. It went to three rides. He beat me in the third ride but before the third and deciding ride he said to me "Well, this is going to be our Olympic Games."

We both recognized that we weren't going to get an opportunity to race against each other in the Olympics. Kopilov was second in the World the previous year, but I had pretty convincingly beat him a number of times in Europe. It was pretty clear to Hesslich and myself that given that it was one Sprinter per country which changed to two given the boycott, that it would have been he and I racing for the Gold.

Aside from winning the Gold, that was, for me personally, the most special race day I've ever had. I beat two of the best Sprinters of the last 20 years all in the same day.

It was like one battalion after another in this war. It was unbelievable. That was a real special race for me. There weren't a lot of people in the stands and no one was watching it on TV, but it got to the heart of competition and just man to man. That kind of competition really meant a lot to me. That year in particular I was riding very well. '84 was my best year, without question.

The boycott was a very ill-advised decision. It was a colossal mistake, making the wrong people pay, using the wrong people as political pawns, which I don't think we've seen before or since in terms of a political decision.

What we're now seeing, as in several Olympiads, is the "home court". The Spanish, in 1992, won 13 Gold medals while they had won 4 in the previous 90 years of competition. The Koreans won multiples of what they'd ever won before in the Olympics. Look at what the Norwegians did in the Winter Olympics. It's just repeated itself over and over again.

No one's ever asked me this, but I believe that it's a heightened intensity level for a year or two prior to the Games if they're coming to your home country. That leads to more intense training day in and day out which leads to better performances and a heightened awareness and intensity level for a longer period of time.

I think it backfires in some guys because there's too much pressure, but for a lot of people it leads to a lot better performances. That definitely was so for me. Everybody knew and was anticipating the Games in LA for two to three to four years out, particularly in Southern California. Every American was certainly gunning for that for a long period of time, every American athlete.

Fun Times

One of the more fun bonding times with the Eastern Europeans was when we were in T'blise in the Georgian Republic of the former Soviet Union.

All the racers were staying at the same hotel. We had just finished a Gran Prix there. It was myself, Nelson, Les Barczewski, Scott Berryman and Hesslich, Huebner and, I think, Kushy and Kopilov and a couple of other guys. It was basically the "Who's Who in Sprinting in the World" at the time.

One of us had brought a Nerf football. There was a huge plaza in the middle of the city where a lot of people congregated. We went down in shorts and cut off t-shirts. I think everyone knew we were there for the Gran Prix event.

We started throwing around the football. Of course, the East Germans knew nothing about how to even throw a football. They'd take it by one end and kind of toss it end over end.

We started, in this huge square, roughly the size of a football field, throwing the football, running patterns and stuff, and of course, after a few minutes we decided we were going to have a game. It was the Americans versus the "Rest of the World."

Everyone took their shirts off and it was kind of like American Gladiators. Midway through the game there were probably 1000 people watching this game intently.

It was hilarious because those guys didn't really know how to play, although guys that good athletically, could run very fast and could throw, once they figured out how to do it.

It turned into a really a competitive game which the Americans did win, fortunately, because we never would have lived down if we hadn't.

I'll never forget Les Barczewski, who was one of the smallest of this group on this day, running a pattern. He was a receiver. Nelson and myself were quarterbacks. Les ran out with Huebner just kind of standing in his way, his feet set in the ground.

Les ran into him and just kind of bounced off of him like a fly! It was hilarious. We were cracking up the whole time.

It was really fun, and the Georgians who were there watching were just loving it. They were cheering us on by the end of the game. It was hilarious. It was great.

Transition

Up through '84 I was going to quit riding at one point. There were all sorts of distractions along the way -- the '80 Olympic experience. I continued because of a desire to find out how far I could go, or maybe a realization that I hadn't reached the top yet, that I hadn't reached my potential, kept me going.

It was a curiosity, I think more than anything. I knew, could feel, could sense, as early as '78, '77, maybe even '75, that I had what it took to be one of the best, that stopping short of that, or letting myself stop short of that, was a real mistake.

I got distracted after '84. I believe I could have continued to perform at a high level, but I made very conscious decisions that were important to me.

Number one was to make money. Number two was to expand my experience beyond athletics into some business areas which I felt would benefit me for my whole life. I'm glad now that I did.

I stopped racing in October of 1989. I hadn't raced particularly well that year. I was fourth in the National Championships. I didn't ride much internationally. We were in the process of moving from Indianapolis back to Southern California, to Newport Beach.

After '84 a big part of my life was more than bike racing. It was representing companies, speaking, doing television commentating, writing for Bicycling, it became a business and a career for me as well as a sport.

Mark's main US opponent in Olympic years was Nelson Vails. Marymoor, 1986

It wore on me that I had other requirements of my time in addition to the fact that I was married and had two kids. I was starting to grow a little bored and starting to look beyond cycling at what I was going to be doing with the rest of my life.

There was a three day event and I was staying at home because the NEC World Invitational was at Dominguez Hills. It was a great event, $100,000 prize money, eight countries.

I was getting ready to leave the house, three hours or so before the race. I had planned, at that point, to continue racing the next year. I was packing up my stuff and I said to Mary, "I have this weird feeling that this is going to be the last day I race my bike." And it was.

I got second in the Keirin event that day. I rode well -- the Keirin was the clinching event for us to take the team title over the Russians and Italians that day.

Over the next month or two I made the decision that I would retire and move on to other things. It was sort of anticlimactic but I sort of just knew in my heart that that was it. I have been pretty much lead by my feelings and my heart about those kinds of things, about major things, about very, very big things in my life.

If you go that way, if you don't waiver from that, I think that you come out okay. You pursue things with such a passion that you can't help but be successful. If it steers you away from something that was a passion, there's a reason for that, and you put yourself on another track with the same amount of passion. That's what I was really looking for, something else which, interestingly, I found that I needed to prove to myself when I went outside the cycling world. I went into the world of investment management and enjoyed it.

Applying what you experience

It was good timing for me for the several years following the Olympics. I was very fortunate to have reaped financial rewards from my success there and effectively leverage my results and who I was, into a role as a spokesperson, which I really enjoy.

I think I was good at it. That's why I was able to be effective and why companies were able to use me. When I deal with the U.S. Team athletes and anyone I come into contact with, I encourage them to think about that, think about how they can do the same thing, translate that experience into a career after the sport.

That's one of the down sides of our sport. It's not, for the most part, an intercollegiate sport. It's tough for an athlete to make a transition. It's tough enough for an athlete to make a transition out of <u>any</u> sport and into the real world.

Out of cycling it's even more difficult, because they don't generally get the educational background or the practical background that can help them in the business world. There are a number of ways to do that.

Number One would be to continue your education while you're riding, and/or, the Olympic Committee has a job program which is reasonably successful but which few cyclists take advantage of.

I speak to them, all the cyclists as a group, and encourage them to do that because it's a great opportunity to build relationships with companies which will last their whole lives.

Too few athletes, and cyclists in particular, maximize the relationships that they build throughout their careers. They just go from one thing to another. In effect, you could be building a great Rolidex of business cards throughout your career if you do it right. I think that's the key.

If you act responsibly, with some minimal effort you can build relationships which you can then call upon when your career is over. You can call someone and say "Hey, would you consider me for a position in your marketing department, or in your advertising department, or in whatever department, in your company?" There's always opportunities if you nurture those relationships as you go.

Now that I'm back in the cycling arena I'm able to bind business with cycling, and that's something I really enjoy.

In terms of competition, I don't see myself competing any more, but I certainly see myself being very close to the world of cycling. I'm involved with what's going on in terms of corporate involvement in cycling, something, something that, following '84, became a big part of my life.

I learned very quickly and first hand how and why companies spend money on the sport of cycling and spend money on athletes. They're

trying to reach a consumer market. The world of cycling and cycling enthusiasts has grown a lot as a percentage of all Americans.

There are a lot of Americans who are cyclists. There are much fewer of them who are really active cyclists, but it would be tough to combine business and cycling if business hadn't grown as much as it has in the last ten or fifteen years. There just wouldn't have been the opportunity to make money and to make a career in that, but fortunately there has been in the sport of cycling, so it's a good time to be involved in the world of sports marketing and cycling.

cycling, whether it was T-Town in the seventies or San Diego in the early '80s. Indianapolis was very, very active for a few years while we were there. Trexlertown off and on, L.A.'s had good times through the '82, '83, '84, '85 years -- I feel like I've been able to live through some great times in track cycling in the last 15 years.

Seattle in **'86**, '87, '88, **'89**, '90, **'91**, had the Nationals three times in those few years and a couple of major events (Goodwill Games, Washington Mutual Grand Prix) that I rode aside from the Nationals. That place rocked and rolled with a lot of people excited about track cycling.

"Intrinsically, track cycling is more exciting than road racing". Mark vs Paul Swift, 1986 U.S. Nationals, Marymoor.

Velodromes

In 1981 San Diego was the track I spent the most time on. It was my home track through the '84 Games. San Diego was a lot of fun in the early '80s. There were a lot of great riders racing, the crowds were good. I remember the 1980 Nationals there, the magic of those times in track

For obvious reasons, I would say that my favorite track is probably LA (Dominguez Hills). It has the most special feelings for me and I spent a lot of time there. More than the Olympics, I spent a lot of training time there, beating Kopilov there in '83 in the 7-Eleven final was a big deal for me.

National Championships with

Nelson, going to a third ride and a photo finish, that was exciting. The last race that I rode was on that track in 1989. I would say that it's not the best track, but it's certainly my favorite.

There are some nightmare tracks, in places you wouldn't expect me to talk about. There's a track in Budapest, Hungary where I won a couple of Gran Prixs. It was about 412 meters and the bumpiest track I've ever seen.

Atlanta has a tree in the middle, it's got a terrible lip coming up from the apron to the track surface, it's very narrow, it's not very steep.

Fortunately there are a number of velodromes, Indianapolis, Trexlertown, L.A., Houston and so on, where you can go and race regularly.

Diet

I never paid a lot of attention to diet. I took multivitamins and amino acid supplements -- it was kind of in vogue to use amino acids to enhance strength gaining ability for a few years. But I was never real fanatical about diet or nutrition. I ate well balanced meals, but I'm a sucker for junk food. Nacho chips -- I could eat those day and night. I would never deny myself that. I feel that you just need common sense habits in the area of nutrition and supplements.

Advice to New Riders

I see a lot of riders are sort of swimming upstream by trying to specialize in something that is not what they should be specializing in.

Big, explosive, muscular guys who are trying to be road riders and smaller, less muscular guys who really love the track and love the Sprints and are trying to be Sprinters.

I could tell these people "You're wasting your time unless you're doing it purely for enjoyment. If you want to be one of the best, hone in on the physiological specialty that is more suited to you."

The first question I ask people to get a sense of their physiology, is what sports have they participated in in the past? What is their vertical jump? -- things that give an indicator of their body makeup.

By asking a few simple questions I can give them an idea which direction they should head. There's so little in the way of access to real quality coaching, access to some of the fundamentals of cycling, that a lot of people just go down the wrong road for a long period of time.

I don't say that they waste their time, because I think they enjoy it, but they could be progressing more quickly by specializing in another area or discipline.

The USCF is doing coaching development seminars, disseminating information to the regional coaches and educating the regional coaches so that there is a Gibby (Hatton) or a Doreen (Smith-Williams), a John Beckman or a Kathy Volski, or whoever, at the various venues around the country to help kids determine where their specialties lie.

Through access to good coaching, kids can learn how to race. If you're somewhat analytical and self-aware I think you can analyze yourself fairly well, but t's tough to do that objectively.

I was able to do that through deductive reasoning, analyzing the races I was doing well in and why.

You can start to figure out "Hey, I'm good at this -- this is what my body can do, this is what it can't do." You have to be realistic.

You can help yourself to determine that by racing enough to see how you perform under different conditions. If you're racing both road and track, you can start to determine what your limitations are, what your abilities are, and what your strengths are.

The problem is, making these decisions has got to be objective, not just what <u>you</u> want. Everyone wants to be the next Greg LeMond.

Some people can be, but not everyone. It's important to be realistic with yourself, saying "I don't think I can do that, but I think I can be the next Nelson Vails."

I played football and I was a running back. I'm six feet, 198 pounds, and I'm a pretty strong guy. I may have wanted to be the next Greg LeMond but I wasn't gonna be the next Greg LeMond because I was just too darn big. My size and my finishing Sprint told me I was a track Sprinter.

It's tough to say, without going in and having some physiological testing, whether you're the next Lance Armstrong or LeMond, because those are very special people physiologically.

I've always said that there were a lot of people along the way who were more physically talented than I was.

I don't think, for one moment, that Nelson or Scott Berryman or a lot of other people weren't more physically talented than myself.

They were certainly stronger. But, I think it was my desire, my ability to

focus, intensity, clear vision, discipline, many years of experience, great pedaling ability -- from years and years of pedaling, I think I was one of the best pedalers around.

That was just the ability to efficiently make the pedals go around, which sounds very simple, but it takes a lot of years and a lot of miles to hone that skill. It's more than just a lot of brute strength, just the agility of pedaling.

It was really more the mental aspects, because I think there's such a connection between what happens physically and your state of mind.

The other thing that I've said many times before: I was never real secretive about training methods because knowing what to do was about a quarter or a third of the battle.

Doing it month in and month out, year in and year out, is much tougher than simply knowing what to do.

The discipline and commitment to do something over and over again and pushing yourself each of those times to do it a little bit better, a little bit faster, a little bit stronger, --that's the challenge.

It's not actually knowing what weight training exercises, what sprinting gears to use -- those things I could tell someone in an hour. All of the mechanical things about training, weight training, stretching, the four component areas -- it's not about secrets.

I could tell you a lot about what I did, about Hesslich, what a lot of the top guys did, but just knowing that is just one, not small thing, but it's insignificant, compared to the ability,

dedication, commitment, to do it. That's the most difficult thing about sports.

Younger kids shouldn't try to specialize on the track. I encourage them to race road <u>and</u> track.

That's why my message to kids would be different than to a 24 year old who's just starting in cycling and thinks he wants to be a track rider.

He's got a much more limited time frame in which to do things, and maybe he's working as well, so he's got to tailor his strategy around where he is in his life, his age and what he realistically has the ability to do. The track is a great discipline, has great events and has great tradition.

There need to be some changes, which will continue to come about, but there are still great opportunities. If you're at or near the top in track racing, there are financial rewards to be had and great satisfaction from all the wonderful things that it brings -- traveling, representing your country, winning medals and all those neat things.

The Future of Track Racing

Track racing has tremendous potential. It's an extremely exciting discipline of the sport, but it was in jeopardy of being eliminated from the Olympics.

The UCI was mandated to make changes to the format and the numbers of people participating. They did that. You're going to have to qualify to be in the Olympics for certain disciplines. If you're the best in your country you don't automatically go in certain track cycling disciplines now.

I don't think track is in jeopardy of

being eliminated in 2000 in Sydney, because the Australians are one of the big track cycling countries, but tradition isn't driving the sport's continued existence. Of interest to the public is television sports.

Intrinsically, track cycling is more exciting than road racing because you're sitting in an enclosed arena. I think real aficionados of the sport love it, but the average person watching it isn't particularly fascinated by it even if it's two of the best guys in the world.

Track has more potential if you add other events like Points Race, Madison, Keirin, and even the Sprints, taking it to two laps.

I've been asked 100 times in my career "Why is the Sprint three laps? Why do you go slow at the beginning?" Because. Because that's the way they've been doing it for 100 years. There's no better answer to that question. There's nothing in the first lap of a Sprint.

Now you've got fewer "sur places" (*Track Stands*), where people actually balance. So I just ask the question "Why?" Why do we need it if it doesn't affect the outcome of the race and it adds another 30 seconds to the lack of action in the event?

They just eliminated the 100 Kilometer Team Time Trial. They just

Gorski with Master's rider Ron Smith. Who's an inspiration to whom? Master's Nationals, 1993, Colorado Springs.

eliminated it. They finally just said "It's gone". It's gone from the World Championships. You've got an event that's been around for 30, 40, 50 years -- they just canned it.

Tandem Sprint is gone too. Actually, that's an exciting event. The problem is that there are so few people who are specializing in some of the track disciplines now that you just don't get enough entrants. You only have six, seven, eight entrants in the event. Six, seven or eight countries that are participating. And you aren't getting it because there aren't races throughout the year.

You've got National Championships and the World Championships, so . . . . Basically there are some definite changes that need to be made

in the composition and the format of track cycling events if it's going to continue to exist, literally.

I don't think that the UCI is going to be able to stop the momentum and trends that are happening in sports. The IOC is looking for exciting events, ones that are going to increase television revenue.

I've been part of the broadcast crew now of the Olympic Games and the television producers don't care about track cycling. They're only going to show it if an American is going to do well, which is very different than their attitude toward the road.

Which runs against what you expect -- track cycling is far more exciting than road cycling.

I don't think it's a matter of personalities, I think that there are other factors. We have World Champions on the track. We have people who are winning on the track. There are more structural, fundamental kinds of problems. I feel if they changed the format, it would be more marketable.

Master's Racing

I'm amazed at the level of competition in Master's racing. When I watched Master's Nationals in Colorado Springs, if I had just walked

up to the rail and didn't know what was going on, I would have thought I was watching the Senior Nationals.

Five years ago that would not have been the case. You knew you were watching the Masters or Veteran Nationals at that point. There were older guys going fairly slow.

Now, the times and the depth of the competition is so great. There are guys who are very serious about it, specializing and training almost full time as Masters.

It's sort of displacing other categories because demographically our population is ageing and more and more people fit into the Master's age category.

Obviously people are trying to stay fit, healthy, etcetera. It's really impressive to me.

It's great to see so many people of that age being competitive. It keeps people young. I think it's wonderful, I really do. I don't know if I will ever compete as a Master, but I think very highly of a lot of the competitors.

I've thought about getting back on the track as does any athlete who finishes, but that level at which I competed spoiled me.

I was used to competing where that was my whole life and winning and losing was everything. I don't know if I'm prepared mentally to go into it to just have fun.

I still ride a lot and fairly regularly, just because I need what exercise does for me physiologically. I don't need what competition brings me emotionally, because I look for other things to do that for me now.

Chapter 6

∞ *Keirin* ∞

The Keirin is a sort of Mass Start Sprint, begun with holders. Riders accelerate into position behind a Pacer who regulates initial speed over the first few laps. Riders often bump and otherwise intimidate each other behind the motor in order to gain a preferred position. When the Pacer pulls off the track, all riders Sprint to the finish.

While this book centers on velodrome racing in the United States, the Keirin event is a Japanese race, imported to the United States after America's most famous Keirin racer, Gilbert "Gibby" Hatton competed in that country for eight years.

The Keirin was first raced in America as a Professional event in 1983 and in the US National Championships in 1991. US women have begun racing Keirin, though not yet as a Championship event. This race is still finding its identity in the U.S.

Marty Nothstein, the first American to win a World title in this event (1994), was fortunate to be coached by Gibby, who reviews his own experiences in the section following this one. Because the Keirin is raced differently in Japan, the United States and in World Championship competition, the USCF Rule Book is presently inadequate as a guide to understanding this event.

Consequently, this description has drawn upon Gibby's knowledge as a primary resource, rather than the USCF Rule Book, in order to compare and contrast what a rider may find in

the different arenas. The USCF Rule Book will likely undergo changes before this event finds its true character in this country. Will it move in a separate direction or will it evolve toward the Keirin as raced in Japan? Perhaps the second edition of this book and future Rule Books will reveal the answer to this question.

History

The idea of riders riding behind a Pacer is not a new one in the history of bicycle track racing. One of the oldest races on the velodrome is the Motorpace event, contested and won at the World level by Americans at the turn of the century.

In that race, bicycle riders rode behind motor-driven bicycles which broke the wind for them, resulting in a ride which was considerably faster than riding a bicycle alone.

One reason for this pairing may be found in the common beginnings of bicycles and early motorcycles which raced together on the old motordromes of the early days. Both motorcycles and bicycles used to race at Los Angeles Coliseum long ago.

Japanese Keirin

The Japanese took the idea of racing behind a pacing vehicle and designed a unique event called the Keirin (pronounced "KAY-ren"). Keirin means "competition wheels" in Japanese. This race, accompanied by betting on competitors, was instituted in Japan at the end of World War II as one means of rebuilding a

The starting line up of the Keirin has taken several forms: parallel, perpendicular, and staggered (seen here). The problem is getting handlers out of the way while giving riders equal opportunity to get on the motor. Vandedrome, 1995

country devastated by World War II. Citizens were encouraged to rebuild pride through competition.

Keirin racing has since become a multi-billion dollar industry which returns a portion of its profits to local municipalities for community improvement. Competitors burst out of stalls like equine racers as bettors discover whether their instincts for picking a winner are correct or not.

Bicycles used in Japan are as basic as bicycles ever were: simple tubing, direct drive, and each exactly the same -- no disc wheels or other aerodynamic aids. The purpose of this is to disallow any mechanical advantage and force

the race results to stem from skills and hearts of the riders alone.

Several riders who have contributed to this book (Gibby Hatton, Nelson Vails and Mark Whitehead) have raced on the Japanese Keirin Circuit. U.S. Sprinter Ken Carpenter is the latest American competitor to have raced in that arena.

Other American riders would like to take on this challenge, but the choice is not up to riders. Racing in Japan is by invitation only. Once a rider is invited he must be invited again each year to continue. Nothing is automatic. Keirin racing in Japan is well-organized and precise.

A Comparison of Keirin Racing in United States, World Championship, and Japanese Venues through the eyes of Gilbert "Gibby" Hatton

No American knows the Keirin like Gibby Hatton. He shares his knowledge here:

Keirin got started in 1948 after we virtually destroyed Japan. They needed something to bring up the peoples' morale, something to perk them up.

Each Prefecture in Japan has a certain number of tracks. A certain percentage of profit from each track goes right back into the state or Prefecture to improve it, for parks, roads or something that benefits the public. Consequently, a lot of the income that Keirin brings goes right back into the community. That's what they wanted to do, rebuild their community after the War, after the atomic bombs.

They also wanted to lift the morale of the people by combining sports and gambling for entertainment. It was very well thought out and all monitor-ed by the government. It's called "MITI", Minister International and Trade. It's all monitored very closely and done very well.

It was begun by a group of businessmen in the Osaka/ Kyoto area who started the first track. In the beginning there were about 40,000 people. It was very successful from the start.

In Japan, not just anyone can become a Keirin rider. Potential riders must go to Keirin School. They must go through difficult testing that is oral, written and physical. 1000 kids try per year and only 250 to 300 per year make it. They are extremely selective.

They don't want some criminal type of guy who's going to hang out with the Acuza (Japanese Mafia) and fix all the races. They monitor all parts of it very closely. It's kind of cliche, but they want only the most honorable

The keynote of the Keirin is the jockeying for position behind the motorcycle. Keirin racing is distinctively different at the Japanese, Worlds and U.S. National levels due to the differences in purpose at each venue. In all venues, riders must get behind the Pacer and cannot pass.

types of individuals who will be very honored to be a Keirin racer. They look at it like you are somebody very special, that you are a privileged athlete. It's a big deal to do something like that. Their top athletes there are as big as their baseball stars. When

Nakano (*10 time World Sprint Champion*) walks down the street, everybody knows him.

When Keirin racing was introduced in the early 80s, the people who made the U.S. rules had never seen it before. They had never been to Japan or to the World's. They sort of made up their own rules. But this has happened before, it's not particularly new.

When the Rule Book says "Match Sprint rules apply," they're talking about impeding the progress of the other riders, that sort of thing. That's a pretty standard rule in track racing anyway. When the guy's trying to pass

you, you can't take him to the rail in any race. Half the Sprint rules simply do not apply to the Keirin.

Even in different venues Keirin is raced very differently. Keirin in Japan, in America, and at the World Championships differs in the use of the Pacer and the structure of the race. There are three different types of tactics in the three different arenas.

• Japan •

In Japan the racing is structured around the **betting.**

The Start

In Japan, each rider is in a little gate, just like race horses. Each of the nine riders sits in a gate and 25 yards up the track is a solo rider with his gate. They're all hooked up by cable to the gun.

When the gun is fired, all the gates are released simultaneously. The back wheel is held until it is released by the gun. The pacing rider has the same kind of bicycle as all other riders. Everything is regulation, all uniforms the same.

Pacer

In Japan, they use a Pacer who is connected with the judge's box by a radio in his helmet which controls the tempo of the race Because of the betting, every rider has to have an equal opportunity.

Tactics

In Japan they have three different

kinds of riders, each with a specific name. Basically they are the lead-out guy, the middle distance lead-out, and the guy who just comes off the wheel at the finish. They have specific names for them. They are not assigned in those positions, it's just in relation to the type of rider each is.

In Japan, Marty and myself, for instance, would be almost the opposite type riders. They use that information to assist in informing the bettors. They tell the bettors what kind of rider each is, what type of placings each has had, the name of their bike, what gearing they're using, and things like that. All that has to be stated prior to the races, just like the horse rags. You know how old the horse is, what his last time for that particular distance was, how much the jockey weighs, how much weight they have added on -- they give you all information in detail so that the bettor has the best and fairest chance to win.

In Japan, riders will ride with their friends or riders who come from their track. The South might ride for the South, the East for the East, and so on. They'll have a couple of different styles of guys who will pair up or three guys will team up.

In Japan they ring the bells for half a lap. The first bell starts at 600 meters, the last one ends at 400, which is one lap to go. There are probably at least a half dozen bells over that 200 meter distance. The bells start "ding . . . . . ding . . . . . ding . . . . . ding" and as it gets closer to one lap to go, the bells speed up "ding . ding . ding . ding". It gets everybody all exited. It's great. They do it the right way!

The Pacers have an ear phone. When the Sprint initiates after the first bell, they tell the pacing rider to get out of the way.

At Worlds and in American racing there's a designated point where they pull off. In Japan you can't pass the Pacer before the first bell or you get penalized. Or, the other rider pulls off (providing it's after the first bell) when the Sprint begins.

In other words, if the first bell is rung and they start attacking right afterwards, the Pacer will swing down off the track. They tell him from the judge's box when he needs to pull off, and they'll tell him to get off quick -- they're coming over the top!

• The United States •
In America there is no betting, so Keirin structured around the **rider.**
The Start
The start in the United States has just changed from riders lining up in a row to riders lined up across the track. That's less confusing. Officials prefer having the Pacer coming along the bottom of the track
The Pacer
In America, the Pacer uses a motorcycle. In fact, everything from a tandem to a 750 cc motorcycle.

The reason we don't use dernys in America is that we have a hard time getting access to them, while motorcycles are much more common here.

In America, riders can ride just about anything. In Indianapolis they use Roger Young's 250 motorcycle. In L.A. they use the big 750. In T-Town they use a little 100. It's whatever anybody has available. 25 to 27 miles per hour is the maximum they are

supposed to go, no matter what kind of vehicle is used.

If the Pacer is on a high speed motorbike and doesn't know what he's doing or goes at too fast a pace, there is not as much opportunity for the tail end riders to be in the race. The big motors give more of a wind break to the riders in the front so they have a superior advantage. The back rider is at a disadvantage because he has less of a wind break.

The object of the race is to give every rider equal advantage, so big motors are not the correct Pacer vehicle for the event.

In the United States, whoever decides to ride at the bike track can do the pacing. In 1994, Roger (Young) was driving the motorcycle. I griped about that because he's a coach of some of the guys in the Final. Someone else should have ridden it, because it's a conflict of interest.

In the United States they just have the one regular bell to signify the last portion of the race.

In the United States we don't have enough riders to have a Keirin circuit like Japan right now. There have been a number of people who have talked about wanting to have it, but we'll see.

There are only two people from the United States who have ever medaled in Keirin at the World level, the coach (Gibby Hatton) and the student (Marty Nothstein).
•The World Championships•
At the Worlds, there is no betting, so it's structured around the **title.**

At the World Championships they use a derny which is limited as to both speed and acceleration. It can go up to

35 miles per hour, but the ones I've seen lately go 25-27 miles per hour.

Drivers are selected according to "X" number of Drivers. They have a lottery to pick who drives each heat and Final. Otherwise, say it's in Italy and it's an Italian Driver, they could get two Italians behind the motor and go like hell and everyone has to chase. They don't want to do that.

At the Worlds they just have the one regular bell to signify the last portion of the race.
Tactics
In the States, when I rode with Wheaties-Schwinn we always rode together and we rode against Team Lycra and a couple of others. It's kind of that way. At Worlds, it's kind of Huebner and Fiedler were riding together, there's always a couple who will pair up. It's not really an individual race. You can ride individually, but it would be to your disadvantage.

Tactics involve not so much blocking as protecting. For instance, if Marty and I are riding together, Marty is a long lead-out guy. My job would be to let him go, but not go 100%. My job would be to lay off of him, watch the back, watch where the attacks come and holler to him to go, "sweep" a little bit and protect the lead-out guy as long as you can.

First, he gets a good placing and then the guy doing the protecting has a good run for the win. The team work goes kind of like that. It's not really blocking, it's more of a protecting type of style.

One basic rule is that you can't pass the motor before the bell. That's supposed to be the rule at World's and in the United States, but sometimes riders pass the motor before the bell and get away with it. If you can stretch the rule and get away with it, you do. If the guy wants to lead it out with 700 meters to go, the other riders don't always mind.

Gibby's advice to the 1994 World Keirin Champion:

If I were to advise someone like Marty how to ride in Japan vs. the United States vs. the Worlds, I would advise him to ride pretty much the same way. I would tell him to ride from the front. His best asset is to go long.

In **Japan**, they go such a slow pace, you could go long from the back. Once the first bell rings, the majority of the tracks in Japan are 400 meters, so you go from the first bell. That would be about 600 meters out. So if Marty were to go from the back I'd advise him to attack early, go to the front, slow it a little bit and watch for the attack.

In the **United States** there's no one strong enough to compete with him so I just tell him to ride at the front, the same way -- attack early and go.

At **Worlds** I'd advise the same, try to get to the derny and go with it, ride the same tactic. Go to the front, watch, and use his throttle control which he's mastered perfectly. He's just trying to counter the attacks, there's not much more he can do. That's his best tactic. Throttle control means you

Paul Swift fights Nelson Vails for Marty Nothstein's wheel.   Paul rode Marty's wheel to the finish, then came around -- not quite enough.
Pushing and shoving and Sprint to the finish -- what more could you ask for?

use enough power and speed to hold the attack off on the hip. That might require the initial acceleration to be 100% for a short amount of time, but once you subdue the attack on the outside, you kind of float with it when they float, kick it when they kick. Just counter their move.

A last minute kick on the part of another rider is always a possibility, but when you get to a certain point if you're so far back you have no chance because all the riders are stacking up. They are stacked up three and four deep coming out of the last turn.

When they tried to attack, Marty just had enough power to sustain the lead. In other words, if you can picture putting him in front of a wave that just broke that has white water, rather than get swallowed by the white water, he had enough power to stay in front. Huebner got blocked in and tried to come up on the inside.

I would give a rider like Ken Carpenter the same advice as Marty, go to the front. Now Paul Swift is a different kind of rider. He is craftier and comes off at the last moment. My advice to Paul would be to sit on, make sure he gets good position, don't leave the inside open and wait for the opportunity after 200 meters to go. He would do well to suck a wheel of somebody like Marty or Ken or Huebner. You have to have all of the elements.

Passing

As a general rule, there are only two logical places you can pass. One is out of the last turn in the homestretch (Turn Four) and the other on the backstretch going into 200 meters. Those are the only two logical places to pass. Any other place, you're going to get hung up into the banking and it defeats the purpose of the track. The track is banked for a specific reason,

not just for looks.

An intelligent racer is going to figure out the advantages and disadvantages of the banking. One main factor is knowing when and how to pass. You can make the track work against you if you try to pass at the wrong place. You end up, first, going further distance, and second, it's so much more difficult. If you pass at the right places, the banking can help you pick up speed due to the downhill transitions.

My three favorite places are in Turn Four going into the bell, in the 200 meter mark area and going into the finish. It happens most out of Turn Four into the finish if everybody waits that long. It's pretty well the same at the Worlds and in Japan. People will try to make a move there or coming out of Turn Two. If you're not there in Turn Four, the race is over.

Gibby Hatton

The United States and the RuleBook

There has been a lot of interest in betting on the Keirin in the U.S. It has been under discussion for some time.

Keirins in the United States are described in the USCF Rule Book as following the same rules as Sprint competition ("sprint rules apply"). Anyone watching a Keirin competition who knows Sprint rules quickly realizes that many Sprint rules simply do not apply to Keirin races. Track Stands and stopping races due to rider contact are contrary to the conduct of the race.

Equipment used in the United States is as varied as the number of riders in any Sprint event. There is no required standardization of bicycles, though certain pieces of equipment such as bullhorns, are not allowed, as in any Sprint event.

Like Tandem Sprints, although Keirin follows Sprint rules according to the Rule Book, it has its own character due to variations specific to this unique event. The Keirin appears to be increasing in popularity as it is a crowd pleaser as well as a challenge for riders. There have only been a few local Keirins for women.

Qualifying

Only Category 1 and professional riders are allowed to compete in Keirins at the U.S. National Championships. Category 1 is a designation found on licenses issued by the United States Cycling Federation.

Riders wishing to sign up for Keirin must show their licenses. If Category 1 is on a rider's license, he may race in the Keirin. This is all the qualifying necessary at present.

While Keirin riders may one day be seeded as they are in Sprints, this is presently not done. Because only high level riders are allowed to compete in this event, they are usually known by officials well enough to sort them fairly evenly. Whether or not this continues remains to be seen.

Qualifying heats determine who moves on to higher levels of competition and who gets the "second chance" of repechage. Procedures here are similar to Match Sprints. The numbers of riders wanting to contest the Keirin are increasing as more riders become familiar with the event. As contact is legal in this race, it is vital that riders have the requisite bike handling skills to compete safely.

Distance/Numbers

The Keirin is a motorpaced event for three of the five laps which usually comprise the race. On the next to last lap, the Pacer pulls off and the race turns into a true Sprint over the final two laps to the finish.

UCSF rules designate the distance as five laps on a track 333m or less and four laps on tracks longer than 333m. The maximum number of riders per heat is nine.

The Rule Book states that "Normally the pacer rides a derny or a motorized pacing bicycle; a tandem may be used when practicable." In fact, motorcycles are the most common pace vehicle seen on velodromes around the United States.

Motorcycles are often fitted with a specially designed bar in back of the rear wheel which has a roller on it so that riders who touch their front wheels to the back of the pace vehicle will not be endangered by the sudden impact this will have on their forward progress.

Local velodromes which offer training with motors on the track may not include this feature, but it is a small price to pay to prevent injury to bicycle riders who may inadvertently bump into the rear of the motor with their direct drive, brakeless bicycle with other riders behind. It is definitely a good idea, especially when riders are still learning.

The Start

In the start of the Keirin, riders line up across the track from the bottom of the track to the top. Position is determined by lot, the same as in Sprints. Each rider is held by a holder who may or may not be an official.

The Pacer (on a derny or motorcycle in the U.S.) circles on the bottom of the track until notified by officials that riders are ready. Usually the official will hold up fingers signifying one lap, two laps, or whatever, to the start.

When the starting gun is fired, riders take off and get on behind the motor. Holders usually push riders off at the start. A neutral start is not necessary.

Sprint Rules

There is no "walking pace" requirement for the first lap in a Keirin, and there is certainly never any need or attempt to go into a Track Stand during this event. No specific rider has to lead at any point or maintain any particular position. Riders can pass or ride alongside any number of other riders.

The only provisions are:

1) the riders *must get on* behind the motor, and

2) they *cannot pass* the motor.

If either of these rules is violated, the race may be restarted or riders may be disqualified. Officials will decide.

The Chief Referee instructs the Pacer as to the position and pace to be maintained. In the early laps, the Pacer holds riders at a speed of 45-50 kilometers per hour. During the next to last lap (in the U.S.), the Pacer accelerates ahead of the riders and moves off the track, leaving riders to Sprint to the finish.

Rules for the Keirin refer to those for the Match Sprint. Many of these are silly if one attempts to apply them to the Keirin (i.e. Track Stands). On the other hand, there is overlap between the two events -- top Keirin riders are also top Sprinters.

As in the Match Sprint, the Keirin involves staying in a draft, conserving energy for the longest time possible until the Sprint begins. This draft is first provided by the Pacer. Once the Pacer pulls off, it is provided by another competitor's back wheel.

The Sprinter in a Keirin race in the United States tries to save his maximum Sprint for Turn Four, into the home stretch, and across the finish line, dropping all other competitors.

However, the Sprint often begins at the time the motor pulls off. The race becomes a free-for-all for two more laps -- kind of an endurance Sprint.

One of the most distinct elements in the Keirin is the pushing and shoving which is allowed in this event, in contrast to Match Sprints, most dramatically when riders are in back of the Pacer. Riders fight for the best place in the draft, either immediately in back of the motor or in back of a competitor who they believe will give them the best ride to the finish line.

Sprinters often win the Keirin, not only because they have the best Sprint, but because they know how to conserve their energy for the maximum effort and they know who will likely give the best ride to the finish.

The skills Sprinters must develop for the Match Sprint are those most heavily drawn upon for the Keirin. Physical interaction between Sprinters is common. Top level bicycle handling skills are mandatory.

The instant reflexes born of years of the "cat-and-mouse" Sprint game come in handy when nine riders are racing at top speed, all trying to stay in a draft until the last possible moment. Sprinters are often the larger riders on the track, too, and it's a lot easier to shove someone else out of the way when you're big and handle your bike well.

The Sprint zone, between the black and red lines, carries the same importance as in the Match Sprint, at least in theory. During the final Sprint, only one rider is allowed in this zone. However, with nine riders contesting this race, who is in the Sprint lane is the least of a rider's concern once they round Turn Four. There are simply too many people in the final stretch to worry about this small zone on the inside of the track.

Riders are intent on passing all others and will follow whatever path that allows them to do that. Usually they are spread across the entire width of the final stretch, from Turn Four through the finish area.

Keirin (Sprint) Formats
Championship format

Championship format sets up rounds in such a way that the fastest riders will meet in the final race. Formulas for seeding any Sprint race are in the USCF Rule Book and will not be reviewed here.

The total numbers of riders who want to ride the Keirin determines how many groups will compete. Competitors are distributed as evenly as possible across heats.

In the early rounds, the top riders advance, while losers compete in repechages, a second chance which offers a path for reentry into the finals for winners, just like in Match Sprints.

In theory, the riders who will arrive at the finals will be those who are the most competitive. As in Match Sprints, those who Time Trial fastest will not necessarily be the winners of this event, as contrary as that may seem.

Round Robin format

A "round robin" format allowing each rider an opportunity to compete against all other riders, is not usual in Keirin competition. However, since Keirin follows Sprint rules which allow round robin format, this would be possible. The winner would be determined by total points accumulated. The Rule Book may be consulted for round robin procedures.

The advantage of round robin type matches would be additional practice in this challenging event by having more opportunities to compete. The number of riders competing in Keirins today would render round robin formats somewhat tedious, but the way Keirins are gaining popularity, this might be a good training routine.

Exhibition Keirins

Exhibition Keirins must follow the format of Championship Sprints, though details may vary. Certain other rules may also vary, such as the necessity of "repechage" and the rider losing twice prior to being eliminated. These things depend on the number of riders and the decision of the venue holding the races.

Stopping a Keirin

In theory, stopping a Keirin once the race has begun follows Sprint rules as listed in the Rule Book. That would allow stoppage in the slow part of the race -- there is no slow part in Keirin racing. In reality, Keirin's are not stopped unless there's an accident, and even then only if it endangers the other riders.

Other rules listed in the Rule Book under "Sprint rules apply" simply do not relate to the Keirin. Track Stand rules are humorous -- no one would think of doing a Track Stand in a Keirin. Touching the track surface or the outside fence or railing is not likely because riders are riding at the bottom of the track.

In the event of a crash, reactions of officials would be the same for any race: if it's dangerous to the riders, the race will be stopped or neutralized. The Rule Book points to Match Sprints for guidance in what to do in the event of mishaps, but with the motor and nine riders, things are just not the same as in Match Sprints. It would appear that rules will continue to develop in response to real conditions and occurrences in races yet to be ridden.

In the Keirin, contact between riders is common, so restarts would not happen for that reason, as they might in Match Sprints.

Riders may not cut others off, but in Keirins everyone is Sprinting all over the track and everyone knows this, so this rule applies a little differently than would be expected between two or three riders of a Match Sprint. As always, a rider may never force another rider off the track.

A rider who is below the Sprinter's (red) line must stay there unless he has "a clear lead" until the finish. All following riders must pass on the right, outside the Sprinter's lane. It is okay for the leader to come out of the Sprinter's lane with a large lead and if there is no hindrance to others, but riders are not usually off the front.

In fact, while Sprint rules theoretically apply, they do not fit well within the dynamics of the Keirin. There are simply too many people on the track for things to be neat and tidy. The bottom line in Keirins is: ride straight and don't cause accidents. If you pass, don't take anyone down as you do. (Try to enforce those neat and tidy rules in a race with nine flailing Sprinters all over the track. Yeah, you bet.)

If the outcome of the race has been significantly altered by some drastic move which caused damage to others, the race might be re-ridden.

However, if it can be as simple as eliminating one offending rider, it makes little sense to "punish" all riders by requiring a re-ride of those who were not impacted by the offender. Officials tend to choose that method which most benefits all concerned, riders and organizers.

Other Sprint Rules
Blocking

Blocking of other riders is possible in Keirin if riders have teamed up. Nevertheless, it is technically illegal to block or interfere with another rider according to the Rule Book.

With nine riders in a race and everyone jockeying for position, determining when blocking is intentional and when a rider is trying to maintain his own position is a quandary. If officials feel that a rider has intentionally blocked another, he can be relegated or disqualified.

Dead Heats

If officials are unable to determine a winner in a particular race, it will be rerun with the competitors who were involved in the dead heat.

Cameras will verify dead heats. If this situation arises during an earlier round, both riders will simply advance to the later rounds. Deciding who actually won is not necessary if several advance.

Mishaps

Mishaps within the first 30 meters are called as a False Start and the race is restarted. As always, the legitimacy of mishaps will be determined by officials.

Disqualifications

If the leading edge of a riders's front wheel moves even with the chainset axle of the Pacer before the Pacer is off the track, that rider shall be disqualified (at least, that's what the RuleBook says).

Race Equipment

The one vital piece of track equipment used for the Keirin is the Pacer. No sponges or cones are used, nothing in the way of competitors whose high speed makes their forward progress unstable and unpredictable.

The Starter's pistol is an instrument of control for violations at any point in any race and can stop the race with a double gunshot.

Bicycle Equipment

Equipment for the Keirin is a standard track bicycle. This may include disc or other wheels, but may not include bull horn bars or aero bars. Keirin bicycles are often Sprint-type bicycles with steeper angles and reinforced stiffness, but may also simply be a standard track bicycle.

Summary

While Keirin rules set the groupings at nine, the trend in the United States has been to group in lesser numbers. While this may be more manageable in some ways, it does not prepare the riders for higher level competition.

Weekly race series at local tracks are offering Keirin races more often, partly because audiences like them and partly because they offer a Sprint race for a larger number of riders.

As with any event, riders training with hopes of participation in a National Championship must have practice in as close to true competitive circumstances as possible in order to acquire the skills which will allow them to be competitive at higher levels. They're learning fast in this race.

Few Sprint finishes on the track are as exciting as the Keirin finish among top riders. Marty Nothstein shows his World Champion style a month before his win. World Cup, 1994

Keirin
Gilbert ("Gibby") Hatton

Gilbert "Gibby" Hatton (nicknamed "The Bear") has a unique place in one of the dynasties of cycling history.

A young up-start named Jackie Simes III battled the great Sprinter Jack Disney for the U.S. Sprint title for several years. Both of these men became mentors for a budding young cyclist called Gibby who began racing as a "Midget" in 1966.

Gibby began his career on the Encino Velodrome. He won the Junior 13-15 Omnium in 1970 and the 16-18 Omnium two years running (1973 & '74). In 1974 he won the Junior World Sprint Championships.

After winning a Bronze medal in Keirin in 1983, he became the first American to be invited to Japan to compete on the multi-billion dollar Keirin circuit. He was invited back for seven more years.

Gibby is now a Master's rider and coaches cyclists on the Junior National and National teams. His home track is Lehigh County Velodrome. No American knows Keirin racing better than The Bear.

Most people back home (Pennsylvania) call me Gil, in California it's Gibby. I was "Gibby when I was a kid.

My dad was friends with Bill Disney a 1960 Olympic Speedskater who rode bicycles in the off-season. We became friends with Bill's brother Jack Disney, a member of the Bicycling Hall of Fame. (*Jack Disney was National Omnium Champion from 1954 to 1958, Sprint Champion 1966 & '68*).

How I Got Started

I began racing at 10 years old. Eventually, Jack became my coach. My dad, Jack Disney and Jack Simes helped me the most to develop as a rider/racer.

My riding style came from my personality and my background. My dad raced motorcycles for 10 years and I started riding a motorcycle when I was eight years old.

My bike handling skills were pretty good by the time I started riding. We got into track when I was ten years old.

The handling skills were possibly there before the actual bike riding. I'd had some experiences where my heart was up in my throat already, a few times on the motorcycle.

Getting on the track, a lot of the bike handling stuff, my father taught me. It was good common sense, and he raced motorcycles for years, so setting the corner up and things like that were something that I learned real fast, right away.

Then everything else followed.

I liked the book *Hearts of Lions* because it gave a lot of credit to my coach and he's probably one of the greatest Sprinters this country ever had. He doesn't get very much credit.

"What we have is virtually a family. There's not one guy who's going to be able to do it by himself. You've got to mold the character and the attitude to be successful.

You get to a certain age, you want to make the world a better place for the kids. Talk to any parent, cycling's a discipline that you learn from, that you can carry on into any aspect of your life."

In fact, a lot of the older riders don't get a lot of credit, and it's absolutely well deserved. The 50s and 60s. They're so caught up on what's happening today. I'm kind of a history buff, I guess. I like to read about Frank Kramer and guys like that and what it was like. There aren't any really detailed publications about their lifestyles and what they did.

It would be pretty interesting to find out what the athletes of the twenties did every day compared to what I know what Marty, our top Sprinter, does. I know what he does every day and it's pretty hard work.

My career has extended from 1966 to the present, from what used to be called Midget to Master's. Along with racing as a Master, I am coaching some Junior National and National Team members. I could easily write a book about my racing experiences over these years, both on and off the bike.

There's a girl in L.A. who has one of my old bikes, Ednita Kelly. She won Nationals on it. It's fun to have someone win Nationals on it again. I won in 1970.

You have to understand the time when I was at my best, 25 years ago. Things are way different now. Training methods and equipment and a good outlook -- I wish I'd had somebody like myself who had grabbed me by the ear.

I probably would have taken a swing at him, but eventually that guy would have won because he was right about what needed to be done. I know all the things not to do.

Velodromes are our working place. If you don't have that attitude stepping into the velodrome then you're not going to succeed at what you intend to do. I think that's a big part of Marty's success.

You have to be focused and you have to have regularity and consistency in your every day program. You should live your life around your training if you want to be successful if you want to be World Class.

I didn't do that. I was just a wild hellion, undisciplined, Southern California kid with a lot of talent. I was fortunate enough to get where I got to go. But I had to move away, too. I feel that contributed to a lot of my later success, getting out of L.A.

It's hard to analyze your own life. Some parts you don't want to admit are true and it's kind of hard to talk about. You're a product of your environment, the place where you live. In that whole big place (L.A.) there are so many things to do.

I think being successful so young was almost a disadvantage. I absolutely took it for granted, being World Champion at 18. With the Federation the kids are much more fortunate now. There's much more organization and a place to go to train. We didn't have that then.

That didn't come about until Eddie came into the country. He demanded his Eastern Block ways and that wasn't

the L.A. way. It didn't work out. At that time I decided to turn Pro.

Turning Pro meant going with Jack Simes and the Eastern people. I was out there in 1976 when it first started.

At that time Jack had the best eight track riders in the country living at Lehigh and he provided everything for us -- good racing, a place to stay for nothing, a cook and food. He had everything. It was like a team.

I call that my second life. I had the youth life which was really successful. Then it was pretty much instructed by Jack Disney and my father and went that way and when I got to be a teenager I wanted to go out and find out about life myself.

A bike wasn't part of my life at that time. I was kind of dabbling with bikes, but I was doing other things. I kind of floated back into the bike game and realized that, hey, that's what I really wanted to do. I was good at it. I wanted to be successful again. So, L. A. was not the place for me to stay. The racing was not here, the style of racing that I liked wasn't here.

It was a real gas and a real turn-on at T-Town, you know? You were somebody there and that's where I needed to be. That was 1980.

Jack sat me down, we had a good long talk. I started to listen because I wanted to do something. I was the one who pretty much had ahold of my destiny. I just went for it.

I started working my way up the ladder. Eventually in '83 I won the bronze in the Keirin at Worlds, so that's when that whole scene started.

From that point on, it was a trip.

Japan

I went to Japan and lived with all these guys. One guy won a couple stages in the Tour de France in '79, another guy was Maertens, they're from the old school. Self discipline was very much involved in it.

They taught me the work ethics of being a professional bike racer and all that. That's where I got all this stuff I have for coaching, all the discipline, the focus, you go to the track to be organized. It's a job. If you want to be at the top, that's virtually what it is.

I was there for eight years. I lived with these guys for almost a year and a half in time in a country where it was very much self discipline and follow the rules and do what you're told in Japanese Keirin. It kind of works under your skin into the bloodstream. That's where it came from.

There wasn't anything before Japan, believe me! So that's where that all came from. It was the environment I lived in at that time and that whole scene. It was the combination of these Euro guys and the Keirin way. Structure. I went eight seasons, consecutively.

I didn't like it all the time. The first year it was a very scary thing. I didn't know anybody, even though I'd been riding for a long time already, it was a very scary, very unsure experience. It was something new, a different country, away from home for ten weeks, and that whole thing. I didn't know any of the Euro guys, it was virtually unturned ground, unturned soil.

I'm getting used to the system and I went there and my whole bike didn't even qualify for the standard! I had to get all new equipment! It was all totally different.

The bikes are real basic in Japan, very basic. They don't even have colored parts, no anodized parts. They're really basic. They have their own rules and regulations for the bike standards for racing. It's unreal because of the betting. Everything is structured around the betting. Everything has to be the same.

You can't even wear socks. Fans may think that's a signal to cheat for something, I don't know. They have a lot of structure, a lot of rules, a lot of regulations. If you have an attitude and you buck the system then you're not going to go back and they're not going to like you. That's something I had to learn a little bit and to be flexible.

My first year I think I didn't have problems with my rebelliousness because I was away. I think I'll always have that because it's part of my nature. I was 25 years old. I tried to get my act together. I wanted to be a responsible professional and really do something with this because it was the opportunity of a lifetime. I didn't want to blow it.

The money was great, that was the first time I ever made real money. It was like a living, like a job, so I was really proud of it.

People would say "Well, what do you do?"

"I'm a professional bike racer."

"You actually make a living racing bikes?"

"Well heck yeah! It's cool!"

All those little elements -- it was a lot of little personal things. The pride of being able to be successful. That was something I always wanted to do.

A Little Help from my Friends

I was invited to Japan because I won the Bronze in the Worlds and Jack Simes had a lot of influence. He helped me get my way over there.

I tell the kids all the time, "You can't go through this sport without a lot of people helping you." There's so many people, and if you start from the beginning it's continuous, people just help you get where you need to go.

The kids are really fortunate today and a lot of them take it for granted themselves, especially at our track (T-Town), we have such a wonderful track there. Pat, Nancy and all of them. The secretaries, it's incredible.

There's no way we would have the development program that we have and be able to develop riders like I have right now without the whole system.

Besides Marty (Nothstein) I have two really good Juniors, super athletes. They have a good attitude. That's something I try to mold right away, first thing. Forget the physical part, forget the riding, the scientific stuff -- forget that.

You've got to mold the character and the attitude. Once you do that, you start seeing that shape up, you're going to start seeing results.

Like I said, it's something that I had to go through life down the line a little bit to learn and to form myself, but once I did, then I was doing pretty good.

Keirin Racing

Japan has changed a little bit now from when I first started. They always had the school there and we always had to do the school, but as the years went on for the international Keirin, the whole system got better.

The first year I went it was ten weeks and we had to go to every city we raced and stay in a hotel, so it cost us more money. During the week the three or four days we didn't race we had to pay for our own hotel.

Once we stepped onto the track and it was time to race we had one day of inspection, what they called Sen-Ken, and then three days of racing.

During those four days we were fully taken care of, but the off days we had to provide for ourselves. The first year we had to live in hotels and pay for it ourselves. As riders, as employees of the Keirin people, we said "Hey, there has to be a better way."

Eventually, at the Keirin school, they have a little sports hotel called Speitel. They have it for swimming and all kinds of sports that they have in the area there. They built us a little wing of ten apartments, so eventually, at the end of the whole thing, we stayed at these places, we actually rented the apartments on the off days.

We paid for our food on those off-days to Speitel, and stuff like that, which was very reasonable. It think it came out, for expenses, for the whole ball of wax, about $2400. Eventually it went down to eight weeks.

The whole thing kept getting better. They kept finding out what works, what cities were receptive to the international athletes. The whole ploy was advertising for the Keirin. That was the ploy of the international Keirin, it still is.

They're using us for advertising for their business, which in 1990 was a 13 or 19 billion dollar business. It's major stuff, and one of their advertising ploys was to have the international riders come and race their best riders to show their Feds that their riders can kick some butt -- and they were damn good.

The competition was pretty intense because of the money. The last couple of years I raced for a quarter of a million dollar purse for one 2000 meter race. That's quite a bit of money for one Keirin race.

You have to understand that it's a business. Guys who were there for four and five years were the favorites of the bettors. It comes down to that. We were there to entice the bettors to pay money on our races, to ride against Nakano, for instance.

You have riders there like Vaarten and myself who have been there four and five years who are fan favorites and then a new rookie guy comes in, unless he's Huebner or someone like that, the fans aren't going to want to see him do well.

They're going to want their favorites to do well. That's the way the system works. Everybody had a chance to win. If you blew your chance, then you didn't win. And that's the way it was.

The first year you aren't going to be the star. You had to earn your popularity. Everybody had to work. I had to work, everybody had to do their job. When it came down to winning money, we had to put the best riders that our ten guys felt would do the best. That's the way it was.

There were three days of racing. The first day was like a heat, the second day was like a semifinal and the last day was the final. We earned points through results.

First place was one point, ninth place was nine points. Usually to get into the large money bracket final you needed eight points or less. It was pretty much decided by the first day. If you got last, there was a pretty good chance you weren't going to be in the final. You would ride the consolation.

To ride the quarter million dollar race, it was the top five guys out of the ten guys at the end of the season. Those were the top point-getters out of the ten foreigners who would ride against the handpicked guys like Nakano, the four out of the top eight in their country. We'd race for the big money.

The Japanese were more interested in the betting, not the personal results of each rider, because we were there on an advertising ploy. We weren't there for them to make us rich or we weren't there for them to help us feed our ego or anything like that. It was a business deal and that's the way we had to look at it.

We had pretty much a half a million dollar business operating there in eight weeks, which is a good chunk of change. It is hard for some riders to understand. The style of life, the way the system works was just the way it was.

To be honest with you, my first year I didn't win a race until I had a good crash in a little town called Oosawada. After that the group kind of got into a little spat and split up. I just happened to be with one of the better guys and I ended up, of the last six races, I won four.

It was unusual things that kind of happened along the way and I was sort of there at the right time. It's the same in business. That's the way it is. The riders split up about too many guys ending up working and some of the other guys ended up winning a lot. That's basically what it was.

A lot of the guys who felt they were working too much couldn't win anyway.

There was other stuff that I don't want to get into. I don't want to go into the personal things about the group, the real nitty-gritty, bottom line kinds of things that went on among the ten guys. It's kind of professional behind the scenes stuff, like the Cowboys locker room stuff. It's a very emotional experience.

I came home and had nightmares for nine or ten days afterwards, cold sweats . . . I came home and had a breakdown. Almost every year.

The traveling, the pressure within the group about different personal and professional issues, it was a lot of different things. You could write a book just on what went on, the underlining of it all. It would probably be pretty interesting, too.

They have a lot of alcoholism in

Keirin, a lot of guys smoke, a lot of things like that among their own athletes, if you can call them athletes. Out of the 4600 probably only about 600 are athletes, I would say. They're like jockeys on a horse.

There are 51 or 53 operating tracks in Japan, which is the size of California. That's why it's a 19 billion dollar business. It's a major deal there. If people only knew -- I would really love to get a documentary going. Like Pumping Iron.

Take someone like Ken Carpenter and follow him and talk to him during the whole thing. I would love to coordinate something like that because I would really know what to get in there and look for. My first or second year some people were there from Canada who were trying to do something, but I never saw it. It would be interesting.

I'd been going there for five or six years and looked myself as someone who really knew how to ride the race. I come here and people who have never seen a Japanese Keirin race are telling me how to ride one. It was very frustrating. I get frustrated with people like that. I just want to walk away.

People in New Mexico who want to start Keirin racing there have never been to Japan to see Keirin racing. They think they know how to run one here. I think I rode 156 Keirins over there. And I had great results. I'm probably still one of the top five guys

"We try to teach everything. All that is part of being a cyclist. A lot of people think you can blow that off. They think all you have to do is be strong and pedal fast. They don't learn anything else."

in results in the sport.

My percentage in the betting, in the combo exacta for first and second place, my percentage was something like 450 for first and second place. Every other race I was getting first or second and I rode one hundred and fifty-something races. I knew the race and I knew how to do it.

The End

Eventually, my job at the end, I didn't have the strength or the speed, I was getting older and stuff, but I knew how to ride my bike real well and I

wasn't afraid. My job was to protect the best guys. Ride behind them and not let the Japanese break the line or get in on the back wheel of our best guys. That was my role the last two years or so, I would say. I was probably one of the best, I'd have to say, at race dynamics.

Keirin Velodromes

Of the 53 or so tracks, I raced at six or seven each year. They were different ones in the beginning. Through the advertising department I'm sure they found out where the most popular tracks were and we eventually started going to the same ones every year. People would go to whatever tracks were in their area. It was like every county having a track. It was all run by the municipality in that area.

They pretty well took care of the track in their area. They all had basic laws and standards that they had to follow, but at each track you had to follow their rules. They had a track manager or boss and he ran the operation, and that's the way it was.

Basically the rules were the same, but certain things might be different. Certain things might be different, but they were very small. Where to bow, sometimes we had to bow right after we got out on the track, sometimes we didn't. Just the little things, but all the basic things of the Japanese Keirin are all the same. Everyone followed the same program.

They usually started at about 11:30. The format of the day of operation was very similar to a horse racing track.

The first race was at about 11:30 and they were the old, old guys, like between, I don't know, 50 years old or so and some young kid just fresh out of school, maybe three months out of the school and was working his way up.

The riders had a points system and every three months they got reviewed. They had a review every three months. You either move up or go down. Everybody had a requirement they had to meet, the riders, the track, everything. Everything's very closely watched.

Throughout the 50+ velodromes they had the same program. They start at 11:30 and there were about 10 or 11 races which went 'til about 4:30, 5:00. Usually we were about between the eighth and tenth race. They'd sort of work up the ladder as far as ability and the better riders were riding at the end of the day.

It was the same type of people you would expect at the horse track. Old guys would be there with their programs, they'd watch you warm up. We'd have an hour warm-up every morning nine to ten. They'd bring the bikes back in and they'd check all the bikes.

That part was really cool, the bike inspection, making sure things were on the up and up, no bad tires, no

"The bike inspection in Japan was really cool, making things were on the up and up, no bad tires, no crummy chains, no out-of-true wheels." Marty never has to worry about his bike -- Gibby takes care of it. (He has a style, doesn't he?)

crummy chains, no out-of-true wheels, everything was right there. They'd have a regular staff of people, say a dozen people, work the bike area every day. They have about 350 employees every day at the track. All the tracks have about this same number of people

running them.

I'd like that kind of inspection in this country, because I'd still be racing, making good money, better money than I'm making coaching! I don't see that kind of racing happening here. People just don't have the minds for it and we don't have the riders for it -- we don't have anybody for it, to be honest with you. I just don't see it happening.

Americans in Japan

Mark Whitehead, Nelson Vails, Ken Carpenter and myself are the American riders who have raced in Japan. Nelson went for three years. Mark went for one year and Ken went for two. Things did not go real smoothly for Ken. I know who the riders are.

The Germans are back and they seem to always be the troublemakers. They're arrogant and have to have control. I really like Ken. He has his personality quirks as we all do, but

he's a great athlete and he's a very hard worker.

I have to attribute some of Marty's success to Ken because when Ken comes around, Marty uplifts to another level of training. I think he got a lot of good work ethics from Ken over the years. They seemed to get along real well.

We saw him before he left and I asked him if he would like to please come out and stay with us this year at T-Town. To help out and help himself. Be part of the team, part of the family.

That's virtually what we have, is a family, right now. That's the way I feel, it's a good stable of Sprinters. Marty, a couple of Juniors, Jack Simes' nephew, he's not really a Sprinter, but he's part of the family. That's part of the philosophy.

If you go through the history of cycling, the success comes from a "stable" or a group of people. You go to France and Morelon has a wonderful stable of Sprinters. You go to Italy and they have a wonderful stable of Sprinters.

It's hard to get people to cooperate with one another, there are so many jealousies and egos to deal with, that's why you don't have it. It's a disadvantage. To have a great stable of Sprinters, you need a group. There's not one guy who's going to be able to do it by himself.

Ken had difficulty being part of a family. He's kind of a loner type of guy, and I think he capped his ability. He could have gone to the next level if he had been part of a family, one that could actually offer something to him.

The System

Many able people have quit cycling, I think due to the system we have here in this country. We're still doing it. The system doesn't provide any incentive for the riders. They do nothing to try to entice young riders to stay in the sport.

What do we offer the kids? Just look at VeloNews and look at the track. That's a good example. They have the Olympic Festival, but there's no track riding. That should be a Junior Development thing, the Olympic Festival, because that's what we're developing, future Olympians. They had it one year.

I can't answer for what these people are thinking or doing. All I can say is my opinion, especially since I've been involved in coaching pretty heavily for the last four years. I'm going to tell you right now that we're not providing any incentive for the kids.

Once they go from Juniors, if you're not up there competing with Marty, you're history. There's no place for you to fit in. They don't provide anything for that middle. And that's why the kids get discouraged.

A lot of it comes down to dollars and sense. For the lot of the younger kids it's pressure from their parents. "You're not going to get anywhere. Bicycles. . . .", you know. "Where are you going to go? The chances of you being on the podium at the Olympics are slim to none . . ." and that's the reality of it.

A lot of people just say "To hell with it. I'm going to go to school, get a job and I'll ride Master's." -- that's more profitable anyway!

People who stay with it, are in it because they have a passion for the sport. They truly love competition.

If you're one of the better riders it's still exciting to get in there and really rub elbows and compete. But for the younger person coming up, it's difficult for them. That transition is difficult. Even for Juniors, because there's no incentive. They provide nothing for the kids to look forward to.

A camp up in Colorado Springs. Big deal. What the heck is that? In reality, where's that going to get you? I've basically stated my opinion. I would say 50% of the Federation's budget is squandered. It's meaningless. The things that they spend their dollars on -- what does it do? Where does it go?

That's the kind of thing I'm really working hard against. Of course you can't go in there and step on toes, it's a lot of politics involved. Because I'm so and so, they're not going to listen to my suggestions, because of something in the past or I'm not going to fit in the system or I'm not the right person to fit that slot -- it doesn't matter if you're doing the job or not, it's just what fits in in their little socialized group.

I think recent changes are different, but I don't think it's any better. I can tell you things I've learned recently that would just take your breath away.

But I'm not going to sit back and criticize. These people are hopefully doing the best they can. It's unfortunate that some people have a very self-centered outlook on everything and they're only in it to make personal gain, not to contribute to the sport and make it better for the future for the young people.

Master's racing

I don't want to support the Master's, I really don't. I love Master's racing, I think it's great, I think it's cool, but I'm not going to support Master's before I support a teenager who has a lot of talent. I won't do it. I think the Federation is stupid. The Board is all Master's people. They're giving $11,000 grants away to the Master's program and how many dollars grants are they giving away to the Juniors program? I don't know of any. The Master's *have* money!

That's why some people stay and some people quit. You have to compete against that. If you have a very negative attitude right off, you're not going to put your all into it. I've known a lot of kids who've stuck with it and really given it everything they have and they still weren't successful because they weren't part of a group. It's just unfortunate.

There are so many things that I want to change. I don't care -- color, creed, where you come from, who you are, if you have talent, I'm going to spend the time with you. That's just the way it is, because I love this sport. I don't love it just to make myself famous, I really don't care if I'm on TV or magazines or what.

If I'm coaching a rider and that rider's successful -- I was happy and shed a few tears just in reading Marty's results every day in the paper and talking to him on the phone. I didn't have to be there to feel the success. Just knowing that I contributed in a fairly major way, that was enough for me. I was successful. I did my job. I know that and that's what's most important.

I'm my best critic. I have to live with myself when I lay down in my bed each night and I'm there looking at the ceiling "Did I do a good job or didn't I do a good job?" Though I do like to get paid and paying for my house payments and buying things for my kid!

Being around the young people keeps us young and vital too. Let's face it, you get to a certain age, you want to make the world a better place for the kids.

For me, I don't need to go out and race. I had my time, I had my chance to knock the world dead. If I didn't do it then that's my tough luck. If I did, then hey, that's great. But I'm not going to ride on it for the rest of my life.

When I have a few beers I might tell a few stories, but that's about it! I don't need to live on something that I did 25 years ago. Who the hell cares anymore? I care about the kids, what they're going to do tomorrow. That's more important to me.

There's no investment in the future at all. I think that's where the Federation is really making they're mistake. I don't know what they need to do. How do you tell them? They have to look at the individual as somebody that they respect enough to listen to and I don't know if I'm that person. To be honest with you I really don't care.

You know what is terrible about it is that every time you read Cycling USA, the Federation publication, and you read VeloNews, every time there's an election for a position on the Board or a position in the governing body, the first thing they write is that they want to help the Junior program.

I could go back home and show you publications of every single time that someone was running for a Board seat, they say they want to do something for the Junior program and they have done nothing for it.

I would really like to grade their position, either periodically or at the end of the year, saying "You can keep your position if you can prove that you've done something to contribute to the sport."

But that will never happen because it's a social thing, it's something that they're doing to get personal gain rather than saying "Hey, the heck with me, let's do something for somebody else."

I just know for a fact that some of the people are not there for the betterment of the sport in the long run in any way, shape or form. They're not there for the long term and I think that's terrible, I really do.

A Wonderful Sport

This sport is a wonderful sport. It's offered me so much that there's no way my parents could ever afford to have me go. There's no way that any school could ever teach me the education that I've learned in cycling.

Those are things that I can offer to my kid that he won't get any place else. It's the experiences, the stories, I

look at it as something that was very positive. It's helped me personally tremendously as far as attitude and everything else.

Talk to any parent, cycling's a discipline that you learn from, that you can carry on to any aspect of your life, it doesn't have to be sports, it can be anything, school or business or family life. The basic things you learn you can carry on. Those are the nice things to learn from it.

The Velodrome

I'm very focused when I'm at the track with my racers. To be honest with you, it's the only way I can work anymore. I want to get things done. We're on a time schedule and you have to be on top of it. Otherwise things don't get done and then you're rushing and you can possibly make a mistake, like forget to tighten a wheel. It doesn't pay.

Things are happening pretty good. It's not me, we have a great staff, we have a great program. I can't say enough good things about our track (T-Town).

The bad thing is when there's too much ice and snow around the track. As far as our goals, our focus, We're definitely looking down the road. We're not only focusing on Marty for '96, but we're focusing on our Juniors for 2000. I think we're going to have a couple more great superstars coming out of our track for 2000. That's the challenge.

Rodale is still absolutely supportive of our track. We're trying to financially and in almost every way, to get away from that. We're building a brand new park across the street with

a three kilometer road course, all kinds of goodies, additions, that we're applying to the area.

Our goal is to make our place an Eastern race regional training center. Eventually we'd like to have housing and every tool we need to provide training and instruction. We want dorms near the track, walking distance.

We always ask "Why do you have to go all the way to Colorado Springs?" Not everybody can afford to go there, not everybody likes it there. It's a great place to go and train and I think it provides a pretty good attitude because the altitude is there, but why do you have to be a permanent resident to get results?

It should be used as a facility to gain peak performance rather than live there. I think we have better racing at our track, we have better criteriums around our area and I think that the attitude that the people have were we live compared to the attitude people get at the Springs -- we call it the Colorado Attitude, we think it sucks.

We have a track, we have the programs there and we're having a road circuit built across the street. Riding in the area is very good. It's very rural. It's building up, but where isn't it building up? It's a long term goal. It's something Pat (McDonough) has been talking about for years and I've been very supportive of.

Teaching bike handling skills to my riders is part of the whole thing. We try to do a lot of mountain bike riding, which teaches you a lot of bike handling skills, balance, positioning yourself on the bike.

Our indoor program teaches riders

how to tumble, the correct way to fall so you don't really hurt yourself. We sacrifice quite a bit, we put a lot of hours into it. In the gym we do tumbling on mats, we roll and all kinds of things.

We try to look at every aspect we can, the smallest, the simplest and the other side of the spectrum. We try to teach everything. All that is part of being a cyclist. A lot of people think you can blow that off. They think all you have to do is be strong and pedal fast. They don't learn anything else.

You know if you're going to compete all the time you're going to end up taking a header. You still make a mistake here or there. You could see in the video of my last crash on the track, a 40 mile an hour T-bone, if you watch my fall I did the first thing we teach the kids and the first thing that I was taught, tuck you're head and land on your back -- that's the strongest part of your body.

If you ding your head up, you're in big trouble. The first thing that happens, everybody reacts normally, something happens, you want to lift you're head to see what's going on or stick you're hand out to break your fall. Those are the things you have to try not to do. I was real lucky that a broken wrist was probably the most serious thing that ever happened to me in 28 years of racing.

In the Keirin racing in Japan they have 6,000 crashes a year. It's something you expect to happen.

The first year they called me a sissy because I didn't have a scar on my collarbone from operating to pin it back together. You were a sissy, a baby, if your body wasn't tattered a little bit. That's just something that's expected in Japanese Keirin. They get up and back to racing or they get hurt, get a concussion, break a collarbone or whatever, then they take time off, I'm sure.

I don't know if they teach falling over there, but I'm sure that they do. The school is so cool, it's so complete, they teach you everything. They have a swimming pool, three tracks, roller rooms, a good gymnasium, -- they have it all, they have everything.

Their thing is the hot tub. The hot bath and you douse yourself down with cold water afterward. That's good for you. They really have it together. I tell people, I really miss it a lot. I look at it like an adventure, like Indiana Jones. Every year was a new thing, a new adventure. We had to race hard against new kids. You had to fight for your status and take your place in line. That's the way it is. It's pretty black and white.

Lot's of riders have a hard time. Nelson had a hard time too. We had a few difficult times. Every guy was there because he was a champion. It's hard to say "You're not going to win today. These three other guys are the ones who are going to have the chance to win." Those are who the people are going to bet on.

If they're betting $100,000 on me and only $10,000 on the other guy, who are you going to want to win? That's what the track wants to do. They want to please the fans because they're the ones who are tossing the money into the system.

If you don't please them, they're not going to come to the track. The

track's not going to make money. It's that simple. You have to understand that. I've tried to explain everything I could, but sometimes it just wasn't enough.

The year Mark Whitehead went over, 1988, I was MVP. I had the most points and won the most money for

it that way.

I was pretty aggressive physically and they didn't want that. It was the way I had to ride. I was put into a predicament, I had no other choice because I didn't have the physical strength that Huebner and guys like that had and I was 34 or 35 years old.

If you watch Gibby and Marty together, you don't see a coach and a rider, you see a __team__, in every sense of the word.

the year. I had something like eight firsts and seconds out of about 19 races. I had an awesome year. It was great memories, something I cherish very much.

When I stopped going I was getting old. I was losing it a little physically and it was time for me to get out of it. I was doing the job the best I could and it got to the point where they were asking me to tone down my radicalness and to do the job and complete it. I couldn't do that. I didn't have the legs or the power to do

It was just time for me to give it up. That's the way it was. I accepted it. Eight years is a long time, I'm not complaining about it.

The Track Circuit

We're trying to help Dominguez Hills and work with them. Pat and I have discussed very thoroughly that each track has its own personality. I think once Dominguez Hills finds its personality and starts working it, it will be successful. Right now Dominguez can't compete with our schedule.

The best World Class riders are going to be at our track, simply because of the tradition. They know that we have decent prize money and they know for sure the racing's going to be there. As far as different times of the year, a late season someplace else (like Dominguez) would be good. October, like a Fall thing. That's when they should have it, a total of 14 weeks, and leave the summer for instruction, for non-licensed riders, for recreation, for the kids -- they could do other things to acquire money, revenue for that particular facility.

They kind of have an advantage because they don't have to deal with the Federation insurance. They have their own insurance from the college. They could have any kind of event that they want out there. They can let anybody ride out there, anybody they want. They don't have to have a license, they don't have to be any part of the USCF. They have an advantage with some things.

I've told Nick Curl, the track director, "Look, you've got to find your personality and you've got to work it. Try things. It took us 16 years to get where we are today. Don't think in three or four years you're going to have some kind of big new thing happening here in L.A. You have to be very analytical about everything you do and take a good look at it."

I think that's the best way for them to do, to keep a very open mind. I told him "Don't count on the Federation to help you with anything." They don't offer that much. That's the problem.

Overall Junior Sprints, licensing has gone down I don't know how many percent, but it's gone down a lot. That's the question I think they should be more concerned about. They should go out an help the younger kids, really develop something. They have so many dollars for development, well damn it, use them! Use the dollars to figure something out.

They supposedly have all these people up there with Ph.D.s in something, I don't know what, because they're not doing the job down here on the ground floor. It's not trickling down here, so I don't know where it's going.

Best Moments

My proudest accomplishments include winning the 1974 Junior World Championships, winning the Bronze medal in the 1983 Worlds and the many National Championship medals I've won.

Coaching

I'm planning on coaching indefinitely. As long as I can have some great athletes to coach. I would very much like to be coaching and follow up on the dream of having that Eastern regional training center.

I'd like to see my athletes carry them through the ultimate goal, especially in Marty's case. We have a really good chance of his being on the podium in '96. I would love to be there holding him (at the start) and at least share his success.

I'm not making a whole lot of money doing it, but I'm making enough that I can still help my wife pay the bills. I'm not driving a Benz or have an extravagant house, but I'm cool where I am.

I'm very content with my life right now. I just wish we had a little more cooperation upstairs. Those frustrating parts of it, if I allow them to, could spoil the whole thing. But I'm not going to allow that. I have to much going for me and I feel if I do that it's going to carry on to my riders. I don't want that to happen.

I see how hard they work and they give me a lot, even my young kids. They give me 110% when it comes to competition and I'm extremely proud of them. That just carries on. It's having that strength in our family. It goes from Marty to my two Junior boys to me.

I have to maintain my emotions and keep them as consistent as possible, because if I don't, they're going to feel it too. We're with each other so much. It has to be a whole positive thing going. It's a flow, it's an aura.

I see some coaches, some days they just lose it. They freak out and consequently their riders are freaked out. If you're doing this at a Championship meet, you're putting a year of hard, hard work at risk on both ends, the coach and the athlete.

If you have a very negative attitude and all that, it defeats the whole thing. It's a pretty difficult task. You have to sit back sometimes and look at yourself.

The person who really helped me out with that is my wife. She's a professional in psychology and a high school counselor and I listen to her. She's helped me out a lot. I ask her a lot of advice on how to do things and handle things and so far it's been working.

I miss the beach in Southern California. Everything else -- don't need it. We'd like Dominguez to have the early season racing, having the best athletes there at the beginning of

Even top riders crash once in a while. Yup, in a Keirin race (T-boned in T-Town, 1991).

the year. I think it's good for the sport. Get the National Team in Southern California to train, that's the best way.

There are a lot of training activities in L.A. There are a lot of good criteriums and track. There's a lot to offer young riders and my kids. They learned a heck of a lot from being out there. I've seen a tremendous improvement in just their overall philosophy of racing and grasping the idea of it.

Velodromes

The tracks in Japan are the best because they're clean, organized and efficient. The track I like least is Northbrook because it's too flat. I've raced in World Championships in Poland, Spain, Switzerland, Italy and France. I've also raced in Japan, Venezuela, Trinidad, Canada and Barbados.

Advice to New Riders

The best way for a rider to begin racing is in local citizen racing events on the road. When riders begin track or any other kind of racing it is a good idea to try all events before focusing on one. Coaching and training is available through local clubs. If there's no track available, find a piece of road that's flat to practice Sprinting.

You have to be a special person to race the track because it's difficult. You need to go to a track with a good racing program and coaches.

If an athlete is looking for money, the track is not the place. S/he should choose another sport such as golf, tennis, or pro baseball. If s/he insists on racing bicycles, ride the road instead of the track if money is important.

Finally, my advice for guys is : women weaken legs!

Master's Racing

Master's racing is a little overrated with all the big team promotion, but it's fun and it gives people a chance to compete as they get older.

I race Masters, I ride about 20 races a year. I won Somerville last year, I beat all the Subaru-Montgomery guys. They spent thousands of dollars on them to come out there.

I wore a 25 year old wool jersey with pockets in the front and all kinds of stuff. I beat Harvey (Nitz) and Glen Winkel.

They were really ticked off.

Chapter 7
ᴼᵛᴼ *Tandem Sprint* ᴼᵛᴼ

Tandem Sprint is possibly the most exciting race on the track. Not only are speeds incredibly high, the riders of this event are usually the large Sprinters. Together they may weigh over four hundred pounds, sitting on a bicycle built to be as light (and strong) as possible.

History

Old time track racers raced on Tandems, so they are nothing new.

Like all track bicycles, track Tandems have no brakes. This, and twice the momentum weight of two riders makes for a scary build up of speed and a scary finish. All the thrills and drama of Sprints with twice the impact -- visually and in all other ways.

Due to the difficulty in assembling a sufficient number of teams and because of the inherent danger, Tandem Sprints have ceased competition as a World Championship event. Tandem races are still held, to the thrill of audiences.

However, they continue to be threatened with extinction in National Championships due to danger to riders. Unfortunate accidents occurred injuring Drivers during each of the 1990, '91 and '92 National Championships. Fortunately, in 1993 and 1994 the event was held with no mishaps and all the usual excitement.

The Team

A Tandem team includes a " Driver", "Captain" or "Pilot" on the front, and a " Stoker" on the back. The Driver has the most control. The Stoker's job is to provide power and information to the Driver.

If the other team is behind, the Stoker has the primary responsibility for watching what's going on to the rear and communicating his observations to the Driver who can then concentrate on driving. During a full-on Sprint, this is vital.

All riders cannot endure the lack of control which is the Stoker's lot. He is literally a back seat Driver with no access to the controls. He must trust the Driver completely -- at least for the duration of the race!

The Driver, on the other hand, must remember that he has a person on the back of the Tandem, not a robot. He also must communicate, yet, at the same time he must react almost without thinking, a requisite of success in any Sprint situation. This is a hard line to walk.

As in any other team, it is very important for the Tandem riders to work out beforehand who will be responsible for what. In the heat of competition there is no time to work out disagreements or new strategies. A team which works together will ride as one, while a team that does not, only handicaps itself.

Driver + Stoker = Power.

Tandem Sprints follow the same rules as Sprints except for the following variations, mostly due to the fact that Tandem bicycles are larger

Tandem Sprint's " Driver With the Most Wins" (4), Paul ("Swifty") Swift, and his two-time National Championship partner (1993&94), Stoker Greg Carlson. Marty Nothstein was Paul's Stoker for two years. Swift seems to have a knack for picking fast partners. A contest between Nothstein/Hartwell and Swift/Carlson would be as thrilling as it gets. Swift is known as one of the craftiest riders on the track.

and therefore require more room to move.

Rules specific to Tandem Sprints
Distance/Numbers

Tandem sprints cover a distance of 1500 meters or the nearest number of whole laps which is nearest to that distance, usually 5 laps on a 333 track. Sprints usually cover 1000 meters, 3 laps.

The rules say no more than four Tandem bicycles are allowed on a track at one time. No more than three are allowed if the track is smaller than 333 meters. In the U.S. it is unlikely that more than two Tandems will be on the track at a time . Higher numbers may occur in World level competition.

Sprint rules

So that the reader will not have to flip back and forth between this and the last section, Sprint rules will be repeated here. As in Match Sprints, Tandem riders are matched in a psychological as well as a physical battle through out each ride.

The Tandem Sprint, like the Match Sprint, involves manipulating another rider into providing a draft from which the eventual winner can "slingshot" to victory. Getting the opposite team to do that, is the cat-and-mouse trick.

Instead of two to four riders, Tandem involves four to eight riders. Same number of bicycles, twice the number of competitors.

At the Championship level "two-up" Sprints (referring to the number of bicycles) are always seen in the finals. Local events also usually only have two on the track at a time.

Qualifying

Flying Start Time Trials are used to seed riders in National Championships. Time Trials for Tandem Sprints take place over one complete lap or 400 meters, whichever is smaller.

Riders are then matched according to established times, fastest with slowest, the same procedure as in the Match Sprint.

Riders line up successively, often with two holders, who may or may not be officials. They are pushed off to ride two laps, during which they get physically and mentally ready to do a maximum effort over the last lap.

As the last lap draws near, the rider's pace increases. Tandem riders will accelerate earlier than Sprinters doing a Time Trial due to the greater mass which must be accelerated.

Like the Sprinters they are, they will dive down the banking of the turn before the timing tape which, in this event, is on the home stretch.

This last minute dive down the steepest part of the track will allow the Tandem team to reach maximum speed by the time they cross the tape in the start/finish area which begins timing in this maximum effort.

Flying Time Trial times are not definite predictors of Tandem Sprint success any more than they are in Match Sprints. Here too, sometimes competitors compete better than they Time Trial.

This may be especially touchy in the Tandem where two riders and their differing competitive instincts are involved and where those instincts can clash. While top-end speed is top-end speed, Tandem competition may more closely follow the workings how two human hearts combine on one vehicle.

Sprint Formats

Race announcements will disclose both format and seeding methods for this event. Riders must be instructed as to whether the event will be held in Championship or "round robin" formats.

Championship format

Championship format sets up rounds in such a way that the fastest riders will meet in the final race. Flying Time Trial times decide matches and the strategy begins.

The formulas for Sprints in the USCF Rule Book are applicable to Tandem Sprint competition, but the numbers involved are so small that seeding is fairly simple. While the same formulas basic to Sprint rules

are applicable to Tandem, they will not be reviewed here.

Numbers common to Tandem Sprint competition are small enough that conduct of competition rounds are comparatively simple.

In theory, the two most highly competitive teams (not necessarily the fastest, but the most competitive) will meet in final competition. Championship format seeding follows UCI rules.

Round Robin format

A "round robin" format allows each rider an opportunity to compete against all other riders.

Round robin is not common to Tandem events as these events are seldom held outside Championship venues unless they are featured at a particular velodrome. If they are held in this format, the Rule Book specifies procedures.

The advantage of round robin type matches in Tandem is that this event is rare enough that availability of practice against varied competitors is excellent preparation for those who want to try their hand at the National level.

Tandem is one of the few events that is largely still a wild card due to the lack of consistency in competitive offerings and longevity of pairings in teams.

Exhibition Tandem Sprints

Exhibition Tandem Sprints must follow the format of Championship Sprints.

The Start

Before teams line up, they will establish their position on the track by drawing lots, same as in Match Sprints.

In 1994, the Silver medal went to Bobby Walthour IV and Michael Hulse.

Teams line up perpendicular to the black line (#1 downtrack) and may position themselves at any reasonable place down or up track. Rules do not dictate lateral position.

Lining up toward the top of the track makes sense because it is easier to accelerate moving down track, but with large, heavy teams and five laps to go, this is unlikely to be a big issue.

Tandem teams usually have two holders who may or may not be officials. Holders may push riders at the start and often do to get this large, heavy duo moving. Often holders will give their riders last minute reminders or other advice as the riders are preparing for the start.

When a team is ready, they notify the official. No one is rushed and each team determines on their own when they are ready for the race to begin.

Tandem Sprints begin with a whistle. The riders at the bottom of the track must lead for the first lap at a walking pace or faster. If one team should pass the other, that team assumes responsibility for being the leader.

If the minimum, walking pace is not maintained for the first lap, the gun will sound and the race will be restarted with the team who moved too slow leading in the re-ride. Once the lead team's front wheel completely crosses the finish line, the Sprint begins.

"Kiloing"

Teams may go faster than a walking pace during the first lap if they choose. In fact, they can Sprint from the start if they want, but they

In 1991, Swift and Nothstein, who had dominated Tandem Sprinting as partners over the two previous years, split into separate teams. This looked like a great contest. The Sprint began but never finished.

The Swift/Silvera front wheel became detached mid-Sprint when the fork separated from the crown. Since the Tandem was originally built for Swift/Nothstein, it might easily have been under Nothstein/Hartwell when it disintegrated.

Swift suffered a broken collarbone, missing trips to Worlds and the Pan Am Games. Silvera was scraped up, but intact.

Nothstein/Hartwell went on to victory over Bell/Tulley in the next round (see 1992, next page).

usually don't. If they do, it is a high risk, a surprise, and it is usually done by riders who think they may have an endurance advantage and cannot match their opponent's speed. It is legal. "Kiloing" is named for the

Kilometer race, a full speed effort over 1000 meters. It is done in Tandem Sprints as it is done in Match Sprints.

The Race

The most common action seen in Tandem, as in Match Sprints, is a "cat and mouse" routine between two teams. Contrasting with Match Sprints, it is not unusual for Tandem teams to have never raced each other in their latest pairings, though this is less true for riders from tracks which promote Tandem racing.

It is not impossible for teams to be ignorant of their own strengths and weaknesses, much less those of their opponents. The planning of strategy is, therefore, all the more challenging.

The race will typically proceed in the same general pattern as Match Sprints: Teams begin with a slow first lap at a walking pace. At the completion of the first lap, the lead team can try to force the following team to take the lead by riding very slow or stopping into a "Track Stand" if it wishes.

Track Stands are quite difficult on a Tandem, but they are possible. It is unlikely that a Tandem team will attempt this maneuver, but again, it is possible. More likely, they will slow to a pace which they think the other Tandem cannot match, hoping that the other team, worried that they might fall over, will take the lead.

Tandem Track Stands are more risky than Track Stands on regular bicycles due to the larger size, the increased weight, and the relative balancing abilities of each rider making up the team. If they fall over, the race must be restarted and it is embarrassing. However, it is a good trick to see a Tandem in a Track Stand. If they pull it off, spectators can't help admiring riders who are able to do it.

As in Match Sprints, Tandem Track Stands are limited to three minutes, but, as indicated, they are unlikely to occur at all, so this is virtually never an issue. If it should ever be, an official would signal the obligated (lead) team that they must proceed.

From the end of the first lap until the finish, anything can happen, according to the skill, riding style and strategies of the teams.

As in Match Sprints the ride may proceed slowly (almost tediously) until the bell is sounded for the final lap, which usually stirs everyone's blood.

The middle laps may see riders at high speeds at any point, moving each other up and down the track. The problem is trying to predict *when* riders will do this.

The "wind-up" begins earlier than in Match Sprints. Acceleration of Tandems is more difficult due to the increased weight of both bicycle and riders and the sheer size of the vehicle. However, as bulk makes it more difficult for one team to accelerate away, it also makes response to such a move more difficult.

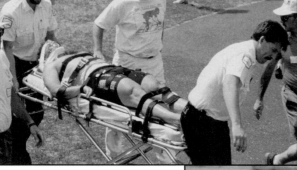

Consequently, a "jump" (quick acceleration) is more likely to happen when Tandems are uptrack and a team can take advantage of the banking to accelerate more quickly. On the other hand, this is of limited value if the other team is also uptrack and ready for just such a move.

As always in any kind of Sprints, just when you think you can relax, a team takes off and rivets your attention once again. In Tandem, acceleration to

In 1992, Nothstein/Hartwell once again found no opponent at the finish line. A mid-Sprint collision (rear pedal to front wheel) sent Bell to the hospital. He laid in a coma for two weeks, outcome uncertain.

After extensive rehabilitation and therapy, Bell went on to pursue a career as a medical professional. Brinker opened a bicycle shop in St. Louis. While both continue to love the sport, this year was one of pain.

Stoker Tom Brinker pays homage to his fallen comerade. Bell and Brinker were National Tandem Champions in '88 and had hoped to enjoy that achievement again. At this point, Bell's <u>survival</u> looked like an ambitious achievement. Brinker was not allowed to continue competition.

top speed is all the more thrilling and powerful (and scary!) From that point it's a matter of watching who can maintain or pull out what top speed to the finish.

If a team breaks away early in the race it is not unusual for them to pull up track and slow down again. During changes in pace, teams get tricky and the speed picks up again.

In International races, things are just as unpredictable, as each country races with its own style.

The zone between the black and red lines, is important for the same reasons in Tandem as in Match Sprint. During the final Sprint, only one team is allowed in this lane.

While this is a highly disputed zone in Tandem as in Match Sprint, the size of the Tandem bicycle does not allow riders the same small space within which to compete. They will tend to give each other more room simply because the machine is bigger, though this is not always the case, especially when a Championship is at stake.

Stopping a Tandem Sprint:

Stopping a Tandem Sprint once the race has begun is addressed in the Sprint section of the Rule Book.

Sprint violations differ during the slow part of the race from those once the Sprint has begun.

Stopping a Tandem Sprint before the Sprint begins:

During the slow part of the race the Starter may stop the race for the following reasons:

1) a rider backs up more than 8 inches (20 centimeters), very unlikely in the Tandem event.

2) a team does a Track Stand on the blue band, a zone they should not be in. Again, very unlikely in Tandem.

3) a rider touches the track surface or the outside fence or railing. This is the most likely of this set of rules to occur in Tandem.

A team which does any of these things must lead when the ride is restarted, as it will be.

Other reasons for stopping the race during the slow part:

4) if a team suffers a mishap (blown tire, falls down, etc.) during the race. If the race is restarted, riders restart in the same positions.

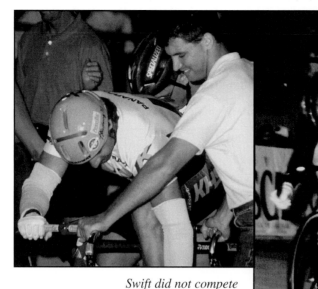

Swift did not compete in Tandem in '92. In '93 he was back, challenging Nothstein once again.

Each Driver had a new Stoker. Master's Sprinter Nick Chenowth was on Marty's Tandem, Sprinter Greg Carlson was on Paul's.

Swift/Carlson was pushed off by Bart Bell one year after the accident that nearly took his life. "Bart's Team" won." It was wonderful to watch a great contest with no tragedy.

5) if a team appears to have a mishap which causes a restart and the mishap turns out not to be legitimate.

While the race is supposed to be restarted without the offender, Tandem races usually only include two teams, so presumably the offending team would simply be eliminated.

6) if an accidental collision occurs before the Sprint has begun.

The race would be restarted with riders in the same positions.

Once the Sprint has begun:

Same as Match Sprints. When the Sprint has actually begun, the following prohibitions apply:

1) a team must not try to overtake an opponent by using the blue band.

2) a team must leave room on the right for others to pass.

A team does not have to leave room on the left, but must not cut off opponents by moving into the Sprinter's lane when another team is already there. A team that moves into the Sprinter's lane in front of another must have *a clear lead*. A team may never force another team off the track.

3) a team which was below the Sprinter's (red) line must stay there until the finish.

All teams following must pass on the right, out side of the Sprinter's lane. It is okay for the leaders to come out of the Sprinter's lane if they have such a large lead that there is no hindrance to others.

4) a team outside of the Sprinter's lane must not make any abrupt motion to stop others from passing or move right, even if it is not an abrupt move, which could cause a fall or a move that exceeds 90 centimeters (the width of the Sprinter's lane). Riders in back of the lead team may pass on either side.

5) the leaders must not move into the Sprinter's lane without *a clear lead* and must not do so when the rear team is overlapped.

If the lead team does this the Rule Book says they must be relegated for foul riding. The lead team is not penalized for accidentally riding below the measurement line or even on the blue band at the finish line.

6) a team cannot deliberately cause a crash (disqualification).

A team shall be disqualified if they cause another team to fall. If a team falls while attempting a move which is illegal, they shall be relegated. The other team is declared the winner whether they cross the finish line or not.

The biggest problem is determining intent of competitors. All of them want to win the race and Tandem Sprints is a race of extremely high tension, power and speed. Decisions in highly competitive contests are always difficult.

Other Sprint rules
Blocking

Blocking of other teams is a common strategy in bicycle racing, but is not allowed in Tandem Sprints. There are unlikely to be more than two competitors, but the rules say there can be as many as four on a track larger than 333 meters.

A team which is boxed in at the bottom may not force their way out. It is illegal to block or interfere with another team. A team which does so will be relegated or disqualified.

If a team has been determined by officials to have "deliberately" caused a crash, they will be disqualified. Interpretation of intentions of a team, much less a rider, is subject to dispute.

In the event an accident is determined by officials to be deliberate, a re-ride omitting the offending team (who is disqualified) will be conducted. If the accident is determined not to have been deliberate, the race will be rerun with teams in the same positions.

No-shows

If a team does not show up at the starting line, the other team must be there ready to race. After showing up at the starting line demonstrating readiness to compete, that team advances to the next level of competition.

Dead Heats

If officials are unable to determine a winner in a particular heat, the race will be rerun with the competitors who were involved in the dead heat.

In National Championship races, the finish line camera aids officials in this decision and they will usually wait for the camera to end any doubt as to the dead heat.

In local events this will not be as likely and officials will make their best guess. Track racing crowds will let them know if they disagree with the official decision.

Race Equipment

Little special track equipment us used for Tandem Sprints. No sponges are used, though teams are expected to stay off of the blue band. Judgment of this type of violation is left to the officials. The Starter's pistol controls violations at any point in the race with a double gunshot signalling a stop of the race.

Bicycle Equipment

Equipment for Tandem Sprints is a specially constructed track Tandem Sprint bicycle. It does not usually include disc wheels and may not include any but standard track handlebars. Wheels are heavier and stronger (maybe "cross 4", 40 spoke).

Summary

Weekly events at local tracks seldom include Tandem Sprints, though some tracks feature this event.

When these races are run, race organizers have latitude in their competition design. Usually local organizers know the teams and their abilities well enough to pair them appropriately and do not run Flying one laps or 400s, but they might.

Riders training with hopes of competition in a National Championship must have practice under true competitive conditions in order to develop appropriate skills. On the local level, opportunities for Tandem racing may seldom exist.

In 1994, Swift/Carlson took the U.S. National Championship for the second year in a row, this time against Walthour/Hulse.

Tandem Sprint
Nelson Vails

Nelson (nicknamed "The Cheetah") is one of the breed of "versatile" Sprinters. He has found success in other events than Sprints which also draw upon his superior Sprinting ability, notably Tandem Sprints and Keirin. He won a Gold Medal in Sprints in the Pan Am Games of 1983. In 1984 he was National Champion in Sprints and won a Silver medal in the Olympic Games.

Also in 1984, Nelson began a three year reign (1984 - 86) as U. S. National Champion in Tandem Sprints. In 1985 he won Silver in Tandem Sprints in the World Championships. Nelson went on to international success as a professional and raced on the Japanese Keirin Circuit for three years. It's always good to have him at the races, the one, the only -- Nelson.

How I Got Started

I grew up in Harlem, New York City. No one knows the real story of how I got started -- I started by recreational riding! The story gets so twisted I sort of make it up as I go along. Lenny Priheim, of Toga Cycles in New York, helped me as both coach and manager.

Before bicycling I did speed-skating, in juvenile years -- early teens. I started hanging out with the bike racing crowd in Central Park, so I started on the roads. In the late 70's I started riding at Kissina Velodrome.

By 1982 I was at the Olympic Training Center in Colorado Springs with Carl Leusencamp as my coach. Trexlertown is my home track because I've spent so much time racing there. When I lived in Indianapolis I spent a lot of time on the Major Taylor track

My racing really began in 1979. In 1980 I raced in my first National Championships, the same year Mark Gorski won his first Sprint title as a Senior.

By 1983 I was almost unbeatable. That year I took Gorski to three rides, at Nationals. Then I took the Gold at the Pan Am Games, my first big victory.

In 1984 I became U.S. National Sprint Champion and was a Silver Medalist in the Olympics. I started riding Tandem Sprints as "Driver" because the United States Cycling Federation asked me to. They wanted a team for the World Championships. My teammate (the "Stoker") was 1981 Sprint Champion Les Barczew-ski.

Throughout the '85 season Les and I trained together, either on road Tandem or road bicycles. That year we were racing against the former World Champion German team. No one expected us to win.

We were so in tune that, going into turn 4, Barczewski yelled "Underneath!" at the exact same time

"A World Class Sprinter pulls a rabbit out of the hat when his opponent thinks he's riding his race. You do whatever it takes to get across the line first without getting disqualified. It takes talent and you can't think about it. I wish someone had told me early on to stay in school and go to college -- get an education. That's my comment to all. I attribute my success to family support."

I dove downtrack. We beat the Germans and won the Silver Medal.

I was US Tandem Sprint Champion from 1984 through '86 (the last year with Scott Berryman), always as Driver. I spent 3 years racing on the Japanese Keirin Circuit, which is by invitation only.

I ended my career as a professional racer. It's like an acting job, when they call you to work, you work, or maybe they won't call you the next time. I had an agent who booked me on the tour.

Tandem Sprints

The secret to Tandem sprint training is for both cyclists to ride together all the time so they get so in touch with each other that they hardly have to think in order to react. Les (Barczewski) and I trained together on a road Tandem 250 miles per week and the other 150 or so miles on our individual bikes, but together.

Scott (Berryman) and I didn't have a road Tandem, but we trained together every day. We were part of the camp and we were one. We were so one that when we had I.D. cards made up we had each others pictures on each others I. D. cards! We took a picture together. We were always in trouble together. We were a great combination.

Those were some fun years that Scott and I were together. We had some great stories, we can't even tell people. Any place around the world, we had laughter and fun, the crying, just the whole everything. The good times and the bad, we shared the camaraderie.

I was always the Driver. It would help for the Stoker to be a Sprinter because of the fast muscle twitch. In order to make a good team you have to

do everything together, warm-up together, drink together, eat together - - the Tandem is like twins.

Both Driver and Stoker need to have a good warm-up on individual bikes. After the warm-up, as far as going out on the Tandem, the guy in the back is always in communication. He's always talking to the guy in the front so the guy in the front won't have to look back.

"Scott (right) and I were so one that we had each others pictures on each others I. D. cards. We were always in trouble together. We were a great combination." Blaine, 1992

He can, of course, but the guy in the back is always looking, always in communication, constantly talking. That way the Driver doesn't have to worry about what he's going to say next. He'll say "They're in the middle of the track. They're moving up the track. They're going a little slower. They're five meters behind us, ten meters, two bike lengths . . . .", whatever the communication's going to be. Basically the Stoker isn't making

up any new information, but the Driver always knows what the Stoker's talking about, whatever the communication terms are going to be.

The Driver is always looking for direction as to where he should be on the track. All that information comes from the Stoker. The Driver can move high on the track or move down, according to what the Stoker says. The Driver is going to look from time to time, but he doesn't have to look as he would on an individual bike.

It's a natural instinct to look and he needs his own point of view, his judgement of what the Stoker is talking about. Like a quick look -- "they're about ten meters back" -- the Driver can take a quick look and guesstimate that ten meters.

The Driver can always stay higher on the track without looking back because he can always ride along the rail and control that straight line. The Stoker's always looking, like "move down to the red line," "move to the middle the track." That way they can control both sides, and the Driver can ride the red line and can hold it because the Stoker's looking.

Getting On and Off the Tandem

Even getting on the bike, we have to get so we don't need help to strap ourselves in. We can get on without someone holding us up. I get on with two feet on the ground and hold the Tandem. The pedals are set already.

My partner gets on and straps himself in while I'm holding him up.

Then, when he tells me he's ready, we shove off. He can pedal while I steer, get in, and strap myself in, left side, right side. My partner is able to strap himself in, left side, right side, and I could still go straight even though his weight went from side to side. Then we get on the track.

When we get on the track, I can look straight while he's looking back and he tells me when it's safe to get on. Then we accelerate, get it going.

Getting off the track, you agree that you're slowing down. They guy in the back is doing a lot of back-pedaling. The Driver's is still in control.

Getting off, we unstrap and he gets off first. He holds me up until I can take one foot out.

You never leave your partner with the bike, you both carry it. The Driver gets on and off with his leg going over the front of the bike. You'll kick the guy in back if you try to put your leg over the back.

The Start

If someone takes you to the line, the Driver can get on first and swing his leg over the back as he would on an individual. Often you see two people shoving off a Tandem, but one person can really do it. It's easier with two people, but, like at the World Championships, only one person may be allowed on the track -- two riders and a coach. Sometimes two people will get on the track, but one will leave before the push off occurs. You don't really need two people to push you off. You pedal. It's not like one team is going to take a flying jump. It isn't going to get going that fast. Not so fast that you couldn't see the reaction and get on it.

The Team

It's really a team thing, it never works when you just put two guys together. It just never works that way because in order to make a good World Championship team, the guys who are in the medal rounds are the guys who rode together all season long. They didn't just get together and say "Ok, let's just get together and practice for a month and do it." Those guys train all summer long so that the Driver knows the guy in the back's weight.

The guy in the back can always look left to right, in fact, he should be able to dance in the back seat and the Driver should be able to go in a straight line, no matter what the guy does in the back. Whether the Driver goes left or right, the Stoker's with him. The Driver shouldn't feel that shift of weight. That's all something that riding together produces naturally.

That's why you can't just throw guys together. If I make a left turn, the Stoker almost knows that, anticipates any move I make, left, right. You ride together enough and you just know, you sense the movement. If someone were sitting in the back and I were driving and we switched places, that person would have done the same thing.

Picking a Partner

In picking a partner, you first pick someone with heart. You pick someone who <u>wants</u> to be back there. They may almost pick you, like "Let me do the back!" Not like the Driver says "You're fast, so I want you on the back." The guy may not have the guts for it. Some guys who might be excellent for it in all other ways may not have the heart for it.

Les was shorter than me and less weight, plus he was a Kilo rider. He worked out great. A good 200 meter time or a good Kilo time would help in evaluating a rider's potential. But then, again, the guy on the back has to want

"At the Olympic Trials in 1992 I flew in, raced the Keirin, took a shower, got dressed, packed my bike and caught the next flight out." Blaine, 1992

to do it. It's not like you pick him and say "Get on." because then the fear is there. The guy on the back has to be fearless.

That's what I enjoyed about Les, he'd pick a fight with the guy on the back of the other Tandem! He'd throw a punch if he had to. He's got to be able to do things. Even cheat. If you can hold the other guy up on the rail and the official can't see it, you can do things like pick your hands up of your bars and put them on the other guy's bars, to hold him back. We were capable of doing little things like that if we had to.

You do whatever it takes to get across the line first without getting disqualified. That's not what I would teach or advise beginning Tandem riders to do, but at the World Championship level, stuff like that went on. "This is not for you to try at home -- these are professional Drivers."

It takes talent and you can't think about it, you just have to do it, sometimes. Les was fearless. It was like "Ok, I've got an extra suit, an extra pair of shoes, an extra pair of wheels, let's go!" That was part of the intimidation. We would let it be known "We've got an extra pair of wheels, an extra suit -- let's go! If we crash we're ready to get up and do it all over again." You didn't <u>care</u>.

It wasn't like "Oh, I don't want to crash on the Tandem!" It was like "I don't care -- let's go!" You let them know. You almost show them "We have an extra set of wheels here, we're ready to do whatever you want." Not like "This is my only set of wheels, I've got to save them." It was more like "Come on, let's do it -- throw some punches." That's what I mean by heart.

Two Sprinters can work, a Sprinter and a Kilo rider can work, they tried it before. They have to have an equal amount of endurance. The Kilo rider may have a little more endurance than a Sprinter, but then a Sprinter can die. It would be good to have an equal amount. Both Tandem guys have to be able to ride a decent Kilo. One can't ride a decent Kilo and one not. It doesn't work then if they go for a long one.

You can't be a Pursuiter and do Tandem. You just can't react with enough fast twitch. There's a real advantage to having raced Sprints and having a feel for Sprint dynamics. Madison riders are not as suitable either, because that's an endurance event. They might do okay if they just went for a long one and held it, because they had the endurance. They'd be Kiloing, getting the Sprint started faster. If it was six laps they'd have to go with four to go, or if five laps, go for three. That way the Sprinters would tire faster.

Two Kilo riders would do well in the Tandem event. Being a Sprinter is appropriate, but Kilo riders have a little better endurance. You get a good team and they can go for three laps, either holding off the competition or catching and passing them -- or for four laps. Plus, they can be ready to do it again eight minutes later.

Some Sprinters don't have the endurance to do it twice in a row, and that's bad. When you get a Sprinters who can't do a twenty-five mile group ride, that's not good.

A Sprinter would have to have a good amount of endurance. He may not ride as fast a Kilo as a Kilo rider, but he has to be up there. Quick reflexes come from training together, from being in tune with each other.

Example: with two and a half laps to go, they know the speed's going to pick up. The Stoker is saying "They're coming, they're coming!" The Driver is anticipating getting out of the saddle and the Stoker with him. It's like one movement. One second later would be too late.

It's that quarter of a second of response. The team is in synch with each other. The team has terminology a typical code, like "up" is a typical word. The Stoker might call that, because he would see the other guys jump on them before the Driver would.

The Driver anticipates, knowing that they're going to get up. It's not like "Up". "Oh, okay, I'll get up." It's more like "Get ready, get ready . . . ." boom!

Once you're out of the saddle, the Driver should be able to have control,

so it takes a little bit more muscle to control it.

When I was riding with Les, we were able to stand up and I was able to go up the banking as if I was on my individual bike and back down, not just straight.

Les was able to be in synch with me knowing that when a Tandem team is going over the top, I was able be up out of the saddle and moving up, holding them off on the rail. Out of the saddle and then dive down the banking,

Nelson looked particularly cool in the Team Raleigh jersey. He did the team proud. Marymoor, 1986

like making a tight left turn, still out of the saddle, but then you're pedaling like crazy. It reverts back to the fact that the guys have to ride together. It makes it even better if you have a Tandem road bike.

If you have a Tandem team with a Tandem road bike, they should be able to win, not by being faster than the other team, but by being more in synch. That little second of no conflict with hesitation would be just enough to get across the line first. The other team may be faster, but the line may come sooner. Sometimes it's the first to react that is the better team. It takes control of the bike and you have to have trust in your equipment.

Everything you do on an individual you should be able to do as one. Jump out of the saddle, jumping down the banking, all the way down the backstretch sitting down or jumping out of the corner, out of the seat, and staying out of the saddle all the way around the corner. That comes from practice, then it becomes natural.

You wouldn't practice with the Tandem without a partner on the back. You need the weight. There's no reason for a rider to practice solo.

The Driver/The Stoker

I was always the Driver because I was a little taller than Les and it worked better. He has driven before with me on the back, but me on the front worked better. The guy on the back wants to be on the back. It's kind of like "You can drive, I trust you." For myself and Les in that situation, he was smarter, he was a smart rider. He say -- I do. I didn't second-guess him. I trusted his judgement.

Example: the Italians had us up against the rail. We were held against the rail. It was my patience vs. his. I had to override his judgement. He was anxious to go. I was like "wait, wait, wait . . ." from my position, from where we were.

If he were driving, he probably would have reacted and we would have lost. They pinned us up and they would have kept us. I allowed them to pin us up and then go, to give us room. Then we took off after them.

By them being in front of us, we were able to chase and pass. When we did pass, they were looking for us to come over the top. At the same time Les said "Underneath!" and I was already thinking that. They were coming up out of the pole, but we already had the momentum and we dove underneath. By the time they looked over their right shoulder, we were on their left shoulder. It was a big track and the banking was not too steep.

The reaction time on a Tandem is about a half a second slower than on an individual bike. It comes with the judgment. It's like a truck with no weight. How much the Tandem actually weighed was never important to me. I didn't know anything about that. We trained on a gear. It was like: "How'd it feel?" "It felt a little small" when we got up to speed. "Well let's go up a gear." "Yeah, that sounds better."

With the Tandem it's so precise, in trusting your equipment, number one, the judgement of your partner, number two, and then the camaraderie. Les and I rode a road Tandem for a whole season. We did road rides, road sprints, so he got used to sitting back there. He could move left to right, he could dance back there and I could still ride a straight line. Not like "Hey, you're making me move around!" He could try to steer the bike and I'd could still go straight.

Scott Berryman was more difficult, but on the other hand, we had enough speed together. Scott was just as heavy as I was, so the weight was more of a problem. That caused me, when I moved, to feel the reaction of the weight. But together we were fast. Reaction-wise, we were not as fast as two smaller guys. We could really get it going, though.

I think it's better if the guys are smaller, not so tall, small and stocky. I'd say it's better if they're smaller than me. I'm 5'9"-5'10". But then, if you're taller but the bike is there for you, that's okay.

I think if you're lighter, like 180 lbs or so, it's less weight to get going, so your reaction time can be quicker. If you can get away faster, even if your opponent is bigger and faster, by the time they catch you it's too late.

Leg speed is important, plus you have to be smooth, not jerky. The Driver needs to do a lot of upper body work to control the bike and not let the bike drift on him. If you can keep it in the pole, you're taking the shorter line.

When you tend to drift, you also tend to slack up on the pedaling. You tend to go "Whooa!" like "We almost lost it!" versus holding it down, like in the individual and pedaling like crazy. It takes a lot more. A place like Minnesota would do that to you, so it

would help to ride a smaller gear on a track like that.

When Les and I were so successful, he and I were together all the time. We trained on our individual bikes together, we did road rides together, we ate together, we roomed together, and that made a good team.

That's why we went straight to the finals when we were underdogs. We were underdogs to win the Gold, and sure enough, we did not win because the Czechs were smaller and faster. We were bigger and stronger, but they were smaller and faster.

I think about that ride even though it's ten years ago. When they reacted, when they jumped, we could react in the same time, but their reaction time was that half second faster. That was just enough for us to come up to a half a wheel, but that's enough to lose, too. That was all they needed, was to win two straight.

If we could react just a little bit faster than them, by the time they'd catch us we'd have already crossed the line. That's what happened in two rides straight. It was like "We know what they're going to do, so we anticipated, we reacted, but it was just enough. They used a smaller gear, like an inch smaller, to get going faster.

Marty Nothstein won the World Championships because he was able to do that. He could ride long, over mountains, he had the endurance. So if he got disqualified and they told him to ride again in five minutes, he could be ready to do it all over again.

That sort of thing helped Les and I in 1985. We had a round when we had to come through the repechage. It

A stylish Nelson calls riders to the line during 1993 Master's Nationals. (Is he a dude or what?) Colorado Springs.

was one of those things where we had just finished riding and had to go against the Italians. They were rested and we weren't, so they called us right

away.

We let the air out of our tires and pumped them back up again, then we walked to the line. We got our composure and our breath back and we had the endurance. Les rode a good Kilo and I was a good road rider. We were ready to go 110% again.

The endurance factor is important in Tandem because you're going to go from 500, probably 800 meters out. That's too much for a lot of Sprinters to handle.

Tandem can be more or less physical than Sprints, it depends on your ride and on your competition. You may have another team that is just as fearless as you, so there you go, there's your fight. There's a good ride, whether someone's going to hold someone up or whether it's going to stay close.

Another thing, a good Tandem team has to be able to throw their bike. Les was real good at that. He was able to throw the bike along with me, he was in synch with that, that one meter before the line. He could throw the bike and not be late. We practiced. We were able to do a Track Stand. Sometimes a win depended on the throw of a bike.

Track Stands on a Tandem

At the World level you see Track Stands all the time. You need to be able to do that if you want the back and you have the front. It was a lot more common at the World level. If you drew the first position and you wanted to ride from the back, you had to be able to do a Track Stand. The Czechs did that. They were able to

115

force us to the front, but we were able to stop also. We just couldn't hold it as long as they, and we had to take the lead. We weren't comfortable, but we were able to do it, we did practice that.

We'd spend a whole training session on practicing Track Stands. It wasn't like you made it up. That was one of the things, we would practice Track Stands and throwing bikes. We'd ride a lap and throw it at the line, ride a lap and throw it at the line. That photo finish could prevent you from going to a third ride. We'd practice moving up and down the track, going up the track, down the track -- just as you would on your individual.

We were even able to get on the Tandem and get in the paceline in the warm-up line. We'd swing up and come back down on someone's wheel, just like on individual bikes.

You have to ride as one, that's the whole idea of being in synch. It's not like the Tandem guys have a lot of power and just pull the paceline around. You swing up the track and go back down on the last guys, just like on the individual. At the same time, that's what helps in training, the guy on the back is always looking around. He looks over his left shoulder, over his right shoulder, and the Driver just rides the straight line.

Strategy

It isn't best to ride from the back or the front particularly. It depends on your opponent. You can't always win from the back and you can't always win from the front. You really have to be able to do both. Just like in individual Sprints, this guy's going to want to ride from the back. You have

to take the position "Ok, fine, let him ride from the back. I have a tactic for him." Sometimes you want the front to stay in the guy's way. Often the first one out of the corner is the first one to the line, but that's not always the case. You've got to be very versatile.

I've noticed a lot of Sprinters, only a handful of them are versatile. It amounts to being on top of your game. You can't always ride at the front. If I know that you like to ride from the front, I'm going to get in front of you and mess you up, mess up your whole tactic. "Ok, you like to ride from the front, well I'm not letting you go. You're not going to be in the front. Just because you want it, I'm not going to let you have it. I can ride from the front or the back." That was one of the tactics that would work on Ken Carpenter. He liked to ride from the front, so you get in front of him with two laps to go and get in his way. Once he's in front of you, you're out of luck. You can't let him do that.

You have a "plan A" and a "plan B" for the front and you have a "plan A" and a "plan B" for the back. That's what makes a World Class Sprinter. You pull a rabbit out of the hat when the opponent thinks you're riding their race.

Strategies are different than in the individual event, for instance, Sprints start sooner. Your reaction time is a little slower. The movement from left to right is a little slower up the track and down the track. The sense of length of the Tandem comes naturally for the Driver. When you're riding slow you know that your wheel is going to be that half an inch further down the

track from the front wheel. It comes with experience. You feel the difference. You won't feel it as much at first, but it come with practice.

It is good practice to have another person ride from the back, moving around back and forth. He's over the top, he's down underneath -- you've got to be able to cut him off or hold him up. He might pull up beside you and you've got to be able to jump and stay with him. Les and I were able to jump and stay up out of the saddle through the corners at full speed and continue down the backstretch.

Another thing that people don't know is that if someone took a flyer and we got really dropped, our strategy would be to fall over. The race would be restarted. The gun would go off and you'd get a restart. The race isn't going to start without you. It's like you're saying to your opponent "Ah-ha! I got you. Try another thing now."

When you don't do a Track Stand the right way and you really need to stay in the front, but you aren't comfortable and you want to get the person in the back to the front, if you're not comfortable and you're over the limit of your spot by the start-finish line, you stop and fall over. You're in the font anyway, so you're going to start from the front again anyway. If you're in the back and you fall over, you're going to have to lead in the re-ride. If the guy in first position and the guy in the back is not ready, he can fall over and then he has to stop and get in the lead anyway.

If you're in the front and you try to get the other guy in the front, but you don't feel comfortable, all you have to

do is fall over and start again. That's something that top riders do and do intentionally because that's part of their strategy.

Velodromes

There's no way some of these riders can't do a Track Stand at Indy. It's so shallow. L.A. is a little difficult, but if you ride the steeper tracks, you should have no fear, but a lot of the guys are not accustomed to that. If you train on Minnesota, everything else is flat!

My home track was Trexlertown (Lehigh). I still consider my home track to be Trexlertown, but I live in Indianapolis now, so Indy -- Major Taylor Velodrome -- is my "second home" track.

As far as my favorite velodrome, I don't have a favorite -- I just show up. It could be a bad or good one, it doesn't matter. Actually, though, Moscow is really my favorite. It's really steep and it's nice and its the best track in the whole world.

My favorite track for Tandem was Switzerland! It's a 333, it's wide and it's steep. It's smooth, and it's really great for Tandem. Any big 400 meter track is good, too. 250 is kind of tight for Tandem. It's more technical and takes more control. You're at that speed and you have to hold the bike down. That's where you're equipment is more likely to fail. The wheels flex more.

Advice to New Riders

"The best way to get into racing?" is a difficult question for a guy like me. If I had it to do over, for me it was timing, all timing. I could have been in jail or dead now. For someone out in some small town wondering about how to get into it, they could contact the Olympic Training Center and find out about their I.D. opportunities -- camps. The Federation and the Regional coaching programs being developed now are one good way. They could also work with their local bike dealer, especially a local pro bicycle dealership. The USCF has information on coaches which they can give to people calling in.

To figure out what event riders might be good at, they should just do them all. If they really want to ride track they really need to be near one. It's pretty hard to train for track without one.

I wish someone had told me early on to stay in school and go to college -- get an education. That's my comment to all. I attribute my success to family support in a big way. That's it.

Master's Racing

I think Master's racing is excellent. They're the supporters of the USCF.

International Racing

One way I'm different or unique among riders is that I get along with all. I don't have any enemies on the circuit. I'm a people person.

And -- the best dressed cyclist on the circuit. I think I got that from racing in Japan. Over there when you show up at the track, you dress like you're going to work. You show up dressed in a suit, your bike, your overnight bag with your pajamas, and your sweat pants, you race, kick butt, then you grab your money, put back on your jacket, and you leave.

That's just like I did at Olympic Trials (1992). I flew in, raced the Keirin, took a shower, got dressed, packed my bike and caught the next flight out.

Whether I get jet-lag depends on how much rest I get. Going to Europe isn't as bad because once I get to Europe I live by night anyway. All of the racing is at night. There's Saturday night racing and Sunday is an afternoon program, kind of for the kids. On Saturday and Sunday there's usually a short program, that's usually like a family day. They run several hours, but it's a short "quickie" entertainment event.

When I'm racing internationally I stay pretty busy and occupied. I have my down times when I would like to catch a plane and come home, but then I have to turn around and come right back.

I probably did well on the circuit because when I was in Europe I lived like a European. Some Americans want to go home. If you're going to make money you have to be willing to follow the program, you have to be willing and ready.

International professional racing is like an acting job, you get work -- you work. If you don't work when they call you to work then you probably won't work the next time. And you want to work. So that's why I'm consistent on my program.

When I'm not doing professional racing I do mountain bike rides and weight lifting. A lot of dates are set. It's already in print. The first couple of them come up and the managers are out there getting contracts for riders. Times of the year for racing may vary. One year I was in Paris in October, the next year I didn't go until the end of the month.

Changes

I would like to see better bike inspection for cyclists. I would like to see a whole new thing done for people that race on the track. I would like to see a total equipment check before every race or before every start. There are a lot of bozos out there who have inadequate equipment.

They used to have that bike check, but I don't know what happened to that. I think the officials are doing a good enough job, I think they're becoming more consistent.

The Future

I will stay involved in the business of cycling in marketing and promotions. It's the life I really know.

"International professional racing is like an acting job, you get work -- you work. If you don't work when they call you to work then you probably won't work the next time. That's why I'm consistent on my program."

Chapter 8

०ᐯ० *Points Race* ०ᐯ०

In a Points Race, riders accumulate points according to their position in the field when they cross the finish line, usually every five laps. Double points are awarded half way through the race and again on the final lap. The rider with the most total points at the end of the race, wins. This event comprises one of the largest fields of riders to compete in the National Championships and is one of the longest continual events on the track.

History

In the races at Madison Square Garden early in this century, points were given to riders at certain times in order to make the races more entertaining and varied in their pace. Riders content to sit in the draft of other riders found "sitting in" more difficult when prizes were offered to winners of Points laps. Either they could not bear to watch others get the prizes or the others accelerated so much that they had to pick up their own pace just to stay in the draft and not get left behind.

In weekly, local races, Primes (additional prizes, pronounced "preems") are often offered to riders for this same purpose, to stimulate competition and add sprints which are less predictable than the every-five-lap schedule.

In National Championships, riders are not offered prizes aside from the awards for the top five places, but Primes and points alike give riders

motivation to work harder during the event and so build the endurance and speed which result in top level competition.

The Mass Start

Up to this point, races discussed have been those beginning with riders held so that they could strap their feet in and otherwise get ready for the ride. Those events placed no more than nine people on the track at the same time, so holders could be on the track with them without much problem.

"Mass Start" (or "mass<u>ed</u> start") races, on the other hand, begin with a large group, twenty, thirty, or even more riders, all beginning at the same time. The "holder" approach is not practical under these circumstances.

Staggering a holder for each rider haphazardly across the start/finish area, then getting them out of the way would be impossible. Having riders shove off as they do in criteriums, getting their feet in the pedals and starting on the narrow, banked surface, would find riders colliding with each other, so neither of these approaches are practical.

Consequently, Mass Start riders begin by lining up at the rail or fence in a long line. Either they take their bikes to the fence and strap in or they ride to the fence and hang on.

Beginning near the front or back of the line is determined by the riders themselves, but is of fairly little consequence due to the way the race

Points Race riders begin their race from the fence/rail.

actually starts and its length.

The Start

Riders roll out from the fence when instructed to do so by officials. They must then roll (*roll*, not ride) around the track for one lap. During this time, they may move to whatever position they want to be in at the start. When the riders come around, at the end of the first lap, they are expected to be grouped together, riding at a fairly slow pace. If they are not, the gun will not sound and the race will not begin until they get it right.

The is why you will not see riders take off in a mad sprint when they leave the fence. The race is not really started yet, and will not start until things are set up correctly.

When the gun goes off, riders can

sprint, watch each other, or begin whatever race strategy they believe will enable them to win.

Distance

The distance of Points Races will vary, but in National Championship events it is usually about 120 laps (40km) for men and 60 laps (20 km) for women. The distance or number of laps or both will be specified in the race announcements and should not change unexpectedly.

Qualifying

Category 1 track and Professional riders automatically qualify for U.S. National Championships. Category 2 riders can qualify through heats which are announced at registration and ridden at Nationals. Qualifiers in the heats ride against the automatic quali-

Riders must come around <u>together</u> on the first lap or the starting gun will not fire.

fiers in the finals.

The Race

Total points accumulated by riders decides the winner.

In National Championship events, this Mass Start race is quite long. Top riders from around the country gain and lose laps, breakaway from the main group and get reabsorbed, and go through leader changes which, lap by lap, lend excitement to this event. The announcer bears the responsibility of keeping the audience informed of point accumulation and who is leading.

Double-Points laps (middle and final laps) will invariably be more hotly contested than any others, so there are moments when the action peaks even higher.

There are many strategies around points accumulation, but riders must also follow certain rules of procedure over the course of the race which allow points to be accumulated. In addition to the order of placings on Points laps, awarding of points relates to where riders are on the track in relation to the main group.

The "main group" is considered the largest group in the lead position.

A rider who has broken away from the main group accumulates points every lap until that rider is either re-absorbed or laps the field.

A rider is considered to have lapped the main group when s/he catches up to the back of it and finds protection in its draft. Once the field is lapped, the rider simply becomes part of the group once more. At this point, the rider must work his/her way to the front and sprint for points like any other member of the main group.

If the number of riders is low and they are spread out all around the track, a rider will be considered to have lapped the field when the Chief Referee judges this to be so. In other words, the lapping rider does not have to catch up with *all* riders in order to be considered a lap "up".

Riders attempting to lap the field are not allowed to get in the draft of riders who are off the back in order to be pulled up to the pack. Riders who are off the front may work together to lap the field or stay away as long as they can, without penalty. Riders are not permitted to sacrifice themselves for another rider. If they do, laps and/

or points will be taken away from their accumulations.

A rider who is off the back and who then gets lapped by the field is still allowed to sprint for points and may continue to do so no matter how many times s/he is lapped.

A rider may be pulled by the Chief Referee if s/he is more than two laps behind and is not judged likely to rejoin the race or be in contention. If a rider goes off the front and laps the field and later gets dropped from the back, s/he does not lose the lap gained until s/he is reabsorbed by the field.

The whole idea behind the Points Race is for a rider to accumulate as many points as possible. The rider with the most points at the end of the race wins.

Points are awarded every five laps in the following order:

1st = 5 points
2nd = 3 points
3rd = 2 points
4th = 1 point
Double-Points are awarded twice,

the first time half-way through the race and the second time at the finish. Double-Points look like this:

1st = 10 points
2nd = 6 points
3rd = 4 points
4th = 2 points

Smart riders revolve their strategy around the Double-Points laps in addition to any other points they may get. A rider who wins the middle and last laps will get 20 points from those laps alone. Riders who take only "normal" laps will have to win four sprints to equal the Double-Points winner's two.

Since riders will be sprinting in every Points lap, it makes more sense to save your energies for the Double-Points laps, but unfortunately, everyone else has this same idea. Consequently, Double-Points laps are going to require a lot more effort than the "normal" Points laps because there will be more riders trying to win those sprints than the others.

Example: riders in National

The field quickly strings out when riders sprint for Double Points!

Championship Men's Points Races, ride 120 laps. This means 24 separate opportunities (every five laps) to accumulate points. Two of these opportunities are for Double-Points, 22 for "normal" Points.

The first four riders to cross the line each get points, so the total opportunities to score *some* points is 96.

There may exist some formula to predict the probability of recurring success in such an event. When a rider is in a race against many other highly motivated, highly trained athletes, the realistic expectation of a win under conditions of such high variability would pretty much seem like a crapshoot.

Incredibly, certain athletes seem to be able to pull out consistent wins or placings in this race, nevertheless. How they do this is a mystery, but is a tribute to their racing savvy in addition to their physical condition. As in many other events, consistency is the key. Riders with good sprints and good endurance appear to do well in this race, but they also have to be smart.

Part of the excitement is trying to keep track of points of the various riders. Totals change every five laps and even more drastically in the middle and at the end with Double-Points.

Mishaps

If a rider has a problem due to equipment or other mishap s/he will be allowed one or more free laps up to

After points laps, the strong riders cruise while those left behind have time to catch up. Indianapolis, 1994

approximately 1 kilometer (three laps on a 333.33 track). If the race is part of a Championship event, free laps are not allowed during the last 2000 meters.

In non-Championship events, referees may allow more latitude, but riders may not receive points during the sprint after the free lap (to discourage resting up for sprints). Foul riding (endangering others) is punishable by warning, relegation, disqualification in the sprint, or disqualification from the race, whatever officials decide according to the severity of the transgression.

If a race must be stopped due to rain or another problem, it is considered over if two-thirds or more of the original distance has been completed. Order of placings is determined by points accumulated at that time. It is possible for the race to be resumed or rerun. It is up to the Chief Referee.

A Points Race is considered finished when the leader crosses the finish line in the final lap. All other riders are also finished at that time, no matter whether they are laps down or not.

If a rider had a mishap during the final 2000 meters, s/he is allowed to keep whatever points were previously accumulated. Any other riders who do not finish the race are considered out of the race.

When the final points are tallied, the number of laps a rider is ahead is considered more important than points when final placings are determined. In other words, if two riders have the same total but one is "a lap up", that rider will be considered the winner.

Otherwise the total number of points determines the winner. If two riders are tied for both points and laps, the winner is determined by who finished first in the most Points Sprints. If there is still a tie, the one who placed higher in the Final Sprint is the winner.

If there should <u>still</u> be a tie, officials will work back through placings in each successive sprint to determine who placed higher the most number of times until the tie is broken. Determinations which require this kind of extended inquiry is unusual, fortunately for officials.

Local Points Race events

Wide variations in Points Race design are common to local weekly races at active tracks. Some of these variations are listed under Non-Championship Events at the end of this section.

One of the charms of non-Championship Points Races is the playfulness with which race organizers might award points on more casual occasions. In addition, Primes are often used at this level to tempt riders into

Finishing sprints are closely contested and can determine the winner even after 60 (woment) or 120 (men) laps. The field is usually much smaller by the finish.

A moment's distraction in a pack can be disastrous (note the sparks!) Indy, 1994

Shelley Matthews was scraped and dirty, no broken bones. Blaine, 1992

unexpected. It's part of our rags-to-riches dreams. The joy of unpredictable thrills in competitions which integrally involve other kinds of unexpected rewards is seen nowhere better than in the Points Race in weekly racing.

In local and regional events, the distances will vary greatly, according to the aims and whims of race organizers. In weekly, low-key events, it is very possible that distance and just about everything else will depend on the number of riders signing up for the race and may change up until the very start of the race. Weekly racers know and understand this. The versatility of the Points Race makes it a classic favorite with riders and spectators alike.

sprinting during non-points laps, spicing up the pace for audiences and riders and throwing confusion into strategy.

Riders seldom object to randomly added Primes thrown in during the course of a Points Race. They may only learn about these surprises from announcers during the actual race.

Sometimes money is collected at various times during the event which is awarded as a Prime. No one, competitor, organizer, or spectators can predict how much this out-of-the-blue Prime might total. With a good announcer stimulating a crowd which is involved with the prizes, these events are very fun, for both riders and spectators.

Another possibility for Primes is miscellaneous donations from spectators. A wise announcer will not refuse these unexpected offerings. They may include a plate of cookies, a half a chicken, a tune-up or any

donated prize. If the donator wants to advertise his/her business cheaply, this is a fun way to get an announcement while contributing materially and adding to the general fun and enjoyment for both audiences and riders.

This kind of activity is especially suited for Points Races because they are long enough to allow for mid-race changes and announcements and because there are definite lulls between Points Laps when riders are resting.

For some riders, Primes may be all they go home with. For these same riders, the total money they can accumulate through Primes may be more than that won by the most successful winner of any race offered on the track that night!

Americans traditionally love the underdog and the

Janie Eickhoff and Karen Bliss Livingston traded off winning women's Points Races for several years. (L - Esther Davis and Lucy Vinnecombe, R - Mindy Mayfield) Olympic Trials, Blaine, 1992

Points Race
Karen Bliss Livingston

Karen grew up in Quakertown, Pennsylvania. Her home track is Lehigh County Velodrome, though she spends much of the year in Gainesville, Florida. She began her cycling career by touring with her father. When she was a sophomore (1983), she joined the Penn State Cycling Club, and the rest is history.

Karen has won the U.S. National Points Race Championship four times, in 1986, '87, '89 and '91. She is one of the most successful Points racers the U.S. has produced. Karen also won the U.S. National Criterium Championships in 1990 and 1994. She took a Silver Medal in the Goodwill Games, 1994. Look for her in 1996.

How I Got Started

When I started riding with my dad it was just me and him more than the extended family. He was never really much of a rider before that, we kind of discovered cycling at the same time.

I saw an ad in the paper for the Penn State Cycling Club and went to a meeting. It was pretty low key, real grass roots. That was before they had any of the collegiate stuff nationwide, I'm guessing '86 or '87.

Jim Young, at Penn State got the ball rolling. NCAA Championships were in Boston in 1993. In 1994 they were in Houston. They include track.

Jim teaches and coaches at one of the Penn State satellite campuses, near Trexlertown and Lehigh velodrome.

A lot of the up-and-coming Juniors go to school at Penn State so they can stay near the track. It's probably the best track program on the collegiate level, although Indianapolis is also offering scholarships at a college nearby, which is a first!

My First Points Race

In the beginning I loved to sprint on the road. Patti Cashman suggested that I try Points racing. I didn't even know what it was until 1986 -- and I won Nationals -- my first Points Race!

I started racing track, I'm guessing, 1984 -- maybe one race, then the next year I raced a couple races. I just kind of jumped right in with both feet at T-Town. I raced whatever Friday night races they had, like Miss-N-Outs, Scratch races, whatever. They may have had some Points Races, but very short versions of them.

Nationals that first year, 1986, was really the first big Points Race I'd ever been in. That year there were so many crashes (three major ones), it was such a bummer. That was my initiation. It got better from there, though.

Racing in Europe

I initially went over to Europe in October and part of November in 1987 with Connie (Young). That was my first introduction to international track racing.

It was a total eye-opener, I'd never seen a track that little! That was in

Ghent, Belgium. 165 meters, I think, and 50 degrees. It was a trip! It's one of the big stops on the Six-day circuit.

It was a whole bunch of firsts that time. My first trip to Europe, my first experience racing against people who didn't speak English, my first time trying to ride on a tiny little dinky track with WALLS for banking. It was very scary. It took me so long to get off the apron! I'd ride by between the first and second turn and I'd look up -- I could put my hand out and touch it!

It was so foreign to me that people would *actually stay up* on this thing. It was like one of those rides at an amusement park. You had to get up some speed on the apron and then go up on the track itself. There was somewhat of a straight-away. That's where you had to get on until you got up more speed, then you could go up.

People rode Pacelines up at the blue (Stayer's) line. You couldn't do a

"I don't think that biologically I am a born athlete. I'm fast, but I'm not the fastest, I'm strong, but I'm not the strongest, I've got endurance, but not the most. It may be that I'm good at putting them all together.

One of the greatest feelings in the world is going to a race, sitting on the start line and saying to yourself "I'm going to win this race" and know that you will."

Paceline down on the Pole line because the centrifugal force is so great, like someone had crawled on your back and was pushing you down into the track, when we started going hard.

That's where the racing was, on the Pole line, but for extended Paceline training it'd be up in the middle of the track.

We went there pretty much every day and we did a couple weekend races. They were just local races. The season was winding down at that point, so nobody was really training and coming up for it or anything, so for Connie and I -- well, Connie knew what she was doing -- but for me, anyway, it was just an experience in learning how to ride the track. There were maybe 10 women and they weren't very good at that point, that time of year, anyway. I never saw any women training, really, just Connie and me.

The next time I went over for track racing, was in '89, with Bobby. We went to the same town and stayed a little longer, about the same time of year. He was doing amateur Six-day races. It was the same kind of thing, but I felt a little more comfortable this time.

Focusing on the Game

That same year I met Bobby, he really helped me get focused, because his whole racing career had been that way. Once I started to get focused, racing took on a whole new meaning. It became an intricate game of mental toughness and scientific training.

I didn't start out with a serious attitude. All I wanted to do was "not get a job" and travel. Bike racing was a way to do that. I could scrape by on winnings and get to the next race.

After a while I started to feel like I could do better than 3rd and 4th places. I began to train hard with Roger and Connie Young.

I love the mental part of the sport. I love being fit enough that I am a serious player and have some type of control of the outcome of a race. One of the greatest feelings in the world is going to a race, sitting on the start line and saying to yourself "I'm going to win this race" and knowing that you will.

Bobby (*Champion in: 1983 16-18 Junior Sprint, 1986 & '88 Madison, 1988 Kilometer, 1988 Olympic Team member*) gave me the most advice

about racing and training on a professional level.

Through Bobby I got to meet more people and do more serious training. I wasn't really afraid anymore to train on the track. It got more fun the second time around.

Toward the end of '88 after he went to the Olympics I really got to know him better. When he got back from the Olympics he didn't have to concentrate so much on training. He could relax, and that's when we really got to know each other. We talked about what we were doing for the next year. He got an offer to ride for Roger's team and I got an offer to ride for Connie's team. So we each signed up with teams that were going to be

training together.

We did all the camps, the men's team and women's team trained together, we started out in California early that year, then onward to Indianapolis, so through the course of that, we spent a lot of time together and developed a relationship -- and life was great!

The Points Race

Ingrid Haringa won the World Points Race two years in a row. She's just amazing. She won the '92 Sprints. At that time she wasn't really a Sprinter, she didn't have as much experience as Connie, but she was SO strong. She would just ride people off her wheel in the Points Race, which is unheard of. She was one I keyed off of.

I guess the difference is that at the International level the speed just dictates everything. If you can maintain the speed and go faster for the sprints, you're up there. But at the domestic level, the National level, it's more about how aggressive you are, how many chances you're willing to take.

You don't have to worry about the speed as much. The size of the packs varies. One year in T-Town there were about 12 women, but last year at Indy we had about 30.

The biggest difference procedurally between the U. S. and Europe

"I didn't even know what a Points Race was until 1986 -- and I won Nationals -- my first Points Race! The most helpful way to train for the Points Race is 1) development of a solid, consistent pre-season training base, 2) lots of intervals on the road and the track, and 3) someone with whom to discuss tactics and training plans."

is where to sprint on the track. In Stuttgart, in 1991, it was a 250 meter track and we sprinted every 7 laps. I guess it was the same in Blaine. It's normally every 5, although apparently they're changing it to every 10.

I've been to three Worlds. I did Pursuit for a couple of years. I only tried Kilo once, in about '86. I didn't see the future in it, because for women there's nothing beyond Nationals. They're going to have the Points Race in 1996. I'm looking forward to that.

Points Race Training

The most helpful way to train for the Points Race is 1) development of a solid, consistent pre-season training base, 2) lots of intervals on the road and the track, and 3) someone with whom to discuss tactics and training plans.

I rack up all the road miles I can, put a good base down. I do stage races early on, road races, crits, for a well-rounded but intense lead-up for two months or so before I want to do well.

Then I'll start getting on the track. I keep some of my road miles, but then put a lot more effort and concentration into speed work. I do intervals on the track, definitely, Paceline stuff, I don't do jumps -- I don't think that's necessary.

Maybe domestically jumps come in handy, but internationally the pace is so high that there's no reason to have a jump! It's negated. So I work on a lot of intervals and motorpacing, Paceline stuff. I do more motorpacing as the Championships approach.

The two years I specifically trained for the Points Race I did motorpacing two times a week, doing a specific workout, not just sitting on the motor, for maybe an hour. I'd do something with the motor, coming around it or under it or racing it to the line, working on recovery, getting back on the motor right after you cross the line -- intervals, things like that.

Some of it is with other people, some is specific to my training. I think at that point it's a matter of "Is there someone who's willing to do that just for you? Is the track going to be empty enough that just you should do it?" It's a matter of logistics. If there are three of us who want to do the same thing, we do it together.

In a race I tend to key off of specific people. I will key off of different people nationally than internationally. The races are entirely different.

On the national level the pace isn't near as high. It's more juggling for position at slow speeds and jumps. There are only three or four women who could win, that really have the combination of power and speed and endurance.

The Women's Points Race is difficult to master on an international level only because there are so few opportunities to race it. The race at Worlds is entirely different than any race anywhere. Women don't have enough opportunity to race in large, Mass Start track events.

Nationally it's harder for different reasons -- feeling comfortable in such a huge pack and getting yourself through holes and taking chances. But Internationally the speed is the dictating factor. You have to be fit, strong and fast. You have to be a really solid road rider.

Racing in Europe

When I went over with the National Team in 1992 we did road races. Ingrid Haringa would sprint for the finish against me, Laura Chara-meda, Karina Skippy (Danish), and a couple other good field sprinters. While she was sprinting she looked over her shoulder and smiled at us.

My first World Championships were in Lyons, France in 1989. That was a whole new experience, because I'd never had a chance to race like that, with so many really good women. I had no idea what it was going to be like. I'd had no training for that style of racing. That was a trip. It was tense, we were all on edge. I was nervous.

People say "Oh, you're so lucky you get to travel." That's true to an extent, but mostly you're uptight because you're racing. You don't get to see the sights, you don't get enjoy life. I hardly remember Lyons. It's not like it's all fun and games. You see the hotel room and that's about it.

I think I learned how aggressive you have to be to perform well at that level. Not aggressive in launching attacks, but aggressive in the pack to maintain your space and shoot for spaces.

There are things that seem to be etiquette in the States -- like not coming up under someone -- that were just out the window over there. It was almost like a free-for-all -- it seemed to me, anyway. Maybe because no one here does that. Nothing was really illegal that they did at Worlds, but it was just all new, because here there aren't as many women who are willing to be that aggressive.

I don't think there's all that much respect for women track racers over there unless you're right up there breaking World Records.

I raced in Belgium and it was pretty poor, but I race in Zurich where there were less women, but they were better. Barbara Ganz was there and a couple of her team mates. They were pretty good. There were less of them, but they were pretty quality riders.

But for the most part, European riders just look like they work hard at everything they do. They have that work ethic look. Like "I'm going to wake up and sweep my whole house and then I'm going to go out and race my bike." You know? They just kind of have that real kind of serious attitude.

I think when it comes to the women there's less opportunity; that there's only a few top spots reserved for the few people who can sort of work their way up and out. For men, you can be a domestique and work your way up, but for women the only way up is to get on the National Team for each country and that's only six women for each country.

Athletic Ability

I don't think I am a born athlete. Definitely not. I look at people like Bobby who I think is . . . I watch him, we try something new together like body surfing or something and he gets it, he just gets it, no matter what. A couple tries, he's in there, he's having a good time, whereas I'm trying it and trying it and getting more frustrated. He can do anything pretty much right away. That's my definition of a natural athlete.

I'm definitely not that way. When I think about my success, it's just that I've stuck with it. When I started cycling it was the same thing, I was really bad. Just *getting a clue* was difficult!

I got into cycling basically just for the social aspect. I stuck with it for that reason, but also because I slowly, slowly, slowly got better. My first race I was off the back, my second race I was off the back. It mean, it wasn't like I jumped in and won my first race. There's no way.

I stuck with it because all my friends were doing it and they said "Oh, don't worry about it, just come ride with us tomorrow." And that was it. So I slowly got better and then it took on a whole new meaning for me.

I was not a successful racer in college. I raced two and one half years or so. I never got good then. My progress was kind of like a stair-step, a series of moments. When I got out of college I learned that I could rest. In college I was working and going to school and riding and doing everything, I never got a chance to recover. When I got out and could get off my feet, not have to run to my next appointment or something, I got better.

The next moment was when I met Bobby. Not like that moment, but I think I was ready, I was receptive to learning about training. I had reached a plateau in my cycling and I was ready to move on to the next level. I think when I met him and he taught me a lot, all that came together at once. That was when I really started to develop -- and *wanted* to develop, part of it was just being ready for it.

I tell a lot of the women around here who are struggling and getting frustrated, "Look, I never was good either. I just stuck with it." If you're just consistent and stick with it, anything can happen. I really believe that if I can do anyone can do it.

I didn't look like an athlete. I was a little bit overweight. I always had some strength, some muscle, but I really didn't know how to use it. I was always an athlete growing up, I did other things, I was a swimmer and I played field hockey. When I was a swimmer I was pretty good, I peaked when I was about 13, though. In field hockey I was never great, but I was okay. Swimming helped my aerobic capacity, but I was never a "complete" swimmer, I didn't stick with it year 'round. I was competitive for a couple of years, I remember getting really into it. I knew about discipline, though I didn't really understand about training.

When I look at myself compared to the rest of the women in the field, I'm definitely one of the strongest in the events that I choose to race. I don't think I'm stronger than the Sprinters, but I don't train for those races.

I think in the events that I race I'm probably overall stronger than the majority of them. I mean just power. To get up short hills and in Sprints. I wouldn't say that I have more mental strength than the majority of people out there. That wouldn't be my top quality, I don't think.

Three women who find themselves on the Points Race awards podiums consistently: Esther Davis, Karen Bliss Livingston and Janie Eickhoff.

I see people like Bunki Bunkaitis as having incredible mental strength. Jeannie Golay has incredible mental strength. My strength is hard to pinpoint for me because I'm really an all-around kind of rider. Maybe that's what makes me a good Points Racer, because you really kind of need all that stuff.

I'm fast, but I'm not the fastest, I'm strong, but I'm not the strongest, I've got endurance, but obviously not the most. I think I have some of all of those qualities. It may be that I'm one of the best at putting them all together.

My weaknesses are probably a couple of things. I think one of them is my hill climbing, which doesn't really relate to the Points Race. That is a definite weakness for me. I know what it takes now for me to be good, but I can never be great, so . . . So that's one.

Another weakness is -- I don't know how to explain it -- not always being aggressive.

I don't think it's so much a mental weakness as maybe just a fluctuation in my training or something. It's a tough one. In a crit I'll always be aggressive, but in a Points Race there are just some days I won't be willing to shoot through that hole or make that move. But it varies. I would never say that about my crit racing, which I feel is my strongest point.

Pressure

The pressure got to me in '92. It was pretty much self-imposed. I was trying to make the Olympic Road Team. I remember I wasn't at all ready for it. I hadn't prepared well, the stress got to me and that affected my training.

I got a huge envelope in the mail from a second grade class in the Midwest that had found my name as someone who might do well in the Olympic Trials. En masse they all wrote me these letters. Normally I would have thought it was really cute, but at that time I felt like "If I don't make the Olympic Team I'm letting all these kids down!" when in reality they were just doing a class project or being nice. It really got to me that year.

Now I can look back and say that was the sweetest thing in the world, but when I received that package I just totally broke down because I just thought of it as being more pressure. It was "Oh, no, look at all these kids who expect me to do well!" when in reality they were just being nice.

I've handled pressure better when I've been prepared in my training. When you're training well and you're fit, the pressure doesn't seem to sink in. It kind of bounces off your "shield of fitness" or something. I think it only gets to you when you're not feeling your best.

Bobby's input for me has been "You overanalyze, Karen. Just do it. So you've had a bad training day, so what? Everybody does. Just get on with it. Take a shower, and start tomorrow." That kind of thing. Whereas I always sit there and mull it over and try to analyze it, over-analyze it, look at it from five different perspectives. He grounds me. He's really focused, really good at not stressing. He's been a role model for me.

And it's been hard because he's been training at the same time I've been training. It's not like I get this unconditional pat on the back every time, because he's been stressed out too, or he's had a bad training day. We've had some ups and downs when we're both training really hard.

"I tell a lot of the women around here who are struggling and getting frustrated, "Look, I never was good either. I just stuck with it."" Karen sprints against Rebecca Everling. Though not a Sprinter, Karen's sprint ability is one of the reasons she's a good Points racer.

Diet

In the years I totally focused on my bike racing I paid a lot of attention to diet. I do other things now and I don't want to get caught up in that because it can be totally all-consuming.

I try to eat a low fat, well-balanced diet, but I'm not going to kick myself for eating cookies. The years I was really focused on training I would kick myself for eating cookies. I take vitamins, more during the season.

My diet is really not varied. I guess being 30, I just know what I can and can't eat. I try to eat foods that make me feel good. That cuts out a lot! I still eat ice cream and cookies and way too much bread, but for the most part for the regular meals I eat lots of pasta, rice, vegetables.

There are things I would never dream of touching, like a Burger King hamburger, stuff like that. That's where I draw the line.

Velodromes

The first velodrome I raced at was Lehigh. That's the primary one. When I was racing on Connie's team I spent a summer out in Indy (Major Taylor). Indy's pretty much the same as Lehigh except it's rounder. The straights aren't quite as long, though it doesn't seem that much different.

Lehigh Velodrome is great because the people there, both the staff and the crowd, **know** bike racing. It's run professionally.

Redmond (Seattle) is a good velodrome for me because it's like riding on the road, it's so big. It's less a Sprinter's track and more a power rider's track.

If there's no track available on a regular basis, find a long, flat stretch and do training there. Intervals, repeat sprints with a group, practice bumping shoulders and tapping wheels, too. Measure out track distances and ride a fixed gear.

Advice to New Riders

The best way for a rider to get into racing is to talk to a local rider/racer to 1) get comfortable on his/her bicycle and 2) find out about group rides. You can learn a lot by talking to people. Get training advice from the *best*. Usually people are willing to help out.

To find a coach or training program, find out what other people in the area are doing. Ask someone who's raced for a while for some coaching advice. Get in touch with the United

States Cycling Federation. They're developing a good regional coaching program.

Because of sponsorships and because sports is now a more accepted profession, people are doing it longer. Because people are doing it longer, they're finding that they're not necessarily peaking when they're 21. A lot of the top cyclists are doing well even into their late 20s, early 30s, even late 30s. Kent Bostick, for instance, (*42 year old 1995 Pan Am Gold Medalist*) wouldn't have been able to do this 20 years ago.

My advice to beginning riders is "Don't Give Up". Even if you don't think you could be great, just keep at it, work hard and be consistent, which is the main one. And then even it you don't turn out to be great, there are so many things you can get from cycling.

I was just telling this woman the other day, I've been riding for 10 years now, and through the course of 10 years I feel like I've been through so many different phases.

Initially it was just to meet people and have a good time, lose some weight, or whatever. As I got better my focus was totally competitive -- how good can I be? what's the best I can be? Excluding my family members, everybody was out of my life and cycling was it. It was a total focus.

That was a real learning experience for me, the fact that I could really do that. I got a lot out of it that year, I learned a lot about myself and I learned the level of professionalism that cycling has.

Also, I think it's important to take some down-time. It's really easy, especially when you're excited and starting something new, to go overboard. It's easy to over-train or get obsessed.

Don't get me wrong, I believe that obsession has its place in training and in sport -- even though that's probably not the politically correct thing to say. But obsession can get you into trouble. I'll give you two examples:

When I began to train harder I never felt like I was doing enough. I'd look around at what other cyclists were doing and thought they were doing more than me, so I'd add more training sessions or more intervals to a training session. It was never enough.

I can say this now because I have the luxury of a couple of years distance on that time, I was grinding myself into a hole. I was always tired and surprisingly I couldn't figure out why.

Now I don't pay attention to how much or what other riders are doing for training. I know from years of experience what works best for me.

For new riders who don't have those years, having someone "on the outside" who is sensible and who knows how much is too much is a valuable person to get to know. It's definitely tough, though, because you're always riding that fine line between too much and just plain solid training.

The other example relates to mental burn-out. That's another one that's hard to detect until you have time to look back.

I began training hard in the beginning of '89 and went right on through the winter and then the whole season of '90. The whole time I spent on my bike -- I never thought not to.

By the winter of '90 I was so blown, I didn't even want to look at my bike. I felt guilty at the time, but I took a solid month off and then spent the winter doing other things like weights, swimming and hiking. When '91 rolled around, I was ready to get going again -- I *wanted* to race.

I don't ever see myself quitting. I may stop racing for a little while, then pick it up again later.

There's so much else to do. Helping other people, getting on your bike and feeling like you know how to pedal! Not the motion itself, but just that you're good at it. After all these years, you get really good at pedaling! It feels good being good at things.

I watch a lot of collegiate people who race here and I think "I was there once" and to watch them and think "if they can only stick with it they'll get better".

You want them to experience that part of it like you did. I really like cycling a lot.

My advice to up-and-coming riders who want to ride the track, is to find a coach. There's a lot to know about track etiquette for training with a lot of people. You must have a track bike, good wheels and three gears to start. Good wheels and tires are very

"I love the mental part of it. Bobby (Livingston) helped me get focused and racing took on a whole new meaning. He's been a role model for me."

important.

The Future

In the future I plan to become increasingly involved with the USCF Women's Cycling Commission.

I also plan to coach locally, race for a few more years, and *always* ride.

Points Race
Mark Whitehead

"Winning an Olympic medal or a World Championship medal was my whole goal in life. Heart has a big part in it. As a coach, I want to instill in my riders the will to push themselves beyond the edge, to push themselves farther than they've ever done. And don't give up. I've never been a quitter."

A "bad boy" of cycling (nicknamed "Meathead" and "The Outlaw"), few can match the passion and versatility of Mark Whitehead, a second generation cyclist, who appears to be becoming one of bicycle racing's most able, albeit controversial, coaches.

Mark's achievements span a wide variety of events, beginning with his Omnium Championship in 1979 as a Junior. He was also U.S. Junior National Sprint Champion in the same year. In 1981 Mark was U.S. National Madison Champion. In 1983 he was National Champion in both Kilometer and Madison. Mark was U.S. National Team Pursuit Champion in '79, '84, and '85. In 1986 he won the Professional Sprint Championship. In 1988 he raced on the Japanese Keirin Circuit.

Today Mark still races well, but he's particularly proud of his coaching success. His Junior riders, male and female, have begun making regular trips to the award podiums. Things are never boring with Mark around!

I was born February 14, 1961 and I grew up in Whittier, California.

How I Got Started

I got to be a good rider because I observed a lot and watched all the best guys. I was very much an observer. I learned how to race and how to position myself.

I got started riding through my father, Pete Whitehead, who used to race. He used to make everyone else work and then he'd win the race. That's where I learned. He coached me when I was first learning to ride through 1975. Then I went on to other people. In 1976 I was coached by Gibby Hatton, through 1979 when I was a Junior. I was very successful. I was also coached by Gibby's dad, Gilbert Hatton Sr. I won three National Championships through that coaching.

Gibby was a World Junior Champion and many time National Champion. I was very lucky to have someone who grew up very close to me. At that time he was in El Monte, only 10-12 miles from my house. That really helped me.

The person who helped me most in my career was my brother David. He was a competitor until 1980. He and I won a lot of races. We competed against Greg LeMond, Jeff Bradley, Greg Demgen -- all the top Juniors in the country for three years, because back then "Junior" was from 16 to 18.

My brother was very good. Actually he was better than I was, but he couldn't handle the pressure. He became my advisor and supporter. He supported me financially from '80 through '82 -- for three years. He motorpaced me and trained me. If it wasn't for him I wouldn't have reached the level that I did.

My parents live in Gig Harbor, Washington. My dad doesn't ride his bike any more. He got fed up. My dad won a Silver Medal in 55+ track Championships in 1986. He trained with me and I told him that he might as well go out being National Champion. He lost the Omnium by one point.

He was like me, the losing took a big toll on him. He had trained real hard for two years with me in Pasadena. Then he went and lost by one point. He gave it up after that. He wanted to be a National Champion, but he didn't make it. The Silver Medal was still good. He was pretty happy, but he's like me, he doesn't like to lose.

I was very fortunate that I knew someone, named Phil Guarnaccia (National Master's Champion) a friend of my father's, who told me that I had to train in the gym to be successful.

I never was really a specialist, I raced everything. The only things I couldn't race was time trials on the road and road racing. I was never really very good at those, but anything else that I ever raced, I was pretty successful. I could race anything I put my mind to. Criteriums were the most fun for me because I was very good at them. I had a good sprint.

My career went from 1979 to 1987. After that I didn't do much. I went to the World Championships and got like 20th racing Pro. At the 1986 Worlds I got 5th in Colorado. Japan gave me a contract (Keirin). I went to Japan in 1988 from March until June.

I was very successful in 1988, independently. I had no sponsorship, I raced on my own money.

In Japan, I raced Keirin. I made a

lot of money, but I was very disappointed in the way that they treated me and in the competitors that were there. But that was just a bad experience of my life.

I wanted to go back because the money was so good, but the other riders didn't want me because I wanted to win and I had to work. There's workers and there's winners. Being a winner all my life and racing to win, I had to get eighth and ninth place out of nine riders continuously, and it wasn't enough. I got very frustrated because I was as good as them, but I was a newcomer. Although I was assigned to be a worker, I got the same amount of money that they did, but I didn't get to win. Money was important to me, but winning was more important.

Best Memories

As a rider I attribute my success to intensity, desire to win, "never give up" and heart. Heart has a big part in it but that's very difficult to coach. As a coach, I try to instill in my riders the will to push themselves beyond the edge, farther than they've ever gone - - and don't give up.

I hate when people give up, that really upsets me because as a competitor I know I didn't give up and just stayed in the field many times and ended up winning the race because the race changes. I just hate quitters, I hate them. I've never been a quitter.

My proudest achievement was personal. My father was a great athlete and he didn't think I could achieve. When I was 14 or 15 we were sitting at the dinner table and I told my dad I was going to the Olympic Games. He laughed at me.

He was a very realistic person. At that time American cyclists were not very good. So that was my big goal through the mid-70s. That was my biggest thing, making the Olympic Team.

As a racer my proudest moment was being the first 18 year old ever to win a Senior title, which I did in 1979 (Team Pursuit). And I also won Junior's at the same time (Sprint & Omnium). That was one of my biggest accomplishments.

But being realistic, I'm so versatile, being able to win stages in the United States tours, winning the Kilo, winning the Points Race, winning the Madison . . . . Most people can't win multiple events. That was very satisfying. I also won Professional Sprints in 1986. As an amateur I won 9 National Championships.

Moments like, in 1983, getting fifth in Zurich in the Worlds Points Race was particularly memorable to me. My whole goal in life was to win a medal in either the Olympics or the Worlds.

I didn't care if it was Gold, Silver or Bronze, I just wanted to get on the podium and be somebody -- be somebody.

Winning the National Championships was important to me as a young rider, but I had accomplished that at 18. I lived in the vicinity where Greg LeMond was and I was on the same Junior Worlds Team in '79 when he won the road and got Silver on the track in the Pursuit, where I only got seventh. I was very, very disappointed.

And so to me, winning an Olympic medal or a World Championship

Mark races against Trey Gannon on the new Vandedrome. Mark's team won the Team Challenge, though a mix-up in points initially gave victory to another team. The program, which aired on PrimeSports in March, 1995 demonstrated Mark's Championship style, both racing and crashing!

medal was my whole goal in life, and getting fifth twice and getting sixth twice, I was just so close, but I just wasn't good enough to be on the podium. That was a very harsh thing for me to go through.

Disappointment wise, my marriage (to Rebecca Twigg) was the biggest disappointment in my life, which financially and emotionally ruined my life. It was a very bad, bad thing for me from '87 on.

Winning stages in the Tour of Texas and winning the Nationals in four different events were my best times. I've been around. I think that that's hampered me and also accelerated me in coaching, because I know what it's like on both sides of the barrel. I know what it's like on the top and I what it's like to be on the bottom of the barrel.

I've started riding again and it's very difficult to know how powerful I used to be. At one time I could just demolish people and now it's more of a struggle. But I have a lot of good friends and people living close that support me. Within five months I came, I would say, 80%. I'm not planning anything for the future, I'm just going day to day.

I'm getting back into it and compete with my friends, but it's very difficult -- I'm not the man I used to be. I'm 34, but still I have fun. I like to play around with everybody. I really know how to handle my bike, I know how to push and shove and play games, so they get mad at me once in a while.

You can ask Danny Van Haute about that. We were Madison Champions in 1983. We would have won in '82 but I crashed real badly. I broke ribs and an elbow and had a concussion, but I still went on to other Championships.

The Points Race

The Points racing event is a potluck event. You have to just keep your peak -- there's a lot of luck involved. From 1980 to '85 I won one, got second in one, got fourth in one, and sixth. It's a very tough event.

I think there was only one rider who repeated, John Beckman, from Oregon. I've won four of the six events

on the track.

The best event ever for me was the Miss-and-Out, but that was a regular track event, not a National Championship event.

Positioning is everything when it comes to winning or losing. In all the Mass Start events, you've got to have positioning, and if you don't know how to position yourself -- well -- You've got to have good legs, too. If you don't have good legs, you aren't going to be in there anyway.

If your mind's working with the good legs and you're an elite athlete, you're unbeatable. Legs and the tactical stuff coming together only happens one out of ten races.

You can't really predict it, but you know it will happen. So if you know where to be at the right time and it gets down to the top six or seven people and you've got good legs, it's like taking candy from a baby. But if you don't have good legs and you know where to be, you're still going to get third or second or fourth.

In a Points Race, where you're racing against 40 or 50 people at a time, you'll never win without a pull or two from your teammates. It just won't happen. It's not being on a certain wheel, you have to ride your own race.

If you're racing 100 laps on a track like San Diego (333.3 m.) for the first

half of the race you're on your own, and then once you've established that you're one of the top three or four guys -- back when I was racing, early in my

Newly crowned National Madison Champion Mark Whitehead has a chat with Eric Heiden at the San Diego Autumn Classic, 1981

career it was mostly friends that came in to help you. You make sure that they chase down the breakaways and stuff like that.

I was always very vocal with all my friends through all my career. Especially in criteriums, Points Races and Madison, and I was very successful in all of them. Coaching and working

with a training partner are different.

Training

What people need to do to prepare for Points Race is motorpace. That's a big thing. And race as much as possible, criteriums, road racing, for endurance and I would say racing is the main thing. Race as much as possible, because every race you learn something.

A couple of months prior to Nationals, it's very individual, but you have to train behind the motorcycle between six and twelve hours per week. That's just going off what I used to do. I lived behind the motor when I was preparing and I raced as much as I could. Racing is the best training. If you can, race as much as possible.

Coaching

I'm happy, I'm making money and I don't have to work now other than coaching. I have a maximum number of riders and I charge a set fee. Now I've got a waiting list.

I've only been coaching since March of 1992. I coached a kid in 1981 when I was only 20. I get very vocal and I get very upset when I feel they're not doing what they're capable of doing.

That's a mistake on my part, by yelling too much. Sometimes other riders who are feeling good are listening to me yelling at my riders and they can take advantage of the situation. They can do what I tell my riders to do and beat them.

Right now my goals are:

#1 -- I only want to coach.

#2 -- I want to take every rider I ever coach farther than they've ever been, which I've already succeeded in doing in 1993 and 1994.

I also want to get myself in shape and show that not only can I coach, but I can compete too, on a lower level than I used to, but to show the people that I coach that I've got heart and I've got drive and I don't quit.

If I put a number on I'm going for the win. If I get 5th, I tried to win; if I get 20th, I tried to win. I've never raced in my home town in my life. The have the Whittier Grand Prix, the Las Portales Grand Prix.

I entered a Public race just to have fun with all my guys, they were laughing at me. I wasn't even in good shape, I weighed 210 lbs, and I struggled, but I stayed with the group and because I'm racing such inexperienced people that I was able to use my head and I won the race.

Then all my people that I coached were more receptive to listening to every word I said, because they knew I wasn't in shape, I didn't train, I only rode my bike maybe 50 miles a week, yet I was able to beat these guys who were in great shape. It's heart, and they understand me now.

I have a variety of riders that I'm coaching. Up-and-coming riders, Masters riders -- many of my riders are Masters, 30 and above. I coach riders who are between the ages of 22 to 27, Senior riders who have some talent and some Juniors. With great coaching they can be someone who's successful.

The guy who I see as having the most potential is my number one guy because he's totally determined. In the Senior class it's make it or break it. If you're between the ages of 20 and 30,

go all out now. At least you'll be able to sleep at night five years from now saying "I did everything I could." Win or lose or Bronze Medal or fifth or tenth, at least you made the attempt and you can sleep at night. You gave it your all. And that's what I try to tell them.

If you don't place top five at Nationals, no one knows who you are. It makes me look very good to coach someone who's never done anything special, no one even knows their name and all of a sudden they're placing.

Coaching Women

I coached a woman for two years who I refused to take to Nationals in '92 because I felt that she was not ready. One year later she beat Connie Paraskevin Young in Sprints. It was pretty phenomenal. She retired now. She's 31 years old, and I coached her for two years.

Now I have one I'm coaching who came in 13th at Nationals. She comes to train once a week and she's improved 20%. She's twenty-five. She made 13th. My goal for her now is to win 5th through 8th. That would be a phenomenal success for me as a coach so that's my goal for her.

Women and men are totally opposite. To coach women is a whole different ball game. It's the most difficult thing I've ever done -- it's as hard as being married. It's very difficult, very, very difficult.

The key to coaching women is probably patience, because they're very, number one, emotional. Number two, I would say that they're not as mentally tough.

I'm a very "mentally tough" coach. I'm very intense and I'm very harsh and I'm very tough, and when I have to deal with women, it's harder for me.

Sometimes I get really ticked off like I did in Indianapolis. It's was a

"Women and men are totally opposite. To coach women is a whole different ball game. It's the most difficult thing I've ever -- it's as hard as being married. It's very difficult." Therese Nugent benefits from Mark's coaching.

fist, but I'll slap them on the back of the head hard. You can even say in this day and age that it's physical abuse, but I slap 'em.

I say "Wake up!" and if you don't, I don't want to coach you, because

difficult thing for me to go through and it's hard. I take coaching women very tentatively. If I get into coaching women I want to be paid for it, number one, and number two, it's very hard. They're just emotional. They can have one bad day and it can ruin them for a month.

Coaching Men

Men can have a bad day and you can hit 'em. I don't mean hit 'em with

winning is not everything, but shooting for winning is what you should do. And if you don't shoot for winning, I don't want to coach you. I don't want to coach somebody that wants to stay in the field.

I've told people "If you get fifth and did everything you can to get fifth and if you got second and you blew it, and were a wimp when you should have won, I'd be more happy with

131

fifth, because you tried and you pushed yourself beyond belief". That makes me very happy.

I've coached a friend of mine for 15 years. He just rode for fun in the group. I said "Why don't you race?" In 1992 he got 12th in the Points Race as a Master, this guy's like 47, and this year in Colorado he got Bronze in the 3000 and he got fifth in the Points Race. Now this guy loves me. He wanted to know when to sign the check.

I didn't do anything unusual, I trained him like I train everybody else. He might have done even better, but there are certain guys that are phenomenally better and it's going to take time.

For me as a coach it's very difficult to classify differences between Juniors, the regular Senior racers and the Masters. It's hard and they're all together. I've got a great group of riders. Everybody's happy that I've been training. And now I can help them on the bike too.

Heartaches

My most disappointing thing is that I've been involved in racing nationally and internationally since 1978 when I represented our country at the Junior World's, yet the United States Cycling Federation doesn't want me coaching in any way because of my personality and my style.

Since 1992 there isn't a coach who's come *close* to my results. People have come to me who have never before placed in the top 10 or 15 nationally. After I coached them, they won medals.

I'm very, very disappointed in the USCF because, in my opinion the two best coaches are Gibby Hatton in Pennsylvania and myself. Because we're motivators, we're trainers, and we push people.

You take a guy like Eddie B. who went through a lot of crap and yet he turned us guys into Super Athletes. I wasn't very fond of him, yet he turned American Cycling around on the velodrome as well as on the road, as well as in the Team Time Trial. I mean he made people great. There's nobody like him right now that is around, and it's a disappointing thing.

Right now Marty Nothstein is the greatest American cyclist besides Lance Armstrong, which -- the track and road are totally separate -- Lance Armstrong is the greatest road rider in our country and the top, number one track rider, is Marty Nothstein. He's been coached by Gibby Hatton since he was 16. He's a double World Champion now, yet the Federation doesn't want to hire the best Sprint coach in the world, which is Gibby. It's disappointing. It's a very disappointing thing that we live in a country that is run by money and politics and they are going to do what they want.

Out of the seventeen riders I've coached since '92, I've had 14 National Medals and 7 Gold, and the Federation doesn't call me, doesn't talk to me. I'm very successful, yet they don't want to hire somebody outside of their Federation who also was an American who competed in 9 World Championship events, including the Olympics -- 8 Worlds and 1 Olympic Games -- and they just don't want to ...... I'm very disappointed, obviously it's because of my background.

I'm who I am, I'm not going to mellow out. I only know one way to coach -- I only know one way -- and that's it. There's not one coach in the United States that's been as successful as I have -- not one. And I'm not going back one year, I'm going back 10!

There's nobody who has coached that many National medalists, and I've only been doing it for two years. Why should I change because I want to be hired by the Federation? I'd be making as much money working for them as I am as an Independent. Why go into that political garbage pail and have to deal with that?

The Federation coaches get pay that is pocket money because they don't pay for anything. I know one who is getting paid as a coach who really isn't really a coach. He has never coached anybody and he has no results as a coach. It's a very sad thing. The Board of Directors obviously don't want me involved or they would be calling me and hiring me --for a lot of money!

I'm a very harsh person and I'm very abrupt, but I get results. In coaching you have to take every person as an individual. You coach them as an individual.

If you have to yell at them and maybe even slap them in the face, which I've done, to wake them up, or you have to consult them as a very slow mannered person. You tell 'em "Think about what you're doing and try harder. Don't give up!" Then you have the other person where you have to yell profanity at them and get mad because they're that type of rider.

Changes

The number one change I would like to see in cycling is the coaching issue. I would say that the favoritism of certain people within the cycling community -- but I feel probably that's everywhere in all parts of the world. But the way that they're handling things is bad. If you don't have the coaching you're not going to be successful. That's all there is to it. You look at all the greatest riders of all time -- they had great coaches.

Maybe the real number one is money, number two is coaching. Money is number one in all of the United States.

Even USCF coaches probably make more money on the side than they do from the USCF, from riders who aren't even National caliber riders, through training programs, diary programs, stuff like that, they 're making more than from the Federation. In my opinion it's a joke and a rip-off.

Some people go at it from a business attitude and they're making a ton of money. They're laughing all the way to the bank.

They even coach foreign riders on the side. They bring foreign athletes to American National training camps and it's disgusting. I get very upset by that. If an American coach is being paid by the Federation, they shouldn't be coaching foreign athletes to beat Americans.

And none of this is discussed in the press. Why shouldn't we know how much a foreign country is paying an American coach to coach a foreign rider? I'd like to know that. It's the most disgusting thing.

Velodromes

My home track was Encino until Dominguez Hills was built in 1982, now that's my home track. That's where I do all my coaching and riding. I rode Encino from 1973 to 1981.

My least favorite velodrome is Trexlertown because they root for foreigners over Americans. My favorite track is right here -- Dominguez, my home track. I've had some good races here at Encino and Dominguez.

The problem with Southern California is that there's no racing on the velodromes any more. There's no racing at Dominguez Hills since I retired in '89. It's disgusting, just disgusting. I go out to a criterium and there's 1000 competitors in all the different events. You go to a track and there's 70 riders.

There's not enough press and P.R. and televised action. All people look at is Greg LeMond and Andy Hampsten and Miguel Indurain and the Tour de France -- and they're dreamin'. For a spectator, track racing's the greatest.

Advice to New Riders

If a rider does not live near a velodrome wants to get into velodrome racing they need to contact someone who knows what they're doing. They need to contact someone who has some kind of experience.

It's not like riding on the street, it's a thing that you have to learn. You have to have a track to learn how to ride track. There's no other way.

Finding a "best event" is up to a coach. I can spot a rider within seconds. I can watch a rider for three, one, two laps and know -- Sprinting you have to have fast twitch muscles and you have to have massive acceleration. If you have slow acceleration but good stamina and endurance you're a Pursuiter, Team Pursuiter or Point racer.

Or, if you have long lasting endurance you can be a Kilo rider. That's the hardest event there is on the track. I've ridden every event there is on the track and there's no event harder.

The trick to Sprints today is pure massive speed and power. Once you get in the top five, then tactics come into it, but it's just raw speed and power.

To up-and-coming riders who want to race track, I would say find a velodrome, find a coach and talk to him.

Master's Racing

Master's riders try harder than anyone I've ever seen. They work a lot of hours, they pay their own money and to watch them at the Master's Nationals in Colorado I was simply super impressed, by the times and by the effort they put out. The effort was very impressive. I was happy because of the nine people who went there, seven who won medals were people I coached. So I was real happy for them.

As involved as I am, getting upset at these things totally disrupts me. I'm the same as I always am. It's very destructive for me to coach a rider and see a rider fall apart that I've coached. I'll go back and it's emotionally rough on me.

I have ulcers. I'm trying to work on it, but I have to be careful. I had them really bad after Nationals. I had to go to the hospital and stuff. But that's just me. And my blood pressure's bad.

But that's just a part of it, it's part of racing. My health is not good, but that's why I'm riding my bike again. I've lost weight and my blood pressure's down. I don't have caffeine any more, and I exercise. I ride every day.

Mark calls lap times to his Team Pursuiters (David Clinger, James Ansite, John Walrod and Kenny Fritts) at the 1994 Junior National Championships.

They won -- Mark was a proud man.

Chapter 9

◥ *Madison* ◥

The Madison is a Team Points Race of riders who alternately throw each other into the action. One rider rests while the other races. As in the Points Race, riders Sprint for Points every five laps with Double-Points in the middle and again in the final Sprint.

History

The Madison is the Grand-daddy of American bicycle racing and is as American as baseball -- I mean, <u>really</u>. It was named for Madison Square Garden, where it was born in 1898 when promoters of bicycle racing were prohibited from allowing riders to ride an inhumane twenty-four hours nonstop. The new law said that the maximum period riders could race was twelve. Promoters, undaunted, responded by forming teams of two riders who each rode in the twelve hour shifts permitted by law.

While the long number of hours has given way to less lengthy contests, the Madison has survived as a distinct race due to it's unique character which simultaneously builds bicycle handling skills, endurance, and sprinting ability in its participants. This unique team approach also adds one more ingredient to strategies similar to the most unpredictable Points Race.

Qualifying

Category 1, 2, and Professional riders may all compete in the Madison at the U. S. National Championships.

In spite of the wide latitude in competitors admitted to the race, there was only one Madison Final, no preliminary heats, at the U. S. National Championships in 1994. This is not a race that attracts vast numbers of riders. If it were, heats would be necessary.

Intentional contact between members of the same team who ride up and down track into and out of a larger race can be intimidating. Top bicycle handling skills are a must.

The Start

As in the Points Race, riders line up at the rail or fence to begin the race with a rolling start.

While all riders line up to receive race instructions, only half of the riders (one from each team) will actually roll around, ready to begin the race. The other half are excused by officials to leave the start/finish area after instructions have been given. They roll out to find a place on the fence away from the start area, somewhere around the track. They wait at the chosen location until the race has begun and it's time to take their turn.

Meanwhile, the first half of the team, grouped in the starting area, will be told when to roll out for the first lap. If they are grouped and moving at a fairly slow pace as they come around, the Starter fires the starting pistol and the race begins.

In the event that riders are not grouped properly or if they are moving too fast, they will be sent around again, until they get it right.

Details of race etiquette must be reviewed with riders before the start

Long time competitor Butch Stinton ('71 & '72 Team Pursuit Champion) shows how to exchange with partner Sean Watkins (right). Bike handling skills learned over many years come in handy in this race. Stinton is still one of bicycling's tough competitors.

of the race. Riders must take care not to get in the way of others during exchanges and when entering and exiting the track.

If riders are required to rest in a specific zone, they must be so instructed by officials prior to the start of the race. If they are prohibited from exchanging during the last lap or last 200 meters of a sprint, they must also be so instructed prior to the start.

The Race

Once the race has begun, the starting riders will race until it is time for the relief rider to take over. The relief rider will swing onto the track from his uptrack position on the fence, partly to take advantage of the track's downhill surface which allows the rider to gain rapid momentum with less effort.

In order for the exchange of competitors to be official, a rider must at least draw even with his partner.

Newer Madison riders are more likely to touch, push or pull their partners until they get the hang of more aggressive actions. Riders are not required to touch their partners at all, but must at least pull even.

Top Madison riders perfect "handslings" which allow the relieved partner to "throw" the relieving rider into the fray, getting up to speed much more quickly than he would be able to by himself. Top riders have techniques designed for maximum efficiency and effectiveness. Practice also helps!

If an "exchange" occurs without riders at least drawing even (a "wireless pickup") referees may penalize the team one lap.

Entering and leaving the racing surface must occur on the Blue Band on either the home or back stretch. An exception to this rule is the Start, where a rider enters the race with a rolling start from the rail.

Relieved riders must stay to the inside of the track until approaching riders have passed. Then they may swing up track and either pedal slowly or hang onto the rail until it is time for another exchange.

Exchanges tend to occur on the straightaways for a couple of reasons: first, the incoming rider can take advantage of the banking from the rail out of the turns to get up to speed more quickly. Second, exchanges are safer on the straights.

The safety factor is not simply a safety issue but also an issue of being able to pass others more easily in an area where speeds are more stable than the corners where banking changes speeds rapidly.

Riders become masters at using the banking for acceleration and deceleration to gain maximum assistance from the physics of the track for both resting and getting up to speed.

With the rapid acceleration and decline in speed, Madisons often appear to be a free-for-all until spectators know how to read the action. Then they become an exhibition of bicycle race artistry with more variables for the rider to keep in mind at one time than any other event.

The rider not only needs to worry about his own riding variables, but he must give equal consideration to those of his partner, using the track to his benefit and working around and among all the other riders and their partners coming and going from the race area. Maximum alertness is required for riders to race efficiently for themselves and not collide with others, including less experienced riders who are trying to do the same.

Scoring

Madisons are scored the same as Points Races. Points are awarded every five laps. Double-Points are awarded halfway through the race and again at the finish.

Points	Double Points
1st = 5 points	1st = 10 points
2nd = 3 points	2nd = 6 points
3rd = 2 points	3rd = 4 points
4th = 1 point	4th = 2 points

Officials are able to keep track of points and laps due to two factors. First, riders both wear the same competition number, so it is the **number** belonging to the team which accumulates points and laps, not a particular rider. Second, both riders must wear the same jersey, which also aids in identification.

Mishaps

In the event of a mishap (crash, equipment failure, etc.) a rider may be assigned to stay alongside another designated rider who is a member of another team in the same position on the track, until his partner returns to the race. The rider must enter and leave the race with his temporarily assigned co-rider.

If a bicycle is damaged, it must be shown to officials immediately. If they verify that a mishap is legitimate, the team affected will not be penalized by a loss of laps. If the team is unable to return to the track within 5 km of racing, the Chief Referee may remove the team from competition.

Reteaming

In the event that one partner of a team cannot continue, whether due to retirement or mishap, the other partner many be reteamed with another rider who has lost a partner. This reteaming is at the discretion of the Chief Referee.

If two teams are combined into a new team, the lower lap count and number of points of the two teams shall be used as a starting point for resumption of competition. If the new team is tied with another team, they will be placed behind that team.

These rules reflect an attempt to be fair to those who suffer setbacks without encouraging riders to take advantage of difficulties, such as rest with no lap penalties, etc. American bicycle racing rules tend toward these kinds of compromise.

The Finish

When the lead rider completes either the specified distance or the specified time, a double gunshot signifies the end of the race. If the race is supposed to finish at a specific time, a gunshot will signify one more lap and the beginning of the final sprint.

Scoring in this race is the same as that in a Points Race, but officials must work a little harder to keep track of riders and their positions. In a Points Race, riders are consistently riding at the bottom of the track in a pack. It is fairly easy to see when someone is off the front or off the back.

In a Madison, the exchanges happen virtually anywhere and both riders are up and down the track continually, so it is a little more visually confusing.

Summary

The Madison is America's own original bicycle race. It was the most popular event in the heyday of velodrome racing. Six-day races continue to survive in Europe and locations around the world, though they are seldom seen today in this country. Track enthusiasts hope to change this, so look for a resurgence of Madison racing on the portable tracks. It is a great training race for development of riders at all levels.

From 1978 to 1983, Madison Championships were held as a distinct event. In 1985, after a year off, they were added to the Senior National Championships where they have been contested annually ever since.

In local, weekly events, organizers can vary the points awards and add all manner of cash, merchandise or other primes if they choose, the same as in the Points Race.

The added factor of team exchanges restricts planned rest time somewhat, during which these kinds of awards would otherwise be available. Local race coordinators can devise all manner of prizes to encourage good racing, to the benefit of spectators.

Madison
Danny Van Haute

Danny Van Haute (nicknamed "The Beast") has served as a role model to many aspiring riders. Watching Danny race, it is obvious that he simply loves racing. He is a magician at finding holes to barrel through, leaving others standing when it looked like he would surely take them down. He coaches with his soul.

Danny was U.S. National Madison Champion in 1978, '80 and '83 and Team Pursuit Champion in 1978, '84, and '85. He was Master's National Champion in both the Pursuit ('90) and the Madison ('91).

Today he continues his competitive career at the Master's level while serving as Assistant US National Team Coach under Craig Griffin for the endurance riders (road and track) including Team Pursuit, Points and Madison on the track.

I was born October 22, 1956 and grew up on the north side of Chicago, Illinois.

How I Got Started

My dad got me started in bike racing in about 1967 as a Midget. They had Midget classes back then. We had races every Tuesday and Thursday nights in Northbrook and Kenosha. My dad was from Europe, from Belgium, and my mom is Dutch, so they knew cycling. Chicago had a lot of people with Belgian backgrounds, coming from Europe to live in the area.

My dad had a lot of buddies and family members in Chicago. We got started like that, from my dad's cycling background. He didn't race. He coached a little bit and went to all the races and was a spectator. He knew all the riders, all the old riders, so he knows all the stories, all the "war stories" in cycling. So that's how I got started, with my dad showing me the ropes.

Aside from the track races were on Tuesday and Thursday nights, there was such good racing going on in the Midwest, you could go anywhere on Saturday and Sunday and race a criterium or a road race. Illinois, Wisconsin, Iowa, Michigan, Indiana, every weekend you had somewhere to go. We'd just pack up the car and go.

My biggest claim to fame back then was third place in the Midget Nationals in Encino, California in 1968. Gibby Hatton won. We've been friends since then. He's one of my best friends now. We talk about once a month. So that was my claim to fame.

It was still a hobby, it was just for fun. I did other things in high school too. I ran cross country and played hockey in grammar school.

I turned down a hockey scholarship at Northeastern to race Six-days in Europe, so I was actually a hockey player too. I weighed 195 one year. I put on a lot of muscle. I was lifting a lot. It was fun.

That year I lived seven months in Europe doing Six-days. I still have

"My strength was that I could do anything on the track. I've done every event and medalled in all of them except Match Sprinting. There are not many people right now who medalled in every event at Nationals."

relatives in Europe, my grandmother still lives there along with uncles, cousins -- my mom and dad go back every other year.

My mom was as enthusiastic about it as my dad. They were very much into the cycling scene, so much so that sometimes there would be three or four riders staying at the house. My mom would cook these enormous meals, seven-course meals for breakfast, knowing the bike riders, plus, it's just the way European women are. "I cook this, that. You eat, eat. ."

A lot of riders loved to come over to our house because they knew they'd get fed well. They didn't mind it. The riders needed it. There are still guys getting paid for racing, but not as many. There are only a handful of corporate sponsored teams right now, back then there were a little bit more, probably 10 or 12.

Now there are only 3 or 4 who are really making a good living off of it. It's pretty sad. We're losing riders left and right. They can't do it on their own and their parents are saying "Hey, wait a minute, time to go to school or do something else."

I have one younger brother. He didn't do any cycling, just the money-making sports: football, baseball, he did all that, all the way through college.

The people who helped me the most were my mom and dad. Then there was my first coach -- probably my dad helping me a lot, not pushing me a lot, but just pushing me at the right times. If he pushed me constantly I wouldn't be in this sport today. But you grow up a little bit

My next coach was John Vande Velde (Senior Pursuit Champion, 1969, '70, '72). He was on the Munich Olympic Team. He was from Chicago too, and he took care of me a lot. Those are the two guys early in my career who guided me the most, my dad and ma and then John Vande Velde took over. He helped me throughout my Junior years and then from '74 to 1980 he was my coach.

As a matter of fact, I think I rode a couple of Madisons with Vande Velde and Jim Ochowitz. I rode with Mike Neel and Vande Velde and Ochowitz because they all grew up in the Midwest too. I was a last year Junior.

Everyone wanted to ride with me. They were just coming to the end of their career and I was just beginning. I had a few opportunities to ride with them and it was fun. Roger Young, Jim Ochowitz, Vande Velde, Ron Skarin, Eddie Van Guise, too.

I made the Junior Worlds Team in 1974 and that's what started it there. I kept on playing hockey to stay fit in the winter time. In fact, I still played hockey when I came out to San Diego.

I was a second alternate on the '76 Olympic Team that went to Montreal. John coached me then. I didn't get to go, only the first alternate did, but they did write it up as "second alternate".

That was Team Pursuit. That was a push that kept me going at that point in my career.

It kept me going until 1980. Then making that Team, well, heck, might as well go until 1984 too! Then there started being money to support it.

Danny (right) with one of his mentors, John VandeVelde. **"There are all kinds of things to do in a Madison, sprinting, chasing, breaking away, sitting on a wheel, you have to have good bike handling skills. There's strategies involved, it's a thinking event. If you have a good prize list, the riders will come, just like "Field of Dreams."**

Actually that started happening in '81. If you're getting paid to do work and ride your bike, might as well continue it. I always say, if someone will pay you to ride your bike, you might as well continue it no matter how old you are.

Eric, Roger and Me

The way it started with me, Eric Heiden and Roger Young was that Jim Ochowitz and Sheila Young lived in Lake Placid and Sheila was the organizer of the speed skating venue

for the 1980 Winter Olympics. They needed volunteers and Roger and I said we'd come help. Connie Carpenter was with us at that time. She's a real good friend of Sheila's. We all stayed at Jim and Sheila's house.

We had the best jobs. Sheila said "Here's your clothing. Get your credentials and work on the ice." We had the best seats in the house. We were right on the ice. Eric and Beth Heiden were getting swamped with reporters every day because of the five medals Eric won that year.

All of a sudden Sheila or someone said "Keep the reporters away from Eric" so Roger and I were sort of like his body guards for a while. So that's how that started.

Then he started racing bicycles.

Speed skaters ride their bikes in the summer time to keep in shape because it is the same muscles, but then Eric wanted to start racing bicycles. So who do you hang out with?

Well, he knew us and he knew Jim, so he said "Hey, I want to race, let's go!" so he and Roger and Greg LeMond and I hung out that year, 1980.

The next year Greg went to Europe while Eric, Roger and I were on the 7-Eleven team. The seven guys who were the original members of the 7-Eleven team were me, Eric Heiden, Roger Young, Ron Heyman, Tom Schuler, Jeff Bradley, and Greg Demgen. Those were the Magnificent Seven. The original guys. And they're all still around, not necessarily racing, but in cycling somewhere. That was a pretty good year, 1980. A fun year.

Eric almost made the Olympic Team in cycling. He got second in the Kilo. Brent Emery won. Eric almost made two Olympic Teams in the same year. He's done some amazing stuff. His attitude in cycling was great. "Let's go ride a hundred miles to here" or he would do interviews and photo sessions for days at a time and not bike and all of a sudden he'd come out and do Paris-Roubaix or something like that. I've known of him doing that.

He's going to med school and Jim Ochowitz would say "Hey, I need you for a couple of weeks in Europe" and Eric would say "I haven't raced in a while" or "I haven't trained for five days" but he'd just go over and do the race and finish. He was a natural. He'd just go over and do the race, start the race and finish.

Then there are other stories, like, hanging out with Whitehead was quite an experience, but some of those stories can't be printed!

In 1985 I became a permanent resident of California. From 1981 to 1985 all my winters were spent in California because it was just too cold in Chicago. I played hockey here in the winter time. I haven't really skated for the last three years -- I have on roller blades, but not the ice. I skated once this year with (son) Trevor.

I did a little speed skating with Eric Heiden in 1979 and '80 and we got to be friends, along with Roger Young and Greg LeMond. We spent the summer of 1980 together after he won his five Gold Medals. The four of us traveled all over the place. It was a good summer. Roger and I were just on the band wagon with Eric after he won his five Gold Medals. It was just a joy ride everywhere. Everybody knew him and he got the royal treatment.

Life Today

I've been cycling all my life. In the winter time I manage a tree farm from October through December. This will be my seventh year coming up. That's the season. In October you start getting things ready for opening day in November.

One year when my career was winding down I decided I had to do something else than just lift weights and ride. I was getting kind of tired of it, kind of burned out. There was an ad in the paper for help at a Christmas tree farm so I went there, interviewed and they hired me. The next year I was the manager, so I've been managing

the farm for about five years.

It works out great time-wise. Now that I'm working with the Federation nothing's happening in the months of November-December.

Other than that my income has just been from cycling, with the big teams that I rode for; 7-Eleven, Schwinn Icy-Hot, Schwinn Wheaties -- those were the days.

We were the first of the riders who got paid to race. It started in 1981 when I rode for 7-Eleven. I was 23. I stayed at home when I was a Junior and three or four years of my Senior years. I stayed at home and raced out of home. My dad and mom helped me out a great deal.

The Madisons -- the Best Training for Racing!

I've done a lot of Madisons. I did 28 Six-days and those are Madison races. Six-day bike races are usually Madison races. I've done 28 of those all around the world. Tahiti, they have a track there, they have a really big Six-day in Tahiti. New Caledonia has a track. I did that Six-day. A whole bunch in Europe, two or three in Canada, but mostly in Europe.

Madisons go back to my background on Tuesday and Thursday nights at Northbrook and Kenosha.

They always had a Madison because number one, it's the best training you can get. It's interval training, you do a sprint, you chase, you get up to the top of the track, you throw in your partner, so you're resting two laps, then you get thrown in again, so it's just intervals, intervals, intervals. The best training. But, also, it's a great spectator sport.

Spectators love the Madison, they came out to see the Madison all the time. We had tons of people in the bleachers at Northbrook and Kenosha. It was amazing.

I won the National Madison Championships three or four times. It is the specialty race for me, I like that the most. I always try to push to put Madisons on, even to this day in San Diego.

The problem is, if you only have four or five teams, it's boring to the crowd. You've got to have 10 or 12 teams. For some reason nobody wants to ride it. I just don't know. They're afraid of it. You've got to start. If it's Tuesday night training night or Thursday night training night, you've got to start somewhere. Someone's got to do it because it's such a good race to watch from a spectators view, plus, it's one of the best races for you to race.

There are all kinds of things to do in a Madison. There's Sprinting, there's chasing, there's breaking away, there's sitting on the wheel, you have to have good bike handling, there's strategies involved, when to pick up your partner -- two laps before the sprint or a half a lap before the sprint --it's a thinking event. You have to *think*, too.

It's not like a Pursuit, where you just go out and do it, you don't even have to think. It's a fun race. I like it a lot.

Scoring in Madisons can be confusing, but you get used to it. What helps is a good announcer who knows what's happening. The announcer in San Diego is really good, Ralph Elliott. He's good. Eddie Van Guise is good,

he knows what he's doing with Madisons. Joe Saling's good, I don't have any problem with him.

I don't know who the announcers in the Midwest are anymore, I can't remember their names. What helps the most about the announcers is telling the audience who's in the lead or who's behind or who's this or that.

All three of those guys were bike racers, so they know what's going on. They know before the officials! They could probably keep the points and officiate the race and still announce. That's how good they are. They can keep the crowd going, telling them what I'm probably thinking, during the race -- "what's Danny going to set up with his partner? how many points does he have?" They just have to keep talking.

There's no low points in announcing the race. One guy shut off the mike for a while. The crowd doesn't know what's going on, so they need to keep talking all the time. There's always something going on. I know what the other rider has to do to beat me, so I can always sense when they're coming over the top or they're coming underneath or just sitting on me. I can pretty well sense that. You've got to think what you have to do, but you also have to think what the other team has to do to beat you also.

Training

The most helpful thing in training for Madison's is doing Madisons and road stuff, short intensity stuff. Both types of things. For Madisons you need all kinds of abilities.

Endurance, because Madison's are long races -- well, not all of them, but most of the ones that I've been in like Six-day racing. They're three, four hours at a time during the day. Even an hour Madison takes endurance, though.

You need speed, so Sprinting, the ability to close gaps, like maybe somebody has a half a lap gap and you've got to close it. So you need everything -- endurance, speed, everything.

People coming on and off the track is not bothersome if you're used to it. That's why we go back to why more tracks need to put on Madisons and why riders are afraid of them. They think it's too confusing.

You have to do a few Madisons in training first, and then you get used to it, you know it. Then it's not a problem at all.

Everybody has a different jersey on, each team has a different jersey, and you know where those guys are. You say "This guy's behind me, so his partner's going to be coming down pretty soon to get thrown in."

So it's not confusing once you understand what's going on. At least, I don't think so. And it's such a neat event. My first experience was "Yeah, put me in there! I want to do that!" Little kids saying "That's relay races, let's do it!"

Race Strategies and Coaching

I think right now we're lagging in strategy and techniques in riding races. The Federation has done so many clinics about psychological aspects of racing, aerodynamics, how to train --

but they never spend time talking about the strategies of racing.

We can have a guy who does a great VO2 on a Turbo Trainer, but we put him in a race and he does nothing. He doesn't know what he's doing. He can be a great Time Trialist but we put him in a pack-style race and he doesn't know anything.

In 1981 Danny was one of the "hot dudes" of the 7-Eleven team which included Roger Young and Eric Heiden. San Diego.

Now the Federation is taking that point too. I'm supposed to do three clinics about strategy and tactics for Juniors, Junior parents -- anybody can come. I'm going to do my three in April. And they're free, the Federation is not charging.

They're saying a lot of coaches and a lot of people know how to train people, but they don't know how to tell them how to ride a race. That's where I come in.

I may not know as much about the scientific stuff, but I do know how to

tell a guy how to race and say "Hey, this is where you screwed up and this is how you should ride the race."

That's why Craig (Griffin) and I make a good team, he knows all the scientific stuff, like "Oh, your heart rate is low today, you're going to ride hard today" or "Your heart rate is really high, like 10 beats high, I think you should stay off the bike today." I'm learning that too now, but with me with so many races under my belt, we make a good team, me and Craig.

With the kids I'm working with at San Diego Velodrome with Doreen Smith-Williams, the AAF program, we have kids now who have been in the program, almost National Team guys, who we've brought up through the levels of "I didn't know how to ride a Paceline."

Now they're almost National Team riders and we have to tell them "Hey, wait a minute, what did I just tell you last week about how to ride a Miss 'n' Out and you just did the total opposite thing last Tuesday. What's the deal?"

"Oh, yeah, yeah, yeah"

Five clinics is not going to do it. Ride the race over and over, every race. Every race you learn something. You've got to keep on telling them. Sometimes it's frustrating.

"I told you ten times and you're still doing this and you still lost the race!"

Best Memories

One of my favorite achievements was winning the 1984 Olympic Trials. That was pretty satisfying since I went into that not being one of the favorites and not being -- I was kind of a rebel and I didn't go with the Federation programs that year so I wasn't really considered a favorite. But I peaked at the right time. In Team Pursuit I was the second guy to be picked.

I won the Points Race Trials so I was automatically going right into the Olympics. They couldn't do nothin' about it, they couldn't kick me out, they couldn't do nothin'. I won the Trials. So that was one of them.

The thing I hate the most is people calling me a "trackie". In a way, that's true, I made all my National Teams, Olympic Teams, Pan Am Teams, and National Championships on the track, but endurance track riders also ride the roads and do criteriums.

I won my share of big criteriums, like Super Week, I probably won three, four or even five criteriums at Super Week. Wheat Thins Races -- I won at least four of those, I've got the trophies right here to prove them. So I have a lot of good moments.

Super Week, Green Bay Criterium there are 10,000 people there and I'm sort of a local boy, from Chicago, things like that. I could probably go on and on about favorite moments, but the one that sticks out in my mind is Olympic Trials in '84. I won more than "just" the race.

I don't ride the 1-2 criteriums anymore. I just do Masters. I just ride two, three hours a day, if that.

I can still win the Omnium just

because I have the smarts to do it. Just because I have the head. I laugh at them and say "You guys do this for a living and I do it part time now, and I can still win the Omnium?" There's something wrong there.

Racing

I don't think I have any particular gift. My weakness when I was racing was probably hill climbing. I can't climb that well. I'm not afraid to do the big hills, it's just that I can't stay with the good climbers, like Andy Hampsten. He just goes up too fast!

That was my weakness. Any time there was a lot of climbing, I was off the back. I could stay with them until the 75 mile mark, but if there was a big climb at mile 80, I was off the back and they would just go a lot faster. They were lighter. My climbing was my weakest.

My strength was that I could have done anything on the track. I wasn't afraid of Match Sprinting. I didn't do great at Match Sprinting, but I didn't train for that. If I'd trained for it I might have done great at it, but I didn't like Match Sprinting that well.

I did everything. There are not many people right now who medaled in every event at Nationals. I've done every event and medaled in all of them except Match Sprinting. That's the only event I didn't medal in.

I medalled in Kilo, Pursuit, Team Pursuit, Points Race -- there are not many guys who have done that. I think Whitehead has done the same. I haven't medalled in Sprints, he hasn't medalled in Pursuit.

I think another guy is Brent Emery, Harvey Nitz -- but now I can't think of anyone today who has medaled in as many events. I'm talking top three places. My versatility is my strength.

Cycling Culture

I would still enjoy doing Six-day races in Europe. I would encourage everybody to go over there. Anybody who has asked me "What should I do in the winter?" I always tell them to go to Belgium or go to Holland and just set up shop there.

It's just the best training, the best experience, the best bike handling lessons -- if they're lagging a little bit on bike handling, they should go there. For road, for track, anything. It's just the best. You can find almost anything there that you need.

Once you get established families are so good to you. They like Americans. They like any foreigners. Americans, Australians, New Zealanders -- they'll find you a place to stay. It's just their nature.

Cycling and soccer are the number one sports there. Here it's baseball, football, hockey and basketball and cycling comes in dead last. Families don't know about cycling as much here, so they're more hesitant to put you up, but in Europe they're like "Yeah, come on over, we like cycling.

We'll put you up in one of our rooms." It's a great atmosphere.

I think the reason I became a top rider is partly just because I like sports. Cycling was talked about all the time. When my dad would have his once a week outing with the boys playing cards or whatever they would talk about cycling and I was there. "What did Eddy Merckx do last week in the Tour?" or this or that. They were listening to the radio all the time during the Tour, to the results. I was brought up in that way.

Now kids watch Tony Gwynn with the Padres and they're out playing baseball every day. That was what was unique about me growing up, I was brought up in that way. My parents and all my dad's buddies were all Belgians and all they talked about was soccer and cycling. I just happened to listen and I'm just sports oriented.

My dad went to hockey games. He had season passes to the Chicago Blackhawks and we just liked sports. My brother is too.

To this day, when he comes over to visit me we have to put on our roller blades and play roller-hockey. Now I have to get him a mountain bike, he's moving to Boulder, Colorado. I was just brought up with it. Not only cycling, but all sports. I'll watch anything.

Changes

I wouldn't change anything about Madison races except put more on! I think the riders have

Regional Coach Danny Van Haute checks out the performance of San Diego Bicycle Club Junior Mark Fitzgerald. When Fitzgerald beat the goal performance time by over a minute, his name was sent in to Colorado Springs to qualify him for training camp invitations. Mark was a happy guy.

Madison teams line up for instructions prior to half the team departing for places around the velodrome. The other half of the team will roll around for one lap and, if they're grouped together when they come around, they'll get the gun and the race is on!

to be more aggressive about that event. They know it's one of the best spectator events but they're afraid to do it. Or they're afraid to fall or whatever. But I would definitely try to put on more races.

That way we get the riders is the way they got them in Northbrook. Riders were afraid to ride it. They'd say "I want to do a Points Race" but Northbrook decided "Hey, we're going to have a Madison tonight no matter how many teams there are. If there are only three teams, we're going to put a race on." And they did.

The riders said "These promoters are serious, they're not going to have what I want to have, a Sprint race or a Points Race. I guess I'll enter the Madison." After two weeks like that everybody entered.

The promoters just took a stand. They just said "We don't care. If there are only three teams we're going to run it and we'll run it all year long like that if you riders don't want to ride." They had a meeting in the infield and said "This is what we want. It's best for you, it's best for the crowd." Even

though three teams is not real exciting, eventually those guys just got on the bike and did the Madison.

Then all of a sudden we had ten, twelve teams against ten, twelve teams and it was exciting. So I would tell the promoters "Hey, just start doing it, you'll get the teams."

Other changes I'd like to see is for us to look at our Junior program and even lower programs than that. Who do we have? Our depth in the Federation is not that good right now.

Who's going to be our Olympic riders in the year 2000? I don't know. Right now our 13 and 14 year olds -- what programs do we have for them? Not many, not at all. Nothing.

We're changing that now. We're trying to do something this year -- Junior I.D. clinics, which are clinics for non-licensees. We're going to put

them to a test and put them on some bikes. If I see somebody who has a great VO2 at 13 or 14 years old I'm going to put him in the direction of a club who will help them, sign up, and see what happens, or tell them about the AAF program. We'll supply a bike at the track and a helmet, and so on.

I think that's the first step, a USCF program for the non-licensed riders. You never know, one out of a hundred. If you get one Lance Armstrong -- one will do it. So that we have to start -- get those kids involved.

That's what the AAF program, the Amateur Athletic Federation has done. We've taken kids out of the barrio and we've put them through classes and they keep coming back. Now one of them is pretty good. His dad bought him a bike and I think he's going to be a good rider.

Now we have a program that I think started two years ago, the San Marcos Migrant Kids. They bus those kids in, about 25 of them every week, they bus them down to San Diego. We put them on a track bike and they do a work out where we teach them how to ride, how to pass people first, then they go race.

If we only get one person out of that group, than that program is successful, plus, we're keeping them off the streets. It's only two hours on the track, but it's another 45 minutes to an hour bus ride there and back, so that's four hours we kept them off the streets.

Velodromes

My home tracks were Northbrook (Illinois) and Kenosha, Wisconsin. I went back and forth every Tuesday and Thursday nights for races. It was good -- we could do four races a week. On the weekends we rode criteriums and road races.

I haven't ridden Minnesota yet, but since Minnesota is pretty much like a European track I'd probably like it, but I haven't ridden it.

My favorite track would probably have to be T-Town. That's a hard question because I grew up in Northbrook and Kenosha and I've had so many good results there and good memories.

A lot of people would probably say that Northbrook only has 18 degrees banking and T-Town is so much better, but I've had such good experiences there and good memories everywhere, it's really hard to say.

I'd probably say, of tracks in the U.S. T-Town, Northbrook and Kenosha are my favorites because they bring back so many memories.

In Europe it would probably be Ghent. Ghent and Rotterdam. Those are my favorites tracks in Europe.

Purely to ride on, without looking at programs or any of that stuff, San Diego's nice. It was falling apart a little bit, but they're fixing it up now. It's in a nice park, Balboa Park. It's open all the time. Some tracks aren't open all the time.

T-Town's not open all the time. I can ride San Diego on my road bike, do a few intervals on the track, not worry about cars, and ride home. San Diego is nice.

Least favorite would probably be a track in Milwaukee that's pretty flat

-- Brown Deer Park. That's probably my least favorite, because if you go really, really fast, you can't hold the turn and you'll slide right off the track. It's flatter than Northbrook.

I've seen guys when I was a Midget and Intermediate, Jim Rossi and all those guys, they would Sprint down

Danny (right) with Erin Hartwell and Marty Nothstein. In a contest of legs, Danny wins "most highly veined from years of competition." Marty plans to claim the title in a few years.

the back straights so fast they couldn't hold the Pole position and they'd slide off the track. It was open (no fence). You don't want to sit in those turns as a spectator! The straightaways would be the best seats.

Advice to New Riders

Riders who want to get involved should ask around for which club in the area has coaches in the club who can guide them to get them started. They should find out if there are any programs at the velodrome like the AAF program.

I don't think you need a $2000-3000 bike to start with. How do you know if a kid is going to like the sport? Yesterday I heard a kid in Northern California is looking for a coach. The parents are buying him a road and track bike which are $3000 bucks just for a frame and the kid is only 16 years old.

That's kind of ridiculous. We don't

even know if the kid likes the sport yet. He's just starting out. It's maybe his second or third year. That's kind of going overboard. But I guess the family has a lot of money. Hey, maybe I should coach him! (laughs)

But I hear things like that and I just roll my eyes. First get him into a club, which he probably is, but I just roll my eyes. To get started anyone interested should just ask around. Don't just take one opinion. See what they have to offer for the kids.

Focusing on a particular event on the track takes time, especially for a 15 or 16 year old starting out.

Mark Gorski was a road rider before he became a Sprinter. Saronni, the Italian Champion, was at the Junior roads in '74 with me as a Sprinter. He got second place to Gibby Hatton in the Sprints and he turned out to be a great road rider. He won Worlds on the road one year.

So even when you're a Junior you don't know. Those are two examples, one of: a road rider who turned into a great Sprinter and the other a Sprinter who turned in to a great road rider.

When you're 15 or 16 I argue the point of "Hey, I want to be a Sprinter. Teach me how to Sprint." "Okay, I'll teach you how to Sprint, but you're going to be a Sprinter when you become 18 or 19." I would wait until you're a last year Junior and then concentrate on one event.

Still, after you concentrate on it you might even change again. You're still young. You might say "Hey, this is too hard to train for a Kilo" or "I want to be a criterium or road rider."

If there is no track nearby, the track workout done on the track can be applied to the road somehow. If you have a good stretch with no cars.

Vande Velde used to tell me "Practice your starts when you come to a stop light. Stop, stand still, then go. Practice your starts that way."

You could do that on the road, no problem. Eventually, like once a month, you have to go to a track and get engaged in a pack-style race, but if you're doing criteriums every weekend, like 100 man fields, that's pretty dangerous too, isn't it?

So you'll learn your bike handling from that, riding criteriums. Then getting to the track won't be a problem. You've had riders on your wheel, beside you, rubbing elbows, elbowing your hip, or this or that. For instance if a guy lives in Las Vegas and he wants to ride the track, can he train for it? Yeah, he can.

But eventually you're going to have to start riding, once a month or once a week, you're going to have to make that trip to the track somehow. If it's not possible then maybe a month before Nationals or so you should get to the velodrome and start doing the weekly races and start training on them. It's not impossible at all.

Master's Racing

My primary career years were all of the 80s, '80 to '90. I've ridden (Category) "1-2" races on the track recently, but it's just for fun. I can still kick some booties. It's fun for the last two years, a lot of the guys come to San Diego to train.

I will still do Master's racing. It's just my nature. I have to race. Today everyone is worried about their fitness. One way I do it is by riding. I still would like to race.

I don't have the time now to train five-six hours a day to be competitive with the "1"s and "2"s. People are doing it -- look at Kent Bostick, he's 41 years old and he's still winning races with the "1"s and "2"s.

With Master's you can train one hour a day. I think I'll always do some type of racing until I'm . . . 60 years old. Hopefully I'll break Vic Copeland's records when I'm 60! Look at that guy. I'll always do something. Number one, I like it, and two, I feel better. Even with Monica (my wife) she has to go run or do weights or do something. We feel much better. We're just used to it. Even during October or November when I'm working at the farm 10-12 hours a day, once a week I get a day off and go mountain biking or I did something.

I just have to get my fix! It's an addiction. Instead of doing drugs I work out, if it's on the bike or running or roller blading or something, just to get my heart rate up. It's kind of rubbing off on Trevor (my son), too.

Good Racing

What I've been thinking about for several years now is, since San Diego has such good weather in the winter time, putting on a Three-day or a Six-day type race here. The Vandedrome was in San Diego and we got the teams, because everybody wants to ride in the winter time.

The Pan Am Games were in March and the National Team was in San Diego in January and February. Everybody rode it. That was a lot of fun. PrimeSports filmed it and it was on TV several times. It will be back again in late 1995.

The Federation has been talking

Throwing your partner into the race can get kind of tricky when you're on 45 degree banking, you're on a direct drive bicycle and you're trying to win a race.

about winter programs, "We should have tracks -- San Diego, L.A., Ft. Lauderdale, that are in good warm weather states -- we should have our riders ride track even in the winter time instead of doing weights or this or that."

If you have a good prize list, the riders will come. Just like "Field of Dreams". If you have a $10,000 prize list, you're going to have the best riders and a full field. It's the same thing in putting on a Six-day.

They don't all handle their bikes like Europeans, but all the Six-day races in Europe are usually on a 166 meter track or 250. We put 12 to 14 teams on a 166 meter track. In Antwerp on a 250 we put 20 teams.

There might be some crashes because people don't all know how to handle their bikes that well. Since we don't have Madisons here a lot, maybe we'll put it down to 12 or 15 teams. Racing the Vandedrome is exciting.

The Future

I'll stay in the cycling industry somehow, whether that's coaching or being a rep or opening a bike shop -- I don't know. I don't see myself from 9 to 5 behind a desk.

I like giving something back to the sport. I plan to keep working with the United States Cycling Federation as a coach.

I started in cycling and it's sort of like coaching in any Pro sport. They were athletes, they came up through the pro ranks and now they're Pro coaches. Basketball, football or whatever Pro sports, that's who I compare myself to.

I started as an athlete, worked my way through, did some great accomplishments that I'm proud of and now it's time to coach. That's what I know best, and I'm still learning to this day about coaching. I have to. I have to start all over now, getting taught.

Now I'm getting taught again by the guys at the Federation. In three, four, five years -- I'll know more, I know that, but maybe I won't have to rely on those guys that much, or maybe I'll be the Head Coach, who knows?

Chapter 10
ᘛᘚ *The Kilometer or "Kilo"* ᘛᘚ

The Kilometer or "Kilo" is a race against the clock over 1000 meters from either a Flying or a Standing start (Standing, in National Championships). Individual effort is pitted against the rider's anaerobic threshold and mental strength. As a tribute to the challenge of this event, riders also call this race the "Killer-meter."

History

The Kilo is a deceptively simple event. It is the "mile" of cycling, the classic distance which provides the ultimate challenge to test the mettle of each competitor. It is both a challenge and an art.

Sprints have their own mission, but the Kilo has become virtually a long, long Sprint. Pursuit challenges the athlete's endurance, but Kilo requires high speed endurance as the athlete "chases" his invisible opponent: the clock.

The Kilo requires all the abilities of the other events, but the athlete is alone in his battle against the final judgement of the clock. There are no team tactics, no opponent's challenge to spur him on. The rider cannot hope that his opponent might do something stupid, lose concentration or any other unexpected variable which, if he can respond, might hand him a victory. The only opponent who might do that is the inner self.

There is no disruption of the purity of what the rider might pull out of the depths of his soul. Once the gun goes off, the rider and the clock are the only factors. Everything else is done.

Has he trained hard enough? With sufficient attention to each sub-skill which he must now pull together into a single "perfect" ride? Will his equipment deliver its promise? Has he prepared all details correctly? Is there some aerodynamic variable he has left out? If he loses in his race against a given time, what must he do differently next time to achieve it?

The Kilometer is long enough to require endurance, short enough to require speed, and technical enough to require imagination. Minor nuances distinguishing a World Record from just another time, become windmills for each Don Quixote. It is short and fast, yet long enough to chop up into parts, each receiving deep analysis by aficionados of the event. It is the ultimate challenge in a tight little package slightly over one minute long.

Distance

The number of times a rider will actually circle a track in this event depends on the size of the track. On a 333.33 meter track the Kilo is three times around. On a 400m track it is two and one-half times around. On a 250m track it is four times around. And so on. No matter what distance the track, a Kilometer is always measured 1000 meters from the start to the finish and permanent markings are made on each track to indicate the start and finish of this event.

Erin Hartwell is one of America's best all-time Kilometer riders. He has been unbeatable in the U. S. National Championships six years running. In 1995 he won Silver in the Pan Am Games. He's ready for 1996.

Qualifying

Each year, qualifying for the different events is subject to change.

In 1994, eligibility for entering the Kilometer at the U.S. National Championships consisted of 20 positions in final competition. Earning one of these positions occurred one of the following ways:

1) The top four finishers in the Kilometer from 1993 qualify automatically. (4)

2) Winners in the nine Regional Cup Races qualify. Plus, the rider with the fastest time of all regions who did not win also qualifies. (10)

3) Another 6 riders can qualify at the National Championships themselves. (6)

This assortment of qualification alternatives is good for several reasons.

First, status is given to having qualified the previous year, acknowledging achievement of top competitors.

Second, the Regional Cup method supports competitions throughout the United States. Competition in the various regions may be uneven due to weather, culture or other differences.

Allowing a tenth rider with a fast time to qualify in spite of not having won his/her Regional Cup recognizes that a rider with the second fastest time in the United States may have unfortunately been pitted against the person with the fastest time in the country. Things like that happen in bicycle racing and it is extremely frustrating for the number two rider.

Third, offering an opportunity to qualify at the time of the event allows other riders to peak, plan or otherwise enter competition for which they may be ready. Who knows what might have happened at their Regional Cup race? Americans have long a tradition of loving this kind of "wild card" opportunity.

And so, U.S. National Championship competition consists of 20 men and 20 women. Whoever rides the fastest five times in each division receives a medal according to finish time order. The winner is simply determined by the fastest time. Simple and tidy. But actually getting to that fastest time, that perfect ride, is a little more complicated.

The Start

There have been two kinds of starts in the Kilo, the Flying start and the Standing start.

The Flying start is no longer recognized in record attempts and is not used in competition. The Flying start continues to be used in 500m and 200m record and in qualifying for Sprints over 200 meters.

The Standing start is used in competition. Riders are held by an Official until the gun goes off. Only Officials may hold riders in this event. The rider must be held neutrally, neither pushed nor restrained. Riders may also be held by a mechanical device which automatically releases the rear wheel of the bicycle when the gun goes off.

The rider must start within the Sprinter's lane, between the black and red lines. The edge of the front tire of the bicycle must be directly over the starting line. The bicycle must be parallel to the lines, pointing neither up nor down track.

Each rider determines when s/he is ready to start. Officials must not rush them or begin before the rider signals his/her readiness. Often riders will take considerable time getting ready for this short, but maximum effort. If a rider should delay the race purposefully for some other reason than taking time to prepare, s/he can be disqualified.

Sometimes riders will have their feet taped onto the pedals to get the maximum contact with the least movement in foot to pedal contact.

For lower level riders these minuscule differences are not of great consequence, but top level riders and coaches are scientists at finding the 1000 small advantages which may determine a win at elite levels. Serious riders look long and hard for coaches and advisors who know of some obscure detail which might give them that extra millimeter.

The Race

Riders used to ride one at a time in a Kilometer. In 1994 they began riding two at a time, starting identically as in the Pursuit. Each rider is, nevertheless, riding only against the clock, not against another rider as in a Pursuit. Riders who ride the exact same time are given the same place.

At National Championships all riders know that this is one quick ride for all the marbles. They take their preparation very seriously. They know that once the gun goes off, it will be too late for any remediations.

Riders generally are attempting target times, usually personal bests, if not the fastest time overall. Top men's times tend to be around 1:05 to 1:10. Top women's times tend to be 1:14 to 1:18. The Men's American record is 1:03.397, set by Rory O'Reilly. The Women's American record is 1:12.298, set by Janie Eickhoff. They are the reference riders for this event.

When the rider is ready, s/he notifies the Official, often with a nod. The flag, red or green, goes up on his/her side of the track. Starters are in the infield, each facing a rider on the home or the back stretch. When flags on both sides are up, "Timers ready . . . Riders ready" is announced to notify everyone that the race will start. Within seconds, the gun goes off.

Usually riders stand into start position when they hear "riders ready." They must be careful at this point <u>not</u> to start pushing on the pedals, beginning a forward motion which will result in a false start. False starts do happen, often because the riders are nervous and know that a milliseconds hesitation might lose them the race.

Assuming the start is good, maximum effort leads to quick acceleration. A common start presently taught is with stiff, straight arms, maximizing power into the pedals. It looks a bit awkward, but seems to work.

Riders accelerate standing up for approximately half a lap, until maximum speed has been reached. Riders then sit in aero position for the rest of the race.

When aero bars first came in, a debate raged as to whether the Kilometer was too short a race for bothering with that piece of equipment. Aero bars were developed for long time trails, this is a power event. Riders have tended to go to aero bars, seeking any advantage to a faster time.

Riders usually hold the second lap pretty well, but the third lap tells the story. Some riders are so highly tuned and practiced that they are artists in their pacing and their knowledge of their own bodies. It is common, however, to see riders "seize up", especially in the last half lap. If it's "your" rider, you send them help with your heart, but they are all alone.

Riders often develop techniques to manage this last period, because it can defeat all other parts of their preparation and their race. They know that if they ride "the Perfect Race" they will be totally exhausted by the time they cross the finish line. The trick is for the point of total exhaustion and the finish line to be in the same space at the same time.

It is not uncommon for riders to go out too fast, with little left by 2 1/2 laps. Another common failing is for riders to cease their efforts before they

For maximum contact, riders may tape their feet.

actually reach the finish line. If this happens, a great ride might get flushed in the last 10 feet. Riders practice pushing *through* (not to, but through) the finish. The great riders find a "kick" to the finish from some gut-level place that true Champions seem to possess.

After crossing the finish, riders are expected to get off the track as soon as possible. They pre-set this fact in their minds prior to the race since they know that rational thought will be elusive at the end. Many velodromes have a warm-up track riders can go to, but some do not. All riders warm down somehow.

All competitors must ride in the same session. If the sequence of riders

is interrupted for any reason (such as rain) the whole event must be done over. Those who have not ridden yet will have the advantage of being fresh for the later session. While riders who must re-ride the very next day are at a distinct disadvantage.

Some believe that a rider is only good for one maximum Kilo effort which renders a second best effort within a week impossible.

False Starts

A False Start is not uncommon among nervous Kilo riders. Rules state that it must be signaled within the first 30 meters by a double gunshot or a double whistle. After two False Starts, whatever happens the third time is final. If the rider False Starts for a third time, he/she is eliminated from competition. Otherwise the race begins.

Mishaps

If any rider suffers a "mishap", the cause will be determined by Officials and a restart may be permitted after the next five riders have gone. If less than five riders remain, the restart is scheduled for 10 minutes later.

A mishap is defined in the Rule Book as "a crash or mechanical accident (tire puncture or other failure of an essential component). However, a puncture caused by the tire coming off due to inadequate gluing is not a mechanical accident, nor is malfunc-

tion due to misassembly or insufficient tightening of any component."

A rider is disqualified if s/he is determined to have intentionally caused the mishap. A rider is permitted two restarts.

The point, for Officials, is to walk the line between the fact of mechanical failure which accompanies bicycle racing and holding riders responsible for properly caring for and preparing their equipment. Riders are on the track with others in Mass Start races where equipment failure can bring down whole fields.

While this is unlikely during individual events, proper care of equipment is a basic requisite for good competition, so there is concern for demanding that riders fulfill their responsibilities while still being fair.

Race Equipment
Sponges

Sponges are important functional pieces of equipment in the Kilometer. They are placed at five meter intervals around the turns to assure that the riders stay at or above the measurement line during the course of the ride. Sponges are placed precisely. Each time a rider hits one, it usually goes flying, revealing that the rider dipped lower than the measurement line.

There is no official penalty for hitting the sponges unless a rider rides below them. However, riding over a hard surface uninterrupted is obviously faster than riding over a soft surface and getting distracted by hitting soft objects. The great Time Trial artists graze each sponge with a breath -- shortest path, least resistance.

The Riders

Kilo riders include a variety of physical types, from the "lean and mean" to the stocky Sprinters. Sprinters to do well since it is a short-distance speed event. Many Junior riders do well in both events. The key is highest speed over a short distance, which would appear to favor Sprinters, but the endurance required by three laps tends to favor those who can maintain a sub-Sprint speed for a longer period of time.

Rory O'Reilly developed a unique approach which allowed him to set World Records. Janie Eickhoff could have an excellent chance for a World Record and a World Championship if a contest for women in the World Championships made it worthwhile for her to train specifically for this event.

Mark Whitehead, Harvey Nitz and Rebecca Twigg have also been National Champions in this event and have held National Records.

Erin shows one reason he keeps winning the Kilometer -- muscle.

Kilometer
Janie Eickhoff Quigley

Janie ("The Pocket Rocket") began her winning record with the 15-16 Junior Women's Omnium in 1985 and repeated in 1986. In 1987 she completed a triple crown, winning Sprint, Pursuit and Points (17-18).

Since then she has been U.S. National Champion in the Kilometer ('89), Pursuit ('90, '91, '94), and Points ('88, '90, '92, '93 & '94). In 1994 she was second at the National Championships in Sprints only to Connie Paraskevin Young.

At the Goodwill Games in 1990 Janie won a Gold Medal in the Pursuit. In 1991 she set a new U.S. National record for the Kilometer (1:12.298 - Standing start). In 1995 she won Gold in the Pursuit at the Pan Am Games. And she is still only 25 years old.

I was born on June 15, 1970 and grew up in Los Alamitos, California.

What is really funny is that when my brother got his first racing bike dad thought it was the next worst thing to a motorcycle! "Doors will get opened up on you!" He gave us the whole spiel on why bicycling's dangerous. "And you shouldn't do . . . and . . . no . . .!"

At the end of the summer the whole family had bikes! We all had these family jerseys. That was the most embarrassed I have ever been. Dad, mom, -- I don't know why we had to do this, but it was something that we had to do.

We all had to wear our family jersey on the family bike ride on Saturday morning. It was a red, white and green jersey . . . people were yelling "Viva la France!" it was like "Italy!" and "Go!" I was 14 at the time. I was just ready to tear this thing off of me and ride home in my brassiere!

My mom used to ride recreationally. She has been the cement in our family because my dad and I would go places. Mom was busy taking care of Kurt (a victim of cerebral palsy). She was the stable component of our lifestyle.

I try to help her sometimes lugging Kurt around. He's close to what I weigh and he's a good bit taller than me and it is a task and a half, that's for sure. He has a good time. He gets so excited at bike races.

Aside from my brother Kurt I have an older brother, Rick. He's 29. He was on the U.S. National Team in Pistol Shooting. Right now he's living in New Jersey. We're not far from each other.

How I Got Started

My father took me to a track race at the Olympic Velodrome following the Olympics and it looked "alright". I was heavy into soccer at the time.

You know how you say a lot of things just to go along with your father, like "Yeah, dad, this is neat, it's okay . . . " He was all excited about it.

I had a road bike and he fixed it up. He found out that there were classes at Encino Velodrome and took me out there. It was like "Okay, dad, just don't spend any money on me, I don't know about this sport."

It was a small class and I was the only girl out there. That was a big incentive. I really started to enjoy myself. How can you pass up an opportunity to ride around a track with other 14-15 year old boys?

It's funny to say because that was probably my initial motivation to be involved with cycling: "Gee, this is sort of fun, there's a whole bunch of guys out here!" It was fun. After a couple of weeks, dad and I went down near Tijuana to get a bike frame. We got a real cheap Benotto. Within a month or so I had my own track bike.

My dad got me hooked up with everybody. He has always been a big part of my training. He liked to talk to the people who have been around a

"Success will come if you love what you're doing so much that you don't even think about denying yourself anything. As long as you have the passion, the desire, the feeling for the sport, you'll work hard. Track riding is like a bug. Once it's bitten you, there's no thrill in comparison. There's not a bad seat in the house. Whenever I watch a race I'm standing on the picnic tables in the infield watching everything that's going on."

while — Gil Hatton, Sr. and Mark Whitehead's father — some of the really old crew in cycling.

When I first started riding I trained in Eldorado Park, which had weekly criteriums. All these old guys would hang out after the criterium and drink beer and dad was always hanging around asking questions, finding out what would be the best thing to get me started. Those two, Simonetti, and some of the others that I knew, explains the good start that I got in cycling.

My mom is very supportive, but it's pretty much my dad who's trekked me around from competition to competition, from training to training and fixed my equipment.

When I was a Junior his enthusiasm drove me nuts. I wished I had just a little bit of freedom. Dad seemed to scare away any chance at a boyfriend. He was everywhere I went.

He was not the Little League parent, though sometimes when I didn't have a good ride I would look over and get this frowny kind of look. But I was the one who wanted to go do the training and go to the velodrome. I wanted to do it, he just helped me.

I've missed out on a lot of things, the normal kids experiences and growing up experiences. Now I'm more interested in those, but the things that I've gotten in exchange far outweigh what I missed. My life is richer in other ways.

Early Racing

I won my first Nationals in Indianapolis in 1985 for Junior Girls, 14-15 Omnium. Following that I was pretty much hooked into the sport. I have a funny story about the Junior Girl's Omnium:

Back then we had three races and the overall winner was the National Champion. In the last race everything was pretty close and I had to finish third to win.

Going into the last corner I was sitting fifth. While I was riding down the straightaway I had this vision of this (Champion's) jersey that had sprouted wings and was flying out of the velodrome. Somehow, I managed to tie for third!

I don't remember at all what went on down the home straightaway, but I remember my vision of the jersey flying out of the velodrome and over the stands. After all these years, it's as clear as though it was yesterday.

When I was going to my first Nationals I thought it was the biggest deal in the world. I was riding for Montrose (Cycling Club) which gave me $100 to go to Nationals. I thought "Oh my God, they expect me to win!" I had all this pressure. For months prior to Nationals I got butterflies when I thought about it. I was such a nut case because I was so nervous. *"They gave me $100 — they expect me to win! Oh my gosh!"* It turned out that they were real happy for me and I didn't know that it was just something they do for all their teammates. Everybody gets $100 for going to Nationals. I was unaware of that.

After winning Nationals in '85 I trained two years straight because I was so excited about it. '86 was a real good year for me, I finished second at the Olympic Festival, then it was strictly Seniors competition, one of the big competitions for Sprinters. I was pretty much considered a Sprinter at that point.

When I was a Junior and early on in Seniors, I really loved cycling. I didn't really have any boyfriends, I wasn't involved with school in high school. I liked to go to the track and I liked the people we'd meet at Eldorado Park on the training rides — that was my social life and I really enjoyed it. I wasn't work to me, I just loved doing it. I think that was a big asset. Riding did not seem like work, I just wanted

to see what I could do and it was fun.

Eddie B., who I admired tremendously, invited me to compete at a U.S./U.S.S.R. competition. That was a real good trip for me because I didn't anticipate how successful I would be. I was real nervous and had no idea what the potential was.

How I Came to Specialize

Following Junior Worlds in '87 Sue Novara suggested I stay in Sprinting. I respected her quite a bit. She had given me good advice on how to prep for Nationals that year and World's. I was a first year Junior going to Junior World's. I had had success, so I continued Sprinting until I won a medal at the World Championships.

1989 was the last year I went to World's to do Sprints and I finished sixth. That was my best finish at World's in Match Sprints. I also finished third in the Points race.

I wanted an event that would complement Points racing that year ('89) for the U.S/U.S.S.R. meet at the Olympic Velodrome (Dominguez).

I had trained for Pursuit for about two weeks with just the previous Sprint training that I had. I was always doing Pursuits and Sprints at the Sundance races. The Pursuits were just for fun and conditioning. With some specific training I was able to break four minutes.

With that in mind and along with the medal at the World's in the Points race I thought "Well shoot, I think the two complement each other, I'd rather do that."

Sprinting is such a high pressure event. It's so technical and there's just so much pressure. I enjoyed it, but I

enjoy Pursuiting more because it really seemed to show the amount of training you put in and I tend to train a lot.

In Match Sprinting if you have one bad move, the race is over with and there's nothing you can do about it. You can go to the repechage and hopefully you'll advance.

With Sprinting, I don't mind hurting, and it was only three laps. Junior women Pursuit over two kilometers. I didn't think it was really too much different than that

The Kilometer

I became a Kilometer rider, when I was a Junior. My father had suggested — and pretty much everybody had suggested — not to be specific in any one event. They advised me to develop a broad range and see what I could do well. They didn't want me to start to emphasize anything in particular. I was still developing and who knows what I might turn out to be? I had always done Kilometer, and had always seemed to do pretty well in them. They take practice.

Technique is especially important. You need to have the proper technique for the Starts because that's a quarter of your race right there. A little less than a quarter of your race is getting up to speed as quickly as you can.

Pat McDonough's really helped me to refine my starting technique. When you're sitting on your bike and you're at the start line you want to make sure you're looking up, like almost to the top of the first corner. You don't want to look down.

In addition to that, you have to make sure that your arms are straight and your hips are sort of forward.

Initially you're not leaning your bike so much, you're using more of your back and your hips — your stronger muscles rather than your arms, which are weaker — to sort of get going. It's hard to explain.

It looks sort of "jarry" or "jittery", it doesn't look as smooth as when you use a little more arm movement.

You want to make sure you're looking up. Looking up like that seems to lock everything into position, I'm not sure what it does, but it's the same thing in speed skating.

You have to learn how hard to go on the first lap. You sit in for the second lap, and whatever you have left for the last lap, you turn it loose and hopefully don't hit that wall on the backstraight.

In the opening lap you want to go all out, but you're really going only 95%, 98%. I put on speed for a good two-thirds of the first lap. Usually standing until I'm entering the third corner on a 250, probably about there. The next lap it's like you just hold it a little bit longer. It's like "go hard" but think a little bit "relax", you're not relaxing, but you're thinking it a little bit.

Usually when you hear that bell your legs are starting to feel a little bit tired, it's like "okay, everything happens," you're just telling yourself whatever it takes to get around. If you're in the corner and you're not holding your line: "Okay, hold your line, hold your line, hold your line . . " Power down the backstraight and going into that other corner, you can focus on holding your line there.

It's just a matter of keeping yourself off the thought that your legs hurt. Anything to distract you from that. It takes a lot, but it seems like for me, once I get to that half lap, it's just "I only have a half lap to go" suck it up and just tough it out.

When you hit the wall, you really have to focus on your pedaling. You can really tell when people hit that wall and they just start pedaling squares. You can sit there in the grandstands watching and your legs just kind of seize up, just agonizing along with that person out there, like, "Oh gosh!" you sort of feel how much that must hurt.

You need to focus on your pedaling and think. If you only have a half lap to go, you tell yourself that you only have a half lap to go. By that time, you only have a quarter of a lap.

The official asks if she is ready. When she is, he signals the other side of the track. At the Starter's gun, the holding apparatus releases her back wheel and she is off. "Pat McDonough's really helped me to refine my starting technique. You want to make sure you're looking up, like almost to the top of the first corner. You also have to make sure that your arms are straight and your hips are sort of forward." World Cup, 1994

Just getting yourself motivated enough to suffer through that last lap, thinking of other things that you like, concentrating on pedaling, breathing, holding your line, coaching your way through that last time — when you're really starting to agonize. You sort of segment each part.

I've never had a particularly fast first lap, but I've always had a really good finishing lap. My finishing lap is probably the strongest part of my whole ride.

Once you know what you're doing, it's an easy thing to push yourself, especially once you're prepared with other training. It's something that you need to keep perfecting, to stay excited about it

When racing, I think it's important to develop, not a ritual, but a pattern for warming up. When you're in a pressure situation, it's those patterns that you rely on. You know what you have to do to warm up and you just get involved in a little regime.

It takes your mind off the pressure because you know what it takes to get warmed up. It doesn't really take any thought, because it's something that's been established.

Once you know how to prepare yourself, you know the motions you need to go through while you're riding. If you get a good start, the second lap you relax, get yourself to go 98%.

Then when you hit that last lap, as you come down that last lap you're progressively feeling worse, but you don't let that get to you. You start thinking of the more technical aspects, like pedaling circles, coaching yourself through that last lap. When you cross that finish line, too many people have too much left. You should have given all you've got.

Training

Through the season I like to do visualization. The closer I get to major competition the more of that I'll do, definitely off the bike.

When I'm riding, I talk to myself, especially in Pursuit when things are going well or if they're not going well — what I'd like to do, or if I'm going out too fast. There are a lot of things I'll talk to myself about. It's all internal.

I think I may not have tremendous ability, but I think I make it up by working real hard. I definitely don't have the stature of the Inga Thompsons or the Rebecca Twiggs. They embody the ideal rider.

I have power, but I've never looked tremendously lean or anything like that. I work real hard. Andrzej Bek was concerned that I work too hard. I guess as I get older I'm kind of drifting away from that attitude, which I know I should.

Each year, getting closer to the next Olympics I'll be refining everything down to where I'll really perfect my own training. Before, it was pretty much just working real hard. I've always been a hard worker

and I think my dad has a lot to do with that. He's a real hard worker also. To a great extent working really hard will result in most of your success, but it's that other little one-third where you really need to be specific about things, conscious of what you're doing. That gets you to that World Championship jersey or that Olympic medal.

Right now I'm focusing more on

Mom and brother Kurt.

Dad has always been Janie's best supporter.

Well, winning yet another National Championship is nice, but a new husband (Ed Quigley) is even better.
He understands all this cycling stuff. Brother Tim is still a competitor.

the Pursuit and track racing, but I do like Stage Races because it's no pressure for me and it's good training. Right now I'll probably use races for training. Stage races and crits (criteriums) and all the road races, but I like to think of myself as a track racer. I don't have that lean physique for stage racing, so I have to assess where I want to go with what I have to work with.

I started out cycling, but from meeting some speedskaters at the Dominguez Hills track I got involved with skating. Paramount ice rink was real close to the Dominguez Hills track. I knew Connie Young and Sheila Young had been speedskaters, so I had to do that too!

I thought that was great to have such intensity throughout the year, whether you're going from cycling into speedskating or what, you had intensity all year, but it wasn't mentally intense because there were different things to learn. You always felt like you were trying to catch up, get in shape for this, get in shape for that, but your intensity never really goes down the whole year. I did that for a couple years.

When I started having knee problems I had to curtail skating. Given the opportunity, I would go back into it, because that's the key, to keep your conditioning up all year around. With speedskating you're not doing the same thing. Training always varies.

Records

In 1989 I won the Kilo at Marymoor during Nationals and the Nationals following (1991) I set a new track record.

When I set the World Record back in Allentown (Trexlertown/T-Town/Lehigh), Erin Hartwell was also there to attempt the track record. It was funny because Pat McDonough pointed out that I had a faster last lap than Erin did! Beaten by a girl in the last lap! But I did, I had a faster last lap than Erin.

It was a World Outdoor Record,

but the U.C.I. changed what is considered a World Record. Now there is no distinction between Indoor and Outdoor. Now it's just the fastest, regardless of whether it's at altitude or indoor or outdoor. (Indoor tracks tend to be faster.)

At Goodwill Games it was nice to win a big competition (Pursuit) on our home soil. I set a new track record there (Marymoor, Seattle) the following year, at 1991 Nationals. In 1989 I had supposedly set a new World record in the Kilo but unfortunately the promoters had not gotten the track certified, so it did not count.

I would expect that whatever track holds Nationals that the track would be certified for new Nationals records or new World records. My record time was not a World record or even a National record, but just a track record because the track hadn't been certified.

I later found out that they had had the opportunity to certify the track, but promoters didn't want to pay the money. If I'd been informed about it the funds could have been driven up somehow. My sponsors might have been interested. I was a little bent out of shape when I realized what had happened.

But, you just have to accept things like that. You have to play the game if you want to play the game. At least that's what I always say.

World Championships

I would love to see a women's Kilo in the World's. I don't see why they don't, they've been talking about for quite a while. The United States has several women who would be good: Kendra Kneeland, myself,

Jessica Greco, Rebecca Twigg — I'm sure if she wanted she could do well in that -- if the U.C.I. decided to have it.

You must be serious about the Kilo before you really try for it. In training you never really push yourself as hard as you could go in an actual race. It's interesting that Rory and I have both set Kilometer records and our birthdays are only 10 days apart. Maybe it's a selection factor for the Kilo! (laughs)

Velodromes

I took some of my first classes at the Encino Velodrome even though I'm much closer to the Dominguez Hills Olympic track.

Encino's pretty much my home because that's where I got my grass roots start. Initially I began with a coach named Paul Schecter. Later I worked with Rick Denman — also Rene Wenzel.

I really enjoy the racing at T-town (Lehigh Velodrome), it's the best racing in the country, but I still always enjoy the little track at Encino. There's nothing quite like the bumps and the little 250 meter track. That one's always been a fun track for me.

Encino has it's own personality. This year they got lights for it, so there has been a lot of refurbishing within the last couple of years.

Three or four years ago we got a real, heavy duty railing. Compared to Minnesota, it's not as steeply banked, it's not as smooth. Aside from work on the apron and more superficial work on it, I think it's pretty much the same track that was laid down in the 60s.

There are so many nice wood tracks in Europe. I just love wood

tracks, especially nice little small ones. A tight, high-banked wood track is just effortless. You can spend more time doing laps and working on technique. I like Minnesota, but I like the indoors, too. I don't like to worry about the weather.

Advice to young women

My advice to young girls who are interested in bike racing —it's a great way to meet young men in black lycra!

Seriously, I would recommend not specializing, try everything. Build the broadest base you possibly can. You'll be drawing from that later when you find what you want to specialize in, when you become more developed, really starting to peak. I think it's real important that you don't burn yourself out on one event.

If you're a track rider you ride the roads, you ride all of the events on the track. That's probably the most important thing. If you really enjoy what you're doing, you're going to work hard at it. As long as you have a passion for it, the desire, a feeling for the sport of riding your bike, you'll want to see what you can do when it comes to competition. Success comes when you love what you're doing so much that you aren't denying yourself anything.

Racing Memories

My most wonderful memory is of my first National Championship. I was so nervous going into that competition I couldn't watch any other races. I sat in a hot van that my father and I drove out to Indianapolis. It had a maximum speed of about 50 miles per hour. We had a small, 14' trailer. Here's the beds, here's the kitchen,

you could just barely turn around.

It was so exciting to go to my first Nationals and win a medal. That vision that I had with the jersey flying away, then chewing my fingernails off waiting to find out if I had won -- it came down to a photo finish. Christine Saxon and I tied. They could not distinguish who actually crossed the line for third place first, so they split the points for third place. I still had enough points to win.

My first medal in the Points race at World's was also memorable. It was such a grueling race. I had gotten off the front with a group of girls and slowly our pack started dwindling down to about three riders.

I swore, every time I looked at the lap cards, the person wasn't flipping them. "It's not getting any shorter!" All of a sudden it was down into the teens. We had maintained over half a lap or two-thirds of a lap, but never made the jump to lap the field. Had we made the jump I would have won, because I had a good 20 points over two other girls who had already previously gotten a lap.

I remember getting off my bike and just dropping on the ground, I was so fried. Then, standing on the podium next to Jeannie Longo. It was just the biggest thrill for an 18 year old.

That was the World Championships in Lyon, France, 1989. Jeannie and Barbara Ganz had gotten off the front. When they got away I think we had gotten off a little bit before that. I was so excited that here I was, standing on this podium and all the people I had admired before and fellow competitors were smiling.

I've always love going over to Europe. I love the traveling part of it. Packing your bike not so much, but going on the trips. I've been to so many neat places, places I never would have been without cycling. I've been to Japan three times, Korea (Soeul) once, Belgium, France, Germany, Italy — there have been so many people and friends and experiences. I've usually been with the Federation on trips and they've always been great.

Japan is neat. This last time I was there, when I went to sign up, one man said "Oh, Jane Eickhoff, Osaka Champion!" People remember all this stuff, and it was really neat. That's the most fun.

When I was there in '91 they had a series of races and I was there for four. They have an overall winner, like a criterium circuit racing. I had won two of the races and won this overall.

I remember sitting near the podium after the last race and signing autographs for over half an hour because there were just swarms and swarms of people. I remember signing this lady's skirt. The people were really into it, it was just great! Those people really know how to put on a race.

I just gotten back from a road race that had television cameras in the helicopters, it was so professional and well organized. Going back to the race in '91, you could set your watch by the schedule, it was so precise. People were concerned about the jobs they did, it was such a treat. Everything was just as it was supposed to be.

Heartaches of the Game

In Germany there was a disaster. We had our program for that day. I had my schedules and I knew what time I had to be back at the velodrome, but they moved up our race schedule, I'm not really sure for what reason.

Maybe they revised the schedule and handed out a new program for that day, but the schedule was changed by 15 minutes. I had been out loosening up from the last ride. I had less than an hour and a half to get ready for the next Pursuit. It wasn't very much time, so I went out to ride and relax.

I thought "Well, I'll come back early just in case I have a little extra time. I heard something about Pursuit and I was in the bathroom. I was walking up the stairs and heard "Women's Pursuit . . something . ."

I said "Craig (Griffin, Pursuit coach), what's going on here?" As I took off my leg warmers I heard "Janie Eickhoff to the start line . . ." I thought "Holy smokes, I haven't even gotten on the rollers yet!"

Those 15 minutes were so critical for me because I had to get back on the rollers, get my leg speed back and refocus on what I was doing. I was caught completely by surprise.

When I lost by about a half a second, all that might have made the difference. Maybe it wouldn't have, but maybe it might have.

That was absolutely the most frustrating experience, just not knowing what I could have done. I was in tears for the longest time. I was real happy with my performance getting a second, but ..

Initially in that ride, in that first kilometer, I lost about three seconds. Then I finally got into my rhythm and was reeling back the times.

We were even with a lap to go and I was just out-kicked. I'm sure it was a combination of physical and mental disruption. I wasn't prepared like I should have been physically — getting back on the rollers, having the time to think about what I wanted to do, visualize getting off the line quick.

Craig kept saying "Take your time, take your time," but it's hard to take your time when you've got an official in your face yelling at you to get on your bike and ride. It was just a weird situation. I'm not sure if it was something which could have been prevented.

You hate to think it might have been a political mix-up since I was riding against a German competitor, that aspect of the sport. That's not why we're all there, but, in a sense, that is why we are there. The spectators and the following that the sport has dictates quite a bit about what's going on. Maybe the reason I'm still in the sport is because I don't let it bother me.

The Federation is there to help you, but sometimes when they're doing what they think is best, everything gets garbled up.

Soviets

The Soviets have always been sort of magnetic. Before the Iron Curtain came down you always sort of wondered what these people were like, but they're good hearted people. You find that experience shoots a lot of stereotypes that you have — it opens your eyes to many new experiences, to the way things really are.

I've always found the Soviets to be very friendly, very helpful. On one Federation trip where they sent us to Europe, to France and Denmark with a coach who wasn't really up to the task at hand and we didn't have the medical equipment and I had gone down (crashed). There was nothing we could do because we didn't have anything to fix me up. I was all road rashed up and no other people would help us, but the Soviets.

Their doctor and their coach came over. They cleaned me up, fixed me up with bandages and it was just really nice. It was awful that the Federation should put us in the position that we didn't have any type of medical aid kit or anything like that, to see that these people were helping us out.

It's funny, too, that sometimes the Capitalist, more Westernized, Western Europeans might not smile at you when you walk by, but the Soviets always smiled. Always give you some sort of eye contact most of the time. It's such a more friendly atmosphere. It's interesting the stuff you pick up.

A lot of the coaches and mechanics are good guys. There's a guy named Jean. Every year I've recognized him and every year he's still there doing the same job. He had been very nice to check my equipment. It's just so enticing, it makes you want to work hard to go back for more.

I met Kathryn Marcel at Junior Worlds in 1989 and we still write. It's those little things where you see the same people at big events. It makes you want to go back to see the people again next year. You want to work hard, to exchange stories, or share smiles.

Coaching

I've never spent much time working with the Federation staff. I've always felt they've been pulled in too many directions.

Griff (Pursuit coach Craig Griffin) had to work with the Men's Pursuiters, Team Pursuiters, Women's Pursuiters, the Women's Points race, the Men's Points race — pretty much everything on the track that's not Match Sprint. That would just spread you so thin that it's real time consuming, real demanding.

If I needed special attention, I didn't want to see myself forced into a certain training regime that might not be right for me. The coaching staff does have good intentions, but the bigger problem is that there is just so much inconsistency in coaching.

The coaches haven't been there for very long periods. There have been quite a few different people — Eddy B., Andrzej Bek, Les Barczewski, Craig Griffin, Norman Shields, I mean it's hard to develop consistency.

Having someone who's seen you race in the past, seen you develop — that's been lacking. Going from one year to the next not knowing who you're going to work with — that's why I've never worked primarily with the Federation.

When I went to Junior Worlds, Pat McDonough was on our trip. I had seen the type of relationships he had with his athletes and thought "Gosh, how lucky!"

Later in '89 I started working with Pat and just stayed with him, going back to Allentown to race with him, to race out there. What I had was working for me and why should I jumble that up trying to work with the Federation?

Janie won Gold at Goodwill Games, Marymoor, 1990

I pretty much do my own thing.

I am working with Craig but I still talk with Pat, too. I want to spend more time in Allentown (T-Town) racing, so I need to get back with Pat. He's worked with me the longest of anybody. We're pretty similar in our expertise on the track. He was a Points racer and a Pursuiter and that's more what I do. We have a real good communication line also.

The Older Rider

Barry Wolf is a rider in the Encino area. He's close to 65. He's amazing. I just hope I'm in half as good a shape when I'm that old. I see that in him and look forward to that when I'm older.

Even when I was starting out younger I didn't see myself as being any different age as anybody else who was out there. I still see myself as the same age but it's different how people view you. I don't really see the age difference.

The Future

Right now I have more control over my career and riding than I've had in previous years.

In Olympic year '92 I was still sort of following the idea of trusting other people with my training and I assumed that they knew better than I did. Sometimes that was not necessarily true.

Now I feel like I'm really gathering more from previous years' experience. "Well, this worked, this wasn't so hot." Sort of gathering the best from everything.

I'd like to compete through '96. I'll be 26 then. I would like to do other things. I might race as a Master for fun. I can see myself doing that. But I want to have kids and I don't know how much time that's going to take.

I will always be a part of cycling. It's been such a great part of my life.

I would love to coach and pass on what I've learned from the people who've helped me.

Besides that I love to eat way too much, so I'll probably be connected with my bike or some form of exercise for the rest of my life!

Track riding has always been so much fun. It's like a bug. Once it's bitten you, there's nothing in comparison to the thrill of track racing.

Whenever I watch a track race I'm standing on the picnic tables in the infield watching everything that's going on, watching the men's races, being involved with the race, or so many things.

You can't miss anything at the velodromes, there's not a bad seat in the house!

Kilometer
Rory O'Reilly

Rory has set two World Records which stood for over eight years. He won a Gold Medal in the Pan Am Games for Kilometer in 1983.

His first U.S. National Kilometer record was for the Standing start — 1:03.397 (1984), which has not been broken. The two World Records were for Flying start, the first for 500 meters — 26.993, and the other for Kilometer — 58.510 both set in 1985.

Rory was U.S. National Kilometer Champion in 1985.

Today Rory coaches and competes successfully at the Master's level. In 1987 he won the Master's National Championship in both Sprints and Kilometer. In 1989 he again won both events. He won the Master's Kilometer again in 1990 and 1993.

I was born in Greenport, New York on June 25, 1955. My family moved to Bellevue, Washington until I was in third grade. Since then I've lived in Santa Barbara except for a few excursions out. During Olympic year (1984) I lived in the L.A. area and in Palo Alto for a couple of years, where I worked as a sales rep.

How I Got Started

I got started in bicycle racing as kind of a two-part thing. I first got a bike in 1971 in the early part of the bike boom. I was 15 or 16.

I started riding with my brother and a couple of friends. One of the guys I was riding with told me about a meeting with this old Italian guy.

This guy started rambling on about the European scene and how he wanted to put together this great team, and racing, and I'd never even heard of racing before. He started talking about training and how he wants everybody to have two bikes, a training bike and a racing bike. The training bike is going to be this heavy old clunker.

He started talking about speeds. "We'll warm up around 25 miles an hour, then we'll pick it up from there and then we'll be going close to 30 . . ." I'm goin' "Well this racing scene isn't cuttin' out for me, because I can't go that fast!"

A few other riders were kind of mulling about and I got the jist that this guy was full of it and none of the other guys could go that fast either! So I got introduced kind of to the local club and riders, a pretty small group of about a dozen people.

I started riding with them every week and got dropped every week, and that went on — this started in the Fall and it went on through the Winter and it was getting close to Spring where I finally stayed up on a ride. I was just pleased as can be. I was literally in the point in every ride of just about puking, "Oh God, just trying to stay with these guys!"

I finally got where I could stay up and they would also regroup at the halfway point, which was real short. The rides were about 25 - 30 miles in length. When I got to the point where

I could stay up I was real happy. I had just made loads of progress. They started talking about racing and how I would be Junior racer, so I found out where there were races and signed up.

The first race I ever rode was the easiest thing I ever did -- I couldn't believe how easy it was. The rides were such the death ride that racing with the Junior ranks was a breeze! I started placing and winning, and from there it just kept on building. After that first year I stopped worrying about how hard the guys would go in the winter time, because they all went slower the rest of the year!

There were one or two riders that were good riders. Mike Celmins was kind of my role model at the time when I started riding in Santa Barbara. The Italian guy was a local character, but as far as getting into racing, he got into importing, but

"While the ride itself didn't hurt, post ride when I did the World Records was the worst I ever felt in my life. I'd always hated Time Trials. A race against the clock. Boring, stupid, something the British do. It was just a whole different world when I started actually plotting it out: what's it going to take to get better? Some riders never realize that it's a game. They think the strongest rider wins, the fastest rider wins, the guy with the best bike, but they never really learn <u>how to play the game</u>."

not for very long.

I started riding in '71, racing in '72. Immediately I got serious. '72 was an Olympic year, and I already had dreams. I wanted to ride the Olympic Trials that year. I'd progressed real quick in winning Junior races and I was riding with the Senior riders around town.

Mike Celmins was a Sprinter and I saw that he was successful. I was naive at that point and I felt that he was someone I should watch. He was probably my biggest role model. After that I pretty much watched the scene and tried to figure out what it was going to take at different points in my riding to get to the next level.

Mike Celmins had been National Champion, Cyril Johnson had been like second in the 10 Mile the year before. He would go on to win either one or two Team Pursuit National Championships, so there were some really good riders. I thought "I can ride with these guys — I can make the Olympic Team!" You have pretty grandiose ideas when you're a sixteen year old just introduced to the scene.

It quickly became evident that I wasn't going to make the Team that year, but I had pretty big aspirations right off, and it was fed by having success right away and having good role models so that I could key off of seeing that they had done well.

The very first people that I started hanging out with were (at that time they had "A", "B" and "C"s) Category "B". I thought that was a great big deal until I started racing. I realized these guys were kind of stuck there. My first year as a Junior I started beating those guys in the local practice races.

I had had very little sports experience. I hated sports in high school and grade school. I didn't like any team activities, I didn't like the people, I was into motorized anything,

especially motorcycles. Somehow bike racing just clicked. I think part of it was the thrills and spills. The success just kind of fed on itself.

It was years and years -- like a decade later -- that I actually liked training. I abhorred training when I first started riding. It was just something that you had to do so you could do well in a race. It was tough starting like I did.

The fact that my brother was there and was doing better than me was this huge incentive. He was a year older. We had sibling rivalry in everything. He would beat me at chess and I'd knock all the chess pieces off. There's eight kids in the family — a good Irish Catholic family. I'm the fifth. My brother was fourth.

I was always self-coached. As I got into college, that's where my education went, P.E. and Exercise Physiology. At a certain point in my life I think I probably wasn't coachable. I had a rebel attitude.

Especially in those days, bicycle racing was such an individualistic sport, that was probably the thing that got me into it. It was as obscure a sport as you could get into, nowhere near the mainstream. It was just all these long-haired drug addicts who were into it. So it really appealed to me!

It's changed immensely since I started. Now it's mainstream people. It's hard comparing the two times.

When I started riding I knew every other rider I would see. It's like growing up in a small town trying to compare it to a big city. Both have buildings and people and they're both cool in their own way. It's not going to

go back to what it was. It was cool then and it's cool now.

Racing

There were two phases in the beginning of my high level racing. My road career, right away when I turned Senior — actually in my second year of riding I was still a Junior and I started doing well in Senior races.

The following year I turned Senior and I won the first Olympic Development Race I ever rode. Right away I wanted to make Senior National Team. I made the National "B" Team.

I had to make it on savvy. I was basically a road sprinter, so I needed things to fall my way. At times when they would hold Trials the courses were just too difficult for me and there was no way I could make the cut.

As I prepared for the '76 Olympics I decided that, since I had a hard time training, the only way, I would go hard enough was to go to Europe and get forced. I could only go hard if I was racing. I couldn't train myself to go hard enough. Races would push you. But when I went to Europe all I did was get sick and injured. I had a disastrous time.

I came back (in '76) for the Tour of Somerville which I had won the year before, probably my first big splash on the National scene. I started

"Bicycle racing was individualistic, as obscure a sport as you could get into -- so it really appealed to me!"

getting press as a regional rider, a guy who was winning some big regional races, but I'd never traveled across the country except for, like, Junior Nationals.

In '75 I won Tour of Somerville and I set the National Record at the time for 50 miles. It was a pretty big win because I won both competitions, the Sprint competition and the Overall. Plus, I was all bloodied up from the day before from a 100 mile criterium in Miami when Roger Young put me down, so it made a good story.

I had borrowed Wayne Stetina's shorts 'cause I'd shredded mine the day before. That was my first splash onto the National scene.

Right before I came back from Europe I was starting to get it going a little better, the weather was starting to warm up and I was starting to get into a little better races. Then I crashed twice right before I came over and I crashed at Summerville. They paid my way back because I was the winner from the year before.

A week later, I went to Olympic Trials and I was just going backwards. I was really frustrated. That would have been my best shot on the roads.

The Trials were held at Lake Seranac and it was rolling courses, ideally suited to me. (Tom) Schuler made the team and that really made me mad because we were very similar riders. If a rider like him could make the team it would definitely have been a good year for a rider like me. I regretted going to Europe at the time, but in the long view, it did show me a lot. I had a hard time staying healthy.

The French scene is a real weird scene because you have to do everything through clubs. It was hard for me to get into all the hard races because the club said "No, I think you should ride this thing . . . ", so that didn't work out well.

The next year I decided I wanted to turn Pro, so I went to Belgium. It ended up the same. I was sick most the of the time. I got strep throat. I've always tended to be sick and injured through my whole life. So, that was kind of the end of my road career.

I came back here and raced, trying to decide what I wanted to do. I thought about trying a 100 K, Team Pursuit, and I played a little bit with trying to

go to some camps with the Team Pursuiters in Colorado Springs.

Kilo became a specialty much later in my career. I started out just riding the roads. There were a few forays onto the track just for the hell of it.

Initially I went to the track because they had a road bike competition at Encino, the only track around at the time. It was a kind of a handicap race or Italian Pursuit, where you chase the other guys staggered around the track. I'd had a Claude Butler track bike before I started racing, so I had the exposure. I started using it a little bit on the track, riding track events, but it was just something I played with.

I didn't particularly like track. I did it because it would help me for racing on the road and because I was successful. My first year I was MIR, Most Improved Rider, on the track as a Junior. I belonged to Santa Barbara Bike Club, at that time called Masse Vittesse, "great speed".

I never wanted to do any Time Trials because I always felt I won on tactics. Then I started realizing I was not only winning on tactics. I was winning because I was so "amped". That allowed me, when I got into a Time Trial, to have success.

How I Became a Kilo Rider

When they had the boycott in 1980, I was thinking "Ah, this isn't workin' out." So I pretty much just kind of bailed out of bicycle racing. In '79 and '80 I got a "real" job and did very little riding. After about a year, I started riding for fun, the first time I'd ever done that in my life. I got enthused about the sport again.

I thought "I don't have the time to

devote to the road. What can I do to get back into it a little bit? Why don't I try something short on the track? Why don't I try the Kilo?"

I made my first stab at it in San Diego in 1980 without a whole lot of preparation though I thought I'd done some things right. I rode a 1:13 and got 11th. I'd already done a 1:13 back in my road days. I thought "Dang, I think I'm doing something wrong."

Then I got 4th in the Points race, and thought "I wasn't even training for that!" but I did well just from knowing how to race. It got my enthusiasm back up again. I still felt that the only way I would be able to succeed was going to be in something short because I didn't have much time.

I thought "Well, if I go for the Kilometer I really don't need to train and I don't need to race on the track. I really don't need to race hardly at all, because it's a Time Trial."

For me that was a big change because I'd always hated Time Trials. A race against the clock. Boring, stupid, something the British do.

When I first started I was lousy in Time Trials, as I always had been. What a stupid event. It reminded me of running track when I was in ninth grade. I hated it.

But, when I started actually plotting it out -- what's it going to take to get better? -- it was a whole different world. For the first time I started delving into the science of the sport and evaluating things much more closely. I had done it during my road racing, but not anywhere near to the degree that I started doing it then. I quickly evolved from that point on.

It was up my alley because I was a road sprinter. I had a good long sprint. I wasn't the fastest guy, but if the race was kind of long and grueling I was faster than the other guys who were in there at the end.

If the real Sprinters were there, they would smoke me. At that time Gibby Hatton and Jerry Ash were riding criteriums. They would all smoke me if they were still there at the end. They were National Champions in the Sprint. I'd never had that kind of speed, I was one notch below that.

Each year I started knocking off more and more time from the Kilo. By '83 I made the Pan Am Team, and '84 I was on the Olympic Team. When I was a road rider it hurt to race the Kilo because my first year as a Senior I rode Kilos for District Championships and things like that. They really hurt.

Once I started racing the Kilo as a specialty the race never hurt. But training hurt severely. It came down to the fact that I was so amped up for the race that factors such as pain just weren't there.

Yeah, I was fatigued at the end and I was breathing really hard, and I just plain couldn't go any harder. I was trying to go just as hard as I could, but I couldn't go any harder. There wasn't that lactic acid pain. There would be after the race, -- my legs would literally puff up in size and they would start aching. If they didn't, I was unhappy because that meant I didn't go fast enough in the ride.

Racing the Kilometer

Track riding is a real educational thing. A lot of people say "Well, the Kilometer, that has got to be a pretty friggin' boring event. It's like watching grass grow. All the rider's doing is just riding against the clock."

But the Olympic Trials in '84, the biggest roars from the crowd were for the Kilometer, because of two things. One was that a portion of the crowd knew the event. The *bigger* thing was that they had timing. Every rider that went off, you saw his splits. They also listed the top rider's splits.

Most of the crowd were people who just wanted to see the Olympic Trials. They didn't know cycling. They put in huge stands in Colorado Springs. People came who had never been around the sport before.

After just a few riders, they started to say "Ah, this rider's starting out fast -- he's dying at the end." So they started cluing into what was happening with the ride. You started hearing the cheers go out as the guy put out a fast first lap, the crowd would get excited. Then you'd see them fade in the end, they would just start hushing.

It kept building. It was staged really well so the riders kept getting faster and faster all the way through the evening.

When I went off, I had never had the kind of cheers I that night, because the splits I did were the fastest all the way through. They were just screaming. It was really exciting for me and for other people who were watching it.

Staging Kilo Races/Gears

Any time you get into any of the competitions, monitoring of time's a must. Whenever they don't have a clock the audience is pretty quiet. It's like "I don't know, did he go faster than the other guy?" "I don't know."

Mark Gorski, my teammate at the time, said "Man, the place just went nuts -- you had more cheers here than I did for the Sprints!" and the Sprints tended to be the highlight event.

Time Trials have to be educational and they have to be staged right for people to enjoy the event. If the audience doesn't know the players, don't know the game, it's foreign.

Even when knowledgeable people are watching riders, it can be deceptive. I have a videotape from my Pan Am ride in Spanish. Mike Celmins (my role model) grew up in Peru, so he knew Spanish real well. He translated as the sports announcer announced the event. He said "Here's Rory O'Reilly, so many meters tall, so many years old"

I started out and the guy said "Well, he looks like he's not really getting that good of a start here." I got my first lap split as I came across and he said "Ah, the fastest split yet!"

So I got into the second lap and he went "Well, it looks like he's fading a little bit here and I think Marcello . . ." (the Argentine's time was the fastest up to that point) ". . .Marcello's time will hold up". Then I came across for my second lap split and it was the fastest. He went "Oh, well, I guess he's still doing okay".

I came into the third lap and he just said "Well, now he's finally *really* starting to slow down here." I come across and I had the fastest time — the fastest split of every individual lap!

What happened is that I rode the biggest gear of anyone, so my pedal cadence was much slower to the announcer's eye. He kept looking at me in reference to all the other riders as they went by pedaling so quickly. To him, it just looked like I wasn't going quite as fast.

It was really rather humorous. Each time he would have to swallow his words, looking at the clock as I came across — "Ah, fast time, okay!" I had a 104 inch gear. By that time I had already settled on that gear. By 1980, 104 was pretty standard for me.

In '81 I decided, since I'd been riding the road and always sprinted in huge gears, I went all the way up to 108 inch gear, which was kind of my road racing sprint gear. I didn't get that good of a start coming off the line, but I felt big gears were more my style. I started playing with gears a little bit more. By '82 I got second at Nationals, just a tick off the win. Harvey Nitz won, I got second, and I was riding 104 inch gear. From then on I pretty much stuck with that gear.

Training

I don't train very much on the track at all. I train on the roads, anywhere, around Santa Barbara, for the most part. There are a couple of places that are conducive to sprinting, generally flat, not real windy, good roads and not much traffic.

The problem with sprinting and with heavy duty intervals is that your concentration is so much on going hard that you need a pretty clear path. I will run into things — cars are the big fear.

I've found that one of the most successful places for both sprints and intervals is along railroad tracks. They have the longest frontage road without a cross street. The cross streets are what kills you. It's not so much traffic on the road, it's traffic coming across.

Track areas are usually flat. There's usually a section that's both flat with good roads and with no intersections. Many cities have areas that are safe and have railroad tracks.

Distances for sprint and interval practice vary immensely, from the very shortest of about 15 meters up to the longest intervals of about five minutes. Going back and forth from distance to time depends on what energy system I'm trying to key on and a little just for plain variation.

Training was always painful for me. You don't have that same high psyche that focuses out everything else like when you're racing.

Doing repeats is extremely painful. For instance, Kilometer intervals, 5 X 200 meters — do 200 meters, take a lap off, do another 200, take a lap off, do another 200 so you break up the Kilo into five 200s, or three 300s, or two 500s. It was always difficult getting through that part of it.

One of the things that helped me was that I had the discipline to make myself do it -- some riders don't. To keep on hammering yourself like that is really hard. I definitely had a tendency toward self-discipline from early on. It probably ties into a competitive nature. I'll put up with things to get to where I want to go. It's that kind of discipline that "makes" you.

Weights

I did a lot of weight training when I was racing. That was probably the big thing I was noted for. Lifting was the key to my riding.

The biggest thing was squats. Dead-lifting, squats, a number of other lifts . . . I was definitely into doing singles, doubles, triples, very low reps, very high weight. I was trying to get as huge as I could.

During the winter time I put on some fat, but a lot of muscle as well. As the season went on I would lose both muscle and fat but I would still gain strength. I had residual strength from all that training.

I lifted all season, up to a few weeks before the event, but I would emphasize weights much more during the winter time. Lifting like that was almost my sole training. I would ride a little bit, but definitely the gym workouts were the real key.

Phasing off was a progression. I would do more and more riding and less and less lifting. Although the lifting would stay very intense, I had fewer sessions and I did fewer lifts. In the winter time I did leg extensions, squats, deadlifts, hack squats, maybe 45 inclines. I'd do a number of different types of lifts.

By the time I was doing my last preparation for the Olympics or another big competition, the squat would be the only leg lift that I did. I did one or two sets. I might only do one set a week as the season progressed. All I was trying to do at that point was maintain as much strength as I could because most of my emphasis then was on the bike. I tried to get very specific.

I didn't do too much upper body stuff. I wanted to have enough strength to really torque on the bike, but I didn't want to have extra bulk.

I usually stopped a couple of weeks before the final peak. My last lifts might be anywhere between one and three weeks before the ride. I went as heavy as I could. The highest I ever squatted was 500, but I was probably not as deep as I should have been. I liked to try to do deep squats, but I started cheating more and more as I got heavier and heavier — trying not to, but if my spotters weren't as good, I could not go as deep.

When I lifted with good spotters - and I did most of my training with powerlifters - I got in my best lifting. That 500 lbs. was probably not an "honest" squat. That was light by some of the other big riders' standards, because I didn't have the mechanics to lift big. I was too long of leg.

You get these guys who are squatty-legged and real thick and they have the mechanics for lifting. I think some people tend to look at absolute numbers as too much of a factor. It's not the absolute numbers but your improvement that is crucial.

Diet

As you get to higher and higher levels you need to do everything you can to optimize things. Diet is a very important factor. People can eat lousy and still perform well. A lot of people tend to dismiss it, but a one percent difference between riders is a huge difference. Guys win events by hundredths of seconds, so it's not something that you can dismiss.

I'm much in favor of people cleaning up their acts when it comes to nutrition. It will allow them to train harder and recover better. Sometimes you get riders who want to put on weight, other riders want to lose weight. A lot of those things can be done with dietary adjustments.

There are no magic foods. I tend toward what most people would consider a real healthy diet, a lot of fresh vegetables and fruit. A lot of people will do fruit, but they don't have enough vegetables. "Power" riders need enough protein in their diets to build muscle mass.

I got to the point that I didn't think I had a healthy diet when I was training for the Kilo, but I did feel it was effective. I had this super high-fat and super high protein diet because it was the only way I could put on weight and the only way that I could lift big numbers in the gym.

I literally force-fed myself. I would take these shakes with ice cream and pour in a bunch of other concoctions. Then I poured straight oil into it. This thing would hit me like a brick. There were probably 1000 to 2000 calories in a glass. I would groan after I drank it. I was force-feeding myself, eating five to six times a day.

I did gain weight and I did gain strength from it, but I didn't feel it was something that was real healthy long-term. I started shying away from it a little farther along in my career. I think there are discipline-specific things that you can do with diet to increase your performance.

The Olympics

I was probably going better in '84 than '85, but I set up badly for the Olympics because of a couple of different things. 1985 was a redemption year of trying to at least get the World Record because I blew the Olympics.

Two things happened in the Olympics. In the event itself, my helmet slid in front of my eyes during the ride — I couldn't see where I was going. I was distracted and I ran over a couple of sponges. I ran totally out of the red line — I was up at mid track.

There's just so little between winning and losing that if you screw up like that, it's all over. I had never raced with that helmet before. I'd ridden in it just a couple of times but it's different racing. You do everything a little differently. You're sweating a little more, you're bobbing a little more when you're fatigued. It was one of those aero helmets. That was a rather big mistake. But I was probably just shooting at a medal, I wasn't really ready to win.

I had gotten sick before the Olympic Trials and I had to do this incredibly fast peak for the Trails. I didn't have enough time to recover by the time of the Olympics, but I thought I would medal.

A combination of two things went wrong. I had three weeks between the Olympic Trials and the Olympic Games. You can look at that time period two different ways: 1) do you want to peak at the Trials and hold that peak through the Olympics so both are very close together with enough time for mental rest? Or 2) do you want to have the events far enough apart so you kind of have two peaks? But that also means having to get up really, really high for the Trials, because if you don't make the team, you don't have to worry about peaking for the Olympics.

Nationally, if they had held the Olympic Trials on a sea level track, I probably would have won, but it would have been much closer. As it was, I was almost two seconds ahead of Harvey in the Trials because I went that much faster than anybody else at altitude (Colorado Springs).

A fast track benefited me because of my big gear and lack of good endurance. The faster the event was over, the better it was for me. I rode my 104 inch gear whether I was at sea level or at altitude. That was the biggest gear that I could use and still come off the line fast. Coming off the line was determined by how big a gear I could use. Whether at altitude or sea level it was going to be the same, because the wind doesn't take effect until you're at speed. *(riders often go to bigger gears at higher altitude)*

The World Records

I rode the Worlds in '85 on a track that was not real quick. I didn't do that well, I think I ended up like ninth or so. I knew, though, that I could probably get a World Record if I was on a really fast track, like Colorado or another high altitude track — maybe Mexico City. I geared things around that. I looked around and found out they had this track in Bolivia at 11,000 feet and I thought "Holy . . . . that's for me!" Speed was my forte and endurance my weakness in the Kilometer. Since I rode a big gear, it was really to my advantage to have a faster and faster track. I needed a fast track to set the records.

The actual World Record was hard. I wanted to go to Colorado Springs and train there before I went to Bolivia. When I finally set a date for doing it, got officials to be there and all this set up, the weather got too cold in Colorado to train. The seasons are opposite. So I had to come back down from Colorado to sea level to keep training. When I went to altitude to do the record, I went to 11,000 feet and had to race right away. It was severe. It wasn't like going to the Springs.

The Springs was bad enough. You ended up with this really nasty hack from doing hard Sprints. You get a little nauseous at the end — but at that altitude just the <u>warm-up</u> was hard.

To get to the top of the track was an effort. When I did the Flying events I was literally out of breath just doing my roll-in to the start. It was severe. I saw right away why the guys who had tried the hour record stuff up there, had all failed. This was a big jump. It could be feasible to live there and adapt. It's hard. At what point does the lack of oxygen become a bigger factor?

For a Sprint event, a high altitude track is definitely going to be to your benefit because oxygen is that much less of a factor. You still need it, but it's not a purely aerobic event. It's much closer to a pure anaerobic event.

While the ride itself didn't hurt, post ride when I did the World Records, was the worst I ever felt in my life.

I decided to start with the shortest events and work up to the Standing Kilometer. By the time I got to the Standing Kilo, the record I didn't get, that was the last event that I went for. That was about the fifth day I was at altitude and it was really starting to take its toll on me. If I had it to do over

"When I did the Flying events (World Record) I was literally out of breath just doing my roll-in to the start. It was severe. I saw right away why the guys who had tried the hour record stuff up there, had all failed. This was a big jump." CO, '93

again I would have tried to do the Standing Kilometer earlier, but it scared me so much because I was having such a hard time at altitude.

I was literally sick — my head just *throbbed*, I was nauseous, for a half an hour to an hour after the last record attempt, to the point where I couldn't be around other people.

Guys would come up to me and say "Are you okay? Can I get you anything?" and I'd just tell them to go away. I just laid on the track for about half an hour. I was really sick.

At that point I was trying to decide what to do. My father had helped me with funding. I talked with him after the last ride and he asked if it would be worth it for me to stay up there for, say, three weeks, get used to the altitude?

I didn't think I could do it mentally. I was so sick and it hurt so much that I didn't think I could put together another ride after a month of training.

It would have helped to adjust to the altitude. I think I might have been able to do it physically, but that mental thing killed me. That was my last ride, definitely, because that hurt so much.

When I got back to the U.S., I wished I could have done it, but I recognized that I couldn't do it mentally. Once I was at that point of saying "I don't have that inspiration to get out there and do it" I wouldn't be able to. You have to have that motivation.

While I did want that record, that's a hard bit of four weeks training that I would have to have done. I was just fried. I didn't get the record that I wanted the most, but it would have been too difficult. I knew myself.

There was a second factor involved in my decision too. My Standing start that year was not good because I'd had back injuries. Both my Flying starts had improved, especially my Flying 1K. It had improved immensely, but I was struggling with my Standing start all during that year because of my back. That was just one more thing.

It was frustrating, but I got most of what I wanted done, so I kind of called it quits at that.

Having World Records helped a lot.

The Perfect Ride

I like Kilo for the fact that it's kind of a "pure" event, straightforward, easy to understand. "This guy just went friggin' faster than the other guy!" and the athlete is usually big and powerful. It can be very impressive to watch some guy just come off the line fast and hold those kind of speeds.

I'm 6'1". Kilo riders vary quite a bit. They'll tend to be bigger than a roadie, but they're usually just a half size down from a pure Sprinter. When I was at my peak I was probably leaner, but I tend to be on the lean side. I have pretty low body fat. There are definitely some huge guys out there.

I guess from there the only other thing that I really wanted to do was put together the "perfect ride".

I felt I knew what I needed to do to get it done and it was just a matter of getting all the pieces there. Stay injury free, stay healthy, have enough support so that I can take the time to train. From there until I quit in '88, that was what I kept trying to do. But you start running into more and more problems.

Putting together the perfect ride is really a step-by-step, growth, both physically and mentally. Different people have different strengths and weaknesses at different points in their lives. You just have to use whatever

you have to your best advantage.

Putting together the perfect ride is a building process. From year to year I try to set an athlete up with a certain goal in mind — actually I try to get them to set the goal, and then I try to refine it.

Looking at each building block, they have to get stronger and faster. For the Kilometer they need a certain degree of aerobic fitness, so it's gathering all of those. It can be so much of a loner event, it's easy to set markers of what you want to do.

You might say, "Well, this year I'm going to do a 1:10, and do a 1:08 the following year, then a 1:07, do a 1:06," and etc. With that in mind, you go about structuring a program so you can do those things.

I think some people think they can jump all the way to the top right away and every once in a while there is that phenomenon who does, but most riders do not make that kind of progress.

They make bigger progress when they first start, but then it's a matter of chipping away at the different points. You either have weaknesses or you just keep building overall. The mental thing is what the person has to show real early. If they don't have that, I don't think you can change it.

Top riders are always there for the big things. Some riders are there for everything. The real top-notch guys are always there for the big rides.

Some riders find a little different motivation as they get older, for different reasons. Some people get motivated when they are bumped off of teams. All of a sudden you see them back in the spotlight again.

Those sorts of things have changed a lot now because there's money in the sport. There wasn't when I first started riding. You never saw older athletes because they couldn't afford to keep at it. They would just ride when they were young and that was the end of it.

Winning

There isn't any magic pill for winning in bike racing. There are a lot of riders who kind of look around for some magic to make them go fast. They think "This guy went fast because of this thing or that." A lot of the stuff is just real basic. Guys go out there and go hard, that's a huge part of it.

If mentally you can't put it together for the big peaks you're just never going to do that. I'm not too sure what makes a person have that ability. If I look at myself I'd say that it's really my only natural ability.

When I went to the Springs and they did all these tests I never tested well physically. That's why I was never much of a favorite of Eddie B. But I had this desire and I was capable of getting up for the big events. I would perform so much better at a big event than I would just weeks before.

Guys in training rides would consistently do better times and beat me, but when the Big Show came I would kill them. Being able to get up for that is a real mental process.

I'm not sure why some people have that but if I look at my natural ability, that was the only natural ability that I think I had. It's a huge factor and it was a big enough factor that it overcame my physical shortcomings.

While the other guys were bigger and stronger and faster, I would get it

together in the end, and that's what it took.

Velodromes

My favorite velodrome is the World Record track, Bol-Alto Irpavi!

In the U.S. it would be a toss-up. Probably still Colorado Springs, but Minnesota track is a great track. It was a delight to go fast on that track. You could close your eyes and go to sleep and just rocket around the bottom without flinching. I've never been known for holding a tight line because I felt that it was more important for me to put all the power I could into the bike. While I don't try to wander all over the track, I don't mind if I wander a little bit because my emphasis is on going fast. On that track (Minnesota) it is so easy you just stay glued. It was probably the first time that I just about rode the stripe for the whole ride.

There is probably no velodrome I wouldn't go to. The slower the track is the less inspiring it is. Northbrook is not that bad. It may be hard to do good times, but part of that is technical, getting through that big, wide turn. It's a pretty fast surface.

Tracks like Seattle used to have a really rough surface, though it's improved a little bit. It's not a real quick track. Dominguez Hills is not a track that I particularly like racing on, because it's windy, so I tend to do a slower time. It gets dewy and wet.

I like tracks where it's hot. I like Houston even though it's not the most rocket-fast. I like it because it's real hot. I'd like Florida because it's hot, but I don't know what the track's like.

I don't really have a home track. The track I trained at the most is

Dominguez Hills, the Olympic track, because it was the closest, fastest facility.

Encino is more of a technical track. Big riders have a harder time getting through the turns fast. I always have to kind of shut off the gas a little bit. Most of the time you don't need to be learning how to shut off the gas, you need to learn how to turn it on.

Advice to new riders

I would suggest that up-and-coming riders keep it fun. A lot of riders lose that. Some of the riders never realize that it's a game. They think that the strongest rider wins, the fastest rider wins, the guy with the best bike wins, but they never really learn how to play the game.

There are so many disciplines in the sport that you can usually find one that is agreeable to you. If you learn how to play the game you can have a ton of fun and it's what I liked when I first got into it.

When I first started riding I realized that I wasn't always the fastest or the strongest, but I could figure out a way to win. There was this tactical aspect. You could get a little bit clever. There was this technological part of the sport, all these facets that, to me, made it fascinating. There was enough danger involved to kind of get you up there, too.

Early on I learned the history of the sport and that made it really cool. It's something that triathlons don't have. At the time *Competitive Cycling* was out. They had stuff on the things going on in Europe in times past. There was a British magazine, *International Cyclesport*, so you get

some of this exposure to the European scene. It became a cultural thing, too.

Traveling was another big hook in me. I just love traveling. I started when I first began racing as a Junior. I went to Nationals with another guy who was a first year Senior. I was out on this road trip when I was sixteen years old and it's just a whole different way of visiting places.

When I went to Europe and different trips to South America, travel was so much different from a vacation. You were exposed to the area in a totally different way. You learned about the people more sincerely.

People would identify with you. I got invited to places I would never have gone to before. I love that part.

My Best Moments

My three biggest highs in my career were:

First, Somerville, because at the time it was the biggest race in the country. It was my first huge splash as far as being a National rider. After that, winning the Pan Am Games was a big push because I had done a really good time and I won the Gold.

Second, the Olympic Trials. The frustration was the Olympics, but the Olympic Trials would probably stand out as a highlight because it was the closest that I ever came to putting together the best ride of my life, any ride. I felt that I had done just about everything I could.

I had gotten sick before the ride and I'd had to do this really fast preparation, but mentally and physically I'd put together that ride as well as I could. It was very pleasing in those aspects.

My goal was to ride the Olympics and do well and quit after that. I probably would have quit if I had just gotten in the ride that I'd wanted to at the time without winning. But when I had the helmet incident, I couldn't quit on that note. At that point, my whole focus changed. I really wanted those (World) records for redemption. They were my third high.

There seemed to be a little bit different drive. Things weren't all for just this one thing. Probably two or three years before the Olympics and riding the Olympics my whole thing was just riding that race and quitting. It made training easier because I knew the training was going to end right at that point.

After that the focus just kind of evolved into something much more — it's hard to describe. It just wasn't that super-narrow beam, that "okay, this is all I'm doing."

Equipment/Goofy Bikes

My unusual looking bikes came from a couple of things, one is that I always liked to figure things out — what would be the best for the situation? From there I would just play with some different ideas.

Also, I welded since I was a kid, so I made my own bikes when I was starting out. Even on the road I had ridden my own bikes during my second - third year. I had sponsors now and again. They gave me a bike and I rode their bike. Then I'd go back to my own bike or I'd have my bike for training and race on one of theirs. I made a few bikes for friends, stuff like that. That gave me the tools to put together whatever I wanted.

In '82 I tried the first of mounting my handlebars on the fork crown. I came to Nationals in Kenosha with my fork crown steering, but it weirded me out so much. I kept thinking "It's mounted here below my headset!"

For some reason I kept thinking through the mechanics "it doesn't make any difference!" but I kept feeling I was going to pull my wheel out from under myself.

I couldn't get over that. Two days before the ride I hacked it off! I just used the standard drop bar because I still had it coming through. I could just add a bar and go down.

That was an interesting scene because no one else had ridden that stuff yet. That was a wild event on that track. I built the whole bike and it was a full size wheel bike but when I got there I just kept feeling uncomfortable.

At that time the biggest part of my training was just doing Kilos. I'd ride Kilo, after Kilo, after Kilo. That was all I'd do for training. I'd go and I'd warm up for 10 or 15 minutes and then do a Kilo. I try to make the warm-up as short as possible so that I was fresh as possible.

When I was doing some of these rides I felt like my foot was too close to the track. I took the bike, tipped it over and put the pedal down, scraping the bottom. I went "Well, I'll be able to lean pretty far without hitting" but I was still nervous that the pedal looked like it would hit.

Finally I did one Flying Sprint and sure enough, I tagged my pedal. "Oh, great, man, what am I going to do? I'm at Nationals, it's the only bike I've got" I started hunting around for

161

a welder in town, somebody who worked on bikes. It was a Sunday. I started calling true welders in the paper and I come across this guy. So I go "Do you do oxy-acetylene welding?" and he goes "Yeah, come on over."

So I go over and the guy works on big rigs! I told him what I wanted to do "What I need to do is unweld it from the seat post, jam my rear stays down and kick the back end of the bike up so my bottom bracket will raise." I said "So I'm just going to unweld these here, bend the whole thing down and then re-weld them farther down the seat post."

So he lights this thing up and he's got this flame that's literally a foot long! I go "You're going to melt my whole bike!" I'm freaking out, and I go "Would it be alright if I just pay you the money for your time of welding and you just let me braze it?" and he goes "Sure!" Then I did what I wanted to do. But that was one fun little adventure.

At Olympic Trials ('92) I was back in Minneapolis riding the same bike I'd ridden in '88, and it was legal then, but I guess they changed the rules. When I got up on the line and they measured my bike it didn't pass one of the international measurements.

I kept trying to fiddle with the bike to get it to pass, adding chain lengths to get the wheel back far enough and it was about half way out the back stay, like a nib hanging on, so I brought it back to the line and it was literally about 1 millimeter too short, so I couldn't ride the race.

I was so mad. It rained out about three-quarters of the way through the event. "Oh, that's perfect!" I thought. "I'm going to be able to ride because they'll have to re-ride, they'll have to re-ride everybody.

I went to the judges and they said "No, you can't do the re-ride because you didn't get on the line." I talked to one of the chief judges and finally got a ruling in my favor.

I went to a local framebuilder and asked "What can I do here?" We

"At Olympic Trials ('92) I was riding the same bike I'd ridden in '88, and it was legal then, but I guess they changed the rules. When I got up on the line and they measured my bike it didn't pass one of the international measurements. I ended up getting fourth, so I was pleased." Blaine, 1992.

welded on another pair of tips on the back of my pair of tips, and got the wheel back farther. In VeloNews or one of the rags, they had a picture of the tips brazed on top of the other one.

I ended up getting fourth, so I was pleased. At that point I was just sort of goofing around, but I still wanted to ride. Either they didn't check that carefully back in '88 or the rules had changed. I think the international rules had changed.

The measurement that I had built the bike around was one of front wheel. This one was rear wheel, like rear wheel to the bottom bracket. The old measurement was in relation to the front wheel.

At the '85 Worlds, right before my ride they had to bend the fork, I mean literally, right before my ride. I got on the line and there was one rider to go before me. They measured my bike and it didn't pass tech. This was my Olympic bike.

They put it in these stanchions right there on the track and bent my front fork until it would pass. Then I got on the line. I was totally wigged. They said "So do you want us to bend your fork?" and I said "Yeah, I want to ride!" It rode a little different, but more, it was a distraction I didn't need. That was my Olympic bike that Mike Celmins built it for me. He was the noted frame builder around town. I did most of the design. He's much more meticulous than I am.

I got a total kick when I saw Obree's thing. I thought "Here's this guy, he's friggin' off the wall, he did the whole thing up himself, this is great!" — you know? Those sorts of things are what add the great dimension to the sport. It is one of the things that takes it beyond something like track and field, well there's pole vault, but in running, well, the shoes have gotten a little better, but big deal. There is this one other little factor.

Some of the designs that come out, like some of the triathlete bars, to me they just looked ugly. It took a really long time and, even now, I still think they look ugly on a bike, these dork bars, but there are bikes that flow really nice and it looks cool. Scott has a bar that drops in from the inside. I've been using those to play with sprinting. You don't have the control but you're in this really low, sprint position with your arms right together. It could get a little hairy if you get bumped around a little bit.

The Older Athlete

If I had unlimited funds again I'd race Seniors again. I still have the motivation when I want to. If someone would pay me $50,000 a year, I think I could ride better than I ever have before! -- if I got healthy, that's a big key.

The problem for the older athlete is that it becomes harder and harder to heal up. On the other hand, I know so many more things now than I did when I was at my peak in my Kilometer racing. I still have enough base and I feel that you keep gaining up until, I would say, upwards of 50. I don't know where that limit is.

I look at people in cycling, the ages that they've done things. Jack Disney — how old he was when he was Sprinting. Some of these powerlifters, when I was really into powerlifting — the ages that they were at their peaks, guys in their mid-forties who set the World Record, squatting 1000 pounds. That's a pure power event, so guys say "Oh yeah, you can build up endurance, but you can't do the short things" — well, it doesn't get any shorter than a single lift! Riders at a World Championship level — I don't know where that cut-off point is, the body actually deteriorating.

Where you can make such strides, while you can't recover as quickly as the younger rider can, you have such a big base that you've built up over the years, so there are pluses that you can keep drawing from. Like when Zoetemelk won the World Championships — look at Bostick, he's going faster now than he was when he was younger. That end of the sport is pretty wide open.

Most people don't have the kind of drive and focus that they had when they were in their teens or twenties or even early thirties. I've learned to focus on certain things now and I'm able to get more productive with certain things that I wasn't able to do at earlier stages in my life.

I gained a lot of things as I got older, but you can keep getting stronger both mentally and physically, so the idea that people are peaking at these really young ages, I don't believe.

I've seen athletes in many sports keep growing. They usually lose their motivation and/or they get injured, Even if you're not injured, you still have to be motivated.

Coaching

In coaching you have to look into those sorts of things, with the different athletes you work with. "What is it going to take with him?" They are all a bit unique, but the same formulas still hold overall.

Learning those nuances is pretty critical. I'm coaching people now. I'm heading toward it as a full time activity again. When I was racing, it was hard for me to coach beyond a certain level. I felt threatened.

Now I don't really care, my racing is something I do for fun. At that point it wasn't. I wouldn't tell rider what it was I did to get to the top when I was racing. "Figure it out for yourself!" "You can pay me and I'll show you a certain part of it, but I'm still not going to show you all of it." I used to say "That's as far as this train goes."

Coaching is a real blast, to be able to draw on the things that I've done. I still tend to use myself as a guinea pig when I want to do experimental things.

It's been a plus to have had some negative experiences, like when I went to Europe, that I draw on when I'm coaching. I don't have any regrets. There were a lot of bonuses that came from it. I probably wouldn't have been coaching or racing as long as I have if things had gone well in '84. I think I would have completely gotten out of the scene. I had no desire.

The Future

I think people used to come and go from the sport more in the past. Now you see riders stick around on different levels. There are a lot of different ways to stay involved. There's much more money in the sport all the way down to the retail level. There wasn't before.

I have two kids, three and five, both boys. I don't care whether my kids race or not.

I would really like it if they did because I love the sport, but I won't push them toward it. I'd definitely encourage it, but if one ends up being a pianist, that's fine.

My father was real encouraging of the different things that I got into in my life, and it was nice having that. That tends to be the same way that I deal with my own kids.

There were a number of times in my racing career when racing was just this solo thing that I did, no other part of my life touched on it, no girlfriend, no friends, no pictures in my room, I didn't want my bike anywhere near. It was something separate, intense while I did it and that was enough.

I liked having political friends, I liked things in the arts and thing of that nature.

I don't know how it evolved, but now everything flows in and out of everything else.

"In coaching you have to look into those sorts of things, with the different athletes you work with. "What is it going to take with <u>him</u>?""

Chapter 11
ᗧ *Individual Pursuit* ᗧ

The Individual Pursuit is a race between two competitors who begin on opposite sides of the track. It ends in two possible ways: 1) when one rider catches the other (hence its name "Pursuit") or 2) when both riders have covered a certain distance: 4000 meters for Senior men, 3000 meters for Senior women and Junior men 17-18, and 2000 meters for Junior Women 17-18. If no rider is caught, the fastest time determines the winner.

There are two big differences between the Kilometer and the Pursuit.

The first is distance. Pursuits are two to four times as long. The second is the method of win. The point of this race is to have your front wheel cross the finish line on your side of the track before your opponent's wheel crosses the finish line on his/her side of the track.

Logically, the times in the 1st/2nd competition will be faster than the 3rd/4th competition. But in Pursuit, if this is not true, medals are still awarded for the levels at which they are contested. In other words, the 3rd/4th competition could result in times faster than the 1st/2nd competition in the finals, but this makes no difference. It is beating your opponent which is the win in this race, no matter what the clock says.

History

Bicycle racing has always involved riders chasing other riders, whether on their way to the finish or around a track trying to lap the field. The contest of riders exchanging leads over a given distance when evenly matched has long thrilled audiences.

While the Pursuit contest is solely against an opponent, the clock is not an insignificant factor. World Record times can be established if they are accomplished.

Formerly, World Record times for the 3000 meter distance were disallowed if they were set during the Pursuit event when two people were on the track. They were only allowed if the distance was covered as a pure Time Trial, one person at a time. In 1993, when Rebecca Twigg set a new World Record over this distance during Pursuit competition, the rules had been changed and her time was recognized as a new record. Apparently officials had decided that 3000 meters was 3000 meters whether one or two people were on the track.

Qualifying

In 1994, all riders could qualify for Individual Pursuit at the National Championships. The top four men and women's times qualified them for the Semifinals.

While this wide-open eligibility would seem to draw every rider in the U.S. for an infinitely tedious rounds of Pursuits, in practicality, it does not. First, you have to have a track bicycle. Second, it is expensive to go to National Championships. With only four final places possible, the logic of

America's 1995 Pan Am Gold Medal Pursuitists, Janie Eickhoff and Kent Bostick ("Bostisauris Rex"). World Cup, 1994.

spending time and energy for one ride which might demonstrate its own inappropriateness precludes vast numbers trying for these few spots.

While qualifying rounds have two riders on the track, each rider is only riding for time and elimination of riders who are passed prior to he leader's final lap. Qualifying rounds seed riders so that they are evenly matched at the time of actual competition.

Competition may consist of Quarterfinals, Semifinals and Finals, depending on the occasion and number of riders. All riders must have a qualifying time. In the first round, the fastest riders ride last.

The Start

Riders are held in a Standing start by officials. There is no Flying start in Pursuit. The holding official must hold the rider neutrally, neither restraining nor pushing him/her, the same as in the Kilometer. Riders begin at the same position on the track as in the Kilometer, front edge of the front wheels over the starting line, and bicycles between, and parallel to, the black and red lines.

The same two officials must hold all riders for a given competition (barring unforeseen circumstances). Officials at the start are responsible for each rider starting the race in exactly the same manner.

Sometimes riders are very nervous and take some time getting ready at the start. Sometimes they appear to play "head games" with each other, forcing each other to wait or even changing their minds after they have signified their readiness.

Coaches may watch riders on the other side of the track and communicate their actions to their rider so that their rider will not have to strain their necks to see what's going on across the track. This also relieves stress on the riders.

The Starter and the Assistant Starter stand in the middle of the track, back to back, each facing one of the riders. As each rider is ready, a red or green flag is raised, one on either side of the track, to communicate this readiness to officials and others on the track.

The Starter then calls " Riders ready — Timers ready . . ." and the gun signifies the start. If there is any problem which should delay the start, officials are expected to be notified <u>before</u> the gun is fired.

Once the gun goes off, timing begins and riders are expected to race to the finish barring an unforeseen mishap.

The Race

Once the race begins, timing is taken at half laps throughout, a big job for officials. Red line markings painted permanently on the track in half laps serve as a start/finish line for each rider.

Riders can receive feedback on their times per lap, but only by one person. The person monitoring time/pace must be either before or after the rider's finish line. Usually, coaches or monitors stand after the rider's finish line. They may indicate the rider's pace through gestures as well as shouting numerical times.

Top riders usually have a fairly accurate idea of what time they are capable of riding and plan in advance to maintain a certain time per lap in order to arrived at the finish in the overall time they seek.

Part of the key to Pursuit is consistency, lap after lap, and staying on the black line the whole time. The coach gives the rider the information s/he needs for consistency.

Riders are not allowed to compete in more than two Pursuits per day, and must be given a minimum of two hours rest between competitions. In unusual circumstances this rule may be waived by the Chief Referee.

In his second ride at World Cup in 1994, Kent tried taking aerodynamics one step further with "The Helmet". (How could he hear his coach give him his splits?) He'll try anything he thinks might work. At age 42, winning National and World level titles is pretty impressive.

Quarterfinals

If competition is offered at the Quarterfinals level, it includes the top eight riders from the qualifying rounds. Fastest and slowest riders are matched using times established during qualifying. Winners go on to the Semifinals, losers are designated fifth through eighth according to finish times.

While the race is over when one rider catches another, the first rider must complete the full distance in order to establish a time used for seeding in the Semifinals.

Semifinals

In Semifinals, riders are again matched fastest with slowest, first vs. fourth, second vs. third. At this level, catching another rider finishes the race. The winner need not finish the distance, but goes on to the finals against the winner from another round.

Finals

Winners of the Semifinals race for the top two spots in the finals. Losers from the Semi's are placed in third and fourth place according to their times. If Semifinals are not used, the top two riders from the qualifying round race for first and second.

The Finish

In Quarterfinals, riders passing riders (who are then eliminated) must complete the full distance in order to establish a time for the later rounds. In the unlikely (but possible) event that two riders have the same time at the finish, the rider with the fastest last lap will be determined the winner.

In Semifinals and Finals, the race is over when one rider passes the other and the gun is sounded.

Mishaps

During the qualifying rounds, riders who have legitimate mishaps (as determined by officials) will be allowed to restart in a later round, either alone or against another rider. The rider who did not have the mishap, must continue the ride in order to establish a time which determines seeding for later rounds.

In Quarterfinals, Semifinals and Finals, if either rider has a mishap within the first kilometer, the race will be rerun. Mishaps at other times are resolved through use of a formula related to where each rider was at the time of the mishap. This formula will not be reviewed here but is presented in the USCF Rule Book.

False Starts

If either rider starts before the gun or if she is pushed, a False Start must be called within the first 30 meters and a re-start occurs. After two False Starts, whatever happens on the third start is final. If the rider False Starts for a third time, s/he is eliminated from competition. Otherwise the race begins.

Race Equipment

A separate set of lap cards and a bell is provided for each rider. A red and a green disk is placed at each rider's start/finish along with markers at a point 30 meters ahead of those discs. This is the zone within which False Starts must be called.

Single red and green flags mark the first kilometer of each ride, double red and green flags mark the last kilometer of each ride. These symbols help the Starter in restarts and everyone

else for information.

Sponges encourage Pursuiters to maintain their ride no lower than the measurement line, as in the Kilometer.

Carl Sundquist and Rebecca Twigg celebrate their Olympic dreams.

Bicycle Equipment

This event has influenced greater changes in equipment design and use than any other track event. The serious riders think of aero tubing, discs, aero bars, helmets and special skinsuits, any physical factor which might allow improved final times. Look at the U.S. National Team for the latest in equip-

ment.

Finally

The Pursuit is a uniquely competitive event as it challenges a rider's endurance and competitive nature at the same time. It is primarily an individual endurance event, but it has become so competitive that speeds accomplished by elite riders are impressive in spite of the fact that speed per se is not the prime issue.

Pursuiters often do well in Mass Start races, such as the Points race and the Madison -- any event where a long distance chase is necessary for the win.

Pursuiters are not normally as competitive in Sprints due to differences in power and up-to-speed demands in that event which are not a focus of Pursuit training. Pursuits require a rider to, first and foremost, concentrate on efficient use of energy for the long run, whereas Sprints demand explosive response.

But, just when you feel you can safely assume that Sprints and Pursuit don't mix, along come Janie Eickhoff and J'Me Carney to force second thoughts on this issue.

Pursuit
Rebecca Twigg

Rebecca Twigg began her career by winning the Junior Women's Omnium in 1979. She then won the U.S. National Women's Pursuit Championship five times, 1981, '82, '84, '86, and '92. She has been World Pursuit Champion five times, 1982, '84, '85, '87, and '93. In 1983 she was second in the World Road Championships.

*In 1984, she was the Silver Medalist in the Olympic Road Championships, but, even more incredibly, she **swept** the US National Track Championships in all major events: Sprints, Kilometer, Pursuit and the Points race.*

In 1986, she won the US National Kilometer Championship and was second in the World in Pursuit. At the Pan Am Games in 1987 Rebecca was a Gold Medalist in both the Road Championship and the Pursuit.

She set an American record which still stands in the Time Trial for 500 meters (Flying start) — 30.642 in 1986. From 1984 to 1991 she held the record for Kilometer (Standing start).

In 1992, Rebecca made a comeback, winning the Pursuit once again at Nationals and winning a Bronze Medal in the Olympic Games.

In 1993 she broke her American record and set a new World Record of 3:37.347 for 3000 meters at the World Championships. She can only be described as: incredible.

I was born in Honolulu, Hawaii on March 26, 1963. My family moved to Madison, Wisconsin for a year and a half and then ended up in Seattle.

How I Got Started

I got started in bicycle racing as a tourist with my mother and sister. We'd go on tours around the Seattle area, San Juan Islands and Mt. Rainier. We belonged to a touring club, Cascade Bicycle Club.

Jerry Baker came to one of the meetings. He's involved in everything. He showed up at one of the meetings talking about the National Championships and how they were going to be in Seattle that summer (1977). He had information about racing, about who to contact and who to talk to . . .

My mother looked into it more than I did. I think that she thought I might be good at it, I was so strong as a touring rider. It was better to have me race against people in races than be dropping her and my sister in touring rides! She saw the schedule, so she pretty much scouted around for everything.

From the start, I used to ride Friday nights at Marymoor and Wednesdays at SIR (Seattle International Raceway), a road circuit training race.

From the first couple months, I raced both road and track. I didn't really prefer one over the other, but I liked the excitement of the track a little bit more.

"Winning is not the most important thing to me, improvement is. It puts too much pressure on you if you say "I have to win." I'm motivated if it's not just for me, if it's going to make other people happy too. My particular gift is concentration. I think I focus better than most people. Otherwise, all I do is do my best."

The first year was probably too much. I didn't know what to do. I got third in the road race the first year in the Intermediate girls and fifth on the track, because I didn't know what to do. I was a little overwhelmed. I had 6 to 10 different coaches telling me what to do right before the start of the race! All well-meaning. "The most important thing is . . . this is all you have to remember . . . ."

I can't say enough for all the people in the Northwest. They really encouraged me and helped me with equipment and all kinds of stuff.

I rode the State Championships on a bike that I borrowed from the Tamura brothers — they own Velocipede and Pine St. Cycle. Jim Garganoff was a key person in helping me. He thought I could be a World Champion the first year I started riding.

Glen Erickson and Kay Henshaw also helped an awful lot. I lived at Glen's house for a couple of months and then moved to Kay's house. Kay was real supportive. We trained together for a couple of years. They were really great.

Some of the races I did at the National level, I'd call Kay at 1:00 in the morning and say "Kay, I can't sleep! I'm afraid I'm not going to do well!" She'd say "Oh, don't worry about it, just let your legs do the work, they'll pull through for you." or something like that. She'd calm me down and gave me more confidence.

Eddie B. was very, very important for getting from the National to the International level.

Harvey Nitz gave me some good tips about Pursuiting and Kilo riding too. He's so into it. He was one of the few riders who was a thinker, who would try new things. I heard about some of the crazy things he did, like putting on an oxygen mask to simulate altitude.

J'Me (Carney) was instrumental in keeping me motivated when I was making the comeback. Everything was so important to him, it made me feel like it was more important to me too. It's a lifestyle.

How I Became a Pursuiter

Eddie B. discovered my talents in Pursuiting at the 1980 Nationals in San Diego. I think Eddie was the Junior coach. He was with the USCF anyway. It was the next to the last day. I still had one more day of the Junior Omnium event left. I had gone back to my hotel a block or two away from the track. It was like 8:30 at night.

Danny Van Haute knocked on the door. He said "Eddie B. wants you to come to the track and ride a time for

World Championships, Colorado Springs, 1986

the 3000 meters, for Pursuit, and see if you can qualify for Worlds. I'm like "Well, okay." So I got all my stuff ready and got out there.

The whole program was over by the time I got a chance to ride. I didn't get a warm-up at all. I just jumped out there on the bike. He didn't coach me at all, I just rode circles. It seemed to take forever. I rode around and around. People were leaving because the program was over and it was late at night. I ended up doing a 4:06. He was

impressed, because the winning Senior Women's time was 4:09!

I guess I had to go under 4:00 to make it to World's, so they still took the Senior Women's winner, Betsy Davis. For a second year Junior, I wasn't that disappointed. It was a thrill to be noticed by Eddie.

At that time I really did both road and track. The next year he worked with me three weeks before the Nationals and did a little more training for the Pursuit. During the Senior Women's Pursuit, I rode against Connie Carpenter in the finals as a last year Junior and won by less than a second. It was really exciting. Eddie always wore a hat. The last lap he took his hat off and he was going nuts, so I figured "He sees something, I'd better go really fast!" and I ended up winning. That was exciting for me.

They took me to Worlds that year, but Eddie couldn't go because it was in Czechoslovakia. Because he had defected from Poland, he was afraid they would pick him up. He couldn't go with me that year, but he went the next year and that's when I won the World's for the first time. I became a specialist in Pursuit because of Eddie

I was still a Junior when Eddie began having me specialize in Pursuit. The way they had Juniors back then, they didn't have specialized events. It

was an Omnium. They had three different events, a short Points race, a very short Scratch race, and a medium length Scratch race.

The Pursuit

There are preparations that I make for the track, but I tend to forget my routine because I only race the track a couple times a year. I have to remind myself what to do.

There have been times when I've felt too much pressure, but then I just tell myself "Well, you're here. You just have to ride it and do your best." That's all there is to it. "You're here. You don't have a way out." Once you get to the start line you're there. You can't back out of it. You gotta do it. It's only 3000 meters long, so it's not like I'm going to have to be hurting that long. The more important the event is, the more important the goal. If it's the World title or making the Olympic Team, "if you really want it, this is where it counts."

I do a lot of road racing because of my sponsorships and because it is such good training. I have a lot of natural speed, but the roads give me the endurance power. I get on the track to do specific events. This year when I got on the track I tried to coast once, but you're reminded real quick not to try to do that!

Mechanical issues have never been a problem for me until the 1994 World's. I had a lot of problems then. My seat slipped, my bars came loose and at one point I found my derailleur was missing. Usually someone has set up my equipment and it's right. I haven't had to worry about it.

I start warming up on the track if

I can. I start riding a gear that is smaller than I will race in. I like getting a feel for the track. Then I might ride the rollers. I basically spin, stretch a little or something. I get to the track at least an hour before the program starts.

When I first start the Pursuit I only think about getting off to a good start. I figure if I start well, then things are off on the right foot (so to speak).

I don't plan a certain time per lap. If I'm up in my time then I might relax. I'd rather hear whether I need to go faster or slower. Then I don't have to actually think during the race, I can just ride. My coach or timer plans my splits and then tells me what to do.

Eddie was really good about keeping track of my splits and also what the other rider was doing. I never watch the other rider. That would break my concentration. I try to just get in tune with my physical self and ride as hard as I can.

I taped my feet in the past, but the shoes I'm using now don't come loose, the velcro is very good, so I don't feel the need for the tape. I've gotten used to the clipless pedals. Carl came out of them during a start during training and broke his collarbone. But Carl's a big guy and he's strong. I have a pretty smooth start and riding style, so I don't worry about coming out — not until something happens, anyway.

I try to do something pretty close to the straight arm start. Eddie had a hard time teaching me that. The idea is to use your back and arms, not your legs. You don't want to wear out your legs in the start.

I stand until I get up to top speed. You don't want to sit down too soon

because then you can't take advantage of gravity and you wear your legs out.

So, you sit down when you're at top speed and you hope you're not in the middle of a turn. On a short track, that's kind of difficult. You might be in the third turn or later. I just concentrate on when I'm at top speed. Whenever I'm there, I sit. On a 333 track it works out pretty well at a half a lap, before you go into the third turn. I can't really remember where I sit down on a 250 meter track.

Once I sit, I think "Get into aero position" on the aero bars. I consciously remind myself to get in aero position. Even at the Worlds I had to tell myself "You're not in the aero bars, get in the aero bars." It's still not automatic. Otherwise, my position is pretty much set up. Other than getting into the bars, I really don't think about my position.

Once I'm sitting and in position I know I'll just grind it out, but I also have to be careful not to go too fast in the beginning. If you do that, you blow up. I try very hard to keep the same rhythm. It's pretty internal. I know my legs are comfortable at certain RPMs. I try to just keep the same rhythm, but otherwise it's just internal. There's a certain feeling I'm looking for. Toward the end of the race I think of maintaining, not dropping my pace. If I have anything for the last lap or two, depending on the size of the track, I just put it all in.

During the race, I try not to think at all. Eddie trained me with hand signals. He'd say "Steady" or "Up" or Pick it up". Sometimes he'd say "Pick it up a little" so I wouldn't overreact.

In 1993 I told the coaches exactly how I wanted them to give me my times. It lets me know what I need to do. I don't want to know the relative times, I just want to know what I have to do.

Probably the biggest mistake beginners make in riding the Pursuit is that they start too hard and then completely die later on. In my pacing, I pretty much have an internal rhythm. Through training I know what a certain lap time feels like. I don't try to go too fast until I know that I can hold it til the end. Usually you don't have any big surges if you're doing it right. You try to pace it.

If I have a really good race, I'm not aware of anything except my coach. I just focus on him. If he says "ease back," or "keep the same pace." or "increase the pace," I just concentrate on my rhythm, more than anything. You don't really think about the pain. You just think about maintaining the pace. I just block it out. Basically I'm there, I have a job to do, and I just have to go out there and do my best.

After the race I warm down however I can, usually on a road bike or rollers, depending on what's available. Sometimes tracks have a warm-up track and sometimes they don't. I warm-down at higher RPMs.

Motivation

I feel the most motivating pressure at the Worlds. I love to ride Worlds. The Olympics is more show. Worlds is kind of like a reunion of people every year. There are always a few more. At lower level races there are more lower level riders, but at the World's you only get the top two or so riders.

I wouldn't say that I plan things. There are certain things I expect of myself. I expect a certain level and I expect to be able to do certain things. But I get to a certain point where I know I can't demand it of myself. I can't demand that I win the Worlds, I can only ask that I do my best and that I keep doing the right things to get there or to get toward that direction.

There's a minimum level I expect of myself. The rest is "Well, if everything goes right . . . then it happens." Basically I head in the right direction and if all goes well I'll get there! It puts too much pressure on you if you say "This is absolutely what I have to do this year."

Winning is not the most important thing to me. What's always been most important to me is improving. There are 100 different ways that you can see improvement. My particular gift, first, is concentration. I think I can focus better than most people. That's really the main thing.

There are other small things that I've brought out more because they help more. Like not being too hard on yourself and only doing the best that you can in training. If everything goes right then it will go right in races. But mostly not being too hard on yourself, not putting too much pressure on yourself, like "I have to win." You know you don't have to, all you have to do is do your best.

In racing, I like to see improvement. If I'm involved with someone, even, like, Eddie, it was very important to him that I won. He made me feel like it was more important that I win. Other people give me more reason, they help me find reasons to want to do well. More motivation, like "This is going to mean something to somebody," so it's not just something for me, it's going to make other people happy too.

Training

The best thing to do to train for Pursuit is riding road and stage races. Pursuiting is an event of fitness. You need to be able to go fast but you need to be able to hold that speed for a long time. Speed comes pretty natural to me. I'm not talking about explosive Sprint speed, but just high speed in general. It's pretty easy for me, so I just need to train the fitness part. Road racing is the best kind of training for that.

Racing is just a better kind of training. If you can't race you just train through it, you do intervals, for Pursuiting you do a lot of intervals. Besides the general fitness and speed, you need to do distance. You need to practice learning — making your body learn — certain lap times.

1993 World Record

My 1993 World Record was not planned at all. I got to the Worlds and I'd been training really hard but I had a hair of lingering bronchitis I caught in July that I was fighting hard to get rid of. I was trying hard to take care of myself and still train and so on, but it was still lingering just a hair.

I traveled over to Norway and felt horrible when I got there. It was probably the first bad travel experience I've ever had. I was there for a few days feeling really slow and horrible.

J'Me was doing a race in Germany or Italy and he wasn't riding real well either because he was traveling all over, by car, by plane, and everything. He was just wiped out. He went to the track early so he could get some track time. He wasn't feeling well on the road. He decided to forfeit his road position, because he had made the road team as well as the track team.

He got to the track and figured out right away what I needed to do. He helped me and basically dug me out of a hole and got me back on track in the next couple of days. Then I just rode fairly well. For me it would have been better if he had been feeling better and raced well also. That was the hard part, seeing him not do well. It almost made me not want to do well myself. I felt guilty that I was doing well.

He got me back on track physically and mentally. I'm not really sure quite what it was, he just helped me get motivated again. Part of the problem was that I wasn't getting a good track workout. I hadn't been on the track for a long time. There were all these people there and it was a steep wood track. There are fewer women in track and it's somewhat intimidating because of the high speeds and the close proximity to other riders. The track just never seemed to be clear enough for my training.

When I'm in Colorado Springs there's hardly anyone else out there. I have the whole track to myself. It's a bigger track and everything, so that was part of the problem. J'Me had me do some stuff on the road to compensate for that.

In the past, if you won a Worlds in World Record time, if there was someone else on the track at the same time, it didn't count. They thought you could be drafting, it could be a teammate or something to help pull you around. This has apparently changed, and it's a good change. They should count World Championship times as World Records.

I heard that they allowed my new World Record and it was during a World Championship that it happened. Breaking World Records after my layoff was a surprise to me. It was more exciting to me that I would be able to go that fast and faster each ride. Winning the Worlds is great, but I was so glad that I wasn't limited by age, that I could still put that fast a ride together and go faster and faster each time.

World Records were not that important except that Jeannie Longo always made a big deal about how she broke all the American records and I had never really thought about records before that. By then I had retired, so I couldn't really do anything.

It was kind of satisfying to break records that she had made a big deal about. She tried to do a record in Colorado Springs and tested positive for amphetamines. She said it was some cold medicine and "The Americans are just out to get me, they're trying to preserve the American record." She can be such a bad sport. I respect her riding ability, but the other things are ridiculous. She thinks people are against her and that's really not the case.

Heartaches

I've lost a couple of World Record times because of officials. In Colorado Springs I tried to do a Pursuit time and I had a front disc on. It was a windy day and I was going all over the track so I didn't even finish the time.

They had a Flying 500 after that so I said "Well, I may as well do that." I did it, but I was supposed to be — and nobody told me this — I was supposed to be below some line, a tape or something, they never really did explain it to me, so I still don't understand. They got the time, but they made me re-do it. It was still a World Record time, but it wasn't as fast as my first time.

I was riding the USA-USSR meet in '87 at Dominguez Hills. I rode a really tough Kilo, I did a 1:13.14. I would have liked to have had that record, but they didn't have the sponges out, so it didn't count. This was a big international meet, right? It's frustrating.

I have found myself involved with politics a little bit, but I try to stay out of it. I have one interesting story.

J'Me gave me my times during Nationals/Olympic Trials (1992) and I won. I wanted him to give me times during the Olympics too. If it worked, why change it, right? He was going anyway because he qualified in Team Pursuit. Some of the coaching staff started making noises the morning before I was going to ride. I rode the Qualifier at 6:00 in the evening.

In the morning it was "We want to talk to you at 1 PM." I showed up at 1 PM, but no one was there. I had an idea they wanted to talk about J'Me coaching me, but they didn't show up.

I was warming up and didn't know all of what was going on, but I guess they took the stopwatch away from

J'Me. He had it for the qualifying and gave me my times, and that was fine. Then something happened — they got pressure from somewhere — so they took the stopwatch away and were threatening J'Me.

They should just want whatever's going to get the best results. They said "He's a rider, not a coach, so he's not supposed to be out there." "Whatever works" was our feeling. J'Me had already told me he'd help me. He didn't want to let me down so he was trying to deal with these people and help me at the same time. That got to be pretty nasty. They didn't put him on the National Team the next year even though he made the Olympic Team in two events. It was politics and I had to get involved in politics then. It wasn't fair at all.

At the Worlds J'Me didn't get to time me even though he turned me around and everything. He didn't try to, he had so many problems, fine. I had one of the National Coaches time me, but it wasn't the same.

The problem is that they are getting money from their sponsors and they are picking the people who are "supposed" to help everybody, they're National Coaches. So it's confirmation that they're doing the right thing and they're coaching the riders to the World Championship title. It's justification for getting money. They're losing the whole point of everything.

Thank goodness Mark Gorski was in there last year. He was an elite athlete, so he understands, but he's still under a lot of political pressure. He knows there's a balance there

somewhere.

You still have to remember that the main goal is to get the best results possible. Everybody's got to work together. EDS came in and they got stationed in Colorado Springs. They

"J'Me gave me my times during Nationals/Olympic Trials (1992). I ended up winning. I wanted him to give me times during the Olympics too. If it worked, why change it, right?" Blaine, 1992

cleaned things up a lot and kind of played watch dog. They can't do everything, but it's somewhat harder for politics to prevail.

Janie Eickhoff's best event is probably the Kilo, but they don't have it at the World's. They should have it. I was on the Women's Commission of the UCI years ago and I suggested that they add it to the Junior Women's World's, but I could only push for one

thing at time, I thought.

The USCF did their political thing and somehow I didn't receive the mail from the UCI Women's Commission. The letters got diverted, they didn't get sent on. They said I was missing meetings so I couldn't serve any more. I don't really like politics that much anyway, so I didn't really fight it.

Best Memories

My favorite accomplishments are probably my earlier ones, it's hard to say. Being at Worlds the first time, before that winning the first National title, I won a Time Trial and a track Omnium.

Even then I liked the track more.

The track meant more to me. Winning the Worlds the first time in 1982, winning the Pursuit as a Junior meant something, but it was a half importance, not a big importance.

With the Olympics it was more an experience. It was something that was exciting just to participate in. Winning a medal was, like, "Well thank God we didn't disappoint everybody!" It was neat just being at the Olympics and having everybody cheering for us, driving to the start of the race two hours beforehand, people waving their flags, having all the banners around the course and all the people . . . . that was exciting. The medal was like "Well, we did our job!" Those were probably the biggest ones.

1984 Nationals was fun. (*Rebecca swept all categories*) I always liked to consider myself a well-rounded person, so that made things kind of complete. It's nice to do things differently. I'm fortunate that I'm not a pure Sprinter or only a very long distance person, that I can kind of "mix and match" and play around with different events.

1993 was disappointing because I knew I wasn't up to the same level and it was really frustrating. I went slower every ride. Inside I was thinking "This never happened before! If I was in my old form . . . !" — it was frustrating. I just didn't have the fitness. I basically took three years off and didn't ride a whole lot -- maybe for a month or so here and there. I had no base. I conjured up fitness at the last minute, but it wasn't enough. The "old miles" stay on you, but not after three years.

We started looking through the

Olympic Team celebration, Blaine, 1992

program reading off a bunch of people who won several Worlds in a row. You don't see their name for a while and then they come back and they win a number of years later, so that made me start thinking.

Toward the end of my "first" career when I retired, I didn't see any other ways to improve except for in other areas of my life and that's what I wanted to explore. I completed an associate degree in CIS, computer information science, and worked as a computer programmer. It was very different.

The 1992 Olympics lured me back into bike racing, because the Pursuit is part of the Olympics. 1996 is a direction. I would never put that kind of pressure on myself, but that's another reason for me to keep going. It's not only improvement, I'm enjoying racing.

Fan Mail

I get fan mail. I didn't get much when I retired, but when I'm doing well, I get more. A lot of autograph requests, more so than before. I got a lot after '84. There are so many "fan"

types in Southern California. In Seattle, you can see somebody really famous walk down the street and it's "Oh, so what." In Southern California they're so much into idolization. With Hollywood, everyone's trained to idolize.

Around Olympic time I had more fan mail, but I still get a lot. Again, it gives me more reason to see why I'm racing. Maybe I'm inspiring somebody or somebody else is happy that I'm doing what I'm doing besides me.

Velodromes

I don't really have a favorite velodrome. Not Colorado Springs because I lost the Worlds in '86 there. The weather's so unpredictable.

My home track was Marymoor, it's kind of cold. I don't really have a home track now. I've lived and trained a number of places. Marymoor's the place where I started, so that's one of the important ones.

T-Town is a big one because they do such a good job of promoting cycling, it's fun to race there. I like Indianapolis. I guess for current racing I probably like those two best.

When they first built Indianapolis in '82 they had the Sports Festival there and had some of the biggest crowds ever. That was part of the reason I liked it there, and it's warm.

There are no velodromes I actually dislike. I rode Alpenrose once and I wasn't crazy about it. The transitions are abrupt and it's kind of scary.

Minneapolis is a nice track. It's fast, but when I was there it was cold. The track itself is great, it's nice to

have a wooden track. Too bad it wasn't covered. I really like the warmer tracks.

Advice for New Riders

I would suggest new riders go to a bike shop that has racing type of equipment. People there usually know more about racing. They would know about club rides, training rides and races. They might even sponsor a team through the shop.

New riders should ride with experienced riders. They should interview them — ask them questions, find out if they want to do it and what they need in order to get into it. Buy a helmet. Shorts are good, you don't need a jersey to begin with, gloves and shoes. Actually you don't even need shoes at first.

My advice to anyone starting in road racing or track racing is: if you have an interest, you never know how good you might be until you go out and try it. The worst that can happen is that you crash, you might get a little road rash, but once you crash you find out "Oh, this isn't so bad."

The hardest part, is going out and trying it. A lot of the tracks have velodrome classes and that's a good place to start. They make it fun, too. As to events, try them all to start with. If you naturally gravitate toward any one particular one, then you can specialize.

The Future

I programmed for a while and I'm okay at it. I'm a good programmer, but I'm used to being the <u>best</u>. It's a hard transition. I'm still trying to find something. I don't necessarily have to be the best, but it needs to be something that I'm so absorbed by that it's really

fascinating.

Programming was fun at times, but it's pretty different. I'm interested in having kids some time down the road.

I don't really have any plans after '96. I wish I knew what I could be really good at besides bike racing. That's really a dilemma. For a lot of top athletes, that is the very best thing they can do, but there comes a point where you have to do something else.

I was a tourist from 1976 to 77. I started racing in 1977 and quit in 1988. I started training again at the end of '91 and began racing in '92. Now it's one year at a time.

Winning is always a pleasure.

Pursuit
Carl Sundquist

Carl has won the Gold Medal in the United States National Individual Pursuit Championships four times, 1985, '86, '87 & '92. He has also been a five-time National Team Pursuit Champion in 1985, '87, '89, '91 & '92.

In 1987 Carl was a member of the U.S. Gold Medal Team Pursuit team in the Pan American Games. In 1993 Carl won Gold Medals at Master's Nationals for Team Pursuit and the Points race. The 1993 Master's Team Pursuit Team set a new National Record for 4000 meters.

In 1994 Carl won a Silver Medal in the World Championships in Team Pursuit. In 1995, he won a Gold Medal at the Pan American Games in Team Pursuit. He has plans for 1996.

I was born November 24, 1961 and grew up in Indianapolis. I was in Florida since 1987. I've relocated to Colorado and Arkansas.

My home track for all practical purposes is Colorado. It's been that way, basically, since 1986. Prior to 1986 it was Indianapolis, but I haven't spent that much time in Indianapolis since then. I'm in Colorado every summer to ride the track up there.

How I Got Started

I got started in cycling back when I was in high school, the winter of 1977-78. I worked at a bike shop where all the employees were really involved in bike racing. Because of my surroundings, I got involved and put together a good bike, but I was also swimming competitively in high school at the time. I didn't stick with cycling as a main objective, but I had a good bike put together and all that.

After I stopped swimming I dusted off the bike, took it out of the basement, and I started riding. I had the advantage of knowing a few people and knowing where the rides were and things like that. I began working at the bike shop because I had a bike stolen and bought a bike there prior to that.

I don't remember exactly how I started racing. Most everybody in Indianapolis was affiliated with a group called the Speedway Wheelmen, one club which is pretty predominant in the city. So I knew everybody. Unless they had out of town connections, they usually rode for that club. They raced track, they did everything.

I raced everything in the beginning. When the track opened in Indianapolis it was very organized. They were smart. I think they brought Roger Young in and contracted him as the racing director. He put together a basic race schedule in the Fall.

They have the Olympic Sports Festival now. They held that in Indianapolis in 1982. Following that, in 1983, Roger began a racing school, so all the local people who hadn't raced before could kind of get a grasp of things. He put together a really good racing schedule for every Friday

"I get angry and I will use that anger in a very positive way to improve my performance. I've tried generating false anger, but it's not the same thing. If you find something that really makes you angry that's relevant, it can help your performance immensely." Early lap, Olympic Trials, 1992

night race. From that I started doing all sorts of different races. I did a little of everything.

If I had to single out one, single individual who helped me the most in my career, it would have to be Roger Young. He was advising me from the beginning of my cycling, so he knows my abilities extremely well. I can always call him up and ask him for advice. I can always rely on him for good answers.

Others have helped me, but in a lesser sense. I saw Eddie B. at the House of Delegates meeting. Seeing how things are now versus how they were when he gave so much of himself, it's beyond a night and day difference now. The Federation is run like a nine-to-five business. That place shuts down. Everybody's tappin' their toes and lookin' at the clock, and it's 10 minutes until five or whenever they're supposed to go home, and that place just vacates. '85, '86, '87 are the years I was there when Eddie was around — I don't know what things were like prior to that, I'm sure they were pretty much the same — Eddie was in the office until 10 o'clock, 11 o'clock at night, we'd go down there, talk to him — he would make the time to spend with you to do what he thought was important to make things better.

It's become "it's somebody else's job", not like Eddie. That was not just Eddie, that was kind of that whole staff back then, '85, '86, '87. The secretaries from the coaching office used to come out to the races. These women would cry when we would have a bad day. They were that involved, they knew us by name. The staff's become so large now that it's very impersonal. I can walk into the administrative offices and there're a hand full of people there that know me, but by and large, most of the people don't.

Specialization

For the first two years I didn't really specialize in anything. As a matter of fact, ironically, at Nationals in '83 I rode the Kilo and the Sprints.

At Nationals in '84 I rode the Kilo, and maybe the Sprints -- I think I rode the Kilo and the Points race.

I didn't ride the Pursuit until Nationals in 1985. I think my time in 1983 was 5:27 and in '84 it was 5:17. In the Fall of '84 I was down in Miami doing a race series, the Coconut Grove race. Back in mid-80s they had two days of one mile time trials. They would take your best time and then

they would have a road race, then they would have the criterium.

In 1984 I ended up third in the one-mile time trial, behind Hugh Walton who had the record (I'm not sure whether he still does or not), and Gene Samuels who is very good at short distances since he's a Kilo rider.

At that point Roger, having seen how I developed on the track for the last few years in Indianapolis, said he thought it was time that I started to specialize. He thought that the Pursuit would be the best thing for me.

In 1985 I did the 7-Eleven Gran Prix. They had it in '83, '84 and '85, I'm not sure about '82. I did real well in those — all the ones they had at the various tracks, the one in Atlanta that year, Trexlertown, and probably Northbrook, I think, also, in Chicago. So I scored a lot of points and I was doing well in the Pursuit as well.

That qualified me for the Final and I went out to Colorado and I was nobody at that point, so I didn't get any assistance from National Team or anything like that, but I did well enough that Eddie (Borysewicz) noticed me and asked me to stay after the Final to train with the National Team. I did real well and ended up winning Nationals that year in Pursuit and Team Pursuit.

That same time trial in Colorado that I did last year, John Stenner ended up beating me by, 23 seconds, I think, but within the first mile my chain came off three times and I had to stop, get off my bike and put it on by hand while I was standing next to my bike. My 30 second man (the person who began the time trial 30 seconds later)

passed me and was way down the road. If that had been a high pressure situation and most people would probably, including myself — it would really negatively affect your performance. I mean, it was not a high pressure situation, I'm doing the Colorado Time Trial, what do I care, I'm not even a resident of Colorado! It was just an opportunity to ride the time trial.

If you start letting little things like that get to you, then, well, for one thing, you're unadaptable. It can't have a positive effect on you.

I do get angry and I will use that anger in a very positive way to improve my performance. I've tried generating false anger, but it's not the same thing. If you find something that really makes you angry that's relevant, it can really help your performance immensely.

I've always felt that I've been a pretty capable and competitive Points racer. The problem is, when you're spending two or three months up on top in Colorado Springs and there's no competition there year in and year out, you tend to lose your focus or ability to — your edge, just as far as decision making.

Strategies and things like that — I hate to use the word "tactics", I think it's vastly overused in sports, I try to use "sports strategy" — but if you're racing every Friday night or every Saturday night, in Trexlertown, Indianapolis, wherever, you know, you develop a certain skill. If you don't continue to practice that skill, it's just like anything else, you know, it's going to get rusty.

That's the reason in the Points

race at World's Robbie Ventura had the ability, the only thing is, he never raced on the International level like that before. He was just in way over his head and next year, whatever he does, he'll be much better from that experience.

On the other hand, Steve Hegg — when was the last time Steve Hegg did a Points race on an International level? It makes a lot of difference. I realized that after I did the World Cup in Denmark, I didn't do diddly-squat in the Points race. I didn't know what the I was doing out there. You have to be doing Points races once a week or whatever, just to kind of use your brain a little bit. Crits are different. The mentality change is so different, as far as chasing down people who attack, on the track as it is on the road.

Most of the tracks are 333, so you get someone who's half a lap up and the field, on a track, they'll wait for the guy just to get tired and come back. In a criterium you're much more likely to have people who try and chase them down or trying to jump up to them. I find the pack is much more compliant as far as solo attacks on the track.

Also, having a Points sprint every 6-7 laps, whatever the case might be, it just effects the way you approach a Points race as opposed to a criterium where you're just going for the finish. Even if they have "primes", it's not like they're accumulating the dollar value of the primes to see who wins the race.

I do the other races like Italian Pursuit and others whenever it's on the program. It's a nice break from the typical Friday night weekly racing schedule which is usually a Miss 'N' Out, a Points race and one of these other races, like "Point a lap" or "Snowball" or Australian Pursuit, Italian Pursuit, or something like that.

It's one of those races that comprises one of the variation races, obviously not a week-in, week-out kind of thing. They're fun, but that has to be one of those races that you can't take too seriously, because usually you can't get yourself paired up with the ideal team, and even if you do, that usually means that most of the other people don't.

Team Pursuit is different in terms of your obligation toward the others and also their obligation to you. Whereas if you do an Individual Pursuit, you live and die on your own. You do a Team Pursuit, you don't want to let the other guys down and you don't want anyone or any two (three of four must finish) of the other guys to be a weak link. That's where you've got conflicts, I think.

Plus, selection for Team Pursuit is very subjective, whereas Individual Pursuit it's cut and dried. That's where you can get into personality problems. God knows how many years Team Pursuit has mockingly been called "Team Dispute" It was nicknamed Team Dispute just for those reasons. This isn't something that's an anomaly, it happens pretty much every year.

You just get high tensions as they decide who's going to ride and who isn't, which is why I was damned glad I qualified for the Individual and not Team Pursuit for the Olympics last year so I didn't have to mess with that. It's not my preference only for those

reasons.

If you can avoid the conflict — obviously somebody's always going to be unhappy. They're always going to think they're better, where in the Individual Pursuit, if you're better then ride faster!

I haven't done Kilo in the past three or four years. I think the last time I did Kilo with any regularity was '89, during those Sundance races, '88 and '89.

Best Moments

"My favorite accomplishment" is a hard one. Sometimes you're flying and, due to circumstances, you have a teammate who's doing something . . . well, one accomplishment was the '88 Olympic Team Pursuit. I was flying there.

I was cranking and it was wonderful revenge for Mark Hodges telling the newspapers I was too slow to make the team. I couldn't find him after the race, but within a half lap I was looking for him. That was definitely one, and probably the most prominent one.

Making the '92 team was so much a relief of pressure, self-imposed pressure to make team, that it wasn't so much a feeling of accomplishment as it was "Oh, God, thank God I did that, now I can get on to the next step!" So, the '88 Olympic ride was one.

Another one would probably be the Points race in the '86 Goodwill Games. I was just crankin', but unfortunately, well, unfortunately for me, I guess, a group of five guys was just the right combination. This was in Moscow at Goodwill Games, huge track if you've ever seen it. Most

One of the last laps, Olympic Trials, 1992

tracks in the States are six or seven meters wide — this thing is 10 meters wide, it's just awful, huge, immense and wonderful. It's 333m around.

The Pole line is the same as far as the radius of the turn and the length of the straightaways, but it's just so big, so wide, the track itself. It's 45 degrees and by the time you get to the top of the turn, you're almost three stories high! If you were going to do a Flying Kilo, basically the first lap is a "gimme."

Anyway, there were a bunch of

people in this race, I mean it's a pretty big field, and Dave Letteri — I'd already been off the front with a Russian guy for a while -- but Dave Letteri got off the front with a Russian, a Czech, and I forget who else, but five guys, and they ended up lapping the field because we were the five strongest teams and nobody was going to chase.

They ended up lapping the field and I was just — it was like myself dueling against the Russians to lead out our respective person who had lapped the field and I was just crankin', I mean Dave couldn't even stay on my wheel. But it was just one of those days when you feel like you just could have . . . everything worked.

The '92 win was good because I think everybody figured I was washed up after I had a crummy '91. I wouldn't necessarily categorize myself as a good pressure rider when introducing myself to someone or describing myself, but looking back in a lot of circumstances I would have to say I am.

I have found myself winning or doing really well — especially, like, at 1993 Worlds. The first ride Matt Hamon rode badly, so I ended up having to do a couple of double pulls, so, somebody's got to do it, I just knew I had to do it. I've always been really good in any timed event, any Time Trial event, regardless of the distance.

The Pursuit

Success in Pursuit is a combination of physical and mental abilities. The mental ability to kind of pace yourself appropriately and I guess you're making goals and things like that and continually evaluating them. I don't know how you can quantify the mental aspects of the Time Trial.

I get a lot of questions from people about how to Time Trial, basically, and you just go out and hammer until you can't ride any more, then you ease up a little bit, then you keep doing it again. There's physical aptitude as well, but, I mean, I don't know why some people just can't Time Trial. I think it's more of a mental thing than a physical thing.

Concentration is important, but you focus on the distance, you focus on the rider in front of you, you're focusing on riding straight, and all these things. But also, a very key thing is just evaluating your current energy expenditure in relation to how much further you have to go and the conditions.

Competing in a lot of other events can prepare you for Pursuit. Last year when I did the Colorado District Time Trial, I had a tailwind downhill on the way out and obviously an uphill headwind on the way back, but I was keeping my heart rate around 170 on the way out because, I mean . . . about the only bit of strategy you can have for a time trial is that you make up so much more time when a course is harder, when you've got to go uphill.

When you'd normally go slower, if you can maintain a higher rate of speed, that's when you're going to make up the big difference. I knew better than to obliterate myself on a downhill tailwind without having anything left for the headwind. That's when you're going to make the most time gained.

I finished up right around 180 heart rate, which is normal for me. I don't normally Time Trial at a real high heart rate. For me that was pretty good, but other people think "Why didn't he have 180 the whole way?" well, because if you had 180 on the way down, you'd be fried when you tried to come back.

I use a heart rate monitor, but more for evaluation afterwards rather than current, just to check monitoring. You can watch like you can a speedo-meter on a computer, but I think it's kind of like a stigma.

If you look at your heart rate and it's at 192 or something like that and if you're still feeling good, then you see the 192, you're going to back off so you don't go anaerobic, when it doesn't matter if you would go anaerobic or not. Depending on your relative freshness or tiredness, your heart doesn't put out the same amount for the same type of effort anyway, sometimes, depending on how tired you are.

There are a lot of factors involved. I can just read myself well enough, I guess, however many years prior to the heart rate, I don't want to say, fad, but the uprise in popularity of heart monitors. Generally I don't, but on the other hand, who's to say that if I didn't start using it more consistently it would start becoming an effective tool?

I have my own routine. My attitude on food and things that are involved with training one way or another is that you just do the best you can. You don't really worry about getting things exactly right because you're going to waste so much energy, create so much stress, by trying to worry about that little micro-thing, that may or may not make any difference anyway.

It's better just to generally do the right thing and just kind of go with the flow that way rather than get real anal and have it just ruin things.

Training

The thing that helps me the most in training for Team Pursuit or the Madison where you're doing high speed, high intensity, short interval type of training. Madison training is so incredibly good for you. You ride just "balls-out" for a lap and a half, two laps, you got a short rest, you just keep doing that just over and over again. It's almost the same as Team Pursuit, a shorter hard effort.

You also get less — well, I don't know if you get less recovery. You get a little bit less, but the speeds are a little bit higher. If you're involved in Madison competition, you're involved in the competition as opposed to the training benefits. Madison training is just phenomenal. It's something you can't duplicate riding by yourself.

You can't get that intensity or the speed just from having somebody throw you in and developing that speed. I do Madisons whenever I can, which isn't nearly enough. You have to find a partner that you want to ride with and who is interested in doing the race.

Velodromes

My favorite velodrome is Moscow. It is so beautiful and so fast. It is just the sweetest velodrome.

Within this country it's a toss up between Colorado and Minneapolis. If the Minneapolis track was in Colorado that would unquestionably be it. The Colorado track has developed too many bumps. Minnesota is so nice and smooth.

Trexlertown is very good for competition, but as far as Pursuiting it's unexceptional.

There are no velodromes I can think of that I wouldn't want to go to. The Atlanta track is pretty rough, but I've gone there for races. Considering how bad and undeveloped track racing is in the States, if there's a big race, people are going to go, it doesn't matter how bad the track is.

I raced in Argentina on a track that was a 135 meter portable track, set up in the mud. It was about 4 1/2 meters wide. It was harder to get from the back of the field to the front of the field than it was to lap the field. The banking was about 40 degrees, not nearly enough.

We were racing on a 49 - 16. I'd never raced there before. I'd done some road races in Uruguay, which is next door. This was just a portable track. They have a concrete track that is, like, 400 meters, but that's just too big for Madisons.

Advice to New Riders

My advice to riders in various parts of the country do a lot of road racing. They have road races everywhere. They don't have track races everywhere. The thing I would recommend is to develop bike handling and pack riding skills. If you can fight your way through the field, you can develop the logic and strategy to ride intelligently in the pack, this is what I lacked coming up in cycling.

I was so strong I never rode with the field, I just rode away from the field and consequently I didn't initially develop my pack riding skills, developing the comfort level. That's one of the most important things.

If you can be with three to four guys in front of you and three to four guys on either side of you, through the turns, setting up for sprints, things like that, that's important.

Step by Step through the Season/through a Pursuit

Early season you do a lot of endur-ance work. You do a lot of races, crits or road, it doesn't matter. Your desire to perform and do quality work is greater than if you're just out training. Your competitors push you better than you could do on your own. You just race as much as possible, wherever they are. If the race is short you ride to or from it to add more miles. The point is not to win but just race hard, whether it's chasing down a break, attacking, soloing, or as much hard work as possible. You want to keep things balanced. You don't want to do all long training or all short criteriums.

You might have three or four rounds of Pursuits during competition, so you do need the endurance, but you also need the speed and intensity. Both aspects have a purpose.

About a month before the event I would try and do Madison races or Team Pursuit workouts because both of those would build your speed immeasurably. Madisons are intense but last a lot longer than Team Pursuit. Both of those races are extremely good. They're basically motorpaced inter-vals. They'll bring you to a very fine peak.

I try to peak for specific events, but my season peak would be for Worlds, not Nationals. If I'm trying to qualify for the Olympic Team, my ultimate goal would be the Olympics, but I would try to reach close to my peak for Trials.

One of the key things I learned in '88 was that while you're training for something that may be three or four months away, it comes a lot faster than you really expect it to. You've got to be acutely aware of that. If you don't do it today, that's one less opportunity that you have to get closer to your goal. It also goes with being mentally prepared.

If you allow yourself enough time, you don't have to look back later and say "Oh, I should have been doing this . . ." It's better to allow yourself more time than to try to cram everything in.

The Federation got into a new training program in 1994 from the East Germans and Australians. It's a lot more intense than in years past. It will help a lot. Because we've had a new program I've been following it much more closely. In '92 I was entirely on my own. I knew what I needed to do to train from past experience. It is refreshing to change the program to something new, though there is a little uncertainty about it, though it is a proven program. I feel good about it.

Say the Olympics are in August. Eight months before the event I'm laying the ground work. Seven months, same thing, there isn't a whole lot of racing going on. In February I'm going harder. I'd be looking forward to the season. Sometimes I've laid off in the winter time, sometimes I haven't. It doesn't seem to have made much difference in the past, which is kind of interesting.

Six months before racing is happening. I'd also start doing some pyramid intervals, 15 min on, 10 min off, 8 min on, 5 min off, 3 on, 2 off, 1 on, 1 off, 30 sec on, 30 sec off, and then start over with another set. I'd do that once or twice a week. I'd also be doing as many group rides as possible and other mileage on top of that.

I train by myself if no one around me is training for the same purposes. At those times I just give myself short term goals, because if you're working on long term goals and there's nobody else around to work with you kind of get lost. Short term goals, two weeks, three weeks, four weeks at a time, works a lot better. Then you just reassess every time you accomplish them.

Five months before, say April, I'm still not worried about getting on the track. If I did it would be for Madisons, Team Pursuits and getting speedwork, but in April you don't need speedwork yet. I'd still be doing a lot of criteriums and road races. Gradually you would still be building intensity and starting to do stage races (over several days). You might do three to four day cycles. You might do intervals one day, moderately long rides the next day, then a rest day. Races make you do long and short intervals.

If you're not in races, you can do pyramid intervals on your own. You can do three minutes on, three minutes off, set of five, maybe a set every hour and a half over a three hour ride. A half hour warm-up, a set of intervals, rest for an hour, do another set of intervals, then a half hour cool down, something like that. Your heart rate should be up beyond your anaerobic threshold.

With four months to go your intervals might be four or five minutes. You look at time more than mileage for intervals, especially in relation to times for Pursuit. You will still be racing regularly, mostly on weekends. If you can, you might race Saturday and Sunday, take Monday easy, Tuesday do intervals, Wednesday do a long ride, Thursday do more intervals, then race Saturday and Sunday again. Average mileage on the weekends might be 80 to 100 per day. If you do a long race that should take care of it, if you do a criterium you should augment it with more mileage.

Three months to go might be in May. Nationals or some sort of selection trials coming up the following month. At that point it's time to start getting on the track. The first couple of weeks in May I would start getting familiar with the track again, riding with the group. If there have been track races around it's fine to have done them, but track racing is not the main focus at this point. If there's a Saturday race, you might get in 50-60 miles in the morning and then race the track Saturday night.

Track racing earlier than May should not be an emphasis. I would not start with Team Pursuit just because it's hard to find other people for that race, so Madisons would be the way to go. If you can do a Madison session or a Points race for an hour, you get that speed and intensity. Your body is getting adapted to riding on the track, the fixed gear, the leg speed, it's really working toward it.

Doing Madison workouts you're doing a lap and a half at a time, which is a lot better than a Team Pursuit pull which is usually a half a lap or sometimes a full lap.

That will build the strength you need for an Individual Pursuit.

Depending on how much practice you have at Indivi-

If you want to learn how to start,

study Pursuiting's top competitors.

dual Pursuit in the past, you need to practice getting lap times you want, getting used to that speed for maybe six lap efforts, doing those as intervals.

You don't need to do the whole 4000 meters. However, if you're inexperienced, it's important to develop consistency on the lap times over the whole length of the race.

Two keys to Pursuit are 1) consistent lap times and 2) holding the black line. Another important thing is position. You have to shove the seat as far forward as you can get and your body as far in front of the handlebars as you can. You will have a cleaner position. You will have a tendency to flatten out your back more. Plus, you need to be more above the cranks rather than behind them in order to pedal faster. Any time you're Sprinting or going fast, you tend to creep forward on your seat. Being more forward is more efficient from an aerodynamic standpoint and also from a power stand-

Efficiency is the name of this game.

point.

You have to get comfortable on the bike so you can ride relaxed. You don't want to use up energy fighting the bike that you could use pushing the pedals. You need to learn pacing. I prefer to do individual lap times rather than ride to a schedule. I've always had a knack for knowing how much energy I have and whether I should go faster or slower.

You should go into the race with a good idea of what kind of finishing time you want to have, then you know what kind of lap times you need to have. My start lap tends to be a little bit slow and my second lap tends to be a little bit faster than my steady pace.

Two months before means that National Championships are probably within that month. You pretty much cut your long rides to one per week. Three months before you probably have those down to two a week. If you're doing a track workout you probably have your two a week on the weekends. You have your rest day on Monday, your intervals on Tuesday, your track workout on Wednesday, back off a little bit on Thursday. You have two good days of quality on the weekend, two on Tuesday and Wednesday. You might make Thursday a moderately long day, maybe 80 miles, but at a relaxed effort. You want to have a little bit of recovery. You don't want to waste yourself.

With about a month to go you need to begin working on your form for your start. You really need to have someone analyze it with you. Seeing yourself, like on video, helps a lot. Having someone tell you something is not the same as seeing it. It's like seeing yourself on TV and having someone say "Oh, you were great!" but you look at it and go "Oh, God!" You are your own worst critic.

If you see yourself do something you can do better, it's there for you to visualize. It's not the same if somebody's just telling you about it.

I'm not a great starter, I don't have the "snap." My first 40 meters doesn't have explosive power. I'll do the "straight arm" start for about the first four pedal strokes, then after that I'll start pulling from side to side with bent arms, just before I get into the turn (depending on the size of the track). Whether it's Individual or Team Pursuit, I've found that if I try to maximize my start, it takes away too much from the finish of my race.

In Team Pursuit, up until the second turn I'm up to a bike length behind everybody else, but from that point until the backstretch I can close that up, so my mid-range acceleration is comfortably strong for me to do that. People panic, thinking I'm off the back, but I also end up sitting down before everybody else. I get up to race speed sooner than other people even though my actual start is slower. This difference is more evident in Team Pursuit. A video camera really helps to see the whole process and correct the mistakes.

With two weeks to Nationals you would cut back on your intervals to one session a week, cut back on your mileage as well, because you need to start making your legs fresh. You're not abandoning the hard efforts. At that point you find someone around to do Team Pursuit or someone who has a motorcycle, to start working on speed. Monday is still a rest day. Maybe you'll ride 50-70 kilometers. Tuesday you'll do one set of intervals,

riding about two and a half hours. Wednesday if you're going to do track training in the morning you'll do simulated Team Pursuit or motor-pacing first, like a lap hard, then two laps behind the motorcycle at race speed.

Do those in sets of 4000 meters just like a Pursuit, giving yourself 20-30 minutes between each set. Do maybe four of those, then a half hour Madison. Thursday just go for a long, leisurely ride, maybe four hours at 20 miles per hour. Keep it flat, flush the gunk out of your legs. Friday either rest or race, that night or that weekend. Don't worry about tacking on extra mileage.

The week before Nationals: Monday a rest day, 40-50 kilometers. Tuesday skip intervals. Go to the track and do another Team Pursuit type workout. Do a 4000 and rest 20 minutes. Four of those. Do the same thing on Wednesday, but also do the Madison, like the previous Wednesday. Thursday back to 60 miles or so, pedaling real easy. Same weekend routine, then you're at Nationals! You've got to travel, things like that.

If you're going to do the Individual Pursuit you're also going to do the Team Pursuit, the Madison and maybe the Points race. Your Individual Pursuit is first and that's your primary objective. In the typical schedule, Individual Pursuit is Wednesday and Thursday.

You may or may not do your race on Sunday, then you might fly to Nationals. On Monday you're there. You do an hour behind the motor at

the track. There will be organized groups at the track. You sit behind the motorcycle. You might do a couple of flying laps just to get used to the track. It might be a different track or a different length than you're used to. You need to get your lap times down for whatever it needs to be for that track. Do a road ride of 40-50 kilometers.

Tuesday you do the same thing as Monday. Wednesday will be qualifying and additional rounds in the afternoon. They may change the schedule around, but it's basically that way the week of the event.

For me, I just want to be in the top four for qualifying. It makes no difference to me if I'm first or fourth. Why expend the extra energy to be first? If you're one of the last eight or so people you pretty well know what time you need to hit.

Worlds you have to go at max-imum pace, but Nationals you don't unless it's for practice. It depends. If you're going to only do Individual Pursuit, you might as well get used to going all out. If you're going to ride several events you might conserve a little bit, do what you need to do to get to the next round and still win.

Mental preparation

Mentally, you want to plan every-thing out as much as possible before you get there. You don't want any of that to go wrong. If it does, you have to go with the flow and realize that nothing is 100% in your control. But, you do as much as you possibly can before the event. I even prefer to plan to cook in my own room than go into a restaurant and sit and wait. I can

think of more comfortable places to sit than in a chair in a restaurant. Plus, when I'm hungry, that's when I want to eat. I don't want to go through the whole routine of ordering. Eliminate all the variables that are out of your control as you can.

When you do things like that you make things more positive. You have less to get down about, to get irritated about. Things go your way a lot better if you can control as many things as possible -- in control of your own destiny, so to speak.

Always allow yourself enough time for things like registration, driving to the track, whatever. Eat early, be smart. If it means you have a qualifying round of 60 competitors and you're in the top eight, you know that it will be a minimum of three hours before your round comes up. Generally I allow seven minutes per round. By the time you get the guys on and off the track, run the race, it's at least seven minutes per ride. You take that into account, you take into account that you could have some scratches.

You don't want to cut it right down to the wire, but you don't want to spend your whole day down at the track. You might get bored, it might be hot, if the track has a tunnel, not everybody's going to fit in the tunnel. If you have to be at the track, the tunnel is your place of refuge. It's cool, it's shady and it's a good place to rest. Unless you really want to watch what's going on in the races, you can hear what's going on over the P.A. system. I don't subscribe to living in the tunnel.

Try to find the hotel that is absolutely closest to the track as possible. If you need to go there you don't need to spend half an hour sitting in traffic. That's another thing you can eliminate from worrying about. In some places there are hotels near the track. That's the ideal.

The Race

On the day of the race I like to go out and do about an hour on the road. Just real peacefully, not even to work up a sweat, just to get the body flowing, to loosen up. It's mental too. Just ride easy, get into your thoughts, visualize your race. Imagine your start. Imagine your first lap time, second lap time, third lap time, and so on. Imagine how you're going to feel. Imagine pushing through that. Sometimes you have to think that you're "better" than the race, that "it's only six more laps, six *stupid* laps. How many times have you been around the track? This is six stupid laps." Things like that. That's what I did in '92.

You should have gone through your race mentally many times. You should have been visualizing the race, relating to how you feel, who you will be riding against, picking it up a little at the end. You're sort of warming yourself up. Also, don't eat less than four hours before your race, easily digestible things, carbohydrates. Your stomach should be pretty well empty by race time and you should start to feel some hunger pangs. Drink a high-carb drink or something like that.

Another thing some people might think is silly, but you need to think about going to the bathroom. You always have that sensation of needing to go to the bathroom five minutes before

your race. Go about an hour to an hour and a half before the race so you won't have that sensation or if you do, it's minimized. I always tried to push for a convenient bathroom in tracks where I had any input. If you find it's a recurring problem, take care of it

You won the Pursuit? Me too! Olympic Trials, Blaine, 1992

somehow. It will distract you from your race and you don't want that.

Unless you're in one of the earlier rounds, don't count on getting on the track to warm up. Take a wind trainer and/or rollers. Either one is good, but tires wear down faster on wind trainers, so you need an extra bike. You don't want to worry about all those variables.

You want to keep moving until the very last possible minute. Ignore what the announcer is saying, ignore what the "go-fer" who comes to get you is saying. If it was up to them,

several people in front of you would all be waiting in chairs. Don't hold up the procession either. The officials are tired, they've been there all day. Put your Pursuit bike up by the start so all you have to do is walk right over. That's why you have an extra bike on a wind trainer or rollers. You want to keep warmed up and not let your body slow down so it's not as much of a shock when you start out. It's enough of a shock to the body just to start, you start to load up on lactic acid.

I warm up really long and gradually, maybe an hour's worth. It's pretty leisurely. I might do ten minutes, get off, go to the bathroom, get a drink, stretch, get back on and pick it up a little more. Then I'll get off, get a drink, get back on, a little bit more, for another fifteen minutes, get back off for another five minutes, get back on for a fairly hard ten minutes closer to race speed. Then back it down, then do a kind of finishing warm up. Heart rate around 130 if your race pace is 180. Something like that. Percentage wise I'd say about 60-70% of your race pace. Light gear, high RPMs, about 120 or so.

I always like to have the sensation that my legs aren't really there but are kind of floating, kind of a lighter than air sensation. You walk right over to the start. You might set your trainer up near wherever your start is. Set up close to there. Minimize your walk. Get off your bike and start the walk over when the competitors ahead of you have about one kilometer to go. That's a little over a minute, plenty of time. You will have acknowledged the "go-fer" several times. If you have

someone assisting you, let them handle this person, leaving you deep in thought. You might listen to rock music or something to minimize your interruptions.

Keep a towel handy to wipe off sweat so you can go to the start line as dry as possible. You feel more fresh. You can keep your mind as much on the actual ride and less on making sure everything's set. I always prefer to do all my bike preparation myself. I always make sure the rear wheel is tight. Too many people have lost races because they have on the wrong gear. They forget to switch the cog after the warm-up or something. Make sure you have the right cog and the right chain ring. This should be done before you start your warm up with an hour to go.

I figure an extra bike is a little more to carry, but anything to lessen aggravation is worthwhile. It will get routine after a while, but you have to keep thinking about your race.

If you're going to drink coke or coffee, your stomach should be pretty empty by the time you race, so you should consume any last liquids about a half hour before your race. That will allow it time to get into your system, but not time to rush out. You want the benefit of it, not the crash afterwards. You also need to bear in mind that when you do an "ergogenic aid" such as caffeine, you do not want to do an amount for your qualifying ride that you will need for your Final ride. It's something you want to build on. A little bit for your qualifying ride, a little bit more for your next round and so on. Save the largest (legal) amounts for when you really need them. Otherwise your body will have already spent that energy.

I'll do a relaxation exercise where I tense up muscles from head to toe, tensing and relaxing, working my way to my forehead, face, neck, shoulders, and so on. Tense and relax two or three times and really relax.

When I'm really ready, I won't take deep breaths, but I'll take a normal breath and expel it forcefully. I'll do that a few times. You want to kind of get a calm aggression to set the mood for your race. You don't want to be thinking negatively, just kind of pumped up. You do a sort of final focus just when you're walking over. You don't look at anything in particular, just do a few exhalations, no deep breaths. You don't want to hyperventilate, that tends to shut you down.

When you get to the line, take as much time as you need to get set. Put your wheels the way you want them. Put your pedals the way you want them. Always mount your bike from the right side. You're then stepping over your bike from a higher point than from the bottom of the track. These are just little things. I place my pedals so my first stroke will take me down the banking so I'm not fighting it. There's no penalty for riding off the track. If I can get a little downhill advantage, I'll do that. I'll place my bike at the top of the pole lane if I can (sometimes officials don't like it). You do whatever you can within the bounds of the rules. Give yourself a little more height. When you do go down hill you don't want a sharp angle, just a very

slight angle, using the downhill for a little assistance.

When you get on your bike, have everything the way you want. The person holding you may be inexperienced and need feedback on how you need to be held to be balanced. You don't want to try to counterbalance the person holding you. You tell them what you need. Surprisingly, the neutral point is not necessarily upright. Often there's a lean, so the holder may have to do a little work. When you're getting ready to start, you don't need to spend that energy trying to balance yourself. Holders need to hold you however you need. Go through your start lap in your head before you get in your "ready" position and before you tell the official that your ready. Know how many pedal strokes you're going to take with straight arms, where you're going to start, where you're going to sit. Anticipate when you're going to get to top speed, when you're going to switch on to the aero bars, and all of that. You want to just concentrate, at this point, on that first lap.

One other thing, before the race, when you're warming up. Listen to the cadence the starter uses when starting other people. The cadence should be about the same for each rider, faster or slower. If you have a pretty good idea of how they're going to do it, you can anticipate the start a lot better.

I usually ride 51-15 on the track, maybe 52-15. Once the actual race starts you do your first lap as you envisioned. When you hear your first lap time, ideally it should be within a couple of tenths of what you planned. By the time I sit down I should be at

the speed I plan to continue through the race. I maintain that for the second lap.

I have to make sure my second lap isn't too fast. I'm really bad off the start line, so to make sure my first lap isn't really off, I end up sort of over-speeding on the second lap. I also do it so that I can sort of take the pressure off the pedals and float and recover on the third lap, getting down to the speed I should maintain for the rest of the way. Beginning riders need to ride Pursuits to get an idea of pacing, to experience the whole distance.

The second lap time tells you how much you have to adjust. If it's within a few tenths, you just keep going the same speed. If it's a half a second or more faster, you can just float, but not a lot or you can lose that little bit of speed. Floating allows you to flush out some of the lactic acid you may have accumulated on the start. Hard effort constricts blood flow through the capillaries, so if you lessen the pressure even momentarily, it allows blood flow to go through the muscles even momentarily, flushing out some the lactic acid. This is going into your third lap.

You're either right on schedule or slightly ahead of schedule for Individual lap times. You should either maintain your lap time or ease up on the pedals slightly to get back to the lap times you want. You will be more efficient by maintaining the same speed than slowing and then trying to pick it up. Ideally you want to keep the same lap time from lap two or lap three until the end of the race, no matter how many actual laps you'll

have to go on the particular track. You don't really know from the first lap time, but the second and third laps tell the story. With the start there can be too much variation over the distance. The second lap is your first full lap at speed, much more representative as to what you need to do from there. Ideally you will be on the mark and will simply continue at the same speed.

It's a lot harder to tell pace when it's a windy day. If it's windy you have to push harder into the wind and recover slightly, float a little with the wind, to try to maintain steady speed. It's sort of like doing intervals. It's harder to keep your speed in the wind. That's what causes most people to have a slower time than going fast in the tailwind and slower in the headwind. It always feels like the wind is about two-thirds of the way around the track -- it never feels like it's just half the track. You just have to just push through it and get whatever recovery you're going to get by floating in the tailwind. You don't try to make up time in the tailwind, you just try to keep an even speed throughout the lap.

Usually around half way you start to feel fatigue. If you have a really crummy race, you might start to feel it by the end of the first kilometer. Usually it's about half way. That's when you have to really start concentrating on your form. Your form, at that point, will make or break you. You need to maintain your position, not sit upright, not let your knees out, keep them pointed in, and be very aware to try and turn circles rather than up - down, up - down.

Smoothness will help. If you're lucky, which happens once or twice a year, you get in this little serendipitous Pursuit. It just never hurts. You just float along and have a great time, both literally and figuratively. It's unfortunate it doesn't happen more, but you feel like you could set a new World Record if you wanted to. If you feel like that in the qualifying you don't go all out because it would cost you later on. But that happens about one out of every 20 times you ride a Pursuit, so that's not something you plan on.

The first half of the race you just keep visualizing, try to keep your lap times constant, and don't even concern yourself with the number of laps. You'll realize with about half the race to go, that you'll be looking at the lap counter. You've got to stay focused on the job at hand rather than the number of laps. I don't worry about the laps until about half way. Once it starts hurting you start looking to see how many laps you have to go.

You try to maintain your focus of form and constant speed, things like that. Worry more about hearing your lap times than about what lap it is. Your laps times may start to increase about half way through. At that time you need to set short term goals within the race. If you're in a 12 lap Pursuit, from lap six to lap three, just worry about maintaining your form and keeping steady.

Don't worry about the last three laps. By that time you just think "It's just three stupid laps!" "It's two stupid laps!" "All I have to do this is just for about 20 seconds!"

When the pain sets in I think about

maintaining form because that's when you get sloppy and it ends up costing you even more. You need to keep your knees in, you need to stay in a straight line, no wavering, keeping your head down, all these little things that add up. You have to let the pain know, as if it's an animate object, who's boss, who's going to control you. Are you going to control yourself or are you going to let the pain control you?

Yeah, it's going to hurt, but you knew it was going to hurt before you started the race. You just have to suck it up and it's only going to hurt for a minute and a half. What is that compared to the years that you've been training? It's not the first time it's going to hurt, it's not the last time it's going to hurt. But it's only going to hurt for a minute and a half and then you're done.

The last lap you have a little over 20 seconds to go. You just have to think to yourself "I can do anything for 20 seconds!" How long is 20 seconds? Not a long time. You have to do something to distract yourself from the pain, whether it's that or counting pedal strokes or anything else. Focus out somewhere else.

Also, keeping track of your competitor, you have the person giving you lap times, you might have another person, what they call "walking the

line," if they'll allow it. If your competitor is 10 meters ahead, he stands 10 meters ahead of the line. He will stand where you will be when your competitor crosses the Pursuit line. So you can see how you compare positionally. That way you don't have to look across the track, which breaks up your aerodynamics and distracts you from riding a straight line. There is a lot of stuff in the way and you may not be able to see them anyway. You want your guy to be past the line -- past is good, before is not so good.

If it's qualifying and you know you're going to make it into the position you want, there's no reason to catch the guy -- unless it's someone you really don't like! It gets more crucial when it's an elimination round. It doesn't matter what the time is then as long as you cross the line first.

I worry more about my lap times than where my competitor is, but there are psychologies relating to competition, too. You can mentally crush your opponent if you go and have a blazing kilometer and are half way into the first turn when they're crossing the Pursuit line, you have that much of a lead, they might just give up. You might be hurting, but they might just give up. It also depends on the other person's personality.

If someone does that to me it doesn't usually bother me because I know they can't keep it up. Then there are the people who do the reverse, who come on like gangbusters at the end. It may be just the way the person rides. There's a little psyching among competitors, but the most efficient way to ride a Pursuit is to ride steady. If you don't do that you're gambling a little. The other guy may have a kick too.

After the Pursuit you want to do a very good warm-down, at least a half an hour. If it's not a night session, get out for a half an hour on the road, real light gears. You might do a few moderate jumps just to put a little pressure and pump the wastes out.

Usually I'll do three warm-down laps if I can along with one out-of-the-saddle acceleration on each lap, less effort each time, to loosen the fluid. Then stretch, then dip in the ice. Massage afterward, if it's available. I take such a long drawn out warm-up I think that does the equivalent, if not better.

I've also been doing an ice bath. It's supposed to help your recovery and your legs. You just dip yourself in it for about seven minutes, waist down. Ice cubes floating like in the Arctic. You do that shortly after you get done with your ride.

If you're only doing Individual Pursuit, take a recovery day following your last ride. Do a 50-60 kilometer ride pedaling real easy. At that point you have a month and a half or two months until the big race. Go back and condense the preceding six months into the following month. You want to get back some of that endurance again. You've gotten yourself to a certain level by doing all these things. You want to get to the next level by sort of "crunching" that into the next month. You go back to the fundamentals as far as endurance and intervals. You do Madisons and Team Pursuit type workouts during that next month. You already developed a certain amount of speed and you're not going to lose that is you keep it up with motorpacing and all that. Work on your endurance again, you don't want to lose that.

With a month to go, go at a pretty high level. Cut back on the endurance but keep the intensity high. With two weeks or a week and a half to go you cut it back. High intensity but with an extremely high amount of rest. At least once a week you need to do a good three or four hour long ride at very low intensity for a change of pace and to flush out your legs.

At the time of the Big Event, everything should be the same except the level of competition should be a little higher. The only thing that should be different is that you'll have to ride harder in your rides. All the preparation should be exactly the same.

You do the same routine on the warm-ups and everything, from a week until the event. Familiarization is the key to lessening stress. If you want cultural differences in foreign countries, save it until after your event. The reason you are there is because of your race. I didn't go to the Olympics to visit a foreign country, I went there because it was a very important race. If you want to play, you play afterwards. You surround yourself with your friends or your group, as much English things for familiarity as possible. Do your own cooking if you can. Take care of yourself instead of adapting to foreign cultures.

You don't want to get frustrated in a foreign country. Americans need to leave a positive impression. You might want to arrive early to learn where things are before time for your event. Go to places where things are familiar. Make yourself as comfortable as possible.

Afterwards I don't really party. Unless you win or unless you've met your expectations there might be a little bit of a letdown. I might go out and have a good time once or so, a relaxing, jovial evening on the town. There may be an occasion organized by the promoters. You might socialize with other competitors. If you want to explore the city, you do it afterwards.

One of the most common things in cycling is: don't stand if you can sit, don't sit if you can lie down. Before the race you should be sitting, relaxing or riding your bike. Otherwise it's hard on your legs.

I don't visualize being on the award stand. That comes if you do everything else. If the weather is bad or I don't feel like it, I just tell myself that if I don't go out today, that's one less day I'll have when everybody else is out there today. You have a finite amount of time to get from your start to your championship. You can rationalize it and skip a day here and a day there, but all of a sudden you have two weeks to go until the Championships and need to have done everything you need to do. There's a confidence factor when you know you're well prepared.

The Rider's Life and the Future

My family has given me only very mild praise because my parents feel that I should be getting on with my life. When I was back in Indianapolis my dad said "Pretty much you've wasted the past five years of your life." That was not too pleasing to hear. I have one older brother. They would rather I pick the conventional path.

Part of the thing that really drives me — and at this point, having done the Olympics, National Championships, this, that and the other — the thing that drives me the most is the fact that before I leave this sport (and, granted, I did think I was going to leave after 1992 anyway, then I reevaluated) I will feel genuinely incomplete if I do not give the performance that is my absolute physical limit.

Granted, that includes training. That isn't to say I could go out tomorrow and ride as far as I possibly could, that's not what I mean, I mean do the full training program, doing everything I can to reach my utmost physical peak, to say "There's nothing further I can possibly do—" and I'm not worried about mechanical advantage, with different bikes and whatever, but as far as training that "—there's nothing that I could do to make myself pedal harder." and that is what I am seeking.

I won't be happy until I reach that.

Carl tries out the new Vandedrome prior to winning Pan Am Gold, 1995

Chapter 12

ᘒ *Team Pursuit* ᘒ

In many ways, Team Pursuit is identical to Individual Pursuit. Each team begins on the opposite side of the track and tries to catch the other before the pre-set distance is covered. The greatest difference is that National Championship competition begins with four riders on the track, allowing a drafting situation which is not available in the individual event. Regulations addressing numbers and drafting reflect the uniqueness of this event.

The basic strategy in a Team Pursuit is for Team members to go as fast as possible, over the shortest course possible (black line), while conserving as much energy as possible (behind teammates).

History

Team competition has been a part of American bicycle racing tradition since 1898 when riders teamed in that uniquely American event called the Madison.

The virtue of Team Pursuit is that it allows yet another factor to become a part of the racing challenge: accommodating fellow team members at all times during an actual race event while simultaneously giving maximum individual effort.

The event is sometimes called "Team Dispute" due to the difficulty in melding the drives and egos of elite athletes into a single unit which depends for top performance on each of its parts.

Even on a team, each competitor has his own thoughts at the start. World Cup, 1994

Any one Team Pursuiter can annihilate the performance of the Team, and all members of the Team know this. Any competitor can have an off-day which blows the race for all others. Whether a bad performance is due to inability or choice is a source of blame and frustration for others who need, and may be giving a top performance that day.

When all members of the Team are together and giving that top performance at the same time, it is as glorious as any individual achievement for each Team member.

The Team

Technically, a Team Pursuit team consists of "two or more" riders. In National Championship events there are four men who race over 4000

meters.

There is presently no Championship Team Pursuit event for women, though there have been exhibition rides at both Nationals and Junior Nationals.

USCF sanctioning requires that parameters for a Team Pursuit contest be specified in the official race announcement and that they be explained to all riders prior to the start of the race. The official race announcement must specify how many riders must finish and on which finisher the final time is taken.

Up to six riders may be entered in a Championship, but no more than four may compete during any one session. Composition of the team may change between sessions, but not between rounds in any single session.

Warmin' up -- as a team. Get into the mental mode.

Qualifying

The organization of qualifying rounds is the same as for Individual Pursuit. In 1994, any Team Pursuit team could try to qualify for the top four positions.

During qualifying rounds, two teams line up across the track from each other in order, number one rider at the bottom of the track, number two in the next position uptrack, and so on.

Teams are only riding for time at this point. Those who are passed prior to the leader's final lap are eliminated. Teams caught *during* the leader's final lap, still get a qualifying time for seeding in further competition, as do all other teams who complete the distance.

All teams must have a qualifying time. Part of the Officials' job is to seed teams of comparable ability. In the first round of competition, the fastest teams will start last.

The Start

In all rounds, each rider is held in a Standing start by Officials. There is no Flying start in Team Pursuit. The holding Official must hold the rider neutrally. All riders in successive rounds must be held by the same Officials during that session on that side of the track, the same as in the Kilo and Individual Pursuit. Officials are charged with making certain that all riders are lined up equivalently.

Teams may choose one of two

A team must start together . . .   *. . . and get into position together.*

methods of lining up at the start: 1) they can line up in a straight line or 2) they can be staggered at a forty-five degree angle, to the rear of each successive rider. One meter must separate riders, whichever method they choose.

Riders always line up from the inside of the track in any Time Trial event, nearest the measurement line which defines their event.

As in the Pursuit, the Starter and the Assistant Starter are back-to-back in the center of the track. As each team is ready, a red or green flag is raised, one on either side of the track, to communicate readiness to Officials and others on the track.

The gun signifies the start. If there is any problem which should delay the start, Officials are expected to be notified before the gun is fired.

Once the gun goes off, timing begins and riders are expected to race

to the finish barring an unforeseen mishap.

The Race

When the Starter calls "Riders ready — Timers ready . . ." riders stand for the gun. When the gun goes off, they begin one of the most difficult phases of this race: the Team Pursuit start which can set the tone for the entire event.

The greatest challenge for riders at this point is to assemble in order into one tight unit of riders, each sitting in the "sweet spot" of the other's draft. Getting in the draft is no problem, it's doing it smoothly while getting up to maximum speed in the shortest possible time which is tough.

If the Number One rider or any other rider along the line takes off too fast, the Team gets split up, and that's hardly the point. All riders must watch each other for pace, taking any advantage forward while not dropping

the rider behind.

It is better to start smoothly, even too slowly, if it means getting the Team lined up quickly and correctly so that riders then have nothing to think about other than hanging on at maximum speed.

There are few fates worse for Team Pursuit than to take off too fast and have to regroup at a point later in the race when the other Team is assembled and maintaining maximum speed.

It's also better psychologically to get a good start since it sets the tone for the rest of the race.

As in Kilo and Pursuit, riders tend to stand for the first half lap, accelerating up to speed before sitting. They remain sitting for the rest of the race.

Teams vary as to when they exchange leadership, and there are no rules as to when or how often this needs to take place.

Exchanges

Usually riders exchange leadership every half-lap. The first rider will basically ride straight when the track curves, swinging up with the increased banking. He will automatically slow in speed due to having ridden up a hill.

As his speed is reduced by the banking, his Teammates pull through on the bottom of the track. As they go by, the rider uptrack now moves down, increasing speed automatically because he is now going downhill. Once he is in the protection of the draft he can rest until it is his turn to pull, usually 1 1/2 laps later.

Riders expend virtually no energy in the exchanges because the banking does the work for them. Their challenge is to move up and down the track smoothly, getting on the back of the Team at the right time with no effort. Some Teams are poetry in motion, others make you cry because they are trying *so* hard and it's just not working.

Riders can receive constant feedback on their times per lap, but only by one person. The person monitoring time/pace must be either before or after the rider's finish line.

Usually, coaches or monitors stand after the rider's finish line. S/he may indicate the rider's pace through gestures as well as shouting numerical

Team members meld into one smooth unit.

times. The Rule Book specifies that this person "may not make any rash gestures of encouragement".

Top teams usually have a fairly accurate idea of what time they are capable of riding and plan in advance to maintain a certain pace.

The science of assembling a team is another of velodrome racing's high arts. Of the four riders, one may serve as "rabbit," like in running races, where one person is there to push the rest of the team to the best time possible. This rider may plan not to finish the race, but to give all he has and then drop out, leaving the other three riders who are not yet spent to maximize their efforts later in the race. While one rider may plan to drop out, it is best if the rider who drops: 1) is the

designated rider, rather than another who was not expected to drop out, and 2) is dropped at the point where he is *expected* to drop, not so soon that others lose his benefit.

The Third Man

Riders are timed on full laps. Timing is taken from the moment the gun goes off to the moment the front wheel of the third rider crosses the finish line.

As the rules reveal, the third rider is the key person around whom the finish takes place. No matter who a third rider is planned to be, race dynamics may force unexpected riders to take full lap pulls or drop out, leaving race strategy at the mercy and the ingenuity of those left to fend as best they can.

No matter what, dropping a third rider is death for a Team. The first two can be way, way ahead of the third rider during the race and it carries absolutely no benefit in final race time whatsoever. Everything revolves around the Third Man. At later stages of the race, this "Third Man" factor is

as important as a good start.

A smart Team will guard it's Third Man at any cost. A "less smart" Team will not watch and will drop the Third Man, not only breaking apart the team, but depriving that rider of the precious draft which would otherwise enable him to get across the finish line faster and sooner. It's painful to watch the dropping of a third rider when you understand the requirements of this event.

Team Pursuit Format

A Team may only participate in two Pursuits per day. The Chief Referee may determine if there is some unusual reason to allow more. In any case, the riders are to be allowed a

A team must maximize efficiency. Used properly, the banking can do a lot of the work in exchanges in slowing and picking up speed.

Passing on the banking is difficult because exchanges are usually happening at the same time. No wonder the U.S. Team got 2nd at Worlds in 1994, this is top, international competition.

minimum of two hours between competitions.

As in Individual Pursuit, Team Pursuit competition may consist of Quarterfinals, Semifinals and Finals. All teams must have a qualifying time for seeding purposes.

Quarterfinals

If Quarterfinals are run, the eight fastest teams from the qualifying rounds are matched on the basis of their times: first with eighth, second with seventh and so on. Winners advance. The four losing teams are awarded fifth through eighth places on the basis of their times in the Quarterfinals.

Semifinals and Finals

In Semifinals the four top teams are matched first against fourth and second against third.

Winners of the semifinals race for the top two spots in the finals. Losers from the Semi's are placed in third and fourth place according to their times. If Semifinals are not used, the top two riders from the qualifying round race for first and second.

A team is considered caught when the third rider of one team draws even with the third rider of another team.

The Finish

A team can win one of two ways: 1) when it catches the other team or 2) when the third rider has crossed the finish line and the gun is sounded. If the second team has not been passed, another gun signifies the second finish.

As in Individual Pursuit, teams that register the same time are placed according to the faster lap times nearest the finish. Three riders must complete the distance to be classified.

Mishaps

The legitimacy of mishaps is determined by Officials. Should a rider have a mishap which is determined not to be legitimate, that rider will be eliminated while the other three riders will be allowed a re-ride.

During the Qualifying rounds, if one rider has a mishap, the others may decide to either stop or continue the ride with only three. If the Team decides to stop, their intention of doing so must be communicated within one lap following the mishap. If the Team continues and finishes the ride with only three riders, their time becomes the seeding time for that Team.

If more than one rider has a mishap during the Qualifying round, the team may stop and re-ride at the end of that round, either alone or against another team which has also had a mishap. In any event, the other Team in a qualifying round must finish their ride for a seeding time.

In Quarterfinals, Semifinals and Finals, if any rider has a mishap within the first half lap, the race will be rerun. If one rider has a mishap after the first half lap, the other three must continue the ride. If more than one rider on either team has a mishap after the first half lap, the Starter shall stop the race and the other team shall be declared the winner.

False Starts

If either team starts before the gun or if he/she is pushed, a False Start must be called within the first 30 meters and a re-start occurs. The rider on the inside of the track, the first rider, is expected to take the lead. If any other rider takes the lead prior to the 30

meter mark, a False Start is called. After two False Starts, whatever happens on the third start is final. If a rider False Starts a third time, the team is eliminated from competition.

No pushing of other riders is allowed in this event. If a rider is pushed, the team is disqualified in the qualifying rounds and relegated to one place lower in other rounds.

Race Equipment

A separate set of lap cards and bells is provided for each team. A red and a green disk is placed at each team's start/finish along with markers at a point 30 meters ahead of those discs, the zone within which False Starts are called.

Red and green flags marking the first and last kilometers are not used in Team Pursuit. Sponges on the blue band encourage Team Pursuiters to ride no lower than the measurement line, as in Kilo and Pursuit.

Summary

The challenge in Team Pursuit is that each team consists of four individual riders, each with his own personal style and rhythm. Accommodating to three other independent riders may compromise the best that rider could do on his own. Doing less than his best is not the keynote of the elite rider.

In this event, doing your best performance does not necessarily mean doing **your** best performance, and that kind of thinking is totally contrary to the competitive temperament. But, Team Pursuiters know that this is the whole secret to their event, so if they are going to win, they absolutely must know that their best interest is the Team's best interest (or they may as well stick to some other event.)

Passing on the back or home stretches is much easier. At this point, the Team Pursuit is over. Note that both teams are down to three men and all are together. World Cup, 1994.

Team Pursuit
Leonard "Harvey" Nitz

Leonard "Harvey" Nitz is one of America's most versatile and prolific Champions. His Senior National Championships and World's placings span 13 years (1976 to 1989) over six top level events — Kilometer, Pursuit, Team Pursuit, Criterium, Madison, and two Points races at the Worlds level. Harvey's three great events are Pursuit, Team Pursuit and Points race. During the eighties he was on U.S. National Championship Team Pursuit teams every year except '85 and '87. In the 1984 Olympics he won a Silver Medal in Team Pursuit team and a Bronze in Pursuit.

At the World Championship level, he has won Silver ('81) and Bronze ('86) Medals in the Points race. He held the U.S. National Record for the 4000 meter Time Trial from 1984 to 1990. In the Pan Am Games Harvey won two Gold Medals for Team Pursuit ('83 & '87) and a Bronze in the Kilometer ('87). In the 1990 Rule Book Harvey is listed in 24 places for his bicycling accomplishments. In 1991, he won the Masters World Cup in Pursuit.

Since turning 35, Harvey has become increasingly involved with Master's racing as a coach.

How I Got Started

I was born September 30, 1956 and grew up in Sacramento, California. I began riding when a friend who lived down the street talked me into going on a double century ride.

My friend was into bicycle riding and he talked me into doing it. I was about 16. I was running track and field at the time. When I ran the All City track meet two weeks after the double century I ran the 440m *20 seconds* slower than normal.

Riding was a lot more exciting than running track and field where you ran around in circles all day long. If you went on a cross country run you ran two miles. You didn't see a whole lot. In bike riding you saw a lot more. I had a $100 bicycle. Back then you couldn't buy a whole lot in a bike. It still had steel cranks.

About a year after the double century I rode my first USCF race, Nevada City. Of course I got lapped. I rode four races that season, in 1973, and I got lapped in all four. The next season, 1974, I raced more seriously. I had no coach. I was just out there riding my bike with no guidance of any kind.

The people who helped me the most were my father and Eddie B. My father supported me as much as he could, considering there were six kids in my family. I was the last.

I had three interests originally: motorcycle racing, bike racing and sailplane (gliding). I had a choice between the glider or my bike. My dad said he'd back me in those two, but not motorcycle racing. I chose bike racing.

"I think the reason I've been so successful is because I've always tried to do my personal best. Winning, to me, was not the all important goal. If my best was second I'd come away happy but if second was not my best, I'd come away very disappointed. In a Team Pursuit it was different. I was scared to death of letting my teammates down. I was <u>petrified</u> of letting my teammates down, more than anything else." CO, 1993

My dad didn't race bikes and knew nothing about bike racing, but he was behind me all the way. He always supported me, but he never pushed me.

I met Eddie B. in 1977 through the Federation. I got along with him personally and I got a lot out of him as a coach. At that time Eddie spoke very little English. He'd only been in the United States a little over a year. Eddie helped a lot of riders. He didn't have favorites, he helped anyone on the National Team who wanted his help.

Track Racing

The track riding just kind of fell into place. I didn't particularly want to become a track specialist. I just seemed to perform best on the track. In track racing you have more control over the outcome. Most of my events, Kilo, Pursuit, and Team Pursuit, were timed events, where tactics were important — a different kind of tactics.

In Points races and other Mass Start races there are a lot more tactics and a lot more luck. And, you have to have talent, it takes all three.

In a Time Trial event on the track it takes talent and strategy to win, but luck is not a real factor. Whereas in a Mass Start race, luck is a major factor -- not the *biggest* factor, but it is definitely a major factor.

In a Time Trial event, you've eliminated one of the major question marks. While it's not a sure thing at all, you have more control over your outcome. If you lose, you can only blame yourself.

I've been to National Championships that were my first track race of the year! And the World Championships were my *second* track race of the year! I'm serious. I had trained on the track before those events, but they were my first track meets of the year.

There were a few years where I did literally no racing on the track. A month before Nationals I'd train on the track to get used to my track bike again -- to remember not to stop pedaling!

Even though I've been doing it for this many years, the first day on the track every year I still go through that. I still have that point where I start to coast. Luckily I never lock my leg out, though. You lock your leg out, you go over, no question about it.

I've never gone over, but I've had to relearn that every year when I get on the track again. Sometimes I went as long as ten months without getting on the track. All of a sudden you get on the track and you think "Oh yeah, I gotta keep pedaling!"

Team Pursuit

For Kilo and Pursuit you can do almost all your training off the track. It's *nice* to train on the track, but you literally can do without it.

For events like Team Pursuit, you've got to train on the track. "Road Team Pursuit" doesn't work. There are many variables: the banking, the timing, getting used to teammates, them getting used to you, the smoothness of the exchanges -- there's a lot of technique. That's a major part of that event.

The most helpful thing in training for Team Pursuit is a big shock — Stage races!

Stage racing is the secret key to Time Trial events. Most of my races were five to nine day races. I consider myself a Pursuitist, and to be a Pursuitist you have to be able to ride the roads.

I don't really consider myself a track racer. Actually, if I had to clarify my greatest talent, it would be road sprints. Out of everything — crits, road races, stage races, anything. I consider myself a road sprinter. Nobody's really classified me as that before.

Training

It's hard to remember all the crazy things I used to try in training. I tried using an altitude simulator. It simulated 6000 feet when you're at sea level. I tried it for a couple weeks, but it was a joke, it didn't work. It didn't make any sense to keep doing it, so I gave it up.

We tried different equipment innovations from the project with Ed Burke and Chester Kyle.

I did other weird training things like ride with one leg. Not for the whole ride, but maybe for a half-hour.

There was a period when I used 180 mm cranks. I used them because I couldn't get up the hill with all the rest of the guys, so I put on the big cranks. It worked on the hills, but the problem was, I had to ride them on the flats too!

Pursuiting, Team Pursuiting, Points racing (and road racing) all seem to go together. In a Points race you have to keep track of where your competition is on the track so you can plan and adjust your strategy. Harvey is real good at that.

I was a Junior at the time and they had Junior gear limitations. I really think they helped my career a lot. I learned that if you're going to make that work you're going to have to learn how to pedal right. You have to learn how to turn some serious RPMs. At that time, in Northern California, the Junior gear limitations were 84.9. I think they're around 93 now. Other places were 88 inches, but ours were 84.9. I think that's a serious mistake of the USCF not to have stricter gear limitations for Juniors. 93 is big.

I rode my first three years as a Senior with 90 inches as the biggest gear on my bike. I didn't ride anything bigger than that until I went to the Red Zinger/Coors Classic at altitude and I found out that gears that little didn't work! You go much faster due to less wind resistance.

I remember many a time when I went to sprint against Davis Phinney in a 52-15 and he had a 53-12. We were neck and neck. It was opposite extremes. But near the end of my career I was in that 52-12 too. As you get older the legs just don't go around in circles like they used to.

I had some goofy spoke patterns that other people didn't have, but they were just experiments, nothing to talk about. I was kind of Mr. Guinea Pig for some of Ed Burke's ideas. The 180 cranks were my dad's idea.

My most "different" training was probably the midnight weight training. I spent many nights at midnight/one o'clock, weight training. There were not enough hours in the day. You'd get up, eat breakfast, go training on the road, come back, have lunch and take a nap. In the afternoon you'd train on the track, go back and have dinner. By the time the dinner goes down, it's time to train and it's midnight!

Sprinters will weight train all year,

After a grueling World Championship Points race, with one lap to go, Harvey unleashed the well known "Nitz kick" to take the last lap and, with double points now added to his score, a Bronze medal. It was unforgettable. Harvey admitted "It hurt."

but most other riders don't. I'd weight train all year up to two weeks before the Worlds. That was normal for Sprinters, but not for other riders.

I remember getting caught all the time in the Olympic Training Center. I brought my own weights into my room. A lot of the time you couldn't get to the gym so I'd do weight training in my room. I'd get caught by Eddie. He'd be walking down the halls

"Lights out!" He'd look in my room with the lights on and open the door and there I was doing squats. "What are you doing? Are you a crazy guy?" But I could always see a difference in my riding when I didn't do them.

My weight workouts were a little different, too. I did full squats, all the way down. I don't believe the theory that you only need to go as deep as you are on your bike. I think you need to go deeper than that for a full range of motion. I squatted 245 maximum, but I only did that once. I generally got up around 220-225. That was all I could do going all the way down. I remember many a time getting stuck at the bottom!

I also didn't believe in doing a lot of upper body weights. That's kind of bad for your overall conditioning, but I felt it was extra muscle mass you had to carry up the hill. A lot of guys believe that's important. I have a picture of me and Greg LeMond with our shirts off, flexing. It's quite hilarious. It's the picture of the "no-muscles."

I did dry land speed skating workouts when no one else was doing them. People would look at me wondering what I was doing. Now it's not that big a deal, but back then no one in cycling did that kind of thing.

I've never slept well, but it was worse when I was training. I was always terrible at shutting my mind down. I'd dream many times of falling off my bike. I'd wake up every time I'd do it. Luckily I haven't had one of those dreams in ten years or so. When I was racing it happened all the time. Maybe that's why I never crashed -- I did it all while I was dreaming!

Actually, I think common sense saved me from crashing more often. I always raced on the conservative side. That meant taking the longer way around instead of diving on the inside taking the shorter route and less chance of making it. If you gambled you did better, but I would take the safer way out, always. Maybe part of my success is because I stayed upright more of the time!

Details

I think I put a lot more focus on training than most people, along with study into the tactics of Pursuit, Team Pursuit, Points race, and the Kilo.

People look at the Kilo and think

you just ride as fast as you can. I've spent 100s and 100s of hours figuring out the Kilo, trying to work the different aspects of the Kilo. People don't realize that there are as many tactics involved in such a simple event.

In Pursuit there are a hundredfold more tactics, and in Team Pursuit a hundredfold more. There are an awful lot of tactics involved in those events that people don't realize exist.

People think there are tactics involved with Match Sprinting. Well, there's no question that there are more tactics involved, it's like night and day in comparison, but I could go and look at the Pursuit and think of all my tactics in the race and all the different things I could do about it for hours on end compared to a Sprinter.

Take a World Class Sprinter and there are ten times more tactics involved in their thoughts and minds. It's all in the extent of your tactics.

We worked with a sports psychologist, Andy Jacobs, in Colorado Springs from '82 to '86. He helped with any problems riders would have. I think it helped us to become a team. It got us to work as one, whereas before we were four individual riders.

Pursuit Sprinters

There are unexpected things about Pursuiters that people don't realize. For instance, during Olympic Trials in '84, there were four different things that the coach looked at: the Flying 200, the Kilometer time, the Individual Pursuit time, and then how you rode as a Team Pursuiter.

You can't just be a good Pursuiter to do Team Pursuit, you also have to have a lot of speed. That's why the coach would look at the Flying 200. We had to do a Flying 200 just like the Match Sprinters. We were traveling at 37-38 miles per hour, which is as fast as a Kilo, but you have to have more than just speed.

The amazing thing about the '84 Olympic Trials was that the second fastest, third fastest and fourth fastest times were turned by Pursuiters. Mark Gorski had the fastest 200 meters. Pat McDonough had the second fastest 200 meters. Brent Embrey had the third fastest 200m. I had the fourth fastest 200m. Nelson Vails had the fifth fastest 200m. Les Barczewski had the sixth fastest 200m.

Three Pursuiters had faster 200 meters than the second fastest Sprinter! This gives you an idea of how fast the Team Pursuiters were. It's pretty funny that Pursuiters could be that fast. And, our times were really close to each other.

The three Pursuiters were within two-100ths of a second of each other. Steve Hegg was the slowest of the Pursuit Team. I think he was the fourth fastest Pursuiter, but he was quite a ways back. The next jump back was quite a bit further back. Team Pursuiters are <u>fast</u>, they're not just out there in Pursuit. Hegg's endurance for Pursuit was incredible.

I think Gorski did a 10.6, McDonough did a 10.61, Embrey a 10.62, and I think mine was 10.64. I think Hegg was back at 10.9 or 11.1. Everybody else was back at 11.2 or 3.

Pat McDonough was the reason we made it to the Finals, from the effort that he made against the other team. We came in at half a lap to go. We were fifteen-100ths down and we won by one 100th. When Pat hit the front it felt like a *rocket*. I swung on the back and thought "Oh my God, this guy is just taking off like a rocket!" I was hanging on for dear life.

Competition Tactics

In the Pan Am Games in 1987 we were behind all the way until the last lap. We were racing Argentina.

In Team Pursuit when you're head to head with another team and you're tight, at that point you have to go for broke and hope to God your team makes it -- stays intact.

At that point you don't pay attention to whether your teammates are going slow or not. You have to go as fast as you possibly can and hope they hang on. If they don't, the race is over, but it doesn't matter because the race is over anyhow.

It's when you're ahead by only half a second and you notice that a teammate of yours is faltering that you have to keep it intact. You then try to protect the faltering rider. When you're behind, you cannot protect the rider a that late date in the event. You have to just bury your head and hope that your teammates will pull through.

Sometimes it may seem like a designated rider will come off, but through the training process, the months of training together, you generally know the abilities of each one of your teammates. You have the idea of how far this rider can go and how fast the fastest rider can go.

When a rider takes a full pull, it's always the rider's decision. When that is discussed before the race, it never occurs. Generally the riders who take the full pull never discuss taking the full pull and the rider who says "I'm going to take a full pull" never takes a full pull. It's kind of hilarious — the rider has no idea how he's going to feel until the event goes off.

That's another thing in Pursuit and Kilo and even in Team Pursuit, I can tell within the first quarter of a lap how well I'm going to ride. When I'm in Turn One and Two I know exactly what I'm going to do by the reaction of my body to the start. I know from the years, the number of Pursuits — I've done so many Pursuits.

You're so in tune with your body, the *littlest thing* that goes on inside your body, tells you "this is the way I'm going to ride." When "that sign" shows up in my body, "this" is what I'm going to do. It changes according to which sign shows up.

It's very disheartening when you start and you get the <u>wrong</u> <u>sign</u>, the one you know is *doom*. And you get it, and you mentally have to bring yourself up more than ever.

In '84 (Olympics) in the Individual Pursuit in the Finals, I got *the bad sign,* in the final ride! It took me two laps to regain composure, to pull myself through that level and to ride over my head. That was a tough one.

That this was the Olympic Games and *there was nothing else*, went through my mind many a time during the ride. Most of the experiences I relate to are Individual than Team.

In competition there are two ways of thinking. One, it's very important in the race to be very focused on what you're doing. On the other hand, it is also extremely important to have knowledge about your opponent.

I've placed a lot of importance on focusing on what I was doing during the race, but also on understanding my opponent before the race. It's the different things they can do — whether he's a fast finisher or a slow finisher, fast starter, steady . . . anticipating what my opponents might do.

In Pursuit, every time you come up against an opponent your tactics ought to be pretty tight. You've got to take each opponent differently. At the National level it's between a half a dozen different riders, but you've got to know the entire field.

It's much tougher when you go to the World Championships. There are a lot of riders there that you've never met.

Teams

National Team Pursuit teams are picked by the coach. National Teams used to be regional. Northern California had a team, Southern California, Oregon, Nevada, whatever. They changed the rules and now you don't have to be from the same district. Then the riders started searching each other out. "Hey Steve, do you want to ride together?"

I knew who would be good teammates through training. It didn't always end up that way, but I remember one year when it was still districts, I joined a district just to get on a team. I changed my district just because I wanted to ride with those guys.

Eddie listened to his riders about teams. He pretty much made up his mind, but he'd listen. At the National level there might be eight guys going for four spots, but after two months of training it was pretty much narrowed down to five or six riders.

Generally it's pretty well known who the Number One rider is, who the Number Two rider is, who the Number Three rider is, and usually the battle is between Fourth and Fifth.

Day after day in training you can feel who has the power, who has the speed, who has the endurance, and you can pretty much rank every rider exactly where they fit in the team.

A lot of times, between the Fourth and Fifth rider, since you can take an alternate, you take the guy, not who performs at the Trials, but who performs consistently for two months. Five guys go, but the day of the race you figure out which four are going to be "The Four".

Very seldom have I seen it falter, but I have seen major blunders a few different times when the wrong four guys were chosen.

I have given my voice where the rider I chose was the wrong rider to ride with, but nobody has ever had a perfect record. The biggest problem in Team Pursuit is personality differences, personality friction.

Best Moments

My favorite moment was my very first Worlds medal, when I won the Silver Medal for the Points race in '81

in Czechoslovakia.

Heartache

In the 1984 Olympics my thoughts in the final ride, during the very first lap, my mind wandered. I couldn't believe that it was happening. (*The 1984 U.S. Olympic Pursuit Team was forced to ride the entire Final for the Gold medal with only <u>three</u> members

"In '84 (Olympics) in the Finals of the Individual Pursuit, I got <u>the bad sign</u>! It took me two laps to regain composure, to pull myself through that level and to ride over my head. That was a tough one. My only thought was: this was the Olympic Games and <u>there's nothing else</u>!"

due to a mishap at the start.)

I said to myself "It's lost. It's over." And then a lap later, going into the second lap I regained my composure and realized "Wait a minute, something could happen to them. I can't quit now. We're going for the Gold!"

I was totally unaware of the people at that point. I regained my composure, I regained my thoughts to the proper thoughts at that point, to give it my

best possible ride. And, I knew that anything can happen in Team Pursuit. They could crash, they could get a flat tire, you don't know.

I was able to hold that thought and regain my composure all the way to the last lap. By the last lap, I knew the race was over, because they had several seconds at that point. I remember thinking to myself at the beginning of the first lap "This can't be happening! This can't be happening!"

That was about the third ride in the Olympic Games with three guys. That was the third time! Steve Hegg and I were the same, but Pat McDonough and Brent Embrey switched.

Kilo vs Pursuit Bikes

A Kilo bicycle needs to be a little stiffer and stronger than a Pursuit bicycle. It still needs the same

aerodynamics.

Generally a Kilo rider sits a little higher in the arm rest area. Getting as far over as a Pursuiter tends to limit your horsepower output. The Kilo requires so much more power output that they don't ride quite so far over. It's kind of a leverage difference. The arm pads need to be a little bit higher for Kilo riders.

There are a few Kilo riders who are still riding the conventional bars and not using the aero position, but I don't think that's wise. The current World Champion still uses old style bars.

But, if you look at the times, out of all the Time Trial times, the Kilo is the one in which times really haven't improved in the last ten years. Pursuit, 40 km, the Hour Record, they've all come down dramatically.

It's more of an aerodynamic problem than an equipment problem. Disc wheels and aerodynamics are two big factors, but when riders went to the aerodynamic position, that was the biggest jump, but it all adds up.

The angles on the bicycles are not different. Mostly the handlebar area needs to be a lot stiffer for a Kilo rider than it does for a Pursuiter. Their start is going to be a lot quicker.

An average start for a Kilo rider is going to be 13.5 to 14.5 seconds, for the first half lap on a 333m track, a Pursuiter will start in 15.5 seconds.

Bostick rides bars with no outrigger bars. He has some great titles behind him, but giving away two seconds on the first lap in a Pursuit can be deadly. Bullhorns are good, with aero bars -- the combination. The benefit of the lateral pull, which allows more power at the start, is worth any aerodynamic loss from their drag effect. You can just make up more time at the start.

Continental Olympic tires are good, they take about 225 lbs or pressure. There are quite a few good discs out there.

Weight is crucial, so they should be as light as possible. Overall, the bicycle should be as light as possible, though you should be careful about not going too light.

You don't want a flimsy bike. In the Pursuit you can get away with some flimsiness, in the Kilo you can't. In the Kilo, the flimsiness will affect the handling, especially on a steep track. In the Pursuit, you're not going fast enough to affect the handling.

Pursuit

The tactics have changed in the Pursuit quite drastically recently. The format has completely changed. Now it's the top 16 to the Gold Medal in the final ride, eliminated very fast.

It used to be five rides for a Bronze medal, now you only have to ride twice. The fastest two riders go to the Finals and ride for first and second. The third fastest time in that group of 16 gets the Bronze Medal. So you only have to ride twice to get a Bronze Medal now. It's a lot easier to go two rides than five.

I can understand why they did it.

They wanted to try and have a little more excitement in the Pursuit and eliminate a lot of the times. They wanted it to be done quick, over with. The other way was not exciting enough. This is more exciting for the spectators.

Roger and Connie Young consult with Harvey about aerodynamics. In the background is Erin Pelke, a Junior rider who is no fool. Who would know more than this group? She's wisely paying attention to the masters.

I would have liked it better because my fourth and fifth rides were very difficult. I was able to ride three rides a lot easier than I could ride five. Other riders have a lot more physical talent to ride five rides easier.

Riding five rounds of Individual Pursuit or four rounds of a Team Pursuit is completely exhausting, the level of fatigue on the body.

Olympic Sprints

"Olympic Sprints" is really an Italian Pursuit. This is an event strictly for Sprinters and Kilo riders. The Pursuiters don't have enough acceleration off the line. They're not going to make up what they lose at the start.

What you're going to want is to start with a Sprinter, then a long distance type Sprinter in second, and a Kilo rider pulling up the last leg.

I've done this event before a few times, even 10 years ago (though they didn't call it Olympic Sprint). I was in last position. It's not a new event. They may be crowd pleasers but from the athlete's point of view it's a corny

event. I was never fast enough at the start. I usually chased for the whole first lap just to get on. Pursuiters don't start fast enough to be competitive.

The problem is that Nationally it's not a contest. You know that all the fastest guys are going to get together. The next three fastest guys are going to be together, and there's going to be this huge discrepancy in time over the teams. The first three places it's not even going to be close.

Internationally it should be fairly close, but I think Nationally it will get boring after watching a few rounds of it. If it's the four fastest teams going at it, that would be exciting, but not 20 teams. It will be more exciting watching the Kilo. The top two or top four will be the big exciting events.

Velodromes

I never really had a home track. San Jose is the closest track to me, but I don't consider it my home track. I don't consider any track my home track. San Jose is the closest track to me and probably out of most of the tracks in the US, I've ridden it least.

My favorite velodrome used to be Colorado Springs, but it's so bumpy now, it's terrible.

I'd have to say Minneapolis (Blaine) is my favorite track now, because it's so smooth. Personally I don't really care too much about the 250, but it's so incredibly smooth.

I prefer a 333m track, but Blaine is the only track in the nation that is smooth enough -- for any event, period.

Smoothness is most critical because of the high air pressure used in tires on the track. Less rolling resistance, less jarring on the body, no question -- the harder, the faster.

Least favorites tracks are probably Detroit and Kissena - they aren't used much now. The Atlanta track is pretty rough. I had a lot of good experiences on the Kenosha and Northbrook tracks. Both of them have major faults, but they're not bad in comparison.

Lehigh is one of the better tracks, no question. It's right there with Colorado Springs.

Advice to New Riders

For a new rider to start racing he/she should get in touch with a local bike race or track club and start doing training rides, training races that they have.

When riders start racing, like at the Junior level I don't think specializing in an event is crucial unless the event totally "jumps out" at the rider. Like "I cannot Pursuit, but I can Sprint."

The average, general rider should get a good perspective of all types of track events for at least a year or two before deciding to specialize in any one event.

Finding a coach is probably the hardest thing, to find a knowledgeable coach who really knows what he's doing. There aren't too many out there. All the riders I'm coaching now have all been directed to me by other people I know.

To new riders I would say it's crucial to get knowledge. Get in touch with a coach who coaches on the track. Not just the basics, there's a little more than the basics that you can learn

Harvey waits for the Points race to begin at Master's Nats. Note the adjustable handlebar stem and the radial spoke pattern on his bicycle wheels. The bike on the right has a "cross two" spoke pattern and conventional stem and bars. Harvey is using "clipless" pedals. Colorado Springs, 1993

from any local coach. He or she should be able to teach you about 75% of the knowledge you need to ride the track. More than that depends on individual goals.

When you want to go from the regional to the National level you're going to need to look for a higher calibre coach. Not necessarily a rider who had been a National rider themselves.

New Pursuiters

If I were coaching a new Pursuiter, I would start with a look at saddle height. Usually they're too high or too low. You start with the saddle height and the saddle position, how far back or forward it is. They're always playing with the rules about where the saddle can be. You have to get the rider low enough. Then s/he has to spend many hours training in that lower position because it takes a lot of time to develop

the ability to transfer the power into the pedals when you're bent over that far.

A flat back is not necessary. The way the back rolls depends on the person's physique. I haven't seen aerodynamic studies saying that a flat back is faster or studies saying that it isn't. The Federation might know about that.

In 1996 look for Steve Hegg and Mike McCarthy to hammer in the Pursuit. Hegg is really focused and getting psyched up for '96.

For the Olympic Games, I hope they go with a builder for the Olympic track who's tried and true. You want an excellent facility for that event.

Incredible Women

I'm coaching a couple of women riders. I've seen some really incredible women's performances.

I remember Marianne Berglund when she first came over to the United States, over ten years ago. I went on training rides with her the same year she won the World's (Road, 1983). She was so incredible. We had about 30 guys, all National Team riders and 7-Eleven Pros on about a 120 mile ride. Coming back into Austin, Texas, we had the hammer down doing 36-37 miles per hour in a cross wind.

We ended up with about six people left -- Marianne was still there! I was just dumbstruck. She was so unbe-

"I've seen some incredible women's performances. Marianne Berglund could have shattered any record." Worlds, '86, La Jolla Grand Prix, 1991.

lievable that she could have shattered any world record at any distance at that time. She could have shattered the Women's Hour Record, the Women's Pursuit Record, the Kilo -- she was so unbelievable that year. Just incredible, that's all I can say.

Another incredible performance I saw was (*Track Sprint World Champion*) Sue Novara, in a field sprint. I got there on the last lap of the Women's race, with Sue in the field. When I got to the finish, Sue came *flying* by. A couple of seconds later, here comes the field!

When did Sue break away? The gap was done in the field sprint! She put 20 lengths on the women in the last 300 meters of the race! The rest of the women were sprinting at 25 mph, Sue was sprinting at 40! It was quite a sight. It was right after she got off the track and she started doing some of the criteriums. There was no woman in the world who come close to the speed that she had.

Even today, you take the best woman road sprinter and Sue was far superior. She was coached by Jack Disney, who was also Gibby Hatton's coach. He had a talent for turning his riders into rocketships. That's the only way I can describe it. I don't know what his secrets were.

I've wanted to call him up and say "Jack, we don't want to lose the knowledge. Since I'm coaching now, let me in on some of the secrets you use to get your athletes to go so fast!"

Success

I think the reason I've been so successful is because I've always tried to do my personal best, the best that I was capable of.

Winning, to me, was not the all-important goal. The important goal was my best. If my best was second I'd come away happy. If I came away with second and second was not my best, I'd come away very disappointed.

In a Team Pursuit it was different. I was scared to death of letting my teammates down. I was *petrified* of letting my teammates down more than anything else. I couldn't <u>stand</u> the thought of letting my teammates down.

Dropping a teammate is not in your mind before the race. During a race your mind has to be clean and clear, and, especially if you happen to be the strongest rider, keeping the team together. I couldn't break it apart. Steve Hegg could.

When the pain sets in I tell myself not to quit now — "This is what I trained all year for!" — pretty straightforward.

It's hard for me to explain, but only my bad races hurt. None of my good races hurt. I know that doesn't make any sense.

For most athletes, winning is everything. That could be a big negative that people can say about me, because winning wasn't everything to me.

The most important to me was doing my best. As long as I gave it my best, that was all that mattered, and that's still true.

Whether I got 10th place, 100th place or 1st place, it didn't matter. The placing wasn't as important as doing my best. Whereas 95% of the athletes out there, winning is everything.

I had desire, more desire than most. If I was to rate myself with regard to different aspects I would rate myself as 60% desire and only 40% talent.

I would say that my desire was much greater than my talent. I would say that my talent as an athlete was only average and that my desire was greater. Wanting it includes the desire for excellence.

Master's Racing

Master's racing is very competitive. The calibre is shocking — how good quality the Master's are, the depths of fields are really good.

The Future

I'm training a lot more consistently than I was for a while.

In the future I plan to continue coaching, enjoying Master's racing and hopefully becoming Director of the San Francisco Velodrome.

The velodrome is still looking good. They're just looking for the location.

Still in his rider's jersey, Harvey gets his notebook and checks his stopwatch as he prepares to coach his riders to victory. Partly due to Harvey's strategies, one of his coachees won Third place in the first Points race he ever entered.

Chapter 13
☺ *Olympic Sprint* ☺
Track Competition's Newest Event

Take three of the fastest men on the track (Sprinters). Line them up, Team Pursuit style, with three other fastest men on the other side of the track. When the gun goes off, each team moves into Team Pursuit position, one in back of the other, accelerating to top speed as quickly as possible.

The first man rides one lap on the front and pulls off. The second continues, pulling off after the second lap. The last man continues for the third and final lap, driving through to the finish.

Is it a Sprint? Is it a Team Pursuit? According to the speed and training of riders, it is a Sprint. According to the rules, it's a Team Pursuit. There will be no track stands, no jockeying for position, no attempts to catch the other guys sleeping. This race is an all-out drag race, dependent for success on speed, teamwork, and constancy. There is no use of the banking as in Team Pursuit, no possibility of half lap pulls.

If you look in the Non-Championship event section, you will see a race described as "Italian Pursuit." If you read the pattern, an Olympic Sprint is an Italian Pursuit, one of the most fun events on the track. Consequently, it should be included under "Time Trials." Try telling these Sprinters that they are doing a time trial. "Ha! they'll say, this is a Sprint! Olympic Sprint!"

It's kind of like the old ad that argues about candy vs. breath mints. This is two (click), two (click), two races in one. Track racing offers no end to variations on its themes. This race will likely offer just enough difference from all other races to present the distinct possibility of a surprise ending.

Marty Nothstein says his "dream team" is Erin Hartwell, first lap, himself second lap and Erin Hartwell third lap! Then he laughs and notes that he and Erin will need to find their third man. While Marty views his team as unbeatable, this remains to be seen.

Logically, the fastest man would win Sprints, but we know this is seldom the case when comparing order of Flying 200 times with order of winning places. The relationship is hardly consistent. There are other considerations when attaching assumptions to race results. The same will be true in Olympic Sprint.

When reflecting on Team Pursuit competition, Harvey Nitz recalls that the 1984 Olympic Team Pursuit team was comprised of men who rode faster 200 meter times than the Sprinters. A strong sense of the unexpected renders a forward look at Olympic Sprint competition very intriguing.

Surprise is the spice of competition. I'm betting on surprises in this event. Men (women?) assemble your teams! Let the games begin!

Bill Clay, Jeff Solt and Erin Hartwell would seem a good combination. World Cup, 1994

Take three of the fastest men on the track (Sprinters). Line them up, Team Pursuit style, with three other "fastest men" on the other side of the track. The gun goes off . . . . .

Is it a Sprint? Is it a Team Pursuit? According to the speed and training of riders, it is a Sprint. According to the rules, it's a Team Pursuit. There will be no track stands, no jockeying for position, no attempts to catch the other guys sleeping.

This race is an all-out drag race, dependent for success on speed, teamwork, & constancy.

Olympic Sprint -- in a nutshell

The Start --
Team Pursuit style

This looks like a race women could do with no problem . . .

First lap --
Bill Clay pulls off

Second lap --
Jeff Solt pulls off

Third/last lap --
Erin Hartwell finishes.

Omnium

The "big Momma" of bicycle racing is the Omnium. Prior to 1965, all National Championships were won as Omniums, none as individual events.

Riders competed in several races, netting points in each which resulted in a total score to determine the overall winner. This approach is still used at all levels of competition, including National Championships. Now it is also called "Best All Around Rider" or "BAR".

The Rule Book lists the Omnium as a distinct race category. Points won in each race need not be awarded equally for all events. If an Omnium is offered, the scoring system is to be specified in the race announcement.

In the case of National Championships, scoring is set at the same number of points for each race. These are: 7-5-3-2-1 for first through fifth places.

In the event of a tie, the tie will be broken by awarding the win to the rider with the most first places. If a tie still exists, the rider with the most second places wins. In the unlikely event that all scores for all races are matched, the tie will be broken by whoever placed higher in the last race of the series or in the last race in which at least one of the riders placed.

Omnium scoring can be used during individual events, for weekly series, as part of club races, for season points totals, and in any other manner of totalling to a larger award. Races can be all at the same location or spread throughout the country. Long term point accumulation shows consistent, superior performances by riders who compete in races over the season and the years.

Published rankings provide a way for riders to compare their overall performances with many other riders. This can assist in other ways, such as selection for National Team, National Training Camps, and many other opportunities.

Other Races

In weekly races at velodromes around the country there are many different kinds of races with many different names. Sometimes these races will be virtually the same as National Championship races, other times traditional races will be altered to add interest. Sometimes an announcer or promoter will dream up some new event just to keep riders on their toes and spectators entertained.

Reviewed below are a sampling of races gathered from velodrome literature and riders' descriptions. There are surely others.

(For others left out, write and describe them for the second edition!)

Mass Start Races

(a.k.a. massed start) races: any race where riders begin from the same point and at the same time and compete in a large field. On the track, Points races and Madisons are two examples of mass start races.

Scratch race / massed start race: Mass start races are the most common on the velodrome in weekly racing, because they allow the greatest number of riders to participate. Variations on this theme can take on many other names.

Scratch races can vary greatly in their number of laps, often 5, 6 or 10 laps in weekly events to keep the program moving. Details often respond to the numbers of riders signed up and are specified by the organizer prior to the beginning of the race.

Primes are also announced if there are any. Lapped riders are usually eliminated from the race. Placings are according to finish at the end of the specified number of laps. Variation is what race organizers determine it to be.

Unknown Distance:

There are few rules to this mass start event except that riders are not notified as to when the race will end. Only one person knows when the end will be. Riders will only know when they hear the bell sounding one more lap.

Riders sometimes "guesstimate" and gamble that the end will come soon, as it might. They ride off the front, hoping that the bell will sound while they are still away. Sometimes they are right.

If the rider is wrong in this gamble, the pack will catch up and s/he will be reabsorbed, often too fatigued to come up with a good sprint at the finish. But that's all part of the fun of the unknown distance. Breakaways make this race much more interesting.

Other times riders just cruise in the pack, waiting for the bell to signify one more lap and set off the final Sprint, which they plan to win. The suspense is constant in this event.

Every once in a while the person picking the number of laps will have a sense of humor and end the race in, maybe, three laps (maybe even one!) Riders do not usually expect it to be that short. The point is the suspense and surprise.

If a rider is off the front at the time the bell is rung, can s/he stay away? The crowd goes wild, and that too is the point.

Miss-and-Out / Devil Take the Hindmost:

This race is a traditional crowd pleaser. On every lap the last rider at the back of the pack is out. Who will it be?

It's not always the slowest rider. Sometimes a top-level rider will inadvertently get "boxed in" at the bottom of the track, have no where to go and find s/he is last. All of a sudden, a top competitor is out. That's the charm of the Miss 'N' Out, you just never know, lap by lap, who the next rider out will be.

The race continues until only three riders are left. Those three riders are allowed one free lap before they sprint for the finish. At that point, the <u>first</u> rider across the line is the winner.

Most races go to the fastest rider, but this race goes to the smartest (who also has a little luck). That rider saves his/her energy for the final sprint by sitting in the pack. S/he is not usually on the front very much, though this is a good place to be to avoid the possibility of getting boxed in. But then the rider is wasting energy breaking the wind for riders behind instead of just cruising in the draft.

Cruising comfortably in the pack seems like a great idea and an easy ride, but even this tactic is risky. It is easy to get comfortable, miscalculating to find that all other riders who were just in back are now uptrack and ahead, leaving the previously confident rider confused as to how they all got up there, as s/he finds him/herself now <u>out</u>.

Smart riders often go "over the top" in order to avoid risking "the box". But sometimes this strategy doesn't work either. Sometimes there is just no place available to move up.

When a favorite accidentally crosses last, it's a sad day for his/her fans. Once the race is pared down to the last three riders, those riders get one free lap to catch their breath before the final sprint determines the winner.

Win-and-Out:

The first rider across on the first lap is the winner in this race and is finished, but the rest of the field is still in the race.

Second place is won by the first person across the line on the next lap, who now is finished.

Third place is won by the winner of the third lap, who is now finished - - and so on down to fifth place.

Then the race is over.

If you're lucky, you live near a track where National Champions train. Here, left to right, Jeff Pierce, Don Scales, Dirk Copeland, Steve Hegg, Danny Van Haute, Kevin Maxey and Tony Olsen. Track champions like Hegg (Gold in Pan Ams, 1983, and Olympics, 1984) left the track for the road and $$. He'd race track professionally if he could (maybe soon he can!) San Diego, 1994

Strategy here is clear: sprint from the beginning to be the first rider across the line. Each lap is a new opportunity to be the first, though each is a successive placing.

Rather than resting at the back until the finishing sprint, this race is a sprint a lap until the first five places are claimed, at which point the race is over.

Point a Lap:

This race is similar to a scratch race because riders ride a predetermined number of laps, but in this race one point is awarded to the winner of each lap until all laps are completed.

At the end, the winner is determined by the rider with (surprise!) the highest number of points. This is another fast race. No rider, unless s/he totally outclasses his/her competitors, wins every lap. With good competition, the leader in points changes several times throughout the race and it is continually exciting.

Snowball:

A snowball tends to get larger as it rolls downhill. In this race, the points total increases with each lap.

The first rider across the line on the first lap gets one point. The first rider on the second lap gets two points, and etc. Points are awarded according to the number of the lap.

The smart rider in this race saves energy for the later laps when the higher number of points will be awarded and those contesting the early laps will be fatigued. The only trouble is, later laps bring out all the smart, elite riders, so the competition is fierce.

In theory, if there are ten laps and no rider gets points on more than one lap, all a rider needs to do is win the last lap to win the race. In reality, one rider usually wins more than one lap and the finish is less certain.

The smart rider doesn't shoot his stuff in the early part of the race, but knows s/he can't depend on winning, say, the last two laps, either. Someone else (likely everyone else!) has the same idea. And that's what keeps it exciting.

Chariot Race:

A chariot race in old Roman days was a no-holds-barred event. It is the same on the track in the Chariot race. For this reason, this race is begun with holders rather than in Mass Start style.

At the sound of the whistle, riders have (usually) one lap to be the first across the line. Then the race is over. The end.

Each holder can push or even throw the rider into the race and possibly the lead. Then the fastest sprint takes it. Quick. Straight to the point. No subtlety about this one.

Handicap Races

Riders are placed at different locations around the track according to their abilities as established by time trial times or other information. The weakest riders are placed first, the strongest riders last.

If properly done, all riders who have been placed according to a handicap "guesstimation" will arrive at the finish line at the same time.

Like the Italian Pursuit, this race allows organizers great latitude in variations to create excitement for both riders and spectators. Riders who would not normally compete against each other can be matched fairly evenly by use of the handicap method.

Other methods of handicapping riders can be used to encourage them to persist over weekly or seasonal programs.

Handicapping requires knowledge and mental planning, so they depend on the level of work organizers are willing to put out.

If promoters want larger fields, handicapping can offer advantages to riders who otherwise wouldn't be able to compete. Some tracks begin a season with handicap racing in order to keep racing low-key early in the season and

to bring out riders who may otherwise not show.

Pursuits

A pursuit race involves individual riders chasing other individual riders. In pursuit races of teams, the front rider is actually pursuing while the riders behind await their turn, resting in the draft. It is this "taking turns in a set pattern" which differentiates the pursuit from other chase situations typical in bicycle racing.

No matter how big the team is or how they are placed, only one individual is actually pursuing one other individual at a time. Others are either pursuing other riders or riding behind, waiting their turn.

Australian Pursuit:

This race is between two or more riders who line up at the rail in staggered locations around the track. All riders begin at the same time when they receive the signal from officials. Each rider us both chased and chasing another given rider at the same time.

The object of the race is to catch the rider in front without getting caught by the rider behind. Each rider who is caught is immediately out of the race. The race continues until one rider catches the last other competitor left on the track. The race might be one big Sprint or it might go on and on, Pursuit-like, until finally the last rider is caught.

Italian Pursuit:

A team pursuit race where two or more teams of any number of riders placed in equal distances (depending on the number of teams) around the track compete over the designated distance.

The front rider leads for a specified number of laps (one or two) and then pulls off, leaving the next rider continuing the competition in successive order until only one rider from each team is left on the track. The last two riders sprint for the finish. The first one across the line wins.

The Italian Pursuit in weekly track programs can take on as many personalities as riders.

One favorite was a race in San Diego comprised of one Midget, one Junior, one Woman, one Master, and one Senior on each team. The teams were matched and staggered as to abilities, the top competitors in each division were not all placed on the same team.

The Senior rider went last. One of the Seniors in this race happened to be Pan Am Gold Medal Pursuiter Dave Grylls, giving the local yokels watching this small-time, weekly race, a magnificent performance at the finish.

Organizers can come up with any assortment of teams. Team Pursuits done in an entertaining way can allow everyone to participate and have a great time.

Adapted National Championship races --- Sprints

Sprints during local events are generally run like Championship races, but their details can be changed by organizers. They are crowd pleasers, but are not always included in weekly programs due to the nature of their small groupings of two to four riders. It takes too long to accommodate everyone. Most velodromes with local

riders training for National, World or Olympic competition will offer Sprints on request.

Points Race

In contrast to Sprints, wide variation in Points race design are common to local weekly races at active tracks with imagination.

One of the charms of Non-championship Points races is the playfulness with which race organizers might award points on more casual occasions. In addition, Primes are often used at this level to tempt riders into Sprinting during non-Points laps, spicing up the pace for audiences and riders and throwing confusion into strategy.

Riders seldom object to randomly added Primes thrown in during the course of a Points race. They may only learn about these surprises from announcers during the actual race.

Sometimes money might be collected at various points in the night which is awarded as a Prime. No one, competitor, organizer, or spectators might be able to predict how much this out-of-the-blue Prime might total. With a good announcer stimulating a crowd which is involved with the prizes, these events are very fun, for both riders and spectators.

Another possibility for Primes may be miscellaneous donations from spectators. A wise announcer will not refuse these unexpected offerings. They may include a plate of cookies, a half a chicken, a tune-up or any donated prize.

If the donator wants to advertise his/her business cheaply, this is a fun way to get an announcement while contributing materially and adding to the general fun and enjoyment of audiences and riders.

The opportunity for this kind of activity is especially suited for Points races because they are long enough to allow for mid-race changes and announcements.

They are also particularly suited to unexpected primes because there are definite lulls between Points laps when riders are resting. For some riders, Primes may be all they take home.

While this may sound sad, for these same riders, the total money they accumulate through Primes may be more than that won by the most successful winner of any race offered on the track that night!

Americans traditionally love the underdog and the unexpected. It's part of our rags-to-riches dream. The joy of unpredictable thrills in competition which integrally involve other kinds of unexpected rewards is seen nowhere better than in the Points race.

Madison

The Madison combines the Points race with Teams of riders. This might seem to lend itself well to variations, but this race can also be so intense that there is never a predictable slack time available as there is in the Points race between Points laps.

No one dictates when riders exchange except the riders themselves and it tends to occur continuously. Consequently, these races are usually run as in National Championships.

Madisons are a great training race for all competitors. A track is fortunate if an expert is available who can teach locals Madison techniques, especially the exchanges, which are the key feature of this event.

Race organizers can assist by designing competition to allow the greatest amount of practice in such a way as to build skills.

The exchanges and dynamics of Team competition can make the Madison a confusing event for those who are trying to keep score. With the constant change of competitors, trying to relate who is ahead of who is virtually impossible for the average spectator. This makes the announcer's role that much more important.

However, with the exchanges, people coming and going up and down the track continually at high speeds and the ever-present threat of danger, this is always an exciting event for local crowds.

Keirin

This event is run the same as in the National Championships except that heats are sometimes divided into smaller groups at the local level than they need to be (5 or 6 vs. 9). The pacer is invariably a motorcycle because that is what most tracks have available, usually through organizers or some other generous soul.

This race is part of a multi-billion dollar industry in Japan and there are strong indicators that it is quickly gaining in popularity in this country.

Kilo / Individual Pursuit:

It would certainly not be impossible for weekly programs to include Kilos and Pursuit, but not likely. These events are too tedious with the average local riders for appeal to crowds.

They can be very exciting if a record is being sought, if Team qualification is at stake or if there is some other reason for these events to take on an excitement which watching

Paul Swift shows the bike handling skills that he developed at his home track in Kenosha, Wisconsin. The contribution of local events reaches to the World level.

one or two riders circling a track ad infinitum simply does not have. So, you will not likely see these two offered very often.

Like Sprints, if local riders are training for major competition, they might be presented on request. More

likely, they might be offered as a part of a special event which is geared toward preparing riders for National or International competition.

Team Pursuit

Ditto. National Championship-type Team Pursuits are seldom run in weekly programs unless it is part of training for a larger event. More likely this race takes on the variations seen in Italian Pursuit. Now *those* are fun.

See Italian Pursuit for variations that can make the Team Pursuit a wonderful event for audience and competitors alike in local, low-key programs without following the rigid procedures necessary in National and World Championships. They just require a little imagination.

The Future

Considering how track racing has changed over the last 30 years, there is no reason to imagine any races listed here are locked into permanence.

All races are traditional in the sense that they include the same elements which have always challenged riders: speed and endurance spiced with a varied structure within which riders can use their intellect to optimize their own performance as well as their interactions with others.

There is no doubt that inventors of new races will offer spectators and riders new adventures in the future which are presently unknown. **Maybe you have some ideas??**

Other aspects of track racing include riders who compete despite physical disabilities. Track racing has seen blind riders on the rear of Tandems, AAF Programs for the Hearing Impaired, and contests involving riders with lost and/or partial limbs.

Charles Dempsey lost part of one leg in an automobile accident. With a an artificial lower leg Dempsey competes on par with those who are missing no parts. While he has competed on the track, Dempsey races primarily on the road.

Robert Picardo

The most notable achievement by a physically challenged athlete on the track is that of Robert Picardo, who has won medals and awards in that arena on equal par with "unchallenged" athletes in Match Sprint, Tandem Sprint and Keirin competition.

He won fifth in the Keirin at the 1992 Olympic Trials and fourth in Tandem Sprint in the National Championships in 1993.

Since that time Robert has been involved with Kayak racing, a sport which draws even more heavily upon upper body strength for success.

Picardo was born with a partial right hand and limited musculature in his right arm and torso. He has made compensations to equipment and clothing in order to gain advantage lost to his unequal structure. He has begun a business to help others realize their dreams.

Picardo has this to say about competition:

"To find the true heart in sport, look to the challenged athlete. Barriers of physical limitations can be broken down to allow an athlete to maximize his/her potential so motivation and genetics become the deciding factors of ultimate performance.

There are no limits to the materials which can be used for adaptations, such as: plastic, titanium, custom machined parts and recycled hardware. I make custom products that are lightweight, realistic and hold up to the rigors of the committed athlete -- straightforward, durable devices that will find years of use among recreationalists, from cycling to paddling, to ice climbing to golf.

Striving for my own peak potential and stifled by equipment that fit "everyone else," I began making adaptive products for myself as soon as I could open a tool drawer. Before that, some terrific people made "add-ons" for me that, at best, let me participate in an activity once or twice before they broke.

What I wanted was to be a *competitor*, to find the highest levels I could attain through desire, genetics and knowledge and never be outdone by some silly physical difference.

In seeing my success I knew others were there, outstanding athletes, possibly with World Class potential, unable to express themselves. They deserve a chance. I work with every individual I help personally, trying to help them realize their goals.

What I feel is important is this: Nothing physical ever held me back and nothing physical should hold others back either.

In the world of the physically challenged athlete, competitors use adapted technology to enable themselves to compete on par with "normal" athletes.

Bicycles are comparatively easy to adapt by disassembling and retrofitting them according to the athlete's needs. This ease of adaptation is changing somewhat with the advent of integrated components.

Cycling is a very symmetrical sport. The grace of cycling comes from symmetry, what I call "linear leverage" or what the Belgians call "antecam", Challenged riders are at a distinct disadvantage with production equipment. Exposure to a retrofitting expert is rare and most riders never go beyond participation.

Those who do, however, will find themselves with satisfaction, a working knowledge of physiology and a "personal athletic inventory" any pro would envy. This leads a "disabled" athlete on a personal path of self discovery, deeper, I believe, than the "abled" athlete. Physically the journey may include development of the undeveloped or underdeveloped

"To find the true heart in sport, look to the challenged athlete. Nothing physical ever held me back and nothing physical should hold others back either." Olympic Trials, 1992

body part as an integral part of compensatory activities.

Unfortunately, the challenged athlete finds many problems outside of sport-specific adaptation. Many people refuse to accept the disabled as an able competitor. An aggressive move in competition can be perceived as lack of control (especially by able athletes who have been beaten!).

The evolution of adapting parts can also be long and, because it is specific to a certain area, painful. There are few rules to follow.

In the end, with their real abilities laid out before them, the challenged athlete will find the true meanings of challenge, sport and competition."

Adapted Tandem grip, 1993

(far left) Fifth in Keirin to some pretty hot Champions. (Robert, far right) Blaine, 1992 Olympic Trials

(middle) Robert (right) cracks a joke as everybody gets ready for the awards photo. He knows which camera to look at. U.S. Nationals, 1993

The Madison, 1992 Olympic Trials.

Standard bars, adapted grip. Marymoor, 1989

Adapted bars, adapted grip. San Diego, 1995

Adapted road bars -- a work of art. 1995

Chapter 15 - Coaches
Coach of Champions
Roger Young

Roger Young is part of the dynasty of Midwestern speedskaters who have so often made their mark in bicycle racing. His father, Clair, was a co-founder of the Wolverine Sports Club with Mike Walden, which provided coaching for speedskating, bicycle racing and cross country skiing. Wolverine members actually built the Dorais velodrome themselves.

Roger's sister is three-time World Sprint Champion Sheila Young Ochowitz, his wife four-time World Sprint Champion Connie Paraskevin Young. Roger himself was U. S. National Sprint Champion in 1973 and has raced internationally for many years.

Roger represents a legendary segment of American bicycle racing history which has had as much impact on the sport in this country as any movement since the Six-day races.

At races you will notice a very quiet Roger Young. He believes that when race time arrives, all work should be done, all riders ready. Still, he will also be ready with his video camera to take back evidence of glory and errors from which his coachees can develop knowledge, skill and learn to "play the game", Roger's favorite game -- velodrome racing.

Eddie (Borysewicz) and I are both sides of the spectrum.

I rode my first bike race when I was three. My mom and dad raced. My dad started off as a speed skater,

so did my mom. Their parents didn't do that. My dad has some stories about my grandfather trying to give him tips. I don't think it was socially acceptable for my grandmother to race.

My mom was already unusual. She wasn't much of a skater, she mostly rode, she was a cyclist. She was into recreational riding and then got into racing. She was real talented. There were four kids in my family, Sheila was second, I was third. The other two were also involved. The youngest in the family was pretty talented and my oldest sister did both speed skating and cycling.

How I Got Started

I was pretty good in science in school. I thought about becoming a vet at one time, but in the meantime I realized while I was in school that I was an expert at one thing more than anything else: sports. It seemed easier to go in the direction of sports than veterinary medicine. I was lucky with sports, because I wasn't talented at football, baseball or basketball, and I probably wouldn't be an athlete if it weren't for my parents involvement with cycling and speed skating. I never had to make a decision between the two, I just put effort into both of them. They were different seasons.

"The thing that makes an athlete most coachable is hope."
Roger and National Champion Jeff Solt. Indianapolis, 1994

We were actually the originators of cross training. There was always that split between when it was too cold to ride a bike and too warm to skate in Michigan. There was always that margin there. Not until I was 17 or 18 did I go directly from speedskating

one weekend to a bike race the next. Most of the time there is a month or so where you're transitioning from one sport to the next.

The transition from cycling to skating requires that you start running. You have to start pounding your skeletal system. Your weight is supported in cycling and it's very traumatic to go from cycling to speed skating without running. You really have to run.

One year my sister won the World Championships one day in cycling and the next day she was out running. Most people are out partying, doing nothing, saying "Well, the work's over for the year. Take a couple of weeks off. But the next day Sheila was out running.

From speed skating to cycling it's a little bit different in that you get on rollers and start pedaling again. It's real difficult in that there's no resistance. Now, fortunately, there's lots of good stuff, like compu-trainers, wind load trainers, things like that, that simulate road riding. Back when I was riding, during that transition, it was the worst time of the year for me because most of the early season races were Time Trials. I hated Time Trials.

"I couldn't wait until it would warm up so I could ride the track. It was more exciting and I'm a ham. I like a full stadium, lots of money, and big time racing." Roger is second from front, Mark Whitehead is the man in black. San Diego, 1981

Racing

I couldn't wait until it would warm up so I could ride the track. I preferred the track to the roads. It was more exciting and I'm a ham. I'm not the person who appreciates the suffering and the loneliness of the long distance runner. I'm a ham. I like a full stadium, lots of money, and big time racing.

I never considered myself as successful as a rider compared to the people I've coached. I wasn't that hot. There were some years that I felt better than others. I guess I started doing really well in 1971. I was satisfied with every year of racing up until 1982 when I injured my back pretty badly. I just lifted something wrong and twisted my back.

From '82 on I raced more for fun, not real intensely. I had a pretty good year in 1990. It was a decent little season, local racing. I won some criteriums, won lots of track races. I had fun riding up through 1990 or so. Now I ride, but I don't race.

Sprints weren't my specialty — racing was my specialty. Sprinting was like putting in golf. It's the short game, and you need to know how to do that. Road riding or long distance racing is the long game. To me, racing was racing. I had to learn and I felt compelled to try to be as expert as any bike race would put upon me. I just like racing.

Sprinting was something you had to do at the end of a race. The first part of a race is just survival. Everything else kind of gets funneled into that one intense moment near the end. I can't say that I'd get excited about the first 100 miles of a road race. You shouldn't be excited. When someone tells me "Seems like you're really interested in Sprinting," -- well, Sprinting is pretty intense. It's intense and you talk about it in an intense way. If you talk about road cycling or endurance riding you talk about it in terms of efficiency and more existential terms.

I can't say that I prefer one over the other, but I like to think that I was pretty good at everything. A Jack-of-All-Trades. I'd race anything. I was fifth in the World's in the Points race. That's the best I've ever done in the World Championships. I've won some big road races in Europe. I was second in a European classic, Het Volleck in 1975. I won lots of small road races in Europe. I won some stage races here in the States. I won the Nationals in the Sprints, I won the Nationals in the Keirin.

The year that Gibby Hatton won

"Mike would tell me what a stupid SOB I was and how lousy I was, but he would make me work hard.. He wouldn't let a good rider be just a rider in and of him/herself. He would say "Hey, go show these kids how to do this.""

third place in the World Championships in Zurich. I beat him that year in the Nationals. I was the coach that year. I was the first U.S. Keirin Champion, I guess.

I've coached some good Points race riders like Frankie Andreu, Dan Vogt, and Jim Pollack. I've had some good Team Pursuit runs, too, even though I was never the National Team Pursuit coach. I've always had just local guys put together and ride pretty well. I was a decent Team Pursuiter. I won Pan Am Games in Team Pursuit.

So, let's see, I won Pan Am Games in Team Pursuit, Fifth in the Worlds in the Points race, rode the Olympics in the Sprints, I rode the Tour of Britain, Paris-Roubaix with the amateurs, second place in Hed Volleck, so I can't say that there's one discipline I didn't try. I was lousy at Time Trialing, no noteworthy results there.

I hated the Motorpace event. I never liked doing that. It reminded me of roller racing, where your legs are going warp speed and it's just real steady. It looks like it goes fast, but the event itself makes the slowest rider out of you that you can possibly imagine. Those guys tend to get pretty slow. So I never really liked Motorpace that well. I liked doing it, but I was no good at it, I should say. I didn't do it that much so there was no worry about my getting slower. You use these huge gears, too, and that tends to slow you down. Low, humungous pie-plates on there. More like pizza plates.

Mike Walden was my coach. My dad helped me out a lot too. They were sort of like Bad Cop/Good Cop. Mike would tell me what a stupid SOB I was and how lousy I was, but he would make me work hard.

My dad was like "Oh, yeah, you're going to do it, you're going to make it. You're going to make the Olympic Team, you're going to win the Nationals!" I'd be going "Yeah, sure, right, dad." But he was right. And Mike was right too. Bad Cop/Good Cop —they're both great guys.

They were the only ones who really coached me. I might have gotten a tip here and there from different people, but that was mostly because Mike and my dad had taught me to learn as much as I could from any

individual, but that was my learning from them, not them coaching me. I just saw what I wanted to learn from different individuals. I just grabbed it. I'm still learning a lot, by the way, that doesn't end. I like to think that I know more and can apply it better than I did before.

"When I was racing, I recognized someone making a mistake and I would take advantage and I would end up winning, or I would end up doing better. Even though it was a pity they made a mistake, I would capitalize on it. Now I do the same thing." Marymoor, 1986

Coaching

Some of my coaching evolved out of necessity. I really loved racing and I had decided to go to Europe and race full time in the indoor tracks. The

American riders who came with me, like Mike Neel, Danny Van Haute, Paul Deem, Mike Moll, guys like that, Dave Bohl, needed some tips. If I was going to race with them I'd try to help them out.

Of course I learned some things from them too, but it was really necessary for me to sit down with them and talk about tactics — what we're going to do here and what we were going to do there. When it came down to helping younger riders in the club, our club was set up like that.

Mike Walden wouldn't let a good rider be just a rider in and of him/herself. They were always in a group. He would say "Hey, go show these kids how to do this." Even when I was sixteen or seventeen. When I was a hot stuff junior Mike would say "Hey, Rog, go show these guys how to do this." or "Demonstrate that" or whatever. So I was already part of Mike's coaching tool at the time.

When it came time for me to start handing out advice it was done in a very methodical way. Obviously I wanted to win bike races and if my partner didn't know how to do something, I needed to teach him how to do it. And it worked. So, positive reinforcement from that encouraged me to take it even more seriously. There are things that I see in cycling that give me the desire, no matter what. I can see some possibility, a bike race lost that should have been won. That really inspires me.

When I was racing, I recognized someone making a mistake and I would

take advantage and I would end up winning, or I would end up doing better. Even though it was a pity they made a mistake, I would capitalize on it. Now I do the same thing. Now I look at someone who should be winning races and I go "Look, I'm going to help you win bike races." I'm still capitalizing on people's mistakes, only now instead of taking advantage as another competitor, I'm helping them defeat the problems that they have.

If I'm coaching people who will compete against each other, they take care of it themselves, I don't worry about a conflict. I give them both my best and let them take care of it. I had a good enough career that I don't need to live vicariously through the riders that I coach. I don't need to do that. Consequently I can look at it as a game and something that's fun for me.

I can look at this Sprinter and that Sprinter and other riders at the same time very objectively, I think, and not get committed to it. If I coach someone, I not only know their weaknesses, I know their competitor's weaknesses too. I study everybody. I don't tell each one what their competitors weaknesses are. If they can't figure it out — I teach a method, too. I teach my riders to be analytical, in the roads, the Points race and the Sprints. If they can't figure it out, I'm not going to push their buttons.

That's part of the anti-vicarious thing. I don't want to get on the podium with the guy. I want them to be up there and say "I put the work in myself, I made my own race decisions. I'm up here. I feel good." That's all I care about. I don't want someone to say "I owe it all to Rog." No way, that would make me feel funky. That would make me feel like "Gee, maybe I should have my college professor up here with me too, now that I'm a successful coach." No way. They taught me what I needed to know and now they're out of the picture. Maybe a good reference, but . . .

I look at what the rider needs in order to win a bike race. Try to help them focus on that. When it comes to the actual race itself they should have known from talking and evaluating what they've done, how things are done properly, just applying, not my methodology, but just sound methodology to what they're doing, they should come up with the right decisions themselves. I don't hedge things. I might give them a hint. I might tell Ken something like "Don't open a door you can't close" which, to some people might sound a little cryptic or encoded, like some sort of message or riddle, but it's pretty straightforward.

That's another thing that's important to riders, to establish a language that's interesting, unique and descriptive so that you don't have to go into some kind of oration to understand what you mean. That was the nice thing about Mike. He had a real specific language that was very colorful. It is very colorful language, but very few people understand it. There's a certain intimacy that comes from that.

When I say something to a rider like "Don't go fencing with somebody's back wheel" he under-

stands what I mean. It's definitely not poetry, but it's about as close as you can get in coaching. It's not novel, they've probably heard it 100 times. It's just like "Ok, I'm going to push button B1 here." It's fun. Again, it's another thing that's fun. And it helps give the riders a sense of security. Things are status quo.

We're still trying to focus on the same things as we should have been focusing on in our training. It's not a new day with all this stuff on the line, it's just the same business. That helps.

There's nothing more rewarding to me than, for instance, when I talk to Connie about training. She raises issues and questions that go beyond what I know and what I've taught her. She's taken a certain degree of knowledge and a certain method and applied it and expanded beyond what I had specifically generated for her, toward her. That's the neat thing.

Mark (Gorski) has done that also, and so has Curt Harnett, and road racers. Dan Vogt, for example, in the Points race, has taken things further advanced than I would explain them to him. It's nice to see. They're making themselves out of it instead of a bunch of Roger Young clones.

The Game

One thing that surprises most people is that what means most to me is the game. "The game's the thing",

as Shakespeare said. I'll find out from the rider how he or she wants to play the game. "What kind of person are you? Are you an aggressive person, are you a conservative person? Are you someone who likes to use their wits? Are you someone who likes to be ballistic or brash or methodical or what? How do you want to play the game?"

When you're well trained and well skilled and you get out into a race, the only thing that differentiates you from other expert, skilled and well trained athletes is your personality and your character. That's what comes out in your racing. That's what you're showing to the public in your racing. The sport itself at the highest level is a very expressive medium. I start there and say "Ok, look. Let's talk about

racing. What kind of person are you? What kind of races are you going to ride? Then it's academic, from there.

The person says "I want to go and hammer everybody. And I want to be the dominant player on the track. I want to be this, and this as far as playing the game goes." That character requires these kind of strategies. Those strategies require these tactics. In order to successfully perform these tactics, you have to have these skills and you have to have this physiological capability. You have to be fit enough to do that.

If you're going to hammer everybody that means you're going to have to do several attacks inside of a points race, not just one big attack and then motor away, but several kinds of attacks.

That means that physiologically you're going to have to be able to go this speed and recover at this rate and you're going to have to be able to handle your bike through the pack to set yourself up to get into position to attack.

Naturally you're going to have to learn how to play that game yourself, too. Everything is absolutely academic once the person decides who they are and how they want to play the game. To obtain those physiological attributes to successfully play the game you want to play, again, it's just a matter of academics. Any exercise physiologist worth his salt can put together a program to give you the anaerobic threshold and the power and the aerobic endurance in order to perform these tasks.

I think the tough thing is deciding how you're going to play the game. That's the tough thing: "Hey, what are you going to do, where are you going to race, what kind of rider do you want to become?" "Well, I don't know."

And that's the most important thing! A lot of people don't ask tough questions right off. They just go "Well, let's go hammer and see what happens. Let's go train and let's go hurt ourselves and climb mountains and then sprint and lift weights and see what happens." "Oh, okay, well, you know, okay, we get this good. Okay, let's see, if we change something, lets's see what happens." Well, let's face it, why don't you just start from the end?

My sister Sheila was one of the smartest, most successful people in doing that, deciding who and what she was doing. She had a muscle biopsy on her leg, that proved that she shouldn't have been a pure Sprinter. Slow and fast twitch muscle fibers were pretty well balanced. It was 50-50 or something like that. But that didn't stop her from doing what she wanted to do or perform in a way that suited her character. She was a Sprinter and she was the World's best. No handicaps or challenges in her physiological makeup were going to stop her from achieving what she wanted to do. What her character said

was "That's the way I am." It's pretty rare to see someone just come up with it on their own and do it. Usually it takes some coaxing. You have to find out what kind of person s/he is and help them discover themselves. It sounds a little flaky, but that's pretty much the way it is.

One of the barbs I always got, even when I was as young as 12 years

Roger gets ready to lead the Keirin race at the 1994 U.S. National Championships.

old, was about levels of riders. Flipping through the Schwinn catalog, I looked at these people riding the Schwinn Typhoons to do the shopping or deliver the mail and everything. I would think "Why are they building a 50 lb. bike for a lady who weighs 110 lbs?" Then you've got a well trained athlete who is on a 21 lb. bike. "Don't they deserve good equipment and a better, more

efficient bike?" Come on!

I've felt that way and I grew up around 99% of riders who just loved the sport, loved to race. Those people deserve to train as methodically and as well organized and reach as high in their potential as they could as an Olympic athlete. I've always believed that. I started a business based on that.

One of the joys of my work in coaching is that I can deliver expert advice to those people who might not ever make it to the Olympics -- most of them won't -- but they deserve the best. They deserve just as much of my attention as an Olympic athlete does because they love the sport just as much. To me that makes a big difference.

Coachability

The thing that makes an athlete most coachable is hope. I would be tempted to say the canned sort of thing like "They've got to want it. And they have to be smart. They have to be talented." No, I think they have to have a profound sense of hope. That's something that can get you so far.

To me, it's kind of the thing that's touching to see because everything else comes from that. The dogmatic belief that hard work is going to make you better. That by doing the right thing you're going to end up winning. That sort of thing. Again, it's not a sense of assuredness, it's just "I hope it's like this, I hope that I can do it, I hope . . ." and there's an area of doubt and lack of confidence that I think helps.

It's almost like, I think it was Eric

Erickson, who philosophized about how most geniuses were neurotics. But in sports and coachability, it's people who have hope who are very coachable. You see people who have loads of confidence, but they don't really have hope.

Those people are difficult to coach because they're not living in the real world. You're never going to help them fulfill that, or it will be more difficult to coach them, to fulfill that. By having hope you realize that people have doubt, so people put that extra work in just to try to confirm what they're not sure of. That takes them the next step.

Then they start thinking of the next thing they're not quite sure of. But they hope that it's right and they hope that, since they put this work into it they hope the coach is telling them the right thing!

That's the biggest element, I think, between someone who's totally coachable and someone who's not totally coachable. Everybody's coachable, it's just that some are more challenging than others.

A personal relationship between a coach and an athlete is not important at all. Yes, you have to understand the person's character and their personality and you have to appreciate them as a human being, but that's not to say that you have to pass judgement on them. You just have to understand them.

In knowing them, you don't have to like them, you just have to know that knowledge will help you realize what they need and fill in the gaps with somebody who's already an

"I use a lot of video tape. I go "Hey, look. Look at the bike race and make your own decisions. Here's the guy you're riding against, look how he rides." "Oh!" Big revelation."

were listening to the conversation you would think we were getting nowhere, but that's not true. We're being patient with each other. Eventually we'll get around to what we want to say and I'll get around to knowing a little bit more about Bill and more about what he wants and things like that. It's important, but only in a very functional way, for me.

I work on visualization, but not in the abstract, only in the practical sense. I don't go for the mumbo-jumbo stuff.

I use a lot of video tape. I go "Hey, look. Look at the bike race and make your own decisions. Here's the guy you're riding against, look how he rides." "Oh!" Big revelation. That's visualization. That's practical visualization. You see someone going from Point A to Point B. So, they say "Ok, if I do this . . ." and they start applying a cause and effect methodology to that visualization and they're rolling.

All you've done is initiated it. You're not saying "Imagine yourself on a waterfall and the water's taking you across the finish line" that kind of bull. I don't buy into that. I do not buy into that, 100%. It works for some people. If I find a rider who is going to respond to something like that, I'm all for it. That's not the way I work. But, again, if I find someone who works that way and responds to it, I will find them a sports psychologist to do that for them. I've had riders who have tried hypnosis.

Coaching Women

There's definitely a difference in gender. Vive la difference. Even

Connie is exceptional, but there are still similarities. I grew up not quite the gentleman that my mom wanted me to be, but if I coach men and women differently, it is probably because I was brought up to communicate with men and women

Connie Paraskevin Young was a World Champion Sprinter before she married Roger, but he still gives her new ideas. Both were speedskaters who have spent their lives as two of America's foremost track cyclists.

differently. To be more polite to women than men, to be more sensitive to women's feelings than men.

I would insult a guy at the drop of a hat. I would not deliberately do that to a woman. I hope that those in the past that I've coached have had similar American values in their upbringing

and appreciated, at least to a certain extent, that I didn't treat them like a guy, that I treated them like they were taught that men should treat them. That is extremely sexist, and I realize that. But, again, I'm in this for myself, too, and I can't bring myself to treat

women the same as men.

Although I expect the same things from them. I expect them to work just as hard. I expect them to learn the same lessons. I expect women to have the same desire to win. I expect them to be as aggressive and as tactical, as witty and skilled. It's just that the way

expert or develop them if they are a beginner. That's necessary, but you don't have to know them all that well or pass judgement on them as a person. You just have to understand what they need. In some cases it's good only to have a certain level of knowledge of someone. That way you can focus more in certain areas.

I don't tend to buy that altogether because I think there's no such thing as too much information about someone. You can always use something to your riders' benefit. A lot of times with some of the good riders we'll talk about the weather and if you

I communicate with them is based on the sociological mores of American society, and I try to maintain that so they know what to expect. It's pretty much from my upbringing and I don't want to compromise on who I am.

If someone said "Hey look, if you started calling all the women that you coach bad names, they'll get better results, I can't do that. I wouldn't do it. That's not me. It wouldn't work with Connie, she'd probably take a swing at me! She'd miss — she's nice. But no, I just wasn't brought up that way.

My mom raced. I know what women can do. I think I understand their desire to compete. But then again, I don't understand their experience and I won't try to pretend to. There's something that I will never understand about a woman's experience, so therefore the way I communicate with them is always with a certain degree of considering that lack of knowledge or that lack of ability to relate 100%.

Problems

The biggest problem I've ever had in coaching is not being with my riders enough. That's been the most aggravating thing, I'd say. I can't be with the riders at every workout and because there's always a chance that I will say "Now I know what this rider needs and I can fix it right now. We'll go and work on it, make it right."

I like watching the assembly line, the work that goes into making the final product. It's like taking a tour of the Chrysler factory when I was a kid. At the end out comes my shiny new car. I just enjoyed watching everything happening. Not being able to do that, it's difficult and I don't like that.

Another frustrating thing is when you do see someone making the exact same mistake over and over again and I can't find a solution to it. I don't have any problems with someone getting beat by a superior rider. But a good rider who is defeated in the same way time after time -- if I couldn't help them find the right way to fix the

Roger consults with Sprinters Paul Swift, Connie Paraskevin Young and "Boko" on the training schedule for the day. Boko takes his training schedule very seriously and wonders if he needs to chase away this pesky photographer so work can proceed.

problem, that would be tough. I'd feel like it was more my short coming.

Riders can't see themselves race. They can see themselves on videotape and stuff like that. They can make some judgement calls with everything in their field of vision, which is anything in front of them. In a bike race 50% of the stuff happens in front of you, 50% happens behind. So guess whose fault it is and guess whose responsibility it is, I should say, if something is wrong and can't be fixed? That's the coach.

The coach sees the whole game and is responsible for being objective. The rider has emotions and fatigue and all this other stuff that's going into the race. They're not the most objective element or entity out there. That's the coach. So when something can't be fixed it is absolutely not the rider's fault. It's the coach's fault. I should say the coach's responsibility, not fault. It's the coach who needs to respond. So it's his responsibility or her responsibility.

I could be with riders more at the ideal training center, a Shangri-la for training and everyone would go there. It's possible that that's in San Diego. All we need is a velodrome down there at the Olympic Training Center. The USCF wants that desperately. We go to Southern California all the time. We need a good, challenging training track down there. Like a 200 to 250 meter velodrome.

That's what we're missing, a track that can challenge the riders' skills enough to make experts out of them. A 200 meter track or a 166 meter track. There's a 140 meter track that's being built in Detroit right now. The one in Atlanta will be 250.

The USCF Today

The USCF is going in a real positive direction. The Federation is becoming less of an administration and more of a service and that's a good thing. It is becoming less of a proctor and more the conduit of information. Less rule oriented and more guidance and assistance oriented.

Everybody over there now, from membership to media is all thinking in terms of "What can we do to help you? Is there any way that we can make the sport better?" rather than "We rule the sport and you've got to come to us for your license" kind of thing. It wasn't so bad before, but it wasn't communicative.

Let's face it, nobody on our coaching staff spoke English at one time. How are you going to communicate with them? Do you think they wanted to go into the field and teach Americans how to coach? I don't. No way.

Now it's much easier to communicate. Not just from the standpoint of the coaching staff, I think the whole

Federation is like that.

The regional coaching program is a new thing, but none of the regional coaches are new to the sport, certainly. Susie Barton is helping them understand their communication and administration tasks, something that real experienced racers like Betsy Davis are just acquiring. Susie is a major benefit in that respect.

They're all going to say different things because they all come from different background, but at least they're all talking about racing when they're supposed to be talking about racing. They're all talking about training at clinics when they should be talking about training. The language should be basically the same. One guy shouldn't be juxtaposing speed work and anaerobic threshold work and another person is not using this language versus that language. We're trying to make that more consistent. It's individual.

There is synergy at the Federation. We need exposure, we need to get the word out. And then media needs to let the constituents of the Federation know what's available for them.

What are the steps to making the Olympic Team? How do you change a tire better? How do you train more properly? That's the type of thing that media's trying to communicate. So there has to be a lot of coordination there.

Most of the clinics at the beginning of the year are trying to teach the riders how to race. There have been lots of clinics and lots of camps and lots of training sessions teaching people how to train.

I wanted to start off the year by running a series of clinics at the Junior Olympic races and a series of clinics at the Regional Cup races, helping riders and coaches learn how to race. It's totally different. A different approach.

I coach all events. I bring a degree of consistency there, so that there will be a common language for road and track, although track relates to different disciplines, the fact remains that power work is power work and endurance work is endurance work.

How to Access Me

Anyone can call me for training advice. I might refer them to the regional coach. I might say "Call Danny Van Haute" You know why? I'm trying to encourage the regional coaches and other people to provide expert advice and expert coaching and guidance. It's necessary for me occasionally to say "I'll give you a few tips here, but contact this person." I'll always try to get people to support their club.

I'm getting more accessible. I'm on "America On Line" now with Bicycling Magazine. America On Line is a computer service like Prodigy or Compuserve. Bicycling Magazine has an area in America On Line.

You could just ask a question or whatever. A lot of people are into it now. Your question will be answered and it will be out there for everybody to read. You could send specific E-mail to me. You say "I want to access this person".

Then there's a live chat room, too, where you can just chat live with people on America On Line. I was on-line last night with about nine people.

We were talking about coffee and titanium versus aluminum and all kinds of junk. We're also going to start a 900 service. You can call once a week and get your training program via the 900 number. It probably ends up costing $5-6 bucks, but it's a deal. I'm pretty accessible.

Roger's latest success story: 1994 U.S. National Sprint Champion Jeff Solt. After beating Marty Nothstein in an unusual fourth ride, Roger gives Jeff a "High-5"

1984 U.S. Olympic Coach
Eddie Borysewicz ("Eddie B.")

I was born March 18, 1929 in Poland -- before the second World War, so it was in a different territory.

Poland was smaller than it had been before. I was born between Lithuania and Byelorussia, what used to be Polish territory. My family had a farm in northeast Poland.

I don't know much about things during World War II because I was born 6 months before it began. It was a very difficult time for my mother. When I was 6 years old, the second World War was over. My toys were guns, bullets, grenades, junked planes and tanks, because we had no other toys. It was very dangerous. Several kids were seriously injured. Mines blew up, grenades. . . .Twenty-five thousand people of the Polish nation died, so imagine.

We were lucky, our entire family survived. My father died from having been in Siberia, from prison. He escaped before the war was over. We experienced discrimination, because the Communists remembered that, the First World War and the Second World War.

Poland is a funny country because everybody's always crossing it. It's a good case for everybody, because Poland has very rich soil, lots of minerals and good industry. It's a nice country. In the 13th century, it was the strongest country in Europe. In the 18th century it was split between Austria, Russia and Germany. From that time on Poland has been in trouble.

Right now is the first time there has been freedom. There was a little peace and freedom after the First World War, only a little peace. Before, Poland extended from the Baltic Sea to the Black Sea. It was a huge country. The older the map is, the bigger Poland was on it.

It was not difficult for me to go from a farm to a University. It was difficult for me to go up to high school because of my father's history. In my place, my little town, we had to emigrate. We had to leave the territory where we lived because Russia started changing the border. The eastern border change took about 30% of the Polish country. So, we went to the western part of Poland which we got from Germany after the split, which made new borders.

First we moved from the place where I was born to the west, to a little town where most of the people knew my father. So, my father and the whole family experienced a lot of discrimination. I was second to the top student in elementary school, but I wasn't going to be allowed to go to the high school. I could have gone to two years of business school and been a driver or something, because I was from "that" family. For this reason,

"I think what has made me a successful coach is that first, I have practical experience as a successful bike rider for a long enough time to learn how hard you must work.

A coach must be honest. He must be intelligent. He must have education and knowledge. He must be incredibly dedicated. He must love teaching. And, he must forgive people."

my teacher sent me to another town where his friend was the Principal of the high school. It was a favor for a friend. The teacher liked me because I was a good student and he wasn't a

Communist. The third move my family made was to Lodz. I was 18.

Lodz was the second largest city in Poland, over 1 million people. At that time it was the strongest cycling district in the country. There was a velodrome in the city and the sport of cycling was very popular. Because I was in Lodz, we raced on the track. My team owned the velodrome. For several years I lived under the velodrome. There were apartments for athletes.

How I got Started

I had been riding a bicycle a lot, but not racing. I started racing when I moved to the city. It's a different system over there. The coach must select you to the team. You cannot just choose to join.

Over there every team, meets three times a week for training with the coach. We met these guys on the road. We knew when they were training

212

because they trained three times a week. We tried to stay behind and then, next time we saw a Sprint, we took off. He could see we were good riders, because when he had everyone sprint up the hill, we were the best. He asked us which team we represented. We said "We represent US! We'd like to be on your team." He said "Okay, sometime next training session." It was just a regular training session. We just proved ourselves and that was how we got started. Three months later, I was third in the Individual Pursuit. I became the best on the team and a year later I won Juniors.

Racing

In my first race I was fourth with 150 starters on the road. So, I impressed the coach and he supported me from that time on. I stayed with that team all my athletic life.

Some people in Europe jump from one team to another, but not everybody. It's much harder to change teams there than here, because riders are dedicated to their teams, but people do change anyway, for the money. I never did that. I was with one team all my life. That's my personality and I am like that. I had fair treatment, very fair. Later I was the highest paid man on the team. I had a leader — I wasn't the leader — and I made more money than the leader because I had to prepare everything for him. I had a good life. Those were the second most beautiful years in my life. That's something incredible — unforgettable. Coaching is nice.

I had my education on the track and I raced on the roads. As a Junior, I was third in the Sprint, I won the Individual Pursuit, I won the Team Pursuit and I was third in the Points race.

We always rode on the road, every weekend and even, sometimes, on weekdays. I was a member of the National Track team. Then, I was member of the National Road team. I received all the education. I was National Champion on the road twice. I was a member of the National Team for six years.

For six years I made a very good living from cycling. I raced within the country and outside the country, representing Poland in International races. When I got finished, I was awarded a Master of Sport. The only riders who received this were me and a three time National Champion who represented our country well. This was based on behavior and representing ourselves well. You have to show you are honorable, that you are educated, intelligent, etc.

The Master of Sport provided free access to the VIP area in every sporting event all the time. It was only for top athletes. It gave special access to any sport in the country. I had a pin and an I.D. When I showed my I.D., I gained access to the VIP areas, at a soccer game, a volleyball game, any game, in any sport. It was an award for having achieved at an exceptional level in athletics. This kind of thing is not available in the United States. It would be nice if it were.

Rider to Coach on Command

When I stopped racing, it was because the Chief of Sports of my city told me I had to. That was the end of my athletic career. Next, I could become a coach which is an enjoyable job, but it was not my choice. I won a National race, on a Sunday, and Monday I was a coach. At that time, I had a Master's degree in Physical Education, a Master's degree in Physical Therapy, and a Master's degree in Coaching and I was a bike racer. I was making a very good living riding a bike.

Our Master of Sport told me he needed me to develop World Champions and Olympic Champions. He didn't need me on the road as a good rider. I was 30 years old, so all my best years were behind me. But, at age 30, you can still be a successful racer. I would like to have had a couple of more years racing, because I had just finished my education.

I had passed my "marriage experience". For athletes, the first-year of marriage is very difficult with the change in lifestyle. I was established. I had finished everything, I had a fresh mind. Now I had a couple of years to concentrate on being a good bike rider, but I had to stop. It was not easy, but I had no choice. I started coaching.

I was always a successful coach in Poland. At first I was a little bit scared because everything was new for me. I knew I could make money by riding my bike. I didn't know how good a coach I was going to be, how good a teacher I was going to be.

Money is not dependent on how your riders do in competition, that's separate. You have a contract. You are paid monthly according to what the contract says. Usually it is for four years, from Olympic Games to Olympic Games. You got increases according to how your athletes performed on another contract. However you negotiated it. You could get a bonus at the end of the year if the team did well. You could get a special bonus.

I didn't have to take a cut in pay when I went from rider to coach. In this case, I was very lucky and people treated me very well.

My first Master's degree was in cycling. My nickname was "Professor" because I was the only one with a Master's degree. They were paying me an excellent salary. They gave me all the opportunity that I needed. They told me I had to stop racing. So, I quickly took the job.

It was a good opportunity. I had everything I needed. I had at my disposal a doctor, a nurse, a mechanic, a masseur, everything.

The first few years I taught Juniors while I rode a bicycle. I was on the bike with Juniors in the afternoon. In the morning I was on the motorcycle.

After a few years, when my best Juniors started beating me in the Sprints, I switched to the motorcycle. That was the end of my riding.

For the next 20 years, I almost never touched a bike. Occasionally, in the last 20 years, I've been on a bicycle maybe 10 times, maybe 15. This year I've had much more time, so I've already been on the bike maybe 15 times. Now I can ride maybe 15 miles, with no pain in the butt. Before it hurt after about a half hour. I enjoy it — I sleep better.

Leaving Poland

I left Poland when I was thirty-seven. I became head coach at age 30.

I raced and coached for two years. I was coaching development riders — Juniors — and it was successful. When I first started coaching, my team won races.

Next I went to another team. Once again, that was someone else's decision, not mine. I started a new team with different competitors. That was a decision of the Chief of Sport of the city. He said that they needed me because the other team almost didn't exist.

He said "We'll give you the opportunity, and we'll give you money. Show us what you can do. We'll pay for your education, we'll educate you, but we need you NOW." I said "Okay" and I was there about nine years, from 1968 to 1976.

My riders were National Champions, World Champions, Olympic Medalists. I was the most successful coach in the country. I had had another proposal when I stopped cycling and started coaching my team in my city. The Federation offered me the job of National Coach in Poland.

I said "No." I have a job with my team. I wanted to test myself — can I develop somebody from that? Over there is a different system, not like here. I had money. Over there you go to school and you recruit candidates. From these candidates, it's your own production.

For two reasons, I said "Thanks, I can't be National Coach." First, I started my work and I wanted to test myself. Can I raise somebody or not? Even if I were a successful coach for the National Team, people would ask me, "Who have you developed?" I'd

have to say "Nobody." They'd say "You took us, our riders. That's not yours." I also didn't want to coach Seniors because that was full time and Juniors was, at that time, part time. That was in conflict with my team, so that was fine.

The National Coach first selects his riders and then does the final preparation. I always had a deep thanks for my teaching experience. Already I had the two years of experience with the Juniors, so I said "I can do something here." Second, I said, "All my friends are on the National Team." The second team was made from the National Team. "They are all my buddies. How I can teach my buddies right now? I am too young and too friendly and I am biased." So, I said, "Forget it."

I quit my job as coach the second of January in 1976. I didn't want to be a coach anymore. I had achieved everything over there. When I quit, after nine years, the newspaper announced that the Federation had offered me the job of National Coach again.

After five years, I had been ready to move to the National Team position. The National Team was very good. But there were a lot of politics and I was not offered the job.

After 10 years, the Team was not as good. The same President offered me the job again. I said, "The first time you offered me the job too early, this time it's too late. I'm burnt out because of politics and other things. I achieved everything I wanted to do, and I don't need to get my hands greasy any more."

I was a teacher in a University. I

was devoted to developing my skills from elementary school to high school, then to the University. It was a very exclusive job over there, very prestigious and very good pay. I only had to work 18 hours.

At one point I had cycling, school, university, -- it was too much. I turned down the National Team position because I was mad at cycling. I got divorced after 12 years marriage, and part of the problem was cycling. So, I said forget it, about the National Team job.

In 1976, I took one year off from school. We could take vacations. I sent a letter to the dean and asked for one year off. I said I wanted to refresh myself, that I was getting divorced, ...etc.

I had done everything Polish people can achieve — the right education, the right job, the right prestige, I had a car, which, over there was very difficult. I had money for other things. Only my marriage got destroyed and I was very upset. I was not a happy guy. My wife divorced me, not I divorced her, so it was very difficult, I have children over there from my first marriage. I was very unhappy.

So, from Montreal ('76 Olympics), I went to the United States. I wanted to see America.

America, to Poland, is the country of heaven. Farm stories are that it is the richest country in the world, which it really is, and the best organized. I wanted to see it. I had been in other countries, in Europe, but I never was in America. I had friends, so I came to visit the States.

How I became U.S. Olympic Coach

While here, I met Mike Fraysee (USCF President) and saw how cycling looked in America. I thought "I can offer a lot to cycling." Mr. Fraysee knew me and knew International cycling and Polish cycling — At this time Polish cycling was the strongest in Europe. It was the best cycling country in the world. We won everything wherever we went. Even in Montreal. In the World Championships in Montreal we were first, second, fourth, fifth and eighth.

Mike Fraysee knew that the Eastern European system is the best system in the world. He knew I was a National Coach over there, National Juniors Coach. So, I met Mr. Fraysee he made me an offer to help his team.

I was hired in 1977 as National Coach. The first year, I prepared a team for Venezuela. I organized training, winter preparation and everything. Beth Heiden was there. She was a skater. I met her and recognized her incredible talent. I met LeMond, Nitz, Paul Deem, those guys, Ken Carpenter… American bike riders were very nice to me. People didn't know much. So, I enjoyed it. I really enjoyed it. That was good, working. That's how everything started.

My second team was the first team in the Olympic Training Center in Colorado Springs. My second team used this facility more than any other sport. We were there beginning in 1978.

When the first training camp was open, I asked that free room and board be provided. Three people came to the training camp in Colorado. One lady never rode a bike before! She only wanted to see the Olympic Committee and get her picture with five rings. She told me what was going on and I said "Keep this secret, don't tell anybody!" She said "I'll help you as I can, with food and drinks. I can even drive the car."

The next year we had about 500 riders during the winter time. It was 90 riders in a rotation and 30 permanent residents. 120 riders in the camp every day. Over 100 riders worked with 3 people. Craig Campbell is a nice guy who was very dedicated. That's why he worked for me too. He worked for the Federation.

I was dedicated. Only dedication and knowledge guarantee you success. It was very difficult to start. I signed a contract, because the American Federation needed me to prepare the Juniors team, for Juniors Worlds. In 1978, in Pennsylvania, was my first success. The year before, the American team was 20th or 21st from 22 teams only the team from Israel was last. The Polish team was second when I was coaching over there.

When my friend came to Pennsylvania I asked him what he was looking for. He said Gold or Silver, everything as usual. That's normal.

He asked me what I was looking for. I told him "Top six." I was more pessimistic. He said, "Oh, you are looking very high." I said, "Why not look high?"

When the race was over, the Polish team was 15th. They had some problems. The U.S. finished third. Now he wouldn't speak to me. He

had been my assistant over there, you see. Next, he told me, "You were born under a lucky star. And, I said, "Yes!" That was very nice.

The president of the Federation, Otto Wenz, Mr. Seubert, Mr. Fraysse were extremely happy. These people were very nice to me. They were the people who hired me.

I really enjoyed them. They were more pleasurable, more helpful, and more happy than after the nine Olympic medals in Los Angeles.

Of course, those were different people. That's life. That's politics. That was in 1977-78.

After one year, I had a contract for the next 4 years. I had signed a contract for one year, because I wanted to be far from my ex-family. It was easier to forget.

I had lots to do, so I worked. I was a 7-Eleven man. I worked from 7 in the morning to 11 in the evening. I worked hard. I enjoyed success, developing athletes. Every year there were more and more medals.

LeMond was Champion. Next was a Silver medal in Mexico. Every year was successful.

Unfortunately we didn't go to Moscow because of the boycott. LeMond was the guy for the medal. The Team Time Trial guys were good, the Stetinas and Doughty (National 100 K Team Time Trial Champions). Bob Cook was good, too. There were several good riders.

The first year I enjoyed. Along with the second year came depression because the language barrier wore me out. But that was fine. More and more I enjoyed it.

1984 Olympics and Controversy

Of all my memories, though Poland was very good for me, the Olympics in Los Angeles was the best, it was unbeatable. It's unforgettable and unbeatable. For me, the Olympic success was really my goal. I reached everything. It was super successful.

Of course, people tried to damage the results, and they did damage them a lot. The controversy was about blood boosting, which was legal. To this time, many teams use this technique and it is untestable.

I didn't tell anybody under me to do blood boosting. I knew about that, what it was. I didn't push anybody to do it. I knew and every member of the Board knew, including the Director and the President. A letter of consent was sent to everyone, including me, so everyone was informed.

I'm not a doctor. They asked me, "Eddie, would that help?"

I said, "Of course."

They asked "Is that dangerous?"

I said, "Danger is everywhere."

If it is professionally done it is not supposed to be dangerous. Millions of transfusions are done every day and help people.

Still, for me today, it's very controversial, because athletes working hard tend to be anemic, and it's their own blood. I take my own blood, put it in a freezer, and I take what I need. It's my body, it's my blood. This medical practice is very popular—transfusions and everything. Of course now there's AIDS and that's different, but still, it's your own blood.

As far as the danger: first, people

don't know what is true. In the Olympic committee people said — that's politician, typical politician — "oh, this is even legal., well, maybe it's not *ethical*." They're not listening to what they're talking about.

Ethics

I was really an "unethical" coach to most countries, because I was smarter in many ways. I looked for all advantages possible for my riders.

For instance, we used helium in the tires. We used over 300 psi while other teams used regular air. We used the lightest tires of anyone. We used the lightest and best bicycles of anyone.

Even the one-piece (aerodynamic) suit was the best. We used the best of everything. We had the best helmets. We had the best performance.

The guys knew we were the best. Before the Olympic Games, we beat everybody in Europe. We beat the Germans, the Russians, and everybody.

We were very lucky in 1984 because steroid testing started in 1983. People didn't have time to come up with different steroids which were not testable in that period of time. We were all on the same wagon. We didn't have a disadvantage.

Before — I don't want to mention the name of the country, there were several cycling countries — like the Bulgarian lifters, 70% of the team was positive for steroids. I believe in cycling many teams also used them, so we had this disadvantage.

In 1984 everybody was scared because of the testing, so we started to beat these guys. Everyone was on the same level in sports medicine. We were clear and those guys weren't. Before, we were behind, and now we came ahead. On many teams, all the best, big guys disappeared. They weren't clean enough.

Later they started testing for testosterone, so people started using growth hormones. When they started testing for growth hormones, people started using natural hormones.

I don't know what people are using right now. If you read VeloNews, Italians fly. All Italians fly. Incredible. Maybe they have some super medicine that is legal. It's legal until they say it's not.

The list of illegal drugs is getting bigger and bigger. So, that's life. It's less enjoyable because sports medicine does a lot. In Professional cycling there's all the money. I enjoy coaching an amateur team more than a Professional team. In a Professional team, the big factor is money. I can be dumb if I have money. I can just buy my riders.

Even with mistakes and a bad atmosphere on the team, I can have the best team or one of the best teams. Even with bad management. Coaching and management are much less important than on an amateur team. Money, for an amateur team, is not a super factor. In Professional racing, if you don't pay a million dollars for LeMond, he won't ride for you. LeMond can ride for the devil for money.

Right now it seems like any top rider will ride for money. It makes a little bit of difference who the manager is. But not much, because there is a contract.

The money factor in amateur racing is not the most important thing in coaching. That is more of a challenge. The money factor is less important. At Professional levels, you already have a devil of a group of guys. You can't change them much. So coaching Professional riders is not as enjoyable. The guy who is looking to be a big shot and can say "I am the coach of the best Professional team" is a lucky guy, because there is money there.

Coaching Track -- Racers and Racing

The coach is supposed to figure out the predisposition of each rider. First, riders have a choice. Second, riders have a predisposition for certain events.

For example, Ken Carpenter. I advised him to do the Kilometer for his main event and Sprints second. He didn't like that. I felt sure that if he listened and dedicated everything to that event as he dedicated himself to the Sprints, he would have been a World Champion. So, I'm not mad that Ken didn't take my advice. I still think he would have been better in the Kilometer, a World Champion, because of his power, his build, and his ability, mentally and physically.

I advised Betsy Davis to do Sprints. She chose the Pursuit. Okay.

For other riders, no problem. For example, Mark Gorski, when I met him, I knew him from Super Week. He was a good road rider. He told me "Eddie, I like Sprints." We checked and found that he did have Sprint ability. He evolved successfully. For Hegg, for Nitz, McCarthy, these

guys went for the best events they were suited for according to the best ability of their bodies.

For example, if I advise "you are a Sprinter" or "you are a Pursuiter". It's very easy to find out. It's through the VO2 maximum capacity and a muscle biopsy. And, of course, your dedication and love for the sport.

Before I became a bicycle rider I was a very successful runner in the 400 meters. According to my coach, I probably could have been a World Champion, but I liked cycling. That's okay. Cycling is okay. You have to do what you enjoy.

Beth Heiden loved skating, yet she was a World Champion on the bike. She did more skating than cycling. What can you do?

Kilo is very difficult event. You have to check ability, speed and your power over the long speed. It's speed for a long distance. That's a combination event. Both Sprinters and Pursuiters can do that event well. That is an event where the two specialists can compete. It's a challenge.

These two groups are absolutely different. Sprinters and Pursuiters are two different categories of riders. The Kilometer is in between, so Sprinters and Pursuiters can compete in the Kilometer.

One Sprinter who is the best Kilometer rider ever is Kopilov, Sergei Kopilov. He was a World Champion in Sprints and World Champion in Kilo. He wasn't beatable.

Next is specialization. I look for a Sprinter with a long Sprint. Kilo riders even win criteriums. Sprinters usually don't.

If a rider came to me and said "Eddie, I don't know which event I want to do" I do testing. Physiological tests are important, especially the VO2 and, for Sprinters, a muscle biopsy. For Pursuiters with a high VO2 who love Pursuit, I wouldn't do a muscle biopsy. Only for Sprinters.

The muscle biopsy gives you some important information, that and the VO2. The higher the amount of fast twitch muscle fiber, the more likely the person can be successful at Sprints. For VO2, the higher the better, over 70 or so, high 70s for Pursuiters.

For Sprinters, VO2 might be 50. They need big muscles. Sprinters are a combination of bike rider, gymnast and lifter. These three things all in one body. They are huge muscled, powerful guys. They must be quick and very aggressive.

Ken's problem is that he is not aggressive enough, by temperament. Ken is normally like a Pursuiter, a calm guy. That and his long Sprint are why I believed he would make a good Kilo rider. It's not too late for him to switch, even now. The Keirin is a good race for him because it is a long Sprint. He does very well in Keirin. His problem is toughness. Keirin riders are aggressive and incredibly tough.

There is a reason our 1984 Olympic Pursuit Team was very fast. Pursuiters are very fast. Kilo riders are Super Pursuit men.

Like Brent Emery, he was an ex-Sprinter and an ex-Kilo rider, and he was on the Team Pursuit Team. Pat McDonough, same thing. Both did Team Pursuit, not Individual Pursuit. Sprinter, Kilo — Team Pursuit.

Kilo riders are very fast in the Team Pursuit. Harvey was a super Kilo rider and a super Team Pursuiter. Harvey liked longer Pursuits, but he could do Team Pursuit too. Hegg was a good Kilo rider and super at Individual Pursuit. And he was a very good Team Pursuiter. Hegg would probably not do as well at Sprints. At Kilo, Pursuit, Team Pursuit, yes. Sprints, no.

The Points race is for Pursuiters and road riders. Fast roadies and Pursuiters. The Madison is the same as the Points race. The Madison is more technical because of the exchanges. It's a Points race, only with two guys making up teams. Technique for the exchanges is very, very important. One miss and you're in trouble. Pursuiters are fantastic for both of these races.

Kilo riders can ride the Points race, but Sprinters are not usually very good in this event. Kilo riders who are also Sprinters can't usually ride those races well. Team Pursuiters who are Kilo riders and Pursuiters do well. Points racers who do well can also do well at Team Pursuit.

Harvey is one of the best in the World. He is best at the Points race, Pursuit, Team Pursuit and Kilo. He is not best at roads because he is not a climber. A road Sprint is a super Points race, so he's very good at that. He rode a super Kilo, a super Pursuit, and a super Team Pursuit.

Harvey is an incredible talent. He's a super man and a super athlete. He's a super person. He's a very kind man. He's honest. That's the guy who is supposed to be a coach. Because of his

"Harvey is an incredible talent. He's a super man and a super athlete. He's a super person. He's a very kind man. He's honest. That's the guy who is supposed to be a coach. Because of his morals, his dedication, his fairness. Harvey is one of the best human beings I've ever worked with."

morals, his dedication, his fairness. That's the man. He should be the National Coach. That's the man for that. Harvey is one of the best human beings I've ever worked with. He's an incredible person. He's an example of good.

What a Coach must be

A coach must be honest. He must be intelligent. He must have education and knowledge. And, he must be incredibly dedicated. He must love teaching. He must forgive people. When someone screws up, he must forgive them.

If you can't forgive people, you can't be a coach. Mistakes happen and it's like you must be able to punch a button on a computer -- the mistake is

gone and you start again. You have to be willing to accept that you must tell people the same thing over and over again. That's the job.

Ability in an athlete is very difficult to develop. New riders who have ability, often don't know much. The more you work with them, the more they know. The coach must be educated. For instance, in Poland, Russia and the East Block you can't become a coach if you don't have a Master's degree. You can only become an instructor. You must have a college degree and a physical education background -- only select people. Engineers, for instance, can't be coaches. That would be an exceptional situation if it were so.

The trend was physical education and Master's, then you could coach. Plus, when you come to a coaching school, you must have a recommendation from the Federation. You must be a high level athlete with the Federation. You must show ability, fairness, intelligence — you must be a good person. You must know psychology. You must know how to teach and judge people. You must know how to present your knowledge. You must love teaching.

Politics

Politics are always a problem. Coaching is a lot of politics. You have a lot of problems when you're winning. Jealousy, always politics.

The worst my time of my life was after my most successful year, 1984, in the United States. My athletes won nine Olympic medals, which is not beatable for any coach, for any team. I had such a hard time with a group of bad people. Politicians. They tried to make this success as minimal as possible.

Money came. There was a position open in the Federation. I worked for $25,000 in the Olympic year. After this the salary was, maybe $40,000. Now coaches get $90,000, $80,000. I worked for $12,000, $15,000, $18,000 and $24,000 and I did everything, without assistants. Now the staff is four times, five times bigger than in my best years.

Why I'm a Successful Coach

I think what has made me a successful coach is that first, I have practical experience as a successful bike rider for a long enough time to learn how hard you must work. I was the guy from the road.

I remember one of my coaches with a college degree who had very little bike riding experience so we ignored him. We used to say "He doesn't even know which side his derailleur is on!"

It has helped me to have as good as possible practical experience. Racing experience helps you a lot. Next, education. I was the best guy in the country and I was on the National Team for six years, and that was a very difficult contest in a sport that was number one (it may have been second to soccer).

I graduated from the best school possible, the Warsaw Academy of Physical Education. It's the second oldest academy in the world with very excellent teachers. I was always thankful for the guys who taught me. They taught me anatomy, physiology, biology, kinesiology, sports medicine, everything.

Finally, I'm crazy about cycling. I'm really too dedicated. That's why I'm now divorced for the second time. I don't recom-mend that everyone follow me, do what I did. Many times for me it was job first, family second.

Of course, that's okay too, I'm not a rich guy, I must make a living. I took every job that I've done in my life and I always did the best job I could. Cycling has been my life from the time I was 18 years old. Not many coaches last very many years, including those in the Federation. I was there twelve years. I was always dedicated.

Even right now, I try to do the best

that I can. In the clinics I try to give them everything I can. All my knowledge, all my experience, I share with these people.

It's more enjoyable to coach lower level riders because coaching is more important to them. Teaching Juniors is the most important of all. Cycling leaders are supposed to teach Juniors. In the Communist system in Poland, the Head Coach teaches the Pros as little as possible (they called them amateurs, but they were Pro level),

Daughter Julia gets a ride.

and spend the rest of their time on development. The riders in the middle were taught by assistants.

I had two assistants for Juniors because we had three groups. I had one group and the two assistants had the other two groups. I controlled everything. It was my workout, my way, under my supervision. I worked with the Pros in the morning and the kids after school.

The best guy must work with the Juniors. They must get the best attention. Right now there is not enough attention to the Juniors. There's Andrzej Bek. And Roy Knickman.

Eddie's son (second from left) Eddie Jr. 1990 Master's Nats

I like Roy. It looks like he wants to do a very good job. I believe he can do it. He's tough, he was a tough Junior. He's back to the old system that worked for him. He's not afraid of that. He has a good education. He was a resident of the Olympic Training Center, he was Junior World Champion, he was a multi-medalist at Junior World's. He was incredible.

He got screwed up. He became Professional too early. He got pushed too early and pushed too much. He didn't reach his potential. Knickman could be much better than he was.

A coach doesn't like everyone. A coach will like teaching one more than another, but he must treat everyone the same. Some people are very selfish, they think in terms of me, myself, and I.

I don't care how fair you are when two athletes are very close and you select one and not the other, one will say "I deserve it" and the other will say "The coach screwed up". When

athletes are riding well, they say "It's me" when problems occur, it's always the coach's fault.

Athletes seldom say thank you. Whoever is looking for that should not be a coach. That's a difficult job. Coaching can be very difficult.

Teaching in school, you have good students and bad students. One does better than the other.

In athletics, it's different. You must be the best. You must make the best athletes. I can write the same program for ten people. Whoever is best is best, whoever is second is second.

We must win. That's the pressure. That's the way. Not "do your job", like engineers or somebody.

There, doing a good job, you're excellent. Here you must be the best. Sometimes you do everything and some little thing screws it all up, like a crash or a mechanical problem, and everything is nothing. This one moment takes 10 years preparation.

Dave Grylls pulled his foot out and screwed up three other guys. It was his fault. He criticized blood boosting because he didn't do it. I will never forgive him this one thing. The other guys too. He was a difficult character. Difficult to coach.

The easiest people I ever coached were Harvey and Rebecca. Some people had problems with Rebecca, I never did. She is the most beautiful and nicest girl.

Those are my roses: Harvey, Rebecca and Steve Hegg. LeMond,

for five years. I will never forget Lance (Armstrong), I will never forget McCarthy. These guys make my days.

Emery was very easy to coach. McDonough I had no problems with. I had some problem with Whitehead. With Whitehead I was the guy who forgot. He was the guy from the camps, from the teams. I always gave him a chance. He had appreciation. He was a different character. Dave Grylls was a different character. Lance is a nice guy. He was young and influenceable.

Coachability

Some riders are easier to coach than others. When you talk to people you recognize who they are. There are coachable people and uncoachable people. It doesn't have to do with intelligence. People can be educated and not intelligent. I've had riders like that.

There are riders who learn incredibly fast and others incredibly slow. Tom Wiesel learns incredibly fast. He was educated at Stanford. He is unbelievably coachable. He is a tough man.

Another rider has a college degree and is educated, but not intelligent. It's just how they are. The one guy just doesn't learn fast. He says "Yes" but he doesn't understand. You repeat over and over and he says "Okay" and a day later he forgets everything.

For me intelligence is making the

Harvey shows Eddie "the Lotus" bicycle and some modifications he's made on his own bike for competition. Still searching for optimals.

right decision and acting right in any situation. Education is different. The intelligent person knows how to act the first time at someone's house. He watches. Maybe he's never been at this kind of party before. He acts like everybody else because he looks at what's going on and he can do it. Another guy can sit with a pot on his head and eat only with a fork. He may have a college degree, but he's not intelligent.

I am still coaching Master's riders. They are a good group. I also have cycling camps. That may be my future.

I enjoy that. Lot's of different people come from all over. Later I will try to develop camps for Europeans, because it is an advantage for them to come here.

I was at the Olympic Training Center in San Diego for the opening and there is no plan for a velodrome there. There is only a plan for a criterium course. That's Mr. Lace. He doesn't want cycling to move. He owns property in Colorado and lives in Colorado.

Cycling is supposed to move to Southern California because that's seventh heaven, not Colorado Springs, although the Springs is good for altitude training. But that's not the base for the winter time and for the whole year around.

The End of USCF Coaching

I lived and worked in Colorado Springs for twelve years. I could have coached longer, I resigned, I wasn't fired. Of course Jerry Lace tried to give me such a hard time that I would resign. I didn't want to fight with him, so I resigned.

Jerry Lace destroyed cycling. When I came on the Board, my main reason was to kick him out, because he destroyed cycling. He damaged a lot. He always took the credit for bringing money.

Money comes because of results, mostly because of the Olympics. He was in the driver's seat. The Federation

gave him too much freedom. Now things are much better without him.

I don't know why things were so difficult with Jerry Lace. Maybe a connection with a couple of people, people who tried to take over the Federation, he was friends with these people — politics.

Good luck to him in skating. He is smart. He is a super-politician. He can take care of anything. He will always tell you what you want to hear and then stab you in the back. That's the guy who hurt me the most. He and a couple of Board members who tried to take over and minimized my success of 1984. For no reason. For hard work.

A vote was taken to stop me from being with the Federation. I was angry and upset. I was unbelievably upset at what people can do.

I was trying not to let these people take over. They were jealous of my success. I was this immigrant Polish guy. People think everybody can do what I did. It is not easy, what I did.

Second, all of a sudden there was money. Nabisco. A million dollars. Money for the job. I made $12,000. Nobody paid attention to that. After the Olympic Games, it was $40,000. That was good money.

By the time of the Olympics, the system was built. The train was running, so all they had to do was jump on the train.

Everybody, like Mark Hodges — it was incredible, that guy, he thought he could do it. He was a bad guy. He was fired after one year. They changed coaches.

Mr. Lace hired another guy from an Eastern block country. He claimed he had the same education as me. He had a high school degree. I have a Master's degree. He was an instructor in cycling, I was a coach in cycling. He started his experience here with me. I had already had ten years experience, with a lot of success. There was a lot of difference between us, like a lot of people.

My wife hated Colorado Springs, so I said that the next year, the Olympic Games, was going to be my last year in the Federation. I wanted to be successful, so I worked incredibly hard.

I was going to quit cycling because my wife was very upset about my job. I spent too much time outside away from home. So I said fine, we could move to Phoenix, she can open a restaurant and I can help her unless I find some job. And we did.

My Supporters

There have been special people who have helped me in my cycling work. The Bek brothers, they're number one. Timothy Kelly helped me a lot. And Carl Leusencamp, who died recently. They were my best assistants. Next was Craig Campbell and Ed Burke, who was with me. And next, my best secretary, Helen.

In the Federation, from a political standpoint, Mike Fraysse, Otto Wenz, Ernie Seubert, Saling — those are my supporters. And, lots of members of the Board of Directors. So many names. Beth (Wrenn-Estes) was

behind me 90%. My first Director, Mr. Prouty, was very fair to me.

Advice to New Riders

My advice to a new cyclist would, above all, be to work very hard, be smart, and be consistent. Be crazy about the sport. The sport must be Number One.

Of course you must have a good

High tech on the track -- Eddie takes a call while holding Harvey Nitz at the line. World Cup, 1991 (While not technically very good (I was losing the light) it's still one of my favorite photos of Eddie.)

body. One may have a good body to be a World Champion and another to be a San Diego Champion.

Or, you can just enjoy riding, not everyone can be a World Champion. Even a guy who has the ability of a World Champion, might not have luck and never make it.

Zoetemelk, at age 39, <u>ended</u> his career as a World Champion. His "best years" he never did that well. Sometimes he won a race. It makes everything possible for many.

One good crash, an injury and psychology and forget it. I remember in one race in Europe one fellow from

the field died who almost got second. He was in a collision.

Danger is everywhere. One of the most dangerous places (and I'm joking), is in our beds. Most people die when they are in bed!

My motto for bike riders is : "Work like a bull, eat like a pig, and sleep like a baby!"

Master's Racing

It's beautiful what Master's riders are doing — sometimes they are too crazy because they're training too hard. That must be sport/recreation. Sport for good health. Some of them take it too seriously and too hard. That's supposed to be sports for health.

Many Masters are finding opportunities to compete for the first time in their lives. It can be a quiet and easy Master's competition, like Harvey, who passed through cycling but still competes for fun.

I understand these Master's who compete for the first time and in their first opportunity, their only opportunity as an athlete. They have to realize the fact of age. Even plastic surgery has its limitations. You can't fix an old engine. It's not a brand new engine. It's very difficult to take, saying "this is all there is for me."

Rebecca still has time to do well. Harvey is a family man. Competition would take too much time and he can't afford it, so he competes for fun.

What American Cycling Needs

What American cycling needs

most now is Juniors. Juniors are development for the future. When I think about work for development in the Federation, I don't see the climate changing. People in the Federation still don't understand development. They don't understand how important the Juniors are.

If I had the power I would put all my efforts into the Juniors program. Competition between schools, between regions, including having regional coaches. I started the regional coaching program, but when I left, it was tabled and started again. My idea was 12 regional coaches, each given the program and responsibility.

I don't know much about the program for regional coaches now in place. For me, the regional coaches here must work free on the velodrome and on the road, minimum once a week.

They must have a base of operations, even if the Federation must pay for it, and they must have video. They must have testing equipment, equipment for setting up position, they must be for support, minimum (it depends on what he's paid) four hours a day, five days a week. They must attend races for selection. That's what I'd like to see.

They must be paid to develop the system from the Juniors level, not from the Seniors level.

Seniors move through this area and he can say "Oh, I have the best team in my area." Juniors are what he actually has <u>developed</u>.

There must be lectures once a week. Work-outs must be, at minimum, once a week on the velodrome, once a week on the road. Or once on the track, twice on the road.

Regional Coaches must also teach club coaches or leaders. The regional coach must teach others, must have the power to accept a race program and the race courses, not the district rep. The district rep and the coach must be the same person.

When there is more money and he has some help, he also needs a computer and a secretary, and not necessarily male or female, but either men or women. It would be regional segments of the Federation.

Every club should have a coach. A bigger club might have a coach for Seniors, for Juniors, for Women, etc. They should have a doctor for the athletes. The Regional Coach should meet with the club coaches a minimum of once a month.

In Poland, the district federation has an officials department, a coaching department and district administration. They sell licenses for their district and pay a fee to the Federation. The top category monies go only to the Federation. Juniors and lower category monies go only to the base and development.

Officials meet every Monday evening and coaches meet every Monday evening. The Regional Coach is the leader in regard to the racing program, problems, — it's a working meeting.

Competition is regional between clubs. Who has the best club? Who has the best rider? best woman? best junior? best vet? People at the meeting make these kinds of decisions, about Tuesday night or Friday night races,

or they might plan for Saturday and Sunday, and the entire year. That's how it's supposed to be.

There must be a system. Without a system, there are no results. When I'm on the Board I will push for that, that's my goal. Right now the problem is a lack of organization.

All money for membership goes to the Federation right now. It must stay in the regions, to develop the regions, not just to support 20 people in the offices in Colorado Springs. It would be better if there were 10 people there and 20 people spread throughout the country. It should not be central, it should be decentralized.

Every area should be a distinct region. There should be competition between regions for the Nationals. The best may be New Jersey, second best Northern California, or best might be Colorado. There should be a trophy or award for the best region. There should be an annual meeting

I have different ideas because I saw my own Federation. The problem is, I don't have much time. For the past two years every Board meeting discussed this crazy new system and other bull. New organization, new system for administration, staff changes and stuff like that.

For all staff there must be authority and supervision by the Board. The coaching staff must have people from the Board who supervise them. The administration must have supervision. The financial area must have supervision.

The Board is too large. I think 12

is good. There are too many athletes. Athletes are not always responsible. They don't know the business. They are too young and too selfish. I think one male and one female is enough. Not 20% like it says now.

The Olympic Committee has better organization, but it's worse in this country compared to others, I think. They are not using this country's

Eddie and USCF Executive Director Lisa Voight. 1991 Master's Nationals

potential. It's ex-retired Colonels and high officers. They're having fun, but they are not athletics people. They are very nice people, but not people with heart to do the best in the world and really be athletic. They aren't using this country's potential.

In other countries the Olympic Committee does much more. The coaches are part of the Olympic Committee. They are more independent. They spend a lot more money for education, for coaching education, for officials education, for the program.

Today

I am on the Board of Directors now only because I want to help cycling. The last two years I haven't had much time because I was managing a Professional team. Now Mr. Fraysse is back. I believe in this man. Together we can do something good. We started this revolution in cycling, he and I. He gave me the opportunity. I have a lot of respect for him for that and I want to help him right now to be a successful president.

Right now, I don't care if I am here or I am in Poland. When I am in Poland, I enjoy myself. When I'm here I enjoy myself. I've almost been in the U.S. 20 years, so it's a long enough time to get used to the language and the culture. I didn't spend one minute in school. I learned language only from people, from riders. I haven't learned English from TV because I have no time for that. I was always on the road, working.

I am Polish. Poland is a nice nation and a beautiful country. There are bad and good people everywhere.

I enjoy living in America. I am proud to be an American citizen. I say I am Polish-American.

I'm very proud of what I have done for American cycling. Personally, I feel very good I've done something. How history portrays me will be up to history.

Some people think I'm a genius, some people hate me because of my position and they're jealous. That's normal, that's life.

Chapter 16 - Announcing
Live Track Race Announcing
Ralph Elliott / M*G*E*

Ralph Elliott has been entertaining spectators at San Diego Velodrome for many years, including the pre-Olympic early '80s. He remains "The Voice" of the San Diego Velodrome.

It's always more fun with Ralph.

Sometimes I'm referred to as Metro Golden Elliott. My motto is *"it's not whether you win or lose but how much fun you have"*. Fun is what I like to try to personify in my delivery of announcing and my life in general. In my dossier I start right out with what I believe: "announcing is probably the single most important element in a successful event."

I have been involved with the sport of bicycle racing for 25 years and provided expert cycling commentary for the past 15 years. By using a combination of enthusiastic delivery and music sound tracks, I introduce newcomers to the sport of cycling and entertain the regulars. Having a top announcer can make or break an event, and I also say that I can turn an event into a happening. That's my view.

How I Got Started

I started getting involved with cycling when I began riding with the American Youth Hostels when I was in Junior High School. My dad gave me a ten speed English racer when I was about 14 years old. I was going to the beach most of the time at that time, but then I started alternating going to the beach and going for bicycle rides

when the waves weren't any good.

I was playing basketball in high school for two years. The third year in high school I didn't make the team, so then I started bicycle racing as a Junior. That grew and then in 1968 I got a Schwinn Paramount and I became a bike racer.

I was California State Road Champion, Rocky Mountain Road Champion, and the winner of the first ever Willows Road race here in San Diego (*now a yearly MGE announcing event*).

Probably my forte was Stage Races. I rode the Red Zinger races which became the Coors races, Tour of Baja, Tour of California, it seemed like the longer and harder the race, the better I did. We rode Tecate-Ensenada and all those.

I raced with Audrey McElmury (1969 World Road Champion). In fact, I've got a great picture of me, Audrey, Dave Wright and Peter Kendall lined up for the Riverside 100 back in 1969. I have a whole bunch of stuff on Audrey, I've got the "Woman Cyclist -- Mother wins World Championship" and this picture of Audrey down at La Jolla Cove from the 1969 Union Tribune. It's in my scrapbook. There are some pictures of me and Audrey.

You see, when I was young, Audrey was our hero. We were Junior

"My motto is "it's not whether you win or lose but how much fun you have." By using a combination of enthusiastic delivery and music sound tracks, I introduce newcomers to the sport of cycling and entertain the regulars. Having a top announcer can make or break an event, and I also say that I can turn an event into a happening." San Diego, 1994

riders and she was this attractive woman who was <u>good</u>. Scott (her husband) was nice too. They were still together. We looked up to them. They were the leaders of our club. They were World Class. We were all part of San Diego Bicycle Club, the only club there was at that time.

When I joined the San Diego Bicycle Club in 1968 I think there were only about 12 members. Audrey, Alan DeFever, Dave Wright, Ed

Renger, a few others. There were only about 1000 cyclists in the whole United States at that time. Bergen can help you with history. He was around then too, of course. (Bob) Zumwalt was out of it then. He was down working at Rohr. That's about all there was of us.

I remember we used to go down to Alan DeFever's house over where the Broderick's house -- Betty Broderick, who murdered her husband -- that was Alan DeFever's house. That's who bought it or it was next door, one of the two. I went over there and checked it out and thought "That's where DeFever lived!" or next door to it.

I distinctly remember that we always had for refreshments -- now these were World Class athletes -- apple cider and doughnuts. Isn't that great? I tell that story to people, they don't believe it.

I started in '68. '69 was my first full year of racing. 1969 was cool. I have this picture at home of Audrey was World Champion, Alan was National Champion, and I was State Champion of California. It's all on this one page. I have that stuff at home in my office. My friends call it, The

Bicycle Museum.

That's how I got involved. Then I started racing more and more. I was State Champion in '69, my first year. I still remember the race. We all went up to King City for the State of California Road Championships. I was a first year Senior.

It was a really tough course and all I remember is that they had this really fast downhill finish and I was always a good downhiller. I made a right turn and in 200 meters was the finish line. So, I told myself that as long as I was the first one through the corner, I could probably win the race. I blasted through the corner as fast as I could. I almost lost control.

For me to do that meant the next two guys, well, they both crashed. They lost control and crashed. I was a good bike handler, so I won the race. I thought "If I'm almost losing it, they're going to dump it." And they did. So I won the race.

How I Became a Track Race Announcer

I was going to Mesa College part time and racing full time until about '77 or '78. I got a teaching credential in Industrial Arts, but then they phased that out. I had been putting on bike races while I was going to college.

I was President of San Diego Bicycle Club. When I got out of college I expanded, putting on more and more races. At one point I was putting on a dozen races a year. That became my full time thing.

I also had a 20 hour per week job at Sears that kind of paid the bills, but I was doing a races all the time. While I was putting the races on, I was also

announcing at my races. Other people wanted me to come and announce at their races, so that's how the announcing thing grew.

Troubles

Then my bike race promotion got so successful that a District Rep named Marilyn Allen didn't think that what I was doing was proper. She wrote that my making money off of the racers was bad, even though she was the District Rep of the USCF, and so she was making money off of them too. She said I shouldn't make money off of the racers, that my races were unsafe, and all these things were bad, yet I would get 1200 racers a day at my races.

I was turning people away, so I think what I was doing was right and that what she wanted was wrong. She made it so bad, she said she'd put me out of business and she all but did. After one Willows race it was so bad that I haven't put on a serious bike race since then except for the cyclocross and a couple of mountain bike things. 1989 was the last big race I promoted. That was Willows Weekend.

I slept for five months after it, I was so depressed. I was going to move to Idaho. I spent two months up there, almost had a house. I got that close, I was out of here. Then we put so much pressure on her that in two years we got rid of her. What happened is that everyone would say "Oh, it's just Ralph, he's having a problem with her," but then after two years everyone demanded her out.

Let me say this about Marilyn Allen. We would never go to dinner or

anything like that, but I think she's a good official. As a professional, I think she's a good official. Interviewing her for the book, you'll get the story of the 1992 Olympic Trials from the horse's mouth. Marilyn says she used to ride, but that was in her Canadian life that none of us know about. She was married to Bill Wild, a former track racer. He's a Commissaire too. I read

Ralph had the hottest programs going. 1986

somewhere that he screwed up some event in Canada, some Nationals or whatever.

Announcing Full Time

Anyway, then I got into the announcing thing full time. I dedicated myself to it. I spent some more money on equipment. I have my big trailer, the photo-finish, that happened in '89 when I gave up on the promotion thing. So now, for the past four or five years I announce almost every weekend at somebody's race.

I began track announcing in 1980. Joe Saling announced at the National Championships in 1980, but I was the Friday night guy at the velodrome. The USCF, like they still do today,

have certain people that they use. It's hard to get these certain jobs unless -- I don't know how you get them. There's so much politics. If you were going to ask the racers who they wanted to come and do their race, 9 out of 10 would want me. The crowd too, for that matter.

So, I have all my stuff and I usually do the weekly races at the San Diego Velodrome. I have done Nationals. I did Nationals in '83 at Dominguez Hills. It was the first time at the National Championships. There was quite a controversy because I use these music sound tracks in my delivery and they usually don't have any music at the Nationals.

The Nationals are usually a boring, drab event and I was trying to spice them up with my style. It got to a point where the officials said "Ok, as long as the racers okay the music, then we'll do it." 99.9% of the racers okayed the music. There was one guy who didn't want it during his Kilo, or something, but everybody else thought it was great.

They may not have it now, I haven't been to Senior Nationals for a while. I went to Master's Nationals in Seattle a couple of years ago and it was so dry and boring. I've done the Master's Nationals a couple of times, and they, of course, love the music.

You go to an event that I'm doing and everyone's laughing and having a good time, it's up-beat. You go to those other ones, it's kind of like a funeral.

I think bike racing should be more fun rather than a funeral. More people do it now, it's more accepted, but your genuine, French-speaking guy, he probably wouldn't like it. Your Olympic or World Championships probably wouldn't like it. I don't know why, it makes it <u>better</u>.

Announcing Events

I'm there to inform the people what's going on, because a lot of people go to the track and it's their first time. I always like to introduce the event, tell how it's done, why it's done, and different strategies that you would use during the event.

Such as, Miss 'N' Out, you obviously don't want to ride at the back, unless you've got a guy who wants to play what I call "the Devil". Sometimes there are riders -- and there are a few that are really good at it, like Danny Van Haute, Mark Whitehead -- these guys love to be the devil.

What they do is, they ride at the back. They're a delight for me, because we work together. They'll sit back there and it will be a close one, and they'll point who it was that was out. I'll start using him as the Devil "Okay, who's Danny going to call out this time? Who's he going to call out the next time? Who's Danny's next victim?" It's really a lot of fun. The crowd loves it when you do that. The Miss 'N' Out, in my opinion, is a showmanship race.

I've been accused by a few officials that, when I call the Miss 'N' Out, that if it was really close I would not call the Devil out, I would call the other guy out that he was choosing if it was close. That's a show race, that's not a World Championship race. That's a for-fun race. If it was close I'd call the other guy out because they're doing the show and the race goes on. But if they were out, I would definitely call them out. When they're that close it's a flip of the coin a lot of the time. Then Marilyn and Jim (Allen) got on my case about that. Then the officials

Yes, Ralph (front) really raced! and still rides. Lemon Grove Criterium, 1982

would pick it.

When the officials pick it, it's not as easy because they hum and they ha, meanwhile the riders are half way around the track and they have to wait for the decision. When I'm doing it, I make a decision and it's done. I'm a Category 4 official. I may go up sometime because now as a Category 4 you don't get to do much. While I have enough, I've been around velodromes for 15 years, I could probably be a Chief Referee or any position on the track just from all my experience and from everything I've seen, but I'm only Category 4. So, that's the really fun thing about announcing.

In the Match Sprints it's the same thing. You want to tell the people what's going on. You introduce it. I always made a big deal about "And now, we're down to the final round . . . it's Nelson, "the Cheetah" Vails. Will he be able to knock off Mark, "the Golden Boy", Gorski?" and all that.

I like to give these guys nicknames and build it up. "And now, here we go . . . in the first ride, who's going to stay alive?" and play all that into it. I think people like that. Put some excitement to it.

For nicknames, some of them just come to me. A lot of these guys have their own. Nicknames are sort of a gift, I guess. You look at a person and you go "Oh, that guy's . . ." whatever. And you come up with something for them. It's kind of like a caricature. You just think of some-thing. I haven't been doing it as much, but I might start doing it again because I'm back on the track Friday nights.

You keep the program going. **A lot of people think events like the Kilo are boring and Pursuits are boring. If you have a good announcer, they're not.** A good announcer on a Kilo can give the lap times. The fans, they're not stupid, they go "Ohhh!" they can tell, "that's a 23. Now a 22 -- we just had the fastest

first lap! We just had the fastest second lap! And now! We have a new time!" you create that enthusiasm and those boring races become more exciting.

A scoreboard helps. Kilo and Pursuit are pretty much the same. The Pursuit's more boring, as we know, because it takes longer. But, again, if the people are into it, if they know what's going on like at Nationals, it's not so bad.

Points races are good, especially if you have a crew of officials who will work with you and keep you updated on the current points standing. You call the lead Sprint. I've got a photographic mind. When four guys cross the finish line, I automatically photograph them in my mind and I can, 95% of the time, tell you the first four people across the line. I remember that shot. Then as they go around the turn I'll say "And, in first place, . . . it was Hayes, it was Peck, it was Kopp, it was Gates." (using a little better delivery than that.)

The officials are constantly keeping their score and they can relay that information to you. They can say "Ralph, we've got the current up-date" and "Oh, okay, give me that information. Okay, the current leaders are . . . Dave Grylls with 23 points, . . . " They need to communicate that to me somehow, verbal, radio, or nearby. There's all kinds of ways to do it.

In the old days I had a guy who was really good at math and he sat there with me and we just did our own. We did our own because they were a little reluctant to give us that information. There was kind of a feud. Everything I say is unofficial. I always say "I'll do the best job I can of keeping you abreast of racing action all night long, but everything I say is unofficial until verified by the race officials." We try to keep it official. The officials we have down there now are all what I call "rider friendly". They're glad to give that information up.

In Match Sprints you have to be careful because there's a lot of good moves made "Oh, there's a good hook . . . " or "Gorski just chopped Whitehead" or whatever. But a lot of times you have to hold back a little bit. A lot of stuff happens, you see a beautiful move down the back side. I'll usually wait three seconds to say "Oh, yeah, he's coming around on the outside" long after he actually came around on the outside.

You don't want to give away race strategy from one rider to the other over the P.A. You could do that. I've never been accused of that. As a racer I always remember what that's like and I think it's unfair, so I always wait a little bit before I announce it. You don't want to give away a tactic. After it's happened, I'd, of course, comment on it. So those are the different events and how I approach them.

The Keirin is kind of new to the United States. A lot of places didn't do them. We have them. They're lined up behind the motorcycle and paced for three and a half laps. Then the motorcycle pulls off and it's a mad dash for 500 meters.

We do a similar thing that's called the 500 meter Sprint and it's just as exciting, you just don't have the three lap build-up. There's no doubt about

it, there's nothing more exciting than watching riders on the track going 40 miles an hour elbow to elbow. That just throws goose bumps over anybody. The Keirin's good for that because it gets them up to that speed, then it pulls off. That's exciting!

I haven't seen much Tandem Sprinting in my announcing. It's kind of a newer thing. Actually it was dead and outlawed when I was racing. They just didn't have it. The Olympics didn't have it, the World Championships didn't have it, then they started bringing it back a little bit. They still don't have it in the Olympics, but they do have it at the World Championships. It's so dangerous. They decided it was too dangerous again. When I was racing it was too dangerous, that's what they said. I don't like to see guys get in comas.

Crashes

Believe me, when I see a crash on the track, I'm not excited at all. It scares me. I don't like it. I like to see 40 mile an hour racing, but I don't like to see anybody on the deck. Believe me, it hurts. I don't go for the crashes. A lot of times there are really gruesome accidents on the track and I'm here trying to keep a lighter side to it.

First we've got to get emergency people on the scene. Then I'll talk about what happens in accidents, maybe why the accident happened, then talk about other things. Then I kind of wean them off to what's coming up next week or talk about some other story while paramedics and other people are doing their thing.

*"In the Match Sprints you want to tell the people what's going on. **You don't want to give away race strategy from one rider to the other over the P.A.**, I think that's unfair. I always wait a little before I announce it." San Diego, 1994*

I'll draw the attention away from that with my verbal delivery and talk about other things -- give away door prizes, talk about what's coming up -- I'll talk about anything except what's actually happening over there in the corner. There are people who would say something in their delivery about "It's wild, it's crazy, you can see blood . . . Come on down!"

I never say something like that. I stress the "It's exciting, it's fast, it's unbelievable what these people do. They're highly skilled, they're highly trained -- don't try this at home." **I don't ever say anything that will give the idea that the reason you**

want to come out here is because people are going to get hurt. I'm against that. I don't like that in any kind of advertising.

A lot of times they'll show advertising "Olympic cycling's coming up" and what do they show? A crash on the velodrome. Why don't they just show two guys going 40 miles an hour, elbow to elbow? That, to me, would be more exciting. The crash advertising kind of makes me mad. I don't go to watch crashes. I like to go to watch motor sports too, because I really appreciate the skills.

I go to Cajon Speedway to watch Demolition Derbies, because they have crashes, but that's what it's about, that's what it's <u>for</u>. I don't appreciate seeing somebody end up in the hospital. I don't go there for that. That's not my personality.

Music & My Delivery

My delivery to the audience is pretty much the same whether it's Master's or Seniors I'm announcing. For Juniors I think you want to be a little more simple, try to be more instructive, maybe. Things that might help them more. Maybe delivery that included, for people in the audience "Hey, you could do this too, and this is what these guys have done to get to this." For Master's I'll play more oldies. I can bring out more stuff that I wouldn't play at a Junior race.

I get my music from a lot of different places. That's an instinct thing. It's an instinct call. It's how I feel, how I want the races to go. For the Kilo I play the fastest, most upbeat thing I can find. If it's Pursuits I play a little more Alan Parsons type of stuff, John Tesch stuff, Tour de France type stuff. In Sprints -- actually NO music works for Sprints. It's one of the races I usually don't play music during. It goes from stop to go. It kind of doesn't work. Any up-beat stuff works for Points races. It's going fast the whole time.

What really doesn't work is if the officials and the announcer are not on the same wavelength, if the officials want to withhold information, they want to withhold results, they want to withhold this or that. They'll change the program and not notify the announcer. They're going by one program and you're going by another.

"Oh, coming up next is going to be the Women's 5K . . . oh, I don't see any women, guess they're . . . oh, the officials . . . oh, guess they're changing that, it's now the . . . uh, . . . Junior's Points race coming up next . . ." I think it might be nice if they could tell the announcer and then he can tell everybody.

The announcer should be a tool for the officials, because he could make their job a lot easier. He can help the riders get ready for their event, he can give results, he can tell times, he can start races, he can give riders instructions -- he can do a lot of things if they'll let him.

What I like to do is, they line up the riders and I'll go through my spiel with the audience of what it's going to be. It's the same speil that the riders need to hear. Why don't we just do it all at once? Rather than they do theirs

and I do mine . . . that's kind of foolish.

They can use the announcer to give the instructions. They can use him to start races -- a lot of times I'll say "Attention riders" and then they'll fire the gun, stuff like that. I think a good rapport between the officials and the announcer is very important. They need to both be on the same wavelength. Officials are usually pretty good. They're there to see that the race is well run. A well run race is usually good for them as well. They are theoretically in charge of how it's going during the meet.

I'll include information from the Rule Book. Sometimes they're pretty slim, like for Match Sprint you can do anything you want as long as you don't impede the other rider! That's the way the rules are written, that's the way I would announce it.

There are other things that are a little more technical. You always talk about, like in Points "In this race we're going to have Sprints every three laps, scored 5, 3, 2 and 1. We count the points up, the rider with the most points wins." We always go through the whole spew on that stuff. If you have a large crowd, you think "there could be a half a dozen people who are here for the first time ever", and the people who already know this stuff will just tune it out anyway.

The Show

Racers are usually no trouble. On a rare occasion a racer may not like the nickname that he or she was given. They'll come by or they'll say "Turn the music down" or whatever. But these are rare. If it's about nicknames, that rider will never get another

nickname, he just becomes a number. That's fine. I'll put my emphasis on the people who appreciate me.

There are some who will work the crowd. That's important. It's kind of a show. There needs to be an interaction between the racers and the crowd. The two should not be apart. I think that's one reason that track races are not going. We have no personalities. Personalities are what bring people back. Look at auto racing and all these other sports. They have these personalities and the media thrives on that stuff. I think it's discouraged and I don't know why that is.

The established powers discourage anything that makes for successful cycling. They hinder the sport more than they progress it. If more people would show personality, we need a few more. I'd love to do the National Track Championships again now. I'd be fun.

Look at your World Championship guys, the Japanese, Danny Clark and those guys. They're great showmen. They all work the crowd like that. That's what brings people back. I think that's why it's more successful. People go "Yeah, I think I'm going to watch Grylls and McDonough do battle tonight at the track."

You need people who are going to go down there and know who these people are. Then they come back week after week. When you go to the ball game you pretty much know all the guys in the playing field, don't you? That's the way track racing should be, in my opinion. You come down every week and "Oh, let's go to the bike

races. Let's see how many times Whitehead's going to be DQ'd."

Showmanship is the key to track promotion. The second thing would be to have races that are more crowd-appealing, such as "Devils" and Madisons instead of Pursuits and Kilos. Getting the crowd out the first race takes a lot of gimmicking. When the San Diego Velodrome was really popular, we had gimmicks. Danny G. was the promoter at that time and he's have the "KGB Feed our Friend Pizza Hut Pizza Night". Everyone who came down there got a free slice of pizza.

At half time they had a deal where you and a partner would feed pizza to each other. The first team to eat a whole pizza would win a party for ten at Pizza Hut. There were ten teams who did it, so that got the audience involved with it. Another time we had "Beach Cruiser Races". We had about ten teams on beach cruisers. You got four of your buddies and it was a relay race around the track.

Another night he had, believe it or not, "Country and Western Night". He had a mechanical bull down there! Whoever rode that bull the longest won a certain prize. He had all these different gimmicks other than the bike racing to get the people to come down there. And of course all these gimmicks had sponsors, different radio stations and stuff like that, who would help publicize the race and get people to come down there.

You would get a market of a certain crowd. That's what radio stations do. So you pick your radio station according to what crowd you wanted to show up. You have to have that involvement. Then you need a set of racers. It has to be built from the ground up. There's no easy solution, but it has to be something people want to come to and that the racers want to race at. I think it's nice to have prizes of some sort every week. I think the bigger the bucks, the more racers will come out. There always has to be that carrot, that incentive to race for. I believe in that.

Danny's still around, he puts on the California Adventure Show at Del Mar. He does that now and he does his writing. He does well. He does his things. We worked together in the '83 Nationals when the San Diego Velodrome Association put the Time Trials on, the road races -- we had 10,000 people out there watching that. And, we put the track races on. We took it up to Dominguez. We lost all of our profits on that.

Some people on the committee wanted to have it at Dominguez. We wanted to have it on our track, but the Olympics were coming up the next year, and they wanted to see that. I was the Technical Director of that project and he was the Promoter of that project, so we worked together.

It's hard, especially in San Diego. In California, well, in San Diego, 20 different events go on every day, every night, every weekend. There's only 52 weekends in a year so that's about 10,000 people trying to get money from not that many people. The sponsorship dollar is spread pretty thin.

If we were sitting in a town like Emmaus, Pennsylvania (home of Lehigh/Trexlertown Velodrome), how many things go on in that town?

Nothing.

Announcing Nationals

I would announce Nationals the same as I always announce. Why not? I think what Nats are lacking are what I do locally. I go to the Nationals and I hear how boring they are.

What I do is anything that's going to enhance it, because the crowd's going to be into it more and that makes the racers into it more, I think. I guarantee you that I can get the crowd "whipped" (that's the term I use) I like to "whip" the crowd -- I really try to get them excited.

We had an Italian Pursuit during Master's Nationals a couple years ago. It was a Pursuit between Danny Van Haute and -- between "the Coach" and "the Student" -- Roger Parenteau.

It was the 3000 meter Pursuit. Both were going for the Pursuit in Master's Nationals. Both were from San Diego. Every lap they were just dead even and I had the crowd whipped.

Every time they came through it was deafening. Parenteau rode his best time in history and the Student beat the Coach. I don't think he's racing any more.

I like seeing the old Champions come back and put bike racing in the

right perspective. That's a lot of fun to me.

Tradition

What I dislike most is starting with something that's an idea, you grow with it, you make it better, and it becomes a real successful thing. That's what happened with Redlands.

They decide that they don't need

For the re-opening of the San Diego Velodrome, Ralph got out his tux. Always in good taste. April 6, 1995

you any more and they go for somebody else. In reality, that somebody else isn't any better.

The person I was replaced with doesn't know any of the local history of the race. He doesn't know any of the local volunteers, he doesn't know anything unique to the event.

He doesn't know about the Redlands "Tunnel of Sound" where I had "Battle of the Fans". He doesn't know any of that stuff.

Those are unique things of me and the race. They did that five years ago when they brought someone else in.

After the race everyone wrote to the newspaper wanting to know where "Our Race Announcer" was.

It hurts me. I put my heart and soul into this thing, I really did, and they slap me in the face.

It's hard for me to be very enthusiastic at the velodrome. It needs a whole new rebirth. They have all these new schemes they dream up.

It goes from one year to the next with one guy's idea this year and another guy's idea the next year. Consistency is very important.

Loyalty seems to be a lost American virtue. When I go to Cajon Speedway to watch auto racing, they've had the same announcer there for 24 years!

I expect to hear that guy. If somebody else was there I'd be upset! It wouldn't be the same.

I go all over town and people come up to me, like at the bank, and say "Hey, aren't you the announcer at the Velodrome?"

"Oh yeah, that's me, "The Voice"" Yeah!

Television Track Race Announcing
Brian Drebber

*Here and there, on ESPN, you'll see Brian Drebber pop up. Most people don't realize that, in his soul, Brian is a hard core trackie with a unique perspective. **He's ready for the future.***

How I Got Started

I moved to Pennsylvania in 1976 after I met Jack Simes and Dave Chauner. They had their OmniSports company, doing bicycle clinics around the country. I stopped in on one in North Carolina on my way to Florida to train. I was racing at that time and lived in Virginia. I started racing in '73. I had come up to Trexlertown in October of '75 when they had had the Grand Opening of the track and had their very first race. Their first season was '76.

I made up my mind in that first race that that was what I was put on this earth to do. If I was going to be a bike racer, it was going to be <u>on the track</u>. I really loved the rough-and-tumble, racing-in-close-quarters stuff -- the speed events rather than going out and slogging along on the road for hours.

Jack and Dave invited me to work out with the team, the guys who were going to be trying out for the Olympics in '76. I sold everything I owned and moved to Pennsylvania. I lived in the house with all the guys who were trying out for the Olympic team and I trained with the Olympic team, even though I didn't quite make the team.

Kilo was the event I trained for, that and Sprints. What I really enjoyed was racing on Friday night. I raced everything. I rode everything, I rode Madisons well, I rode Sprints okay.

I raced against Jerry Ash and Leigh Barczewski and those guys. There were three or four guys that were better than me -- Gibby, Leigh, Jerry. I was a lot stronger than most of the Sprinters and a lot faster than most of the strong guys, so I was right in the middle somewhere. A good middle distance guy, Madisons, Miss-N-Outs, things like that, I was really good at.

In 1976 when I was racing we had a big post-Olympic meet after the games in Montreal. A bunch of the riders came down to compete at Trexlertown. Including Morelon, Tkac, the Olympic Sprint Champion, and other guys. Dave Chauner was the regular velodrome announcer. He got laryngitis or somehow lost his voice.

They scrambled around to find another announcer. They got John Reoch, Miji Reoch's husband. With all due respect to John, he didn't do very well. It pointed up a need to have an "understudy" or someone else in case this happened again. They started auditioning a number of people -- basically anyone who was <u>warm</u>! I was one of the ones who tried. They figured I never shut up and I was working at the track anyway. I helped build a lot of the improvements

"There is a trend toward track cycling as a media event, for three reasons: First, we love it, Second, we're successful at Worlds, Third, MONEY!" Brian Drebber, World Cup, 1994.

because I was a carpenter by trade some years ago.

So, I started announcing on Tuesday nights in 1977 when I was still racing on Friday nights. Friday was the Pro-Am night and Tuesday was the locals. And that's how I started. Little by little I guess I showed a

proficiency for it and eventually promoters of other races and criteriums nearby began to ask me to come and do their races.

Late in the season after I got through with racing I did a couple of announcing jobs. I went out to Arizona and did a big women's race in 1977, the "International Women's Challenge." The organizer burned KLM airlines and other people for a lot of money, so it was a scandal at the time, but it was a great event.

In 1978, I made the decision that I was going to have to get a job and be a responsible person. There was no money in the sport at that time and I was raising my daughter by myself. I had left her with my sister down in Virginia when I moved to Pennsylvania. Donna, my sister gave me that couple of years to get it out of my system and I did.

I went back to working full time as a carpenter and whatever I could do to make a living and bring my daughter up. In the spring, when cycling started coming around, rather than training and racing again, I started announcing on weekends as sort of a side job.

Little by little, through the late '70's and through the '80's, until about 1988, I did P.A. announcing. I was the "Voice of Cycling." I did all the major events; the World Championships, the Coors Classic for nine years, all the big stage races and criteriums -- whatever, all over the country.

I started Event Services which is still out in Colorado. Beth Estes and Al MacDonald run it now. I founded the company with Artie Greenberg. Eventually it was sort of a hostile takeover -- I essentially got fired by my own company. You don't want to hear that whole story. Somehow as a majority stockholder and President of the company I got fired.

I've gotten over it. They say the best revenge is living well, and I've certainly done fine. I wish them all the luck in the world. We parted and that's just water under the bridge.

The first television job I did was in 1978. We had the National Championships at Trexlertown and a local PBS station came in and produced a show of the Nationals that aired nationally on the Public Broadcasting System.

Dave Chauner and I co-hosted the broadcast since we were the two announcers at the track, though Dave had pretty much given up announcing by that time and I had pretty much taken over. Dave and Jack and Omnisports had started doing other things. The first job I did for ESPN was the Mayor's Cup, the old Nabisco-Wheat Thins Mayor's Cup races back about 1987.

The Difference between Live and TV announcing

The most obvious difference about broadcast announcing is that there is no live audience. I can relate to movie and television actors who crave going back and doing theatre. That really sums it up. There really isn't a lot of difference in the mechanics of it, but the fact that there's no audience feedback doing television, you don't get that instant gratification. You don't get the electricity and the feeling of complementing the event and having people applaud, stand up out of their chairs and go nuts.

I'm sitting up on a scaffold somewhere with a headset on watching a monitor and it's a parallel universe. We feed off that energy, but I'm not contributing to it. The event, the energy, the ambience, all that natural sound and applause and all that is part of our show when we do a television broadcast. We have microphones all over the place and we pick up a lot of that noise and everything, but I'm not helping make it happen. I'm not contributing to it.

We're just looking at it through a television camera and listening to it though microphones. It's very second-hand. It isn't really isolated because we're there, at least most of the time. Occasionally we do events for television where we're not there.

For instance, the 1993 World Championships. We took raw footage from Norwegian television, the host broadcasters. We edited it down to a one-hour show and then voiced it all over in the studio. I was never there.

In 1994, I wasn't there again. Whatever happened, happened without me or anyone actually being there. Whatever coverage of the World's showed up was done post-production. It was "posted" in the studio somewhere. For the viewer at home, that's pretty transparent. People are easily fooled. "Oh, yeah, we were there!" Part of the skill, the professional talent, is to simulate that sort of live action when, in fact, it's all posted.

In the Tour DuPont we do a half-hour show about a five hour race. Anyone who thinks about it for more than about one and a half seconds would go "wait a minute, this can't be live." but while they're watching it they might be fooled into thinking it was live at first.

On the other hand, that's not the best example because the real race may be finishing outside the booth where we're voicing the early part of the show, so that's a little more live than some. But the main difference is that there's not that direct feedback, that audience feedback. You make a little joke, people laugh. You say something that you think complements what's going on and people react. Or you impart some little piece of information and people look at each other and sort of go "Oh, wow!" so you get to feel what happens.

The only time I get to feel that is if I happen to be sitting in a bar or at somebody's house when we're watching a television show that I've done. Then people will react.

Broadcaster as P.A. Announcer

Having the broadcast announcer be the same person as the P.A. announcer is a technical problem. We run into it a little bit at Trexlertown. I go up there and I do announce on Friday nights occasionally during the season. I was up there a couple of times this year.

If it happens to be one of the nights that we're taping for television, then it sounds really weird when I go in and do the commentary in the studio and it's very obviously the same voice doing the live announcing in the background. It's a technical thing that's a little ugly.

Plus, television proceeds at a different pace. It starts and stops a little differently than a live event does, although with track cycling it's pretty much a one to one relationship. At least it's very close, because track cycling starts and stops. The riders come to the line, they race, then they ride around while we show a replay, then they get off their bikes and it's over with while we go to commercial. It actually works out great for a track race, but you'd never be able to do that for a road race.

Track Races on TV

There have been quite a few track races on TV this year. **I definitely feel like there is a trend toward track cycling as a media event**, for three reasons:

First, we love it

Number one, there are a few of us out here who are trying to make that happen. We feel very strongly about track cycling. We love it, believe in it and think that it's just great. But that's probably the third most important reason.

Second, we're successful at Worlds

The second most important reason is that track cycling as a sport, as an event, is beginning to really come up again. It's really starting to become more popular. I think the Federation is putting more effort into it. We're in a cycle right now where we have athletes who are having international success. We're becoming World Champions and so on. With Marty, Rebecca, Janie ...Connie P.... there are a number of track cyclists who, in the last half dozen years or so have really accomplished some wonderful things.

They've always done that to a certain extent, but now the Federation is starting to realize that "Hey, out of every $10.00 that we spend, we're putting $9.50 in the road program and we get Lance Armstrong who wins the World Championship." The only guy to have won a World title going back to Greg LeMond. Ten years is a

long time to have gone back between road titles. Well, the women won the Team Time Trial, too.

The point is, they put 90% of their money into the men's road program, another $.75 into the women's road program, $.15 into everything else and $.10 into track cycling. Out of that $.10 we get, out of the seven medals we won at the 1993 World Championship, four of them were on the track. And that was an aberration. **Almost every time we come home with medals, they're on the track, not on the road.** We didn't win any road medals in Japan. We came back with a couple of track medals.

Now the Federation is beginning to say "Now wait a minute. This track thing is a better investment." For a sponsor, a medal is a medal. They don't know that road cycling is a bigger, more powerful arm of the sport. All they know is that a Gold medal is a Gold medal. An Olympic Champion is an Olympic Champion forever. It doesn't matter what sport or what event.

They're starting to realize that their investment is paying off a lot better in track, so they're starting to put more resources into it. Plus the fact that now a days, with the World Championships and the Olympics in '96 being open, the job for the Cycling Federation with regard to the road is really going to be nothing more than a developmental arm.

The athletes that represent the United States are all going to be Pros. Why have an amateur National Team? You don't need it. You don't need an elite program. You need to develop

those riders to get them to the point where the trade teams take them over. Then all you do is use your selection process to pick the Pros that are on trade teams to represent their country at the World's just like every other country does.

The job of the Federation with regard to the development of elite amateur athletics is beginning to diminish, especially with regard to the road. They can continue to support the track program because there are no trade track teams. There are very few athletes who are well sponsored through trade sponsorship. You don't have Saturn and Coors and all that carrying riders who are known as track specialists.

I think that's going to change. I think the trade teams are going to start paying a little more attention to having track riders. It's funny, you know, what comes first, the chicken or the egg? These guys are starting to get on television more, that means a lot to sponsors. It all begins to feed on itself.

Third, MONEY

But the most important reason that track cycling is on television is because it's much more cost efficient to produce track cycling. Getting into the television business, the way in is through the looking glass. It's Wonderland. Nothing makes sense in the television business. Trust me! Little, if anything, makes any sense at all in the television business. The reason why most things are done elude most of us who have a certain kind of logic. But, once you understand that, you work within that system.

Track cycling is very cost

effective. Very inexpensive to produce. You can produce an hour of track cycling <u>way</u> cheaper than you can produce an hour of road cycling. You drive a truck up to the edge of the track, you throw some wires out the door, you hook some cameras up on the end, and there it is. With the roads you have to have motorcycles and wireless microwave transmission, helicopters flying overhead -- it's a technical nightmare.

Imagine trying to transmit live while you're still traveling down the road. The stuff they're bringing out for the Tour de France is literally millions of dollars worth of equipment. It's great for the people who produce the technical equipment, but the people trying to pay for it don't think it's all that swell.

Cycling's one of those sports that doesn't have the ratings to warrant the expense. The ad revenues don't justify the kinds of ratings that cycling has, whether it's track, road or anything. It's pretty meager, so you have to come to the game with your own sponsors, in a lot of cases. That's what the Federation has done with the National Championships. They've brought EDS to the table, ponied up their own money and made it happen on TV. Hopefully the rewards will be there.

How Riders Can Get Media Attention

The best way for a up-and-coming rider to get media attention, and it's cynical to say this, but the best way is to have a really spectacular crash! Coat your body in some liquid nitroglycerin and then burst into flames, and you'll make ESPN Sportscenter. You'll get your 15 minutes of fame! There are always publicity angles beyond what you do on your bicycle. It's always been difficult for cyclists in any arm of the sport to get a lot of publicity.

To get my attention, as a television broadcaster, the guy has to be a competitor, has to be capable of winning. That's what competition's all about.

Let's assume we have a room full of winners. What does it take beyond that? For television it takes some personality. **You have to be able to deliver that 15 second sound bite that we all live and die by.** You walk up and you put a microphone in a guy's face and you don't expect him to go "Uh-huh. . . " **You expect him to repeat the question you've asked him in the way of answering it.**

When you go up and say "That was a terrific ride", you compliment the guy, and you say "How do you think you won?" The guy will answer "I won by making such and such a move at 200 meters and" blah, blah, blah, "and then I threw a little hook at him coming out of the final turn and I held on and won by half a wheel and it was really great! *And the first thing I'm going to do is call my mom back home!*"

You've got to say something to relate to the average schmoo who's sitting there with his beer in his hand and his bag of pretzels. So **it's personality, speaking clearly and understanding that when I come up with a microphone and a television camera, *they're not talking to me.***

It may sound like I'm asking a

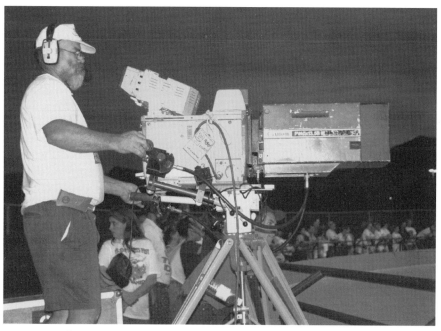

Camera man, World Cup Finals, Colorado Springs, 1994

really stupid question, but bear with me, answer the question, pretend you're talking to some guy who's never seen this before. Keep that in mind.

Most of the guys are very good about it now. They've grown up with television, they've seen how it works and a lot of them are actually media trained, especially on the big teams.

You go to guys who are on Motorola, Coors and teams like that and they've all been through media training. They've all been instructed how to answer questions, you can see it.

In my 20 years in the sport, it used to be a very common thing -- I can remember interviewing one rider after a race. I said "So, you just won the world's biggest bicycle race, how do you feel?" You want him to display some emotion or relive the moment.

He said "First I want to say that we have some wheels and tires for sale in the back of our car. Anybody who needs some good stuff, come over and buy it from us." Then he looked at me as though "Now what was the question again?" That wasn't the cool thing we were looking for with an audience out there waiting to hear about the race.

Riders need to be themselves. If a rider doesn't have a personality, that doesn't mean he needs to go out and invent one, but everyone has <u>some</u> personality. Track guys are bubbling fountains of personality, most of them.

First they have to create their accomplishment. Then they have to be open and even though the people at home may not be able to relate to the sport or to them as athletes other than with admiration, if they're human, if they display emotion, talk about their

mom, their sister or "Boy, I sure wish my dog was here -- he's my best friend, he goes with me on all my training rides." People at home are going "Aww, isn't that neat?"

Taking classes in communications, acting or that kind of thing isn't something I would discourage people from doing, though I'm not sure it's necessary to spend a lot of time doing that. People need to spend their time in the way they feel it will be best spent. There's no problem at all with being your own P.R. guy.

Role Models

I remember Brent Emery, in 1984, was Mr. Self-Promotion. Sometimes it got a little much, but he knew that no one else was going to do it for him, so he had to do it himself. He had pins made "Go for the Gold in '84 -- Brent Emery" and was handing them out to everybody. He was always self-promoting.

Nelson's like that, Nelson Vails. He's wonderful. He understands that no one else is going to toot his horn, he's got to do it himself. Occasionally someone else will come along and build him up, but pretty much, if you're going to get ahead in this world, you've got to do it yourself.

Taking classes, getting involved with public relations, things like that, are good places to start. Being part of teams who teach how to handle the media is also good, as well as studying the guys who are good at it.

Davis Phinney is Mr. P.R. Davis will stand there and answer the same question from 29 local TV guys after he wins a race and 29 newspaper guys if they happen to be around.

After all these years, Connie is an old pro with the media. Marty is learning fast how to negotiate the perils of the media waters in a multitude of cultures and languages.

Look at Michael Jordan if you want to get an idea of a guys who's really good at what he does in terms of publicity and P.R.

He sits there and answers the same stupid question about 50 times. "Well, when do you think you're going to hit your first home run in baseball?" The local news guy from Dipstick, Iowa asks him that question because he needs it for his news, then the next guy -- it's like a receiving line of guys who come up and ask him the same question day after day, night after night, when he was playing basketball before and now. He sits there and patiently answers every one, over and over.

Guys who aren't trained to do that are going to get tired of it. They're going to look up at the guy asking the question and make him feel stupid for asking. They're going to flick him off and nobody wins.

There was a guy on TV the other night asking about something the guest said he wouldn't respond to. The guy kept pushing and pushing and eventually words were exchanged and it got ugly. Those of us in the media can be as guilty of provoking situations as athletes are of being unable to deal with them. It's good and bad.

Sometimes guys who do well are not able to express themselves when they do well.

The flip side is that guys who do poorly are not always able to express themselves. That losing locker room interview is a tough one, for both the journalist and the athlete. But you have to learn to deal with both the good and the bad, and it's a learning process.

You can learn by observing those who are good at it. Classes and courses help too.

Soundbites

One of the best things to do is to repeat the question that you're asked. Cleverly. If someone says "That was a great victory, tell me about it" when you go to edit the interview, the response needs to be a complete statement. It can't be just an answer without knowing the question.

Nine times out of ten, when you go to do what's called the "soundbite", it's only going to be the guy's answer, not your question. It's a real good thing for riders to understand, especially for TV.

It isn't so important for newspaper guys, because they can write their own lead to it. They can pull quotes out and put them any way they want. They have the luxury of being able to massage their words over a period of time, but if you walk up to a guy and you have one chance to get him to say something that's going to make it on the air, then it's nice if he says it in a complete statement.

Say it's windy and rainy. If I walk up and say "Did the conditions today affect the race?" If he says "Yes, they did." I can't use that answer on the air. If the guys says something like "The conditions today were really horrible and I feel they affected the way I had to ride the race, I had to be much more conservative. I had to play a waiting game and when I got close to the finish line I was able to get around the guys who were tired and that's how I won." That's a beautiful little 15 second thing

that you can drop in with no set up or anything. That gets him on the air.

If a guy gives an answer that we can't use, he may have just won the race, but it's not going to make air. It's going to hit the floor every time. Part of that is my job. Part of my skill as an interviewer is to go there and get an answer from a guy that we can use. But it's a pleasurable experience at the level that I work most of the time if these guys are good at it. If I can go up and ask these guys a question and know they're going to work with me, I'm much more likely to approach a guy if I know he's going to give me a good answer that I can use.

More Role Models

In drag racing, there's a guy named John Force. John Force is probably the best interview in any sport, of any person I've ever seen ever. It doesn't matter what you ask him, he's going to come up with something a little off the wall, it's going to be really energetic, it's going to make great television. I know that guys who cover drag racing just love to go up and ask John something because everything he says is going to make air. He's unbelievable as a role model. He's really amazing.

In cycling there are guys like that too. Certainly Davis Phinney is one, Steve Hegg is good, Malcolm Elliott is good, though he's a little dry. Davis will throw his head back and laugh or sigh, there's going to be some punctuation, some animation. Davis is retired now.

Bigger-than-Life Trackies

The thing I like best about track racing is this. People think about the Tour de France and about how grueling it is and all that stuff. They look at bicycle racing athletes and may go to an event and stand next to a guy like Greg LeMond. He just looks like a pretty ordinary guy. You put him in street clothes and walk him down the mall and nobody's going to turn their head and look at him.

But you walk Michael Huebner through a mall with a sleeveless shirt on and shorts and people are going to look! Track guys are much more physically impressive guys. They're specimens. That's a "hook" that I've tried to use to sell the idea of track cycling to television producers and so on. These guys fit more into the mold of what Americans think of as athletes.

We always look at guys like Carl Malone in the NBA, or Shaquille O'Neal, because he's almost a freak. He's larger than life, he's larger than us. That's certainly more true of track cycling guys.

You look at someone like Curt Harnett, he doesn't look like the average guys walking down the street. He's a little "more of". He's also great with media. I'd put Curt up there with Phinney. If you want a track guy who makes for a good interview every time you talk to him, it's Curt. He can be a goof-ball. He's going to always be loose and glib, even when he's really focused and concentrating and has his race face on, his personality comes out. He allows himself to be fun and say and do neat things.

I've seen him jump up on the podium and do a little tap dance, a little pantomime, a little soft-shoe, while he was waiting for the other guy to get up there. Everybody chuckled.

He can be a goof-ball when he wants to be. He always plays to the crowd, always. He's a showman, he really is. He's a pro and he's a showman. He plays right to the crowd.

Cliff Halsey did that when he was racing. No body lit up Trexlertown like Halsey. All the girls would go

← Photographers of many track events, Casey Gibson (Cycling USA) and Mike Gladu (VeloNews). They know a lot about that technical stuff! Indy, 1994

crazy when he rode by. All the guys would slap their girlfriends "What are you looking at?" because he was big and handsome. California guy, always tan, tall, all the things all the guys wished they were and all the woman wished they had. He played to the crowd just great. All he had to do was just look up in the stands and the place would go nuts. He was good at that, too.

Another person was Danny Clark. He didn't really play to the crowd as a

The Japanese take their track cycling very seriously. They did an <u>exemplary</u> job of covering World Cup (1994). They were great. The woman being interviewed (lower right) is Hashimoto Seiko, Champion speedskater and cyclist.

personality, but he was a consummate showman on his bike. He would make every victory look like it was the end of the world.

He was capable of winning by 15 bike lengths, but he would time it so he won by four inches. He'd do a desperate lunge at the end. The crowd would be on their feet all the way through the last turn. The collective intake of air would probably stop the earth spinning on it's rotation. Everybody would gasp as he came through the last turn and wiggled through a few guys to win by two inches at the line.

He "somehow" managed to do it again and again. He was head and shoulders better than anybody out there. He always treated his competition with respect, never made them look bad. He always won in the most dramatic fashion possible. Instead of doing it the easy way, he'd always do things the hard way, making it look tough. Bike racing and every other sport is entertainment, it isn't *War and Peace.*

The Portable Tracks

The portable tracks will make a positive impact if they provide a venue that people can go and see. Whether it will ever be like it was in the '30's, I doubt it. Some people think Six-day bicycle racing can make a come back as entertainment.

In Europe Six-day races are very popular. Jack Simes talks of bike racing in Madison Square Garden again. I'd love to see it, but I'm not going to hold my breath. Vande Velde's new portable wooden track could be the kind of thing people really enjoy. It is very

exciting. The smaller the track, the neater, visually, it is. The steeper, the smaller, the better. It's like the old "riding around in the barrel" at the county fair. "How do they do that? Why don't they fall off?"

I raced on a little 140 m. track that Dale Hughes used to have in Detroit. We all called it "the little board track" because it wasn't permanent, it didn't have a location. I announced a Six-day they had at Michigan State University in an arena. I raced on it in a Madison in Detroit. 140 meters, 57 degrees, 8 seconds a lap! It was neat. It was like riding around the walls of your den! It was really tiny.

Cameras for Track Coverage

I think there were seven cameras for World Cup. There was one up on the roof, there was one on the top of the Grand Stand at the Pursuit line, there was one next to the announcer, one in the fourth turn, the boom camera, one or two hand-held cameras down inside the track, and one on the backstretch. Seven is a very good number to cover track.

In Trexlertown we did five shows which have aired on Wednesday nights on Prime. We do those with four cameras. We have a camera in Turn One, another between One and Two, a camera outside of Turn Three, and a hand-held camera moving around inside.

Sometimes we use a little palm-corder, a handicam, as a fifth camera. We mount in on the judge's stand and aim it at the finish line to get any close finish line shots. Or we might put it on the motorcycle for pacing the Keirin right into the riders' faces. Those shots

are all pasted in post-production.

There's a certain quality that needs to be used for broadcast quality. Most of the Sony Handicams, the Super VHS home video and the High 8 cameras, the little High 8, not regular 8, work really well. It's the camera itself, not so much the media. It's the way the camera processes the images.

Sony makes one that costs about $3000. It's what they call a "three-chip" camera, but it's just about the size of one of the palmcorders, about the size of a small loaf of bread, maybe two English muffins. The pictures it puts out are every bit as good as one of the Sony professional Betacams. It doesn't have the lens capability, it doesn't have the optics, but within what it will shoot, the quality is every bit as good.

A friend of mine who's a producer uses a bunch of those when he does beach volleyball. It's made it so much cheaper for him. One of those big cameras will cost you $1000 a day or more to rent, plus the guy who runs it. You might end up spending $1300-1400 a day to run one of those big Sony Betacams. He uses them mainly for what we call the "lock-down" shots, meaning there's no operator.

He'll mount one straight across the net, or he'll mount one way up high somewhere showing the whole court, and it sits there and just chugs away. Nobody has to zoom it or focus it, he just locks it down and there it is. He'll use three or four of those plus three or so Betacams that move around with operators.

He can get seven or eight cameras for the price of four or five. It doesn't

cost him any more and the quality of the broadcast is enhanced by a factor of several, but the cost is not. He may not really save that much money, but he's able to put a better product on the air for the same money. Better quality, a more interesting show.

If I sit with people and tell them what's happening during a show, they understand the difference better. It goes back to the fact that a lot of what we do on television is very transparent to the viewer at home. They don't know it's magic. How it's done isn't obvious to a lot of people watching television at home . It's fascinating.

Motion pictures are still shot on film and despite all the advances in television cameras, film is still a superior medium for processing an image. Subtleties of light and color are richer on film than on video. All the top motion pictures are still shot with film, but all the soap operas and TV programs are shot on video. It's a flatter, two dimensional image. It doesn't have as much depth and richness as an image on film. It's just flatter, there's no better way to describe it. But the advancement is amazing. Special effects are a whole other area. They are really amazing.

The TV Announcer's Life

My work is them calling me and me calling them. I call to solicit work when I know something's happening and they call me because they know me now. I've developed some momentum. Maybe one day I'll get like Phil Liggett. He doesn't call anybody! He figures "If they want me, they'll call." He never calls and solicits anything.

Nothing's set for '96, but I didn't know anything about doing '94 Track Nationals until about three weeks before it happened. I found out about the World Cup about the same time. I think a lot of that came together about the same time, the television stuff. The event, obviously, was going to happen, but the television production came together kind of late.

The Future

I started out doing television in cycling only. I figured out two things pretty quick: Number one, I like doing television. I feel like I'm good at it and I like doing it, so I want to keep doing it. I've found what I want to do with my life. Secondly, if I'm going to have a long career doing television, it isn't, presently, at least, going to be as a Cycling Color Commentator, which is how I started out, being the "expert analyst" for cycling fans.

I had a long conversation with John Beckman, who's trying to get into the business. I said "Look John, I'm not an overnight success. It took me fifteen years to get into the business." People think "Oh, Drebber just waltzed into the business and all of a sudden he's everywhere." I'm living the realization of my goals right now, I'm where I want to be in terms of working in the business. All I'll do now is more of different things.

I'm already known pretty well through the business as a guy who can do any sport. The niche that I've carved for myself is "I do the sports that Bo don't know." I don't do baseball, I don't do football, I don't do basketball. No one will ever call me to do those sports, probably. If they did I'd probably turn them down anyway.

There are a million guys out there who think that they're going to be the next Chris Berman or the next Al Michaels. I don't want to be either one of those guys. I want to be me. What I do is go to different events in totally different sports and do what I do for all those different sports and do them well. Professionally, the things that I'm interested in are: everything!

I can go to a stock car race, to a bodybuilding event, to a track cycling event, to a triathlon, and do all those things on four consecutive days. I'm interested in and inquiring about all those things to learn about them. The skill that I've developed over fifteen years is a lot of acquired skill.

You don't just sit there with a director screaming in your ear that a commercial break is coming, you're in the middle of a sentence and the guy starts counting you down "ten, nine, . . ." and you've got to somehow finish your thought and smoothly transition into a commercial while doing it exactly on his count. That's one of the skills I bring to the table.

I don't think any of us are going to get rich out of this. Gil (Gibby) is in that same category. He probably could have gotten into something else that would have made him more money, but that isn't what gets him out of bed every morning.

Now that Marty won the World Championships they have a bigger lever to pry with in terms of things they want to accomplish. Gil said immediately after Marty won that if he was going to win again next year, they still have a lot of work to do. Next year the World's are on a small track again, so the training will be different. Instead of training for big horsepower and top end it's got to be more quickness and acceleration. Tactics are different on a small track than a big track.

My God-given talent is probably my voice and a fairly good command of the language, parents who taught me the language properly. Beyond that it's just been a lot of hard work. But fun -- I wouldn't trade it for anything.

I'll continue to do cycling because that is what burns down in my belly. Track cycling is what I like the best. I'll always do that.

Everybody thinks I'm making a lot of money. I'm just another guy with my lunch pail trying to make my mortgage payment and put food on the table, just like everybody else, but I'm happy. I love getting up in the morning and going to work.

There are plenty of guys making lots of money who are miserable -- I'm not one of them!

Nobody gets in this camera's way. As the spectators at World Cup '94 line the fence, this boom camera misses none of the action. It went wherever the riders went, up, down and all around.

Chapter 17
Velodrome Director
Pat McDonough

Pat McDonough is a seven time National Champion and an Olympic Silver Medalist. He began his career as a Junior National Champion, winning the Kilometer in 1978 and the Points Race in 1979. He was National Madison Champion in 1982 and National Champion in Team Pursuit in 1981, '82 and '85. In 1985 he also won the Points Race. In the 1984 Olympics he won an Olympic Silver medal, thrilling a stadium full of 1000s with one of the great Team Pursuit performances of all time.

Pat has been Director of Lehigh Velodrome, in Trexlertown, Pennsylvania, the most active track program in the country, since 1989.

How I Got Started

I was born July 22, 1961 and grew up in Long Beach, CA. I was involved in short-track speedskating before I began bicycle racing. At that time there was a very well known club in ice skating circles called the Mora at Iceland in Paramount.

In June of 1974 there was a criterium in Cerritos, about a half a mile from my house. A lot of the people who skated also raced bicycles. They told my dad and I we ought to go look at it, that it was good training. It was one of the old industrial park criteriums common at that time.

I joined the Paramount Bicycle Club and rode with them the first few years. I was a smallish kid, not just my height, which never changed a whole lot, but I was real small for my age. I wasn't too impressive my first couple of years of riding, I didn't ride track my first two years, I just rode the road.

Back then, Encino was the only track in Southern California. San Diego hadn't been built yet, nor Dominguez Hills. It may have seemed like a long way to drive an hour and a half from San Diego, but today we get people racing at Trexlertown who drive from Virginia, three and a half hours away.

I went to Encino because they had special sessions with track bikes and riders who gave basic instruction. I went out there one Saturday and I was the only guy. Dave Mulica of the South Bay Wheelmen, a member of the '72 Olympic Team, took me around and I got involved in their program. I was able to borrow their bikes to race for the first couple of months.

To be honest, cycling was my second sport for a long time. It wasn't until I was in my Junior years that I really got into it.

The first year I won a Junior Championship was in 1978, here at Trexlertown. Then I rode the Junior Worlds, again at Trexlertown. It was the first time I won a Championship and the first time I represented my country, both at Trexlertown.

I went back to California and skated, but that was the last year,

"I likely get a half a dozen to a dozen people every year inquiring about building a velodrome. They'll say "We're going to make money." "Wow, you are?" I'll ask them, "Tell me how! I want to know too."

I'm working to ensure that the track is going to be here for another 20 years."

because I felt I had to make a choice. My dream had always been to go the Olympics and at that time short-track indoor skating, wasn't in the Olympic Games. I felt I had a much better chance if I rode a bike, so the winter of 1979 was the last year I skated. I was one of many people who did both sports at that time.

Back then, bicycle racing didn't even start until April. There was not a race to be found, even in California. In March, Time Trails would start. Then, in the first week of October, everything would shut down. There was no racing and here was another sport that utilized the same major muscle groups (skating).

If you take a look at a skater's position, it is very similar to a rider's position. The knees are bent, the crouch -- it's pretty simple to imagine a bicycle underneath a skater.

In cycling, the "I-T" band, the muscle that goes from the hip and along the outside of the leg, gets tight in a lot of people. You see people trying to stretch that all the time.

In skating, when you push out with your leg, you really stretch that out. You use a lot of the same muscles and connections, but you're using them in a different manner. You're strengthening them by fully extending them and using them differently. It can be an advantage, especially for somebody who is young, who's developing physically. We're trying to develop that.

Skating's tough, because it usually takes a couple of years for somebody to develop to the point where they can get a good workout. The in-line skates offer a wider balance point, so that people can generally, within a very short time, get a good workout on them.

My Influences

A lot of people helped me in the early years. Buddy Campbell, Ted Ernst, Jerry Mulrooney, who ran a lot of the Schwinn shops back then and was a sponsor of the Schwinn-Paramount team.

One of the neatest things, when we were racing, happened at Encino before a lot of guys took off for Trexlertown. You could go out on any given night and watch Gibby Hatton and Jerry Ash Match Sprint! Ron Skarin, Ralph Therrio and Paul Deem raced there -- it was the 1976 Olympic Team! It was basically a bunch of Californians and Leigh Barczewski. Those guys all raced at Encino and Chuck Pranke ran the show.

Early Racing

Chuck put on racing with all these great cyclists. We had enough good cyclists at that point to put on two or three Senior classes, a Women's class, and a Junior's class. My group, the Intermediates usually didn't get to ride as much.

Chuck started a program in the Saturday races where the Intermediates would come out 2 or 3 hours before the program started and have a series of races. Then we'd take a break, eat or whatever, and come back later for the evening session and race a couple of races.

It was a Points series and Pranke personally went out and got Campy grouppos and all kinds of things, prizes for the points series for the whole year. It was great because when he was doing that stuff, I decided I liked track more than road and that was the direction I wanted to go. That

was fun -- my personal battles with Mark Whitehead.

Mark and I grew up within about 10 miles of each other. We're the same age. The first bike race I ever went to in my life, I knew nothing about bike racing. It was probably the closest I came to winning that whole year as a Midget. It was a parking lot criterium on about a half mile course.

I came from speedskating. We were in this little pack. They rang the bell, and I went. When they rang the

"My dad kept me going . . . "

bell in skating it was time to go, but it was a very short distance. Mark sat on my wheel the entire last lap and just came around me right at the finish. That was my first experience with Mark. What I found out later is that that was Mark's first licensed bike race too. He had raced a bunch of other races, but that was his first as a licensed rider.

Chuck Pranke was a tremendous influence at the track in the early days, but if I'm going to give credit to anybody, I'm going to give credit to my dad.

My dad kept me going at the beginning when I was racing as a first year Intermediate. I was scrawny, I didn't even weigh 100 pounds yet. I was very little. I was being beaten by guys who were 15-16 years old. There were kids in the field who were shaving and I wasn't even 100 pounds! It wasn't real close.

My dad kept my spirits up. He told me "We're in this for fun. Don't worry about it." later on, when I was improving, he was there and he always has been. There's definitely no doubt about it, if anybody has affected me in this sport -- and a lot of very good people have -- it's really my old man who made it happen for me. He didn't know any more about the sport in the beginning than I did.

My experience at Trexlertown with coaching is that if the parents don't have an interest, this sport is very difficult. I know very few elite riders whose parents weren't behind them. (though sometimes they can be too supportive.)

Harvey's dad was great. As far as

the way Harvey was able to analyze things and stuff like that, it became real obvious why, when you met his dad. He's a chip off the old block. There are many things I found out later when I quit riding and found some old East European magazines and whatever I could beg, borrow or steal, and I showed them to Harvey and he said "Wow, I didn't know I was doing the East German stuff!" It was funny seeing Harvey's hair-brained ideas elsewhere.

How I Became T-Town Velodrome Director

Trexlertown has a tremendous amount of history for me. I came to T-Town in 1978 with my dad, won my first National title here as a Junior in the Kilometer, was named to the Junior World Team that year, and rode for the U.S. for the first time. I was just turning 17.

After the Junior Worlds in the late '70s, most of the top riders in California had moved out here. The track was new. Robert Rodale's enthusiasm for the sport and financial commitment were unparalleled. There were about 10-15 guys from around the country that they housed for free. Jack Simes ran the track back then.

They housed the riders, fed them, and gave them coaching jobs. Back when sponsorship was virtually non-existent in this sport, these guys were being supported. It was easy for them to get the best guys here.

During that time a lot of other riders came to spend the summer. Several of them would get together and rent a row house. I told my dad I wanted to stay here to race and he agreed. It was a very big change in my life, all of a sudden I was far away from my family and spending the summer alone as a 17-year-old, making my own decisions.

I came back here in 1980 with Gibby, <u>really</u> on my own, with about two nickels to rub together. He and I made a go of it for two or three years before I began to make my final preparations for the Olympic Games in L.A.

I moved out to L.A. for the second time with my wife-to-be. After the Games, we got married. A few months after we had our first baby, we decided that the area where we could afford to <u>live</u> in L.A. was not a great neighborhood to raise a family. That was 1986.

So, I had been in T-Town in '78, came back in '79 and moved to Pennsylvania in 1980. I stayed for '81 and '82 and spent '83 and '84 on the road getting ready for the Games. '85 I spent in L.A. and in 1986 we moved back here again.

I called up Dave Tellyer, who was running the track at the time, and told him I was coming back out there. He said great, they had a program where they were trying to get the local kids ready for Nationals. They had just lost their coach and they needed one.

He could also get me work in the Bicycle League and maybe the Air Products program. All of that ended up being $2,000-3,000 for the whole summer.

I knew there were a lot more races where I could get my wheel in and make a couple of bucks here and there. Within a couple of weeks during the

summer there's a $10,000 prize list within a three or four hour drive of T-Town. That's the reason we get people here from all over the world.

So, I moved back here in '86 and started up the coaching program. I was planning to do the same in '87. I planned to keep racing for a couple more years. I really didn't plan on going to the '88 (Olympics) at that point.

I busted up my collarbone pretty bad at the track. I was going all out and got taken down real hard. It was busted in two or three places. It was a prime race. I was in a group -- $250 to lap the field. One of the riders in the front decided he didn't want me coming around him, so he took me to the rail. He felt as bad about it later as anybody else. It happens.

Then we had Nationals here that same year. I spent all my time getting the kids ready and the group did better than it ever had before.

At the same time, right after Nationals, the person who had been in the Technical Manager position told me that he was leaving. He didn't want to just tell Dave he was leaving. I told him I was really interested.

While I had won some titles in the sport, I had never made any money. Here was an opportunity for me to stay in the sport, do some other things I wanted to do and get paid for it! I jumped on the opportunity. After the '88 season, Dave stepped down as Director. At the time, I really *didn't* want the job.

I think we went three months without a Director. I didn't have any business background. I knew a lot

about the sport and cared about it.

Finally, some of the Board members and I talked about the possibility of getting someone to run the business side of things while I ran the racing side of it, the coaching side. The board met and then told me that they only wanted one guy to do it and they wanted <u>me</u> to do it. I could only think "*I don't want to do it.*"

I got called into Bob Rodale's office. I went in thinking "Okay, I'm just going to tell him. This is what I want to do. All I want to do is coach. I don't want to get involved in the business. I don't think I can do it, I don't think it would be fair to the track." -- I had it all lined out.

Forty-five minutes later I'm shaking Bob Rodale's hand, thanking him for the opportunity to run the velodrome! The best laid plans of mice and men . . . .

He told me "Hey, I'm not asking you not to make a mistake. I understand you're going to make them. Don't even worry about that." He told me in no uncertain terms that he felt I was the right person and that I could do the job.

I immediately went into panic mode, as I usually do when things like this happen, and spent the better part of the next six weeks, from 9 AM to about 2 or 3 AM, going through files, reading everything I could, trying to take a crash course in *everything that we did*. I struggled through the next year or two.

In retrospect I would say that what Bob saw was probably two things. 1) He saw that I really care for this place. I have a true love for the velodrome

here. A lot of neat things happened to me here. Winning National titles, representing my country, you name it, this place has been a big part of shaping who I am.

From that standpoint, 2) I feel a big responsibility in getting back to it. That's not something that, if you bring in a business person, you can make happen.

I'm not saying everybody can learn how to run a business, that would be foolhardy, but we have a Board that oversees us, making sure that the same mistakes aren't made again and again. It came down to Bob Rodale saying "You're the guy." '89 was my first full season as Director. Now I'm getting ready for '96 (Olympic Trials will be held at Trexlertown).

Sponsorship

The most difficult thing I've had to deal with is sponsorship. Sponsors are both waiting to be approached and needing to be developed.

What we're attempting right now at T-Town is to develop more sources of support for our livelihood than just one, even though that one has been wonderful.

The key to success is to be in a position where you have a number of important players to support the business. If, when Bob Rodale died, the Board had decided that velodrome racing was not what they wanted to do, we'd be done.

Right now we're in the process of setting up a trust fund to provide for future security. Bean counters question why the company still supports the velodrome.

We want to set up a trust where we can start taking donations. Rodale can make donations as part of a supportive group and not have to bear the full burden as the primary supporter.

When the trust fund gets to a certain level, employees could start coming off the payroll at Rodale and we could start supporting more of our own expenses.

The likelihood is that our offices are going to be moving out to the track, so we need to do some of those things anyway. Right now we're housed in Emmaus, about eight miles from the track, in one of the Rodale buildings.

My Best Advice

I likely get a half a dozen to a dozen people every year inquiring about building a velodrome. In the eight years that I've been here, two of them have been built.

They say "We're going to build a velodrome. We've got this and we've got that . . . . I need some information on how you run things since you're the best place." They'll say "We're going to make money."

"Wow, you are? " I'll ask them "Tell me how! I want to know too." I think we could make money too, but we'd have to run things very differently.

What I usually suggest is that it's relatively easy to bring funding together to build something. That's something that a lot of people have an interest in. But it's very different for people to donate to maintain things. The glamor isn't quite there. Certainly, not only for maintaining on

a physical nature, but maintaining the facility from the standpoint of over-seeing, ensuring programming and ensuring that other people are going to be there.

What I've told people (no one yet has taken my advice, but I'm waiting for someone to do it) is one of two things: a) add a million dollars to the plan that you need or b) cut the venue by a million dollars. Make the venue a little less extravagant.

Take that money and create a trust fund. With the annual profits of the trust fund you can ensure that there will be a permanent staff, on-going programming, and some other things.

Yeah, a park may be willing to do it now, but within two or three years the park's going to say "Yeah, but we can't afford it anymore, so see you guys later."

This has happened in Indianapolis and some other places. Instead of that, the money would come from the trust. It's going to be there every year.

The more people who donate to the trust the better, even to the point where, when profits happen, they get dumped back into the trust. The tracks in the future are going to have to think of that and it doesn't preclude the tracks that already exist from doing that.

Pat shows Janie her latest Pursuit time. U.S. National Championships, 1994.

What made T-Town different, what "made" this track, is that Bob Rodale supported it at a level that this sport -- in fact, cycling in general -- had never been supported before in this country. He did that for a number of years.

The first three years, the entire Olympic Team trained here. After '76,

Anton Tkac, who won the Sprints in Montreal, came down here and raced.

The first couple of years they spent a lot of money -- they spent more money than I spend now -- but they created a "personae" around this place. They created an awareness for people around the country and around the world. They all knew about this track. It enabled the Directors who came after to do a lot of things that would not have been possible without that high level of support and that continued support on a different level.

What I'm trying to work on is ensuring that the track is going to be here for another 20 years. While we're trying to do some things on a physical level, we're also working on the structure of how we're governed, how we're funded.

It might take 10 years to get there, but if we have a trust that is able to pay for the majority, if not all the expenses of the staff by then, we'll be a great position to continue. Rodale can be a sponsor just like anybody else and they won't have the whole burden. I really see that as the way for tracks.

The beautiful wood track in Minnesota cost more than two and one half million dollars (*note: Blaine was built for the 1992 Olympic Trials*). Considering what's happening with it, or rather, what's not happening, would they have been better off raising more money in the first place or down-sizing what they wanted to do, to ensure that there's going to be activity?

We have been able to do things here that other tracks can't do. I don't have to worry about the bottom line from the standpoint of my salary. It's part of what we have been building upon.

It might make better sense to charge people more for certain services, but we have built this place to give as much service to as many different people as possible, whether they could afford it or not. That's why our development programs are free of charge. We go out and get sponsorship to cover those expenses.

In addition, I don't have to worry about my people putting in extra time because that's taken care of. Another track might look at it that, in addition to their own expenses, the event cost, the promotional cost, the additional venue cost that you might have, there's the track overhead. On top of that they may have to deal with those same issues from a staff perspective.

We are looking at ways that we can use a trust to continue to keep programs free. The most successful program besides ours is the AAF (Amateur Athletic Foundation). That's a free program. What makes our program so unique is that support, the feeling of: "I can try this!"

There's a tremendous amount of expense in bike racing today. If we can come up with ways to try it without having to spend any money or with the support of additional sponsorship, it's easier later on for them to open up their wallet in other ways.

The land and the forming of the job to build this track was donated by Bob Rodale, but it was finished with county dollars.

I'd say it was half completed when the county came in to finish it up fin-ancially. The contracts were already signed. Bob turned over that land plus some adjoining land for a park.

The American Track Racing Association (ATRA)

We are trying to create more communication among tracks through our new association. At this point we're calling it the American Track Racing Association, "ATRA" (maybe Gillette will be a sponsor!) *(laughs)*I guess I'm responsible for starting it. I felt very strongly that the tracks, at least those who had staff, needed to meet. We all went out to Colorado Springs on our own dime and the Federation put us up.

Professional track Directors were invited. We've put our notes together, and sent them to all the track directors. We would like to put together a national calendar for track cycling.

We're also working on a concept for a series of races that would be held throughout the year. Each of us is going to put on what we call a "pilot" race to see if we can organize and accomplish things that we all agree need to be done.

There are plenty of areas of disa-greement, but at the meeting, when we felt we were running into one of those areas, someone would put their hand up and say "Next subject!" We figured if five or six of us couldn't agree on a subject we weren't going to be able to get very far with the other tracks in the country.

Tracks represented at the meeting were Nick and Tim from L.A., Dick Kelly from Indianapolis, Barclay Kruse from Minnesota, and John Vande Velde with the new portable track. Kathy Volski from Houston was invited, but she got caught in the flood. Walt (San Diego) was irate not to be invited. Colorado Springs was invited but didn't make it.

The first meeting was small because if we tried to bring all track directors together, 15 people who didn't know each other wouldn't be able to get as much done. Each person at the meeting was given certain responsibilities for the organization.

Only professional track Directors were invited. The problem with non-professional track directors is that if one of them convinces the rest of us that he can get the logo together for the USA Grand Prix, then all of a sudden something happens to his business and he doesn't do it, he's a volunteer. He's not paid to do it.

We want to get this thing off the ground. We need to move quickly and the best way to do that is to keep the group small and manageable at first, a group which could host major events right *now*.

We don't want the group to stay small. We're getting things organized and taking it to everybody. Each one of us who attended the meeting accepted a level of responsibility to do certain things.

The national track calendar will go to all of the tracks. They're going to be given ten working days to respond and add their events to the calendar. It's not going to be possible for some of them.

Portland ran a Six-Day race. I didn't know they had any plans to run it until I saw it in VeloNews about three weeks before it ran. A track like that can't afford to run ads for months. We've convinced Cycling USA and we're doing the same with VeloNews, to print our calendar separately so there's a distinct track calendar. These are things that we want to coordinate among the tracks.

We can get these things done if we all work together. We'll also send a packet on to Lisa Voight and all the people in the Federation including the Board.

We want the association run by the velodromes themselves. If you look at most sports, the venues run the sport. The USCF might say "We're giving this support to that track cyclist" or "We're making this track bike" or we're doing this or that.

What needs to be supported is the specific places where you can <u>do</u> this kind of racing. That means only about 20 places in this country, of which only six are suitable for international competition at this point.

That doesn't mean that if other tracks get the funding that they cannot also do this soon. They can update and change. We can add to that, but at this point less than one third of our existing velodromes are suitable for international competition.

From that standpoint alone we need to start supporting our venues better and ensuring that the venues we do have continue. We need to organize.

There might have been a better way to do it. It would have been much better if we could have been part of the House of Delegates meeting. We're in the process of coming up with an annual meeting where all velodromes are invited. Then we can do our annual calendar session.

Next we'll put a small board together which will meet one other time per year. We'll look at proposals from all the tracks. We want to effect legislation. We want to organize to the point where we have a national mailing list and a national newsletter specifically for track cycling.

The more organized we are, the more attractive we're going to be to sponsors and the cyclists themselves.

There's no doubt that the Cycling Federation and the USOC recognize a responsibility to track cycling -- that's where all the World level medals are being won. If we stay as separate voices in the wind, that responsibility will never be fully realized.

If we get organized, it will make it easier for them, and that's fine. We want their financial support and if that will be more effective by getting organized, then so much the better.

That's what the meeting was about. We wanted to be sure that within a week we had contacted and talked to every velodrome in the country.

Eventually track cycling needs to be as strong as any other arm of the USCF. Those are the long term goals. There are a lot of things that need to be worked out. That's one of the reasons we're putting together this pilot race program

More than anything we want to get information from and to all the tracks. What does each track charge for sponsorship, for this and this and this? For us to centralize that kind of information so we're able to put

together a package, it's going to take a little time. We all agree this sport has potential. It just needs to be focused and developed.

Format

One of the things that hurts us in the media on the US front is that Americans are used to a simplistic format. Track cycling is hard for beginners to understand.

I guess you could say that football's not exactly a simple format event, but it's standardized.

If I watch a football game, it doesn't matter what stadium I watch it at, it's going to be four quarters, this long. At tracks, everyone's running whatever program they're running.

Certainly for a national series the format should be standardized and interesting for spectators, easily televisable, well photographed, easy to understand and one that has some kind of outcome.

One of the problems is that you go to your basic bicycle race and every race is a race, but what does it mean? If it's an Omnium, are the spectators informed as to the fact that it's an Omnium? If they are, are they informed as to what's happening out there *because* it's an Omnium?

An Omnium may not be the right format for a televised race unless it's something like the top four or five guys go on to race in the final race.

Pat shouts times to Janie Eickhoff in the Pursuit, Olympic Trials, 1992. In 1995, Janie won Pan Am Gold. Good job!

You have an Omnium to determine who's going to race in the Final. The Final is it -- it's the *Final*. Even though I might have won three out of four in the Omnium races, I got fifth in the final race, I got fifth place. That's the way it goes.

We're trying to think of a format that can be televised, that has interest for a number of people and basically is a commercial formula.

Most of the track Directors have found that when you go out and try to run an Olympic style event, it's difficult because you get a large group of people who are cyclists who want to do this. You can't show people a Pursuit on TV.

Even World Records are only

"maybe" exciting. I've never seen a Pursuit on TV that's exciting. I've seen a ton of Pursuits that were exciting if you were there. You just can't see it well enough on TV. Even on a split screen, it's so hard to tell where they are in relation to each other.

(note: sounds like a media /photography problem)

Even my Olympic Pursuit, I know how exciting it was to be there, but it didn't look that great on TV. I was <u>in</u> it, so I was prejudiced, but even then, a good Pursuit on TV isn't as exciting as a mediocre Keirin.

The basic thing about it is that people understand the Keirin even if they don't understand anything about it. They ring the bell and the first person across the line wins.

We need to translate more of that into our sport, spectator-friendly events. That doesn't mean everything has to be Sprint oriented, either. The events are going to be put together in a way to attract people from the media. All you need at a track is one person.

There's no doubt that the next year or two, we're going to have Sprints because we have the World Champion (Marty Nothstein). That's going to add credibility to the series immediately.

If the World Champion shows up to race the series and they advertise the series and that the World Champion will be there and everything else -- WOW!

Chapter 18
Rules and Officials

Rules in cycling can vary, depending on the level of competition and the location of the event. The United States Cycling Federation (USCF), located in Colorado Springs, CO, is the body which governs cycling in the United States under the umbrella of the U.S. Olympic Committee. The Union Cycliste Internationale (UCI) governs cycling internationally.

Riders competing in the United States follow USCF rules. If the event is international, whether in this or a foreign country, UCI rules and procedures prevail. As is logical, most of the rules are the same. Differences may be explained by the fact that the UCI, as the higher level body, can change and amend rules without the permission or agreement of the USCF. The USCF is a member of the UCI and has as much input (but no more) as any other member.

Some UCI rules may not be enforced in domestic competition because they are viewed as particular to international competition. Others may be too new for the USCF to have effected changes here as yet. In any event, USCF rules should not be in conflict with those of the UCI. When US athletes go to international competition they need to review any differences since they are responsible for knowing them. In addition, officials have their own RuleBook interpretation materials which riders never see (hmmm . . .).

The 1994 Rule Book devotes 11 of its 140 pages to Track Racing, including both National Championship and other track events. The first section gives clear specifications on track markings applicable to any track of any size, which serve as reference for starting and finishing the various events.

The second section reviews rider conduct in Mass Start events (Points and Madison) which apply to riding the track in general. Most of the rules have been set down for safety as well as guidance in how the events differ. Organizers of events must notify riders of any requirements not in the RuleBook.

Officials have the job of enforcing the RuleBook. Reviewed here are responsibilities of various officials and

Officials take a break between the action. World Cup, 1994

their positions as set down in the USCF Rule Book. In local events more variation is expected and tolerated, but at the National Championship level things are more strictly enforced since outcomes at that level can be a deciding factor in an athlete's career, especially if the National Championship is also the Olympic Trials.

For the most part, officials are people who have been involved in cycling for a long time and truly love the sport (= low pay). Officials are expected to be as impartial as possible for the sake of fair competition. Sometimes riders and their fans debate this impartiality when they receive an adverse ruling. At those times officials are viewed as human beings who have prejudices and foibles just like anyone else -- (but until someone invents a computer that can unfailingly judge a Sprint, we'll just have to "make do" with what we have.)

Local venues are great practice for higher level competition for referees as well as for competitors. Dominguez Hills, 1994

Officials

There are seven categories of officials covered in the Rule Book: the Chief Referee, Assistant Referees, the Starter, Scorers, Judges, Timers and Registrars.

All USCF officials are categorized according to training and experience. Each official must work his/her way up the ladder to positions of increasingly greater authority.

Lately officials are further differentiated on the basis of "Road" or "Track" designations. Velodrome enthusiasts are very happy to see this recent change as track events are considerably different than road events.

Registrars

Responsibilities of the Registrars are clerical. They must actually see each rider's valid racing license. They verify the identity of the rider (as well as possible) and, most importantly, that the riders are signed up for the correct <u>level</u> of race.

As noted under qualification for

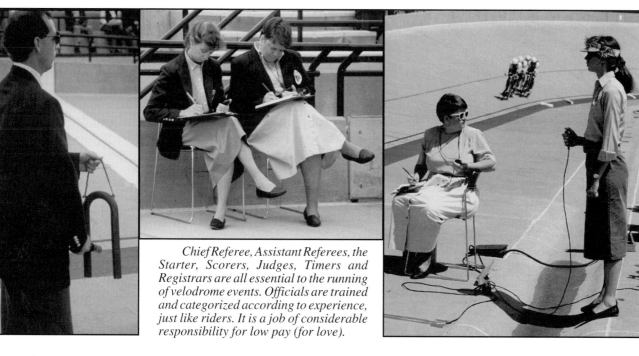

Chief Referee, Assistant Referees, the Starter, Scorers, Judges, Timers and Registrars are all essential to the running of velodrome events. Officials are trained and categorized according to experience, just like riders. It is a job of considerable responsibility for low pay (for love).

the various events, some are strictly according to category. If a "Cat 4" rider wants to ride in an "Cat 1" race at the National level and tries to sign up, the Registrar is responsible for telling the rider that s/he is not eligible.

Registrars are usually very strict about licenses. Riders who have not yet received them in the mail or who leave them at home generally can't ride. It's fairly cut and dried. The reason for this is that the rider may be under some sort of suspension or other ruling where the license has been withheld and the rider cannot be allowed to ride. Registrars are responsible for seeing that rules related to participation are enforced and one of these involves riders actually showing their licenses. The only exception is by appealing to the Chief Referee.

Officials know that accidents ("My dog ate it!") can happen, but they also expect riders to be responsible for themselves. Unfortunately, riders have been known to try to get away with not having a valid license, so officials get even more strict.

Timers

If timed events are offered, as they are at the National Championships, Timers are essential. They don't just sit there with a watch, they are also responsible for knowing what times must be kept for what events. There are two ways of timing track events, by hand and by machine.

There is a Chief Timer who is responsible for coordinating the efforts of the other Timers. Wide variations in timing must be resolved by the Chief Timer into a viable and final official time.

At least two Timers must be on duty recording separate times with watches that give time in .01 seconds. The watches must be accurate to one second every 48 hours or better. The Rule Book states a preference for more than two timers. All times will be averaged into a final time to 0.1 (tenth) second. If one of the times seems off, it may not be discarded unless the Timer who took it says that it is not a valid time (maybe s/he was distracted or knows s/he didn't react quickly enough).

If the timing is done by automatic timing equipment, the timing equipment operator is responsible as an Assistant Timer and reports to the Chief Timer with results from that equipment. Machines must record to .01 (hundredth) second for most races. Those 1 kilometer or less must be recorded to .001 (thousandth) second.

"Adequate" hand timing must be in place for back-up and verification of the automatic timing. The reason for this is that depending on machines is only as reliable as the machines. Riders who ride their best race only to find that they have no finish time are pretty upset, so this safeguard is generally appreciated.

(Marilyn Allen notes: "At most events, the Chief Judge acts as Chief Timer")

Judges

Judges are responsible for picking the order of finishers in a race. The Chief Judge is the final determiner of finish order, but this is directly reflective of the work of the judges since it is impossible for any one person alone to pick finish order. Some races are difficult even with all judges doing their best work because the finishes are so close.

Photofinish cameras are always found at National Championship and other top level events to assure fairness and break finishes which appear to be ties, if possible. The person operating the finish camera acts as a judge in that position and reports to the Chief Judge with either finished film or order-of-finish information, as instructed. After any protests and appeals have been processed and finalized, finish film will be returned to the race organizer.

Riders are assigned as many places as required according to race rules. In the event of ties, riders are assigned equal placings.

Scorers

Scorers are responsible for keeping track of laps gained or lost during the progress of a race by each competitor. At the end of the race, scorers report laps gained or lost for each rider to the Chief Judge. Scorers are also responsible for operating lap cards and bells for races in which they are appropriate.

Starter

The Starter is usually the guy or gal with the gun. A whistle can also be used, but the Starter's pistol is more

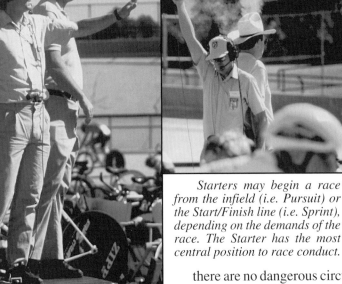

common, especially in higher level events such as a National Championship.

The Starter's position is key because s/he is responsible for giving many last minute instructions which the riders must follow. Often Starters will look long and steadily at riders, asking "Do you understand?" knowing that sometimes riders are so keyed up

that they aren't hearing a word they're saying.

Starters call riders to the line, remind them of distance and any special rules, and notify them as to the location of the finish line if it is different than where the rider starts. They do a final visual check of equipment and riding attire to assure

Starters may begin a race from the infield (i.e. Pursuit) or the Start/Finish line (i.e. Sprint), depending on the demands of the race. The Starter has the most central position to race conduct.

there are no dangerous circumstances which can be foreseen. If the Starter determines that a rider's equipment is dangerous or attire is not correct, the rider will not be allowed to start until the appropriate action is taken. Even such details as end plugs in handlebars should not escape the Starter's notice.

The Starter notifies other officials of an impending start, verifies that a "clean" start has occurred and stops the race if it has not. A good Starter can make the event move right along

or can allow it to lag. A good Starter is a real attribute to a smooth, flowing event.

Assistant Referees

The Assistant Referees advise the Chief Referee as to infractions and other circumstances which require judgement. The Chief Referee cannot be at all vantage points around the track and so must depend on other eyes and judgements.

Assistant Referees report rule violations whether the riders involved protest or not. They are responsible for seeing that rules are obeyed. Rule infractions are to be written, signed by the official making the judgment, and submitted to the Chief Referee for enforcement. While the Chief Referee can rule another way, this tends to counteract the purpose of having Assistants, so generally this is not done. The Chief Referee relies on Assistants.

It is not uncommon for several officials to get together to confer on questionable circumstances involved in a possible infraction. A big event will see a Race Jury making important decisions.

Rulings, unfortunately, are not as

clear-cut as developing a set of rules might intend.

Rules sometimes include "intent" of a rider as a factor and this is not always easy to determine. As noted, officials have a mandate to impartiality. Sometimes an official who is responsible for a particular section of the track, for instance, might not have been able to see an occurrence as clearly as an official standing in another vantage point.

The last category of official is the Top Dog, the Big Banana, ...

The Chief Referee

The Chief Referee is the big cheese on the track. S/he is responsible for the overall event as relates to rules and their enforcement. The Chief Referee's powers are quite comprehensive. S/he not only enforces rules, but s/he also *interprets* them. That is a heady level of power.

If an issue is not specifically covered in the Rule Book, the Chief Referee can institute his/her own ruling (also known as "can make it up"). Fortunately Chief Referees are usually selected with care. It is hoped that rulings necessary without the guidance of the Rule Book will be accomplished with knowledge, experience and wisdom.

The Chief Referee can take any measures deemed necessary to complete the task of racing while assuring the safety of all involved. The Chief Referee can penalize or recommend the suspension of riders who disobey rules or commit offenses. S/he can interpret input given by Assistant Referees in light of their position on the track and their experience levels.

The only measure a Chief Referee cannot take against a rider is suspension, though this can be recommended. Decisions of Chief

Junior Champion Ednita Kelly has her bicycle "rolled out" by an official to verify adherence to Junior gear restrictions. This bicycle used to belong to Gibby Hatton. Ednita isn't riding a bicycle, she's riding history!

Referees under the rules is final pending protests.

Duties of other officials can be assigned by the Chief Referee for each event and varying types of authority may be assigned to them.

Payment of officials, insurance charges, etc., must be completed by the Chief Referee who submits an invoice to the race organizer and receives a check with which to take care of business prior to the end of the event.

A wide variety of other clerical work must be completed by the Chief Referee, including incident reports, race reports, a check for insurance charges, a copy of race results, a list of any unlicensed riders, and release forms signed by riders. Incident reports must be submitted to USCF offices immediately following the race. Within five days, the District Representative must receive other paper work which is forwarded to the USCF "promptly".

The only circumstances under which a Chief Referee can also be a member of the club putting on the event is if no one else is available.

Officials' Fees

When officials fees are reviewed it may be a source of wonder that anyone willingly accepts the important responsibility and hard work in these positions with such low hourly pay. The most any official can get (the Chief Referee) is $150 per day.

That may not sound too bad until you consider the level of responsibility that this position entails. It is certain to involve many more hours than those in a single day, plus, the nature of high level events is that they may go far longer than 8 hours.

If the event is a low level event, a Chief Referee will only be paid $40 for however long the day lasts and however many hours it takes to organize things and complete paper work.

Officials receive "free" trips to the events they serve and food or money for meals. They also receive "basic housing" if they must stay overnight. But it's not your average "get rich quick" scheme, and officials don't exactly live the good life. They must love the sport. The ones who do are around year after year after year. USCF personnel and riders get to know them and know how they view different issues in the various events.

Politics

While officials are pledged to impartiality, this does not necessarily relate to how rules might be interpreted. Some may interpret one way, another a different way. Often experienced riders already know what they can "get away with" if certain officials are on the job. Sometimes the official in question is a regular on the rider's home track and has ruled in a certain way on a certain issue consistently.

In this respect, experienced riders have an advantage which inexperienced riders do not have. In Time Trials, this may be more cut and dried, but in an event such as Sprints much more diversity is seen in rule interpretation.

Politics plays a part, not necessarily because of anyone's intentions. Rules are left open to interpretation so they are also left open to differing perceptions. If you watch velodrome racing over the years, you will see what appear to be miscarriages of justice, the same as in all sports and all situations in life. If you enter the fray, you may become a casualty of politics and it is good to understand this from the outset.

What can be done? Individuals, clubs and other interested parties need to continually fight to correct injustices and change rules that need changing.

New enthusiasts are needed to become part of yet another area within this sport which needs people. People who are willing to spend the time and energy to continue elevating bicycle racing to its highest levels of performance by developing excellent judgement. Judging of an event takes years of practice with experienced supervision. Some people will have a better "eye" than others.

All competitors should feel confident that equal opportunity and fairness to all competitors will be enforced by the officials who control their destinies. Those who have fought the fight for years get worn out and need reinforcements. If you fall in love with this sport, this is another area that needs your abilities!

There are many low key essential jobs to be done at all levels.

An Official's View
Marilyn Allen

Marilyn Allen was asked to give views of officiating specifically due to her role as Chief Referee at the 1992 Olympic Trials. She is a highly experienced and highly qualified official. She is also a UCI Commissaire, a status reserved for those authorized to officiate at international levels. She has some definite opinions on officiating and officials.

Her husband Jim is also an official and interjects some additional points.

How I Got Started

My brother competed, so I saw my first bike race about 43-44 years ago. In those days in Victoria (British Columbia, Canada) a fair number of people raced. Torchy Peden (famous Six-day rider) came from Victoria, so cycling was a fairly popular sport in that area.

I had seen my brother compete and became involved myself as a competitor. I raced for about five years, both road and track. In those days women were not allowed to race on the track in Vancouver in Mass Start events. They thought that was too dangerous for women. We could ride Kilos or Pursuits, but we couldn't ride any Mass Start events or Sprints.

I rode flat track events at that time. I did ride the 250m, 45° banked track in Vancouver. Many years later I did a lot of motor pacing on it. Unfortunately, it was torn down about 10-12 years ago. Now there are two in

B.C., one built for the Commonwealth Games, one still being built.

I had a gap of about three years when I was a spectator. At that time I was in nurse's training. I still went to races and I rode a little bit, but I couldn't get the time off to compete. My first husband was a competitor. I went out to races so I was always there. In those days there was no training for officials. The first training started in 1972 in Canada. In the United States they may have started later than that. People who became officials in the fifties and sixties were just people who were around the sport and who volunteered their services. A lot of them had been ex-competitors who were offering something back to the sport.

I think that's why there was a lot of frustration for athletes who raced in the sixties and seventies, because those people weren't trained properly as officials, they <u>weren't</u> impartial, and they frequently had a motive for being there -- often they were related to someone who was competing. I don't know that things were more political, I think they had the right intentions, but they just didn't have the expertise

Marilyn Allen confers with Barclay Kruse during Olympic Trials/U.S. National Championships, 1992

that's available now. When you think of a sport that's been around for 100 years and officials have only been trained for 20-25, you can understand why the riders' attitude toward officials isn't always the most favorable.

The other problem that I see is that riders often learn the rules from other riders. This system has been passed on over a long period of time. The riders from the sixties taught the riders who raced in the mid-sixties, who taught the riders who raced in the

seventies. What they taught them may not have been as much the <u>rules</u> as the rules as they interpreted them. Sometimes there's a gap between the actual rules, the way the riders interpret those rules, and the way the officials interpret those rules. There is a rule that disappeared in the mid-sixties that riders still refer to in Sprinting.

Understanding the Rules

The RuleBook is confusing, it's not easy to understand. Many riders don't have anyone actually teaching them. Coaches focus on teaching riding skills and technique and not on the rules. It would be to the advantage of the coaches and the managers if they went through Officials Programs so that they have a better understanding of interpretations.

Recently the national coaches asked Al MacDonald, an international Commissaire, to speak to them so they would have a better understanding of how they should deal with officials at the international level because they don't know. They don't understand the protocol. They may have the international RuleBook, but I'm not sure they understand the process. This creates problems for them.

(husband Jim interjects:) It's not so much the rules, as how they should interact with the officials. It's all well and good that they know the specific wording of the rule, but you have to know how to work with the people involved and processes that have been set up over the years. If you go in wanting to do it your way and they've been doing it another way for 20 years, your way is not going to be the right way.

(Marilyn) Americans have a really bad attitude, and I don't mean people from the United States, but <u>North</u> Americans, that "well, this is the way we do it, so this is the way it should be done!" The Europeans don't like that. Riders feel a great deal of frustration and they don't know where to go, how to get the answer they want or their problems solved for them. Frequently they go to the wrong people, perhaps other riders, and don't get the right answers.

I came from a different system in Canada. There are some bad things about it, but there are some good things. One of the positive things was that anyone who wanted to be a National Coach or Team Manager had to go through an officials seminar. They didn't have to pass it, but they had to attend. At first, it was a threat to the officials because the knowledge base was theirs and they wanted to protect it, but they found that it made their jobs much easier. The officials didn't get frivolous protests. The coaches/managers understood the rules and when it was appropriate they protested.

When it wasn't appropriate, they weren't in your face. It made a big difference. It would be beneficial for coaches and managers to do. It's not passing the course, it's sitting in on them and learning so that they understand where we're coming from as officials.

A coach who's coaching an international rider would benefit the most from an international officials' class because, I hate to say it, but national rules don't always coincide with international rules. They're close, but there are some "fine nuance" type things that are different. The major difference comes for the manager, how to deal with people at the international level. A manager at an international event deals with things differently than at a local event. It's a matter of learning the protocol.

(husband Jim) A good example of riders not knowing the rules is when Rebecca Twigg went to the Time Trial (Nationals) without a front brake. The officials were trying to stage people, trying to get them off on time. You try and notice equipment, but things are moving pretty fast and you have to get them set up. If someone had noticed that she didn't have a front brake, she could have been prevented from starting. She won the Time Trial, but she could have been prevented from starting. She got a one-minute penalty which didn't change the outcome, she still won. It is important that the riders know the rules, especially if the riders are self-coached.

(Marilyn) Had the riders noticed

Marilyn's husband Jim has also been an official for a many years.

at that point, they could have gone up and said "She doesn't have a front brake, she can't start" and she would have had to get a different bike up there or gotten a brake on it. She wouldn't have been allowed to start and her start time would have gone by.

(Jim) That's a rule that hasn't changed since I've been involved. This is a rule you would think the rider would know because she had been involved in that particular aspect of the sport (Time Trials). "I don't need the front brake -- it's more weight."

(Marilyn) I believe she was <u>very</u>

well coached, that she knew exactly what she was doing. It's my understanding she had more than one bike there and they simply may have gotten away with it.

(Jim) But if the person on the starting line had said "You can't start" she would have had to get off her bike, go get her other bike . . .

(M)..which would have disrupted her preparation . . .

(J) and at some point in time -- they were doing 30 second starts -- she could have started later.

(M) Riders who protested after she'd ridden, protested too late. If they had protested at the start, she would have been prevented from starting. But the same thing happened with the riders as happened with the officials -- they hadn't noticed it, so she started. Some coach probably noticed it when she finished or when she was on the road. At that point it's a little late to do anything.

Why Become an Official?

We probably became officials because we've been around the sport so long and we felt that we wanted to give back to it. We could see a void that needed to be filled. One of the things that came out at a Cat 1 officials class is that a lot of us who work at a very high level like to bring order to chaos. You want to see things done fairly.

There are a lot of riders who came out of the fifties and sixties and maybe even early seventies who felt that things were not fair, and they weren't. If you were from San Diego and you went to LA, you probably didn't get a fair deal. The LA riders, when they came to San Diego, may not have gotten a fair deal. That's just how things were done. There was no concept of fair play. Your local club got a better deal. I hate to say it but it still occurs, but we're striving to get away from that attitude.

Those of us who were around in that era and saw it as a bad thing wanted to see it change. I think one of the biggest changes you're seeing, is getting away from that regionalism and moving toward a more common basis throughout the country. Instead of "Well this is the way we do it here . . ." it's "Well, how do they do it in T-Town? How do they do it in Houston? Colorado Springs? Let's all do it the same way."

Unfortunately officials presently don't have meetings where they attempt to standardize things. It would be a major expense to do that.

One of the things that has helped the most is the Category 1 seminars that started six or seven years ago. It brings high level officials from all over the country into one area. Everyone goes through the same program. Whether you go out of it with the same information, is up to you. As well as giving you the same information, it allows you to talk to other people from other areas. A lot of times you decide that what you've been doing *is* right. You meet people from different areas. So then, even though the riders say to you "That's not the way they do it in . . .", you know it frequently is. They just don't

want you to do it that way, so they'll try and bluff you. It's part of the game.

(Jim) We had an interesting experience at a bike race in Redding. A bike rider came up to us and said "Well that's not how we do it in San Diego!"

(M) He said "Last week in San Diego I got to ride without a license." I said "Which race was this?" He started telling us about a stage race. I said "Gee, that's funny. I was appointed as Chief Referee. That race got cancelled because the organizer didn't have any permits. So now you've competed in a race that was cancelled by the USCF, an illegal event. What did you say your name was?" He walked away.

Changes

If I could make one change in officiating I would make it more professional. The image the sport projects has a lot to say about the way we officials conduct ourselves. Even at the lowest level events, we need to be professional. We need to dress professionally and we need to be professional in our approach to the athletes. The only way you get respect is by earning it. You can't demand it. How do you get respect? By being fair and professional in what you do. Sometimes at a lower level you may think "Oh well, it's just a local race." You shouldn't treat it that way.

I guess if I could change, not just officiating, I would bring the coaches and managers in and have them attend the seminars. I'm not sure they feel it's necessary, but we can learn from each other.

(Jim) In the European scheme of things, all participants, not just riders and officials, are licensed. Announcers, promoters, mechanics, drivers . . . Some of them just have to pay a lot of money to get the license, but the mechanics and trainers have to take instructional courses just like the officials. You're not at a bike race unless you're licensed to be there.

(M) The press, even, is licensed. That way if there is a problem, they can remove them.

(J) They don't yank the press licenses because they want those people there.

(M) But when the press gets in there and start to change the outcome of the race, that's not allowed. They allow them to get really close, to get really good pictures, but there are times when they're not allowed to be there. The European press don't argue about it. In North America they don't understand.

At Dupont, Chief Referee is saying "No, you can't." They couldn't understand. The Chief Referee commented, "What is with these American press people? Why don't they understand that I'll give them everything I can, but they'll change the race if I let them go through now."

Officials categories

One thing that many people don't understand is there are many levels of officials, just as there are many levels of riders. When you go to a local bike race, you may not have top level officials It depends on the level of event you're working as to the level of efficiency and proficiency of the

officials. You may be lucky and have high level officials working in your district, who are going to be working local events because then other officials will learn from them.

You can go out and work 20 events and learn 20 lessons. Or, you can go out and work 20 events and learn the same lesson 20 times. If you're working in an area where there are not many people around who have more experience than you, you tend to learn the same lesson 20 times. Bike riders tend to do the same thing. Their experience is based on what happens to them. Sometimes they repeat the same thing again and again, they don't learn from it.

When you look at the officials and you say "How well trained are they?" you have to look at the level. You can't just say they're good or they're bad. I wouldn't expect a Category 4 official to know what I know. I wouldn't expect someone who's been around the sport a year to know what I know in 37. You have to look at categories, experience levels, and whether the person has had a chance to work at other than the local bike races. That makes a difference.

The training programs that are in place right now are good. One of the problems with the training programs is, if you're scholastically bright you can pass the exams. Sometimes those same people don't do well at the practicum. Or they may not deal well with the riders. They may not see what's developing in the bike race because they haven't got the experience.

(J) It's not possible to teach

common sense.

(M) That's another thing that can be a problem. But I think the programs that are in place now are good programs. There has been a dramatic amount of growth within the officials in the last 10 years or so, since a lot of these programs have been implemented.

Al MacDonald has been a major force in implementing these programs. Both Al and Beth (Wrenn-Estes) were on the Board of Directors. With the two of them on the board they were able to see that programs got implemented for officials. They developed the Category 1 class. Then Al had the Category 2, then the Category 3 and 4 programs developed.

Now, instead of someone standing in front of you reading the rules, you actually get some practical applications. You need to know the rules, but you have to also know how to work the bike race. They need to say more than "this is the rule when you're working in the pit", they have to tell you what you have to do when you're there. How do you work so you can implement that rule? Telling you that you have to put the rider in at a certain point is fine, but if you don't know where he came out, you can't put him back in. You've got to have some tools to enable you to do those things.

(J) Other sports refer to that particular aspect of the sport as the "mechanics". For example, if it's football and it's the kickoff, where do the officials position themselves? In basketball, if it's a fast break, how do you handle things? If it's this situation, you do this. As the Cat 1 course has gone, more and more top level officials throughout the country have seen what the mechanics <u>should</u> be in "this" particular type of situation within the race and they have fed that down to the lower level officials so the mechanics

Yes, Al MacDonald, that low key, friendly guy checking out the photo finish, is actually a high level official.

are starting to filter down.

(M) That's one of the problems when you get into the scholastically bright or gifted person. They can study the RuleBook and they can quote it back to you, but put them in the caravan and expect them to be able to deal with pro managers, team managers, and maybe they can't do it. Seeing it on paper and dealing with it as it happens are two different things.

There are a lot of differences between track officiating and road officiating, but I think the biggest one is that on the road there is a lot of time when you don't have to be super-intensively focused. Things are just rolling along and it goes from a broad focus to an intense focus back to a broad focus. It changes constantly. On the road you have a chance to recover from things. You have a chance to make decisions. Things happen during the race and generally you don't have to do anything about it until the end of the race, which may be hours from now.

On the track, things happen very fast. It's very intense, very highly focused. It requires an awful lot of concentration for a long period of time. Riders are concentrating for minutes at a time. Officials are concentrating for hours at a time. It is also much more of a show, in front of the spectators at all times.

(J) Criteriums are a lot like track racing. In road racing you're talking about point to point, large 12 to 25 mile loops.

(M) The focus, concentration, being in front of the crowd, all those things that require a professional, more intense focus are there with criterium racing. You do have a little bit more time to deal with things, the race may go on for an hour. Track races may only be minutes long. It can be exhausting doing track racing.

Fatigue

The other thing people don't realize is that you're there from one o'clock to four in the afternoon, and you're there from seven to ten. They don't understand that before you get there at one o'clock you've probably put in three hours worth of work. When you leave at four, maybe you get something to eat, maybe you don't, and you frequently work until you come back at seven. There's a whole lot more behind the scenes work that is being done than there is at a single day road race.

I've had people who have been riders who have worked as coaches and managers for teams who have become officials and worked at National Championships. They work one and say "I'm not doing this again. I'll work it as a coach or a manager, but not as an official." It's so intense. You get very little sleep. At the end of the week you get edgy and irritable. You've probably been in the hot sun and haven't been getting meals regularly. Stage racing can be the same.

Pay for Officials

I came from an era when we didn't get paid. When I first started you came out and volunteered your services. I've promoted bike races and I've coached, but officiating is my love. But I did come from an era when you didn't get paid. You did it because you enjoyed doing it. You wanted things to be fair for everybody.

When they started talking about

paying officials, I pushed for it. One reason is that I felt if someone is paid, even if it's a token amount, it's an obligation. It's more of an obligation than if you come out and volunteer. You feel more responsibility.

I'm not sure we're getting paid fairly. You can go out and work a Category E race, from seven o'clock in the morning until seven at night, dealing with 1000 bike riders and get paid $25. I could go and work an event that takes two to three hours in the afternoon and get paid $150. Is that fair? I don't know. Maybe it required more expertise, more knowledge, but I'm not sure that we're breaking it down as fairly as it could be. I don't have any suggestions on how you could change it.

(J) There have been lots and lots of legislation proposals to key time to the fee and the number of riders you have, but there are a large number of promoters on the board and they don't want to pay more. I'm not sure pay is going to do anything but put another $10 in someone's pocket.

(M) Another thing is that you've probably spent several hours preparing before you even get there. You'll probably spend another evening doing your report. It's not like it's just 12 hours, it generally ends up being more like 18 or 20 hours. If you start charging a lot of promoters a lot more money, you're not going to have races. There's a breaking point.

I get frustrated with promoters who pay the riders $10,000 but complain when they have to pay officials or they cry about travel money or "Do we really have to give you lunch?" "Well no, you want us to stay focused for 12 hours, not eat, and expect us to do well?" Often the last race of the day is where we really need

Officials measure and set up the Start Finish area prior to Goodwill Games, 1990. Officials do many things riders know nothing about both before and after competition.

to be the most focused.

I understand, from having promoted events, that there's a really fine line. I don't think the complaint is with the local race run by the local club. They're trying to run enough races to recoup their money and can make a little for the club.

What we're talking about is the promoter who's a "semi-promoter" who offers a semi-reasonable prize list but doesn't see the benefit of having sufficient officials or officials of an adequate level.

Legal Issues

Another thing we're dealing with is the liability issue. There are a number of officials who have gone through the court room and it's not pleasant. I'm not sure that they pay us enough for that responsibility.

(J) I haven't heard of anybody who gets paid for going to court except maybe Les (Earnest) who may get paid by one party or the other as an expert witness.

(M) One of my frustrations with bike riders is that they don't accept responsibility for their own actions. If I do something stupid and injure myself, why would I sue the promoter and the Federation? Some of the things are not the responsibility of the promoter. You're in a dangerous sport, accept responsibility for that and act accordingly. If you don't want to be involved in something dangerous, then go somewhere else and play some other game.

Some officials may be more conscientious than the riders like because of our concerns about liability.

Being an Official

One of the most difficult things for officials is learning to judge Sprints.

I think it helps if you've done some riding. For someone to learn to judge Sprints they have to spend hours and hours and hours watching. Watching the maneuvers. What is the end result of that maneuver? When is the person out of contention? Different rules apply for the slow part of the race than for the fast part of the race. In a "three-up" Sprint, when you get into the fast part of the race and you're near the end of the race, if one of those riders is 50 meters behind the other two, you forget about him. You don't even look at him because he's out of the bike race, out of contention. You have to learn to see and focus on those riders still in contention.

I teach officials to watch the movement of the wheels on the track rather than focusing on the body movement. If you watch the wheels you will also see what the bodies are doing. You have a better perspective of how much movement there really was by watching how much the wheel moves up or down the track.

Another thing is not to get too close to the track. If you get too close you can't see things properly. You don't want to be too far away but people who stand too close can't see things the same way. They miss things. You have to step back a bit and observe calmly.

If someone gets injured, you go to them and you deal with them, protect them. When you start working at a higher level you don't go to the rider who's injured, you go to the bicycle. That's one change that occurs when you're dealing with different levels. It's not that I don't care about the rider, but my job is to get the bicycle to make sure nobody gets his hands on that bike before the officials get a chance to examine it. We examine it for mechanical problems. It depends on the event, but we check the bike to see what happened, what caused the incident.

In a Sprint you probably don't need to do that so much. In a Points race, a rider who has an incident has a certain amount of time to get back on his bike if it's a valid incident. If it's not, he has to get back up right away and loses laps.

In Kilo or Pursuit, if a rider has a valid mechanical, they frequently get another chance. Sprinting is different. Generally if an incident occurs it might be a blowout, but generally it's a crash because riders get tangled up with each other. The bike isn't a priority because you have a pretty good idea why they crashed. In other events it is essential because they don't get to restart if it's not valid, or they lose laps. There are different interpretations and it's important, at a higher level, to understand that.

Assignments

Once a person has reached a certain level, they're considered qualified. One of the things I teach people from the time they enter the sport: Get your experience as a Category 4. If you make a mistake as a Category 4 official, just like a Category 4 rider, people are more forgiving. Spend more time at the Category 4 level. Don't move up before you're ready.

The other thing I stress is: If you're not comfortable with an assignment,

say "No." Or, if you know you've gotten a particular assignment, say as a Starter, then go out and get as much experience as you can before you go and do the job . I would rather have an official who's a Category 3 who's had a lot of experience and is confident doing a job than a high level official who doesn't care anymore and has stopped learning.

The Chief Referee has little control over who works on the crew. It depends on the event. If you're going into a National Championship race, they assign key positions and then there are local people who work other roles.

(J) There are three or four people who are assigned. The Chief Referee, the Chief Judge, the Starter on the track, the Race Secretary, or sometimes the technical services people. The USCF assigns them.

(M) They're assigning five to the track and eleven to the road, but it changes, depending on the budget. Another reason is that they have more people that are trained and are capable now.

At Olympics or World's you may see twenty or twenty-five people. A lot of times they're window dressing, but they're also getting experience. The more exposure to ways that other people do things, the more you learn.

One frustration I have with both riders and officials is that I'm tired of people indicating "It's owed to me." I think if you want something, you have to actively seek it out and you may

have to do it at your own expense. People can say "I never get selected for anything." They need to travel to races at their own expense. Everybody has a learning curve and it's really important that we get as much opportunity to learn as we can. If you

Officials conferring, Olympic Trials, 1992 (Marilyn, left)

deny yourself that opportunity to learn, you're not being fair to the athletes. By the same token, athletes have to learn as well. The athletes need to learn that officials are really striving to become professional. They're really striving to be fair.

One of the frustrations for riders is that they don't see calls as being consistent. They see that "last week it got called this way and you've made a different call this week." They don't

know that last week the Chief Referee was a Category 4. They don't know that maybe the Chief Referee didn't get the same information. Why didn't he get the same information? As a Category 4 official he may not have realized that he needed to put somebody in the back-straight to watch the Sprint. Maybe he put somebody there but he didn't get the same information because he didn't ask the right questions.

(J) Or, maybe an official didn't show up last week. Last time it happened in Turn 3 and this time it happened in Turn 1.

(M) Riders see things as being called differently -- often times they are different. It might be an identical situation but the experience level of the official might change the call that was made. It may have become a part of their learning curve.

International Officiating

At an international level, World Championships and Olympics, Commissaires are assigned internationally by the UCI. The USCF selects the Commissaire Adjoint, or Assistant Officials, who go in as the "window dressing." I think it's interesting that a lot of people are so focused on this coming Olympics and see that as their only goal as officials.

They're going to get in there and they're going to be treated like a Category 4 official again, or worse. They're at a different level. They won't be a part of the decision making process. They won't even be asked for their opinion. The UCI Commissaires don't care about the opinion of the local officials.

I guess there's a certain status to being able to say "I've worked an Olympics." What's more important to me is to be able to say "I feel that I did a good job." I think that's what every official needs to look at. What ever level you're at, perform to the very best of your ability. You will grow and you will learn and you'll be better. But you have to critically self-examine.

I'm not sure we offer officials enough positive reinforcement or enough negative. You really need to implement the evaluation process through the earlier stages of officiating so that people don't get to be a Category 1 official with bad habits they've learned early on.

Evaluations

(J) The Federation has 22 high level officials who have been trained as evaluators. They go in and watch the races, see how the officials do the mechanics, do the trivial jobs, rules interpretations, and make sure they're within standards. Most people get average or better evaluations. Few people get bad evaluations. You have a very hard time marking people down because there aren't many mistakes

made, especially at a Nationals.

The best part of doing that evaluation is sitting down with a piece of paper with all this stuff on it. You mark down different levels for different parts of the jobs. You sit down with them and talk about it. I've been on both sides of the process. That's the best feedback the officials get as to how they're doing and how

"Riders ready . . . Timers ready . . . " Indianapolis, 1994

they compare with other officials (according to that particular evaluator.)

The more times they're evaluated and the more of these discussions they have, the better idea they're going to get of how they compare with other people and what areas they're really good in and what areas they're not. Even really good officials have weak areas. It might be just how they interact with the other officials.

(M) One of the things I teach new officials is that you want to do every job. You want to get experience in everything. You will not want to do everything. Eventually, you're going

to want to become more specialized, but you need to know all the jobs. If you become a Chief Referee you may need to explain how to do something. If you haven't done it you're going to have a hard time explaining to that person so others understand what you want.

Budgeting for Officials

(J) The last time I looked at a budget for the USCF it was four and one half million dollars. Fifty thousand of it was for officials. That isn't a lot. That was two years ago, I don't know what it is today.

(M) There's a tremendous amount of money spent on athletes and athletes programs, as there should be, but our sport will never become newsworthy, saleable to the TV until officials learn to do things in a consistent manner and to be really professional about what they do. If we can't do a good job and keep things running the way they should be run, TV isn't going to be interested. It doesn't matter how good our bike riders are, you'll see a 10 second clip on the news and that will be it.

Most people don't understand our sport. The Team Pursuit is being eliminated and the Olympic Sprint is being added. The UCI is very aware that they aren't getting their share of the market. They're trying to bring events into the sport that people will enjoy watching.

(J) There's been a change in Europe. All the broadcasting in Europe was sponsored by the government. There was no advertising. That's changing. Sponsors of bicycle racing who couldn't advertise on TV can now advertise on TV. So now are they going to put their money into TV or are they going to put their money into bike racing teams? What do you think? What do they do here? Where do they get their bang for their buck? So the people in the UCI are under pressure to improve their events so that the events are marketable, not just a bike racing event and no other place to put our money. Now they can put it into the broadcast medium, so there's competition for those dollars. Things are changing.

(M) I think you will see the same events at Nationals for a while. One of the reasons they'll do that is because the UCI has a habit of changing things. "We'll take this out and see how it goes. Well, it didn't work so we'll put it back in." So the USCF will wait for a little while and see if this is really what the UCI is going to do.

We're Human

One of the things that riders have to understand about officials is that we're human and we make mistakes. We try not to, but generally if we have to make a decision, it's because the riders made the first mistake. One of the things officials have to understand is that riders get off their bikes and sometimes have a real adrenaline rush. They can be agitated and upset, but you've got to talk to them. You have to let them know that you will listen to them.

Riders need to understand that when they approach officials they should do it with a certain amount of respect. You don't see football players screaming at and berating officials. You don't see soccer players doing that. Baseball players do it. But for the most part there's a certain line, a certain respect level.

Whether you like the way we're doing things or not, you have to allow for that to occur. You don't necessarily have to respect me, but don't be rude to me (as an official) because it tends to get you off on the wrong foot right away. Very often the call will not go your way, whereas if you have a manager speak for you or if you can wait until you're a little calmer and speak quietly, you will tend to get the ear of the person much more readily.

(J) Top level officials will often just turn around and walk away or tell you to come back later when you've calmed down so that they don't have to do something that they don't want to do. It's usually the manager in baseball who's kicking the dirt. If they touch the referee there's a large monetary fine as well as suspensions. That's why they kick dirt. Especially in baseball, that's part of the show, the interactions between the umpires and managers. If you look at the materials that baseball puts out in training their officials, they look at that as part of the show. In the Pro leagues, certain things are part of the show, so it's okay.

(M) When officials gather to make a decision in a high level event, there's generally a Jury, three or five people making a decision. It's not one person arbitrarily making the decision. If a rider comes up to me and says "The seeding's done wrong" you go over, you look at it, it's right or it's wrong. But if it's a call that has to be made, number one, you gather because you need to get the information from the people who saw the incident. Number two, there's a Jury that will then make the decision based on the information that they get.

(J) If you're at the track and you're the Chief Referee, in the normal course of events the Chief Referee makes the decision. If the Chief Referee saw what happened and feels certain about what s/he saw, s/he'll make his/her call. If s/he's not 100% certain or if someone else was in a better position, s/he'll go ask them. If I have a decision to make, I want to be fair to the rider, so I will ask every official who could have seen it what they saw. I take what I saw, what they tell me, and I make a decision based on all that information. Generally at the Nationals level there's a Jury.

(M) The Jury will probably be made up of the Chief Referee, the Starter, the Chief Judge, and maybe two other people. It's very possible that the Chief Referee and the Starter were positioned where they could see the incident, but then maybe not. You may need to go people who saw it and ask "What did you see? What is your impression of what occurred? If you get input, and you trust the official who's giving you information, then you base your call on that information. If you don't know them or their level of expertise, you try not to put them in a position where they're going to be giving you key information.

(J) You may have a sliding scale of weight you attach to each person's opinion based on their level of experience and what they've done in the past.

Officiating requires a lot of concentration for long periods of time. U.S. National Championships, Indianapolis, 1994

(M) After I've worked with people I'll know their strengths and weaknesses and I will appropriately assign them. I won't put them where I figure they're going to make a mistake. I don't want that. I want the best people in the best positions. As a Chief Referee you try to gauge that beforehand. Sometimes you don't know the people, so you have to ask them "What have you done? Who have you worked with? What position are you comfortable in?" Sometimes their perception and your perception are different, but you have to live with it.

You do ultimately have to consult your officials. If you don't and you start arbitrarily making all your calls independent of them, you will not have that crew working for you again. I've gone to races and worked for people that I've decided I'm not working for again because I don't like their style or philosophy. That's acceptable.

As a new official you've got to work with everybody because you need to learn how to do things. The way you do that is by watching people who do it well and also by watching people who don't do it well (just don't do it that way). But, you've got to work with everybody. As you get more experience and get to a higher level, then you can choose a little bit more as to who you want to work with.

I've done what I've wanted to do in the sport, so if someone asked me to work as a Starter for someone I didn't like, even at a National Championship, I would say "No." I would be miserable all week and I won't do a good job and that's not fair to the riders.

Ultimately you're looking for the best, safest, fairest event for the rider. Whether the riders realize that or not, that is what we try to do.

Chapter 19 - USCF
The United States Cycling Federation (USCF), the Union Cycliste Internationale (UCI), and the RuleBook(s)

Competitive cycling has always had rules, just like any other form of competition. In the beginning, rules were simply agreed upon by competitors "first one to that tree wins". As cycling became more popular, increasingly complex rules evolved to increase both interest and challenge.

The Beginning

The first organization for bicycle riders was the League of American Wheelmen (LAW), begun in 1880 when most bicycles were the High Wheelers which look so quaint today.

With Six-day races, when cycling became a business, rules were made by promoters of velodrome racing to organize the event for presentation to audiences. Initially it was "ride round and round for twenty-four hours -- see who drops and who doesn't" -- a rather primitive competition.

An official governing body was needed to administer the logistics of professional racing, and business interests drove this organization. The National Cycling Association (NCA) began offering championships in 1895 for professionals and in 1899 for amateurs. Many riders entering the NCA's professional ranks began with the amateur organization.

The fact that an agency was needed to both promote the sport and protect the riders, was evident from the beginning. Promoters had money to

make. There was no insurance to protect injured riders and no responsibility for the promoter to pay for medical care. If a rider couldn't ride, another would take his place at the starting line.

Law suits so common today were not the mode in the early days. Riders were expendable, the same as coal miners, factory workers and others. Riders who were "box office draws" were less expendable than others, but many of the advantages in place for today's riders weren't in place in the early days.

The Beginnings of the USCF

In 1921, the American Bicycle League of America (ABL or ABL of A), a non-commercial, grass-roots organization, began offering its own championships outside of the governance of the NCA.

After 10 years of racing, the ABL did not hold championships (1931-34), but resumed in 1935. In 1942, World War II interrupted competition by both the NCA and the ABL. No championships were held in '42, '43, or '44.

The National Cycling Association never recovered after the war, despite an attempt to revive the Six-day circuit in the early 50s. Some say the death of the NCA was the real cause of the

The offices of the United States Cycling Federation (USCF), Colorado Springs, Colorado

death of the Six-days and that its demise really began in the loss of commercial support and business and personal difficulties of promoters during the depression.

ABL championships resumed in 1945. By the time attempts were made to revive the NCA amateur championships in the early 50s, it was too late and they ceased forever after two years. The ABL of A had become the dominant organization for championship racing in the United States.

While support was virtually nonexistent, riders persisted in competing wherever there was something resembling a track. As reflected in the memories of those who were there (see Chapter 4,

History), those who rode the track made do with whatever was available. If a real track was too far away, riders and coaches mapped out distances on the road to train over equivalent courses.

The USCF

In 1976 the ABL was renamed the United States Cycling Federation. The USCF has a somewhat convoluted history, attempting to respond to competitive cycling in both professional and amateur arenas, imposing changes and legislation on the sport as it has interacted with international influences. It now encompasses amateur and professional cycling, both on and off-road, including velodrome racing.

The USCF and Velodrome Racing

The Velodrome chapter (Ch. 2) charts the revival of present day velodromes. Of the 21 tracks on the list, six tracks were built in the 60s; four in the 70s; five in the 80s; and three in only the first <u>half</u> of the 90s (total -- 18). As usual, several others are reportedly in the works, including the certainty of the 1996 Olympic Velodrome in Atlanta.

Americans are winning more World Championships and bringing home more medals in track racing than in any other segment of bicycle racing. The USCF is wisely allocating increased support and attention to this highly technical and most successful specialty.

Europe and the Union Cycliste Internationale (UCI)

The bicycle has enjoyed continual popularity and daily use by members of all levels of society in Europe. Some of the world's most famous races and most famous tracks are located in Europe. From the earliest day, Americans have sought competition overseas. Some of the most famous European bicycle builders have enjoyed fame and fortune in a culture where the fine craftsmanship of experts is revered as much for its tradition as for the exquisite beauty of its products.

Both the UCI and the International Olympic Committee are located in Switzerland. They act as governing bodies for all bicycle racing throughout

USCF Director Lisa Voight and EDS's Dick Wyles

the world. The United States Cycling Federation is a member organization of the United States Olympic Committee. Both organizations are located in the same U.S. town, Colorado Springs, Colorado.

Under this authority, the USCF trains, enters, and underwrites expenses for athletes who participate in the Olympic and Pan American Games. Accordingly, USCF athletes benefit from the following programs of the USOC: athlete support, coaching development and education, drug control, grants and insurance administration, the Olympic Training Center, sports medicine, and sport science and technology.

The RuleBook

The USCF assumes the responsibility of both supporting and protecting riders by organizing competition in the United States, utilizing the USCF RuleBook to educate bicycle racers on appropriate race conduct and a wide variety of factors, from basic fees, to equipment, to rules for each contested event -- even to clothing appropriate for officiating -- on the track, the road, and off-road, amateur and Pro.

The RuleBook is a most educational little volume. Much of the factual information in *No Brakes!* has been taken (not copied) from that source which offers its information to any who wish to use it. While it is copyrighted, copy privileges are offered to all users who acknowledge their source.

Rules of Bicycle Racing, published by the United States Cycling Federation is a most informative publication. The world of bicycle racing in the United States (and *No Brakes!*) would be in sorry condition without this most helpful and impressively complete booklet.

It is available to any who purchase a racing license or who send the appropriate fee which, in 1995, is still only $3.00! Surely an all-time great bargain for some of the most comprehensive information on bicycle racing in the world.

Get yours -- license or no! Address:

U.S. Cycling Federation
One Olympic Plaza
Colorado Springs, CO 80909

1-719-578-4581

The Coaching Offices of the U.S. Cycling Federation

USCF Director of Event Marketing and Communications Steve Penny

It's always a challenge to determine the direction of an organization like the United States Cycling Federation because there are so many demands that need to be met. Everybody wants things.

This organization serves a lot of different individuals and groups which have different goals and interests. Racing members, officials, mechanics, sponsors, clubs, race promoters are even further distinguished among Master's, Junior's, Elite, men, women. Across the board, it is easy to see that there are all types of people looking for services from the USCF.

It's a huge umbrella organization which strives to establish a direction, meet the goals that it has, and satisfy the membership.

The current pressure focuses on increasing the racing population which has plateaued in the last few years. Growth has occurred in the last few years with the increase in popularity of mountain bike racing, but the challenge is to grow again within the racing population. This requires growth from the entry level athlete, meaning the Junior level athlete or the person just beginning to race. We are developing programs to satisfy their needs at whatever level they want to compete.

By the time an athlete is established as an active racer, the issue becomes at what level are they going to be competitive and what are their goals in the sport? The only way in which we can continue to develop elite athletes is to provide greater access to the sport for the younger age groups, which is among our top priorities. Programs such as the Lance Armstrong Junior Olympic Series, regional racing program, and the Fresca Cup are examples of providing increased exposure and racing experience at the grass roots level.

People have to work together to keep athletes involved in bicycle racing at whatever level they are comfortable. The incorporation of the USCF, the National Off-Road Bicycle Association (NORBA), and the U.S. Professional Racing Organization (USPRO) under the USA Cycling umbrella fosters cooperation at the elite level of racing. Currently, we have an affiliation with the National Bicycle League, a BMX organization, which helps both parties.

Everyone is represented at one level or another with the UCI (Union Cycliste Internationale) by one organization. Being able to represent all levels of cycling holds great promise and advantages.

Recently, the vision of the USCF has been to broaden its representation of cycling on a larger scale in America. We want to be the leader within the

"The USCF serves a lot of different individuals, groups, types of groups. When you distinguish between racing members, officials, mechanics, sponsors; different groups: Master's, Junior's, Elite, men, women -- across the board, there are all types of people looking for services from the USCF. It's a huge umbrella." (Thanks for your help, Steve!)

industry with regard to the organizations that promote cycling. We want to foster growth within bicycle groups and to increase the emphasis on bicycle racing. We are going to continue to look for new ways to do that and to try to meet the needs of the racing population.

Velodrome racing

Velodrome racing specifically provides a wide range of appeal and benefits to a cyclist with regard to:

a) athletes can be rather selective about their preferred style of event. You can compete in an individual event like the Pursuit or go head to head in the Sprints. Or, you can race in a pack, in a Points race or other team events. And,

b) track racing offers benefits from

an educational point of view in training athletes for riding skills, form, and bike handling in a safe, captive environment rather than trying to practice things on the road.

A fixed venue like a velodrome offers other advantages as well, particularly with respect to spectator appeal. We are looking into increasing the activity at the velodromes around the country by providing coaching, regional programs, and other local incentives the give people more of a reason to race on the tracks.

The only limitation is the number of velodromes that actually exist in the U.S. and the conditions of some of them. There's a great deal of inconsistency with respect to how they're managed and the infrastructure available at the facility.

Recently, the concept of portable velodromes has drawn a great deal of attention. John Vande Velde and the Vandedrome has become an attraction which is trying to make portable racing viable. Dale Hughes has previously owned a portable velodrome and is currently building the track which will be used for the 1996 Olympic Games. This will also be a portable track and able to be moved to different locations after the Games.

Building a Velodrome

Anyone interested in building a velodrome can contact the USCF for plans and architectural specifications for the track. We are always willing to do whatever we can for people who contact us.

The traditional length of the tracks has been 333 meters, but lately the 250 meter wood tracks have begun to become more popular for international competition. This has a tendency to produce more exciting racing, particularly for the Match Sprints and pack races (Madison). The old Six-day tracks were smaller. The World Championships in Sicily were conducted on a 400 meter track.

New velodromes have no direct contract with the USCF. We do not exert control over any velodrome in the country, but we are definitely willing to work with all of them. Interaction with the Federation typically focuses on accredited coaching programs, competition programs, National Team participation in events, and possibly National Championships or international events.

When new velodromes are built, it is advisable to consult with the USCF. Ft. Lauderdale felt it was very important to have a signature event upon their opening to help establish the facility. The USCF awarded the 1994 EDS National Master's Track Championships to demonstrate our confidence and appreciation for opening the track. It was a "Thank You" for the county's commitment and may have helped get the lights up a little quicker!

While the USCF can initiate pro-

USCF Executive Director Lisa Voight

grams to help develop cycling at the local level, it takes a strong local group to implement programs and foster growth and participation. The commitment from the community to the facility is very important.

Racing and the Velodromes

The USCF works very closely with our local organizers in promoting our National Championships. We have developed a partnership with our organizing groups which provides title sponsorship of these events and brings the necessary services to the event. This allows the local organizer to spend more time and effort on promoting and marketing the event.

For National Championships, we want to insure that a certain level of results are provided and expertise is available for timing and results. We have contracted with various groups to do that and this is a service we provide for the promoting organization. We also bring a good race announcer, the necessary officials, and a variety of other resources for the promoter.

Some velodromes have their own timing and results systems which helps them promote better events. T-Town, the Marymoor velodrome, Indiana-

polis, and the Colorado Springs track all have some form of timing system installed at their tracks. These tracks have developed budgets through their racing programs and clubs which helps them afford some of the infrastructure for their events. The velodromes with full-time staffs also have a certain luxury.

One of the challenges in event promotion is actually "building" an event. We are just now beginning to develop a formula for promoting the Nationals and being in Indianapolis for a few years has helped accomplish this. It takes more than working with an organization for 8-12 months to be effective in building an event. The learning curve is too dramatic when an event moves from year to year. Remaining in a city for more than a year at a time also helps establish a legacy for the sport in that community.

The Final Four (college basketball tournament) was held in Kansas City for many years before they started traveling it around. The reason they were able to move it around was because they had built such a successful event. They developed a formula that worked for the event.

We try to match a variety of elements when selecting a location for National Championships. A market like Indianapolis has the potential for large crowds and a variety of peripheral events around the races. It is also a good market for our title sponsor, EDS.

If it is right for the city and right for the USCF, it leaves a very positive image and gives us an event of which we are proud. It also allows more promotion of athletes in the area. Look at the success of some of the Indiana athletes at the 1994 event -- that's a vital part of what our program represents.

There are many variables taken into account in selecting a venue for National Championships. Each year, depending on the nature of the competition, a variety of elements are taken into consideration. These include the condition of the track, the promoting organization, support of the community, proximity to athletes, history of National Championships at the facility, and other items.

Our goal is to help people develop a loyalty to track cycling which creates an interest to develop their own events. T-Town has been very successful at this. Each track needs to work at developing their own following for races on an annual basis. We have one of the best velodromes in the world in Minneapolis and we are looking for way to help them develop a regular racing program.

Media / International Success

The value of success among our elite athletes can not be underestimated. Athletes who are successful in international competition attract attention, which is important for the marketability and viability for the sport.

Looking at the direction and success of our current elite athletes is very encouraging, particularly among our track athletes. Watching Marty Nothstein, Erin Hartwell, Rebecca Twigg, Janie Eickhoff, the Pursuiters, and everyone else succeed breeds a greater feeling of success and optimism. It helps to sell programs

and promote the events in which they compete.

We're putting a great deal of emphasis on Project '96 from both athlete preparation and promotion aspects. This is a rallying point for the entire country through the 1996 Olympic Games and gives us the ability to measure our success. The progress of the Team Pursuit over the past few years is a direct indication of this program -- an integrated approach to preparing our athletes, building the necessary equipment and letting people know about it.

Track cycling lends itself to being a bit more media friendly than road races. All of the events are self-contained and easily watched. Athletes are readily available in the infield and easy to interview. Capturing images for television is a little easier, especially if a full-scale production is planned.

Track cycling can be a very marketable property. Signage is very visible at the velodromes and the audience is captive. It requires less money to produce a high quality event and is much easier to organize within the venue. Many of the venues have concession areas and large fields or parking areas where trade shows and festivals can be developed.

The difficulty lies in educating the public and the media about the events, but over time this can be accomplished. It is less expensive to televise than road racing, but track racing can also be more difficult to televise in certain respects. No one has yet figured out a good way to televise Individual Pursuits and many

people do not know enough about what they are watching to really enjoy the subtleties of the sport.

Race announcing is very important at a track event. A good race announcer can help educate the crowd and the media as well as add to the enjoyment of the event. Traditionally, the race announcers have limited their interaction with the race, kind of like tennis. This direction came from the UCI. One thing that has become obvious is that a good track announcer can really get the crowd going. (*see Ch. 16*)

At the 1994 Track Nationals and at the World Cup finals in Colorado Springs, the track announcers did a fantastic job of announcing the race action, not interfering with the event, but fostering, *increasing* the enjoyment of the event. Brian Drebber has an outstanding reputation for getting the T-Town crowd to make things happen. But at the Worlds or the Olympic Games this type of interaction is not permissible and probably rightfully so.

(*ed: Sounds like the USOC is missing a media opportunity!*)

For a new journalist, track cycling is not an easy sport to watch for the first time. People we bring in like to watch bicycle racing, but still do not

Brian Drebber says "If you want a track guy who gives a good interview every time you talk to him, it's Curt." Steve arranged for Curt Harnett to promote World Cup on the radio. It must have worked -- the turn-out was great!

As Steve (top left) consults with his staff, the media truck sets up.

understand it. They have a certain degree of fear in having to write about something they do not truly understand and it is the responsibility of the promoter and the athletes to help the media. Polite assistance is always

The World Cup of track cycling and Champions cups, Colorado Springs, 1994. World level competition and international interaction enrich the lives of everyone involved.

resources. This provides benefits to both sides of the relationship. We can do things more cost efficiently for some companies and relieve them of certain up-front costs. Additionally, by combining the resources of each corporate sponsor, products and marketing programs can be developed which help everyone involved.

Being the USCF allows us to centralize certain efforts, such as television advertising, print advertising or direct mail marketing.

We represent an opportunity to accomplish business objectives at a value that may not otherwise be available. It becomes very important to listen to one another in order to accomplish these things.

EDS

EDS is actually our business and technology partner. We have learned a great deal from EDS in a variety of ways.

EDS has played a vital role in helping us coordinate Project '96, which is our plan for success in 1996 and beyond. It is the development of new equipment, new technologies that will benefit cycling.

The important thing is to realize

appreciated by the reporter who is not quite sure of what to write.

At all of our national and international events we always have a media director to help the press understand what's happening on the track. Materials and results are provided to help them gain the necessary information.

It does no good for the media to attend an event and not understand what is taking place. Each media person is different and it is important to communicate with them. It's a matter of making the media a priority and taking the time to realize that a serious effort is required to gain the support and attention of the press.

Sponsors

We continue to learn more about interaction with corporate sponsors. There is always a certain level of

partnership with any sponsor that is involved with your organization. You have to understand each other's goals and objectives in order to effectively do business together. The closer you work with them, the better the level of understanding which develops between you and their organization.

We've had sponsors in the past who were only interested in having an affiliation and being about to gain visibility for the US Team. Others are more interested in sponsoring cycling. The real benefit comes when you are able to combine resources and develop programs which mutually satisfy each company's marketing goals.

We're just now learning how we can maximize the visibility for corporate sponsors with the Cycling Team or the USCF organization and how we might capitalize on their

Master's Sprinter Nick Chenowth, held by Coach Skip Cutting (past National Sprint Champion), gets ready to Sprint against Marty Nothstein. As EDS's Sports Marketing Director, Nick has been instrumental in formation of the partnership between the USCF and EDS. (Good Sprinter, good Coach/Sprinter!)

259

International athletes are not the only ones who get the goodies. The growth of the Master's division has been phenomenal over the last 10 years. Master's Nats, 1992.

that this will not only be an equipment advancement, but also an improvement in the knowledge we have about training techniques and practices.

EDS has been very willing to interact with all of our sponsors in the development of technology which services the U.S. Cycling Federation and the U.S. Cycling Team. EDS has developed a variety of technical products which have assisted in the advancement of our training practices for elite athletes, as well as given us

new ability to provide greater service to our membership

EDS developed the event registration system which we used at our National Championships. We are looking at a way to develop a results system as well.

This could become very helpful to promoters who could contact the USCF for an event registration and results program which could be installed on their lap-tops at little cost to them.

EDS has provided us with something that would have cost considerable dollars for the USCF or other race organizers to implement and develop.

Other Sponsors

We are pretty flexible about how we work with people, depending on their goals and reasons for wanting to be involved with the USCF. We have developed a two-tier sponsor identification program, of sponsors and suppliers.

The most important aspect to effectively managing your corporate relationships is listening to how you can continue to improve the partnership and looking for new opportunities that are unique to your organization.

Corporations are responsible for showing a profit and everything must contribute to that bottom line. There has got to be some kind of return that justifies that expense.

It is important for promoters to remember that corporations are not

donating money for the sake of being nice. This is someone who is trying to accomplish a business objective.

As a promoter, you must understand what is necessary to satisfy that business objective and/or and the relationship. Essentially you are in the middle of a business deal. Understanding and meeting a company's corporate objectives can help you maintain relationships over a longer period of time, and bring in other companies to work with you as well.

Successful business partnerships sell each other. Having EDS say "Yes, we are working with the USCF and they are doing a great job. We are excited and this is why we are involved. This is how we think you should be involved." can go a long way in brining in other sponsors.

For a company of EDS's stature to walk into another sponsor's presentation with the USCF carries a great deal of weight and has considerable impact on the prestige you bring to the table.

The point is to be sure you understand the business goals and objectives of any sponsor with which you are connected and work to satisfy these items. If you do not, you do not give them any reason to continue working with you.

Growth

The success our athletes have experienced at the World Championships will help make U.S. Cycling a more competitive force in the marketplace. It allows promoters to sell more prestige in their marketing efforts.

It's great to have the credibility of having five World Medalists coming

USCF Executive Director Lisa Voight shows Pursuiter Dirk Copeland the fulfillment of his dreams (his new Olympic jersey). Blaine, MN, 1992

to an event. It establishes the link for the media. Spectators are more interested in attending the event.

Athletes with World Champion or Olympic medals are much easier to promote. This helps the other athletes as well because all of a sudden they are finishing less than a wheel-length behind the World Champion.

Getting athletes to attend an event requires direct contact with their coach, agent, or themselves, depending on the athlete. Sometimes it is necessary to have an incentive for this athlete relative to their accomplishment in the sport.

This could be in the form of a good prize list, paid expenses, or other attractive enticements. Essentially, the athlete realizes his or her presence helps the promoter generate additional revenue for the event.

Growth at the velodromes has to come from within the cycling community in that city. These facilities need to become self-sustaining and continued efforts must be made to increase the marketability of the sport at the local level.

This is the impetus behind the regional program which is designed to provide mechanisms for local coaching programs to use. Hopefully we can continue to work together in accomplishing our mutual goals.

The Year 2000

In the year 2000, the USCF will continue to represent cycling more fully, both nationally and internationally. We want to establish professional racing at the level of other professional sports organizations.

Our goal is to establish U.S. Cycling's properties similar to what Major League baseball, the NFL, and the NBA have done with their sports organizations. These sports have experienced great success because of the mainstream nature of their activities. Elementary schools, YMCA Youth League programs, the Boys and Girls clubs, intercollegiate athletics, all contribute to the popularity of other sports.

Sports like gymnastics, figure skating, and track and field have all thrived on successful clubs. Cycling has thrived on successful clubs as well and there are some great clubs in this country.

We have to develop more consistency, however, which will foster more growth and success at the club level.

The clubs are a vital part of the entire organization. Teams like L.A. Sheriffs have a huge commitment to the sport, from the grass roots to the professional level.

Bicycle racing needs to become an integral part of a community's identity, just like the high school basketball team. The challenge is that bicycle racing requires more of a commitment and a bit more of an involvement at the local level.

Everything you see in other sports developed at a grass-roots level. Little League Baseball and Pop Warner Football are successful because of the commitment made by the parents. We have to work together to bring more people into the sport and keep them active at the local level.

Lest we forget, amidst the ambition and the hype, where the future comes from . . . .
. . . . . . it may come from a clinic offered during Nationals in Indianapolis hosted by Champions and international competitors Roger Young and Nelson Vails . . . .

. . . . or it may come from an anonymous road race in Carlsbad, California where Regional Coach Danny Van Haute has just passed by a future World Champion in a gaggle of children who just rode their first bicycle race.
They're out there -- waiting. . .

Chapter 20
Photographing Velodrome Racing
Sandy Sutherland

A number of other people might have written this section with considerably more technical expertise than I. However, I wrote it because:

1) while I have had training, I consider myself a "common person" photographer, a person who just wants to get the picture, not someone who obsesses on technical detail. This section is addressed to people like me: parents, interested racers, friends, lovers and a broad spectrum of fans (a.k.a. "real people," not professional photographers).

Aspiring technicians will find greater satisfaction in technical books and training which are far more extensive than this entire publication, much less this chapter. I offer a view of photographing bicycle racing, from the heart with only a few numbers.

2) I took almost all of the photos in this book. It would seem silly to have someone else write this section with my photos illustrating.

3) I refer you to several bicycle track race photographers for technical expertise: Mike Gladu, Casey Gibson and John Pratt are three that I keep bumping into at world level events. Marianne McCoy, Nelson Machin and Randy Briggle are three more. I'm sure there are many others whose names I don't know. The rule here is the same as always: *you can learn something from everyone.*

4) I know what I want to communicate in this section, and it is this:

The Joy of Photographing Bicycle Races

I have come to believe that no one has a better time at the velodrome than me. Win or lose, if I get good photos, I'm happy. There is no pressure on me, no rules save my own, no political involvement. Whether I have access to the inside of the track or not, I know great photos are mine, as long as my batteries hold out, the light is available, and I pick a spot where something is happening -- and that's pretty hard <u>not</u> to do on a velodrome.

Every mom and dad, every friend and lover, wants to take decent photos of their loved one on the track -- but it's not easy. There are different things to look for in each event.

The absolutely most basic thing in sports photography is to 1) **focus** (usually on the ground) where you plan to take the picture and, 2) when the riders get to that place, 3) **push the button!** It's that simple. Well, almost. The most obvious and probably easiest place to start practicing is at the finish line (<u>but</u> **don't** <u>drop anything on the track and</u> **don't** <u>interfere with riders!</u>).

Then go home, have the film developed and decide what kinds of other shots you'd like based on how successful your last ones were. Voila! You're a sports photographer!

No matter how many years go by, it will always be challenging and you'll never really know what you'll end up with until you see the prints.

USCF Executive Director Lisa Voight (left) and me, Master's Nats, 1993. (Thanks for your help, Lisa, Steve Penny and USCF! This book thanks you too.)

Cameras/Numbers

It is always said in photographic circles that it is the photographer, not the camera, that gets great pictures. This is mostly true, but certain choices allow better photographic results than others.

Photography is filled with numbers. Like lines on the track, once you understand what they mean, everything makes more sense. Certain combinations of numbers work better than others. The numbers that don't work need not be discussed. What you want is to: 1) stop action enough to see it and 2) have "your" rider in focus.

Most people will have automatic cameras which select one or more numbers for you. While "auto every-

thing" seems like a good idea, it doesn't always work like it should. There are two issues primary to photography that determine the outcome, the first concerns how much distance is in focus and the second relates to the speed of the subject.

Aperture Priority

With "aperture priority" cameras, <u>you</u> choose the "depth of field" numbers, usually located on your lens, ("f/" numbers like f/22, f/16, 11, 8, 5.6, and so on) and the camera selects the other number (speed). The bigger the "f/" number, the more will be in focus. The smaller the "f/" number, the less will be in focus.

With bicycle racers coming across the line at 40 mph you would need to be pretty quick in anticipating the moment your rider is at <u>the</u> focusing spot with a small depth of field. With a greater depth of field, your rider is more likely to be in focus within a range of several feet.

As the light changes, an aperture priority camera will change it's selection of shutter speed. Before you know it you may be shooting with a shutter speed of 60 or less which will not allow stop action in bicycle races. You may have plenty of depth of field, but with everything blurry, it doesn't matter.

While you can sidestep this by constantly re-checking your numbers with a light meter, it's hard to remember to do this in the "heat of battle", so speed priority works better.

Speed Priority

With speed priority cameras, <u>you</u> select the speed, usually located on the top of the camera (numbers like 1000, 500, 250, 125). The camera selects the "depth of field" for the best exposure.

In sporting events, where speed is an important factor, it makes more sense to use a "speed priority" camera or to select the speed setting if the choice is available. While today's cameras have all sorts of alternative settings including a "sports" setting, these programs are not as dependable as selection of the correct speed.

250 shutter speed is about as slow as you can go in bicycle racing to pretty well stop action. 125 is risky, but possible if riders are going slow or if you "pan" (move the camera along with the movement of the rider) so the rider is clear, though the background

may be blurry. It depends on what effect you're trying to get. 500 and up is better, but then you get into an increasingly small depth of field, depending on how much light you have, so choices must be made. It's a matter of balancing all numbers.

Film

In direct line with stop action (or not) is film speed. The common speeds you see in drug stores are 100, 200 and 400 (25, 64 are too slow, 1000 is too "grainy".) 100 works fine on sunny days, 200 works, and 400 is great when the light is fading -- more grain, but a better photo. It's all a trade.

Choosing 100 ASA film will more likely result in some movement recorded in your photos, wheel motion and more. If you like the feel of how that looks, 100 ASA will give it to you. Evidence of motion in such a high action sport is appropriate. It's a difficult thing to plan, but the effect communicates part of what the sport is all about. Stop action is for those *slow* sports like football and baseball. Bicycle racing *moves*. The deciding factor needs to be what result <u>you</u> want to look at later.

400 ASA allows better stop action, and many photographers use this. Professional film is better quality than regular film (duhhh . . !), but is also quite a bit more expensive. Photographers constantly argue over methods of lessening grain. Investigate those methods if you wish.

Slides

Slide film is more expensive than print film. As original transparencies go, it is easier to see what is on a slide than what is on a negative. Reprints

are more expensive made from slides but enlargements from slide film have richer colors, especially 8 x 12's and up. Reviewing slides is easier and storage of them is more space efficient. When you see a slide you want to blow up, that IS the "negative" (so to speak) so you don't need to go try to find it.

Print film

Print film is cheaper to buy than slide film. It's hard to see what's on negative film, so you will need prints of the whole roll. Unless you watch for the specials, this can get expensive. However, there are <u>far</u> more specials for having negatives reprinted and enlarged than slides. The colors are not as brilliant, but the difference may not be significant to you.

The trouble with negatives is: there's nothing worse than thinking "I want an enlargement made of this picture -- now where <u>is</u> that negative?" Looking at and organizing negatives can be a nightmare. It's <u>much</u> easier with slides.

The fact is, the small 3 x 5 and 4 x 6 size photos look pretty good whether from print or slide film. It depends on your reasons for taking the photos to begin with. If you don't take a lot, it probably doesn't matter. If you take a lot of photos the significant thing is what you're going to do with them and how you prefer to work with them. Pick one.

Lenses

Heck with the camera and the film, a lot of your success can depend on your lens. A fast lens can help you a lot with low-light and stop action. The lens speed is usually printed on the end of the lens. Standard 50 mm

lenses that come with cameras are usually f/1.8. You can "buy up" to 1.4, a faster lens. The smaller the number, the wider the lens is capable of opening, thus the more light will register on the film. You <u>will</u> notice the difference with that faster lens.

Zoom lenses are often f/4.5-5.6 or so. These are fairly slow and as the light dims you notice it in your pictures. You swear there is plenty of light and you get home to dark photos. Splitting with the BigBucks for a faster zoom is a tough decision because they are very expensive, but it does make a significant difference.

What I Use

I use three lenses (lately) which seem to work well most of the time in the day time (other than the standard 50 mm lens). On my Canon I have a 35-105 (f/4.5-5.6) which I use quite a bit for close shooting. For Sprints, especially, I change to my 75-300 (4-5.6) because the best Sprint action may be at the other end of the track. On my Nikon I have a 180mm, 2.8 lens which I adore except that I don't have as much freedom in distance as my 75-300. These work well for a wide variety of situations. If I were sitting in the stands I would rely exclusively on my 75-300. On the Vandedrome 153m. track I use my 35-105 almost exclusively.

Except at night.

Flash

If I had a choice, all my shooting would be in the day with lots of light coming from Turn One on a white track offering "fill" light to the riders faces. Unfortunately, much track action happens back-lit and at night.

Flash theory is addressed in the technical books. The significant thing is how far you are away from your subject. In bicycle racing, you'd <u>better</u> be some distance away (unless you're up close on a small track with barricades), so you need a strong flash that throws a lot of light.

The camera will have a specific shutter speed designated for use of a flash. The camera must be set on this number or you will get partial illumination over the width of your shot (it will look funny).

Canon has a "125" flash synchro speed, signified on the camera. Nikon requires the speed for flash be set at 250. Since 250 is better for stop action, the Nikon is best for night shots. It makes a big difference in the quality of night shots to have a fast lens.

The Canon, therefore, is my choice by day when there's plenty of light, the Nikon for night shooting.

Unless you're a techno-freak (and this chapter is not written for them) you will not have endless choices. Once you know what you're doing you can break out the BigBucks and increase your range of alternatives, but consult experts and the technical books -- it depends on what you're trying to do. Once you decide that, things get more predictable.

If you have an aperture priority camera that's fine, you need to check your light more often -- **don't forget!** The camera speed needs to be 250 or higher (125 if action is slow), which means your aperture will probably be 5.6 to 8 unless you use ASA 400 and have a faster lens. Don't select f/22 with ASA 100 and a f/5.6 lens and

expect to get great photos. f/11 and 16 will work on sunny days, but <u>*the number you really need to watch is the shutter speed.*</u>

Whatever you try, it helps if you know what numbers were chosen at the time of the action. You don't want to get home and say "Let's see, did I shoot that at 125 or 500?" My advice is, pick a number and see what shots you get before you go trying out other possibilities. If you want to experiment, write the numbers down so you can judge the results. Part of your success will be getting to know what choices will net what results.

I usually shoot at 250-500 and f/5.6-11, 16 if there's lots of sun. I'd pick 250-500 at f/11-16 if I could, but sometimes there just isn't enough light. Faster film and lens speeds do help.

News Photographers / Huge Lenses

You will often see photographers with huge lenses at Championship events. They are probably newspaper and magazine photographers. Track specialists don't tend to use these, sports photographers in general often do. What's the difference?

First, often news photographers have huge lenses available to them for events such as football and baseball where most of the shooting is a) at a distance and b) from off of the field, maybe elevated so they have a clear shot. Second, news photographers are not usually used to the mobility demands of photographing velodrome races.

Those huge lenses are not inappropriate, it's just that they limit the kinds of shots you can get. They are great for those long shots toward the finish line

from deep in Turn One and the super close-up photos, but they have limitations for general racing.

Velodrome race photographers are closer to the athletes, whether they are on the infield with the event going on 360° around them or shooting down the banking with riders 10 feet away. Velodrome photographers are much more likely to move around to various locations for different events. Carrying a huge lens and setting it up under these circumstances means two things. First, while you're hauling and getting set up, many great shots are lost. Second, people are much more likely to walk in front of you because of the distance you must keep between you and the subject, so you lose more shots and get generally frustrated. (Third, you're totally exhausted at the end of the event if you last through it at all!)

What you find too is that some of the great shots are 10 feet away -- great if you have a zoom, lost if you have a fixed 400mm. If you only want a certain kind of photo, that's okay.

So don't envy those with huge lenses or feel you need one. You don't (neither do they!) "Quick on your feet" is the rule in velodrome racing, whether you're inside or outside the track. Mobility is essential -- that's another reason velodrome racing is so challenging. You can't just stand and shoot -- you have to actually think and respond!

What You Can Use

You can spend thousands of dollars on equipment, but most people don't want to have as much invested in their cameras as they do in their **cars!**.

If all you have is the standard aperture priority camera with the 50 mm or short zoom (i.e. 35-70) lens, don't feel like you need to run right out and buy a new camera. A longer zoom lens does help in a sport where you will be so many distances from your subject.

You can start anywhere though, because in the beginning what you will need to work on most is your timing and visualization. Those don't cost any money. It is, however, simply hard to get close enough to take good shots of racing with a 50 mm. If you're going to buy anything, buy a zoom.

Whatever equipment you have, you will adapt to it and if you have any talent or drive you will get good shots with almost whatever you have. Just shoot and let your results tell you what to do next.

I do not recommend instamatics unless that's really all you have and the moment is important -- memories are far more important than technical details. Even the $10 film-in-the-camera cameras are better than *no* photos of memorable moments. The image will be very small on the film unless you get <u>really</u> close-up. But you can do that, too.

Another common saying in photographic circles is that if you take a ton of photos, you're bound to get a couple of good ones. That works! You don't <u>care</u> about the bad ones. The trouble with a sport like bicycle racing, and the thing that makes it so challenging, is that you never know when a great shot will present itself. You have to always be ready. If you try to decide what will be good or what won't, the shot is gone while you're making up your mind. The action happens so fast that you just have to do your best and know that something will turn up.

I can't really tell you what choices to make, I can only tell you which ones I've made. If you have no preferences, use mine or ask some authority. I don't pretend to be one. All I know is I get home from an event and if I get three or more (to me) great photos per year, I'm thrilled. I usually end up with hundreds of shots per event, no matter how small. At National Championships I usually end up with over 1500 shots. You just never know when the Great One will show itself. When it does, it's worth everything! However, it is possible to plan to some extent according to what event you have at hand.

Events

It helps if the photographer knows where the "hot action" is most likely to take place during a given event. Every spot is a gamble.

The finish line is an obvious place, but if you know the races, you can get great shots from almost any place. Some action captured on film relates to a specific race, such as Madison exchanges where riders grab and throw each other. Some shots, like a single rider on the track in race position, could be from any race, any moment, any time period (except if aero bars are on the bike, it has to be a Time Trial!)

No matter what, if one location on the track doesn't feel right, it's not that far to another spot that might produce

better results, whether you're on the infield, the perimeter of the track, or in the stands.

In every event, there is a start and a finish. The start of any race allows leisure in getting a portrait or a "scene". The finish is usually so fast that you're lucky to get anything at all. You certainly have no time, at the finish, to recognize whether the shot will be good or bad. When your rider is coming across the line, shoot! Figure out later whether or not you threw away 25¢.

SPRINTS /Match Sprint

Match Sprints are a great event to photograph. You just never know what's going to happen or when. They are wild cards. Sprinters are great to photograph from the moment they arrive at the track to the moment they leave. Sprints are a very emotional race. The riders are usually like race horses, jittery and high strung, not necessarily off the track, but certainly when they're getting ready to race. Don't expect to talk to them when they're competing because their heads are not available (unless they've won -- somehow congratulations are always acceptable!)

There are many different aspects to a Sprint. There's the mental focus while the rider is waiting his/her turn. There's the choosing of the lot which tells whether the rider will be up or down track. There's the mental thing while being held by the holder (unless you're Bill Clay -- he doesn't need any of that silly stuff!). There's the moment of dropping onto the handlebars. The shove off. The cat and mouse first lap.

But no! A rider may take off and try to "Kilo" (ride fast for three solid

laps) his opponent! The challenges up and down the track as one rider attempts to catch the other off-guard. The moment of sprint! Will he/she be able to hold it? Will they crash into each other (if they do, get the shot!)

Coming around Turn Four in the final Sprint is a great spot. Shooting down track from the outside is good shooting. And -- can you get that moment of truth when both front tires are on the white area of the finish line at the same time? See the photos of Hill and Harnett in the Gallery section for a "hot action" Sprint.

Favorite spots for Sprints: 1) the finish line <u>area</u>, start and finish, inside or outside. 2) Turn Four, inside or outside 3) "getting ready" events, psyching up, drawing lots, preparing. 4) between Turn 2 and the 200 meter line (sometimes the Sprint will start there).

Watch for: the start, Track Stands in the first lap; falling over in a track stand; testing each other up and down the track; the Sprint, especially over the last 200 meters; contact between riders (illegal in Match Sprint); intimidation activities which may result in crashes, especially when the Sprint begins; riders throwing their bicycles at the finish; (and, for a real challenge) a photo finish with both wheels on the line!

Keirin: same areas, but more involvement with the motor. Starting line up; getting on the motor when it comes around; lined up on the motor (who is where?); physical contact between competitors (legal in Keirin) which might lead to crashes; the time when the motor pulls off (usually

between Turn Two and the 200 meter line on a 333 m. track; anywhere in the final Sprint; finish line bicycle throw.

Tandem Sprint: similar to Match Sprint. The same riders are probably using similar tricks, though it takes longer to get the vehicle to speed and the race is usually five laps as opposed to three. The position of the Stoker (in back) makes for some interesting photos. The danger in this event makes it very unpredictable.

MASS START RACES

Both Madison and Points are Mass Start races. The starts are conducted differently and the Madison has rider exchanges. Points accumulate the same, double at the middle and end.

Initially, all riders will report to the fence or rail. Points race riders shove off and come around grouped together on the first lap, getting the gun. Madison teams split up after assembling at the rail. One half move to staggered points around the velodrome, the other half ride one lap together as in the Points race. Officials signal the start and the race begins.

The accumulation of points during competition is similar, but riders tend to be much more spread out in zones around the track in the Madison than in the Points race. Teams tend to exchange in the same general area several times consecutively. Effort must be spread somewhat evenly between partners, because the race is a long one. Riders exchange at will.

Exchanges will most likely happen coming out of Turn Two and Turn Four and into the straightaway. In 1991, the Champion Carney brothers exchanged often out of Turn Two and into the backstraight. In 1994, Champions Copeland/Durso exchanged often between Turns Four and One, later in the homestraight.

Whoever you're photographing, watch them for a few laps to see what they tend to do. Of course, once you figure it out, they'll change to a different spot!

If you're feeling physically fit, you can run to either side of the velodrome to get exchange shots which are pretty dependably on the straights. Exchanging on the turns is more risky.

Whether Madison or Points race, riders will be going hardest at the bottom of the track. Sprints will occur half way through each race and at the end for Double Points.

Crashes are more likely during these high stress times, so don't forget, this work is not without dangers. If you're on the outside of the track, you're in a safer position, but on the infield you must keep in mind that a rider crashing into you at 40 miles per hour will likely hurt you. Be careful and don't get in anybody's way.

Favorite spots for Points races: 1) the finish line area, start and finish, inside or outside. 2) Turn Four half way through and at the finish when Double Points are being contested. 3) anywhere around the track when someone is trying to lap the field or bridge a gap. 4) anywhere there is a background feature you want to photograph with a lot of riders in the shot.

Maybe a shot into the stands, maybe the scoreboard, velodrome sign or sponsor advertisement in the background. If you want a commercial shot of a velodrome scene with a lot of riders, these are the races. They'll be going on for a long time, so you can walk around and do set-up shots. If there are any celebrities in the crowd, get them in the fore/background!

Watch for: start activities, especially riders lined up at the rail; Sprint sessions, whether for Double Points, getting off the front, bridging a gap or ? ; riders uptrack resting, waiting for someone to take off; "portraits" in a crowd of your guy/gal. **Madison:** same as above, but the start has some riders at the line and some not. The most significant challenge is trying to photograph the exchanges. Those are good for a workout and will keep you busy the entire race!

TIME TRIALS
Kilo/Pursuit

These events are most distinct by how many laps (opportunities) you have to get photos. In the Kilometer you usually have three laps (maybe four, depending on the track), to get the rider on film. It is the same for women and men. A Kilo is a Kilo.

In the Pursuit you probably have nine (for women) or twelve (for men) laps to get one or more photos. This is for a 333m track. On a 250 track you will have twelve and sixteen laps, accordingly.

Photographically, the starts of these are always good. Riders take time to make sure their equipment is okay. They sit if they have to wait, sometimes with coaches giving last minute advice. They may tape their feet in or need to re-tape their numbers. Janie Eickhoff spoke of her "rituals" in preparation for her everts. These allow the rider to go into "concentration mode". "Race faces" are interesting (especially Janie's).

One particularly tricky spot in Time Trials is immediately after the gun has gone off. If anything weird is going to happen, this is often when. Riders are putting tremendous effort into their starts. Sometimes equipment will break. Sometimes riders will pull their foot. Sometimes a rear wheel will come loose. You just never know. You may record a technical position problem that the rider would want to correct if they could see themselves start. Videos will capture this kind of thing in a different way.

In both races, riders will be standing, building speed for approximately a half lap. Sometimes it is good to be on the other side of where your rider starts so you can get either the rider still picking up speed (but actually going fast, as opposed to the start) or in the middle of the transition of hands from the drops to the tuck position on the pursuit bars. Those are kind of tricky to get. Once they settle in their seats, shots are more the same except for the face, which often gets more strained as the effort goes on and especially toward the end.

The Kilo requires a stronger effort for more of the race, so facial contortions and "grunt" efforts are more evident throughout this race. The biggest change you'll see in the Pursuit is that in the beginning riders will look somewhat relaxed, but by the end they will have that "pain" expression that makes for great photos (unless they are of Rebecca Twigg -- she looks effortless the whole time!)

You won't have much time in the Kilo, but the Pursuit allows time to practice getting the rider in focus and experimentation with "grueling portrait" kinds of photography. They are going fast enough that getting a clear shot with accurate focus is still a challenge. It is good practice time, and you have enough time between shots to think a little.

The finish is always maximum effort. You might practice getting them at the <u>moment</u> they cross the finish line. This is a timing thing that improves with practice. Mike Gladu, a photographer for VeloNews, is really good at it. I have a tendency to shoot too early, partly because I am interested in the effort, and sometimes riders relax at the finish line.

Favorite spots for Time Trials: 1) the finish line <u>area</u>, start and finish, inside or outside, 2) backstretch, during the start when riders are just in the process of sitting from the Start or putting their hands onto the aero bars, maybe one on, one off, 3) outside the track, shooting across to get both riders and the Starter in the shot, all at the same time. Maybe at the moment the gun goes off, shooting smoke into the air as both riders expend maximum effort.

Watch for: the rituals of Time Trial starts, almost as "heavy" as Sprints. Riders taping their feet, putting on double straps, etc. Watch for unusual equipment -- more likely in Time Trials than any other event -- like goofy bikes, helmets, rubber suits, weird handlebars (see Bostick's bars), who knows what? This is The Event of Equipment Innovation.

Team Pursuit/Olympic Sprint

These events have a lot of similarities. Multiple riders doing maximum efforts means that there is more likelihood that something will break or that something will happen. One rider fell down at the start zipping up his suit. Another fell when his stem bolt broke, about three strokes off the line. You never know. Be ready.

The duality of individuals who are also part of a team is intriguing. Each must interact with his teammates as he simultaneously focuses within himself. The start is always full of action. Like Kilo and Pursuit, riders are usually standing for the first half of the lap while they SMOOTHLY (we hope) transition into their appropriate places in the team formation.

Team Pursuit: Once the team is in place, things become much more regular. At that point, what you can depend on is the exchanges up and down the banking on the turns, mostly every half lap, though maybe an occasional full lap. Then you watch for whether the team can stay together and for how long.

Once they drop one team member, that's fine, but then the remaining three must a) not drop the Third Man and b) finish together. Catching them passing another team (or getting passed) is a heartbreak or joy, as is losing the Third Man (depending on who you're rooting for). Three must finish together.

Olympic Sprint: As riders move into team formation they must also be accelerating to maximum speed. This is the tricky part and is the most essential part of the race. Riders cannot depend on the laps of the future to compensate for any slowness in getting together at the start. Every millisecond counts. The first rider is only available photographically for one lap, then he's gone. The next rider is only there for two laps. One more lap and the race is over. The end. The move of each rider off the front is significant, but not tricky. The hot stuff here is the start.

Favorite spots for Team events: 1) the finish line area, start and finish, inside or outside. 2) the first half lap. 3) the exchanges, Turns Two and Four for Team Pursuit, the Homestretch for Olympic Sprint.

Watch for: unexpected things at the start, action in the first half lap, lead exchanges, Team Pursuit--all three or four riders finishing together or losing the Third Man, exhausted riders at the finish.

Other Events:

While what has been discussed so far has been Nationals events, there are many shots available at local races which get at the heart of track racing. The more practice you get at local races, the better prepared you are when the "Big Event" arrives. Timing and anticipation are important. You need to stop, from time to time and look for unusual shots. They are there if you just look.

Another factor in getting great shots is straight luck (but it helps if you're prepared.)

Crashes and Other Disasters

There is a classic philosophical problem in photojournalism concerning placing on record other people's pain and disaster. The uninitiated ask "How can you be so cold as to keep shooting when people are hurt or in pain?" You will need to find your own comfort level.

Some riders like seeing the scene later at a time when they are not in a state of shock. If you don't take it, you may get the lament "Oh, you should have taken it!" Others deeply want no reminder of the incident, ever!

The beginning of the Team Pursuit in '84 was not Dave Grylls' favorite moment (*"Olympic Nightmare"*, see Gallery) and is likely one he wants to forget. Nevertheless, the moment was inadvertently caught on film. If it were an invasion of privacy, it would be different, but this was an event that occurred before thousands of people and is hardly a secret.

Any shot represents different things to different people. Every time I look at *Olympic Nightmare*, I realize Dave pulled his foot and the Gold was lost, but those are only the technical details. What I really see is three magnificent riders (McDonough, Nitz and Hegg) who showed the proudest hearts athletes can display to thousands of spectators who will never forget their performance. It's a great photo because it has a history (and tragedy) accompanying the moment, for the main player and for others on the team. That is what photojournalism is all about.

On the other hand, recording personal moments that become available to you is accompanied by a moral responsibility to respect your subject(s). What can you live with?

On the other hand, if you get a personal shot during a national event before 100s or 1000s, especially if it's a sad but great shot, the photo may be a great one for its message or a lesson to be learned.

All this moral stuff is a huge responsibility and one that should not be taken lightly. These are lives that you're shooting. Respect them.

Magazine Work

Sending photos to magazines can be a frustrating experience, especially when you got a great shot, you know they should print it, and you get back a note saying "This does not meet our needs at this time." What are they talking about? Can't they see this is a great shot? It is aggravating.

If you should decide that bicycle race photography is something you want to pursue, others can tell you more about how to pursue it for money. Be prepared for finding other ways to support yourself than the life of a full time bicycle race photographer. Ask Casey Gibson and Mike Gladu what they do.

Doing it on your own terms is the best. Sending photos you know are special to people who don't understand is frustrating. It becomes a matter of artistic control. If you love bicycle racing and photography, you will do it no matter what. Supporting it becomes a matter of independent enterprise.

The Bottom Line

Winning a race can't be better than snagging a great shot, and no magazine can offer a greater reward than looking at your own great shot. The Pulitzer Prize is a journalistic award given for capturing significant moments on film. The actual photo may be technically outright bad, but that doesn't matter because that is not why the award is given. It is given for <u>significance</u> of a moment frozen in time. Those shots are worth so much more than money. They are kind of like stopping and capturing time.

Go to a photo exhibit that has "arty" photos and a photojournalistic section. While the "arty" photos may be beautiful, they are often rigid. The photojournalistic photos *move*. No one posing or trying to be anything.

Ansel Knew

Ansel Adams spoke a lot about "pre-visualization": what do you want the photograph to look like? If you know that, you can select or seek advice on what equipment might help you record the vision. If you have little idea of what results you want, look at bicycle racing books and publications for ideas.

Ansel isn't famous for discussions of "post-visualization", but taking shots and evaluating them later provides that opportunity. You meant to do *that*. Why didn't it come out like that? Thinking through what you were trying to do and figuring out what you have to do differently to have more success is a very worthwhile activity. It leads to pre-visualization the next time you're on the track. It's an on-going challenge.

Think you don't have enough light? Shoot anyway and see what you get. If you don't try, you'll get nothing. If you try, maybe you'll get something great or just a poorly recorded memory of someone's great moment which otherwise would not be on record at all. It goes with the territory.

Cartier-Bresson

Henri Cartier-Bresson was not a sports photographer, he was a photojournalist, yet he was more. He played with motion in his photos (some including bicycles). He took pictures from odd angles. He wasn't afraid of investigating his own sense of the unknown. He answered an internal imperative to explore. He spoke of the "decisive moment." In sports there are many decisive moments. If you're lucky you will catch a few of them.

Trying to capture a part of yourself in relation to a subject matter over which you have no control is a mysterious challenge. If you can do it, you are putting yourself in photos of the world around you. It's almost a contradiction. Photographic style reflects you.

Grabbing a shot on the run and taking risks as to whether decent photos will result makes it an adventure. Cartier-Bresson did that. His vision of the beauty available from where he happened to stand was reflective of his unique mind. In the end, pleasing yourself is the best reward.

This is especially true if you have imagination and are recording the human spectacle, not just riders riding hard. It's the ultimate souvenir because it's specific to your interests. Nothing is ever wasted (that's one of those laws of physics -- hey, ask a physicist to explain it!)

How to Get Great Shots

The main characteristic you must have to get *great* shots is patience. They are virtually a gift. You can't ask the riders to pose for you during competition -- they're a little busy and re-rides are out of the question. The more you try, the better you will get at "assisting" the fortuitous great shot.

Make sure the racers are as large in the view finder as possible unless you have a reason to do a more distant shot. No matter how close you are and how large the riders seem at the time, they usually look smaller when the film is developed.

Often shots are more interesting when part of a rider is out of the picture than when all bodies and bikes are in it and you are farther away (hey, maybe you want one of those big lenses after all!)

You might select <u>any</u> rider (if you don't have a favorite) and just try to take that person's picture, with everyone else in or out according to wherever they happened to be when the shutter was hit. Also, this isolates the "depth of field" zone so you don't get confused by trying to figure out who all is in focus and who all isn't.

At first, you'll do fine just to get one person in clear focus moving at 35 miles per hour. **Practice, practice, practice!**

Often, permission is not given, even in local track events, for photographers to be on the infield unless they are doing some specific work. This is due, in part, to safety considerations. This is not unjustified.

Some of the best shots are from the outside of the track anyway. The position just on the other side of the track from the finish line is excellent, and up into Turn One.

Shots down the banking from the ends of the track are also excellent. At some tracks, like Blaine, this is not possible without a rented boom because there is no place to stand. At other tracks, like Colorado Springs, you can grab good shots from just about any place around the track. T-Town has an overhead walkway, other tracks don't, so those shots communicate where you were.

In races like the Madison it is advantageous to be on the infield if you want to run back and forth, but this is not necessary. From the outside mobility is much more restricted, especially during popular events.

If you know the races, you can get great shots from almost any place even though getting through the crowd may require patience.

It is really a good idea, in the beginning, to try many different locations with the specific intention of finding out where you prefer to be. Roaming is the best.

And Last --

I'm always surprised that there actually are images on the film! It's so joyful just to see them, it's kind of like giving birth 1500 times per event (well, sort of).

To those who love this sport, we each serve it in our own way. We all have our place and our function. If you get involved, it will pay you back over and over, throughout your life. That's its addiction.

If you are a velodrome photographer, you have a *double* addiction. It couldn't be more gratifying being a double World Champion.

Favorite Shooting Spots per Event

1 - my favorites
2 - still good
3 - not a favorite
4 - good shots may be there anyway.

Flying 200s -- 200m line and Turn 4, in or out, absolutely.

Shooting Spot	Match Sprint	Keirin	Tandem Sprint	Points Race	Madison	Kilometer	Individual Pursuit	Team Pursuit	Olympic Sprint	Other track events	The Event itself
Inside, Start/Finish	(1)	(1)	(1)	1	1	1	1	1	(1)	(1)	Entry.
Outside, Start/Finish	1	1	1	1	1	2	2	1	1	1	Anywhere activities
Inside, Homestretch	1	1	1	1	1	(1)	(1)	2	2	1	are going on. Special
Outside, Homestretch	1	1	1	1	1	2	2	3	3	1	people. Last row
Inside, Backstretch	2	2	2	1	(1)	(1)	(1)	2	2	1	panorama shots. Interviews.
Outside, Backstretch	3	3	3	1	1	2	2	3	3	1	Award ceremonies.
Inside, Turn One	3	2	3	3	4	2	2	1	1	2	Media. Riders
Outside, Turn One	1	1	1	2	3	2	2	1	1	1	arriving, getting ready.
Inside, Turn Two	2	1	1	3	2	2	3	(1)	1	Watch the action	Behind the scenes
Outside, Turn Two	4	4	4	4	3	4	4	2	2	Go where changes occur	action. Parents.
Inside, Turn Three	2	3	2	3	4	2	2	2	2		Kids with hope in
Outside, Turn Three	3	4	3	4	4	4	4	3	4		their eyes. Everybody
Inside, Turn Four	1	1	1	(1)	3	2	2	1	1	1	having a
Outside, Turn Four	2	2	2	2	4	4	4	2	2	1	good time.

| | Sprints | | | MassStart | | Time | Trials | | | Other | |

(*1 for Start/Finish and 3 for Homestretch means that there may be photographic Start/Finish activities, but the race itself may be better from another area.*)

And, sometimes shots are simply best where other people are NOT.

World Amateur Champion Track Medalists from the USA 1888-1992

1888	Buffalo, NY	
	3 mi	1. H. Crocker
1893	Chicago, IL	
	M Sprint	1. Arthur Zimmerman
		2. J. Johnson
		3. J.P. Bliss
	10 km	1. Arthur Zimmerman
		2. J.P. Bliss
		3. J. Johnson
	Motorpace	2. Albrecht
		3. Ulbricht
1899	Montreal, Canada	
	M Sprint	2. E. Peabody
	Motorpace	1. J.A. Nelson
		2. Goodson
1900	Paris, France	
	M Sprint	2. John Henry Lake
1904	London, England	
	M Sprint	1. Marcus Hurley
1912	Newark, New Jersey, USA	
	M Sprint	1. Donald McDougall
		2. Kaiser
		3. Diver

While professional track racing flourished in the 20s and 30s, there was little incentive or opportunity for amateurs. A lone figure stands out in the history of US track racing during this time:

| **1949** | Copenhagen, Denmark | |
| | M Sprint | 3. Jack Heid |

In the 50s and 60s the world of track racing was a desolate place. Family tradition and role model Jack Heid combined to light another man's fuse:

1968	Montevideo, Uruguay	
	M Kilo	2. Jack Simes II
(1969	Brno, Czechoslovakia	
	W Road	1. Audrey McElmury)

While primarily a road rider, McElmury repeatedly chose international over domestic track events, breaking ground for those who followed. Flood gates opened with the legendary midwestern speedskaters whose influence continues through Connie Paraskevin & Roger Young.

1972	Marseille, France	
	W Sprint	3. Sheila Young
1973	San Sebastian, Spain	
	W Sprint	1. Sheila Young

1974	Montreal, Canada	
	W Sprint	2. Sue Novara
	Warsaw, Poland	
	JM Sprint	1. Gibby Hatton
1975	Liege, Belgium	
	W Sprint	1. Sue Novara
		3. Sheila Young
1976	Mendrisio, Italy	
	W Sprint	1. Sheila Young
		2. Sue Novara
	W Pursuit	3. Mary Jane Reoch
1977	San Cristobal	
	W Sprint	2. Sue Novara
1978	Munich, Germany	
	W Sprint	2. Sue Novara
	Tandem Sprint	2. Jerry Ash, Leigh Barczewski
1979	Amsterdam, Holland	
	W Sprint	3. Sue Novara
1979	Buenos Aires, Argentina	
	JM Pursuit	2. Greg LeMond
1980	Besancon, France	
	W Sprint	1. Sue Novara
1981	Brno, Czecheslovakia	
	W Sprint	1. Sheila Young-Ochowicz
	M Points	2. Leonard Harvey Nitz
1982	Leicester, England	
	W Sprint	1. Connie Paraskevin
		2. Sheila Young-Ochowicz
	W Pursuit	1. Rebecca Twigg
		2. Connie Carpenter
1983	Zurich, Switzerland	
	W Sprint	1. Connie Paraskevin
	W Pursuit	1. Connie Carpenter
		2. Cindy Olavarri
	Wanganui, New Zealand	
	JM Pursuit	3. Roy Knickman
	JM Team Pursuit	2. Tim Hinz, Roy Knickman, Kit Kyle, Craig Schommer
1984	Barcelona, Spain	
	W Sprint	1. Connie Paraskevin
	W Pursuit	1. Rebecca Twigg

1984	Caen, France	
	J M Kilo	2. Craig Schommer
1985	Bassano del Grappa, Italy	
	W Sprint	2. Connie Paraskevin
	W Pursuit	1 Rebecca Twigg
		3. Peggy Maas
	Tandem Sprint	2. Nelson Vails, Les Barczewski
1986	Colorado Springs, Colorado, USA	
	W Sprint	3. Connie Paraskevin
	W Pursuit	2. Rebecca Twigg
	M Points	3. Leonard Harvey Nitz
	Tandem Sprint	2. Kit Kyle, David Lindsey
1987	Vienna, Austria	
	W Sprint	3. Connie Paraskevin Young
	W Pursuit	1. Rebecca Twigg
		3. Mindee Mayfield
1987	Bergamo, Italy	
	JW Sprint	1. Janie Eickhoff
	JW Pursuit	1. Janie Eickhoff
1988	Ghent, Bel	
	W Pursuit	3. Mindee Mayfield
1989	Lyons, France	
	W Points	3. Janie Eickhoff
1990	Maebashi, Japan	
	W Sprint	1. Connie Paraskevin Young
		2. Renee Duprel
	M Pursuit	3. Mike McCarthy
1991	Stuttgart, Germany	
	W Sprint	3. Connie Paraskevin Young
	W Pursuit	2. Janie Eickhoff
	W Points	3. Janie Eickhoff
1992	Valencia, Sp	
	W Points	3. Janie Eickhoff

Beginning in 1993, amateurs and professionals compete together at the World Championships (see next page)

| **Key:** | M -- Men | J M -- Junior Men |
| | W -- Women | JW -- Junior Women |

National Professional Track Champions of the United States of America

Track Champions 1895-1941
Run by the National Cycling Association

1895 Eddie Bald	1911 Frank L. Kramer	1927 Harris Holder
1896 Eddie Bald	1912 Frank L. Kramer	1928 Fred Spencer
1897 Eddie Bald	1913 Frank L. Kramer	1929 Fred Spencer
1898 Tom Butler	1914 Frank L. Kramer	1930 Cecil Walker
1899 Tom Cooper	1915 Frank L. Kramer	1931 Cecil Walker
1900 Major Taylor	1916 Frank L. Kramer	1932 Cecil Walker
1901 Frank L. Kramer	1917 Arthur Spencer	1933 George Dempsey
1902 Frank L. Kramer	1918 Frank L. Kramer	1934 Willie Honeman
1903 Frank L. Kramer	1919 Ray Eaton	1935 Willie Honeman
1904 Frank L. Kramer	1920 Arthur Spencer	1936 Willie Honeman
1905 Frank L. Kramer	1921 Frank L. Kramer	1937 Mathias Engel
1906 Frank L. Kramer	1922 Willie Spencer	1938 Albert Sellinger
1907 Frank L. Kramer	1923 Willie Spencer	1939 George Shipman
1908 Frank L. Kramer	1924 Arthur Spencer	1940 Mickey Francoise
1909 Frank L. Kramer	1925 Fred Spencer	1941 Tom Saetta
1910 Frank L. Kramer	1926 Willie Spencer	

Run by the U.S Professional Racing Organization (USPRO)

Track **1983** Trexlertown, PA

Sprint -- Gibby Hatton   Keirin -- Roger Young
Points Race -- Dale Stetina   5km Pursuit -- Jeff Rutter

World Professional Championship Track Medalists of the USA 1895-1994

Year	Location	Event	Medalist
1895	Cologne	Sprint	2. George A. Banker
1898	Vienna	Sprint	1. George A. Banker
1899	Montreal	Sprint	1. Major Taylor
			2. T. Butler
		Motorpace	2. H. MacLean
			3. Boake
1904	London	Sprint	1. Iver Lawson
		Motorpace	1. Robert H. Walthour
1905	Antwerp	Motorpace	1. Robert H. Walthour
1909	Copenhagen	Motorpace	3. Nat Butler
1910	Bussels	Motorpace	3. Robert W. Walthour
1911	Rome	Motorpace	3. James F. Moran
1912	Newark, NJ	Sprint	1. Frank L. Kramer
		Motorpace	1. G. Wiley
			2. Elmer L. Collins
			3. James F. Moran
1983	Zurich, Switzerland	Keirin	3. Gibby Hatton
1992	Valencia, Spain	Pursuit	1. Mike McCarthy

Beginning in 1993, amateurs and professionals compete together at the World Championships

Year	Location	Event	Medalist
1993	Hamar, Nor	W Pursuit	1. Rebecca Twigg
			3. Janie Eickhoff
		M Keirin	2. Marty Nothstein
		W Points	3. Jessica Grieco
1994	Palermo, It	M Sprint	1. Marty Nothstein
		M Keirin	1. Marty Nothstein
		W Pursuit	3. Janie Eickhoff
		M Team Pursuit	2. Carl Sundquist, Mariano Friedick, Adam Laurant, Dirk Copeland

Sources: 1990 &1994 USCF RuleBooks, Cycling USA

Olympic Track Medalists from the USA 1900-1996

1900   Paris, France
Sprint   3. John Henry Lake
1904   St. Louis, Missouri, USA
1/4 mile   1. Marcus Hurley
                            2. Burton Downing
                            3. Edward Billington
1/3 mile   1. Marcus Hurley
                            2. Burton Downing
                            3. Edward Billington
1/2 mile   1. Marcus Hurley
                            2. Burton Downing
                            3. Edward Billington
1 mile   1. Marcus Hurley
                            2. Burton Downing
                            3. Edward Billington
2 miles   1. Burton Downing
                            2. Oscar Goerke
                            3. Marcus Hurley

1904   St. Louis, Missouri, USA (cont.)
5 miles   1. Charles Schlee
                            2. George Wiley
                            3. A.F. Andrews
25 miles   1. Burton Downing
                            2. A.F. Andrews
                            3. George Wiley

1984   Los Angeles, California, USA
M Sprint   1. Mark Gorski
                            2. Nelson Vails
M Pursuit   1. Steve Hegg
                            3. Leonard Nitz
Team Pursuit   2. Dave Grylls, Steve Hegg, Pat
                            McDonough, Leonard Nitz, Brent Emery
1988   Seoul, South Korea
W Sprint   3. Connie Paraskevin Young

1992   Barcelona, Spain
M Kilo   3. Erin Hartwell
W Pursuit   3. Rebecca Twigg

1996 Atlanta, GA--Write it in as you watch it !!

Sprint -- Men --   Women --

Kilometer -- Men --   Women? --

Pursuit -- Men --   Women --

Points -- Men --   Women --

Team Pursuit --

Olympic Sprint --

Pan American Medalists from the USA 1959-1995

1959   Chicago, Illinois, USA
M Sprint   2. Jack Disney
M Kilometer   1. Allen C. Bell
                            3. D.D. Staub
Team Pursuit   1. Rich Cortwright, Charles Hewett,
                            Robert Pfarr, Jim Rossi

1963   Sao Paulo, Brazil
Sprint   2. Jim Rossi
1967   Winnipeg, Canada
Sprint   3. Carl Leusencamp
Kilometer   2. Jack Simes III
10 mile   3. Tim Mountford
Team Pursuit   3. Wesley Chowen, Michael Cone,
                            Skip Cutting, William Kund

1971   Cali, Columbia
Kilometer   3. Cliff Halsey
Team Pursuit   3. David Chauner, Michael Hiltner,
                            David Mulica, John VandeVelde

1975   Mexico City, Mexico
Sprint   1. Steve Woznick
                            3. Carl Leusencamp

Kilometer   3. Steve Woznick
Team Pursuit   1. Paul Deem, Ron Skarin,
                            Ralph Therrio, Roger Young

1983   Caracas, Venezuela
Sprint   1. Nelson Vails
                            2. Les Barczewski
Kilometer   1. Rory O'Reilly
Pursuit   1. Dave Grylls
Points   1. John Beckman
Team Pursuit   1. Brent Emery, Dave Grylls,
                            Steve Hegg, Leonard Nitz

1987   Indianapolis, Indiana, USA
M Sprint   1. Ken Carpenter
                            2. Mark Gorski
 W Sprint   1. Connie Paraskevin Young
                            2. Renee Duprel
M Pursuit   2. David Brinton
W Pursuit   1. Rebecca Twigg
M Kilometer   3. Leonard Nitz
Team Pursuit   1. David Brinton, Dave Lettieri,
                            Leonard Nitz, Carl Sundquist

1991   Havana, Cuba
W Sprint   2. Julie Gregg
                            3. Jessica Grieco
M Kilometer   2. Erin Hartwell
M Pursuit   2. Dirk Copeland
W Pursuit   1. Kendra Kneeland
Team Pursuit   2. Chris Coletta, Jim Pollak,
                            Tim Quigley, Matt Hamon

1995   Mar del Plata, Argentina
M Sprint   1. Marty Nothstein
W Sprint   2. Connie Paraskevin Young
M Pursuit   1. Kent Bostick
W Pursuit   1. Janie Eickhoff
M Kilometer   2. Erin Hartwell
W Points   1. Janie Eickhoff
Team Pursuit   1. Carl Sundquist, Zach Conrad,
                            Mariano Friedick, Adam Laurant,
                            Christian VandeVelde

Senior Amateur National Track Championships 1899-1952

Run by the National Cycling Association

1899 Frank L. Kramer	1910 Frank Blatz	1920 Fred Taylor	1930 Dominick Tuccillo	1940 Buster Logan
1900 Willie Fenn, Sr.	1911 Frank Blatz	1921 Bobby Walthour, Jr.	1931 Arthur Rose	1941 Bob Stauffacher
1901 Marcus L. Hurley	1912 Donald McDougal	1922 Willie Grimm	1932 Amos Hoffman	(World War II)
1902 Marcus L. Hurley	1913 Donald McDougal	1923 Willie Fenn Jr.	1933 Eddie Miller	1951 Dave Rhoades
1903 Marcus L. Hurley	1914 Harry Kaiser	1924 Paul Croley	1934 Robert Lipsett, Jr.	1952 Ronald Rhoades
1904 Marcus L. Hurley	1915 Hans Ohrt	1925 Charles Winter	1935 Albert Selinger	
1905 Matt Downey	1916 John L. Staehle	1926 William Coles	1936 Mickey Francoise	
1906 Charles Sherwood	1917 John L. Staehle	1927 Jimmy Walthour, Jr.	1937 Mickey Francoise	
1907 Willie Vanden Dries	1918 Gus Lang	1928 Charles Ritter	1938 Mickey Francoise	
1908 Charles Stein	1919 Charles Osteritter	1929 Sergio Matteini	1939 Howard Rupprecht	
1909 Percy Lawrence				

Senior Amateur National Track Championships

Run by the Amateur Bicycle League of America, now the United States Cycling Federation

Senior Men Omnium 1921-1964

1921 Arthur Nieminsky, NY	1936 Jack Simes, Jr., NJ	1951 Gus Gatto, CA
1922 Carl Hambacher, NJ	1937 Charles Bergna, NJ	1952 Steve Hromjak, OH
1923 Charles Barclay, CA	1938 Albin Jurca, WI	1953 Ronnie Rhoads, CA
1924 Charles Winter, NY	1939 Martin Deras, CA	1954 Jack Disney, CA
1925 Edward Merkner, IL	1940 Ferman Kugler, NJ	1955 Jack Disney, CA
1926 Edward Merkner, IL	1941 Marvin Thompson, IL	1956 Jack Disney, CA
1927 Jimmy Walthour, Jr.	1942 not held	1957 Jack Disney, CA
1928 R.J. Connor, DC	1943 not held	1958 Jack Disney, CA
1929 Sergio Matteini, NY	1944 not held	1959 Jim Rossi, IL
1930 Bobby Thomas, WI	1945 Ted Smith, NY	1960 Jim Rossi, IL
1931 not held	1946 Don Hester, CA	1961 Jim Rossi, IL
1932 not held	1947 Ted Smith, NY	1962 Jim Rossi, IL
1933 not held	1948 Ted Smith, NY	1963 Jim Rossi, IL
1934 not held	1949 James Lauf, MD	1964 Jack Simes III, NJ
1935 Cecil Hursey, GA	1950 Robert Pfarr, WI	1965 changed to individual event contests

Senior Women Omnium 1937-1969

1937 Doris Kopsky, NJ	1955 Jeanne Robinson, MI
1938 Dolores Amundson, IL	1956 Jeanne Robinson, MI
1939 Gladys Owen, NY	1957 Nancy Neiman, MI
1940 Mildred Dietz, MO	1958 Nancy Neiman, MI
1941 Jean Michels, IL	1959 Maxine Conover, WA
1942 not held	1960 Edith Johnson, NY
1943 not held	1961 Edith Johnson, NY
1944 not held	1962 Nancy Burghart, NY
1945 Mildred Dietz, MO	1963 Edith Johnson, NY
1946 Mildred Dietz, MO	1964 Nancy Burghart, NY
1947 Doris Travani, MI	1965 Nancy Burghart, NY
1948 Doris Travani, MI	1966 Audrey McElmury, CA
1949 Doris Travani, MI	1967 (contested as individual events)
1950 Doris Travani, MI	1968 (contested as individual events)
1951 Anna Piplak, IL	1969 Audrey McElmury, CA
1952 Jeanne Robinson, MI	1970 from 1970 on, track events
1953 Nancy Neiman, MI	were contested as individual events
1954 Nancy Neiman, MI	for both men and women

U. S. National Champions -- Men 1965-1994

Senior Men -- run by the "Amateur Bicycle League of America" until 1976, when it became the "United States Cycling Federation" (USCF)

	Match Sprint	Pursuit	10 mile / Points	Kilometer	Madison	Tandem Sprint
1965	Jack Simes III, NJ	Skip Cutting, CA	William Kunde, CA			
1966	Jack Disney, CA	Dave Brink, CA	Jim Rossi, IL		Early Madison	
1967	Jack Simes III, NJ	Dave Brink, CA	Steve Maaranen, OR		Championship locations	
1968	Jack Disney, CA	Dave Brink, CA	Steve Maaranen, OR		1978 Kalamazoo, MI	
1969	Tim Mountford, CA	John VandeVelde, IL	Jack Simes III, NJ		1979 Encino, CA	
1970	Skip Cutting, CA	John VandeVelde, IL	Bob Phillips, MD		1980 Northbrook, IL	
1971	Gary Campbell, CA	Mike Neel, CA	Hans Nuernberg, WI	Tim Zasadny, IL	1981 Encino, CA	
1972	Gary Campbell, CA	John VandeVelde, IL	Bob Phillips, MD	Steve Woznick, NJ	1982 Trexlertown, PA	
1973	Roger Young, MI	Mike Neel, CA	Mike Neel, CA	Steve Woznick, NJ	1983 Indianapolis, IN	
1974	Steve Woznick, NJ	Mike Neel, CA	Ralph Therrio, CA	Steve Woznick, NJ		
1975	Steve Woznick, NJ	Ron Skarin, CA	Leroy Gatto, CA	Steve Woznick, NJ	Madison Championships were	
1976	Leigh Barczewski, WI	Leonard Nitz, CA	Ron Skarin, CA	Bob Vehe, IL	held separately from 1978 to 1985,	

All competitions listed here were contested as amateur until 1993 when the U.S. National Championships were opened to both amateur and professional competitors.

(changed to) **Points Race**

	Match Sprint	Pursuit	10 mile / Points	Kilometer	Madison	Tandem Sprint
1977	Leigh Barczewski, WI	Paul Deem, CA	Nelson Saldena, NY	Jerry Ash, CA		
1978	Leigh Barczewski, WI	Dave Grylls, MI	Ron Skarin, CA	Jerry Ash, CA	Danny Van Haute, Il/ Roger Young, MI	
1979	Leigh Barczewski, WI	Dave Grylls, MI	Gus Pipenhagen, IL	Jerry Ash, CA	Bruce Donaghy, PA/ Dave Grylls, MI	
1980	Mark Gorski, IL	Leonard Nitz, PA	Scott Hembree, CA	Brent Emery, WI	L. Nitz, PA/ D. Van Haute, Il/ R. Young, MI	

when they became a part of regularly contested US National Championship events.

(The US did have Tandem Sprint competitors prior to 1984. In 1978, Jerry Ash and Leigh Barczewski (see Sprint and Kilo, 1976-79) won Silver at the World Championships in Munich, Germany.)

Tandem Sprint

	Match Sprint	Pursuit	10 mile / Points	Kilometer	Madison	DRIVER	STOKER
1981	Les Barczewski, WI	Leonard Nitz, PA	John Beckman, OR	Brent Emery, WI	Ron Skarin, CA/ Mark Whitehead, CA		
1982	Mark Gorski, CA	Leonard Nitz, PA	John Beckman, OR	Leonard Nitz, NY	Dave Grylls, CA/ Pat McDonough, PA		
1983	Mark Gorski, CA	Leonard Nitz, PA	Brent Emery, WI	Mark Whitehead, CA	Danny Van Haute, IL/ Mark Whitehead, CA		
1984	Nelson Vails, NY	Steve Hegg, CA	Mark Whitehead, CA	Leonard Nitz, CA	-- no Madison competition in 1984 --	Nelson Vails, NY/Les Barczewski, CO	
1985	Mark Gorski, CA	Carl Sundquist, IN	Pat McDonough, CA	Rory O'Reilly, CA	Chris Gutowski, IN/Frankie Andreu, MI	Nelson Vails, NY/Les Barczewski, CO	
1986	Scott Berryman, CO	Carl Sundquist, IN	Frankie Andreu, MI	Bill Drysdale, CA	B. McDonough, CA/Bobby Livingston, GA	Nelson Vails, NY/Scott Berryman, CO	
1987	Scott Berryman, CO	Carl Sundquist, IN	Dan Vogt, IN	John Hays, CA	Darroll Batke, CO/David Lindsey, CO	David Lindsey, CO/Russell Meade, CO	
1988	Ken Carpenter, CA	David Brinton, CA	Frankie Andreu, MI	Bobby Livingston, GA	B. McDonough, CA/Bobby Livingston, GA	Bart Bell, TX/ Tom Brinker, MD	
1989	Ken Carpenter, CA	Steve Hegg, CA	Craig Schommer, CA	Erin Hartwell, IN	Bryan McDonough, CA/Jim Pollak, IN	Paul Swift, WI/ Marty Nothstein, PA	
1990	Ken Carpenter, CA	Steve Hegg, CA	Jim Pollak, CA	Erin Hartwell, IN	Mike McCarthy, NY/Kevin Peck, CA	Paul Swift, WI/ Marty Nothstein, PA	
1991	Ken Carpenter, CA	Dirk Copland, CA	J'Me Carney, PA	Erin Hartwell, IN	J'Me Carney, PA/Jonas Carney, PA	Marty Nothstein, PA/Erin Hartwell, IN	
1992	Ken Carpenter, CA	Carl Sundquist, FL	J'Me Carney, PA	Erin Hartwell, IN	Pat Warner, IN/Claude Gerard, FL	Marty Nothstein, PA/Erin Hartwell, IN	
1993	Marty Nothstein, PA	Kent Bostick, NM	Dirk Copeland, CA	Erin Hartwell, IN	J'Me Carney, PA/Jonas Carney, PA	Paul Swift, WI/Greg Carlson, IN	
1994	Jeff Solt, CA	Kent Bostick, NM	Christian VandeVelde, IL	Erin Hartwell, IN	Dirk Copeland, CA/John Durso, NJ	Paul Swift, WI/Greg Carlson, IN	

1995 -

Team Pursuit
(originally competition was regional)

1971	Mike Celmins, Fred Davis, Ron Skarin, Butch Stinton	(CA)
1972	Cyril Johnson, Ron Skarin, Tom Sneddon, Butch Stinton	(CA)
1973	John Chapman, Dave Chauner, Joe Saling, Steve Woznick	(NJ)
1974	Les Luczy, Dave Mulica, Ron Skarin, Ralph Therrio	(CA)
1975	Rene Averseng, Chris Haley, Ron Skarin, Ralph Therrio	(CA)
1976	Paul Deem, Kevin Lutz, Paul Murray, Ron Skarin	(CA)
1977	Bob Allen, Paul Deem, Kevin Lutz, Ron Skarin	(CA)
1978	Scott Andrews, Mike Cavanaugh, Scott Holzrichter, Danny Van Haute	(IL)
1979	Paul Deem, Scott Hembree, Kevin Lutz, Mark Whitehead	(CA)
1980	Paul Deem, Bruce Donaghy, Leonard Nitz, Jeff Rutter	(PA)
1981	Bruce Donaghy, Pat McDonough, Leonard Nitz, Jeff Rutter	(PA)
1982	John Beckman, Dave Grylls, Pat McDonough, Leonard Nitz	

1983	Steve Hegg, Dave Letteri, Leonard Nitz, Jay Osborne
1984	Kit Kyle, Leonard Nitz, Danny Van Haute, Mark Whitehead
1985	Pat McDonough, Carl Sundquist, Danny Van Haute, Mark Whitehead
1986	Frankie Andreu, Steve Hegg, Dave Letteri, Leonard Nitz
1987	Tim Bengston, Dave Letteri, Matt Rayner, Carl Sundquist
1988	Steve Hegg, Dave Letteri, Mike McCarthy, Leonard Nitz
1989	Darroll Batke, Steve Hegg, Leonard Nitz, Kevin Peck, Carl Sundquist
1990	Jonas Carney, Steve Hegg, Mike McCarthy, Jim Pollack
1991	J'Me Carney, Chris Coletta, Matt Hamon, Jim Pollak, Tim Quigley, Carl Sundquist
1992	J'Me Carney, Chris Coletta, Dirk Copeland, Matt Hamon
1993	Chris Coletta, Dirk Copeland, Maiano Friedick, Matt Hamon, Adam Laurent
1994	Matt Hamon, Mariano Friedick, Adam Laurent, Zach Conrad
1995 -	

U. S. National Champions -- Women 1965-1994

Senior Women -- run by the "Amateur Bicycle League of America" until 1976, when it became the "United States Cycling Federation" (USCF)

	Sprint	Pursuit	Points	Kilometer
1967	Nancy Burghart, NY	Nancy Burghart, NY		
1968	Nancy Burghart, NY	Nancy Burghart, NY		
1969	Championships were held as Omniums this year			
1970	Jeanne Kloska, NY	Audrey McElmury, CA		
1971	Sheila Young, MI	Kathy Ecroth, OR		
1972	Sue Novara, MI	Clara Teyssier, CA		
1973	Sheila Young, MI	Mary Jane Reoch, PA		
1974	Sue Novara, MI	Mary Jane Reoch, PA		
1975	Sue Novara, MI	Mary Jane Reoch, PA		
1976	Sheila Young, MI	Connie Carpenter, WI		
1977	Sue Novara, MI	Connie Carpenter, WI		
1978	Sue Novara, MI	Mary Jane Reoch, PA	Mary Jane Reoch, PA	
1979	Sue Novara, MI	Connie Carpenter, WI	Mary Jane Reoch, PA	
1980	Sue Novara, MI	Betsy Davis, NJ	Mary Jane Reoch, PA	
1981	Sheila Young, WI	Rebecca Twigg, WA	Connie Carpenter, WI	
1982	Connie Paraskevin, MI	Rebecca Twigg, WA	Connie Carpenter, WI	
1983	Connie Paraskevin, MI	Cindy Olivarri, CA	Betsy Davis, NJ	
1984	Rebecca Twigg, CO	Rebecca Twigg, CO	Rebecca Twigg, CO	Rebecca Twigg, CO
1985	Connie Paraskevin, MI	Betsy Davis, NJ	Collette Gernay, GA	Ellen Braun, VA
1986	Maria Wisser, PA	Rebecca Twigg, WA	Karen Bliss, PA	Rebecca Twigg, WA
1987	Connie Paraskevin Young, MI	Mindee Mayfield, MI	Karen Bliss, PA	Ellen Braun, VA
1988	Connie Paraskevin Young, MI	Mindee Mayfield, CO	Janie Eickhoff, CA	Peggy Maas, CA
1989	Connie Paraskevin Young, MI	Mindee Mayfield, CO	Karen Bliss, PA	Janie Eickhoff, CA
1990	Renee Duprel, WA	Janie Eickhoff, CA	Janie Eickhoff, CA	Sharon Penn, WI
1991	Renee Duprel, WA	Janie Eickhoff, CA	Karen Bliss, PA	Lucy Vinnicombe, FL
1992	Connie Paraskevin Young, MI	Rebecca Twigg, CA	Janie Eickhoff, CA	Amanda Henry, CA
1993	Lucy Vinnecombe, FL	Janie Eickhoff, CA	Janie Eickhoff, CA	Lucy Vinnicombe, FL
1994	Connie Paraskevin Young, MI	Janie Eickhoff, CA	Janie Eickhoff, CA	Karen Dunne, IN
1995 -				

> Women have participated in exhibition Madison, Keirin, and Team Pursuit races, but have not yet enjoyed these events as a separate competition. Women have participated in Tandem Sprint in mixed pairs Master's events, but not in Senior competition. Women's competition in Olympic Sprints is not presently scheduled. Women are ready for their own Kilometer at the Worlds.

LOCATIONS

of track championships run by the Amateur Bicycle League of America, now the United States Cycling Federation

1921	Washington, D.C.	1934	not held	1947	Philadelphia, PA	**1960**	Milwaukee, WI	1973	Northbrook, IL	1986	Redmond, WA
1922	Atlantic City, NJ	1935	Atlantic City, NJ	1948	Kenosha, WI	1961	Milwaukee, WI	1974	Northbrook, IL	1987	Trexlertown, PA
1923	Chicago, IL	1936	St. Louis, MO	1949	San Diego, CA	1962	St. Louis, MO	1975	Northbrook, IL	1988	Houston, TX
1924	Buffalo, NY	1937	Buffalo, NY	**1950**	New Brunswick, NJ	1963	Chicago, IL	1976	Northbrook, IL	1989	Redmond, WA
1925	St. Louis, MO	1938	Chicago, IL (AAU)	1951	Columbus, OH	1964	New York, NY	1977	Redmond, WA	**1990**	Trexlertown, PA
1926	Philadelphia, PA	1939	Columbus, OH	1952	New Brunswick, NJ	1965	Encino, CA	1978	Kenosha, WI	1991	Redmond, WA
1927	Louisville, KY	**1940**	Detroit, MI	1953	St. Louis, MO	1966	Northbrook, IL	1979	Northbrook, IL	1992	Blaine, MN
1928	Kenosha, WI	1941	Pasadena, CA	1954	Minneapolis, MN	1967	Portland, OR	**1980**	San Diego, CA	1993	Indianapolis, IN
1929	Newark, NJ	1942	not held	1955	New York, NY	1968	Encino, CA	1981	Trexlertown, PA	1994	Indianapolis, IN
1930	Kenosha, WI	1943	not held	1956	Orlando, FL	1969	Detroit, MI	1982	Kenosha, WI	1995	Indianapolis, IN
1931	not held	1944	not held	1957	Kenosha, WI	**1970**	New York, NY	1983	Carson, CA	1996	Trexlertown, PA
1932	not held	1945	Chicago, IL	1958	Newark, NJ	1971	Portland, OR	1984	Trexlertown, PA	1997	???
1933	not held	1946	Columbus, OH	1959	Kenosha, WI	1972	Kenosha, WI	1985	Indianapolis, IN	1998	???

U. S. National Junior Boys Track Champions 1922-1994

Junior 16-18 Boys Omnium

1922	Charles Smithson, DC	1931	(not held)	**1940**	Harry Naismyth, NJ	1949	Donald Clauson, WI	1959	Jack Simes, III, NJ
1923	Samuel Dowell, OH	1932	(not held)	1941	Andrew Bernadsky, CA	**1950**	Harry Backer, CA	**1960**	Bobbie Fenn, NJ
1924	William Honeman, NJ	1933	(not held)	1942	(not held)	1951	Vaughn Angell, UT	1961	Alan Greico, NJ
1925	Walter Bresnan, NY	1934	(not held)	1943	(not held)	1952	John Chiselko, NJ	1962	Alan Greico, NJ
1926	Chester Atwood, DC	1935	David Martin, NJ	1944	(not held)	1954	Robert Zumwalt, Jr., CA	1963	Jose Nin, NY
1927	Ted Becker, IL	1936	David Martin, NJ	1945	Spencer Busch, NY	1955	Pat DeColhbus, NY	1964	Tony McMillan, CA
1928	Bobby Thomas, WI	1937	Furman Kugler, NJ	1946	Don Sheldon, NJ	1956	Dave Staub, CA	1965	Peter Senia, NY
1929	Tino Reboli, NJ	1938	John VanDiest, OH	1947	Joe Cirone, Jr. CA	1957	Perry Metzler, NY	1966	Dave Johnson, WI
1930	George Thomas, WI	1939	Frank Paul, UT	1948	Donald Clauson, WI	1958	James Donovan, NY		

Boys 13-15 Omnium

1967	Peter Milward, WI
1968	Jesus Portalatin, NY
1969	Nelson Saldana, NY
1970	Gilbert Hatton, CA
1971	Les Barczewski, WI
1972	Les Barczewski, WI
1973	Stan Kostuck, WI
1974	Bruce Donaghy, NJ
1975	Chris Springer, CA
1976	Jeff Bradley, IA
1977	Marcello Palazzo, IL
1978	Rob Krippendorf, WI
1979	Dave Lettieri, PA
1980	Tim Voelker, IA
1981	Craig Schommer, CA
1982	David Brinton, CA
1983	Marcello Arrue, CA
(format change)	

Boys 16-18 Omnium

1967	Peter Senia, NY
1968	Gary Campbell, CA
1969	Gary Campbell, CA
1970	Jesus Portalatin, NY
1971	Ralph Therrio, CA
1972	Nelson Saldena, NY
1973	Gilbert Hatton, CA
1974	Gilbert Hatton, CA
1975	Kurtis Miller, CA
1976	Chris Springer, CA
1977	Chris Springer, CA
1978	Eric Baltes, WI
1979	Mark Whitehead, CA
1980	John Butler, PA
1981	Russ Dalbey, CA
1982	Dave Letteri, PA

Boys 15-16 Omnium

1984	Marcello Arrue
1985	Tom Brinker, MO
1986	Albert Hale, CA
1987	Jonas Carney, NJ
1988	George Hincapie, NY
1989	George Hincapie, NY
1990	Brandon Lyon, MI
1991	Mariano Friedick, CA
1992	Andrew Coletta, IL
1993	Matt Young, PA
(format change)	

Boys 13-14 Omnium

1988	Frank Ventura, WI
1989	Mike McKenna, WI
1990	Kenneth Fritts, CA
1991	Rene Saenz, NV
1992	Joaeph Masser, NJ
1993	Andy Hardwick, TX

Boys 10-12 Omnium

1991	Carlos Rice, FL
1992	Mark Conley, CO
1993	Chad Milliken, CA
1994	John Brant

Junior National Championships

Junior National Championships were first contested in 1922 as an Omnium. In 1976 a Pursuit competition was added for 16-18 year old boys; in 1977, the Kilometer; and in 1978, Sprint and Points. Prior to 1988, Junior Nationals were held along with Senior competition. Since 1988, Junior National Championships have been held as a separate event .

Categories have continued to expand. In 1994, competition was offered in many different categories in an effort to encourage up-and-coming cyclists. Many names of Senior National Champions can be found in records from the Junior division.

Boys 16-18 Pursuit		Boys 16-18 Kilometer		Boys 16-18 Sprint		Boys 16-18 Points	
1976	Andy Weaver, FL			*(format change)*			
1977	Andy Weaver, FL	1977	Bruce Donaghy, NJ				
1978	Grant Handley, CA	1978	Pat McDonough, CA	1978	Mark Gorski, IL	1978	Jay Osborne, GA
1979	Jeff Rutter, PA	1979	Peter Kron, IL	1979	Mark Whitehead, CA	1979	Pat McDonough, CA
1980	Mike Rosenhaus, NJ	**1980**	Matt Francis, CA	**1980**	Matt Francis, CA	1980	Johm Butler, PA
1981	Dave Lettieri, PA	1981	John Waite, CA	1981	John Waite, CA	1981	not held
1982	Dave Lettieri, PA	1982	Craig Schommer, CA	1982	Joe Chang, WI	1982	not held
1983	Roy Knickman, CO	1983	Kit Kyle, IL	1983	Bobby Livingston, GA	1983	Roy Knickman, CO

Boys 17-18 Pursuit		Boys 17-18 Kilometer		Boys 17-18 Sprint		Boys 17-18 Points	
1984	Frankie Andreu, MI	1984	Paul Swift	1984	Paul Swift, WI	1984	Aaron DeRuntz, CA
1985	Mike McCarthy, NJ	1985	Sean Tulley, CA	1985	Steve Zeigler, LA	1985	Aaron DeRuntz, CA
1986	Mike McCarthy, NJ	1986	Marcello Arrue, CA	1986	Marcello Arrue, CA	1986	Jamie Carney, NJ
1987	Erin Hartwell, IN	1987	Tom Brinker, MO	1987	Tom Brinker, MO	1987	Neil Fraser, CA
1988	Adam Payne, GA	1988	Jonas Carney, NJ	1988	Marty Nothstein, PA	1988	Christian Young, NJ
1989	Brett Reagan, CO	1989	J.D. Moffitt, Jr., PA	1989	Marty Nothstein, PA	1989	Jonas Carney, NJ
1990	George Hincapie, NY	**1990**	George Hincapie, NY	**1990**	Zac Copeland, CA	**1990**	George Hincapie, NY
1991	George Hincapie, NY	1991	John Luvkulic	1991	Scott Skellenger, CA	1991	Paul Abraham, CA
1992	Paul LeBlanc	1992	Mike Witty, WI	1992	Mike Witty, WI	1992	Nick Feid, TX
1993	Mariano Freidick, CA	1993	Kenneth Fritts, CA	1993	Shawn Washburn, PA	1993	Jason Hall, OR
1994	John Walrod, PA	1994	Sky Christopherson	1994	Kenneth Fritts, CA	1994	Eric Jacobson

In (1994), categories for Juniors were expanded in order to offer more opportunities for success to budding competitors.

New Event!   **All 1994**

Boys 17-18 Team Pursuit
1994 David Clinger, James Ansite, John Walrod, Kenny Fritts

	Boys 2km (like Pursuit)		Boys 500m (like Kilo)		Boys Sprint		Boys Points
10-12	John Brant	10-12	John Brant				
13-14	Ryan Miller	13-14	Ryan Miller	13-14	Ryan Miller	13-14	Ryan Miller
15-16	Barry Wilcox	15-16	Brian Sitcer	15-16	Brian Sitcer	15-16	Kevin Gordon

1995 -

U. S. National Junior Girls Track Champions 1968-1994

Girls 13-15 Omnium
1968	Jean Saldana, NY
1969	Jackie Disney, CA
1970	Jackie Disney, CA
1971	Jackie Disney, CA
1972	Carole Brennan, MI
1973	Janie Brennan, MI
1974	Dana Scruggs, IN
1975	Connie Paraskevin, IN
1976	Connie Paraskevin, IN
1977	Jacquie Bradley, IA
1978	Jacquie Bradley, IA
1979	Brenda Hatlet, WI
1980	Sue Schaugg, MI
1981	Rene Duprel, WA
1982	Celeste Andreu, MI
1983	Celeste Andreu, MI

Girls 16-18 Omnium
1976	Jane Brennan, MI
1977	Connie Paraskevin, MI
1978	Connie Paraskevin, MI
1979	Rebecca Twigg, WA
1980	Maria Wisser, PA
1981	Maria Wisser, PA
1982	Jolanta Gorai, NJ
1983	Mary Farnsworth, CA

(format change)

Girls 15-16 Omnium
1984	Debbie Newell, CA
1985	Janie Eickhoff, CA
1986	Janie Eickhoff, CA
1987	Jessica Grieco, NJ

Girls 17-18 Omnium
1984	Rene Duprel, WA
1985	Celeste Andreu, MI
1986	Robin Coon, CA

(format change)

Girls 16-18 Sprint		**Girls 16-18 Pursuit**		**Girls 16-18 Points**	
1987	Janie Eickhoff, CA	1987	Janie Eickhoff, CA	1987	Janie Eickhoff, CA
Girls 16-17 Sprint		**Girls 16-17 Pursuit**		**Girls 16-17 Points**	
1988	Debra Cohen, IL	1988	Jessica Grieco, NJ	1988	Jessica Grieco, NJ
1988	Debra Cohen, IL	1989	Jessica Grieco, NJ	1989	Jessica Grieco, NJ
1990	Jessica Grieco, NJ	**1990**	Jessica Grieco, NJ	**1990**	Jessica Grieco, NJ

1988	Denise Mueller, CA
1989	Susan George, PA
1990	Crystal Waters, CA

(format change)

Girls 13-14 Omnium		**Girls 15-16 Omnium**		**Girls 10-12 Omnium**		**Girls 17-18 Sprint**		**Girls 17-18 Pursuit**		**Girls 17-18 Points**	
1991	Amber Holt, CA	1991	Jeanne Farrell, VA	1991	Tiffani Glowacki, WI	1991	Denise Mueller, CA	1991	Kiersten Johnson, PA	1991	Denise Mueller, CA
1992	Erin Veenstra, WI	1992	Nicole Reinhart, PA	1992	Tiffani Glowacki, WI	1992	Chris Witty, WI	1992	Susan George, PA	1992	Jeanne Farrell, VA
1993	Ednita Kelly, CA	1993	Amber Holt, CA	1993	Rebacca Veenstra, WI	1993	Nicole Reinhart, PA	1993	Susan George, PA	1993	Nicole Reinhart, PA
				1994	Meranda Seely, CA	1994	Amber Holt, CA	1994	Nicole Reinhart, PA	1994	Stephane Derr, PA

(format change)

In (**1994**) categories for Juniors were expanded in order to offer more opportunities for success to budding competitors.

All 1994

Girls 500m (like Kilo)		**Girls Sprint**		**Girls 2km** (like Pursuit)		**Girls Points**	
10-12	Meranda Seely, CA			**10-12**	Meranda Seely		
13-14	Jillian Payne, CA	**13-14**	Sara Sorenson	**13-14**	Sara Sorenson	**13-14**	Jillian Payne, CA
15-16	Ryan Kelly, MN	**15-16**	Jennie Reed	**15-16**	Jennie Reed	**15-16**	Ryan Kelly, MN

1995-

U. S. National Junior Track Championship locations:
Prior to 1988 Junior and Senior Championships were held together.

1988	Trexlertown, PA
1989	Colorado Springs, CO
1990	San Diego, CA
1991	Houston, TX
1992	Indianapolis, IN
1993	Trexlertown, PA
1994	Redmond, WA
1995	Houston, TX

U. S. National Masters Men's Track Champions 1983-1994 ▬▬▬

		Sprint	Kilometer	Pursuit	Points	Omnium
1983	36+	Joe Pignataro, NJ	Robert Lea, MD	Robert Lea, MD		Skip Cutting, CA
	46+	Jack Hartman, NV	Ronnie Palazzo, CA			Jack Hartman, NV
1984	36+	Joe Pignataro, NJ	Jim Montgomery, VA	John Payne, GA		Jim Montgomery, VA
	46+	Robert Zumwalt, CA	Robert Zumwalt, CA	Jerry Nugent, MD		Larry Dierem, MD
	56+					Robert Pfarr, WI
1985	36+	Joe Pignataro, NJ	Jim Montgomery, VA	Tim Loose, PA		Bob Phillips, MA
	46+	Robert Zumwalt, CA	Robert Zumwalt, CA	Gunter Thomas, MD		Allen Bell, NJ
	56+					Robert Bergan, CA
1986	31+					Larry Desario, FL
	36+	Joe Pignataro, NJ	Michael Leach, MI	Andrew Buck, PA		Larry Desario, FL
	46+	Robert Zumwalt, CA	Robert Zumwalt, CA	Joe Saling, NJ		56+ Lloyd Rake, NJ
1987	31+		Rory O'Reilly, CA	Ken Nowakowski, IN	Ken Nowakowski, IN	
	36+	Xavier Mirander, FL	Michael Leach, MI	David LeDuc, NC	David LeDuc, NC	
	46+	Robert Zumwalt, CA	Robert Lea, MD	Robert Lea, MD	Joe Saling, NJ	56+ Barry Wolfe, CA
1988	30-34	Jim Martin, TX	Ken Nowakowski, IN	Mike Osborne	Dale Luedtke, CA	
	35-44	Mike Cavanaugh, IL	Roy Simonson, WA	David LeDuc, NC	Bob Muzzy, CA	
	45-54	Jack Simes III, PA	Jack Simes III, PA	Jack Simes III, PA	Robert Lea, MD	55+ Dick Poor, NJ
1989	30-34	Rory O'Reilly, CA	Rory O'Reilly, CA	Tom Fritschen, WA	Ron Hinson, NC	
	35-44	Nick Chenowth, TX	Dale Luedtke, CA	Bob Muzzy, CA	Bob Muzzy, CA	
	45-54	James Montgomery, WA	James Montgomery, WA	James Montgomery, WA	James Montgomery, WA	
	55+	Larry Galka, CA	Dan Babbitt, WA		Dan Babbitt, WA	
1990	30-34	Brian Moore, IN	Tony Vincenti, CA	Danny Van Haute, CA	Tom Broznowske, CA	
	35-39	Xavier Mirander, CA	Rory O'Reilly, CA	Roger Parenteau, CA	Paul Pearson, CA	
	40-44	Bobby Phillips, MD	John Elgart, CA	Brad Wallace, CA	Robert Barney, CA	
	45-49	Thomas Weisel, CA	Victor Copeland, CA	Robert Schaub, CA	James Montgomery, VA	
	50-54	Robert Zumwalt, CA	Robert Zumwalt, CA	Joe Saling, NJ	Joe Saling, NJ	
	55-59	Bill Walter, CA	Larry Galka, CO	Dan Babbitt, WA	55+ Larry Reade, NY	
	60+	Lloyd Rake, NJ	Robert Bergan, CA	Alan Ashmore, PA		**Madison** (all ages)
1991	30-34	James Baker, AZ	Clark Rasmussen, Jr., OR	John Frey, NM	Benjamin Swann, CA	Paul Pearson
	35-39	Nick Chenowth, TX	Roger Parenteau, CA	Roger Parenteau, CA	Paul Pearson, CA	Danny Van Haute
	40-44	George Geier, IN	William Berezny, PA	Kenny Fuller, CA	David LeDuc, NC	
	45-49	Victor Copeland, CA	Victor Copeland, CA	Victor Copeland, CA	Robert Barney, CA	
	50-54	Thomas Weisel, CA	Thomas Weisel, CA	Joe Saling, NJ	Daniel Wulbert, CA	
	55-59	Richard Widmark, IL	Clark Rasmussen, Sr., CA	Clark Rasmussen, Sr., CA	Hector Monsalve, CA	
	60+	Robert Bergan, CA	Alan Ashmore, PA	Alan Ashmore, PA	Robert Bergen, CA	
1992	30-34	Jeff Solt, CA	David Rosenthal, CA	Benjamin Swann, CA	James Woods, WA	**Madison** (all ages)
	35-39	Don Scales, CA	Don Scales, CA	Kent Bostick, NM	Thomas James, OR	Butch Stinton
	40-44	Butch Stinton, CA	James McCarthy, CA	Kenny Fuller, CA	Butch Stinton, CA	Phil Buhl
	45-49	Joe Pignataro, NJ	Dale Harless, WA	Dale Harless, WA	Glenn Erickson, WA	
	50-54	Victor Copeland, CA	Victor Copeland, CA	Victor Copeland, CA	David Spangler, CA	**Team Pursuit** (all ages)
	55-59	John Creed, CA	John Creed, CA	Robert Kaye, WA	Robert Kaye, WA	Tom Bain, Kent Bostick,
	60+	Dick Poor, NJ	Dick Poor, NJ	Dick Poor, NJ	Dick Poor, NJ	Clark Metcalf, Dave Spangler

U. S. National Masters Men's Track Champions (cont.)

		Sprint	Kilometer	Pursuit	Points	Madison
1993	30-34	Jeff Solt, CA	Jeff Solt, CA	Chris Carlson, TX	Carl Sundquist, FL	Matt Chambers
	35-39	Larry Nolan, CA	Rory O'Reilly, CA	Larry Nolan, CA	John Frey, NM	Glenn Winkel
	40-44	Butch Stinton, CA	Thomas Bain, TX	Kent Bostick, NM	Kent Bostick, NM	
	45-49	John Conley, CO	Mickey Allen, TX	Kenny Fuller, CA	Robert Evans, CO	**Team Pursuit** (all ages)
	50-54	Victor Copeland, CA	Victor Copeland, CA	Victor Copeland, CA	Victor Copeland, CA	Kent Bostick, Chris Carlson
	55-59	Paul Yazolino, CA	John Creed, CA	Daniel Babbitt, WA	Nicholas Van Male, CA	Dave Spangler, Carl Sundquist
	60+	Richard Stein, CA	Lawrence Galka, CO	Ron Smith, CO	Dick Poor, NJ	
1994	30-34	John Waite, CA	Chris Carlson, TX	Chris Carlson, TX	Curtis Tolson, KY	**Madison** (all ages)
	35-39	James Joseph, NY	Don Scales, CA	Leonard Harvey Nitz, CA	Carl Westergen, FL	Butch Stinton
	40-44	Butch Stinton, CA	Kent Bostick, NM	Kent Bostick, NM	Jim Hetherington, FL	Phil Buhl
	45-49	Joe Pignataro, NJ	Jerry Woodruff, CA	Glen Norton, WA	Mickey Allen, TX	
	50-54	Victor Copeland, CA	Victor Copeland, CA	Victor Copeland, CA	Victor Copeland, CA	
	55-59	Paul Yazolino, CA	James Kloss, CA	James Kloss, CA	Robert Kaye, CA	
	60+	George Hansen, NJ	George Hansen, NJ	George Hansen, NJ	George Hansen, NJ	

U. S. National Masters Women's Track Champions 1983-1994 ━━━

Women's 36+ Omnium

1983	Leslie Nitz, NY
1984	Judy Layton, NV
1985	Ellen Dorsey, PA
1986	Elise Harrington, MI

Women's 31+ Omnium
Elise Harrington, MI

		Sprint	Pursuit	Points	Kilometer	Omnium 40+
1987	31+	Alice Church, NY	Elise Harrington, MI	Meg Berry, CA		
1988	30-39	Debbie Hendrickson, CA	Linda Elgart, PA	Meg Berry, CA		Camilla Buchanan, VA
1989	30-39	Debbie Handrickson, CA	Mary Beth Novak, CA	Maryann Kusina, OR		Camilla Buchanan, VA
1990	30+	Sherry Malotte, WA		Janice Gaines, OR		
	30-39		Liz Heller, MO		Sherry Malotte, WA	
	35-39		Betsy King, FL		Betsy King, FL	
	40+		Camilla Buchanan, VA		Camilla Buchanan, VA	
1991	30-34	Juliana Nowlan, CA	Juliana Nowlan, CA	Juliana Nowlan, CA	Juliana Nowlan, CA	
	35-39	Linda Stein, CA	Jackie Norton, WA	Meg Berry, CA	Jackie Norton, WA	
	40+	Betsy King, CA	Betsy King, FL	Betsy King, FL	Betsy King, FL	
1992	30-34	Sherry Malotte, WA	Eileen Furey, OR	Andrea Carden-Greenfield, WA	Suzanne Timerman, NY	
	35-39	Elizabeth Davis, NJ	Carol Ann Bostick, NM	Carol Ann Bostick, NM	Carol Ann Bostick, NM	
	40+	Alice Church, FL	Betsy King, FL	Betsy King, FL	Betsy King, FL	
1993	30-34	Sharon Penn-Lichty, FL	Rebecca Hart, IL	Linda Petry Kruse, TX	Suzanne Timerman, NY	
	35-39	Carol Ann Bostick, NM	Carol Ann Bostick, NM	Carol Ann Bostick, NM	Carol Ann Bostick, NM	
	40+	Alice Church, FL		Nancy Bruce, WA		
	40-44		Betsy King, FL		Betsy King, FL	
	45+		Nancy Bruce, WA		Nancy Bruce, WA	
1994	30-34	Jill Gianettoni, CA	Beth Mundy, FL	Linda Kruse, TX	Linda Kruse, TX	
	35-39	Carol Ann Bostick, NM	Carol Ann Bostick, NM	Carol Ann Bostick, NM	Suzanne Timerman, NY	
	40-44	(40+) Alice Church, FL	Betsy King, UT	40+ Nancy Bruce, WA	Betsy King, UT	
	45+		Lynn Joslin, FL		Lynn Joslin, FL	

U. S. National Track Records

Time Trial -- Flying Start

200m	Senior Men	10.283	Ken Carpenter	Maebashi, Japan	8/20/90
	Senior Women	11.289	Connie Paraskevin Young	Colorado Springs, CO	8/5/88
	Junior Boys 14	12.065	Mike McKenna	Colorado Springs, CO	8/3/89
	Junior Boys 16	11.37	Kenneth Fritts	Colorado Springs, CO	8/3/89
	Junior Boys 18	10.499	William Clay	Colorado Springs, CO	7/91
	Junior Girls 14	13.251	Erin Veenstra	Indianapolis, IN	7/28/92
	Junior Girls 16	11.85	Chris Witty	Colorado Springs, CO	7/91
	Junior Girls 18	11.666	Nicole Reinhart	Quito, Ecuador	7/26/94
500m	Senior Men	26.993	Rory O'Reilly	La Paz, Bol-Alto Irpavi	11/12/85
	Senior Women	30.642	Rebecca Twigg	Colorado Springs, CO	8/16/86

Time Trial -- Standing Start

500m	Junior Boys 14	36.827	Brandon Lyon	Colorado Springs, CO	8/3/89
	Junior Boys 16	35.272	David Valade	Colorado Springs, CO	8/3/91
	Junior Girls 14	41.26	Ednita Kelly	Trexlertown, PA	8/12/93
	Junior Girls 16	38.229	Ryan Kelly	Redmond, WA	7/31/94
1 km	Senior Men	1:03.397	Rory O'Reilly	Colorado Springs, CO	7/6/84
	Senior Women	1:12.298	Janie Eickhoff	Trexlertown, PA	6/14/91
	Junior Boys 18	1:05.446	Shawn Washburn	Quito, Ecuador	7/25/94
	Junior Girls 18	1:15.517	Joany Copeland	Blaine, MN	6/24/92
2 km	Junior Boys 14	2:32.439	Ryan Miller	Redmond, WA	8/1/94
	Junior Boys 16	2:24.92	Glenn Milano	Colorado Springs, CO	8/3/89
	Junior Girls 14	3:00.449	Sara Sorenson	Redmond, WA	8/1/94
	Junior Girls 16	2:44.687	Jennie Reed	Redmond, WA	8/1/94
	Junior Girls 18	2:34.049	Margot Quandt	Quito, Ecuador	7/27/94
3km	Senior Women	3:37.34	Rebecca Twigg	Hamar, Norway	8/20/93
	Junior Boys 18	3:31.50	Tim Quigley	Moscow	7/8/89
4km	Senior Men	4:31.44	Mike McCarthy	Maebashi, Japan	8/20/90
5km	Senior Men	5:45.51	John Frey	Colorado Springs, CO	10/9/91
	Senior Women	6:40.61	Carolyn Donnelly	Colorado Springs, CO	10/29/90
10km	Senior Men	5:45.51	John Frey	Colorado Springs, CO	10/9/91
	Senior Women	13:31.15	Carolyn Donnelly	Colorado Springs, CO	10/29/90
20km	Senior Men	23:53.43	John Frey	Colorado Springs, CO	10/9/91
	Senior Women	17:12.40	Carolyn Donnelly	Colorado Springs, CO	10/29/90
1 hour	Senior Men	49.947km	John Frey	Colorado Springs, CO	10/9/91
	Senior Women	44.028km	Carolyn Donnelly	Colorado Springs, CO	10/29/90
50km	Senior Men	1:02:00.20	John Frey	Colorado Springs, CO	10/9/91
	Senior Women	1:08:26.24	Carolyn Donnelly	Colorado Springs, CO	10/29/90
100km	Senior Men	2:09:11.31	Kent Bostick	Colorado Springs, CO	9/13/89
	Senior Women	3:04:58.95	Patricia Jones	Indianapolis, IN	7/23/90

4km Team Time Trial

Senior Men	4:18.68	Steve Hegg, Jim Pollack, Mike McCarthy, Carl Sundquist	Maebashi, Japan	8/23/90
Master's Men	4:31.87	Kent Bostick, Dave Spangler, Carl Sundquist, Chris Carlson	Colorado Springs, CO	7/16/93
Junior Boys	4:29.886	Kenneth Fritts, Christian Vande Velde, Matt Young, John Walrod	Quito, Ecuador	7/27/94
Junior Girls	5:18.135	Laura Reed, Joany Copeland, Susan George, Stephanie Owen	Trexlertown, PA	8/13/93

Master's Time Trial -- Flying Start

200m Men	30+	10.525	Jeff Solt	Colorado Springs, CO	7/13/93
	35+	11.123	Rory O'Reilly	Colorado Springs, CO	7/13/93
	40+	11.222	Nick Chenowth	Colorado Springs, CO	7/13/94
	45+	11.34	Victor Copeland	Colorado Springs, CO	8/21/93
	50+	11.34	Victor Copeland	Colorado Springs, CO	8/21/93
	55+	11.687	Paul Yazolino	Colorado Springs, CO	7/13/93
	60+	13.260	George Hansen	Ft. Lauderdale, FL	7/15/94
Women	30+	12.252	Carol Ann Bostick	Colorado Springs, CO	7/13/93
	35+	12.252	Carol Ann Bostick	Colorado Springs, CO	7/13/93
	40+	12.733	Alice Church	Colorado Springs, CO	7/13/93
500m Men	30+	27.869	Jeff Solt	Colorado Springs, CO	7/17/93
	35+	28.921	Rory O'Reilly	Colorado Springs, CO	7/17/93
	40+	28.967	Vic Copeland	Colorado Springs, CO	7/17/93
	45+	28.967	Vic Copeland	Colorado Springs, CO	7/17/93
	50+	28.967	Vic Copeland	Colorado Springs, CO	7/17/93
	55+	36.414	Lawrence Galka	Colorado Springs, CO	7/17/93
	60+	36.414	Lawrence Galka	Colorado Springs, CO	7/17/93
Women	30+	32.249	Carol Ann Bostick	Colorado Springs, CO	10/16/93
	35+	32.249	Carol Ann Bostick	Colorado Springs, CO	10/16/93
	40+	33.47	Betsy King	Colorado Springs, CO	8/10/93
	45+	43.756	Sandra Sutherland	Colorado Springs, CO	7/17/93
1km. Men	30+	1.00.971	Jeff Solt	Colorado Springs, CO	7/17/93
	35+	1:01.754	Vic Copeland	Colorado Springs, CO	7/17/93
	40+	1:01.754	Vic Copeland	Colorado Springs, CO	7/17/93
	45+	1:01.754	Vic Copeland	Colorado Springs, CO	7/17/93
	50+	1:01.754	Vic Copeland	Colorado Springs, CO	7/17/93
	55+	1:17.003	Lawrence Galka	Colorado Springs, CO	7/17/93
	60+	1:17.003	Lawrence Galka	Colorado Springs, CO	7/17/93
Women	30+	1:07.923	Carol Ann Bostick	Colorado Springs, CO	10/16/93
	35+	1:07.923	Carol Ann Bostick	Colorado Springs, CO	10/16/93
	40+	1:11.91	Betsy King	Colorado Springs, CO	8/10/93
	45+	1:29.172	Sandra Sutherland	Colorado Springs, CO	7/17/93

Master's Time Trial -- Standing Start

1km Men	30+	1:04.271	Jeff Solt	Colorado Springs, CO	7/13/93
	35+	1:06.912	Rory O'Reilly	Colorado Springs, CO	7/13/93
	40+	1:07.85	Vic Copeland	Colorado Springs, CO	7/13/93
	45+	1:07.85	Vic Copeland	Colorado Springs, CO	7/13/93
	50+	1:07.85	Vic Copeland	Colorado Springs, CO	7/13/93
	55+	1:14.237	John Creed	Colorado Springs, CO	7/13/93
	60+	1:11.341	George Hansen	Ft. Lauderdale, FL	7/15/94
Women	30+	1:14.278	Carol Ann Bostick	Colorado Springs, CO	7/13/93
	35+	1:14.278	Carol Ann Bostick	Colorado Springs, CO	7/13/93
	40+	1:17.935	Betsy King	Colorado Springs, CO	7/13/93
	45+	1:20.137	Nancy Bruce	Colorado Springs, CO	7/13/93
3km Men	30+	3:24.60	Kent Bostick	Colorado Springs, CO	10/16/93
	35+	3:24.60	Kent Bostick	Colorado Springs, CO	10/16/93
	40+	3:24.60	Kent Bostick	Colorado Springs, CO	10/16/93
	45+	3:40.75	Kenny Fuller	Colorado Springs, CO	7/14/93
	50+	3:38.624	Vic Copeland	Colorado Springs, CO	8/18/94
	55+	4:01.74	Lawrence Galka	San Diego, CA	8/28/91
	60+	4:06.628	George Hansen	Ft. Lauderdale, FL	7/17/94
Women	30+	3:37.34	Rebecca Twigg	Hamar, Norway (Wld Rec)	8/20/93
	35+	3:59.99	Carol Ann Bostick	Colorado Springs, CO	7/14/93
	40+	4:07.19	Betsy King	Colorado Springs, CO	7/14/93
	45+	4:15.86	Nancy Bruce	Colorado Springs, CO	7/14/93

ʘᴠʘ **Velodromes of the World** ʘᴠʘ | ** courtesy UCI+ **

North America
United States of America
United States Cycling Federation   1-719-578-4581
Mike Fraysee, President
Lisa Voight, Executive Director
One Olympic Plaza
Colorado Springs, CO 80909 U.S.A.

GA - Olympic (Atlanta)	**250m.**	**wooden, ±45°**
WA - Marymoor,	400m	concrete, 25°
OR - Alpenrose (priv)	269m	concrete, ±45°
CA - Hellyer Park	333.75m	concrete, 22.5°
Dominguez Hills	333.33m	concrete , 33°
Encino	250m	concrete, 28°
San Diego	333.33m	concrete, 27°
CO - Colorado Springs	333.33m	concrete, 33°
TX - Houston/Alkek	333.33m	concrete, 33°
MO - St. Louis **	1/5 mi.	asphalt, 28°
LA - Baton Rouge	333.33m	concrete, 30°
GA - E. Pt./Dick Lane	323.13m	concrete, 33°
MN - Blaine	250m	wood, 45°
WI - Brown Deer	1/4 mi.	asphalt, 23°
Kenosha	333.33m	concrete, 23°
IL - Northbrook	382m	asphalt, 17.5°
Vandedrome Portable	126-153	wood, 53°
IN - Major Taylor/Indy	333.33	concrete, 28.5°
MI - Dorais **	333.33	concrete, 26°
PA - Lehigh/T-Town	333.33	concrete, 27°
NY - Kessina **	1/4 mi.	asphalt, 17°
FL - Piccolo/Florida	333.33	concrete, 30°
IL - Shakopee (demol)	200m	wood
MI - Madison Velo (demol)	133.33m	wood

** denotes unraceable tracks

Canada
Canadian Cycling Association
333River Road
Vanier, Ottawa, KIL 8B9

B.C. - Victoria (1994)	333.4m	concrete, 30+°
B.C. - Burnaby, B.C. (10/'95)	200m	wood/indr, 43°
Alb - Edmonton (1978)	333.6m	concrete, **
Calgary (1976)	400.15m	concrete, 39°
Man - Winnipeg	400m	concrete, 43°
Ont - Fonthill	155m	
Que - Montreal ('76)(demol)	285.7m	wood/indoor
Ont - Delhi (demol)	120m	wood/indoor

Mexico

Mexico City, Olympic ('68)	333.33m	wood, 39°
Mexico City, Centro Dep.('72)	333.33m	concrete, 34°
Monterrey	333.33m	concrete, 39°
Leon	333.33m	concrete, 38°
Guadalahara	400m	concrete, 38°
Saltillo	333.33m	concrete, 36°

Western Europe
Austria

Bregenz	450m	concrete
Vienne	250m	wood/indoor

Belgium

Anvers Sportpaleis ('55)	250m	wood/indoor
Liege Rocour (1950)	454.5m	concrete
Gand Blaarmeersen ('88)	250m	wood/in-out
Gand Sportpaleis	166.6	wood/indoor
Elewiyt	400m	asphalt
Zensd	450m	concrete

Denmark

Aarhus	333.33m	concrete
Odense	333.33m	concrete ('88)
Copenhagen	370m	concrete ('55)
Forum	190m	wood ('76)
Ordrup	368.2m	concrete ('87)

Finland

Helsinki (1972)	400m	concrete
Turku	333.33m	asphalt

France

Alsace,		
Colmar	356m	concrete
Strasbourg (1992)	333.33m	asphalt
Aquitaine,		
Aire sur Adour	333.33m	concrete
Bayonne	500m	concrete
Bordeaux (1989)	250m	wood/indoor
Damazan	400m	concrete
Mont de Marsan	375m	concrete
Mourenx	400m	concrete
Pays de Loire,		
Angers (1991)	300m	concrete
Chateaubriant	250m	concrete
Coueron	250m	concrete
Guemene Penfao	333m	concrete
La Roche sur Yon	454m	concrete
Les Sables d'Olonne	500m	
Lucon	362m	concrete
Nantes	500m	concrete
Noyant la Gravoyere	245m	concrete
Pontchateau	250m	concrete
Renaze	336m	concrete
St. Nazaire	250m	concrete
Auvergne,		
Aurillac	550m	concrete
Clermont-Ferrand	500m	concrete (1985)
Commentry	477m	concrete
Lurcy Levis	250m	concrete
Vichy	500m	concrete
Bourgogne,		
Auxerre	333m	concrete
Dijon	250m	concrete
Montceau les Mines	250m	concrete
Bretagne,		
Cleder	350m	concrete
Fougeres	250m	concrete
Guipavas	400m	concrete
Guingamp	250m	

Henanbinen		concrete
Lesneven	252m	concrete
Lorient	416m	concrete
Loudeac	303m	concrete
Melgven	370m	concrete
Plelan le Grand	250m	concrete
Plouasne	365m	concrete
Plouzane	333m	concrete
Quintin	273m	concrete
Rennes	403m	concrete
St. Brieuc	400m	concrete
St. Malo	250m	concrete
Vannes	400m	concrete
Champagne Reims	399.3m	concrete (1973)
Sedan	300m	concrete
Cote d'Azur,		
Hyeres-Toulon	250m	wood, 48° ('89)
Dauphine-Savoie,		
Eybens	250m	concrete
Grenoble	250m	concrete
Grenoble Vel d'Hiv	210.5m	wood/indoor
Flandre-Artois,		
Aire sur la Lys	500m	concrete
Bruay la Buissiere	400m	concrete
Grande Synthe	333m	concrete
Lens	350m	concrete
Lillers	500m	concrete
Roubaix	500m	concrete
St. Omer	412m	concrete
Valenciennes	481m	concrete
Franche-Comte		
Besancon	453.9m	concrete (1979)
Lons le Saunier	420m	concrete
Valentigney	400m	concrete
Ile de France		
Aulnay-sous-Bois	454m	concrete (1950)
Champagne-sur-Seine	250m	concrete
Croix de Berny		
Paris Bercy (1984)	250m	wood/indoor
Paris la Cipale	500m	concrete
Paris Insep	166m	wood/indoor
St. Denis	250m	concrete
Languedoc Roussillon		
Ales	400m	concrete
Branoux les Taillades	252m	concrete
Carcassonne	456m	concrete
Lorraine		
Commercy	285.7m	concrete ('85)
Luneville	500m	concrete
Lyonnais		
Lyon	333.33m	concrete ('89)
Rochetaillee	200m	concrete
St. Etienne	400m	concrete
Normandie		
Alencon	250m	concrete
Caen	400m	concrete ('84)
Deauville	450m	concrete
Equeurdreville	400m	concrete
Grand Couronne	200m	concrete
Le Havre	250m	concrete

Le Neubourg	450m	concrete
Le Val St. Pierre	250m	concrete
Lisieux	330m	concrete
St. Lo	401m	concrete
St. Pierre sur Dives	350m	concrete

Orleanais

Blois	285m	concrete
Bourges	250m	concrete
Briare	400m	concrete
Descartes	250m	concrete
Henrichemont	333m	concrete
Le Blanc	390m	concrete
Le Grand Pressigny	339m	concrete
Montargis	250m	concrete
St. Amand Montrond	400m	concrete
St. Denis de l'Hotel	333.33m	concrete ('85)
Salbris	333m	concrete

Picardie

Beauvais	250m	concrete
Creil	454m	concrete
St. Quentin	400m	concrete
Senlis	333m	concrete

Poitou Charlentes

Angouleme	333m	concrete
Bressuire	250m	concrete
Chatellerault	453m	concrete
La Rochelle	329m	concrete
Loudun	180m	concrete
Marans	245m	concrete
Rochefort	437m	concrete
Saintes	378m	concrete
St. Pierre d'Oleron	315m	concrete

Provence

Cavaillon	400m	concrete
Marseille	250m	concrete
Port de Bouc	454m	concrete
Vitrolles	333m	concrete

Pyrenees

Foix	250m	concrete
L'Isle Jourdain	375m	concrete
Mountauban	413m	concrete
Muret	250m	concrete
Tarbes	250	concrete
Villemur	433m	concrete
St. Servan sur Mer	240.45m	B+ton ('50)
(?) Brest Ponaulcoise	333.33m	concrete (1993)

Germany

Augsburg (1988)	200m	wood/indoor
Berlin, Seelenb.	171m	wood/indoor
Weissensee (1971)	333.33m	B+ton
Deutschland (1963)	208m	wood/indoor
Schoneberg	333.33m	wood
2000 - projected	250m	wood/indoor
Bielefeld	333.33m	concrete
Bocholt	333.33m	concrete
Brandenburg	385m	concrete
Bremen, Stadthalle	166.7m	wood/indoor
Buttgen	250m	wood/indoor
Chemnitz (1971)	318.25m	concrete
Cologne, Mengersdorf	250m	wood ('90)
Cologne, Sporthalle	166.66m	wood/indoor
Cottbus (1993)	333.29m	epowit
Darmstadt	394.65m	asphalt
Dortmund, Westfalen	200m	wood/indoor
Dortmund	400m	B+ton
Dresden, Barnsdorfer	400m	concrete
Dudenhofen	250m	concrete
Erfurt	333.33m	concrete
Forst	399.5m	concrete
Frankfurt, Main	400m	asphalt
Frankfurt, Oder	285.7	wood/indoor
Fredersdorf	333.33m	concrete
Gera	250m	concrete
Gottingen	400m	asphalt
Gutersloh	400m	spurtan
Halle Saale	399.85m	concrete
Hamburg	250m	concrete
Hannover	333.33m	wood
Hassloch	333.33m	concrete
Hildesheim	400m	asphalt
Lank Latum	200m	asphalt
Leipzig, A. Rosch	400m	concrete
Leipzig	400m	asphalt
Linkenheim	333.33m	concrete
Luckenwalde	250m	asphalt
Ludwigshafen	333.33m	concrete
Magdeburg	400m	concrete
Mannheim	333.33m	concrete
Merseburg	373.9m	asphalt
Munich, Oly. Radstad.	285.7m	wood/part in
Munich, Oly. Halle	200m	wood/indoor
Munster, Munsterland	153m	wood/indoor
Niederporing	333.33m	concrete
Nordhausen	454.5m	concrete
Nurnberg	400m	concrete
Oberhausen, Baden	333.33m	concrete
Oschelbronn	200m	wood
Plauen		
Rostock	250m	concrete
Saarbrucken	333.33m	concrete
Schopp	400m	asphalt
Singen	200m	concrete
Solingen	384.7m	concrete
Stuttgart	285.7m	wood/indoor
Wuppertal	500m	concrete
Zittau		
Zickau	454m	concrete

Great Britain

Birmingham	403m	asphalt, 13.5°
Brighton	579m	asphalt, 15°
Brodsworth	402.3m	
Calshot	146m	wood/indr,52°
Cardiff	459.9m	concrete, 25°
Carmarthen	405.4m	asphalt, 20°
Clay Cross	332.8.	grass
Coverntry	402m	asphalt, 15°
Dorset	534m	Macadam
Dundee	402.3m	asphalt
Glasgow	380.2m	Macadam
Halesowen	402.3m	asphalt
Liverpool, Kirkby	485m	asphalt, 25°
London, Herne Hill	450m	B+ton, 28°, '93
Ile de Man	404,2m	Macadam, '61
Welwyn	461m	asphalt, 26°,'60
Scunthorpe (1964)	485.1m	asphalt, 29°
Manchester (1976)	466m	polymer/cim.
Manchester (1994)	250m	wood/indr, 42°
Mansfield	405m	asphalt, 13°
Leicester (1978)	333.33m	wood, 37°
Edinburgh (1986)	250m	wood, 44°
Middlesbrough (1990)	455.8m	asphalt, 21°
Newcastle-under-Lyme	399.7m	asphalt
Nottingham	464.8m	asphalt
Portsmouth	534.6m	asphalt
Poole	534m	asphalt
Harlow	197.5m	wood
Reading	459.15m	asphalt, 11°
South Shields	401.55m	asphalt, 29°
Southhampton	160m	wood/indoor
Southhampton	480.1m	asphalt
Wolverhampton	458.6m	asphalt

Holland

Alkmaar	250m	concrete
Amsterdam (1979)	494.1m	concrete
Amsterdam, Sloten	200m	wood
Apeldoorn	250m	concrete
Oudenbosch	200m	concrete
Rotterdam (1983)	200m	wood/indoor

Italy

Busto Garolfo (1988)	380.6m	asphalt, 47°
Crema	329m	concrete, 32°
Dalmine (1987)	374.4m	concrete, 33°
Mantova	449.2m	cem/plas 13°
Varese (1968)	446m	concrete, 40°
Milano, Vigorelli ('86)	397.5m	wood, 42°
Ascoli Piceno	333.33m	asphalt, 39°
Avezzano	333.33m	concrete, 32°
Barletta (Bari) (1993)	333.33m	concrete. 36°
Bassano del Grappa('71)	400m	cem/plas 38°
Cavezzo	373.9m	concrete, 49°
Cento	396.4m	concrete, 19°
Civitavecchia	465m	concrete, 34°
Donada	333.33m	concrete, 30°
Farigliano	350m	asphalt
Ferrara	333.33m	concrete, 35°
Firenza (1982)	333.33m	concrete/synth 40°
Forano	250m	concrete, 32°
Forli	400m	R+sine, 37°
Fornacette	300m	concrete, 24°
Fierenzuola d'Arda	394m	concrete, 33°
Genova	450m	concrete
L'Aquila	450m	concrete, 30°
Lanciano Chieti (1992)	400m	concrete, 34°
Marcianise	285.7m	synth, 45°
Milano, Palazzo (1976)	250m	wood/indoor
Molinella	433.3m	asphalt
Montallese	326.1m	asphalt
Montechiarugolo	400m	concrete, 15°
Monteroni di Lecce ('74)	333.33m	wood, 40°
Napoli (1963)	595m	concrete
Noto	345.5m	concrete
Padova	330m	concrete, 26°
Palermo	400m	cem/synth
Pesaro	507.8m	B+ton, 45°
Pescantina	340.3m	concrete, 37°
Pordenone	400m	concrete, 34°
Portugruaro	395.4m	concrete, 33°
Rome, Olympic (1959)	400m	wood, 34°
Quartu Sant Elena	333.33m	concrete,
Sestu	203m	concrete, 30°
Torino	392m	concrete, 36°

Norway

Hamar (1993)	250m	wood/indoor
Halden	300m	asphalt
Levanger	400m	asphalt
Savallen	400m	asphalt

Portugal

Algarve, Tavira	400m
Algarve, Lovle	400m
Lisboa, Halveira	400m
Ribatejo, Alpiarca	400m
Aveiro, Sangalhos	333.33m
Gaia Oporto, Canelas	400m

Spain

Province, City		
Alava, Vittoria	250m	asphalt
Alicante, Castalla	250m	asphalt
Alicante, Novelda	350.3m	concrete
Alicante, Sax	347.7m	asphalt
Avila, Avila	400m	asphalt
El Tiemblo	320m	concrete
Baleares, Algaida	250m	concrete
Baleares, Campos	250m	concrete
Baleares, Palma	250m	concrete
Baleares, V. Bonany	325m	concrete
Barcelona, Igualada	158.5m	concrete
Barcelona, Mataro	200m	concrete
Barcelona, Barcelona	250m	wood, 42°
Cadiz, Chiclana	250m	concrete
Castellon, Benicasim	250m	concrete
Castellon, Mules	357m	concrete
Castellon, Vall de Uxo	420m	asphalt
Castellon, Burriana	250m	concrete
Ciudad Real, Argamasilla	333.33m	beton (?)
Ciudad Real, Manzanares	400m	concrete
Ciudad Real, Tomelloso	250m	concrete
Ciudad Real, Valdepenas	333.33m	beton (?)
Alcazar San Juan	250m	beton (?)
Cordoba, Posada	250m	concrete
Granada, Armilla	500m	asphalt
Guipuzcoa, San Sebastian	285.7m	concrete/indr
Huelva, Bollulos	200m	concrete
Lerida, Lerida	235m	asphalt
Madrid, Alcala d'Henares	400m	concrete
Madrid, Coslada	400m	concrete
Madrid, Alcobendas	400m	concrete
Madrid, Madrid	200m	wood/indoor
Madrid, San Sebastian	250m	concrete
Madrid, Torrejon	250m	concrete
Madrid, Madrid	250m	wood
Murcia, Torrepacheco	250m	concrete
Navarra, Tapalla	250m	concrete
Salamanca, Salamanca	333.33m	concrete
Segovia, Madrona	333.33m	concrete
Sevilla, Herrera	250m	concrete
Sevilla, Dos Harmanas		
Tarragona, Tortosa	250m	concrete
Tarragona, El Venorell	180m	concrete
Tarragona, Campo Claro	250m	concrete
Tarragona, Mont Roig	250m	concrete
Tarragona, Vilaseca	250m	concrete
Valencia, Alcudia	250m	concrete
Valencia, Algemesi	200m	concrete
Valencia, Silla	250m	concrete
Valencia, Valencia	250m	concrete

Valladolid, Valladolid	250m	concrete
Vizcaya, Berriz	250m	concrete
Vizcaya, Fadura	420m	asphalt
Vizcaya, Zalla	250m	concrete
Zaragoza, Zaragoza	250M	concrete

Switzerland

Geneva, Queue d'Arve	166.66m	wood/indr,51°
Zurich, Hallenstadion'72	250m	wood/indoor
Zurich, Oerlikon	333.33m	concrete ('82)
Lausanne	250m	concrete

Japan

Japan Keirin Association
c/o Nippon Jitensha Kaikan Bldg.
9-15, Akasaka 1-Chome
Minato-Ku, Tokyo - 107,
Japan
Sosuke Hanaoke, President

Velodromes 1 - 50 are for professional Keirin competition, 51 - 70 are for amateur races.

Each year more than 40,000 Keirin races are held across Japan.

1. Hakodate	400m	29°
2. Aomori	400m	32°
3. Taira	400m	29°
4. Yahiko	400m	32°
5. Maebashi	333.33m	36°
6. Toride	400m	31°
7. Utsunomiya	500m	25°
8. Oomiya	500m	26°
9. Seibuen	500m	26°
10. Keioukaku	400m	32°
11. Tachikawa	400m	31°
12. Matsudo	333.33m	29°
13. Chiba	500m	24°
14. Kagetsuen	400m	30°
15. Kawasaki	400m	32°
16. Hirastuka	400m	31°
17. Odawara	333.33m	35°
18. Itou	333.33m	34°
19. Shizuoka	400m	30°
20. Ichinomiya	400m	33°
21. Nagoya	400m	34°
22. Toyohashi	400m	33°
23. Gifu	400m	32°
24. Oogaki	400m	30°
25. Toyama	333.33m	33°
26. Matsuzaka	400m	31°
27. Yokkaichi	400m	32°
28. Fukui	400m	31°
29. Ohtsubiwako	500m	25°
30. Nara	333.33m	33°
31. Kyotomukomachi	400m	30°
32. Wakayama	400m	30°
33. Kishiwada	400m	30°
34. Koushien	400m	28°
35. Nishinomiya	333.33m	32°
36. Tamano	400	30°
37. Hiroshima	400	33°
38. Hofu	333.33	34°
39. Takamatsu	400	33°
40. Kanongi	400	30°
41. Komatsuzima	400	29°
42. Kouchi	500	24°

43. Matuyama	500	22°
44. Kokura	400	29°
45. Mozi	500	27°
46. Kurume	400	28°
47. Takeo	400	32°
48. Sasebo	400	31°
49. Beppu	400	33°
50. Kumamoto	500	29°
51. Hachinohe	333.33	36°
52. Shiwa	333.33	34°
53. Oomagari	500	23°
54. Shinjyo	400	33°
55. Miyaginohara	400	31°
56. Matsumoto	333.33	34°
57. Japan C.S.C No. 1	333.33	33°
58. Japan C.S.C No. 2	400	31°
59. Keirin School	400	31°
60. Kansai C.S.C.	400	31°
61. Akashi	400	29°
62. Miyazaki	400	31°
63. Uchinada	400	33°
64. Oota	333.33	34°
65. Kagoshima	400	31°
66. Yamanashi	400	31°
67. Kurayoshi	333.33	33°
68. Okinawa	333.33	32°
69. Kourakuen	400	32°
70. Izumizaki	333.33	38°

According to the UCI, all Japanese velodromes are asphalt with the exception of OOgaki, Fukui and Hiroshima which are concrete, and Maebashi Greendome, which is an indoor, wooden track.

In addition to those listed above, the UCI lists the following:

Abeno-Ku	400m
Bofu	333.33m
Chofu	400m
Iwaki	400m
Kahoku-gun	400m
Kitakyushyn	500m/400m(?)
Maebashi	400m
Muko	400m
Nichikanbara-gun	400m
Nishinomiya	400m
Otsu	500m
Senboku-gun	500m
Sendai	400m
Shuzenji-machi	400m/333.33m(?)
Tagata-gun	400m
Tokio	500m
Tokio-Hachioji	400m
Tokorozawa	500m
Yokohama	333.33m

Eastern Europe

Bulgaria

Kazanlyk	333.33m	concrete

Estonia

Tallinn	400m	concrete

Czechoslovakia

Brno (1974)	400m	concrete
Louny (1959)	446.7m	B+ton
Pardubice (1974)	507.1m	concrete
Plzen (1959)	399.8m	B+ton
Prague (1974)	333.33m	concrete

Prague	161m	wood/indoor
Bratislava (1974)	354.2m	concrete
Prostejov (1974)	300m	concrete

Georgia
Tbilissi, V+1 Central	400m	wood, 39°, ('72)
Tbilissi	228m	concrete, 40°

Greece
Athens	250m	wood, 42°
Rodos	400m	concrete

Hungary
Budapest (1972)	412m	concrete

Lithuania
Klaipeda	250m	wood

Poland
Lodz	400m	concrete ('56)
Varsovie	333.33m	
Szczecin	400m	
Radom	500m	
Zirarduv	300m	
Kalisz	500m	concrete
Kracovie	434m	concrete
Wroclav	200m	concrete

Romania
Bucharest	400m	concrete

Russia
Moscow, Olympic ('80)	333.33m	wood/indoor
Moscow (1963)	400m	concrete
Moscow	250m	wood
Toula	333.33m	concrete
Saint Petersburg	333.33m	concrete
Noguinsk	500m	concrete
Groznyi	500m	concrete
Rostov	250m	concrete
Lepetsk	280m	concrete
Jaroslavle	333.33m	concrete
Penza	333.33m	concrete
Irkoutsk	496.5m	wood

Slovenie
Kranj	370m	asphalt
Preson (1992)	333.33m	concrete, 21°

Ukraine
Lvov	250m	wood/indoor
Kiev	500m	wood
Kharkov	333.33m	concrete
Simpheropole	333.33m	concrete

Central/South America

Argentina
Buenos Aires	140m	wood/indoor
Buenos Aires	333.33m	concrete
Buenos Aires KTD	333.33m	concrete
Salta	333.33m	concrete
San Juan	400m	concrete
Mendoza	333.33m	concrete
San Rafael	333.33m	concrete
Barilocha	333.33m	concrete
Bahia Blanca	250m	concrete
Mar del Plata	500m	concrete
Mar del Plata (proj.)	250m	concrete
Gonzales Chaves	145m	wood
Jauregui	200m	concrete
Junin	333.33m	concrete

Rosario	400m	asphalt
Rosario Fray Belr.	333.33m	asphalt
Esperanza	250m	concrete
Rafaela	250m	concrete
Reconquista	333.33m	concrete
Rufino	333.33m	concrete
Vanado Tuerto	250m	asphalt
Corral de Bustos	200m	concrete
San Francisco	400m	concrete
Cordoba	250m	concrete
Rio IV	250m	concrete
Sta. Rosa/LaPampa (under const)	333.33m	concrete

Barbados
Brightown (1970)	500m	concrete, 27°

Bolivia
La Paz (1978)	333.33m	concrete
Cochabamba (1993)	333.33m	concrete, 28°

Brazil
Belo Horizonte	250m	concrete, 45°
Curitiba	333.33m	concrete, 40°
Sao Paulo (1979)	285.7m	concrete, 45°
Parana	333.33m	concrete, 45°

Chile
Curico	250m	concrete
Santiago	333.33m	asphalt
Vina del Mar	500m	concrete
Valparaiso	250m	asphalt, 45°
Pontarenas	333.33m	concrete
Talcas	438m	concrete

Columbia
Bogota	400m	concrete ('86)
Cali -- A. Galinda	250m	wood ('71)
Medellin -- Antioquia	249.4m	concrete ('74)
Medellin -- C. Rodriguez	250m	concrete ('83)
Pereira	333.33m	concrete ('86)
Cali -- Alcides Nieto	250m	wood ('86)
Duitama	250m	concrete ('90)
Bucaramanga	250m	concrete ('92)
Arauca	250m	concrete
Baramquilla	250m	concrete

Costa Rica
San Jose (1994)	333.33m	concrete, 30°

Cuba
La Havanna , (1991)	333.33m	epowit, 38°

Dominican Republic
Santo Domingo (1974)	333.33m	concrete, 43°

Equador
Cuencas	333.33m	concrete, 21°
Quito	333.33m	concrete, 42°
Tulcan, Carchi (1992)	333.33m	concrete, 38°

Guadeloupe
Baie-Hahault	333.33m	concrete, ('91)

Jamaica
Kingston	500m	concrete, 27°

Panama
Panama City	250m	concrete

Puerto Rico
Coamo (1979)	333.33m	concrete, 48°

Trinidad-Tobago
Arrima	440m	asphalt, 33°
Parasico	500m	concrete, 38°
San Fernando	333.33m	asphalt, 27°
Port of Spain	445m	concrete, 27°

Uruguay
Montevideo	333.33m	concrete, 38°
Mercedes	330m	concrete, 42°
Paisandu	333.33m	concrete, 42°

Venezuela
Acarigua	333.33	concrete, 47°
Barquisimeto	400m	concrete, 45°
Caracas	333.33m	concrete, 47°
Ciudad Bolivar	333.33m	concrete, 47°
Coro	333.33m	concrete, 47°
Cumana	333.33m	concrete, 47°
Maracaibo	500m	concrete, 45°
Maracay	333.33m	concrete, 47°
Maturin	333.33m	concrete, 47°
Puerto la Cruz	333.33m	concrete, 47°
San Cristobal	333.33m	concrete, 47°
Valencia	333.33m	concrete, 45°
Valencia	333.33m	concrete, 47°
Valencia, MaximoRomero '94	333.33m	concrete, 42°
Valera	500m	concrete, 45°

Austral-Asia

Australia

Australian Cycling Federation Incorporated
Maureen Robins, National Administrator
68 Broadway   Mr. Peter T. Bartels, Patron
Sydney, N.S.W. 2007
Telephone: 61-2-281 8688 Fax: 61-2-281 4236

The ACF says: "There are three indoor, wooden velodromes in Australia. A fourth is to be built in Sydney for the **2000 Olympic Games**. Expected completion: late 1997. All other velodromes are either concrete or asphalt. All states have a number of flat tracks, in the vicinity of 150, though all are not in use."

Queensland
Blackwater		
Brisbane (1982)	333.33m	concrete
Brisbane	400m	asphalt
Bundaberg		asphalt
Caboolture		asphalt
Cairns	400m	asphalt
Ipswich	333.33m	asphalt
Mackay	400m	asphalt
Maryborough		asphalt
Mt. Isa	400m	asphalt
Nerang		asphalt
Rockhampton	333m	B+ton
Townsville	333m,	B+ton
Toowoomba		asphalt
Warwick		asphalt

Western Australia
Perth,SpeedDome, 1989	250m, wood/indr, 42°	
Collie		

New South Wales
Sydney -- 2-400m concrete, 1-250m concrete, 1-333.33m asphalt, incl. Canterbury, Dulwich Hill

Sydney for Olympic Games, 2000	**250m, wood/indoor, projected**	
Aubury	400m	asphalt
Bathurst	400m	asphalt
Camperdown	285m	concrete
Canberra	290m	concrete

Canberra	400m	concrete
Casino	400m	asphalt
Coffs Harbor	400m	asphalt
Cootumandra	400m	asphalt
Dubbo	400m	asphalt
Glen Innes	400m	asphalt
Gosford	500m	asphalt
Goulburn	400m	asphalt
Grafton	400m	asphalt
Hunter District	400m	concrete
Hurstville	400m	concrete
Illawarra	265m	concrete
Inverell	295m	concrete
Lidcombe	400m	asphalt
Marrylands	400m	asphalt
Mudges	400m	asphalt
Muswellbrook	195m	concrete
Newcastle	250m	concrete
Orange	400m	asphalt
Tamworth	400m	asphalt
Taree	295m	asphalt
Wagga	400m	asphalt
Wollongong		
Moama, built 1993	285.7m	concrete, 25°

South Australia

Adelaide, Superdome,	250m wood/indoor (1993)	
Adelaide	400m	concrete
Mt. Gambier	250m	concrete
Pt. Pirie	500m	asphalt
Whyalla	250m	B+ton

Northern Territory

Alice Springs	333.33m	concrete
Darwin	400m	asphalt

Victoria

Ararat		
Ballarat		
Bendigo	500m	B+ton
Echuca		
Leongatha		
Maryborough		
Melbourne	one 250, one 333, + 2, B+ton	
Northcote		
Coburg,		
Brunswick		
Blackburn		
Shepparton	333.33m	concrete
Wangaretta		
Warragul		

Australian Capital Territory

Canberra

Tasmania

Burnie	450m	asphalt
Devonport	490m	asphalt
Exeter	400m	asphalt
Georgetown	350m	asphalt
Hobart	400m	asphalt
Latrobe	450m	B+ton
Launceston,Silverdome,	285.7m.	wood/indr ('86)
Longford	350m	asphalt
Rosebury	400m	asphalt
Sheffield	440m	asphalt

New Caledonia

Noumea	333.33m	B+ton

New Zealand

Invercargill, Kew Bowl	321,2m,	concrete, 28°,'60
Christchurch, Denton Pk	400m,	concrete, 42°,'73
Christchurch, Eng. Pk.	406.9m	asphalt
Wanganui, Cooks Gdns	404m	asphalt, 26°, '83
Auckland, Manukau	285.7m	concrete, 25°,'89
Levin	420m	asphalt, 25°
New Plymouth, Rugby Pk	440m	asphalt, 20°
New Lynn, Olympic Pk	446m	asphalt, 20°
Palmerston, No.Mem.Pk	452m	concrete, 35°
Te Awamutu	469m	asphalt
Temuka	400m	asphalt, 10°
Wellington, Haitaitai	333m	concrete, 35°
Taupo, Owen Delany Pk	333.4m	asphalt, 20°
Feilding, Johnson Park	401m	asphalt, 12°
Timaru, Caledonian Gr.	484.9m	asphalt
Tinwald, Tinwald Spts	396m	asphalt, 24°
Nelson, Trafalgar Pk	520m	asphalt, 12°
Blenheim, Athletic Pk	455m	asphalt, 15°
Waimate	355.8m	asphalt, 5°

Tahiti

Papeete	400m	concrete

Near East

Armenia

Erevan (1965)	250m	concrete

Azerbaijan

Bakou	333.33m	concrete

Croatia

Zagreb	400m	concrete

Iran

Tehran	333.33m	concrete

Kazakhstane

Alma Ata	333.33m	wood

Kirguizstane

Bichkek	333.33m	concrete

Lettonie

Ventspils	250m	wood

Lebanon

Beirut	500m	concrete

Ouzbekistane

Tashkent	333.33m	concrete ('84)
Namangane	333.33m	concrete

Tadjikistane

Leninbade	333.33m	concrete

Tunisia

Tunis	400m	concrete

Turkey

Adana		
Ankara		
Balikesir	500m	concrete
Konya	500m	concrete
Istanbul, 2000	400m	concrete

Africa

Algeria

Alger (1990)	400m	concrete, 38°
Annaba (1990)	500m	concrete, 34°
Oran	250m	concrete

Ivory Coast

Abidjan	435.9	concrete

Lyberia

Tripoli (1979)	400m	concrete
Tripoli (under construction)		concrete

Morocco

Casablanca	332.8m	B+ton

South Africa

Border

Amalinda, E. London	500m	asphalt
Pt. Elizabeth, oval	500m	B+ton
Pt. Elizabeth, Galvandale	500m	B+ton

Natal

Kings Park	333.33m	B+ton
Durban, Ilovo	500m	B+ton
Pietermaritzburg	500m	B+ton

Nothern Orange Free State

Harmony Gold Mine	500m	B+ton

Northern Transvaal

Pretoria,Pilditch	500m	B+ton
Pilditch	250m	B+ton
Mamelodi	500m	B+ton
Attridgeville	500m	B+ton
Bapspontein	500m	B+ton
Pietersburg	500m	B+ton

Southern Transvaal

Johannesburg, Hector Norris	490m	B+ton

Western Province

Belville (1992)	250m	B+ton
Paarl	500m	B+ton
Cape Town, Green Pt	500m	B+ton
Mitchells Plain	500m	B+ton
Worchester	500m	B+ton

Western Transvaal

Krugersdorp	500m	B+ton
West Driefentein	500m	B+ton
East Driefentein	500m	B+ton
Libanon	500m	B+ton

Indo-Asia

China

Beijing (1989)	333.33	concrete
Beijing -- 2000 (projected)		wood/indoor
Chang-Chung		
Changping		
Taiyuan (1991)	333.33m	concrete
Columbia		
Korea		
Inchon	333.33m	asphalt
Seoul	333.33m	wood
Dae Gu	333.33m	concrete
Weug Jung Bu	470m	concrete
Weug Jung Bu	333.33m	concrete
Na Ju	333.33m	concrete
Jeon-Ju	333.33m	concrete

India

Bombay		
New Delhi (1982)	333.33m	concrete

Indonesia

Djakarta

Maylasia

Ipoh (1989)	250m	wood
Kuala Lumpur	333.33m	concrete

Bicycle Racing Terminology ◉▽◉

"The ABC's (attacks, blocks and chases) of Bicycle Racing" published by the USCF describes bicycle race terminology as "a dialect blending English, French, Italian and Californian". Hanging around bicycle racing fans pick up terms pretty quickly, but in case you've heard some that don't make sense to you yet, here's a compendium: (from the USCF and other sources)

attack -- a hard effort off the front, attempting to get away from other riders.

B.A.R. -- Best All-around Rider. Rider with the highest accumulation of points given for places in each event. Also known as an Omnium.

block/blocking -- getting in front of other riders, usually to allow a teammate to get away from the pack. Blocking is especially important during the final stages of a race to set up a win or finishing sprint for a teammate.

blow up -- become unable to ride any more, exhausted.

biff -- crash

bonk -- run out of energy to the extent that riding becomes very difficult or impossible. Also "hitting the wall".

box -- in the middle of a group with no way to move to a new position.

boxed in -- unable to execute race strategy because there is no way to move out of the middle of the group.

break/breakaway -- to make a gap or get away from the pack or main group of riders. A bold move in longer races unless done in a group. Those in the pack can conserve energy by drafting off each other. A lone rider in a break early in a long race is usually thought to be crazy or foolish. Sometimes riders with little hope of winning will break just to get attention or make the race more interesting. A contender takes a big chance unless in a track race s/he

succeeds in lapping the field. Then s/he is a "lap up" on the field.

bridge -- usually "bridging a gap". Making progress by moving from one group to the next one in front. This takes a lot of energy, but is worth it if the front group stays away from the pack.

chase/chase group -- riders chasing a group in front which has made a gap.

chop -- to move **down** track, cutting off another rider. A "hook" moves up the track. (see "hook") An illegal move, impeding the forward progress of another rider, done as a threat or intimidation. The rider who does it can be disqualified or relegated. In a Points race, a move like this can take down the whole field.

clincher -- tire with a tube which has a ridge of wire or Kevlar hooking into the rim of the wheel. These used to be used strictly for training because they couldn't match the high air pressure of sew-ups, but today they are made for higher air pressure and are found in races. They won't roll off the rims like sew-ups that aren't glued on well.

derny -- vehicle used in the Keirin race to pace riders.

disc/disk wheel -- a wheel with solid sides, not spokes, built for superior aerodynamics. May be a little heavier than spoked wheels, but cut through the air better and lend a "flywheel" effect to the ride. Origin-

ally used for Time Trials only, but now seen in all races.

domestique -- French term referring to a rider who sacrifices his/her individual achievement for the benefit of a teammate. A rider may be assigned specific tasks to perform during a race to assist the designated "winner" or highest achieving (presumably strongest) team member. This term is more commonly used on the road.

door -- a space a rider can move into. "Shut the door" means blocking another rider's movement.

drafting -- riding behind another rider who breaks the wind for the rider behind in order to save energy. This is illegal in individual time trial events, but is basic to most competitive racing on both track and roads. It is a major competitive strategy. All other things being equal, those who use it are much more likely to win than those who don't due to the great energy-saving advantage to the rider behind.

echelon -- a group of riders staggered so that each successive rider gets optimal draft from the one in front. Echelons may be almost side by side or lined up behind each other, depending on the direction of the wind.

field -- the main group, also known as

Derny used to pace Keirin riders. This one belongs to USCF Coach Andrzej Bek. Cool, isn't it?

the pack, bunch, peloton.

field sprint -- a sprint to the finish line by the main group or pack. Position in the field is very important during the final sprint. If you can't get by, it doesn't matter if you're the fastest rider or not. This is where blocking by teammates can be a great advantage. The rider who is back in a large pack approaching the finish line with no teammates is in trouble in a field sprint.

force/push the pace -- riding faster, forcing others to ride harder to keep up. Sometimes riders will do this to test the possibility of a breakaway. Sometimes a lesser member of a team will do this to wear out non-team members in order to give an advantage to a teammate who is probably on their wheel, expending little effort compared with surrounding riders. Sometimes just a rider having fun!

float -- pedal with light pressure, using little energy.

fred -- a new and inexperienced rider or someone who does not seem to know what he/she's doing. Also known as a duffus (do-fuss) or a geek.

gap -- (noun) distance between a rider or riders and the main group. verb: to move away from the group. Similar to a break, but usually a shorter and maybe more temporary move. It may precede a break if the pack does not respond to the fact that a gap exists.

half-wheel -- (verb) constantly staying slightly ahead of another rider, especially in training. It can be very irritating.

hammer -- riding hard for whatever reason, often in a bigger gear.

hammerhead -- a person who likes riding hard. This person is popular with those who like taking advantage of a free ride, but not with those who do not want the pace to be forced.

hand sling -- a move used to throw a teammate into a Madison race on the track. It is also a change of partners who are taking turns competing.

handicap -- placing riders at successive distances around the track to take away advantage of stronger riders and even out the competition. On the roads, a handicap is a time differential given to slower riders, also to make competition even.

hanging in -- barely staying in the race by drafting on the back of the pack.

hook -- an illegal move, moving the other rider **up** track impeding his/her forward progress, done as a threat or intimidation. The rider who does it can be disqualified or relegated. A "chop" is moving them down track. (see "chop")

interval -- ride hard, often for a specified distance or time, as a training regimen. (see attack)

jump -- accelerate quickly, out of the saddle or sitting down. In Sprints a jump is usually standing up and accelerating with maximum effort to drop the other competitor for the win. In Points races a competitor may stay seated so other riders are not alerted to the jump until it is too late. Jumps are part of training for bicycle racing because a good jump is a distinct advantage in getting away from other riders in any race.

kick -- a final burst of speed during the final, sprint portion of any race.

lead-out -- a sprint off the front of the pack to benefit a teammate. The second rider will slingshot off the draft provided by the leader, accelerating even faster, especially for a win.

mass start/massed start -- a race where all competitors start from the same general area at the same time without holders.

minute man -- the rider one minute ahead of you in a time trial.

Motorpace -- also known as "Staying" (hence the "Stayer's line" on the track). An event primarily done in Europe in which a rider rides behind a motorcycle, derny or motorized bicycle in competition as a team with the driver.

We knew these podiums would come in handy. We need to get out there and hammer. Michelle, push the pace in the paceline on the pole while Bobby practices jumps uptrack. Paul will probably take a flyer. Vic, you have good snap, get out of the saddle and lead him out over the top. Joany, you're bonking today, so don't blow up, just sit in and spin. No hooks or chops, and be careful you don't pull a foot. Those roadies look like squirrely freds, so attack if they try to hang on. After some two-by-two motorpacing we'll do some tempo work on the rollers. Everybody understand?

This is different from the practice of motorpacing as a training technique.

motorpacing -- training in the draft of a motorcycle maintaining a high speed, allowing a rider to practice riding faster than he/she could alone or behind another rider. Motorpacing is said to be the quickest way to build speed fast.

Nats -- US National Championships

Omnium -- a group of races contested for the "best overall" award, usually on the basis of points. (see B.A.R.)

open the door -- allow another rider to get through.

out of the saddle -- standing up on the pedals, off the bicycle seat

over the top -- pass other riders on the upper (right) side of the track.

paceline -- a line of riders all going the same speed on the bottom of the track warming up for competition. They are usually single file and the leader changes regularly, usually every lap or half-lap.

pick-up -- change of partners, usually in a Madison.

pole line -- also known as the measurement line. The black line at the bottom of the track by which the measurement of the track is taken. Sometimes the area below the Sprinter's line is simply called "the pole".

prime -- from the Latin (those Italians again) "prima," meaning first and hence the pronunciation "preem." A prime is a prize given to the first rider across the line at a given moment in the race. Primes can be surprises announced to the riders in the midst of a race in order to stir things up a bit. Sometimes top contenders will go for the primes, other times they will save themselves for the win and allow other riders to take the primes. Sometimes riders will go for primes because they know this may be the only opportunity they will have to win anything, depending on the competition.

pull -- taking a turn at the front of the pack, breaking the wind for others. Taking a pull is considered appropriate etiquette, especially in longer races. Riders who refuse to take pulls may be looked down upon as wheelsuckers who are selfish, trying to take unfair advantage of others.

However, often those who take no pulls are the ones who have more energy left at the finish to win the sprint. Wheelsuckers are not respected for their race conduct, but they are respected for their placement on the podium.

roadie -- riders who prefer to ride or race on the roads.

rollers -- three cylinders attached by rails and a drive belt which fit the wheelbase of a bicycle. Rollers are the classic home or in-place training and warm-up devise. Other equipment has since been invented which holds bicycles securely as the back wheel goes around. The later devises are less likely to allow riders to fall. Some riders swear there is no workout like a roller workout and that more modern devises do not take their place.

scratch -- the full distance in a handicap race, ridden by the strongest rider (the "scratch rider") who is placed last. In a Scratch race, everyone begins at the same place at the same time and rides the same distance.

sew-up/tubular -- a tire which is sewn around the tube, providing strength which allows maximum air pressure to be pumped into the tire. The tire and tube are then glued to the rim of the wheel.

These tires can roll off of the rim if not glued on very securely, as opposed to clinchers, which will not roll off, but cannot take as much air pressure.

sitting in -- see drafting

Six-day -- an indoor track race, especially popular in Europe, which lasts for six days and is contested by teams of two or three riders, often raced like Madisons. The winners either cover the most distance or win the most points.

slipstream -- the "sweet spot" behind a rider where the most energy is saved while drafting.

snap -- ability to accelerate quickly.

spin -- pedaling at high RPMs, such as 90's and up. 60 RPM is considered very slow, 200 *very* fast! As discussed in training, spinning is riding at high RPM with little effort to build quickness.

spun out -- hitting an RPM rate that does not allow the rider to attain maximum speed, but not having a big enough gear to go faster. On a road bike, riders can equip their bike with a higher gear to shift to if they find themselves

"spun out," but track bicycles only have one gear. Track bicycles need to be equipped with the correct gear according to the rider's strength and RPM ability so that s/he can race as fast and as efficiently as possible.

squirrel -- an unstable or nervous rider who does not hold a line.

take a flyer -- accelerate off the front all of a sudden.

tempo -- riding at a fast pace.

track bicycle -- a special bicycle used for racing on the velodrome with only one gear and no brakes. These bicycles usually have steeper angles and a higher bottom bracket than a road bicycle to allow the pedals to clear the banking of the track.

Direct drive action allows riders to control speed by pushing or resisting forward motion on the pedals. There is no coasting on these bicycles and riders must remember not to lock their legs or they'll end up on the ground! They are extremely light and responsive.

trackie -- riders who prefer to ride or race on the track.

trackstand -- balancing in place on a bicycle. This is often seen in Match Sprints in order to unnerve the competition and/or force the rear rider to the front.

The USCF RuleBook has now set a limit on trackstands to 3 minutes. At the signal of the Starter, forward movement must be resumed.

Track stands still add excitement and allow top riders to demonstrate their expertise. There is always the distinct possibility that even top riders will fall over!

two-by-two -- a training formation used a lot in Europe where riders train side by side.

UCI -- **Union Cycliste Internationale** the international organization, based in Switzerland, which governs cycling around the world.

USCF -- United States Cycling Federation, the governing body of bicycle racing in the United States. See Chapter 19.

velodrome -- the place where we all go to watch the most exciting bicycle racing on earth! Velodromes are banked tracks, usually built of concrete, but sometimes of special wood. Maximum banking is on the turns. The straightaways are compara-tively flat. Degree of banking varies from eighteen to fifty-something. See velodromes section for more information on tracks in the U.S.

wall -- as in "hit the wall" -- unable to perform anymore.

wheel sucking/sleigh ride -- drafting on another rider's wheel to save energy.

wind it up -- accelerate to top speed.

zone -- go deeply into yourself.

Another kind of "hitting the wall" is riding the steepest tracks!

Paul Swift rides the Vandedrome.

Gallery — *of my favorite shots*

It was just a local Spring race series at Dominguez Hills (1994), no big Championship. The boy was the son of 70s racer Lon Benson. He must have "worked" with no protest from Gibby for 20 minutes. I could never have set this shot up. Watch for those gifts. They may be where you least expect.

← One of America's greatest **past** Champions, Gibby Hatton, works on the bicycle of America's **current** double World Champion Marty Nothstein with America's **future** -- ?? -- Champion? mechanic? This is bicycle racing in a nutshell. One generation teaches the next. I call it:

Gibby and the Kid

↓ Curt Harnett had just won the Gold Medal for Sprints at Goodwill Games. I couldn't believe my good fortune when Curt rolled up 10 feet from me (outside the railing going into Turn One) to share the moment with his mom. I had noticed the woman with the Canadian flag earlier, but had made no connection. I couldn't help thinking:

He's Got His Gold, She's Got Hers.

I mailed a copy of this photo to: "Curt Harnett's Mom, Thunder Bay, Ontario." It got there. Good job, Canadian Post Office.

289

1986 World Championships Colorado Springs, CO

↓ I recognized Nelson Vails from the 1984 Olympics and Southern California racing. When I first saw him, he was talking to various people, doing his P.R. thing.

A little later I looked over and noticed him out of the spotlight, giving his undivided attention to this boy with the sweet face. No cameras were around and Nelson wasn't playing to the crowd. He was just patiently listening to a boy who wanted to communicate with one of America's heroes.

I thought: **Nelson Vails Always Has Time For His Fans**

The Great Gibby Hatton

↑ You don't need to be in any particular place to get great shots. I could hardly get this one because crowd control marshalls were trying to keep the view of the crowd unobstructed. I had to crouch down low, which turned out to give me an even more interesting perspective. Don't get discouraged, look for the angle. Railings can be an asset to a composition.

This shot was in Turn Two, during a very slow part of the Sprint between Gibby Hatton and the great Japanese Sprinter, 10 time World Champion, Koichi Nakano. This was the last year he won Worlds. If I had known who Nakano was at the time, I might have focused on him, but I didn't.

This was **The Great Gibby Hatton** I had heard so much about.

Triumph and Tragedy

These two shots were triumph and tragedy for everyone, including the photographer.

↓ From the beginning of the Games, the **1984** Olympic Team Pursuit Team was plagued by endless problems.

At long last they were in the Finals, Dave Grylls replacing an ill Brent Emery. This was it, the last race, the race for the Gold. They knew they had the speed. They were experienced and ready. The flags went up, the gun went off, the riders were released.

But wait -- what's this? The top holder knows that something is wrong. Coach Eddie B. has just hit the stopwatch and does not yet realize. Dave Grylls' toestrap has come lose and he's "pulled a foot!" Grylls looked around, convinced that there would be a restart. There was none. The US had lost the Gold before it left the starting line.

Knowing that anything can happen in bicycle racing, the three remaining Team members, Nitz, McDonough, and Hegg persevered, losing by milli-seconds. As Australia gloried in its win, the US Team had given one of the great track performances of all time, unforgettable for the 1000s of spectators who witnessed their proudest effort of the heart.

1984 Olympic Games, Los Angeles, California

1992 Olympic Trials, Blaine, Minnesota

↑It was the Finals for the **1992** US National Sprint Championship and an Olympic berth between Ken Carpenter and Paul Swift. The first ride, Carpenter had beaten Swift. The second ride, Swift took a flyer and Carpenter was unable to catch him.

Last ride and winner take all. With about 150 meters to go, Swift behind, Carpenter pulled uptrack out of the Sprinter's lane. Swift moved forward as Carpenter moved back downtrack. Swift, seeing a collision but refusing to back off, went onto the BlueBand. By Turn Three he was riding the black line. Going into Turn Four, Carpenter came downtrack into Swift twice, pushing him onto the Blue Band again. Coming out of Turn Four, as Swift pulled ahead. Carpenter's front end came into Swift's pedal and he went down.

The tragic irony is that Swift appears to emerge as conqueror. He had ridden the race of his life at the moment of truth. He was disqualified on a technical ruling, that he had advanced on the Blue Band during the Sprint. Watching the video, I know what I think. You decide for yourself. No reride was allowed. Carpenter's win was tarnished by a controversy which placed him on the Olympic Team. He didn't complain. Swift refused to accept the Silver medal. He felt he had won the Gold.

Photographically: Sports Illustrated asked all photographers if they got "the" shot. I was the only person who said "Yes". After sitting on my photo for 2-3 weeks making it too late for other publications, SI returned it. They had cost-effectively used one by their own photographer of Ken being hauled off on a stretcher. Do you think it was more effective than this? I know what I think.

Photographically: Using an unfamiliar camera, I got an exceptional shot, but almost got nothing because the settings so overexposed the film. Always shoot right after the gun goes off. You never know what might happen.

Number Four

"I'm talking to my psychic today" I said to Jeff Solt, "do you want me to ask him anything?"

"Yeah, ask him if I'm going to Europe," Jeff replied, frustrated by uncertainty. And so, I did.

"He's already qualified, I don't know why he's worried about it," Ralph, my usually jolly English psychic, answered. "I see five people going and Jeff is number four."

Oh, right, I thought, as if the USCF is going to send FIVE people to Europe. Ha! They never even send three. Well, it was okay, Ralph didn't know anything about bicycle racing.

A couple of weeks later, Marty Nothstein and Paul Swift had qualified one and two. A ride-off was going to be held for the unprecedented third spot. The USCF was indeed going to send three people to Europe. Red letter day! This photo is the finish of that contest and one of my favorite photos of all. Note that Solt's wheel is <u>off</u> the ground.

After Bill Clay was declared the winner I realized: that made Jeff Number Four. Hmmm. . . Well, still, they never send five people, and there was no fifth rider.

Later, the word came. Jeff went to Europe -- along with EDS Sprinter Trey Gannon, number five.

That is my "stranger than fiction" psychic story and it's absolutely true. →

Taken from the inside, Dominguez Hills Spring racing series, 1994

Meg Berry Begins the Throw

← Meg Berry was a familiar sight on the track in the eighties, usually in the Sprint and the Points Race. She was experienced and knew all the tricks (she still does), including details like how to throw your bike at the end of a race. Sometimes that alone made the difference between triumph and defeat. Berry was taking no chances.

On this occasion it was the 1986 Southern California District Championships. The San Diego track had been newly resurfaced. The starkness of white against dark gives the shot strength. This was taken from the outside in Turn One.

The Look of a Champion

I had first noticed "the look" in a photograph from Goodwill Games, 1990. It was as though she had left this world and was now in a place no one could reach. Judging from Janie Eickhoff's record and performance, it reflects her personal power and determination to effect a win.

(How does she do that?)

But There Were Light Hearted Moments, too.

At Goodwill Games, between sessions, the American Champions were getting a little restless. Giant Sprinter Ken Carpenter (6'4"?) picked up little (5'1"?) Janie Eickhoff's ultra small bicycle and began to ride it around the track. Janie, not to be outdone, picked up Ken's giant bicycle and barely able to straddle the top tube, hopped on it to catch up with him and finish the ride around the track.

World Cup, Colorado Springs, CO 1994

Ken Carpenter

Ken Carpenter cut a dramatic figure during his five-time National Sprint Champion years. From 1988 through his move to professional racing in 1992, Ken was virtually unbeatable.

At San Diego Velodrome in the early days, Ken got beat a lot. But, he stayed with it and rode his way to the top. After two years on the Japanese Keirin circuit, Ken retired from bicycle racing. He remains immortalized in a couple of favorite shots.

At Goodwill Games, Ken paid his respects to Soviet Sprinter Belostetski. They could have been just a couple of guys hanging out. It was international relations at their best.

A lot of wars could probably be prevented if leaders would simply ride around a track together and just discuss the situation!

At Goodwill Games in 1990, Roberto Chiappa was a 19 year old Italian Junior Sprint Champion. Today he is one of the best Sprinters in the world and considerably thicker. *This shot was from the start/finish area, outside.*

This was shot in between sessions from Turn One, outside during warm ups. Watch during off times for those special shots. Use the rail.

Last Look

The 1992 Olympic Trials was to be the last Nationals Ken would race as an amateur. Winning here would mean a trip to Barcelona as a member of the Olympic Team.

I went early to take a photo of the elegant sweep of the new Minnesota (Blaine) track.

As I planned out my shot and laid down on the track to take it, Ken walked up to the start/finish area to plan strategy, get in the mood -- whatever.

As he walked to the very top of the track, I thought "This is too good to be true!"

While Ken courteously thought he was out of my way, he gave me one of my favorite shots.

At the **1986 Southern California District Championships**, Ken was still just a young hopeful. In this Sprint with Mark Garrett, final Sprint fisticuffs sent Garrett to the ground. The final ruling is unknown, but Garrett took a good fall and walked away. On the sidelines was ex-Sprinter and Coach Gary Scheutz. He knew how that felt and reacted accordingly.

Garrett still races and works as an officer with the California Highway Patrol. If you get caught speeding, you might try "But Mark, I was practicing my Sprint!" (Yeah, like he'll let you off.)

Shot from Turn One, outside.

"Where'd He Go?" (oh sure, Ken, try and look innocent.)

Teams are basic to bicycle racing. They often have characters of their own due to the characters on them. Photographic series can capture some of this feeling as you notice similar emotions in the various shots. Doing a theme series is sort of like collecting a milieu, what you're seeking is better found over several shots rather than just one.

Team/theme work

↑ Being part of a team can be very rewarding. Andre Magannam (left) had done some criteriums, but wasn't so sure about this track stuff. He was talked into trying it by his teammates. After Master's Nationals 1993 he decided track racing may not be so bad.

Realizing that Andre had a chance for a medal at a certain point in the Points Race, Coach Harvey Nitz shouted directions for Subaru Montgomery teammate Tony O'Brien to help Andre by pulling him around on his wheel. That way Andre could rest during the race while maintaining his speed -- classic Points Race strategy which Harvey knew well. Tony, a strong rider but not in contention, assisted Andre to his first medal in his first track race. Teammate Jerry Malone shares Coach Harvey's pride in a job well done.

Subaru Montgomery (now Montgomery Bell) is based in San Francisco, but these three are San Diego guys, the very unique Ron Smith, the already immortal Vic Copeland, and John Creed, "Mr. Chart House/Islands" restaurants. (Guess that's where they get all that energy.)

When Push Comes to Shove

← Taking up-close photos of riders in hot competition is challenging. You have to sacrifice seeing the race or watching what is happening until you see the photos later. You have no time to say "Oh, that's interesting, I think I'll shoot it. Let's see, focus on the rider in the middle . . . . " By that time the riders have probably circled the track twice more and finished the race.

Instead, it's more like: "Here they come! I think they're in focus right a . b . o . u . t . . . <u>NOW</u>!" -- you hit the shutter <u>just</u> when they hit the predesignated spot on which you have already focused. You get whatever you get. The closeness tends to be interesting, and sometimes you actually get action that you would have chosen if you had been able to choose. Other times it's a bust and the shot is a dud. That's the race photographer's life. The surprise is half the fun.

You do get better at picking what will more likely produce excitement, such as this race, a Keirin. There is much more likely to be contact because it is allowed and you know riders often fight for the motor's wheel, especially early in the race.

I knew there was a camera on the Canadian rider's bicycle, but I didn't' know there were <u>two</u> cameras in the race until I saw this photo. Often you will see things in photographs that you didn't notice at the time you were taking the picture -- a strong argument for just shooting happily away and just seeing what you get later.

This was shot from the infield on the backstretch because the light was better on that side (the lovely Seattle "Golden Glow" was happening). You can't always decide where the light comes from. Sometimes you'd like them to turn the track around so you can get better lighting on the photo you want to take. Most tracks were obviously not designed with best lighting for photographers in mind. Often Start/Finish areas are either back lit or in the shade. Better lighting would seem to be beneficial to officials too, though the riders might just have light in their eyes. (You might think about that in the future, track site designers.)   →

Goodwill Games Photographers

Goodwill Games, Marymoor, 1990

← The Goodwill Games was a great time. Curt Harnett took Sprints, with Gary Neiwand second and Ken Carpenter third.

Unexpectedly, Ken picked up Curt as the Canadian National anthem was being played. I could only entitle this:

I May Have Been Third, but I Can Still Lift Over 200 lbs with One Arm!

That Champion Behavior

As disappointing as it is for an athlete to lose in competition, it's always nice to see good sportsmanship. A fair battle between worthy opponents is what sports is all about.

Italian rider Roberto Chiappa did not make it to the award stand in the 1990 Goodwill Games (he was only 19 at the time), but he today he shows the best of sportsmanship in honoring his opponents, win or lose.

In the top photo Chiappa honors countryman Fredrico Paris, who he has just beaten. His actions say: "He is a great rider -- and I beat him" (ergo: I am all the greater for having beaten a great rider).

In the bottom photo he adds honor to the victory of Gary Neiwand of Australia by acknowledging his own defeat. This act says: "He had to be a really great rider if he beat <u>me</u>" (ergo: I will be all the greater when I beat him next time).

By honoring his opponents, Chaippa honors himself.→

World Cup Finals, Colorado Springs, 1994

The Sprint begins.

Hill (Aus) vs. Harnett (Can). World Cup Finals, Colorado Springs, Colorado, 1994

Uh-oh, riding the blue band is a no-no. Sometimes you're forced down by your opponent. Officials will rule later -- can't stop the Sprint now.

Ride 'em up . . . .

. . . . . ride 'em down . . .

The Joy of Sprinting -- International Style

Yes, one of these guys won, and I have the finish photo, but, when you love to watch great Sprinting, who wins is kind of beside the point.

The joy of the chase is the joy of the race. This race was great.

← Therese Nugent and Karolyn Smith collided at the end of a Sprint in Turn Four. I was at the finish line waiting to get the finish shot. As I took these photos, I appreciated my auto-focus (Canon) camera, because I had just focused on the finish line, 15 feet away. I don't think I would have gotten all of these without it. Therese and Karolyn were probably 50 meters away. But, I just pointed and shot four times.

I have no idea why the third shot came out significantly darker than shots 1,2 and 4. The camera saw something I didn't see. It illustrates the frailties of automatic cameras. I did not change the settings at all. (Explain that, Canon, I'm supposed to get a perfect exposure every time!)

↓ Mike McCarthy goes down at Goodwill Games in 1990, 10 feet away from me. I did not have an autofocus at that time, but I had just focused on the start, also close. Mike's stem bolt broke (see second photo). When you hear something funny, SHOOT! Figure it out later. Maybe you get something, maybe you don't. Don't stop and watch, you can't help the rider. The only good thing to come out of it may be a great shot. (Nikon or Canon, 50 mm lens)

Crashes

Seattle Film Works prints and slides -- these are from slides. Dominguez Hills, 1994

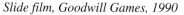
Slide film, Goodwill Games, 1990

Crashes can happen anywhere and at any time. Experienced riders are more likely to be in less crash-likely spots, have quicker reactions and possess the bike handling skills to stay up even when most riders would not. However, all riders know that crashes are just part of bicycle racing. Coaches teach their riders how to fall to avoid injury.

Cr*ash*es

This crash occurred just after I had walked in. Standing on the outside, between Turns One and Two (not a favorite spot), I heard a funny sound all the way at the other end of the track. I turned my lens to 105, and shot. If I had had my 75-300 lens, I would have gotten a better shot, but that's life.

The rider in question had apparently gotten physical (legal in Keirin racing) with Paul Swift. If you're going to try out your Keirin techniques, don't try them with the best bike handlers in track racing unless you've had a lot of experience and know how to fall. The rider ended up with a broken collarbone and a punctured lung (due to the fall). The angle of his arm in the third shot looks ominous.

These shots show riders what to do when a crash occurs. If you can, ride uptrack (Scott Skellinger moving up), because you know the rider will be sliding down. If you can't go up (Dave Bittenbender at the bottom), speed up and get by. Good save by the rider in red uptrack.

Finish the race -- you can't help the rider.

Notice that emergency medical personnel, seated at the table, are grabbing gear and starting toward the rider.

Print film, Dominguez Hills, 1995

In 1991, daddy Ron Storer's ear was the most interesting thing around the velodrome.

By 1992, bicycles were looking like a lot more fun

No matter how crowded the track, groups of people comprise individuals who each have their own thoughts.

Mood

1991 and 1992 Nationals, Marymoor and Blaine

US Nationals, Indianapolis, 1993

Timers Ready. Marymoor, 1991

Dave Bittenbender's track bike goes for a bike ride. Marymoor, 1991

Mood

Sometimes you get shots that, well, you don't really know why you like them, but you do.

If you see 'em, shoot 'em.

Bad weather between sessions, US Nationals, Indianapolis, 1993 (don't ride on wet tracks -- you'll slide down.)

Nick Chenowth and Marty Nothstein get the treatment. Indianapolis, 1993

World Cup Finals, Colorado Springs, CO, 1994

The End

"*Whew! Glad that's over with!*"
Refs go home after a strenuous 1992
Olympic Trials. *Blaine, MN*

Renee Duprel
I had to have you in here somewhere.
Wave goodbye, Renee. US National
Sprint Champion, *Marymoor, 1991*

In her section, Janie's advice to young women is: *"It's a great way to meet guys in black lycra!"* I like the way Janie thinks.

One thing about Sprints, they build great thigh and gluteus muscles. I couldn't resist this trio of World Class ### Buns

It's not where the inspiration comes from, it's what you do with it that's important.

Legacy

Each generation leaves a legacy for those who follow. Mary & Fred "Cappy" Capicchioni were instrumental in the building of the 7-Eleven Olympic Velodrome in Colorado Springs. Here Fred pauses for a photo as, in the background, a beneficiary of his legacy begins his race. *Colorado Springs, 1993.*

All this bike racin' makes me sleepy. . . . Blaine, MN, 1992

Goodbye Phil, we miss you.
See you later. With love.

Goodnight.
US National Championships,
Marymoor, 1991

And . . . that's it!